THE GREAT
DIY BOOK

PROJECTS FOR THE HOME AND GARDEN

THE GREAT
DIY BOOK

PROJECTS FOR THE HOME AND GARDEN

MURDOCH BOOKS

contents

workshop
basics

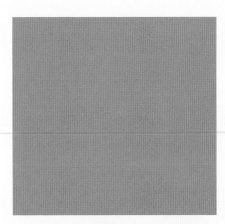

YOUR WORKSHOP

TOOLS

BASIC TECHNIQUES

BUILDING WORKBENCHES AND TOOL STORAGE

contents

your workshop

your workshop

SETTING UP YOUR WORKSHOP

You'll spend a lot of time in your workshop, so make an effort now to ensure that you'll be comfortable and safe. A functional workshop is one with sufficient work space, storage, power, light and ventilation.

A tidy, well-organized workshop is the dream of many an amateur or professional craftworker. A corner of your home or garage is all that's required.

PURPOSE

The set-up of your workshop will depend on its intended uses. Some will require a general area for basic tool storage for simple repairs around the home and garden, while others might want a special-purpose layout to cater for their hobby.

LOCATION

If you are fortunate you may have a studio, shed or garage you can dedicate to your needs or hobby. The space available will dictate the layout of your workshop, so very careful planning is necessary to make it as efficient as possible. If you are an amateur

motor mechanic you'll require at least a one-car garage, but if you make delicate wooden miniatures, between four and six square metres in the corner of a spare room may suit you. In all cases it is important that your workshop is well organized, well lit, well ventilated, safe and easy to clean.

LIGHTING

The work area must be well lit, as poor lighting can lead to poor work. Windows in the north wall will supply good daylight without direct sunlight, and this is ideal for woodworking. If a window is not available, skylights that use a flexible silvered tube to direct the light are excellent alternatives and simple to install. For those times when artificial lighting is needed, 150-watt halogen floodlights are preferable: fluorescent lighting, while popular, is not a good workshop lighting system because it distorts colours and gives rise to a phenomenon called the stroboscopic effect, when a rotating part spinning very fast appears to be stationary. This is a serious safety hazard when you are using variable-speed machines, such as routers, drills and lathes. Place lights so they are either directly over the workbench or to one side. Never place lighting so it shines in your face or behind you, as this will cast shadows on your work.

VENTILATION

Cross-ventilation is ideal, so if possible locate your main work space between a door and a window. If your work is dusty or you are likely to use solvents or other vaporous chemicals, cross-ventilation with the air flow from your back is preferable. This, together

with an appropriate face mask, will provide reasonable protection from airborne substances. Consider fan-assisted ventilation if you are unable to get a good cross-flow of air. If you are in a cold climate where doors and windows are kept closed and the room is often heated, ensure that the air in the workshop moves around by using a fan-forced air-circulating system, preferably with an easy-to-clean filter.

Adhesives and paints can give off fumes, so cross-flow ventilation is very important as it helps to disperse fumes, and it also helps to set adhesives and paints. When you are working with timber, the air should be dry to prevent the timber warping or swelling.

LAYOUT

Primarily you will require a sturdy, flat work surface, such as a wooden bench or table, and sufficient space to assemble and manoeuvre your projects. If your work space will be shared with other activities, consider a folding workbench and lockable folding board for tool storage. In a small space, a wall-mounted bench or a bench with storage underneath will be more useful. If you are lucky enough to have a large, dedicated workshop, a free-standing workbench will give you the greatest flexibility.

You will probably need some kind of vice fitted to your workbench, so think about where you will place it and how much clearance you will need for the type of projects you will be working on.

If you have any fixed machinery, such as a table saw, drill press or lathe, try to arrange them so that movement between the various workstations with your projects is easy and relaxed. The floor surface should be given a lot of thought, especially if you will be standing for long periods, and it should be easy to sweep and keep clean. Cover or eliminate low spaces under cupboards and shelves, where dust and dropped items can hide and be difficult to recover.

Have your tools within easy reach of your work space, each with its own place to ensure that you can always find the equipment you need. The worst place to store tools is on the 'big shelf'—that is, the floor. Most hand tools lend themselves to being stored on a folding board. A low, open shelf under the workbench or nearby is fine for storing portable electrical tools such as a drill or circular saw. The upper limits of the tool storage area must be no higher than you can comfortably reach, and frequently used tools should be stored at bench height or above, to eliminate unnecessary bending.

The practical and convenient workshop layout shown at right was originally designed for a practitioner of fine woodwork. You may note the following points of interest:

- The folding board with all its tools, the small drawer unit and the various shelves are all close and convenient to the workbench.
- The bandsaw, the most often used of the set machines, is also nearby.
- The windows are well located, giving maximum natural light; which is supplemented by several small halogen floodlights (not shown).
- The set machines are positioned to avoid direct sunlight.
- The area between the bench and the roller door is adequate for assembling large items.

ELECTRICAL SUPPLY
Pendant general-purpose electrical outlets are convenient and safe. Hanging above the work area, they keep the cords of portable tools away from the workbench

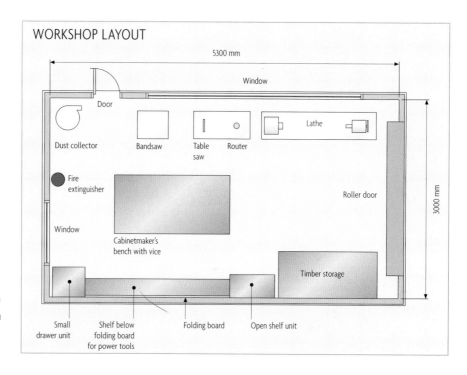

WORKSHOP LAYOUT

5300 mm

Window

Door

Dust collector   Bandsaw   Table saw   Router   Lathe

Fire extinguisher

Roller door

3000 mm

Window

Cabinetmaker's bench with vice

Timber storage

Small drawer unit   Shelf below folding board for power tools   Folding board   Open shelf unit

or floor, where they might accidentally be damaged or tripped over, as well as providing a greater working range for the tools. You may also need to install extra lighting, which should be placed over your work areas and aimed carefully so as to eliminate annoying shadows and dark spots.

Ask your electrician to provide sufficient circuit capacity for additional outlets that may become necessary later, and ask about special-purpose outlets or circuits that may be required if you intend to use machinery or welding equipment.

Ensure you have enough power outlets, that they are conveniently placed around the work area and are fitted with an earth leakage cut-off device for safety. Small power tools such as jigsaws and drills are rated up to 750W (1HP) and require 5-amp fuses, but large power tools such as band-saws, drill presses and radial arm saws usually require 13-amp fuses. Any electrical work should be done by a qualified electrician.

SAFETY
Keep your work area clean and tidy, not only so it will be a pleasant place to work, but for safety and health reasons. Always observe good working practices, such as wearing the correct safety gear and using tools for the purpose for which they were designed. Be alert and protect yourself, your family, friends and anyone else who may have reason to enter your workshop.

Eye protection must be worn whenever the job requires it, such as when using a router, grinder, power saw, lathe or any high-speed tool. Good ear muffs or ear plugs are essential when you are using noisy equipment: hearing damage often does not become apparent for some years after the damage is done. Disposable face masks provide sufficient protection from ordinary dust, although cartridge-type dust masks should be worn if you are working with toxic fumes or extremely fine dust. Pay attention to the manufacturer's directions when using the mask, and if your work requires the use

SAFETY EQUIPMENT

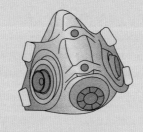

Safety goggles Eye protection is essential when using power tools.

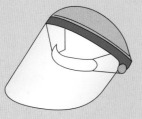

Safety mask A full-face mask may also be useful to protect against small flying particles.

Ear plugs or ear muffs Disposable ear plugs provide effective protection against hearing damage. Some may find ear muffs more comfortable and effective than ear plugs.

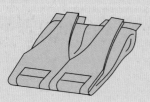

Overalls and hairnets Fitted clothing helps prevent loose fabric and hair being caught in machinery.

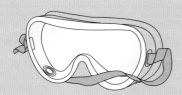

Cartridge face mask More efficient than a disposable mask and ideal for working with toxic products.

Gloves Provide some protection against accidental injury, but must not be worn near rotating machinery.

Work boots Solid shoes with non-slip soles.

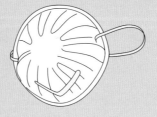

Dust mask Disposable dust masks effectively keep wood dust out of the nose and mouth.

of noxious substances, check the product label for necessary safety precautions.

Safe, comfortable footwear is a must, and protective clothing such as a pair of overalls is vital when the environment of your workplace becomes, or is likely to become, contaminated with dust or other substances. Fitted clothing and a hairnet will also help prevent loose items of clothing or hair becoming entangled in machinery.

Fixed machinery must have safety switches such as no-volt releases and emergency stop switches. No-volt releases automatically turn off the machine's on–off switch in the event of a power failure, ensuring that the machine does not start up again unexpectedly when power is restored. An emergency stop button is usually a large red knob that stops the machine when it is pressed. As an additional feature, many of these switches must be manually reset before the machine can be

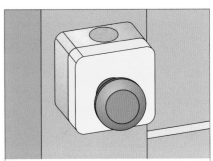

Press your knee against an emergency stop button to bring machinery to a quick stop.

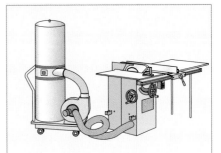

Place a small industrial dust collector with flexible hoses on a trolley and connect it to fixed machinery.

started again. Test these devices regularly to ensure that they will not let you down in an emergency.

If your work creates a lot of dust it would be wise to invest in a dust-collection system. All wood dusts are potentially dangerous, particularly dusts from MDF and particle boards. A simple solution for a small workshop can be a domestic vacuum cleaner, but if you make a lot of dust or you work in a large area, a piped system to each machine is ideal, or you can use a mobile collector that can be wheeled about the workshop to wherever it is needed.

Keep a fire extinguisher and first-aid kit on hand for emergencies.

WORKBENCH

While an old table may be strong enough for small projects, you will need a strong bench for most woodworking. The bench should be about 850 mm high, with the legs braced to prevent spreading. The top should be of thick timber able to withstand blows, especially near the front edge. A thinner timber can be used at the back or middle to form a well where tools can be safely placed.

A portable folding workbench may be an option if space is a problem. It can be folded away when not needed and carried to the worksite. The top is split in two halves which can be moved in and out to operate as a vice.

Accessories for the workbench include adjustable bench stops for planing against, bench hooks to aid with cross-cutting, a mitre box for cutting angles, a drawer for storing tools or hardware, and a woodwork vice. This differs from engineering vices as it holds the work beside the bench, not above it, and has timber jaws to protect the job. Trestles, ladders or steps are also useful.

STORAGE

Correct storage and care of tools will keep them in good condition. Tool racks or folding boards will protect them and help you keep track of them. A well-designed folding board is a great asset in any workshop. The board can be custom-built to suit your tool collection and the available space, and there is a wide variety of purpose-made hardware to mount the tools. Many tools come in a storage box when purchased. Even if this is cardboard, it will serve well for some time. If tools are not going to be used for a while, put them away, especially at the end of the day.

Keep hardware in its packaging until required—it is designed to protect the fittings and keep the parts together. Keep screws and nails in clearly labelled boxes.

BASIC TOOL KIT

There is an enormous range of tools available but you can build up your kit gradually, purchasing tools as the need arises. For best results, always buy recognized brands.

A few basic tools are all you need to get started:

- claw hammer (570 g)
- smoothing plane (no. 4)
- marking gauge
- combination square
- steel tape (3 m)
- three bevelled-edge firmer chisels (10 mm, 18 mm, 32 mm)
- cross-cut saw (650 mm long)
- tenon saw (300 mm long)
- nail punch (3 mm)
- set of twist drills
- set of screwdrivers (slotted, pozi, cross)
- oilstone
- cork sanding block
- variable-speed power drill
- jigsaw

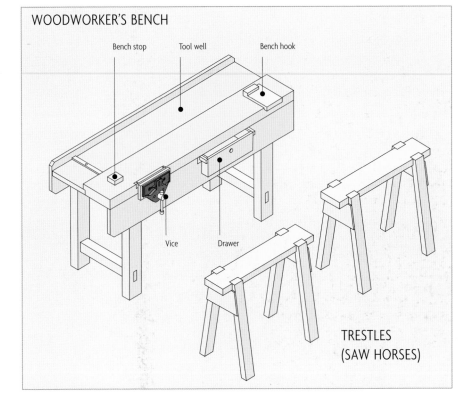

WOODWORKER'S BENCH

Bench stop

Tool well

Bench hook

Vice

Drawer

TRESTLES (SAW HORSES)

tools

tools

TOOLS FOR YOUR WORKSHOP

Using the right tools for the job will make your work easier and the time spent in your workshop more pleasant.

BUYING TOOLS

Build up your tool kit gradually, purchasing tools as you need them. Price is often a good guide to quality and it is worth paying a little more for a tool that will give a lifetime of service. The following lists are intended only as a guide, so adjust them to suit your needs.

BASIC WORKSHOP

- Workbench
- 100 mm engineers vice with removable wooden jaw pads
- 450–570 g claw hammer
- 300 mm combination square
- 8 m retractable steel tape measure
- Soft lead pencils
- Hacksaw
- 600 mm general-purpose handsaw
- 300 mm tenon saw
- 12.5 mm portable electric variable-speed drill
- Basic twist drill set (1–13 mm)
- Masonry bits (5, 6, 6.5, 8, 10, 12 mm)
- Countersink bit
- 150 mm pliers
- Retractable knife with replaceable blades
- Several screwdrivers (slotted-head, cross-head)
- Three 100 mm G-cramps
- 200 mm adjustable spanner
- Basic wood chisel set (3, 6, 12 mm)
- Mallet
- At least one plane (No. 5/jack plane)
- Spirit level
- Nail punches (several sizes)
- Pair of trestles
- Cork sanding block
- Spade drill-bit set (6–25 mm)
- Fine/medium oilstone

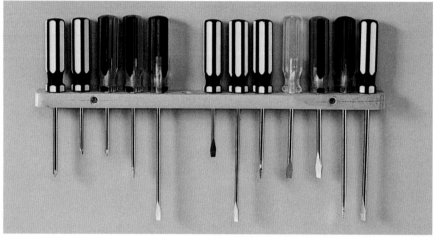

A collection of well-maintained hand tools is the basis of your workshop. Buy tools as you need them to ensure that they are exactly right for the job.

GENERAL WORKSHOP

To the basic list, add:
- 340 g ball-peen hammer
- No. 3 smoothing plane
- Low-angle block plane
- Hone and lubricant
- Marking gauge
- 300 mm steel rule
- Centre punch
- Coping saw
- 250 mm second cut file with handle
- Cold chisel
- Three 1000 mm sash cramps or cramp head sets
- Plug cutters (9, 12 mm)
- Portable electric jigsaw
- $1/3$ sheet orbital sander
- 10 mm battery-operated (cordless) drill

ADVANCED WORKSHOP

To the basic and general lists, add:
- Drawing board, A3 size

- T-square
- 60/30-degree set square
- 45-degree protractor
- 180-degree protractor
- Mechanical pencil, leads and eraser
- Sliding bevel gauge
- Mitre gauge
- 600 mm rule
- Mortise gauge
- Dovetail gauge
- Dovetail saw
- G-cramps, various sizes
- Cabinetmaker's scraper
- Wood chisels (8, 16, 20 mm)
- Complete set of twist drills
- Pincers
- Staple gun
- Pin hammer
- Long-nose pliers
- Complete screwdriver set
- Web cramps

CHISELS

A woodworker's chisel is a hand-guided cutting tool used to shape timber by paring away waste. It is also used to create joints and recesses to receive hardware. Chisels are manufactured from fine-grained tempered steel and are bevelled on one end to produce a cutting edge. They range in size from 3 to 50 mm.

CHISELS

Mortise chisel

Firmer chisel: square edge

Firmer chisel: bevelled edge

Paring chisel: bevelled edge

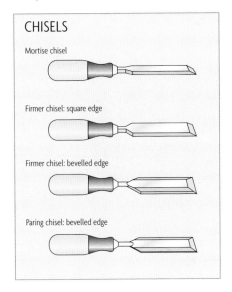

FIRMER CHISEL

This is a strong chisel used for general work and to remove large amounts of material. The blade is comparatively short and thick, and may be square or bevel-edged. A firmer chisel can be driven by hand or hit with a mallet. The bevelled-edge firmer chisel is the most useful chisel. It can be levered against to remove waste.

USING A FIRMER CHISEL

When chiselling, always keep the job secure in a vice or cramps, and never have your hands or any part of your body in front of the cutting edge. Ensure the chisel is sharp (see page 30 for the correct way to sharpen it).

1 To cut a groove or housing with a firmer chisel, put the job in a vice, hold the handle (bevel down) in one hand and strike it with a mallet, removing the bulk of the waste.

2 Turn the job around and repeat from the other side, gradually levelling the housing. Turn the chisel over (bevel up) and hold it between the thumb and fingers to guide the cut. Pare away the waste and smooth the bottom by moving the chisel from side to side using a slicing action.

PARING CHISEL

This chisel is used for light work and finishing, so accuracy is required. The blade is long and thin with the edges either square or, more commonly, bevelled. This chisel should only be driven by hand—one hand applying pressure to the handle while the other holds the blade and guides the cut.

MORTISE CHISEL

For extra-heavy work, this chisel is ideal. It has a square edge and a thicker blade than other chisels, and the blade tapers along its length. It is used for cutting mortises and levering out the waste. It may be driven by hand or struck by a mallet.

GOUGES

Gouges have a flat, medium or quick curved face and curved cutting blade.
- Firmer or out-cannel gouges are ground on the convex (outside) face and used for detailed carving and hollowing out shapes and designs.
- Scribing, paring or in-cannel gouges are ground on the concave (inside) face and used for cutting around curved shapes such as mouldings.

CHISELLING TIPS

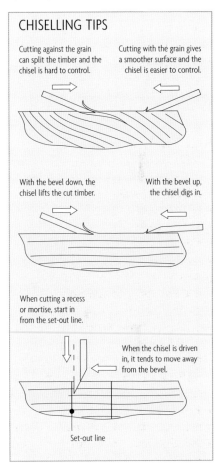

Cutting against the grain can split the timber and the chisel is hard to control.

Cutting with the grain gives a smoother surface and the chisel is easier to control.

With the bevel down, the chisel lifts the cut timber.

With the bevel up, the chisel digs in.

When cutting a recess or mortise, start in from the set-out line.

When the chisel is driven in, it tends to move away from the bevel.

Set-out line

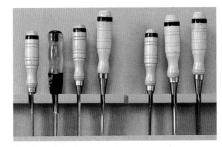

Storing chisels correctly ensures they stay sharp.

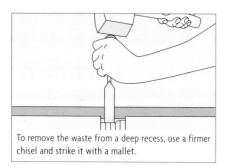

To remove the waste from a deep recess, use a firmer chisel and strike it with a mallet.

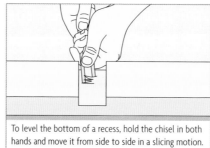

To level the bottom of a recess, hold the chisel in both hands and move it from side to side in a slicing motion.

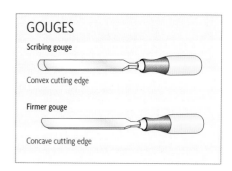

DRILLING TOOLS

Most carpenters use power drills, but there are hand-operated types that may be used if power is not available. All drills are used in conjunction with interchangeable drill bits.

BRADAWL

A bradawl is used to make a hole to help start the thread of a screw. Place the flat edge across the grain in the desired position and force it into the timber with a back-and-forth twisting motion to cut the fibres.

HAND DRILL

The hand drill is used with twist bits up to 8 mm in diameter. It drills either timber or light metal (use a centre punch with metal). There is a larger hand drill called a breast drill.

To drill a hole, hold the top handle with one hand and apply pressure straight down. If you tilt the tool as you drill, the bit may break.

When drilling hardwood, the bit may clog up with shavings. To clear the hole and bit, move the drill in and out a few times.

BIT AND BRACE

This drill, with its larger cranking action, provides greater leverage for drilling through timber. It is available with or without ratchets, which allow you to drill in confined spaces as the brace can rotate in either direction by moving the collar on the crank which engages the ratchet wheel.

The chuck jaws are generally slotted to hold both parallel and tapered shank bits. When inserting a bit, turn the outer case of the chuck until the bit will fit between the jaws. Place the bit well down in the centre of the chuck. Tighten it with the bit held central and firm.

To use the bit and brace, centre the bit and apply pressure to the head of the brace. Rotate the crank clockwise. Check the bit is at 90 degrees to the surface. Drill the hole until the point of the bit just comes out the other side. Continue rotating the crank in the same direction without any pressure and pull back. This will remove the waste from the hole. Now drill in the same way from the other side, using the small hole made by the pointed centre as the guide. Prevent splitting by clamping a piece of scrap timber at the back and boring through both.

DRILLING AT AN ANGLE

To help maintain the correct angle and ensure the bit starts in the right place, clamp a guide block (made from a piece of timber with the correct hole in position) to the work. A depth stop may also be used to ensure the hole is the correct depth.

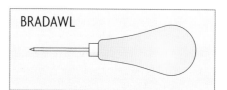

GOUGES

Scribing gouge

Convex cutting edge

Firmer gouge

Concave cutting edge

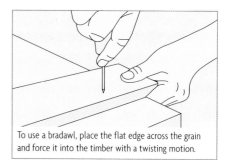

BRADAWL

To use a bradawl, place the flat edge across the grain and force it into the timber with a twisting motion.

MAINTENANCE

Keep tool mechanisms free from grit and dust. Dust in the gears or bearing will make them stiff to operate. A little lubricant may be needed.

DRILL BITS

- Auger or centre bits are used mostly in the brace. They are used for boring deep holes with and across the grain. The sharp point of the bit has a screw thread that guides it and helps pull it through the work. Augers

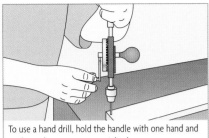

To use a hand drill, hold the handle with one hand and apply moderate pressure straight down.

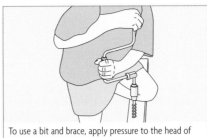

To use a bit and brace, apply pressure to the head of the brace and rotate the crank clockwise.

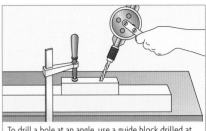

To drill a hole at an angle, use a guide block drilled at the correct angle. Clamp it to your work piece.

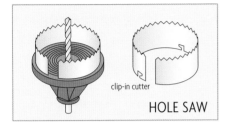

clip-in cutter

HOLE SAW

can be single or double twist, with or without side cutters (spurs). The spur cuts the fibres off around the outside edge of the hole and provides a clean finish, especially important in cabinet work and when drilling softwoods. The twisted shank carries the waste timber out of the hole. The tapered end on the shank provides a firm grip for the chuck. Flat augers are often referred to as speed

bores or spade bits. They are used for fast cutting and leave a rough-edged hole. They must be used in a power drill.

- Expansive bits are used in a brace for cutting large or odd-sized holes. They have the same cutting action as augers, but can be adjusted in and out to bore any size hole from 12 to 75 mm. Large holes can also be cut with a cylinder-shaped bit called a hole saw, which is attached to a power drill.
- Twist bits are mainly used for metal, but they also work well in timber. They are used in hand drills or power drills. The straight shank must be held firmly in the chuck, or it may slip and break.
- Countersink bits are used to recess the head of a screw into timber. There are two

main types. The rose bit is used in hardwood and the snail bit in softwood. These bits are used by hand or in a brace. Special bits can also be used in power drills for metal and timber. Only light pressure is required to countersink the hole.

- Tungsten-carbide bits are very hard-wearing and are used for drilling masonry. Avoid overheating the tip, as the carbide will separate from the mild steel shaft. These bits can be resharpened only with a special grinding wheel.
- Drill and countersink combination bits drill a pilot hole, shank clearance hole and countersink in one process. Some are restricted in depth but others are adjustable. A separate bit is required for each gauge screw.

HAND DRILLS

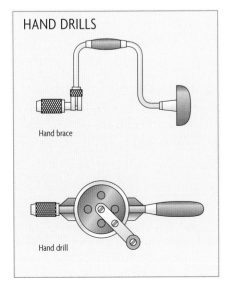

Hand brace

Hand drill

DRILL BITS

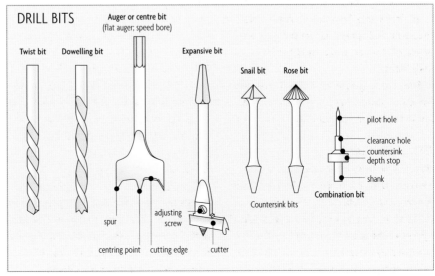

Auger or centre bit
(flat auger; speed bore)

Twist bit   Dowelling bit   Expansive bit   Snail bit   Rose bit

pilot hole
clearance hole
countersink
depth stop
shank

Combination bit

Countersink bits

spur
adjusting screw
centring point   cutting edge   cutter

FILES AND RASPS

Files are used to shape and finish materials such as metal, timber and plastics.

TYPES
Files and rasps come in a range of different shapes: flat, half-round, round, square, triangular and needle for extra-small, fiddly jobs. Surform files have detachable blades.

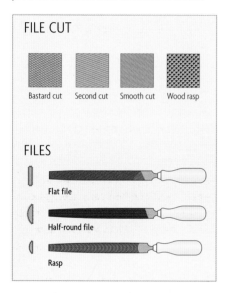

FILE CUT

Bastard cut   Second cut   Smooth cut   Wood rasp

FILES

Flat file

Half-round file

Rasp

The teeth can be single- or double-cut. Single-cut files have teeth in one direction only; double-cut files have two rows of teeth crossing. Some have single on one side and double on the other. Files are classified by the number of teeth per 25 mm.

Rasps have much coarser teeth and are used predominantly for rough cutting or shaping timber. To shape a job, start with a coarse file known as a 'bastard', then use a medium-grade or second-cut and finish with a smoothing file.

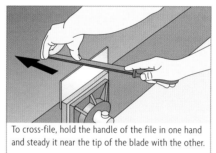

To cross-file, hold the handle of the file in one hand and steady it near the tip of the blade with the other.

USING A FILE OR RASP
1 To cross-file, keep the file flat on the surface. Applying slight downward pressure, push the file forward with slow, even strokes the full length of the job. Don't apply pressure on the return, as this will result in excessive wear on the teeth.

2 To draw-file, hold the file at 90 degrees to the surface and move the file back and forth along the surface. This produces a smoother finish.

To draw-file, stand at the end of the job. Holding the file at 90 degrees, move it back and forth.

GAUGES

The marking gauge is used to mark lines parallel to an edge or face into the surface of timber. Use it only where the timber is to be cut, never on a finished surface.

MARKING GAUGE
The marking gauge has two main parts—the stem, which has a steel pin or spur near one end, and the stock, which slides along the stem and is secured with a thumbscrew.

To set a marking gauge, loosen the screw a little, slide the stock along the stem the required distance from the pin and partly tighten. The distance is best measured with a rule. The setting can be adjusted by tapping either end of the stem on the bench. Tighten the thumbscrew and recheck the measurement.

Hold the gauge firmly, with the stem resting on the surface of the timber and the stock against the edge. Rotate it towards you until the pin touches the timber. Press lightly on the gauge and slowly push it forward so the pin marks the surface.

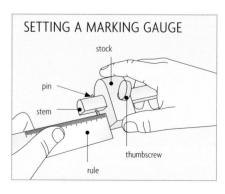

SETTING A MARKING GAUGE

stock

pin

stem

thumbscrew

rule

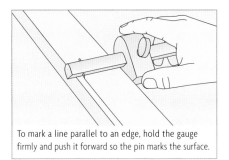

To mark a line parallel to an edge, hold the gauge firmly and push it forward so the pin marks the surface.

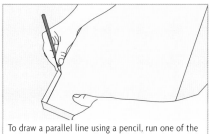

To draw a parallel line using a pencil, run one of the fingers of your hand along the edge of the timber.

MORTISE GAUGE

The mortise gauge is similar to a marking gauge but has two pins for marking mortises and tenons.

PENCIL GAUGE

A line can be drawn parallel to an edge using a pencil gauge, which does not score the surface. Either run one of the fingers of the hand in which the pencil is held along the edge of the timber, thus maintaining the distance required, or use a pencil and rule or combination square.

HAMMERS, PUNCHES AND NAILS

Two hammers form an essential part of any woodworker's tool kit: the claw hammer and cross-pein hammer. Both are used to drive in nails.

HAMMERS

The size of a hammer is determined by its head weight. The hardened face is slightly convex (rounded) so it is easier to strike a nail and prevent the hammer marking the work badly.

- Claw hammers have claws at the back of the head. They can be pushed firmly under the head of bent or unwanted nails to lever them out. The two common size ranges are 450–570 g (16–20 oz) for site fixing or bench work, and 620–680 g (22–24 oz) for construction and building work.
- The cross-pein or Warrington hammer is used for light joinery work, to start small nails or panel pins. It is useful for nailing into corners. A smaller type is used for very small pins and tacks. These hammers range in size from 100–400 g (3.5–14 oz).

MALLETS

The wooden mallet is used to drive chisels and to assemble joinery work where a metal hammer would damage the surface of the job. A rubber-head mallet may be used to knock joinery together but not to strike chisels or other tools. Take care using mallets as they may bounce back and cause injury.

USING A HAMMER

1 Keeping a straight wrist, hold the hammer near the end of the handle. With your other hand, hold the nail steady and rest the head of the hammer squarely on the nail head. The handle should be horizontal when the nail is vertical.

2 Tap the nail lightly to get proper aim and to start the point of the nail. Using wrist,

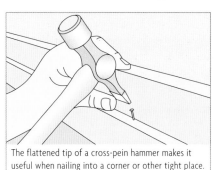

The flattened tip of a cross-pein hammer makes it useful when nailing into a corner or other tight place.

elbow and shoulder action, continue to hit the nail squarely on the head. Sharp, glancing blows may bend the nail. Moderate force will drive the average nail into most timber with three to four blows. Use a nail punch to drive the nail home.

Never use the side of the hammer for striking nails. Keep the face of the hammer clean and bright so the head won't slip off the nail and damage your job or your fingers.

PURCHASING A HAMMER

Choose a hammer to suit most of the jobs you do. It should not be so heavy that you

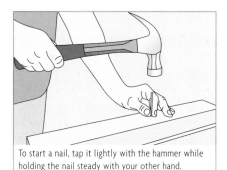

To start a nail, tap it lightly with the hammer while holding the nail steady with your other hand.

TYPES OF HAMMERS

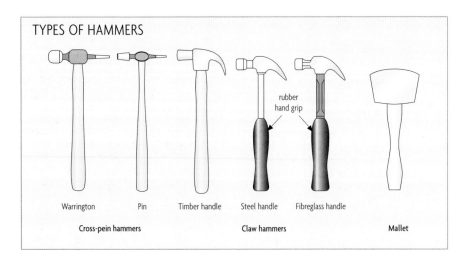

Warrington   Pin   Timber handle   Steel handle   Fibreglass handle   Mallet

rubber hand grip

Cross-pein hammers   Claw hammers

COMMON NAILS

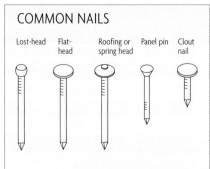

Lost-head   Flat-head   Roofing or spring head   Panel pin   Clout nail

PINCERS

NAIL PUNCH

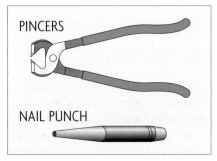

need muscles of steel to use it, or so light that you have to hit nails too often to drive them in.

On a claw hammer, look for claws that have a sharp vee for a tight fit around the nail. Ensure the head is firmly attached to the handle. Check the balance. If the hammer feels comfortable and you can swing it easily, then it is probably right for you.

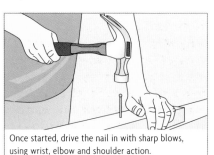

Once started, drive the nail in with sharp blows, using wrist, elbow and shoulder action.

NAIL PUNCHES

A nail punch is a tapered, hardened piece of steel used to set the nail below the surface of the timber.

When new, the tip is concave (cupped) to fit the nail head and prevent it sliding off. There are different tip sizes for different nails.

To use the punch, first hammer the nail to within 2–3 mm of the surface. Grip the punch with thumb and forefinger. Rest the tip on the nail with the index finger pressing against the side of the punch, ensuring the punch is directly in line with the axis of the nail. Use the hammer to strike the head of the punch to drive the nail 2–3 mm below the surface.

EXTRACTING NAILS

The position and size of the nail will determine the extraction process. Long nails may be pulled from the work with the aid of

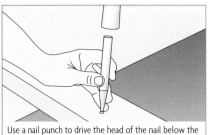

Use a nail punch to drive the head of the nail below the surface. Steady the punch on the head with one finger.

Use the claws on the hammer to extract a nail, placing scrap timber under the head to increase leverage.

A nail can also be extracted using pincers, but again use scrap timber for leverage.

a crowbar (also known as a wrecking bar or case-opening bar).

When using a claw hammer, ensure the claws are pushed firmly under the head of the nail. Pull the handle until it is nearly vertical. Unnecessary force may break the handle. To increase the leverage and relieve the strain, place a piece of timber under the head and continue. This will also prevent damage to the surface of the job.

Pincers may be used to draw out small nails. Place the jaws around the head of the nail and lever it out. A piece of timber will increase leverage and prevent bruising the job.

workshop basics

NAILS

HEAD TYPE	PURPOSE
Lost-head	For general-purpose use in construction or cabinetmaking.
Flat-head	For joining thin materials to timber and softwood frames. The width of the head gives greater holding power. 12–150 mm long.
Roofing nail	Galvanized nail for corrugated roofing. It has a spring washer under the head and may also have a neoprene washer under this. Older types have lead washers. 75–150 mm long.
Clout nail	Galvanized nail, a shorter variety of the flat-head. It has a much larger circular head and is used for fixing thin sheet material. 12–50 mm long.
Panel pin	Small, slender nails with a conical shaped head for finer work. They leave a very small hole when punched. 10–50 mm long. A smaller variety, called a 'brad nail', is also available.

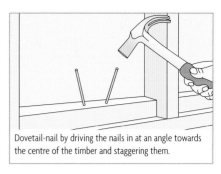

Dovetail-nail by driving the nails in at an angle towards the centre of the timber and staggering them.

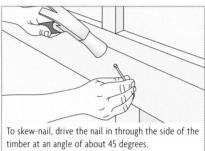

To skew-nail, drive the nail in through the side of the timber at an angle of about 45 degrees.

NAILS

Nailing is the quickest and most economical method of fastening timber together. Today, most nails are made from wire, usually mild steel, although other metals are used for specific situations (for example, copper nails for boat-building). Most nails are left bright, but they may be hot-dip galvanized, nickel, zinc or cadmium-plated for use in areas of high moisture. Galvanized nails are for exterior use.

Nails come in a wide variety of head shapes for particular purposes (see table above). Other types of nails include staples, escutcheon pins, cut tacks and corrugated fasteners.

The point of a nail is pyramid-shaped to force the fibres apart. This may split the timber sometimes. Blast types may be used for fibrous cement sheet—they punch a hole through it.

The thickness or wire gauge of a nail is stated in millimetres. The shank may be square or round. For greater holding in softwood, end grain or chipboard, use an annular, helical or twisted shank nail.

When ordering nails, state the length and gauge in millimetres, head type, material the nail is made from and the quantity in grams or kilograms. A typical nail order would be 2 kg of 100 mm x 3.75 mm galvanized mild steel lost-head nails.

The length of a nail is important to gain the maximum hold in the timber. When nailing across the fibres, the nail should be 2–2.5 times the thickness of the timber, and when nailing into end grain it should be 2.5–3 times the thickness.

NAILING METHODS

Face-nailing and skew-nailing are the two most common methods of nailing timber together.

Face-nailing

Face-nailing means nailing through the face of the timber. Do not nail too close to the edge or use nails that are too heavy, as this may split the timber and reduce holding power. Nails rely on friction for their holding power—the greater the friction, the greater the hold.

For greater strength you can 'dovetail' the nails. Drive the nails in at an angle towards the centre of the timber, staggering them to minimize the risk of the timber splitting.

When nailing close to an edge or end, use a thinner gauge nail. To reduce splitting near an end, turn the nail upside down, place it in the correct position and give it a tap. This will flatten the point of the nail and form a cup to receive the nail in the surface of the job. Turn the nail over and drive it in the normal way around. In timbers such as hardwood it is a good idea to drill a pilot hole first. To create it, drill a hole slightly smaller than the nail through the face of the top piece and just into the top of the bottom piece. Then hammer in the nail.

Skew-nailing

Skew-nailing is used when you need to nail through the edge of a timber, when otherwise you would need a very long nail. Drive the nail in through the side of the timber at an angle of about 45 degrees. Stagger the nails and drive them in from both sides of the timber. This method of nailing is used extensively in construction work.

LEVELS

The traditional spirit level is used to test work for level (horizontal) or plumb (vertical). The stock or body of older levels is made from timber, but newer ones are aluminium.

PARTS OF A LEVEL

The body of the spirit level has one or more vials used to see if surfaces are level. The vial is a glass or plastic tube filled with fluid and a vapour bubble. Two graduation lines on the vial are spaced to suit the length of the bubble. When the spirit level is level, the bubble rests exactly between these lines.

USING THE LEVEL

The surface to be levelled should be straight so the level will not rock. Place the level in the centre of the job and adjust one end of the work so the bubble is between the lines. The bubble rises to the high end.

When you think the work is level, turn the level around end to end. Place the level back on the work in the same position. Check the bubble again. If the level is accurate, the reading will be the same.

If not, the level may require adjusting.

For levelling over larger areas, place a straight edge (a piece of timber with both edges perfectly straight and parallel) along the work. Use the level in the centre of the straight edge.

Over large distances, a string line and line level may be used. A more accurate method is the water level. This is a clear plastic tube filled with water that is often used for levelling around corners.

TESTING FOR PLUMB

To test work for plumb, the spirit level has vials at the ends. Place the spirit level in the centre of the work and check the bubble as before.

Another method for testing for plumb is with the plumb bob. A plumb bob is a shaped metal weight attached to a string.

When it is suspended from the job, the weight holds the string vertical.

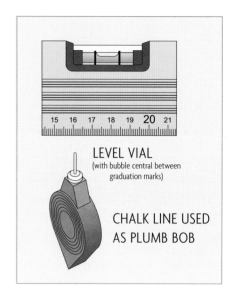

LEVEL VIAL
(with bubble central between graduation marks)

CHALK LINE USED AS PLUMB BOB

PLANES

The plane is used to produce a smooth surface on timber before it is sanded. Depending on the type of plane used, the finished surface may be flat, curved or moulded. Most planes are similar in use, although they may differ in appearance.

TYPES OF PLANES

The main types of planes with adjustable iron are the smoothing plane (the most common), the jointer plane (the longest) and the block plane (the smallest). Other planes have specialized uses. Each plane has a sole, a handle and a cutter.

- Smoothing planes are often referred to by a number. The larger the number, the larger the plane. Half numbers indicate

the width of the blade. For example, planes labelled 4 and 4.5 are the same size, but the latter has a wider blade. A long smoothing plane is called a jack plane. If sharpened correctly, a smoothing plane will produce a flat, even surface ready for final sanding.

- Jointer planes are ideal for large surfaces. They are used for planing the edge off long boards to be joined or for large

surfaces such as table tops, which must be perfectly flat.

- Block planes used with one hand and the cutter set at a lower angle are very handy for small, fiddly jobs.
- Rebate planes are used to produce or clean up rebates.
- Moulding combination or multi-planes have cutters that are interchangeable to match a variety of timber mouldings.

BENCH PLANES

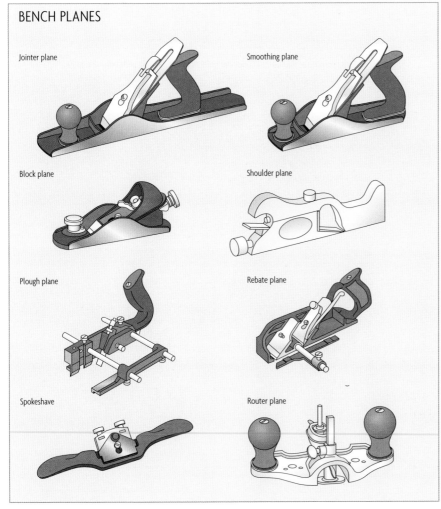

Jointer plane

Smoothing plane

Block plane

Shoulder plane

Plough plane

Rebate plane

Spokeshave

Router plane

- Router planes (sometimes referred to as 'Granny's tooth') are used for levelling the bottom of grooves, housings or trenches to a set depth.
- Spokeshaves may have either a flat or round face and are used to smooth concave or convex shapes.
- Shoulder planes are used for cleaning up rail shoulders that have not been cut true.
- Compass planes have an adjustable base plate for use with convex or concave shapes.
- Plough planes are similar to multi-planes, and are used only for small grooves or rebates in timber.

USING A PLANE

1 To plane the surface of timber, secure the timber on the bench. For wide timber, use a bench stop or a block that is slightly thinner than your job, nailed to the bench. For narrower timber, use a vice. Set the plane to take off a fine shaving and place it flat on the surface with the cutter off the end of the timber.

To start planing, stand with your weight on your back leg and exert pressure on the knob of the plane.

Push the plane forward, transferring pressure to the back of the plane and your weight to your front leg.

PLANING IN PRACTICE

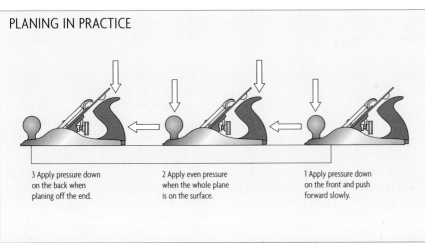

3 Apply pressure down on the back when planing off the end.

2 Apply even pressure when the whole plane is on the surface.

1 Apply pressure down on the front and push forward slowly.

SHARPENING PLANES AND CHISELS

Cutters become worn and chipped and require grinding and honing to restore them to good condition. A plane blade needs to be ground at an angle of 20–25 degrees and honed a further 5 degrees. For chisel blades the grinding angle is 25–30 degrees with honing a further 5 degrees.

GRINDING

If using a bench grinder, set the adjustable rest to the required angle. Hold the cutter, with the bevelled edge down, between the index fingers and thumbs of both hands. Position the cutter on the rest and move it from side to side across the full width of the cutting edge. Do not grind too quickly or leave the cutter in one position too long, as this will burn the metal. Cool the cutter frequently in water. Keep fingers well away from the grinding wheel, and wear safety glasses at all times.

HONING

To obtain a fine cutting edge, hone the cutter on a sharpening stone (oilstone). They come in coarse, medium or fine grade, or a combination. Choose a stone that is coarse on one side and fine on the other. Slipstones, with a rounded edge for inside curves, are also available.

Sharpening stones need to be lubricated with oil during use to prevent them clogging. Use neat's-foot oil, a light machine oil or a 50/50 mixture with some kerosene, but don't use linseed oil, as it clogs the stone.

Apply sufficient oil to the side of the stone you are using so it remains wet. Place the ground edge flat on the stone. Raise it slightly (about 5 degrees—honing guides are available to give the correct angle) and, applying an even pressure, move the cutter back and forth along the stone, ensuring the edge stays flat.

Lift the blade and check that a fine burr has appeared on the back edge: the blade is now sharp. This burr will need to be removed to produce a fine cutting edge. Lay the blade flat on the stone with the ground side up and move it up and down. The burr may also be removed by slicing the cutter through a piece of scrap timber, although you will still need to rub the back of the blade on the stone.

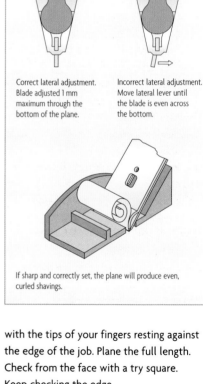

ADJUSTING A SMOOTHING PLANE

1–3 mm

Correctly set back iron

shavings wedged between are choking the plane

Poorly fitting back iron

1 mm

blade uneven

Correct lateral adjustment. Blade adjusted 1 mm maximum through the bottom of the plane.

Incorrect lateral adjustment. Move lateral lever until the blade is even across the bottom.

If sharp and correctly set, the plane will produce even, curled shavings.

2 Press down on the front of the plane and push forward slowly, taking a fine shaving from the end of the timber. As the plane passes over the timber, apply an even pressure to shave the entire length of the timber. When nearing the end, release the pressure on the front but maintain it on the back to plane the full length.

3 Place a straight edge across and along the timber to show up high spots. The edge of the plane may be used as a

straight edge. Plane down the high spots, continually checking until a flat, even surface is obtained. Apply a face mark for identification.

-- To plane the edge requires more care. Keep the plane straight and square to the face. Sight along the edge of the timber and select the hollowed edge (it will straighten more easily than the rounded one). Use the longest plane possible. To guide the plane, place your thumb on top of the plane at the front

with the tips of your fingers resting against the edge of the job. Plane the full length. Check from the face with a try square. Keep checking the edge.

5 To straighten end grain, hold the plane as before with a finger at the front to guide the plane, and work in from both ends towards the centre. (Otherwise the grain will split when you are planing off the end.) The plane must be sharp and set to take off a fine shaving.

PORTABLE POWER TOOLS

Power-driven tools make work easier for the woodworker, as they will do the job in less than half the time of hand-operated tools. An increasing selection of battery-powered tools, complete with a plug-in charger, is available, and most will operate on standard domestic power.

SAFETY

Portable power tools are dangerous. Use them with extreme care. Read the instruction manual supplied with the tool, and follow these safety guidelines whenever you use them:

- Always follow the manufacturer's handbook regarding safety and correct operation.
- Never use faulty tools.
- Never use tools with faulty or frayed leads.
- Never lift tools by the lead or disconnect by pulling the lead.
- Keep leads away from cutters.
- Keep cutters sharp.
- Disconnect the power supply before adjusting the tool.
- Allow tools to reach full speed before working with them.
- Never use tools in wet conditions.
- Avoid dropping tools.
- Never use tools for any purpose they were not designed for.
- Wear appropriate safety clothing and equipment.

POWER DRILL

The most used power tool in the workshop is the power drill. All drills are much the same, regardless of size and make. They have a motor, a trigger switch and a chuck to hold the bit. Jaws within the chuck hold the drill bit in place and prevent it slipping when locked. The jaws are locked with the aid of a chuck key, turned clockwise to lock and anti-clockwise to unlock.

Most drills have a pistol-style hand grip with a trigger switch that can be locked. Some are supplied with a second adjustable hand grip directly behind the chuck.

The body houses the motor and at the front is the gearbox, which regulates the speed and functions such as hammer action.

Purchasing a drill

When buying a drill, choose one that suits your needs. Battery drills are handy but not as powerful as power drills. A drill will be more useful if it has more than one speed—a low speed for metal or masonry and a higher speed for timber. Variable speed control lets you select the speed for any job, especially when using screwdriver bits. Some also have torque setting, so more or less pressure is placed on the screw head.

The chuck size refers to the size of the drill bit shank that will fit in the drill. Generally, the more powerful the drill, the bigger the chuck (a 500-watt motor could have a 10 mm chuck, a 700-watt motor a 13 mm chuck). Either of these would suit the average woodworker.

Impact drills or hammer drills are best for masonry. Unlike normal rotary drills, where the bit remains locked in the chuck and rotates, the bit in these drills vibrates in and out while rotating. The effectiveness of this action relies on the force you apply to the drill. This action may be disengaged to drill normally.

Some drills, especially battery-powered drills, have a reverse rotation for removing screws. Drills may have many accessories that can convert them to other uses, such as disc sanders, buffers, grinding wheels and even jigsaws.

A vertical drill stand drills holes straight and to a required depth.

Operating a drill

Select the appropriate bit for the job (see Drill bits on pages 22–23). Never use auger bits with a lead screw as this will jam and/or overload the motor. Instead, select spade bits that can be used on high speed. Always use tungsten-carbide bits for masonry.

When placing a drill bit in the chuck, ensure it is in the centre and turn the chuck key clockwise until the jaws have tightened on the drill shank. Remove the chuck key. Some drills have keyless chucks.

Select the correct speed for the bit and job. Smaller bits require a higher speed than a bigger bit. The harder the material, the slower the speed.

When drilling holes over 8 mm in diameter, use a drill with a side handle for greater control and to help prevent injury should the bit jam.

POWER DRILL HINTS

- Using a punch to create a starting point will prevent twist drill bits wandering.
- Keeping the drill running until it is removed from the hole will help clean out any waste. Move the drill back and forth while drilling masonry or hardwood to help clear the hole and drill bit.
- When drilling ceramic tiles, place masking tape over the area to be drilled to prevent the drill wandering. Never use the impact or hammer action on tiles, or they will crack.

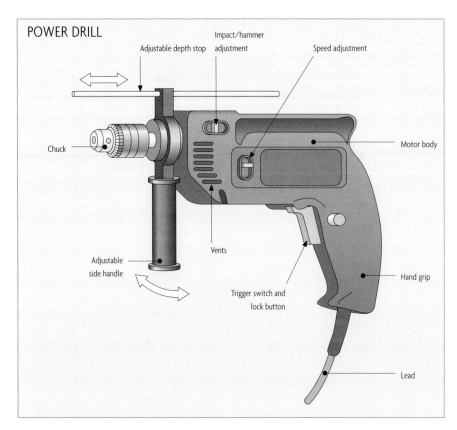

POWER DRILL

Adjustable depth stop

Impact/hammer adjustment

Speed adjustment

Motor body

Chuck

Adjustable side handle

Vents

Trigger switch and lock button

Hand grip

Lead

Preparing to cut

Measure and mark the cutting line on your job. Fit the appropriate blade for the material you will be cutting. Set the depth to 5 mm more than the thickness of the material. For cross-cutting, position the job on trestles or other stable support with the waste side on your right, overhanging one end. This allows the weight of the saw to rest on the material. The job must be held firm and this can be achieved by any of the following three methods:

- Hold the saw in your right hand and place your left knee on the job.
- Clamp the material to trestles.
- Nail blocks of timber to the trestles on either side of the job to make a channel for it to sit in.

If the job is small, nailing it down while cutting will probably provide the greatest stability and safety.

For cutting along the grain, use the last two methods only—the timber will normally be too long and narrow for the first method.

When using your saw:

- Never wear loose clothing that may get caught in the saw.
- Remove all nails, bolts and grit from second-hand timber.
- Ensure the guard works properly.
- Never use a saw on which the blade has been damaged.
- Use the correct sharp blade for the work at hand.

Cutting procedure

Stand slightly to the left of the job to avoid kickback. Secure the work (see above). If ripping material, use the rip fence supplied or clamp a straight edge to the job to guide the saw. Place the saw baseplate flat on the surface of the material and line up the notch at the front of the plate with the cutting line so the blade doesn't touch the material.

Remember to secure your work in a vice or cramp, and maintain a firm grip while you are drilling. Keep the drill at the required angle. Changing the angle while drilling may break the bit or make an irregular hole.

If drilling all the way through a piece of timber, clamp a block of scrap timber to the back of the job. This will help prevent the back splitting when the drill breaks through the other side.

CIRCULAR SAW

Circular saws are used to make straight cuts through timber, metal or masonry. They come in a range of sizes from 150–250 mm (the diameter of the blade governs the depth of the cut).

When purchasing a circular saw, think about the type of material you are likely to

be cutting, and select a saw that is able to cut through the material in one operation.

Saws generally come supplied with a combination blade for ripping or cross-cutting, although special ripping or cross-cutting blades are also available. A blade with tungsten-carbide tips will provide a cleaner cut and last longer between sharpens. Also available are metal and masonry-cutting discs.

The saw is fixed to a baseplate which can be raised or lowered to change the depth of cut. It is held by a locking lever or nut. The baseplate may also be tilted up to 45 degrees to the side for angle (bevel) cutting; some can go up to 55 degrees. On top of the baseplate is a fixed guard that covers the saw blade; beneath is a retracting guard that must operate freely at all times as the saw moves through the work.

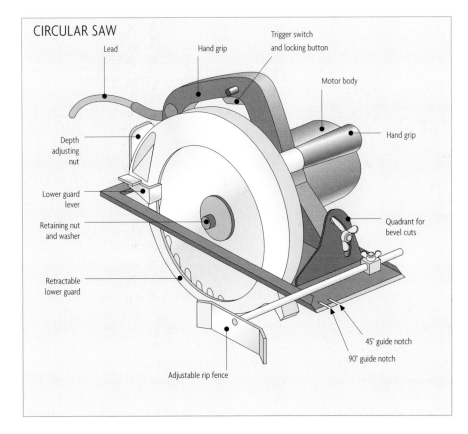

CIRCULAR SAW

Lead

Hand grip

Trigger switch and locking button

Motor body

Hand grip

Depth adjusting nut

Lower guard lever

Retaining nut and washer

Quadrant for bevel cuts

Retractable lower guard

45° guide notch

90° guide notch

Adjustable rip fence

When cross-cutting with a circular saw, use your knee to hold the work. Line up the notch with the line.

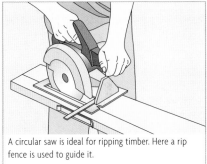

A circular saw is ideal for ripping timber. Here a rip fence is used to guide it.

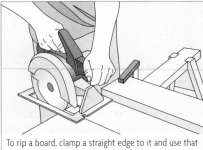

To rip a board, clamp a straight edge to it and use that as a guide for the circular saw.

Start the saw and allow it to gain maximum speed before steadily pushing it forward along the cutting line. Keep the baseplate flat on the job until you have completed the cut and the waste has dropped. Turn the saw off and allow it to stop rotating. Check that the bottom guard has returned before placing the saw on the ground or bench.

Changing the blade
Always unplug the saw before changing the blade. The saw blade is held in place by a retaining nut. To prevent the blade moving while you undo the nut, engage the locking device (if fitted) or place the saw on a piece of soft timber and push the blade into it until the teeth are embedded. Undo the retaining nut in the direction of the saw rotation and remove the old blade. Clean the washers and flanges, and replace the blade in the reverse manner.

Maintaining the blade
Blades that are sharp are most efficient so keep them free of dust and timber resin. Sharpening blades, however, is probably best left to a professional, especially blades with tungsten-carbide tips, as they require special grinding. Talk to your local tool supplier to find a saw doctor.

SANDERS
Power sanders can be used to shape and remove timber, although to achieve a fine finish the work must be completed by hand sanding.

Disc and belt sanders remove large amounts of timber quickly. With practice, you can use them to produce a large flat surface or curved work. A flexible disc attachment may be used with a power drill.

The most useful power sander is the finishing sander. The orbital or reciprocating action will produce a fine, flat surface that will need little hand finishing. It uses the same abrasive paper used with a sanding block, either half or quarter sheets.

The sanding paper is stretched across the base and held by spring-loaded clips. Take care when selecting the abrasive paper, as coarse grades may damage the surface.

FINISHING SANDERS

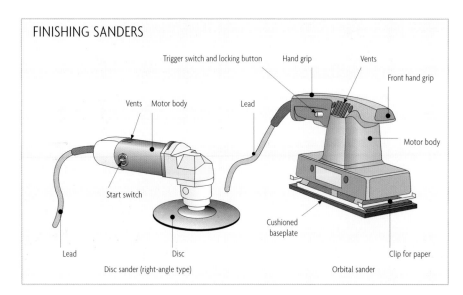

Vents
Motor body
Trigger switch and locking button
Hand grip
Vents
Front hand grip
Lead
Motor body
Start switch
Cushioned baseplate
Lead
Disc
Clip for paper
Disc sander (right-angle type)
Orbital sander

When using an orbital sander, use long, overlapping strokes forward and back, always along the grain.

Operating the sander

Start the sander before placing it on the job. This will prevent jumping, which could damage the surface. Some sanders have an on–off locking button so you don't have to hold the trigger on manually while you work. Hold the sander with both hands, one on the trigger handle and the other on the front handle. Place the sander flat on the surface and, with light pressure, guide it slowly backwards and forwards over the work. Too much pressure will wear out the abrasive paper. Keep the sander moving evenly. Do not sand too much in one place, as this may create a depression.

Clean the sander regularly with a soft paintbrush or an air compressor, if you have access to one.

JIGSAWS

Jigsaws are used to cut curved work. By changing the blade, it is possible to cut a wide variety of material. Jigsaws come in many styles and sizes, some with dual or variable speeds. The smaller, light-duty saws are used for thin material such as plywood. Heavy-duty types can cut most material, from thin board or metal to thicker timber.

Most jigsaws have an adjustable baseplate for bevel cutting and come supplied with a ripping fence. The cutting action may vary from reciprocating (straight up and down) to oscillating (oval). The oscillating action is used to cut steel and other hard materials.

Operating the jigsaw

Secure the work, as vibration is a problem, especially on thin sheet material. Select the appropriate blade and fit it. Blades are relatively inexpensive to replace, so throw out blunt blades. If you have a dual-speed model, select the appropriate speed.

Mark the cutting line and place the baseplate on the surface in line with it. With the blade just off the material, start the saw. With the motor at the correct speed, slowly push the saw with a firm forward motion. Never force the blade, as it may wander or break. Keep a moderate downward pressure on the saw to stop it lifting from the surface.

On internal work, such as cutting a circular hole, draw the shape on the surface. Make a starting point by drilling a hole the size of the blade on the waste side of the line. Insert the blade in the hole and work towards the cutting line, gently turning the

JIGSAW

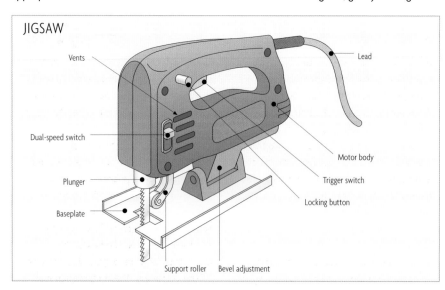

Vents
Lead
Dual-speed switch
Motor body
Plunger
Trigger switch
Baseplate
Locking button
Support roller
Bevel adjustment

To start a hole for a jigsaw, use a power drill with twist bit to drill a hole on the waste side of the line.

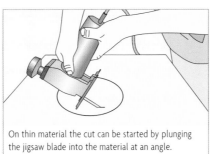

On thin material the cut can be started by plunging the jigsaw blade into the material at an angle.

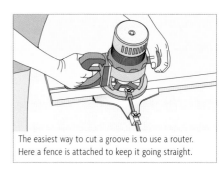

The easiest way to cut a groove is to use a router. Here a fence is attached to keep it going straight.

ROUTER

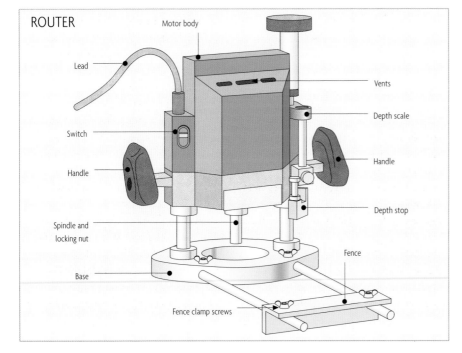

Motor body
Lead
Vents
Depth scale
Switch
Handle
Handle
Depth stop
Spindle and locking nut
Base
Fence
Fence clamp screws

A groove can be cut using a router and jig. Experiment on scrap timber so the width of the groove is correct.

saw to follow the shape. A circle-cutting guide may be purchased for your jigsaw.

On soft timber or thin material such as plasterboard, you can cut a hole without drilling a starter hole by plunge-cutting. Rest the saw on the front of the baseplate and tilt it forward until the blade clears the material. Turn the motor on and lower the saw into the material, maintaining firm pressure. Complete the cut in the normal way.

ROUTERS

The portable electric router shapes joints and moulds on the edge of timber using jig (guide) attachments and cutters. Routers range from laminate trimmers to large plunge routers for heavier work. Consult a dealer for the type best suited to your needs.

There are more than 200 types of cutters, from straight to elaborate; some have ball-bearing guides, some don't. These are mainly for cutting along the edge and require a guide to run the router against. A guide fence or wheel can be attached to the baseplate of any router. Without a guide the rotation of the cutter and the timber grain makes

it hard to control the router. Cutters are high-speed steel or tungsten-carbide tipped.

Operating the router

Fit the appropriate cutter (check the manufacturer's handbook). Fix any jigs or guides to the router or work. Start the motor and allow it to gain full speed—be careful, as the power of the motor may twist it out of your hands. Rest the base-plate on the work. To obtain a clean cut, the router should run at high speed; if it is too slow, it may create friction and burn the material. Hold onto the router firmly with both hands. Move it into the timber to make the cut, working from left to right so the cutting edge is fed straight into the timber. Keep it firmly pressed against the jig to eliminate any chatter.

When routering all sides of a piece of timber, router the end grain first to prevent the end splitting.

Routers may be mounted upside down on a table for easier working.

SANDING BLOCKS AND PAPER

Sanding blocks and abrasive-coated paper (commonly called sandpaper) are used to produce a fine, smooth finish on timber.

SANDING BLOCKS

Sanding blocks are small pieces of cork or other soft material around which a piece of sanding paper is wrapped. Using a sanding block not only saves your hands, it helps maintain an even pressure on the sanding paper and avoids rounding the edges of your job.

When you are ready to sand, wrap a piece of sanding paper the same width as the block around it and place the block on the surface of the timber at 90 degrees to the direction of the grain. With an even pressure, move the block back and forth.

Hold the block at 90 degrees to the grain, or a splinter may be caught between the paper and the block. Circular or cross-sanding scratches the job.

To clean up timber that has a moulded shape, it may be necessary to use a small block in the reverse shape, otherwise the shape may be distorted when sanding by hand.

SANDING PAPER

The coat or grit of sanding paper comes in fine, medium or coarse and has a numbered coding. The higher the number, the finer the grit: for example, P16–P60 is coarse (for shaping timber), P80–100 medium, P120 and above fine (for giving a final finish). These coats are applied in different densities. On 'open-coat' the grit is spaced further apart and so reduces clogging. 'Close-coat' has grit closer together for a finer finish.

When sanding, start with a coarse grit and work through to a finer grit to produce the required finish. Fold or tear the sandpaper into a manageable size, and replace it when it becomes worn or begins to tear.

When sanding hold the block at 90 degrees to the grain and move it back and forth, applying even pressure.

If the paper clogs, it may be cleared by shaking or tapping the back to loosen the dust. For an even finer finish, raise the grain by wiping it over with a damp cloth. When it is dry, give a final sand with fine paper.

When sanding end grain, the fibres will sometimes lean in one direction (rub with your finger to determine the direction). Sand only in this direction, not back and forth.

SAWS

A saw is used mainly for cutting solid timber or panel products, although there are other saws for different materials. There are traditional handsaws as well as power saws to suit different jobs.

PARTS OF A SAW

The traditional handsaw has a handle at one end of a thin, flexible blade, which varies from 550 mm to about 700 mm long.

The teeth vary in size and shape according to the type of saw. The size is quoted as a number of teeth per 25 mm, so a 7-point saw has seven teeth per 25 mm. The fewer the teeth, the faster and rougher the cut. Each tooth has been bent out on alternate sides of the blade to provide a 'kerf', or clearance for

the saw. The space between the teeth is known as the gullet. This allows the sawdust to be carried out of the cut.

HANDSAWS

- The ripsaw is the largest handsaw used for cutting along the grain, a technique known as ripping. The teeth have 3 to 6 points. There is a half ripsaw with more teeth.
- The cross-cut saw is used for cutting across the grain. The teeth cut like a series

of knife blades that sever the fibres. They range from 5 to 9 points, and the blade is about 650 mm long.

- The panel saw is used for cutting panels, manufactured boards such as plywood and chipboard, and for finer work. It has 9 to 11 points; the blade is about 550 mm long.

BACKSAWS

These saws have a parallel blade with a reinforced back of steel or brass over the top

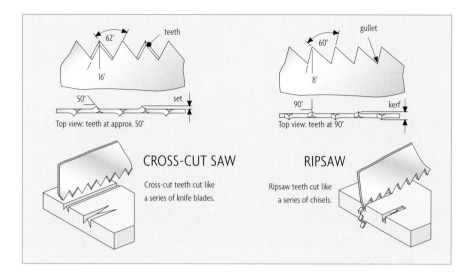

CROSS-CUT SAW

Cross-cut teeth cut like a series of knife blades.

RIPSAW

Ripsaw teeth cut like a series of chisels.

edge. This adds stiffness and weight to the saw. The teeth are cut and set as on a panel saw, only finer. These saws have between 10 and 14 points.

- The mitre saw is the largest of the backsaws and is used with a mitre box to cut mitres and other angles.
- The tenon saw is a middle-sized backsaw used for finer work. The teeth are more vertical and are sharpened like the cross-cut saw.
- The dovetail saw is used for cutting with or across the grain on very fine joints or small beads. Smaller than a tenon saw, it has three handle types: closed, open or straight grip.

CURVE-CUTTING SAWS

- The coping saw has a spring steel frame with two levers for altering the blade position, and a handle that turns to lock the blade in position. This saw is used for cutting intricate shapes, inside and outside curves, or scribing joints. Keep the adjusting levers parallel while maintaining the correct tension on the blade.

The blade should never be forced, as it is easily broken (blades are inexpensive). It is placed in the frame with the teeth towards

the handle—the cutting action relies on pulling, not pushing as with other saws. Keep the blade square to the work. Don't cut too quickly.

- The fretsaw is similar, but the blades are generally not adjustable. The blade is thin enough that it can be turned in any direction.
- The keyhole or compass saw has a narrow, tapered blade with cross-cut teeth designed to cut a variety of building materials. When cutting internal curves, drill a hole through the work on the waste side of the line to get the saw started.
- Other saws used for curved work include bowsaws for larger curves and padsaws for smaller jobs.

HOW TO USE A SAW

All timber, whether being ripped or cross-cut, must be held firm. This applies whether you are holding the work by hand, vice or cramp, and your job must be supported during the sawing process. Work only on a steady surface and avoid excessive vibration. Use trestles to support longer pieces, with only as much timber overhanging as you need.

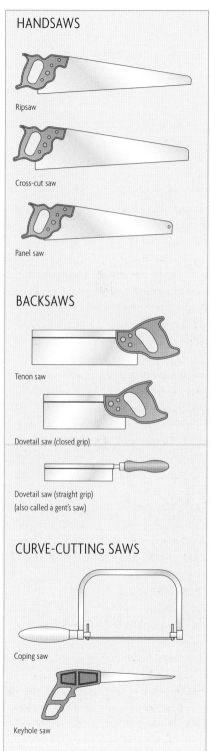

HANDSAWS

Ripsaw

Cross-cut saw

Panel saw

BACKSAWS

Tenon saw

Dovetail saw (closed grip)

Dovetail saw (straight grip) (also called a gent's saw)

CURVE-CUTTING SAWS

Coping saw

Keyhole saw

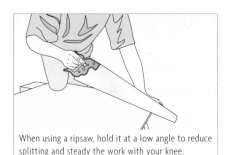
When using a ripsaw, hold it at a low angle to reduce splitting and steady the work with your knee.

The coping saw with its fine blade is used for cutting curves. The work is held steady in a vice.

A keyhole saw is used for cutting inside work. Drill a hole on the waste side of the line to get it started.

If the saw cuts badly or slowly, it is blunt. Never force the saw. Jamming a saw into timber will distort the blade and render it useless. Watch out for nails or screws: the saw will cut them, but you'll then have to resharpen the saw.

Most carpentry saws have one handle so one hand is left free to hold the work. To steady your work when cutting on trestles, rest a knee or foot on top of the timber. If cutting in a vice or using cramps, the job should be held as close as possible to where it will be cut to avoid the saw jumping, which makes cutting difficult and dangerous.

Hold the saw with your forefinger pointing towards the blade. This gives better control. To start a cut, mark the cutting line with a pencil. Place the saw on the waste side of the line at a low angle, holding your other hand at the end of the timber next to the line. Rest your thumb against the blade to guide the saw.

Pull the saw backwards a little to make a slight cut, then push forward the same length. Repeat a few times, gradually increasing the length of stroke. Once the cut is 20–30 mm long, bring your hand back to steady the timber. Raise the angle of the saw to about 45 degrees for cross-cutting or 60 degrees for ripping.

Move into a comfortable position and use full, steady strokes with only light pressure. Let the saw do the work. Position your body so that the saw, forearm and shoulder are at 90 degrees to the work and you can see the line to be worked. If the cut runs out of square (undercut), your piece may end up the wrong size.

To prevent the saw binding when ripping timber, place a thin wedge in the cut to keep the kerf open. Don't twist off the waste with the saw blade, or the underside may split off.

Cross-cutting

When cross-cutting, support the weight of the offcut when you near the end of the cut. Lower the angle of the saw and cut steadily.

When cross-cutting a veneer surface board, lower the angle of the saw to minimize the amount of break-out on the bottom of the board. To cross-cut small sections of timber mouldings and joints, hold the timber against a bench hook or in a mitre box and cut with a tenon saw.

When using a tenon or dovetail saw, keep your thumb against the blade and raise the handle so the saw cuts the far edge first. Draw the saw back to start the cut, gradually lowering it as it cuts.

To cut square, square a line around the timber and cut down about 3–4 mm on all sides. Then keep turning the timber, cutting a little deeper on each side in turn. The saw will follow the cuts already made. Alternatively, score a fine line around the timber with a sharp knife or chisel, then remove a small section of timber on the waste side to form a groove in which the saw can run.

Timber mitre boxes are used to cross-cut timber at 45 and 90 degrees. They are used in the same way as a bench hook, but you don't need to use your thumb to guide the cut as the box will do it. Adjustable metal mitre boxes may be used to cross-cut timber at any desired angle.

Curve-cutting

For curve-cutting, place the timber vertically in the vice as low as possible. In some cases the timber can be held horizontally with cramps: even if it has to be moved during cutting, the sawing will be easier. Start the saw cutting horizontally and follow your set-out lines. Keep the saw square to the face of the timber.

For internal cuts drill a hole through the timber on the waste side of the line. Push the blade through and, if using a coping saw, replace it in the frame. You may have to turn the blade at an angle within the saw frame to cut to the required shape.

MAINTAINING SAWS

Generally, the only parts of the saw requiring maintenance are the handle and teeth. After some use the saw will become blunt and need resharpening and/or setting. This should be done professionally: ask your local hardware store to recommend a saw doctor.

When it is not in use, stand a saw on its handle leaning against the bench or trestle. When you have finished using it, protect its teeth by placing a protective sleeve over them. A piece of plastic pipe with a split down one side is quite effective.

workshop basics

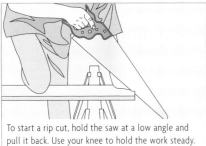

To start a rip cut, hold the saw at a low angle and pull it back. Use your knee to hold the work steady.

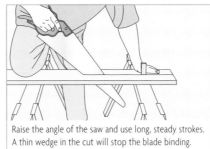

Raise the angle of the saw and use long, steady strokes. A thin wedge in the cut will stop the blade binding.

MITRE BOXES

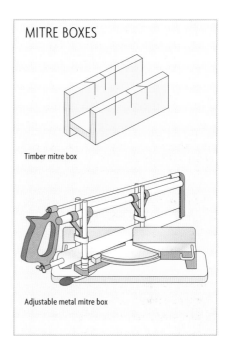

Timber mitre box

Adjustable metal mitre box

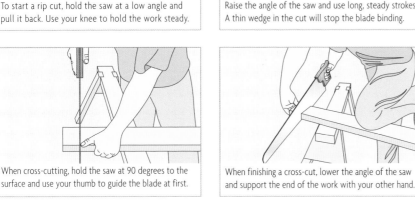

When cross-cutting, hold the saw at 90 degrees to the surface and use your thumb to guide the blade at first.

When finishing a cross-cut, lower the angle of the saw and support the end of the work with your other hand.

FIXED MACHINERY

The following fixed power tools are among the most frequently used in a do-it-yourself workshop. While they make some jobs easier, anything these machines can do may also be done with well-maintained hand tools and a little more time and effort.

There is an ill-advised tendency for some beginners to rush out and buy fancy gleaming machines so they can do the job easier and better. The beginner may also take advice from well-meaning friends and eager salesmen that this machine, or that, is a definite 'must have'. Nothing could be further from the truth.

There are many classes and small schools operated by reputable woodworkers, and beginners should avail themselves of these services. These classes will stress the vital safety precautions to be taken when using woodworking tools, especially fixed machines. Highly detailed advice will be given about eye and hearing protection, together with instruction in the correct use of face

masks for respiratory protection against airborne dusts and fumes.

BANDSAW

The need for a bandsaw will be felt, early on, by most beginners, and the purchase of a suitable machine must be given serious thought. The bandsaw is an upright saw with a narrow steel blade, able to make curved as well as straight cuts. Bandsaws are usually referred to by the diameter of the wheels, and the most suitable size for the hobbyist woodworker is a two-wheel machine with 300 mm wheels. Reputable manufacturers will usually supply an owner's handbook, which will deal with the adjustment of the machine and the many safety aspects, but

without very much information about the use of the saw itself.

Beginners' woodworking classes or expert private tuition are the best ways to learn how to correctly and safely use a bandsaw.

TABLE SAW

Table saws are often high on the beginner's 'want list' and here, too, great care and

SAFETY TIP

When using a lathe, drill press, router or any other spinning tool, it is important that woodworkers who wear their hair long tie it back or contain the hair in a net or close-fitting cap.

BANDSAW

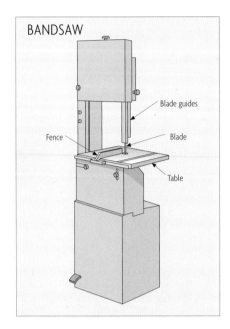

Blade guides

Fence

Blade

Table

TABLE SAW

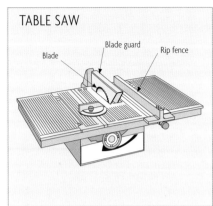

Blade

Blade guard

Rip fence

DRILL PRESS

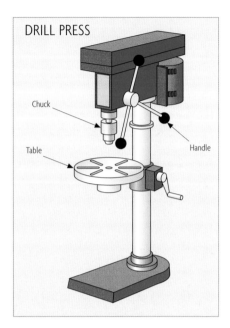

Chuck

Table

Handle

ROUTER TABLE

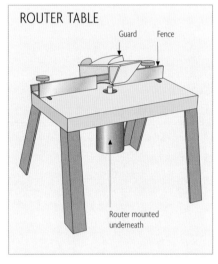

Guard

Fence

Router mounted
underneath

restraint must be exercised. These machines, in the hands of an experienced operator, are extremely versatile tools. Used by the inexperienced these saws can, and do, become lethal weapons. The exacting adjustment of the table saw's various components is vital for the safe and efficient use of the table saw.

Table saws vary greatly in size, from tiny machines with 100 mm diameter saws as used by miniaturists to the monsters seen in sawmills. The one best suited to the beginner would have a blade of about 250 mm diameter. Free-standing models are available, but a benchtop version will meet the needs of most hobbyists.

ROUTER TABLE

The advent of the router and its improved affordability has made the life of the hobbyist woodworker much more interesting. It is a very versatile tool, and in the freehand mode it is possibly as safe as a woodworking machine can be. The router can be used freehand with suitable fences and bearing-guided cutters to do the jobs of many other

workshop tools, such as planing, shaping and even sawing.

Today, routers are often mounted under a table top, with the cutter projecting above the table top. With fences and guides it becomes a very useful machine. Known in this form as a table router, the increase in the danger factor is possibly tenfold. It becomes, in effect, a miniature version of the industrial machine known as a spindle mounter, which is considered by many to be the most dangerous woodworking machine of all. If you are a novice in the use of a router, you would be well advised to take lessons before purchasing one for your workshop.

DRILL PRESS

Drill presses have become almost irreplaceable in the hobbyist workshop, and are relatively safe if the necessary precautions are understood and followed.

The drill press is usually bench-mounted, but large floor-standing versions are available. The drill bit is held in a chuck attached to the lower end of a revolving shaft which can be raised and lowered by a handle projecting from the side of the machine frame. The machine is fitted with a table that is adjustable vertically and horizontally about the machine's vertical circular support column and can be tilted in excess of 90 degrees either side of the centre line. The work piece can be firmly held to the table with cramps, which allows the drilling to be controlled with great accuracy and versatility.

Always follow the drill press manufacturer's instructions regarding the speed of the drill for different materials you may be using, and exercise the same care as you would with your portable drill.

BENCH GRINDER

The bench grinder is an important tool and is relatively safe if the necessary safety procedures are followed. The bench grinder consists of an electric motor with a shaft at each end. These shafts are fitted with grinding wheels which enable you to keep your tools in good condition, ultimately saving you money and making your work easier.

The machine will be fitted with adjustable tool rests and toughened glass safety screens. The tool rests should be adjusted very close to the spinning wheels so your work-piece cannot become jammed between the tool rest and the spinning wheel— a dangerous thing to happen. The wheels must run true, and there are dressing tools or stones for this task. If a wheel becomes chipped, cracked or damaged, it must be discarded immediately.

LATHE

The wood lathe is a very popular machine and is available in a bewildering range of styles and sizes. The lathe is used to hold and turn a piece of wood, while a cutting tool such as a gauge or scraper chisel or parting tool creates details in a piece of timber. It is used to make round things of extraordinary variety and artistry. When choosing a lathe, check that the clearance between the headstock and the bed of the lathe is adequate for the diameter of the work you intend to do on it.

Special tools are needed for woodturning, and you can also find classes to instruct you in the skills and methods required to make turned projects.

SAFETY TIPS

You may already be familiar with these machines and their uses, but it is important not to allow familiarity to lead to unsafe working practices.

- When using any piece of machinery, fixed or hand-held, follow the manufacturer's instructions at all times, and always make sure you understand the correct safety procedures.
- Never attempt to fix or modify any of these machines yourself. Contact a qualified electrician or the manufacturer's representative to carry out any repairs or adjustments that are not covered in the owner's manual.
- Use fences and safety guards whenever they are fitted. Refer to the machine owner's manual for their correct adjustment.
- Always use safety glasses and hearing protection when using fixed machinery, and be alert for possible hazards such as dust, loose clothing or long hair.

BENCH GRINDER

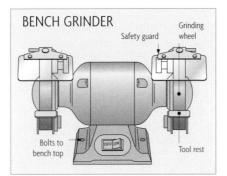

Safety guard — Grinding wheel — Bolts to bench top — Tool rest

HINTS

For best results when using a bandsaw, keep the blade guides close to the work piece.

Use a push stick, not your fingers, to guide work pieces through a table saw and to clear material away from the blade.

Remove as much waste timber as you can from your work piece before using a shaping tool such as a router or lathe.

LATHE

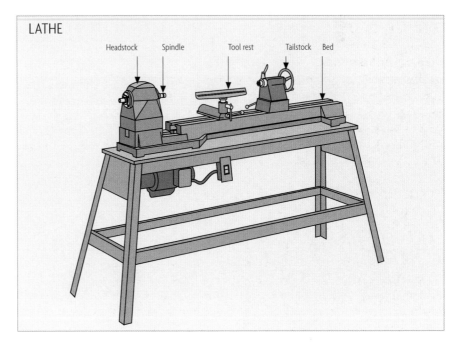

Headstock — Spindle — Tool rest — Tailstock — Bed

SCRAPERS

Woodworking or cabinet scrapers are flat pieces of steel with a cutting edge that will remove a very fine shaving when pushed over the surface of timber.

SHARPENING A SCRAPER

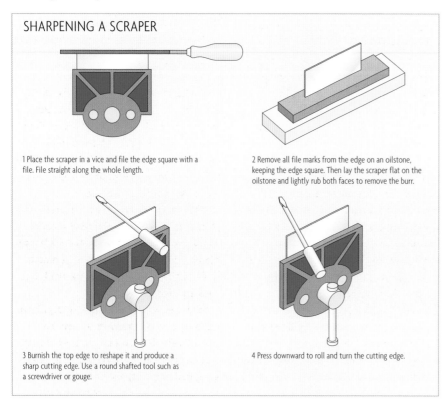

1 Place the scraper in a vice and file the edge square with a file. File straight along the whole length.

2 Remove all file marks from the edge on an oilstone, keeping the edge square. Then lay the scraper flat on the oilstone and lightly rub both faces to remove the burr.

3 Burnish the top edge to reshape it and produce a sharp cutting edge. Use a round shafted tool such as a screwdriver or gouge.

4 Press downward to roll and turn the cutting edge.

CABINET SCRAPERS

Hold hand cabinet scrapers with both hands. Place fingers over the face and press the thumbs firmly into the back of the scraper, flexing it slightly.

To use the scraper, place the edge on the surface of the timber at a low angle. Firmly pushing it forward, remove a shaving. Adjust the angle of the movement as necessary.

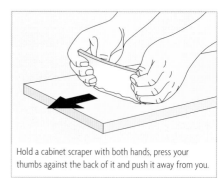

Hold a cabinet scraper with both hands, press your thumbs against the back of it and push it away from you.

SCREWDRIVERS AND SCREWS

There are different types and sizes of screwdrivers and each one will only do a small number of specific jobs successfully. Using the wrong screwdriver may result in damage to the job, the tool or the operator.

SCREWDRIVER TYPES

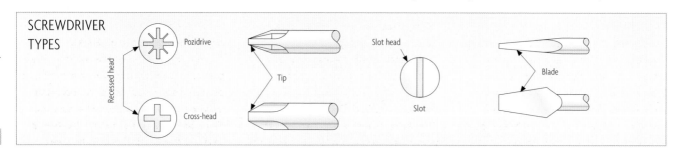

Recessed head — Pozidrive — Cross-head — Tip — Slot head — Slot — Blade

workshop basics

COMMON SCREWDRIVERS

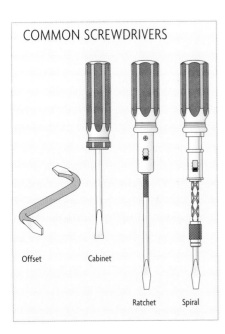

Offset   Cabinet

Ratchet   Spiral

BASIC SCREWDRIVER KIT

BLADE SIZE

Qty	(slotted)	Length
1	4–6 mm slot	150 mm
1	6–8 mm slot	200 mm
1	8–10 mm slot	250 mm

TIP SIZE

Qty	(Cross/Pozi)	Length
1	No. 1 recessed	150 mm
1	No. 1 recessed	200 mm
1	No. 2 recessed	200 mm

TYPES OF SCREWDRIVERS

Screwdrivers may be hand operated or power-driven. Hand-operated ones have a timber or plastic handle, a steel shaft and a blade or tip at the end. A power screwdriver or drill has a screwdriver bit inserted.

You will need five or six screwdrivers of varying size, blade and tip types. They should include the three basic types of tip:

- slotted, with a flat blade for standard headed screws;
- Cross-head, with a cross-shaped tip for screws with recessed heads;
- Pozidrive, similar to cross-head but ground at a different angle to allow greater pressure to be applied to screws without damaging the head.

Cross-head screwdrivers may be used on Pozi screws, but take care not to damage the head, as the recess in the head and tip do not match exactly. Never use Pozi screwdrivers in cross-head screws as they will damage the head or tip.

Screwdrivers may be purchased individually or in a kit. They are selected by the length of the shaft and size of the blade or tip. Slotted screwdrivers are measured by the width of the blade in millimetres. Cross-head and Pozi tips are measured by the diameter of the shaft, which is quoted as a number from 1 to 3 (3 being the smallest). The table (at left) shows a basic kit.

A screwdriver blade or tip should fit the screw head exactly, reaching the bottom of the slot or recess. If it is too wide it will damage the surrounding timber when driven in, and if too narrow, it may snap or twist the slot or recess, making the screw difficult to drive.

Common screwdriver types are:

- cabinet, which has the blade the same width as the shaft;
- ratchet, which can be used with one hand and turns screws left or right on the blade;
- spiral, which turns as the handle is pushed in a pump action;
- offset, which has a lever-type handle and is used in confined spaces.

Other specialized screwdrivers are available, but they are not common.

USING A SCREWDRIVER

Using a screwdriver correctly needs practice. You may need two hands to get started: one

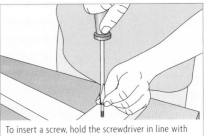

To insert a screw, hold the screwdriver in line with the screw and steady the head of the screw.

on the handle and one steadying the blade and screw. To avoid injury, never have any part of your body in front of the screwdriver.

Before inserting a screw, always drill a pilot hole to guide it and relieve any friction. Failure to do this may result in damage to the screw and/or screwdriver.

When you have positioned the screw, place the screwdriver in the head in direct line with the screw, otherwise the blade may slip off. Apply an even, downward pressure while turning clockwise. Continue until the head is pulled up tight.

To loosen old screws clogged with paint or rust, first clean the heads to ensure the screwdriver will fit properly into the slot or recess. Place the screwdriver into the head and give it a light tap with a mallet to jar away any rust. This may have to be done several times while turning the screwdriver.

A range of screwdriver blades and tips can be used in braces or variable speed drills. Slotted blades are hard to control, so select cross-head or Pozidrive in this situation.

MAINTAINING SCREWDRIVERS

Apart from a small amount of lubrication on ratchet types, there is little maintenance required to maintain screwdrivers.

The blades on slotted screwdrivers should have cross-grinding marks for greater holding power. If they are burred or rounded, restore them with a file or grinder, but ensure you shape both faces the same and that they are square so they fit the head of the screw correctly. Never overheat the blade as this will weaken the strength of the steel. These blades can be reshaped several times.

Cross-head and Pozi tips require more care to restore as there are four sides to be shaped exactly the same. Hold the shaft in a vice and use a hand file. The angles on these tips will not withstand more than a few attempts at filing. You may find it better to replace the tool.

Screwdrivers are not levers or chisels and should never be hit with a hammer. Incorrect use can bend the shaft, damaging the blades or tips or cracking the handle. Shafts can be straightened, but if you crack a handle you may find that it is cheaper and easier to replace the entire tool.

SCREWS

Screws give greater holding power than nails as the threaded shank cuts its way between the timber fibres. Screws are used to fix joints as well as to secure hardware and fitments. They are usually made from mild steel, brass or stainless steel, and are available in a variety of finishes such as galvanized, florentine bronze, nickel, cadmium and zinc-plated. The heads may be slotted, recessed (cross-head or Pozidrive) or bolt type.

When ordering screws, you will need to know the following:

- Purpose: the material you will be fixing to, such as wood or metal.
- Quantity: the number required. Screws are normally boxed in 100s or 200s, depending on size. Most suppliers sell smaller quantities in sealed plastic bags called 'blister packs', or on cardboard cards.
- Length: the amount the screw goes into the timber. Screws range in length from 6 mm to 150 mm.
- Gauge: the diameter of the shank given as a number. The higher the number, the

bigger the diameter. Screws range from 1 to 20.

- Type: head type as well as the type of drive. You may also need to state the thread required.
- Metal: the metal the screw is made from.
- Finish: any surface coating.

The most common size for screws is from 12 mm x 4 gauge to 100 mm x No. 12.

An example of how to place an order for screws would be 100 only 50 mm x No. 8 cross-head countersunk steel wood screws.

SELECTING SCREWS

You need to select a screw according to the type of material you will be joining. With softwoods you need to use a longer screw with a thicker gauge than you would need to get the same holding power with hardwoods. There is less holding power in end grain than cross grain, so the screw will need to be longer.

Another consideration is the thickness of the two pieces of material being joined: you don't want the screw to come out the back of the job. While there is no hard and fast rule, the screw should be long enough to penetrate the bottom piece of timber by the thickness of the top piece, for example, to hold down a 25 mm piece of material, use a 50 mm screw.

BORING A HOLE

When you have selected your screw and a screwdriver that suits the size and type of screw, drill a clearance hole completely through the top piece of timber to match the diameter of the shank of the screw. On the bottom piece of timber, drill a smaller pilot hole at least half the depth of the clearance hole. This smaller hole gives the thread of the screw a firm bite.

If you are using a countersunk screw, the top of the hole will need to be countersunk to receive the screw head. Use a countersunk bit attached to an electric drill or place the bit in the clearance hole and turn it by hand. Twist it several times to create a recess for the head. Avoid countersinking too deep. Test the depth by inverting the screw and inserting the head into the countersunk hole.

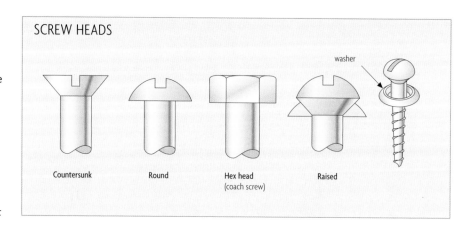

SCREW HEADS

Countersunk

Round

Hex head
(coach screw)

Raised

washer

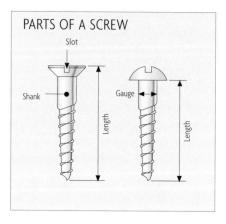

PARTS OF A SCREW

Slot

Shank

Length

Gauge

Length

Store unused screws in a jar and label for future use.

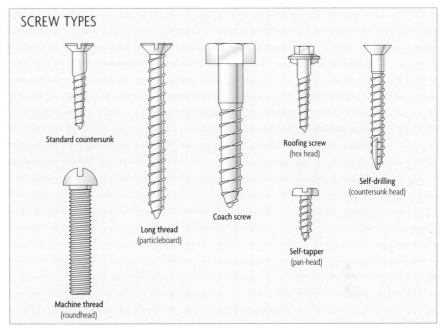

SCREW TYPES

Standard countersunk

Roofing screw (hex head)

Self-drilling (countersunk head)

Machine thread (roundhead)

Long thread (particleboard)

Coach screw

Self-tapper (pan-head)

COMMON SCREW TYPES	PURPOSE
Countersunk head	Head finishes below the surface. For general timber work.
Roundhead	Head finishes above the surface. For thin sheet material and where head should be seen.
Raised head	Combination of countersunk and round head. For fixing hardware and where appearance is important. Can be used with cup washers for fixing thin sheets.
Long threaded	Countersunk embedding head; thread spaced apart for greater holding power. For chipboard.
Coach screws	Square or hexagonal head. For heavy work, such as fencing or pergolas.

SQUARES

Components that are not square will not fit together neatly, and the job will look rough. Always test them with a square.

TYPES

- To use the traditional carpenter's square (try square), hold the stock firmly against the job with the blade over the face or edge to be tested. Sight between the blade and work. If the blade is not parallel to the job, it is not square. Some try squares have a 45-degree angle on the stock near the blade for setting out and testing mitres. A square may be used to test internal and external corners.
- For larger jobs, use the builder's or roofing square. This is made from a single flat piece of steel.
- More versatile is the adjustable combination square. The blade length can be adjusted and secured in place by a locking screw. The stock may also be used to set mitres as it has a 45-degree shoulder at the top. The adjustable blade may be used to test the depth of recesses or as a pencil gauge. Common features are an adjustable blade 300 mm long with gradients, a level vial and a scriber in the stock.
- An adjustable sliding bevel may be used to set out or test a required bevel or slope on timber, especially in roofing or dovetail work.

HINT

Assuming the sides of a box or frame are parallel, you can test whether your job is square by measuring the diagonals. If they are the same, the job is square.

TESTING A SQUARE

For accurate work, a square should be 'square'. Be careful not to distort it, and never use it as a hammer. To test the accuracy of your try square, make a line across the face of a straight piece of timber while holding the stock firmly against the edge. Turn the square over. If the blade lines up with this line, the try square is accurate.

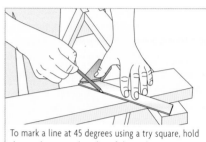

To mark a line at 45 degrees using a try square, hold the stock against the edge of the timber.

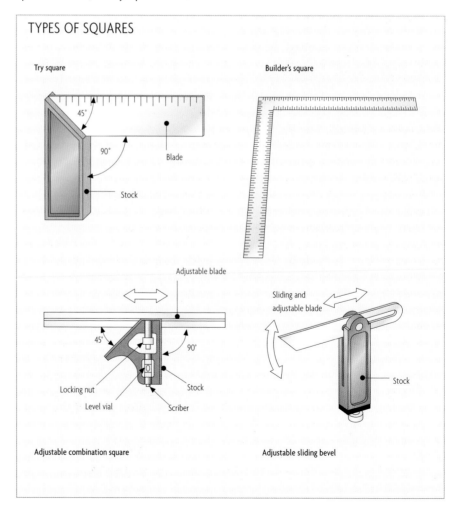

TYPES OF SQUARES

Try square

45°

90°

Blade

Stock

Builder's square

Adjustable blade

45°

90°

Locking nut

Level vial

Stock

Scriber

Adjustable combination square

Sliding and adjustable blade

Stock

Adjustable sliding bevel

workshop basics

TESTING AN EDGE FOR SQUARE

TESTING A TRY SQUARE

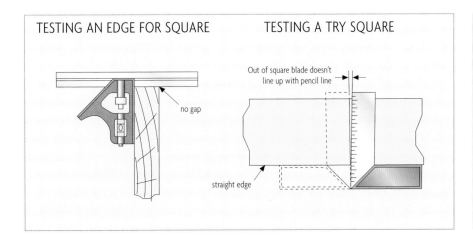

Out of square blade doesn't line up with pencil line

no gap

straight edge

OIL AND WAX

- A little oil or wax can be used to protect tools from rust if they are stored for long periods.
- If a plane squeaks when in use, try a little wax or oil on the bottom. This may be transferred to the work, and it will need sanding before finishing.
- To reduce friction when using a saw, rub the side of the blade with light oil or wax.
- Wax or soap may be used on screws to reduce friction.

TAPES AND RULES

Tapes and rules come in a wide range of shapes and sizes, but only two are needed for most work: a folding rule and a steel tape.

TAPES

Steel measuring tapes have a flexible blade that is spring-loaded to retract into the case. The case may also have a belt clip and a locking device to prevent the blade retracting.

Tapes are usually marked in millimetres, centimetres and metres, and range in length from 1 to 10 m. The measurements may be printed on both sides of the blade. Replacement blades and springs are available for good-quality tapes.

By taking good care of your tape, you can lengthen its life:

- Keep it dry so the blade and spring don't rust.
- Never let the blade retract at speed, as this may snap the hook rivets.
- Don't drop the tape, as this may snap the spring, crack the casing or damage the hook.
- Don't bend the blade, as this can split or break the spring steel.
- Keep the spring lubricated with a light machine oil.

RULES

Folding rules are made from boxwood or plastic, with four sections hinged together with brass or stainless steel fittings. Most are 1 m long, but shorter sizes are available. Plastic rules are generally more durable.

Your rule will last longer if you don't whip it around or bend it excessively, as this places extra stress on the hinges. Always fold the leaves in the direction of the hinges.

MEASURING TOOLS

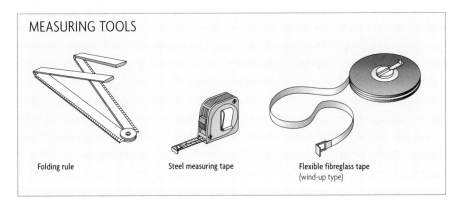

Folding rule

Steel measuring tape

Flexible fibreglass tape (wind-up type)

MEASUREMENTS

In carpentry, measurements are taken in millimetres or metres, not centimetres. For example, a nail may be 75 mm, not 7.5 cm, and timber is purchased in 300 mm increments, not 30 cm ones.

basic techniques

basic techniques

TIMBER

Using the right tools for the job will make your work easier and the time spent in your workshop more pleasant.

SAWING METHODS

The two main methods used to convert a log into usable boards are plain-sawing and quarter-sawing. Plain-sawing is most common because it produces a large number of boards from a log, including a good number of wide ones. The boards have growth rings parallel to the face, and the rings are prone to cupping or warping as each face shrinks at a different rate. These boards tend to cup away from the heart side.

Quarter-sawing is less common as it produces fewer boards. These boards have growth rings at right angles to the face and are a higher quality with even shrinkage on each face. They are more expensive.

HARDWOOD OR SOFTWOOD

Timber is classified as hardwood or softwood according to its growth structure: it bears no relation to how hard the timber is. For example, Western red cedar, meranti and balsa are hardwoods, but they are fairly soft. Hardwood trees have broad leaves, while softwood comes from cone-bearing trees such as pine and fir with needle-like leaves.

Hardwood is best suited to external work and construction as it withstands greater stress than does softwood. Well-seasoned (dried) softwood is mainly used for framing or lining boards. Although treated pine can be used externally quite successfully, it will not have the higher stress rating of hardwood. Both hardwood and softwood can be used for furniture if they are seasoned well. Always take precautions by wearing a dust mask and goggles when using treated timber, as the preservatives used can react with your skin or cause other illnesses. The offcuts of treated timber should never be burnt because the fumes are highly toxic.

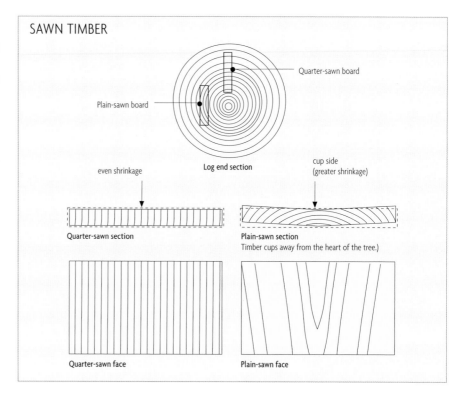

SAWN TIMBER

Quarter-sawn board

Plain-sawn board

Log end section

even shrinkage

cup side
(greater shrinkage)

Quarter-sawn section

Plain-sawn section
Timber cups away from the heart of the tree.)

Quarter-sawn face

Plain-sawn face

PURCHASING TIMBER

Timber can be purchased either sawn or 'planed'. Sawn timber is rectangular or square, and the surface will be rough: it is regarded as raw or unfinished. Sawn timber is used for general building construction and is available in both seasoned and unseasoned timbers.

Timber used for most projects is planed or shaped timber. This means that it has been machined but needs to be further smoothed by planing or sanding. Planed timber can be P1S (planed one side), P1S & P1E (planed one side and one edge), moulded (machined to a profile—for example, bullnose), or PAR (planed all round). PAR timber has a smoother surface and requires minimal sanding.

The process of planing timber reduces the finished size of the actual timber. For example, a piece of sawn timber 100 mm square (its sawn size) will finish from 90 to 92 mm square when planed. You have to keep this in mind when ordering your timber.

Timber rarely comes supplied in the size required for a particular project. It may still need to be reduced further by cutting and/or planing. Your timber merchant may offer this service for an additional fee.

Timber is readily available in lengths ranging from 0.9 m to 6 m in increments of 300 mm. The width and thickness of timber ranges from 10 mm to 200 mm. Although lengths, widths and thicknesses greater than these are available, they may have to be specially ordered.

SELECTING TIMBER

Timber is selected for a job by its grading. Visual grading is made according to its appearance.

- Select or no. 1 grade is free of knots and has straight grain. It is used for high-quality cabinet work.
- Select merchantable grade has straight grain and some knots, and is used for door and window joinery.
- Merchantable grade has larger knots and wavy grain, and is used for frame construction.
- Standard or building grade has larger knots and sloping grain, and is used for battens and bracings.
- Engineering grade is free of defects and has straight, tight grain for high-quality structural timber.

Stress grading refers to the structural strength of the timber (the amount it will bend) and is shown by a 'C' number—the higher the number, the greater the strength.

Defects in timber

The grain in timber may be either wavy or ribbon, with knots and gum pockets. These may be regarded as defects or as features that can be worked and polished. Seasoning can also create defects in timber that will, in some cases, make working with it difficult.

Ordering timber

When ordering timber, you need to provide the timber merchant with certain information if you are to get the timber you need. This consists of the following:

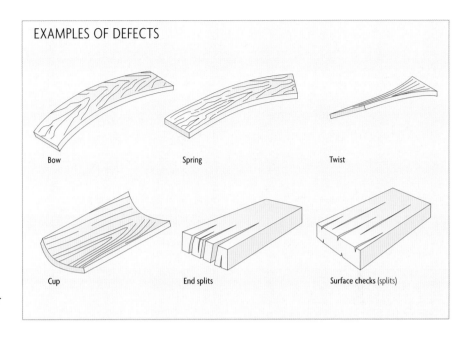

EXAMPLES OF DEFECTS

Bow   Spring   Twist

Cup   End splits   Surface checks (splits)

- the section width and thickness, for example, 100 x 50 mm
- the length, for example, 1.2 m
- the condition, for example, PAR
- the species, for example, parana pine
- the number of pieces
- the stress grade (construction work).

BUILDING BOARDS

Timber products such as particleboard from pine trees, hardboard (masonite) from hardwood trees and medium-density fibre-board (MDF) were developed for reasons of economy. They are manufactured from forest-thinning waste such as branches and sawdust that would otherwise have been burnt. They are cheaper than solid timber, and are available in large sheet sizes.

There is a variety of finishes available, from plain synthetic and natural timber veneers to plastic laminate or melamine. These products have no obvious grain, and most have an edge that can be machined to any shape, although particleboard needs an edge finish such as veneer.

- MDF is used in craft projects and for skirtings and architraves as it machines well and sands up to an excellent finish ready for painting. It does, however, contain chemicals that can cause skin problems for some people. Always work out of the sun, wear gloves and protect your eyes, nose and mouth from the dust.
- Take care when nailing or screwing near the edge of particleboard as it may split. Fixing into the edge of the board also creates a problem as the particles will pull out very easily. MDF and hardboard are less likely to be damaged in this way.
- Plywood consists of an odd number of veneers glued together, the number varying from three to thirteen. Alternate layers have the grain at 90 degrees, with top and bottom layers running in the same direction. Plywood is stronger than particleboard, and nailing and screwing near or on the edge poses no problems. Cutters such as saws keep their edge longer with plywood, whereas MDF, particleboard and hardboard dull cutters very quickly.

- Blockboard, sometimes referred to as 'solid core', is timber laminated together to produce a wide board. It is covered with two layers of veneer on each side. The first is placed at 90 degrees to the timber; the second is a better quality veneer running in the same direction as the lamination. Blockboard is mainly used for solid flush doors and cabinet work in thinner sections. It has largely been replaced by particleboard.

FINISHING TIMBER

Any finish applied to timber is only as good as the preparation beneath. The timber must be seasoned or the paint or lacquer may peel, blister or crack. Any surface faults in the timber should be repaired before the finish is applied.

- Remove scratches with fine abrasive paper or use a scraper.
- Steam out bruises in bare timber by placing a damp cloth over the area and applying a hot iron.
- Fill chips or cracks with slivers of matching timber glued down with PVA adhesive, or use a wood filler. For traditional finishes use a coloured beeswax, otherwise choose a filler to suit your job. They come in a wide range including acrylic (water-based), linseed putty and solvent-based.

Timber is best stored in a dry and well-ventilated area away from sunlight.

TIMBER JOINT CONSTRUCTION

There are scores of joints that can be used to join timber. The skill is in fitting the pieces together precisely to form a joint that functions properly and is able to withstand the stresses required of it.

TYPES OF JOINTS

There are three main types of timber joints—box joints, framing joints and widening joints. Box joints are used for drawers and cupboard shelves, framing joints for window sashes and doors, and widening joints to join timbers for panels.

Many joints can be used for more than one purpose, for example, butt joints are used in all three categories.

PREPARATION OF TIMBER

Even planed timber may require some preparation.

- Cut the timber slightly overwidth and thickness to allow for planing. Do not cut the length yet.
- Choose the best side (face). Plane it the full length. Check it with a straight edge. When it is straight, apply a face mark with a pencil.

- Plane the face edge. Check with a straight edge and square from the face side. Plane the cupped side to straighten it. Mark the face edge.
- Using a marking gauge, scribe a line for the thickness required all round. Plane to this line as necessary. Check with a straight edge.
- Repeat on the side for the width. Now set out for length and joints. Work from the face side and edge.

STEPS IN SETTING OUT TIMBER

Always take care when setting out the timber. Allow enough timber for waste from saw cuts, planing and joint construction. Work from the face side and edge marks. On frames and cupboards, keep these marks facing in for greater accuracy. To help sort out which piece goes with which, number them on the face side as you cut so side 1 goes with end 1.

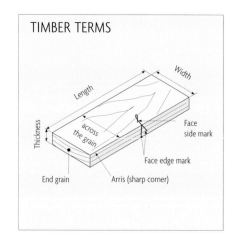

TIMBER TERMS

Length · Width · Thickness · across the grain · Face side mark · Face edge mark · End grain · Arris (sharp corner)

If setting out identical parts, align them carefully and set out across all of them. This ensures the marks are identical on all. When setting out moulded or rebated sections, ensure there is one left-hand and one right-hand section.

BUTT JOINTS

These are the simplest of all joints. They can be used in box, widening or framing construction.

CONSTRUCTION

Cut the ends of the two pieces square and place them together. Fix with screws or nails.

Adhesive may be applied to the joint before fixing to increase its strength. Butt joints in framing may also be strengthened by fixing

a nail plate or corrugated fastener over the outside, or a timber block may be fixed to the inside.

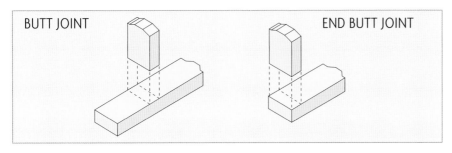

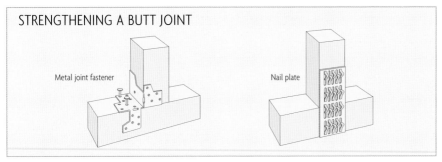

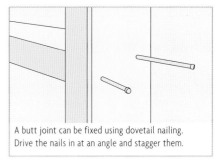

A butt joint can be fixed using dovetail nailing. Drive the nails in at an angle and stagger them.

Butt joints rely on fixings for strength.

DOWELLED JOINTS

Dowels may be used to add strength to a joint. They provide a shearing strength to the joint and rely on adhesive to hold it together. Dowel joints may be used in framing joints (furniture), box joints (cupboards) or widening joints (panels).

CONSTRUCTING A DOWEL JOINT

1 Accurately cut all components to size. Set out the position of the rail on the face side and edge of the stiles.

2 Mark the centre lines for the dowels at the ends of the rails. This must be at least half the thickness of the material in from each edge. For wide rails, more than two dowels may be required.

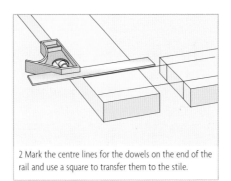

2 Mark the centre lines for the dowels on the end of the rail and use a square to transfer them to the stile.

3 Lay the stiles and rail face side up. Using a try square, transfer the centre lines onto the stile. Number and mark each joint.

4 Square these marks across the face edge of the stiles and ends of the rails.

5 From the face side, gauge a line across the centre of the timber to cross the set-out lines. This represents the centre of the dowel holes.

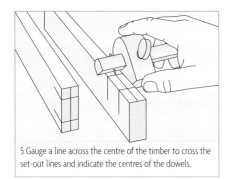

5 Gauge a line across the centre of the timber to cross the set-out lines and indicate the centres of the dowels.

6 Using a power drill with a twist bit attached, or a hand drill with an auger bit attached, drill the holes straight in all the pieces. Make sure the drill bit has a long centre point and clean cutting spurs. When drilling into cross-grain the depth of the holes should be about two and a half times the diameter of the dowel and in end-grain three times the diameter. Leave approximately 2 mm clearance at the bottom of each hole.

7 Countersink the top of the dowel hole to remove any fibres. This also helps when inserting the dowel and provides an adhesive pocket for greater strength.

DOWELS

Dowels should have a groove down the side to allow any extra adhesive to escape when the joint is assembled. If the dowels do not have a groove, plane one side flat to achieve the same result. The ends should be tapered (chamfered) to permit easier assembly and prevent the dowel tearing the inside of the hole. Again, if the dowels are not tapered, file or sand them to a tapered shape.

USING DOWEL CENTRES

Set out and drill the rails of the joint. Place dowel centres in the dowel holes. Line the rail up with the set-out lines on the stile and push together. The points on the

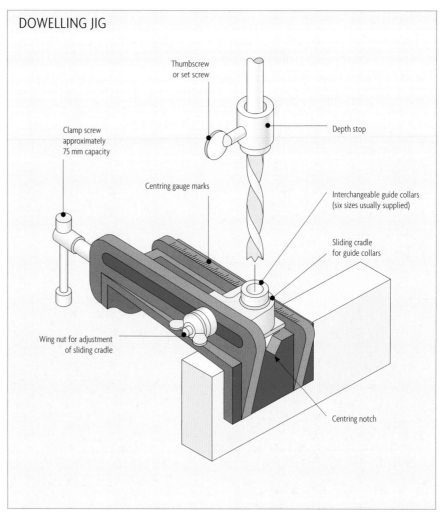

DOWELLING JIG

Thumbscrew or set screw

Clamp screw approximately 75 mm capacity

Centring gauge marks

Depth stop

Interchangeable guide collars (six sizes usually supplied)

Sliding cradle for guide collars

Wing nut for adjustment of sliding cradle

Centring notch

centres will mark the position on the stile. Drill on these marks. An alternative way of locating the centres is to drill holes in a guide block and clamp it in place as a guide when drilling.

USING A METAL DOWELLING JIG

A metal dowelling jig makes locating and drilling the dowel holes simpler. In box joints, a dowelling jig can be used for the end grain but will not work on the face of wide boards.

1 Set out centre lines on the face of the material where the dowel holes are to be.

Select the appropriate drill guide and place it in the jig.

2 Line up centring guide marks on the side of the jig and lock the sliding cradle in place.

3 Place the jig over the timber. Line up the centring vee with the centre lines of the dowel holes; tighten.

4 Fix the depth stop on the drill bit at the required length.

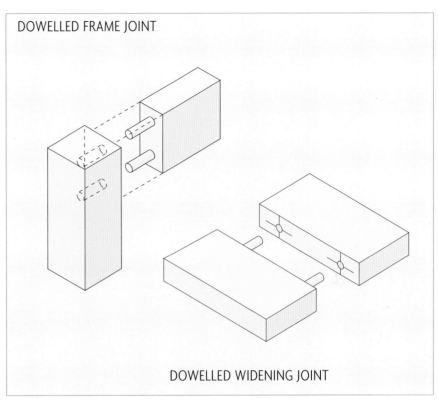

DOWELLED FRAME JOINT

DOWELLED WIDENING JOINT

A dowelled joint is neat but strong

WIDENING JOINT

To obtain a wider piece of timber, two pieces the same thickness may be joined on edge with dowels.

Hold the two pieces of timber face to face in a vice, with the ends carefully aligned. Square a line across the face edge to mark the centre line of each dowel. Gauge a line across each of the centre lines in the middle of each edge. Where these lines cross each other is the centre of the hole.

HOUSING JOINTS

A housing joint is used as a corner or intermediate joint where one end meets the face of another. It is based on a butt joint with a shoulder to provide extra strength and is used in framing (house) or box (cupboard) construction.

TYPES

The main types of housing joints are stopped housing joints, which look like a butt joint but are stronger; corner housing joints; and stopped corner housings.

Corner rebate and stopped rebate joints are made the same way, but two-thirds of the material is removed.

CONSTRUCTING A HOUSING JOINT

1 Set out the housing on the face of the material. The distance between the two lines is the thickness of the other piece. Square the lines across the face and down both edges.

2 Use a gauge to mark the depth of the housing between the lines on the edge. The depth is generally one-quarter to one-third the thickness of the material. Mark the waste.

3 Use G-cramps to hold the work down firmly. Saw the shoulders on the waste side of the line to the depth required. If it is a wide housing, make a few intermediate cuts inside the waste to help break the grain and make chiselling easier.

4 Chisel out the waste from both sides and check the bottom of the housing for flatness. A hand router may be used to even the bottom of the joint.

5 Test for fit. If the piece is too tight, it may need to be eased by planing. Check for square.

6 A housing joint may be secured by any one of the following methods, or by a combination of them:

- gluing and clamping until the adhesive is set
- screwing through the face of the outside piece
- dovetail-nailing through the face of the outside piece
- skew-nailing through in the corner.

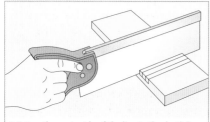

3 Cut on the waste side of the line to the depth line, making intermediate cuts in wider housings.

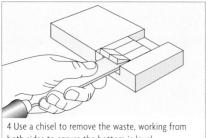

4 Use a chisel to remove the waste, working from both sides to ensure the bottom is level.

A housing joint is quite strong.

HOUSING JOINTS

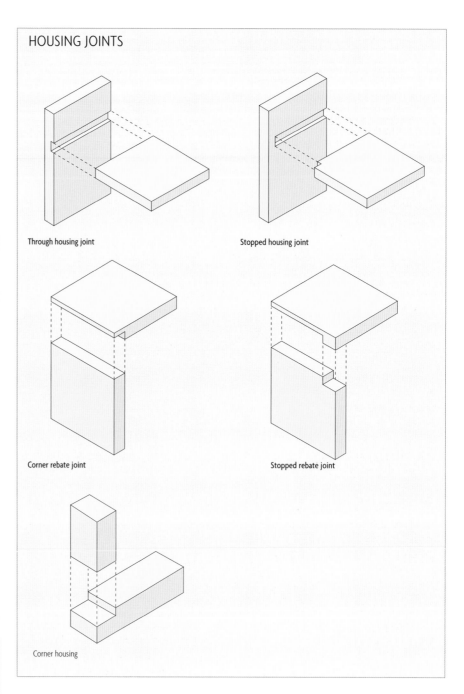

Through housing joint

Stopped housing joint

Corner rebate joint

Stopped rebate joint

Corner housing

BAREFACED TONGUE AND GROOVE JOINTS

This is a combination of a housing joint and a rebate joint, the housing restricting the movement of the joint. It is used in furniture construction and window reveals.

CONSTRUCTION

1 Square the ends of both pieces of timber. Set out the shoulder line on the end of one piece, coming in from the end by the thickness of the other piece. Square across the face side and down both edges. This line is the barefaced side of the timber.

2 Square a second shoulder line back towards the end. This should be one-third the thickness of the timber and down both edges.

3 Gauge the depth of the groove (one-third the thickness of the timber) on the edge between the two shoulder lines.

4 Cut the shoulders down to the gauge line with a tenon saw. Remove the waste with a chisel and check for flatness.

5 With the gauge set as before, mark a line across the back face and across the edges of the other piece.

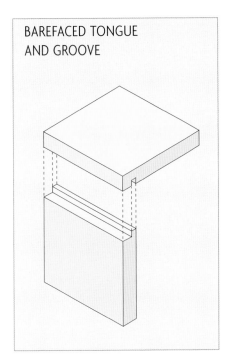

BAREFACED TONGUE AND GROOVE

HINTS

- Joints such as a barefaced tongue and groove joint can be easily constructed using a router and jig, either just for the groove or for both groove and rebate. See page 35 for the correct techniques when using a router.
- If the fit of the tongue is a little tight, plane the face of the tongue to obtain a snug fit, or rub it with abrasive paper.

6 Gauge from the face side towards the end on each side and across the end. Saw down to the gauge line with a tenon saw. Don't cut too deep, as this will weaken the joint.

7 Chisel in from the end to remove the waste. Check for fit and adjust the joint as necessary.

HALVING JOINTS

Halving or half-lap joints are framing joints used to join timber on edge or on flat. The joint is constructed by removing equal amounts of timber from each piece so they finish flush on top and bottom.

TYPES OF HALVING JOINTS

There are six main types of halving joint: cross, corner, stopped, mitre, dovetail and end.

- Cross halving joint. This is used to allow two pieces of timber to cross each other without having to cut one in half. It is constructed in the same way as a housing joint, with half the material removed from each piece. The width is made to suit the width of the intersecting piece. The halving is removed from the top of one piece and the bottom of the other.
- Corner halving joint. This is made with laps that intersect at 90 degrees. A tee halving is similar, with one housing and one lap. It can also be made as a stopped halving joint.
- Mitre halving joint. This is used when the top face of the timber has a moulding on it. By mitring the top of the halving, the mould returns around the corner.
- Dovetail halving joint. A dovetail halving joint has a wedge (dovetail) cut on the lap, either both sides or on one side. The joint will only come apart if the top piece is lifted out of the socket. The pitch for the dovetail is usually 1:6.

- End halving joint (scarf halving). This joint is used to join timber end to end by overlapping the pieces together. The length of the lap is equal to the width of the timber. The joint requires some support for it to have any strength.

CONSTRUCTING A CORNER HALVING JOINT

1 Square the ends of both pieces of timber. Square a line across the top face of one piece, coming in the width of the other. Repeat on the underside of the other piece. Square the lines down the edges of both pieces of timber.

2 Set a marking gauge to half the thickness of the timber and mark a line around the ends and both edges of both pieces. Mark the waste on the top of one piece and the bottom of the other.

3 Hold the timber on end in a vice at 45 degrees. Rip down the waste side of the centre line until the cut reaches the diagonal point. Turn the timber around and continue cutting carefully while gradually lifting the handle of the saw until the cut reaches the shoulder line on both edges.

4 Remove the timber from the vice and lay flat. Hold firmly against a bench hook or clamp the job down.

5 Cut the shoulder to the ripped saw cut and remove the waste. Any unevenness in the lap should be cleaned out with a paring chisel. Check for flatness.

6 Repeat the cutting on the other piece of timber.

7 Check that the two pieces fit together well and adjust as necessary using the paring

chisel. The joint should be square, flush, free of wind and have no gap.

8 The joint may be fixed with nails or screws, and it may be glued to add greater strength.

HALVING JOINTS

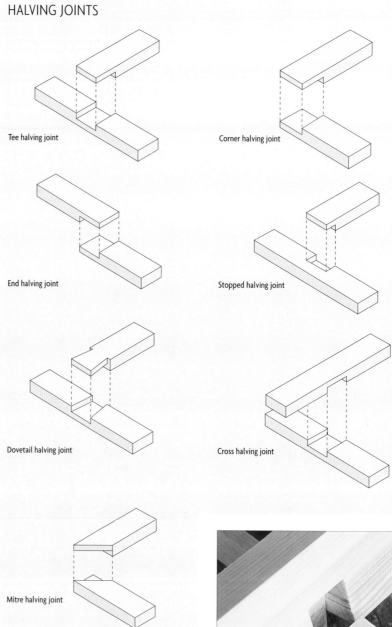

Tee halving joint

Corner halving joint

End halving joint

Stopped halving joint

Dovetail halving joint

Cross halving joint

Mitre halving joint

The halving joint is similar to the housing joint

MITRE JOINTS

A mitre joint is used at corners to hide the end grain, and so that a moulded shape continues around a corner.

TYPES OF MITRE

To create a mitre, the angle at which two surfaces meet is bisected. In a true mitre this is 90 degrees and so each surface is cut to 45 degrees, but the angle may be obtuse or acute. Mitre joints constructed using materials of different thicknesses are known as 'offset' or 'bastard' mitres.

CONSTRUCTING A TRUE MITRE

1 Set out the length of the material, keeping in mind that if the mitre is inside a corner, the length is measured on the long face of the mitre. If the mitre is on the outside of a corner, the length is measured on the short face but allow for the thickness of the joint.

2 Once the length has been determined, mark a 45-degree line on the edge or face where the angle is to be cut.

3 Using a combination square, square a line across each side of the timber.

4 To cut the timber by hand, use a mitre box with a fine-toothed saw such as a tenon, panel or mitre saw. Hold the work firmly against the back of the mitre box when cutting: if it slips it will result in an uneven cut and a poorly fitting joint. If cutting freehand, take care to follow the set-out lines on all sides of the work. If you have one, a power mitre saw will provide a very accurate cut.

5 Place the two pieces together and check the fit. You may be able to adjust it by planing the surface of the mitre. Hold the work firmly and use a fine-set, sharp plane.

6 If the joint is to be nailed, start the nails in both pieces by laying them flat and nailing

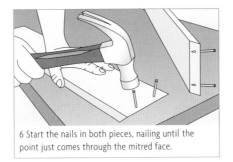

6 Start the nails in both pieces, nailing until the point just comes through the mitred face.

7 Drive the nails in the overlapping side first as the weight of the hammer will cause the joint to pull up.

through the external face until the point just comes through the mitred face.

7 Apply adhesive and hold the joint firmly, with one side slightly overlapping the other. Drive the nails in the overlapping side first. As the nails are driven in, the weight of the hammer will cause the joint to slip. The surfaces should line up. Nail the other side and punch the nails. Check for square.

8 If you have a small gap because your mitre doesn't line up, rub over the open corner of

the joint from both sides with the round shaft of a screwdriver. This will push the fibres over on the outside and hide the gap. If the gap is too wide, you may have to re-cut the joint, or you can fill it with filler.

9 To add strength to a mitre joint, you may glue a block on the inside as long as it is not seen. If appearance is important, a loose tongue placed inside the joint or veneer keys across the joint will give extra strength. On flat mitres, dowels or tongues may be placed inside the joint.

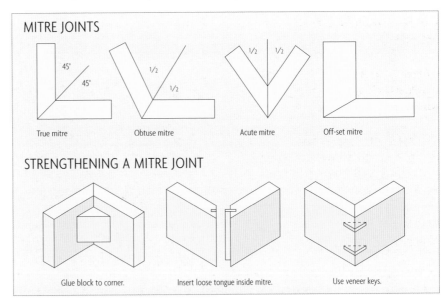

MITRE JOINTS

45°   45°   True mitre

½   ½   Obtuse mitre

½   ½   Acute mitre

Off-set mitre

STRENGTHENING A MITRE JOINT

Glue block to corner.

Insert loose tongue inside mitre.

Use veneer keys.

SCARF AND SCRIBE JOINTS

A scarf joint joins timber end to end, while a scribe joint is used where one piece of moulded timber is butted against another.

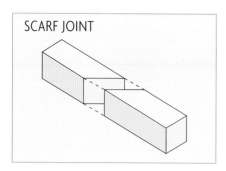

SCARF JOINT

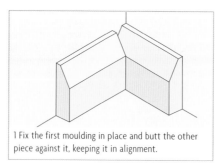

1 Fix the first moulding in place and butt the other piece against it, keeping it in alignment.

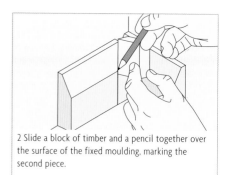

2 Slide a block of timber and a pencil together over the surface of the fixed moulding, marking the second piece.

SCARF JOINTS

A true scarf joint joins timber end to end with bevels cut on the end of each piece of timber so that uniform thickness is maintained.

SCRIBE JOINTS

A scribe joint is used where one piece of timber with a moulded or irregular shape, such as a moulded skirting or quad moulding, is butted against another in a corner. If the timber moves back while it is being fixed

against the wall, a gap may appear, but it will be less noticeable than with a mitre joint.

1 Fix the first moulding in place. Butt the end of the other piece against the fixed moulding, keeping it in alignment.

2 Slide a small block of timber and sharp pencil together over the surface of the fixed moulding. The pencil will mark (scribe) a line on the face of the moulding to be fitted.

3 Cut along the scribed line. Check the fit and adjust as necessary.

Detailed mouldings

Fix the first piece in place and use a mitre box to cut a mitre on the end of the other piece. The line formed by the moulded face and mitre will show the shape needed. Cut along this line with a coping saw or fretsaw.

BRIDLE JOINTS

A bridle joint is used where two pieces of timber meet on edge, either at a corner or an intersection (for example, the corner of a window sash or where a table leg meets a rail).

TYPES OF BRIDLE JOINT

The most common types of bridle joint are the corner bridle and the tee bridle. The joint relies on adhesive for strength but may have a timber dowel or metal star dowel pin inserted through the joint to give it added strength.

BRIDLE JOINT

1 Set out as you would for a mortise and tenon joint (see steps 1–4 opposite),

but divide the thickness of the material by three to find one-third. Mark the waste on both pieces. On one piece, the centre will need to be removed. This is called the socket. On the other, each outside piece will need to be removed, leaving the pin.

2 Rip all the pieces to the shoulder line on the waste side. Cut the shoulder with a tenon saw to reveal the pin.

3 Working from both sides, remove the waste from the socket with a mortise chisel or coping saw.

4 Check for fit and adjust as necessary using a chisel. Apply adhesive to the surface of the joint. Check for square. Use a G-cramp to hold the joint while the adhesive sets.

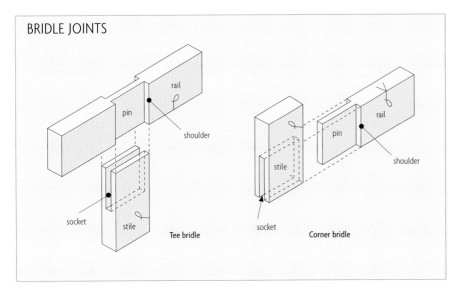

BRIDLE JOINTS

Tee bridle — rail, pin, shoulder, socket, stile

Corner bridle — stile, pin, rail, shoulder, socket

For best results, ensure the chisel is very sharp

MORTISE AND TENON JOINTS

The mortise and tenon joint is used in framing where two pieces of timber meet at a corner or intersection. It is probably the strongest of all the framing joints used in joinery and is used to construct doors, window sashes and furniture.

TYPES OF MORTISE AND TENON JOINT

The two main types are the common mortise and tenon joint, and the haunched mortise and tenon joint.

The haunched mortise and tenon joint is used at corners. The mortise and tenon are reduced to about two-thirds of the width of the material. A haunch is left next to the tenon and fits into a small groove near the mortise. The haunch helps prevent the rail twisting.

COMMON MORTISE AND TENON JOINT

1 Locate the position for the joint on both pieces of timber and square these marks around the timber. The marks represent the width of each intersecting piece. The tenon will be on the end of the rail and the mortise will be through the stile. A little waste should be left on the end of the tenon for cleaning up the joint.

2 Select a chisel that is as close as possible to one-third the thickness of the material. Set a mortise gauge to the same width as the chisel and gauge the mortise in the middle of the stile between the set-out lines. Work from the face side. If you prefer, use a marking gauge set to one-third of the thickness of the stile and work from both faces.

3 In the same way, gauge the tenon at the end and down both sides to the shoulder lines on the rail.

4 Place a support piece of timber in the vice, high enough to clamp the stile on edge. Clamp the stile to the support piece close to the set-out on the mortise.

5 Chisel the mortise, starting about 3 mm in from each end, being sure not to damage the end of the mortise when levering out the waste. Make sure to chisel straight by keeping the edge of the chisel parallel to the face of the stile. Make the first cut straight down with the ground edge of the chisel towards the centre of the mortise. Repeat at the other end.

6 Make a number of second cuts with the chisel at a slight angle, with the ground side down. Lever out the waste. Once down 5 mm, make a series of larger clearing cuts and lever out the waste. Continue down about halfway through. Turn the timber over and come in from the other side in the same manner.

7 Once the bulk of the waste has been removed, clean the mortise and cut back to

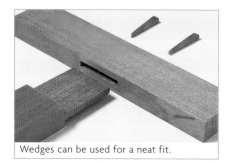

Wedges can be used for a neat fit.

the set-out lines by paring straight in from each side.

8 Rip the tenon, cutting on the waste side of the line and cut the shoulders with a tenon saw.

9 Test for fit and adjust as required. The shoulders of the tenon should fit neatly against the stile and finish square and free of twist.

10 To lock the joint, wedges may be placed on both sides of the tenon. The clearance for these is made in the mortise. From the outside of the stile, chisel the ends of the mortise about two-thirds of the way through at a slope of 1:8. The wedges are cut at the same slope.

11 Glue the joint and clamp it up tight. Check for square. Apply adhesive to the wedges and drive in firmly. Saw off the excess wedge and clean up the adhesive when set.

OTHER MORTISE AND TENON JOINTS

Mortise and tenon joints for sash and door construction differ slightly from the haunch mortise and tenon, although the technique for constructing them is the same. A rebate and/or a moulding is run on the inside to take the glass or panel.

When making a mortise and tenon joint in timber that has a rebate on it, keep the face of the tenon in line with the edge of the rebate. One shoulder on the rail is left longer

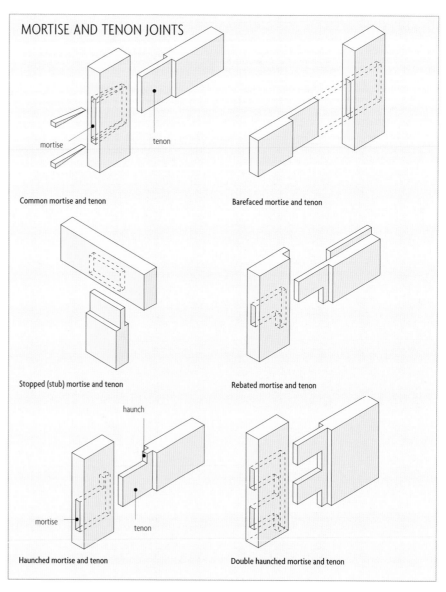

MORTISE AND TENON JOINTS

mortise

tenon

Common mortise and tenon

Barefaced mortise and tenon

Stopped (stub) mortise and tenon

Rebated mortise and tenon

haunch

mortise

tenon

Haunched mortise and tenon

Double haunched mortise and tenon

(the depth of the rebate) and the other short to fit against the top of the rebate—hence the name long and short shouldered mortise and tenon joint.

Mortise and tenon joints for timber with mouldings have a scribed shoulder to match the moulding. Alternatively, you can remove the moulding from the edge of the mortise and mitre or scribe it to match the corresponding piece.

Other types of mortise and tenon joints:
- barefaced—for door construction
- bevelled haunched—designed to hide the haunch
- double haunched—for wider sections of timber such as door bottom rails.

All these joints may be either through or stopped, so no end grain is seen on the outside of the stile, or they can be wedged and pinned.

workshop basics

WIDENING JOINTS

Wide, good-quality timber is becoming harder to obtain and is very expensive. These wide boards are also prone to excessive movement, making them difficult to work with. Widening joints are used to join narrower boards together on edge to create a wide panel for table or bench tops and panelling in doors.

PREPARATION

Before you begin to construct a widening joint you need to follow certain procedures:

- Select quarter-sawn timber where possible. It is less prone to movement across the face than plain-sawn timber. If plain-sawn boards are used, place them with the heart sides on alternate surfaces.
- Avoid putting quarter- and plain-sawn boards together in the same panel.
- Never mix different species of timber if they aren't seasoned (dried) properly. They will move at different rates and will split.
- If possible, arrange all the pieces so the grain lies in one direction.
- Always bring the timber to its correct size before jointing.
- Always use a good-quality adhesive.
- Match any grain or colour in the timber if the work is to be polished.

WIDENING BUTT JOINT

1 Lay all the pieces out with the face up. To help match the pieces up later, mark the edges to be joined with a continuous pencil line across the joints at an angle.

A loose tongue and groove joint.

2 Plane the edges true and test for fit against the corresponding pieces. Line the ends or the pencil lines up each time.

3 Check that there is no gap and the surface is flat. If you try to close gaps with a cramp or by filling them, the joint will split later.

4 If planing short lengths, place both pieces in the vice face to face and plane both edges together. The edges do not have to be square, as the angles will complement each other.

5 Prepare the joint as you would for a butt joint (see page 53) and apply adhesive. Rub the two surfaces together with a downward pressure, forcing out the excess adhesive and creating a suction between the surfaces.

OTHER WIDENING JOINTS

Other widening joints reinforced for extra strength and alignment are prepared the same way. They include:

- dowelled edge joint
- tongue and groove joint
- rebate joint.

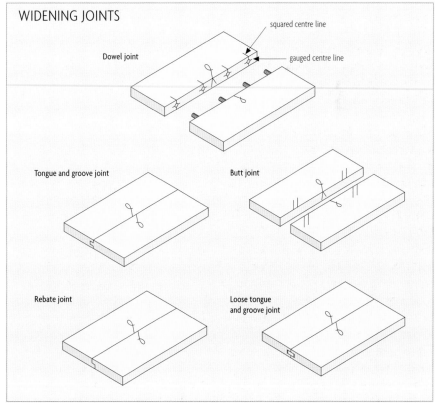

WIDENING JOINTS

squared centre line

gauged centre line

Dowel joint

Tongue and groove joint

Butt joint

Rebate joint

Loose tongue and groove joint

GLUING AND CLAMPING

Gluing and clamping are an important part of the woodworker's work, without which many items would lack strength.

ADHESIVES

Adhesive adds strength to the job by holding the work fast so that it cannot be pulled apart easily. Always wear protective gloves when working with adhesives, and follow instructions on the package for safe use. Clean excess adhesive off the job before it sets as it can blunt plane blades and clog up sanding paper.

PVA (polyvinyl acetate)

PVA is a general-purpose woodwork adhesive. While still wet it can be wiped off with a damp cloth. It has excellent gap-filling properties and needs clamping for a short time only. It sets in about an hour. PVA is quite strong and will adhere to almost any porous surface. It bonds permanently but is not heat- or water-resistant. Apply it to joints with a brush, but for larger flat surfaces dilute it with water and apply with a roller. Being water-based, PVA will shrink while it is setting.

Contact adhesive

Contact adhesive bonds on contact. Apply it to both surfaces, and when it is touch-dry place them together. It is used to bond plastic laminate or veneer to chipboard. No clamping is required. It cleans off with thinners.

Contact adhesive is flammable. Use it in a well-ventilated area to reduce the effects of the fumes. It is not recommended for outside use, as it is not waterproof or heatproof.

Epoxy adhesive

Epoxy adhesive is the strongest woodworking adhesive and the most expensive. A two-part resin adhesive, it doesn't shrink as it sets and won't soften with heat or creep under load. It is waterproof and bonds most materials, porous or not, except thermoplastic (PVC or perspex). It is suitable for outside use. It will clean up with thinners when wet.

Hot-melt adhesive

Hot-melt adhesive bonds almost anything, including many plastics. It generally comes as a stick that is inserted into an electric glue gun. Apply it, press the work together and hold for 30 seconds. No clamping is needed. It cleans up with thinners.

CRAMPS

Cramps come in a wide range of styles and sizes—those without a screw action are often called 'clamps'—but usually only a couple of types are required. Always place a small scrap of timber between the jaws and the work to prevent bruising the timber when pressure is applied.

GLUING AND CLAMPING TECHNIQUES

Before gluing any project make a trial assembly without adhesive. Clamp it if necessary to check the joints and the overall size.

If all is correct, pull the project apart, taking care to keep the pieces in order. Set up the gluing area and have cramps already set out on the bench to the correct width.

Assembling a frame

Using a brush for even coverage, spread adhesive on both sides of the joint and assemble the work quickly. Wipe off excess adhesive and place the job in the cramps.

Apply an even pressure to close the joints. The cramps should be square and parallel to the work.

Keep the cramps as close as possible to the joint. Check the rails are parallel and adjust as necessary. Measure the diagonals: if they are the same, the job is square. If not, a sharp tap on the end of the stile may move it. If necessary adjust the cramps.

If the work isn't flat across the surface, tap any parts that are kicked up with a mallet and block of timber. If this fails, you may need to ease off the cramps or to clamp a block of timber across the job.

Assembling a panel

Using a brush, apply an even coat of adhesive on both edges. Position a cramp at each end of the job and no more than 300 mm apart. Check the ends are flush and pencil marks align. Apply light pressure with the cramps. A cramp over the top will even up pressure and help prevent cupping.

Tighten the cramps evenly. Remove excess adhesive and allow the job to dry. Ensure the surface is flat, flush and free of twist.

CRAMPS

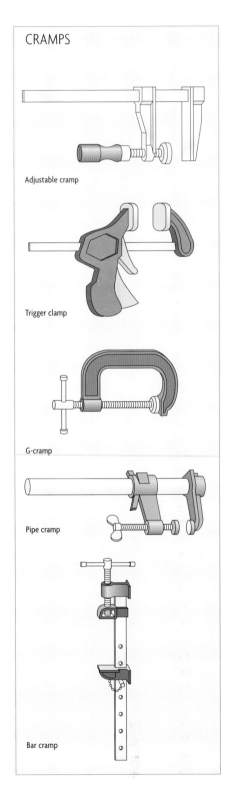

Adjustable cramp

Trigger clamp

G-cramp

Pipe cramp

Bar cramp

It is worth investing in a number of different-sized cramps, rather than just one. Also, if you are working on large projects, more than one cramp may be needed at a time.

building work-
benches and
tool storage

building work- benches and tool storage

FOLDAWAY BENCH

If your workshop area is shared with other activities or even with the family car, then this bench will suit you. When not in use, it folds down to take up a space of less than 100 mm from the wall.

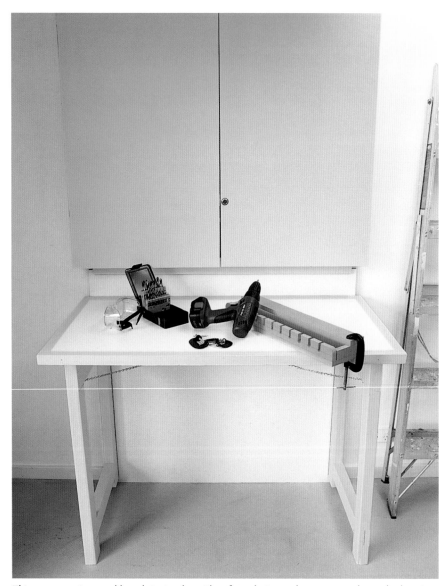

This space-saving workbench is sturdy, with safety chains and stoppers to keep the legs in the open position while you work.

TOOLS

- Builder's square
- Pencil
- Tape measure
- Handsaw
- Three 100 mm G-cramps
- Two 1000 mm sash cramps
- Portable electric drill
- Drill bits: 4 mm, 6 mm, countersink; masonry bit (if required)
- Screwdriver (cross-head)
- Ruler or other straight edge
- Marking gauge
- Chisels: 12 mm and 18 mm bevelled-edge wood chisels
- Mallet
- 200 mm adjustable spanner
- Safety glasses
- Hearing protection
- Dust mask
- Gloves

FIXING THE WALL CLEAT

1 Take the two pieces of timber that will form the wall cleat and cut them both to 1100 mm long. If you want to use the folding board featured in the photograph on page 88, assemble a 'T'-shaped wall cleat. If you are only using the bench, modify the cleat to be 'L'-shaped as shown in the diagram on page 70. Glue and clamp the two pieces of the cleat together. The wall panel sits behind the lip of the cleat but is not fastened to it.

2 Check the construction of your wall and determine the type of fastenings required (see page 72). Drill suitably sized holes through the middle of the two thicknesses of timber in the wall cleat. Stand the wall panel against the wall with the long edge horizontal and position the wall cleat above it. When you are sure that it is level, insert a pencil or pointed instrument through the holes in the cleat to mark the position of the fastenings on the wall. Remove the wall cleat and drill pilot holes for the screws or wall plugs, then fasten the cleat securely to the wall.

3 Having mounted the wall cleat correctly you should be able to take hold of the wall panel close to the floor and lift it forward and out from under the wall cleat, and completely away from the wall. This enables the completed bench to become a free-standing portable bench, or to be wall-mounted, as you choose.

PREPARING THE WALL PANEL

4 Lay the wall panel flat on an even surface and measure 900 mm from the bottom edge. Using a pencil, square and straight edge, mark a horizontal line across the wall panel on both faces. On the back face, mark another line parallel to the first one but 16 mm below it. Along this line, mark out eight evenly spaced screw holes 160 mm apart and 15 mm from each edge. Use a 4 mm bit to drill pilot holes for the screws. Countersink the holes on the back of the panel.

PREPARING THE LEGS

5 Check the timber you have selected for the legs is square and measures 66 x 41 mm (planed size). Mark off the lengths required for the front and back legs and side rails,

MATERIALS*

PART	MATERIAL	FINISHED LENGTH	WIDTH	NO.
Wall cleat	38 x 25 mm hardwood PAR	1100 mm		1
	75 x 25 mm hardwood PAR	1100 mm		1
Wall panel	18 mm MDF	1150 mm	1000 mm	1
Panel cleat	50 x 38 mm hardwood PAR	1200 mm		1
Top	32 mm laminated MDF	1136 mm	570 mm	1
Lipping (front)**	38 x 38 mm solid timber PAR	1200 mm		1
Lipping (side)**	38 x 38 mm solid timber PAR	570 mm		2
Front leg	75 x 50 mm solid pine PAR	868 mm		2
Back leg	75 x 50 mm solid pine PAR	750 mm		2
Rail	75 x 50 mm solid pine PAR	500 mm		4

Other: Sixty 38 mm x No. 12 wood screws; twelve 50 mm x No. 12 wood screws; eighty 16 mm x No. 8 chipboard screws (or size to suit hinges); PVA adhesive; two 700 mm piano hinges; one 1100 mm piano hinge; four to six masonry bolts OR wall-fixing screws as required (see page 72); 3 mm galvanized chain or 8 mm sash cord and rubber or wooden blocks (optional).

*   Finished size: top 1200 mm x 600 mm; height (to bench top) 900 mm. Timber sizes given are nominal. For timber types and sizes see page 112.

** The 38 x 38 mm lipping will give a reasonable fit, though the planed timber will be slightly narrower than the MDF. Alternatively, select 50 x 38 mm timber and plane it to the thickness of the laminated bench top, or increase the size of the MDF bench top to 1200 x 600 mm and omit the lipping entirely.

leaving the thickness of a saw cut between each length. You will need two front legs at 868 mm each, two back legs at 750 mm each and four rails at 500 mm each.

6 Lay the front and back legs together with 66 mm faces up and the top ends of the back legs exactly 84 mm from the tops of the front legs. Clamp them together with sash cramps or large G-cramps. Mark a line across both front legs with a pencil and square, level with the top of the back legs. Mark a second line 66 mm below this one across all four

legs. Mark another line 84 mm from the bottom of the front legs, across all four legs, and a parallel line 66 mm up from this one.

7 Remove the cramps, and with the square and pencil mark the joint edge lines across the narrow sides of each leg. Set a marking gauge to half the thickness of the legs, and scribe the middle lines of the joints.

8 Lay the rails with 66 mm faces up and ends aligned and hold them together using suitable cramps. With a pencil and

7 Use a marking gauge set to half the thickness of the leg and rail timber to scribe the centre line for the joints.

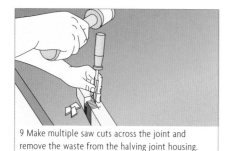

9 Make multiple saw cuts across the joint and remove the waste from the halving joint housing.

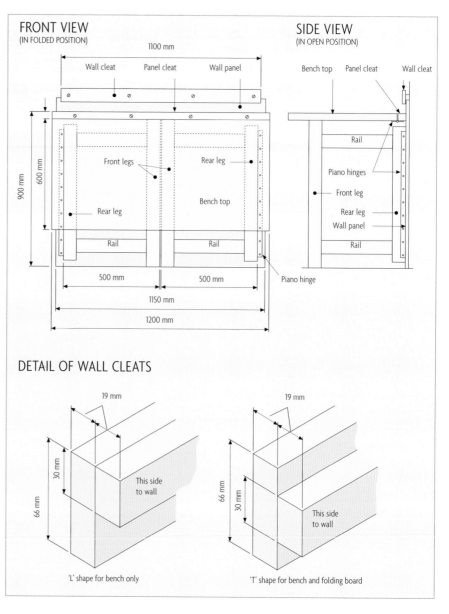

FRONT VIEW
(IN FOLDED POSITION)

1100 mm

Wall cleat · Panel cleat · Wall panel

900 mm
600 mm

Front legs · Rear leg

Rear leg

Bench top

Rear leg

Rail · Rail

500 mm · 500 mm

1150 mm

1200 mm

SIDE VIEW
(IN OPEN POSITION)

Bench top · Panel cleat · Wall cleat

Rail

Piano hinges

Front leg

Rear leg

Wall panel

Rail

Piano hinge

DETAIL OF WALL CLEATS

19 mm

66 mm
30 mm

This side to wall

'L' shape for bench only

19 mm

66 mm
30 mm

This side to wall

'T' shape for bench and folding board

square, mark a line 66 mm in from each end, across all four rails. Remove the cramps and use a square and pencil to continue the joint edge lines onto the narrower faces of the rails. Use the marking gauge to scribe the joint lines around the three sides of each end.

9 Use a saw to make cuts in the waste part of the joints, cutting through the material down to the scribed centre lines. The more cuts you make, the easier it will be to remove the waste with a chisel and mallet.

10 Check the joints for fit and, if necessary, ease the shoulders with a bevelled-edge chisel until the joints fit well and are square. Mark and drill pilot holes on each end of the rails, with two 38 mm x No. 8 screws offset diagonally for each joint. Glue and clamp the joints in place, then insert the screws.

11 Lay the wall panel on a stable, flat surface, and onto its front face lay the gate legs in closed position as shown in the plan, 95 mm from each outer edge of the wall panel.

Make sure there is a gap of 10 mm between them and that they are square to the edges of the panel. Clamp them in place. Position the piano hinges and, using 16 mm x No. 8 chipboard screws, screw the hinges to the wall panel and then to the legs. Check that the legs open easily and the wall panel and leg assembly stand square.

MAKING THE WORK TOP
12 Cut the timber lipping to size and set aside the longer (front) piece. Take the two side pieces and determine which is the outer face of each. Mark a line with a marking gauge down the centre of these and, on this line, mark three screw holes 40 mm in from each end and in the centre. Using a 6 mm drill bit, drill and countersink holes for

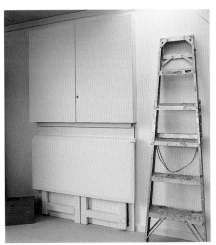

The workbench and tool cupboard fold neatly against a wall, leaving the space free for other activities.

the 38 mm x No. 12 wood screws. Apply adhesive to both side pieces and use sash cramps to secure them to the side edges of the bench top. Ensure that the top of the lipping is level with the laminated bench top. Repeat the process for the front lipping, with evenly spaced screw holes starting 60 mm from one end.

13 Cut the panel cleat to 1200 mm. Lay the bench top face down on a flat, level surface and lay the panel cleat along its rear edge. Position the 1100 mm piano hinge along the joint and screw into place with 16 mm chipboard screws.

14 Apply a line of adhesive to the rear face of the panel cleat and clamp it to the front of the panel with its top aligned to the line marked at 900 mm. Fix in place using 38 mm x No. 12 screws inserted from the back.

15 Check that the legs and the top swing open easily. Fit restraints of chain to prevent the legs being opened beyond 90 degrees, and add wooden blocks to the underside of the bench top to keep the legs open when in use.

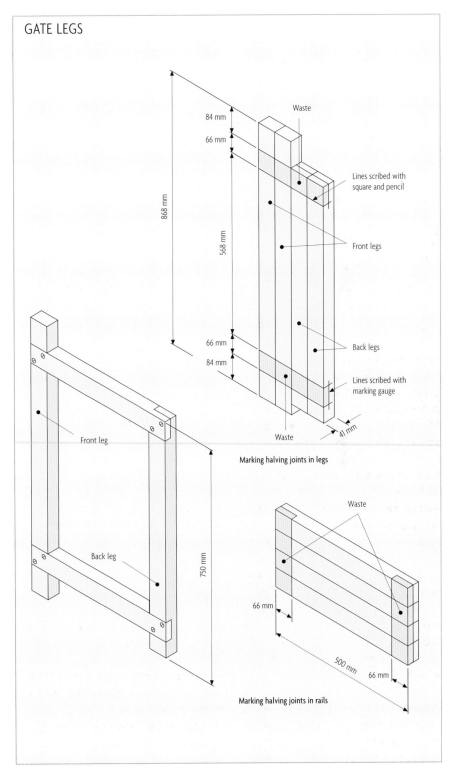

GATE LEGS

84 mm
66 mm
868 mm
568 mm
66 mm
84 mm

Waste
Lines scribed with square and pencil
Front legs
Back legs
Lines scribed with marking gauge
41 mm
Waste

Marking halving joints in legs

Front leg
Back leg
750 mm

Waste
66 mm
500 mm
66 mm

Marking halving joints in rails

WALL CONSTRUCTION

CONCRETE OR BRICK WALLS

These are also known as masonry walls. To make secure fastenings in these walls will involve the use of plugs or expansion bolts. Wall plugs come in various types and sizes and may be made of plastic, fibre or aluminium. The commonly used Rawlplugs are extruded plastic and come in different sizes to take different gauges of screws. You may use ordinary wood screws once the wall plugs are in place.

Expansion bolts are ideal for heavy-duty purposes and operate on the same principle as wall plugs, only the plug and bolt come as a single unit. Pre-drill and countersink holes spaced evenly on the item you want to mount on the wall, then use a nail or other narrow spike to mark through the holes where you will need to drill into the masonry, being careful to avoid drilling into mortar joints or cavities. Using a masonry bit and, with your portable electric drill set on low speed and hammer action, drill a hole of appropriate size in the wall to accept the plug or expansion bolt you have chosen.

TIMBER-FRAMED WALLS

First find the studs to fasten into, either by tapping with your knuckles or using an electronic stud finder. This will determine the position of the holes for the screws on the item you want to mount on the wall. If you are not sure, use a fine drill bit to drill into the wall—you will be able to feel the resistance of the timber. Mark the centres of the studs and measure the distance between them, then carefully transfer this measurement to your item. Drill and countersink the holes on the item you want to mount as usual, then insert the screws directly into the wall studs. Use Nos 10–12 wood screws at least half as long again as the thickness of timber you are fixing to the wall.

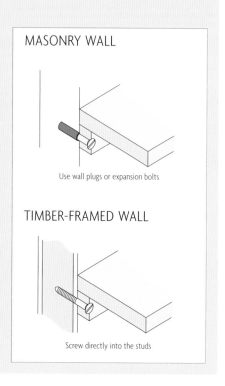

MASONRY WALL

Use wall plugs or expansion bolts

TIMBER-FRAMED WALL

Screw directly into the studs

CABINETMAKER'S BENCH

For those who are fortunate enough to have a large space in which to work and want a good size bench, this robust workbench will provide many years of service.

1 Cut the leg pieces and then plane the sawn edges smooth to ensure a good fit between the two pieces.

CONSTRUCTING THE LEGS

1 The legs are made in an 'L' shape which reduces the volume of timber (and therefore the cost) without reducing the strength.

With a tape measure and pencil, mark each of the four lengths of 200 x 38 mm leg material into one 110 mm wide piece and one 75 mm wide piece (the completed leg assembly will have approximately equal sides). Rip down the length of each leg with a handsaw. Plane the sawn edges smooth and straight.

2 Draw a pencil line parallel to and 15 mm in from one edge of each of the wider pieces of timber. Mark four evenly spaced screw locations along these lines (25 mm from one end, then at 270 mm intervals) and, using

a 10 mm drill bit, drill (counterbore) holes 10 mm deep. Complete the pilot holes with a 6 mm drill bit to suit the No. 12 screws. Apply adhesive to one long edge of the 75 mm wide leg piece and clamp it against the back of the pre-drilled edge of the 110 mm wide piece. Complete the assembly by screwing in four 50 mm x No. 12 wood screws. The counterbored holes will be plugged at a later stage.

BUILDING THE SUBFRAME

3 On a flat, smooth surface, lay out the six pieces of timber that make up the bench top

TOOLS

- Tape measure
- Pencil
- Handsaw
- Low-angle (block) plane
- Jack plane (if required)
- Square
- Portable electric drill
- Drill bits: 6 mm, 10 mm, countersink bit
- Screwdrivers (cross-head)
- Two 100 mm G-cramps
- Two 300 mm G-cramps
- Drill stand and 10 mm plug cutter (optional)
- 18 mm bevelled-edge or firmer chisel
- Mallet
- Hammer
- Safety glasses
- Dust mask
- Hearing protection

This bench was built out of hoop pine—a stable, resilient timber of medium hardness which is cost-effective for a bench of this type. The top can be re-planed many times to counter the inevitable wear and tear.

and check the width and length of the assembly (finished size will be 1800 x 960 mm). The final dimensions of the subframe should be the same as this measurement. Number the top pieces 1–6.

4 Cut the end rails to 900 mm (that is, the width of the bench top, less twice the thickness of the rails). On each rail, 55 mm in from the end and parallel to the end, mark a line with the pencil and square. On this line, 35 mm in from each edge, mark two screw holes, adding another in the middle. Counterbore and drill these screw holes as for the legs in step 2.

5 The solid (110 mm) face of each leg will be the end face. Determine which way is

up on each leg and mark the top with a pencil mark. On each leg, 50 mm down from the top, mark a line with a square and pencil around both faces, square to the corner edge. Spread adhesive over the area of the end face where it will be covered by the rail. Align the rail with its top edge along the 50 mm line and its

end aligned with the side face of the leg. Clamp it in place with 100 mm G-cramps. Insert and tighten the 50 mm x No. 12 screws.

6 You will now have two leg/end rail assemblies. Check that the legs are square to the end rails.

7 Cut the side rails to 1800 mm (that is, the length of the bench top). On each rail, 50 mm and 100 mm in from the ends and parallel to them, mark a line with the pencil and square. On the first line, 40 mm in from the top and bottom edges, mark the locations for two screw holes and add another in the centre. On the second line, mark two screw holes 60 mm in from each edge. Counterbore and drill these five screw holes as before. Apply adhesive to the area of the leg side face that will be covered by the rail, and align the side rail upper edge to the 50 mm line marked on the leg and its end to the outer face of the end rail. Clamp it in place and insert the 50 mm x No. 12 screws.

8 With the bench subframe complete and standing on a flat, level surface, once again check that it is absolutely square by taking measurements diagonally from each corner. If these measurements are equal, everything is square. A small error in the order of 5–10 mm in a structure this size would be tolerable.

9 Take a measurement between the inside faces of the legs parallel to the end rails, and cut the support rails to that length, less 4 mm (approximately 836 mm). With a 6 mm twist drill, drill two evenly spaced pilot holes about 20 mm in from the edges at each end of the support rails (being careful to avoid meeting other screws already in the assembly). Apply adhesive to the inside face of the legs that will be covered by the rails. Clamp the support rails in place so that the upper edge of the rail is level with the tops of the legs and insert the 50 mm x No. 12 wood screws.

MAKING THE BENCH TOP

10 Lay one of the bench top pieces in place so its outer edge is aligned with the outer

workshop basics

MATERIALS*

PART	MATERIAL	FINISHED LENGTH	NO.
Leg	200 x 38 mm solid timber PAR	860 mm	4
Top	175 x 50 mm solid timber PAR	1800 mm	6
Side rail	200 x 38 mm solid timber PAR	1800 mm	2
End rail	200 x 38 mm solid timber PAR	900 mm	2
Support rail	100 x 38 mm solid timber PAR	836 mm	2

Other: 50 mm x No. 12 wood screws; twenty-four 100 mm x No. 12 wood screws; PVA adhesive; contrasting material for plugs (19 mm solid timber PAR) or purchased 10 mm plugs; woodworking vice and stop block (optional).

* Finished size: 1800 x 960 mm and 900 mm high. Timber sizes given are nominal. For timber types and sizes see page 112.

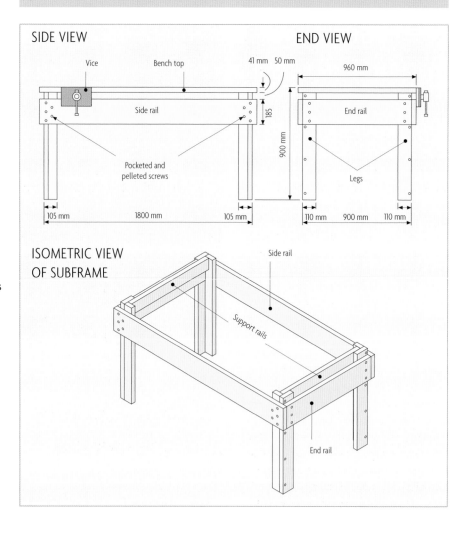

SIDE VIEW

END VIEW

Vice

Bench top

41 mm   50 mm

960 mm

Side rail

End rail

185

900 mm

Pocketed and pelleted screws

Legs

105 mm   1800 mm   105 mm

110 mm   900 mm   110 mm

ISOMETRIC VIEW OF SUBFRAME

Side rail

Support rails

End rail

face of the side rail, and one of its ends is aligned with the face of the end rail. Clamp it in place with 300 mm G-cramps. With a straight edge against the face of the other end rail, mark the finished length of the top piece. Check this measurement is the same at the other side of the bench, and cut all the top pieces to that length.

11 Mark a pencil line along the centre of the top edge of each of the support rails. Lay each top piece in turn in place and use a square to transfer to it the location of the support rail centre lines. On the top piece that you marked as number 1, locate a screw hole on the line so that it will be over the centre of the leg (75 mm in from the end and 45 mm in from the edge), and another hole the same distance (45 mm) from the other edge of the top piece. Repeat at the other end of the top piece. Counterbore and drill screw holes as before, then screw the timber in place with 100 mm x No. 12 wood screws.

12 Lay out the rest of the bench top pieces and mark screw holes in the same positions as for the first piece, ensuring that the outer screw on number 6 will enter the top of the leg as for number 1. Counterbore the holes and firmly screw all pieces in place. Where the screws enter the end grain in the top of the leg, remove each screw, fill the hole with PVA adhesive and reinsert the screw to ensure a secure fastening.

FINISHING

13 Using a low-angle plane, bevel any unwanted sharp edges on the legs, rails and bench top.

14 Using a drill press and 10 mm plug cutter, cut plugs from any contrasting soft wood to cover all the external screws. A plug cutter is not suitable for a hand-held drill, so if a drill press is not available, dowel or ready-made

13 Bevel any unwanted sharp edges on the bench top and subframe with a low-angle plane.

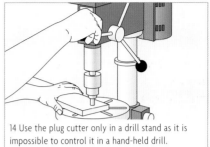

14 Use the plug cutter only in a drill stand as it is impossible to control it in a hand-held drill.

BENCH TOP WITH TOOL WELL

Old-fashioned cabinetmaker's benches had a tool well—a sunken area used to prevent tools falling off the bench and being damaged (or causing damage). Many people find that the tool well becomes a receptacle for rubbish and tools that would otherwise have been cleaned up and put away, so it has been left out of the bench on page 73.

However, if you want to add a tool well, this diagram shows how it may be done. When fitting the bench top as described in step 12, omit the second and third timbers, leaving a space of approximately 320 mm (the width of two top pieces) between the first and fourth planks. Turn the bench upside down and measure the distance between the support rails, then cut two 200 x 50 mm pieces of solid timber (PAR) to that length, less 5 mm. Secure these two boards to the edges of the bench top boards with 75 mm x No. 10 wood screws, after first gluing them together. Fit four short lengths of 175 x 50 mm timber (PAR) to fill the gaps in the bench top at the ends of the tool well, securing them with screws from the underside of the tool well and into the top of the support rail.

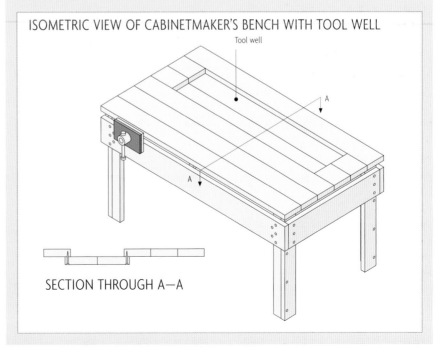

ISOMETRIC VIEW OF CABINETMAKER'S BENCH WITH TOOL WELL

Tool well

A

A

SECTION THROUGH A—A

15 After the glue has set, level the plugs and trim off any excess adhesive with a firmer chisel.

plugs can be substituted. Apply a little PVA adhesive to each plug and, placing a piece of scrap timber over the plug to prevent damage to the work top, use a hammer to tap it in.

15 Allow a couple of hours for the adhesive to set, and then trim the plugs and any excess adhesive off flush using an 18 mm firmer chisel and mallet.

16 A woodworking vice like the one shown in the photograph above right is an optional accessory that many woodworkers will find useful. To accommodate the permanently mounted vice, cut a clearance in the top edge piece and the side rail near one end of the bench. Counterbore and plug the holes for the bolts as for all of the other bench top screws, noting that the counterbored holes and plugs will need to be larger.

17 The adjustable stop block, pictured above right, is fitted through the bench top just behind the support rail. Measuring 60 mm square and 300 mm long, the block is secured in the appropriate position by a bolt and wing nut. Cut a vertical slot approximately 150 mm long and the same width as the bolt in the bottom end of the block and remove one screw from the end rail to accommodate the bolt. Adjust the block as required.

You might like to mount a vice and stop block on your bench. If necessary, cut a clearance from the side rails and hide any mounting bolts with timber plugs.

USING THE BENCH TOP FOR METAL WORK

If you intend to do any metal work on your cabinetmaker's bench, fit a small engineer's vice with a sheet of metal underneath to prevent metal cuttings from becoming embedded in the bench top or your project.

Secure the vice with bolts through the metal plate and the bench top. Both the vice and the metal sheet can easily be unbolted and demounted from the bench when more space is required for woodwork projects.

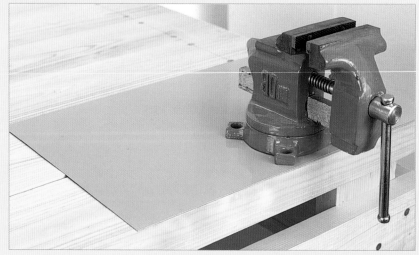

This picture shows how you may mount an engineer's vice and protective metal plate on the bench. Bolt the vice securely in place before use.

workshop basics

BENCH WITH STORAGE

When you have adequate floor space but wall space is at a premium, a bench top mounted on a storage cabinet may suit your needs. This storage unit has drawers and shelves and can be fitted with racks for planes, chisels and screwdrivers if desired.

TOOLS

- Jack plane
- Pencil
- Three sash cramps or cramp head sets and wooden bars
- Builder's square
- Tape measure
- Portable electric drill
- Drill bits: 4 mm, 5 mm, 6 mm, countersink
- Two 100 mm G-cramps
- Screwdriver (cross-head)
- Panel saw
- 3–5 mm chisel and mallet
- Sanding block
- Dust mask
- Safety glasses
- Hearing protection

ASSEMBLING THE TOP

1 Order the lengths for the bench top planed all round, but a bit overlength. Lay them out on a flat surface and arrange the growth rings in the end grain so that they alternate as in the diagram on page 78.

2 The top is made by edge gluing boards together to make up the size required. Check the fit of each board with its neighbour. There should be no gaps between them, but if there are, reduce the gaps to a minimum with a jack plane, being sure to maintain the squareness of the edges. Mark the top face of each board with a soft pencil and number them 1–4.

The bench top is made of hoop pine and is mounted on a storage box of 16 mm MDF. If there is a gap left at the top of the drawer box, cover it with a small piece of leftover MDF, as shown here.

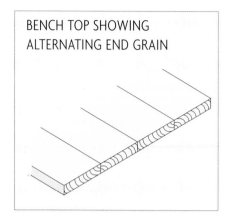

BENCH TOP SHOWING ALTERNATING END GRAIN

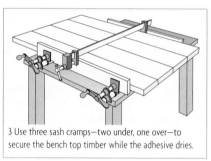

3 Use three sash cramps—two under, one over—to secure the bench top timber while the adhesive dries.

3 Apply adhesive to each of the joining edges of the boards and bring them together without delay. Use two sash cramps under and one over to clamp the boards together. Meanwhile, with 100 mm G-cramps and some scrap timber, ensure the edges of the boards are held tightly together with a flat profile. Tighten the sash cramps to an even pressure, and remove the scrap timber before any excess adhesive causes it to stick to the bench top. Leave the bench top to dry overnight.

ASSEMBLING THE BASE

4 Your supplier will be able to cut the larger pieces of MDF to size for you, or you can mark them out and cut them yourself. Take the two 630 x 870 mm pieces of MDF for the end panels of the base and measure 92 mm from the bottom edge. With a pencil and straight edge, mark a line across, parallel to the bottom edge. Along this line, mark screw

MATERIALS*

PART	MATERIAL	FINISHED LENGTH	WIDTH	NO.
Top**	225 x 50 mm solid timber PAR	1400 mm		4
End panel	16 mm MDF	630 mm	870 mm	2
Base panel	16 mm MDF	630 mm	1168 mm	1
Plinth (side)	16 mm MDF	630 mm	100 mm	2
Plinth (front/back)	16 mm MDF	1232 mm	100 mm	2
Mid panel	16 mm MDF	770 mm	1168 mm	1
Dividing panel	16 mm MDF	770 mm	420 mm	1
Fascia	16 mm MDF	1200 mm	75 mm	2
Front shelf	16 mm MDF	420 mm	648 mm	2
Rear shelf	16 mm MDF	1168 mm	150 mm	2
Shelf cleat	25 x 25 mm solid timber PAR	150 mm		2
Drawer side	140 x 12 mm prefabricated	400 mm		8
Drawer front/back	140 x 12 mm prefabricated	478 mm		8
Drawer base	4 mm MDF	370 mm	448 mm	4
Drawer front	16 mm MDF	520 mm	164 mm	4
Top mounting cleat	75 x 38 mm solid timber PAR	750 mm		2

Other: PVA adhesive; 50 mm x No. 8 chipboard screws; forty 25 mm x No. 8 chipboard screws for shelf supports and drawer runners; eighty 30 mm x No. 8 chipboard screws for drawers; sixteen 20 mm x No. 8 chipboard screws for drawer fronts; twelve 45 mm x No. 12 wood screws for cleats; ten No. 10 wood screws of varying lengths for bench top; twenty-four brass shelf-support plugs; four pairs of drawer runners; four drawer handles and appropriate screws; abrasive paper.

* Finished size: Bench top 1400 x 840 mm and 910 mm high; storage cabinet base 1200 x 630 mm and 870 mm high. Timber sizes given are nominal. For timber types and sizes see page 112.

** Timber of these dimensions (225 x 50 mm) may be hard to find and expensive, although it makes a solid and sturdy bench top. If necessary, substitute six lengths of 150 x 38 mm solid timber PAR and adjust your measurements as required.

holes 40 mm in from the front edge, then at 110 mm intervals (six screw holes in total). Use a 4 mm twist drill and countersink bit to drill countersunk holes from the outside face of the end panels.

5 Clamp a straight piece of scrap timber to the inside face of each end panel so that its lower edge is exactly 100 mm from the bottom edge of the panel. Spread adhesive on one end of the 630 x 1168 mm base panel

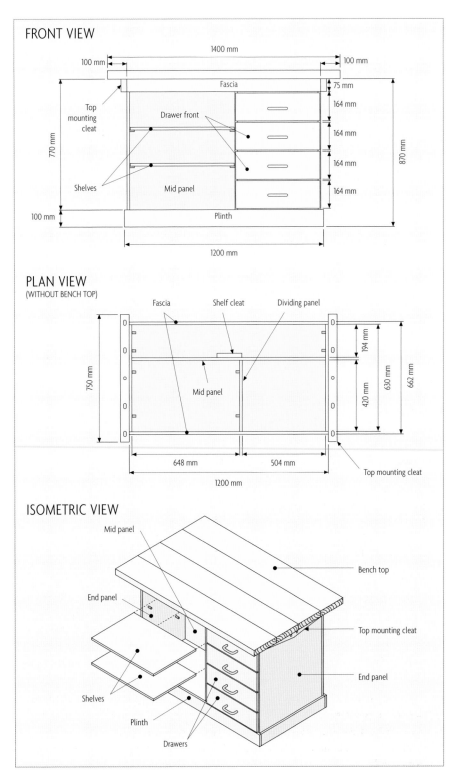

FRONT VIEW

1400 mm

100 mm | 100 mm

Fascia

75 mm

164 mm

Top mounting cleat

Drawer front

164 mm

770 mm

164 mm

870 mm

164 mm

Shelves

Mid panel

Plinth

100 mm

1200 mm

PLAN VIEW
(WITHOUT BENCH TOP)

Fascia   Shelf cleat   Dividing panel

194 mm

750 mm

420 mm

630 mm

662 mm

Mid panel

648 mm   504 mm

Top mounting cleat

1200 mm

ISOMETRIC VIEW

Mid panel

Bench top

End panel

Top mounting cleat

Shelves

End panel

Plinth

Drawers

and position it against the scrap timber so that its top face is 100 mm from the lower edge of the end panel. Insert the 50 mm x No. 8 chipboard screws from the outside face of the end panel to secure and repeat the procedure for the other end panel. Remove the scrap timber.

6 Take two 630 x 100 mm lengths of MDF for the plinth. Mark a line 8 mm down from the top of each plinth and parallel to the top edge. Mark five screw holes in each plinth piece, starting 55 mm in from one edge and then at 130 mm intervals, checking that these will not align with the positions of the screws that hold the end panels to the base. Drill and countersink the holes. Spread adhesive on the inside face of the plinth and clamp it to the lower edge of the end panel. Fasten in place with 50 mm x No. 8 chipboard screws.

7 Take two 1232 x 100 mm lengths of MDF for the plinth and, 8 mm from the upper edge, draw a line parallel to the edge. Mark nine screw holes, starting 66 mm in from one edge, then at 140 mm intervals. On each end of the plinth, mark a screw hole 8 mm in from the end and halfway between the two edges (50 mm). Drill countersunk holes.

8 Spread adhesive on the front edge of the base panel and the lower front edges of the end panels and lay on the plinth piece, so that both ends are flush with the outer face of the side plinth pieces. The top edge of the plinth piece should be flush with the top face of the base panel. Screw into place with 50 mm x No. 8 chipboard screws, and repeat the procedure for the back plinth piece.

STORAGE MODULE
9 Check that the mid panel is a snug fit between the end panels and that its top

PLANE STORAGE

One drawer of the bench can be modified to store planes. Cover the bottom of the drawer with waxed baize and fasten small battens at appropriate intervals on the drawer base, to prevent your planes moving when you open and close the drawer.

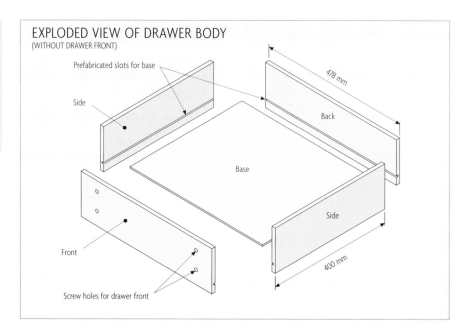

EXPLODED VIEW OF DRAWER BODY
(WITHOUT DRAWER FRONT)

Prefabricated slots for base

Side

Back

478 mm

Base

Side

400 mm

Front

Screw holes for drawer front

edge aligns with the top edges of the end panels. Position the panel 420 mm in from the front edges of the end panels. Mark lines on the end and base panels on either side of the mid panel, then remove the panel. Symmetrically mark and drill a number of screw holes (about fifteen, five on each end and five across the base) centrally between these lines. Countersink the holes from the outside face of the end panels and from underneath the base panel. Apply adhesive to the edges of the mid panel, position it between the marked lines and insert the 50 mm x No. 8 chipboard screws to secure the panel in place.

10 Take the 420 x 770 mm dividing panel and check the fit. Mark a line square to the front edge and 504 mm from the right end panel. Align the dividing panel so its right-hand face is flush with this line, ensure that it is square with the mid panel and the base, and mark lines on both sides of the panel as you did for the mid panel in step 9. Mark and drill eight screw holes (five on the mid panel and three on the base) centrally between these lines and countersink them from the back of the mid panel and from underneath the base panel. Apply adhesive to the back and bottom edges of the dividing panel, position it between the marked lines and insert the 50 mm x No. 8 chipboard screws to secure.

FASCIAS AND SHELVES
11 Take the two 1200 x 75 mm fascias and clamp them to the top of the storage

assembly so that the ends are flush with the outer face of the end panels on both sides. On the front piece, use a pencil to mark the position of the dividing panel and square a line across the front face of the fascia at the mid point of the dividing panel. Square a line 8 mm from each end, and on each of these three lines mark two screw holes approximately 20 mm in from each edge. Remove the fascia from the assembly, drill and countersink the holes then, applying adhesive to the edges of the end and dividing panels where they will meet the fascia, replace it and insert the 50 mm x No. 8 chipboard screws. Repeat at both ends of the back fascia.

12 In the end and dividing panel on the left-hand side of the module you will need to drill a series of blind holes to take the movable shelf support plugs. To ensure that the shelves are evenly spaced, cut a batten of scrap timber 770 mm long and mark a line down its centre. Mark one end of the batten as the base and mark and drill 4 mm holes right through the batten along the centre

line at 200 mm from its base, then at 50 mm intervals up to 600 mm from its base. Place the batten against the end panel so the holes are approximately 100 mm in from the mid panel, ensure the batten is square to the base and drill through the holes in the batten. Fit the twist drill into the chuck so that the amount of drill protruding is equal to the thickness of the batten plus the desired depth of the blind holes (approximately 12 mm). Repeat on the dividing panel and again 100 mm in from the front of the cabinet. Cut shelves from MDF and try them to see that they fit.

13 The same scrap wood batten may be used to drill blind holes in both end panels for the narrow shelves at the rear of the storage unit. Place the batten with one edge against the mid panel and drill one set of holes, then locate the second set of holes approximately 60 mm in from the back edge of the end panels. Because of the length of these narrow shelves, the 16 mm MDF is likely to bend. To prevent this, secure short lengths of 25 x 25 mm cleat to the mid panel, centrally

HINT

Drill pilot holes for all screws to be driven into MDF, especially into the end grain, to avoid splitting the board.

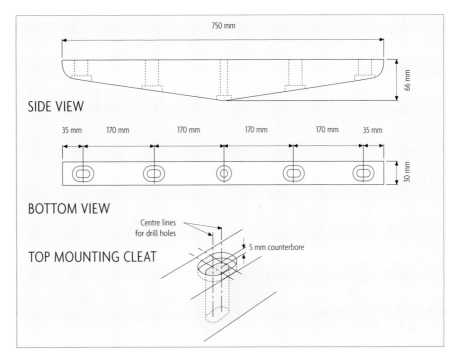

between the end panels and with the top of the cleats in line with the top of the shelf support holes you have drilled. Use the scrap wood battens to help you mark the position of these cleats and secure them with 25 mm x No. 8 chipboard screws.

ASSEMBLING THE DRAWERS

14 The drawers are assembled from prefabricated drawer section available from most hardware stores in 2400 mm lengths. Drawer runners are also available at most hardware stores and come in many sizes and types, so select a 400 mm runner of a type that suits your requirements. Cut eight side pieces of drawer section 400 mm long and eight front/back pieces 478 mm long. Adjust the width of the drawers if necessary to suit the type of runners you have selected, following the manufacturer's instructions. Mark and drill with a 4 mm bit four evenly spaced countersunk screw holes 6 mm in from each end of the 400 mm pieces. Partly assemble a drawer body and check the size of the drawer base before cutting four bases from 4 mm MDF.

15 Apply adhesive to the ends of the side pieces and assemble the drawer bodies, inserting the bases into the prefabricated slots before fitting in the fourth side. Use 30 mm x No. 8 screws to secure. Once the drawer is assembled, remove one screw at a time, insert adhesive in the hole and replace the screw, tightening firmly.

16 Following the manufacturer's instructions, attach the drawer runners to the inside of

the cabinet with centres approximately 168 mm apart. Attach the remaining runner hardware to each drawer body, following the manufacturer's instructions.

17 Mark and drill two screw holes 60 mm in from each end and 60 mm apart on the inside of the front panel. Countersink the holes on the inside. Cut four drawer fronts from 16 mm MDF, each measuring 520 mm by 164 mm.

18 Mount the bottom drawer body on its runners and position a drawer front with an 8 mm overlap on each side edge and a couple of millimetres clearance from the base of the cabinet. Use 100 mm G-cramps to clamp the front to the body before withdrawing the assembly and drilling pilot holes for the 20 mm x No. 8 chipboard screws. Screw the drawer front to the body.

19 Return the completed drawer to the cabinet and position the next drawer above it. Allowing a 3–4 mm gap between the

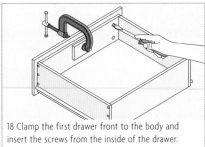

18 Clamp the first drawer front to the body and insert the screws from the inside of the drawer.

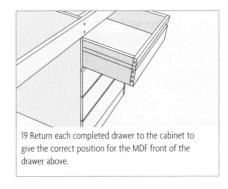

19 Return each completed drawer to the cabinet to give the correct position for the MDF front of the drawer above.

drawer fronts, clamp the next drawer front to the body and assemble as before. To attach the top drawer front, partially screw the holding screws through the front of the drawer body so the points project outwards slightly and press the MDF front against the screws to mark the correct positions. Drill pilot holes in the MDF, then remove the top drawer body from the cabinet to attach the drawer front. When all fronts are attached, mark and drill the positions for the drawer handles, drilling right through the drawer front and body. Firmly screw the handles in place.

ADDING THE TOP

20 Take the two top mounting cleats and taper the edges if you like, as shown in the diagram on page 81. Cut away the waste with a saw and dress the sawn faces with a plane, rounding over the ends at the same time. Mark holes with centres approximately 35 mm from each end of the cleat, then at 170 mm intervals (this will place one hole directly in the centre of the cleat). These holes should be drilled vertical to the top edge of the cleat and all except the centre hole must be elongated to allow for the expansion and contraction of the timber top. Use a 5 mm twist drill

to make two pilot holes, one either side of the centres you have marked, then remove any material between the two holes with a very fine chisel. Counterbore the holes to a depth of around 5 mm using a 10 mm twist drill and making elongated holes as before.

21 The cleats are attached to the end panels with adhesive and 45 mm x No. 12 wood screws. The holes for the screws that fasten these cleats to the MDF panelling should be countersunk on the inner face of the end panels. Mark screw holes at 60 mm from each end of the panel and also at 170 mm from each end and 280 mm from each end. Clamp the cleat to the end panel and ensure that the marked screw holes will not interfere with the counterbored holes for the top fastening screws. Drill pilot holes with a 6 mm drill bit. Apply adhesive to the inner face of the cleat and clamp it to the end panel. Insert the screws.

22 Allow the adhesive holding the cleats to the cabinet to dry, preferably overnight. Once the adhesive has set, lay the bench top

on the MDF cabinet and align it square. Use No. 10 wood screws that are approximately 15 mm longer than the depth of the pilot holes in the cleat; that is, two 40 mm screws at each end, two 50 mm screws and one 60 mm screw in the centre. Insert the screws centrally in the elongated slots and screw the top down firmly. Check that all is square, then loosen each screw off by half a turn. Do not use adhesive to secure the bench top to the cabinet.

23 Use a saw and plane to level the ends of the top timbers and slightly bevel all edges with a block plane. A little sanding here and there may be needed to create a pleasing finish.

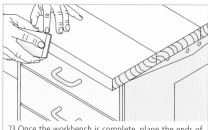

23 Once the workbench is complete, plane the ends of the bench top square and finish with a little sanding.

WALL-MOUNTED TOOL CUPBOARD

The ideal storage place for all your tools, this cupboard is constructed using rebate joints on all corners and housing joints for shelves and divisions. It is hung on the wall by split battens, so it can be lifted off and taken to a job site if required.

CUTTING OUT

1 Decide where you want the shelves and divisions to go in your tool cupboard. The inside of this cupboard has been set up with one main shelf, above which are two vertical dividers with two small shelves attached to the outer side (see diagram on page 85). You can alter this arrangement to suit your tools, but remember to add 12 mm to the desired

lengths of the shelves and dividers as each end will be set 6 mm into a housing joint.

2 Cut all material to size using a handsaw or jigsaw; for greater accuracy, use a mitre box or electric mitre saw. Use a smoothing plane to square up the ends and a square to check for accuracy. Stack each section together and ensure all parts are cut out.

2 Cut all material to size. Using a mitre box such as this ensures greater accuracy when cutting.

This tool cupboard is easy to make and hang, and will keep your tools safely locked away when not needed. Each tool hangs in its own place, making them easy to locate and keep in good condition.

TOOLS

- Panel saw
- Tenon saw
- Jigsaw (optional)
- Coping saw (optional)
- Mitre saw (optional)
- Mitre box (optional)
- Portable circular saw (optional)
- Tape measure
- Pencil
- Square
- Electric router (optional)
- Router bit: 18 mm straight
- Chisel: 18 mm
- Portable electric drill
- Drill bits: various sizes
- Hammer
- Nail punch
- Smoothing plane
- Electric sander (optional)
- Cork sanding block
- Screwdriver (to suit hinges)
- Dust mask
- Safety glasses
- Hearing protection

MATERIALS*

PART	MATERIAL	LENGTH	NO.
Side (centre/doors)	25 x 150 mm pine PAR	900 mm	6
Centre top/bottom	25 x 150 mm pine PAR	888 mm	2
Door top/bottom	25 x 150 mm pine PAR	435 mm	4
Divider	25 x 150 mm pine PAR	558 mm	2
Main shelf	25 x 150 mm pine PAR	876 mm	1
Small shelf	25 x 150 mm pine PAR	176 mm	4
Door shelf	25 x 75 mm pine PAR	423 mm	2
Split batten	25 x 75 mm pine PAR	900 mm	2
Centre back	6 mm plywood	900 x 900 mm	1
Door back	6 mm plywood	900 x 450 mm	2

Other: PVA adhesive; 40 mm lost-head nails; 25 mm panel pins; abrasive paper: two sheets of 120 grit; two 900 mm piano hinges; two 50 mm barrel bolts; hasp and staple lock; 25 mm x No. 6 roundhead screws; 50 mm x No. 8 countersunk screws; 6 x 6 mm beading; tool mounting clips.

* With doors closed the cupboard measures 900 mm high, 900 mm wide and 276 mm deep. Timber sizes given are nominal (see page 112).

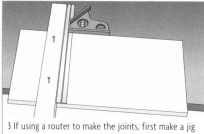

3 If using a router to make the joints, first make a jig by fixing a scrap piece of timber at right angles.

5 Adjust the router bit to cut 6 mm deep and cut the housing joints, being sure to be accurate.

CUTTING THE JOINTS

3 Select one side piece and use a tenon saw or router with 18 mm bit (see page 35) to cut a rebate 12 mm deep on the inside face at both ends. Repeat for the other sides.

4 Select the two sides for the centre section. Place them side by side on a flat surface and set out the housing joints for the shelves. For the main shelf, measure up from the bottom 300 mm and square a line across both pieces at this point. Measure up a further 18 mm

(the thickness of the material) and draw a parallel line. These two lines represent the width of the housing joint.

5 Carefully cut the housing groove 6 mm deep (one-third the thickness of the timber). Then repeat this process on the other side piece.

6 Set out the positions for the small shelves at even spaces (or to suit your needs). With the two side pieces placed side by side as before, transfer the position from

one to the other. Remove one of the side pieces and place a divider in its place, with the top of the divider 12 mm down from the top of the side piece (as it will be set into the top piece). Square the small shelf marks across onto the divider and repeat with the other side and divider. Cut the housings using a saw and chisel, or with a router.

7 Set out the housing joints in the top and the main shelf by placing them side by side on a flat surface and measuring 170 mm in

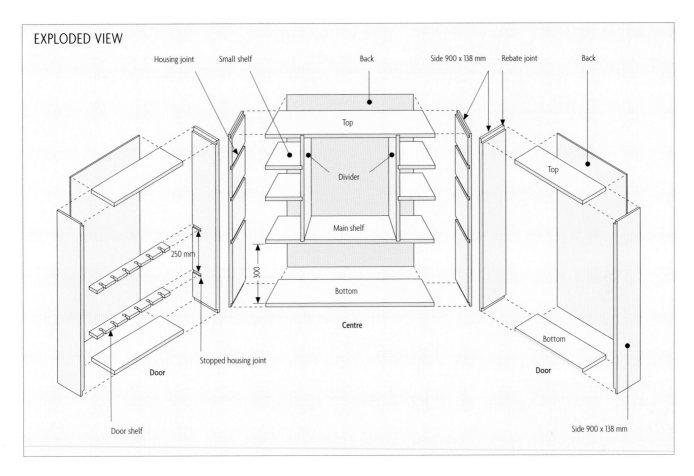

EXPLODED VIEW

Housing joint · Small shelf · Back · Side 900 x 138 mm · Rebate joint · Back · Top · Divider · Main shelf · 250 mm · 300 · Bottom · Centre · Stopped housing joint · Door · Top · Bottom · Door · Side 900 x 138 mm · Door shelf

from each end. Square a line across at this point and another a further 18 mm on (the thickness of the material). Cut the housing joints.

THE DOOR SHELVES

8 To make the slotted shelves to hold screwdrivers, files or chisels, drill holes the required distance apart (about 50 mm) into the centre of the door shelves and then cut slots from the holes to the front edge with a tenon saw. The holes and slots may be of varying sizes to suit the tools.

9 Take the two sides of one door and set out stopped housing joints for the slotted shelves, measuring up the required distance from the bottom, and allowing enough space

between (about 250 mm) to get the tools in and out. Lay the two side pieces side by side. Measure across from the back edge the width of the shelves and mark a line parallel to this edge where the housing will stop. Mark all four stopped housing joints, making sure the sides make a pair (one left-handed and one right-handed). Cut out the housings, being careful not to go past the stopped end. Square the ends of the housings with a chisel, and check the fit of each shelf.

THE CUPBOARD

10 To assemble the cupboard, work on one housing joint at a time, applying adhesive and then nailing through the joint using 40 mm lost-head nails. Begin with the centre

section: take one divider and fix one small shelf, then the other. Repeat for the other divider. Fix the dividers to the main shelf and top.

11 Apply adhesive to the housing joints and the top rebate joint on one side piece. Fit the side piece to the shelf assembly and nail through the outside into the end of each shelf. Then nail through the top piece into the rebate joint. Fix the other side to the unit in the same way. Stand the unit on its top, and glue and nail the bottom in place by nailing through the timber into the rebate joint.

12 Assemble the doors using the same method as for the cupboard.

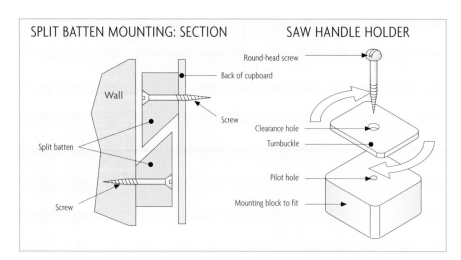

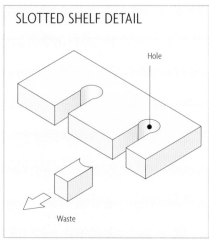

SPLIT BATTEN MOUNTING: SECTION

Wall
Split batten
Screw
Back of cupboard
Screw

SAW HANDLE HOLDER

Round-head screw
Clearance hole
Turnbuckle
Pilot hole
Mounting block to fit

SLOTTED SHELF DETAIL

Hole
Waste

13 Lay the centre section on a flat surface and plane any of the joints flush using a smoothing plane. Check the section is square by measuring the diagonals. Apply light pressure to the longer diagonal until it is square. Apply adhesive to the edge and place the plywood back in position. Fix it using 25 mm panel pins 40–50 mm apart, nailing to all sides, shelves, dividers, top and bottom. Neaten the edges by planing and sanding the whole job. Repeat this on the two doors.

THE DOORS

14 Although the tools to go on the doors are lightweight, the doors will still carry a fair amount of weight, so piano hinges are best, although butt hinges will do. The leaf of the piano hinge is 12 mm wide and 1 mm thick. Run a rebate down the full length of the side pieces of the cupboard and on the hinge side of the doors (the 12 mm will be on the edge of these pieces). Fix the hinge in position with the screws provided (usually 16 mm x No. 4), placing one in the top and bottom and one in the centre on each side. Check the operation of the door, adjust as required and fix all the screws.

15 To hold the door shut, use barrel bolts on the inside of one door, top and bottom. On

the other door fit a lock or a hasp and staple with a padlock.

TOOL MOUNTINGS

16 For small tools use commercially available tool-mounting clips or hooks. To hang the saws and level, glue on blocks of timber cut to the inside shape of the handle and attach a turnbuckle made from scrap ply or timber and fixed to the handle block with 25 mm x No. 6 roundhead screws (see diagram above). To hold the squares use pieces of timber with a rebate in the back edge the size of the blade.

17 To prevent tools falling off the shelves, pin small beading (6 x 6 mm) along each

MANUFACTURED BOARDS

Two types of manufactured boards are commonly used, chipboard and MDF.

- Chipboard, made from timber chips bonded together, is rarely used in its raw state, but it also comes with a melamine or timber veneer. To give a good finish, exposed edges need to be covered with a matching edging material.
- MDF (medium-density fibreboard) is an ideal material for building furniture, as you can use a plane and router on it and it doesn't need finishing, although it will take a surface treatment if desired. However, it does contain chemicals that can cause skin problems in some people. Always work out of the sun. Wear gloves if you have sensitive skin, and protect your eyes, nose, mouth and lungs from the dust.

shelf. Don't glue it, as you may need to move it later. Fix a small piece of beading across the shelf where the planes will fit. This will help protect the blade from damage by keeping the edge up off the shelf.

FIXING TO THE WALL

18 To make the split battens, set the circular saw at a 45-degree angle and rip a 900 mm piece of 75 x 25 mm timber down the centre of the face to produce two pieces of timber the same width with a bevel on one edge. Make two sets of battens, one to go at the top and one at the bottom of the cupboard. Drill clearance holes through them corresponding to the centres of the unit sides and (for the top batten only) the two dividers.

19 Lay the unit face down and position the battens 75 mm in from the top and bottom, ensuring that the bevel edge of each batten is on the bottom and the wide face is on the outside. Drill pilot holes through the clearance holes in the battens into the cupboard and fix using 50 mm x No. 8 screws.

20 Decide where you will hang the cupboard and the distance from the bottom of the cupboard to the floor. Place the remaining half of each batten against the ones fixed to the cupboard. Measure the distance up from the bottom of the cupboard to the lower edge of each pair of battens. Add this

measurement to the distance from the bottom of the cupboard to the floor and mark the positions on the wall. Fix the battens to the wall with the bevelled side upwards, using at least three 50 mm x No. 8 screws for each and ensuring the battens are level and in line with each other. If you are fixing the cupboard to a framed wall, make sure the screws have solid fixing into the frame. If you are fixing it to a masonry wall, use plastic wall plugs or other patented fastenings.

21 Lift the tool cupboard onto the wall just above the battens and slide it down until it rests neatly and firmly on the battens.

22 If desired, apply a finish of your choice (see below).

POSITIONING THE TOOL CUPBOARD

When deciding where to hang your cupboard, consider how easy it will be to get the tools in and out. There should be enough clearance so that the doors will open at least to a right angle. The cupboard should not be placed so high that you can't reach the tools or so low that you can't place a workbench under it. Placing it so that the bottom is approximately 1200 mm off the floor or 300 mm above your workbench is ideal.

FINISHING YOUR PROJECT

PREPARATION
- If there has been any major bruising of the timber, remove the dents by covering them with a wet rag and ironing over the rag. The steam and heat will penetrate the timber and swell the grain. This process may need to be repeated a couple of times if the bruising is bad.
- You may need to use a scraper to remove scratches that go across the grain properly. Sanding the scratches out is not always successful and can leave a large, unsightly hollow.
- Fill the nail holes and any other gaps in the outer face with wood filler.
- Give the surface a good sand with 180 grit abrasive paper. If you are using MDF, take care not to sand the faces too hard, as this will make them furry, but do work hard on the edges. Use good-quality wood filler to fill bruises or holes that may be visible after finishing.

PAINTING
- If you are painting your project, first apply a coat of primer/undercoat so that the timber is well coated. This also makes it easier to sand back to a smooth finish. Apply two coats of the top coat of your choice, remembering to sand between each coat with 180 grit abrasive paper.
- If you are using MDF, choose a good-quality undercoat that has been specially formulated for use with MDF.

APPLYING LACQUER OR VARNISH
- If you are planning to stain, varnish or lacquer the project, make sure you remove all excess adhesive before applying the finish, or the finish will not penetrate through into the timber and you will be left with white blotches.
- First apply a sealer coat of your chosen finish and allow it to dry before sanding it with 220 grit abrasive paper. Apply the final coat using a good-quality 75 mm brush for large flat surfaces, and always brush in the direction of the grain. Use a well-wetted brush, and work from one end to the other with full strokes if possible. Move the brush slowly over the surface and watch the material flow from the brush. In some cases a third coat may be necessary. If so, sand between coats and clean the dust off before applying the final coat.

SMALL LOCKABLE CUPBOARD

In a shared work space a small wall-mounted lockable cupboard is a great idea for storing tools. The one shown here is ideal for mounting above a workbench.

Almost all types of hand tools can be mounted on this type of folding cupboard. The fact that this one is lockable is useful for security and for ensuring a neat and tidy appearance in a workshop that may be shared with other activities.

TOOLS

- Pencil and tape measure
- Handsaw
- Jack plane
- Rule and pencil
- Square
- Portable electric drill
- Drill bits: 4 mm, 5 mm, countersink bit
- Screwdriver (cross-head)
- Two 300 mm G-cramps
- Dust mask
- Safety glasses
- Hearing protection

PREPARING THE PIECES

1 Cut the MDF panels to the sizes indicated, and plane the edges smooth and square. Alternatively, your supplier may be able to cut the pieces to size for you.

2 On the back face of the back panel, draw lines parallel to the edges 8 mm in from each side edge and the top edge. Do the same 28 mm and 194 mm up from the bottom edge. Mark six screw holes along each horizontal line, starting 75 mm in from the edge and continuing at 210 mm intervals. Mark five screw holes along the two vertical lines, beginning 100 mm from the top edge and continuing at 200 mm intervals. With a 5 mm bit, drill the holes and countersink them from the back face of the panel.

3 Take both 1000 x 100 mm side panel pieces and identify the inner face and the top end with suitable markings. Using a square, mark a line 8 mm from the top edge. On this line mark two screw holes 35 mm and 70 mm from the front edge then drill and countersink them. Measure up 28 mm and 194 mm from the bottom edge and use the square to mark lines parallel to the bottom edge. Drill and countersink two screw holes on each of these lines as before.

ASSEMBLING THE CABINET

4 Apply adhesive to the back edge of one side panel and butt it up against the back panel, flush with the side edges. Clamp it in place with large G-cramps, then insert the screws from the back. Next take the top panel, apply adhesive to its back and end edges and position it flush with the top edges of the side and back panels. Clamp and screw as before, and repeat for the other side panel.

5 To ensure the correct alignment for the bottom and shelf, take a piece of scrap timber and clamp it so the top edge is exactly 186 mm from the bottom edge of the back panel (8 mm below the centres of the pilot holes for the screws) and square. Apply adhesive to the back and end edges of the shelf piece and align it so its bottom face is against the edge of the scrap timber. Insert the 50 mm x No. 10 screws from the back panel. Remove the scrap timber and again clamp it so that its top edge is exactly 20 mm from the bottom edge of the back panel. Apply adhesive to the back and end edges of the bottom piece, and align it against the scrap timber as for the shelf. Insert the screws and remove the scrap timber.

6 On the back face of the back panel 36 mm down from the top edge and 56 mm up from the bottom edge draw lines parallel to those edges. Along these lines at approximately

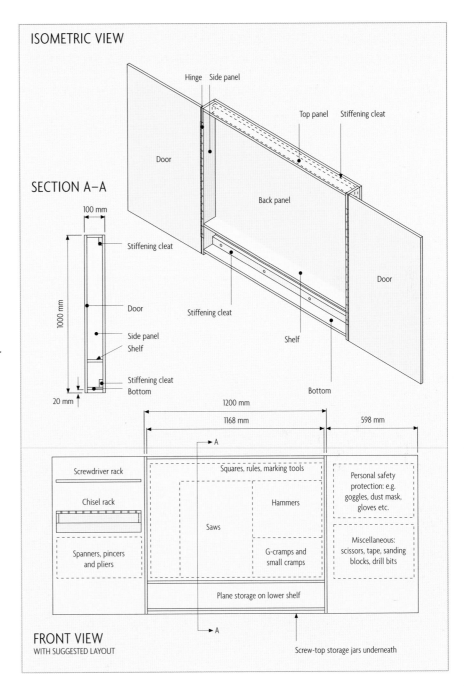

150 mm from each end and in the centre (600 mm) mark, drill and countersink a screw hole with a 5 mm bit to suit the 25 mm x No. 10 wood screws. Apply adhesive to one 41 mm wide face of a stiffening cleat and

position it inside the unit against the top and upper corners of the box. Clamp it in place and insert the screws. Repeat with the second stiffening cleat, placing it in the angle formed by the top face of the bottom shelf

MATERIALS*

PART	MATERIAL	FINISHED LENGTH	WIDTH	NO.
Back panel	16 mm MDF	1200 mm	1000 mm	1
Side panel	16 mm MDF	1000 mm	100 mm	2
Top/bottom/shelf	16 mm MDF	1168 mm	100 mm	3
Door	16 mm MDF	1000 mm	598 mm	2
Stiffening cleat	50 x 25 mm timber PAR		1168 mm	2

Other: Forty 50 mm x No. 10 chipboard screws; two 710 mm piano hinges; twenty 16 mm x No. 8 chipboard screws or appropriate size for piano hinges; PVA adhesive; six 25 mm x No. 10 wood screws; six mounting screws or bolts to suit wall type; two brass barrel bolts and suitable screws; locking mechanism and suitable screws; hooks, eyes, brackets appropriate for your tools; paint and pencil for shadows (optional).

* Finished size: 1000 x 1200 mm and 132 mm deep. Timber sizes given are nominal. For timber types and sizes see page 112.

and the back panel and securing with adhesive and screws as before.

THE DOORS

7 Lay the unit on a secure flat surface and position the two doors so they are flush with the side and top panels. There should be a small gap of about 4 mm between the inner edges of the doors. Use a straight edge or builder's square to check that the bottom edges of the doors are level with the bottom edge of the back panel. Using 300 mm G-cramps, clamp the doors in place and mark the position of the 710 mm piano hinges with a soft pencil on both the side edges of the doors and the side panels of the box (145 mm from top and bottom

edges). Remove the doors and use a builder's square to carry the markings from the side panels onto the edges.

8 Place the piano hinges between the markings on the front edge of the side pieces and fasten them in place with 16 mm x No. 8 chipboard screws. With the hinges open, replace the doors on the box, clamp the doors in place and fasten the remaining side of the hinge to the outer edge of the door with the chipboard screws.

LOCKS AND BOLTS

9 To hold the doors shut, use barrel bolts on the inside of the left-hand door, fixed so that one bolt locks upwards into the top of the

cupboard and the other locks downwards into the top of the bottom shelf. Use a small spacer block behind each bolt, to ensure that the bolt enters the cabinet shelf a little back from the edge, making it more secure.

10 Decide on a position for the locking mechanism, and fit it according to the manufacturer's instructions. We have used a key-operated lock but a simple hasp and staple with a padlock attached to the outside of the doors is also suitable.

MOUNTING ON THE WALL

11 Determine the construction of the wall on which you intend to mount the cupboard. For a sturdy mounting, four bolts should pass through each of the stiffening cleats, unless you are mounting the cupboard over the foldaway bench (see page 68). In that case, the extended edge of the back panel sits inside the lip of the T-shaped wall cleat and it is not necessary to screw or bolt through the lower stiffening cleat. If it is a masonry wall, fastening bolts may be inserted at 75 mm from one edge of the cabinet, then at 350 mm intervals through each stiffening cleat. If you are drilling into a hollow wall and need to position the fasteners according to the location of the studs, it is possible to remove one or more of the screws holding the stiffeners to the back board once the adhesive has dried overnight.

FINISHING

12 Clips and hooks designed to hold specific tools are readily available at hardware stores. Square hooks of different sizes are ideal for holding many tools, which often have holes in their handles for just such a purpose. Custom-made racks, such as the chisel and screwdriver racks on page 93, can also be mounted in this cupboard. However, if you want to use the plane rack (see opposite), you will need to modify it slightly: an

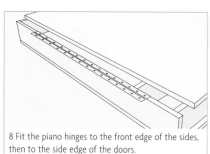
8 Fit the piano hinges to the front edge of the sides, then to the side edge of the doors.

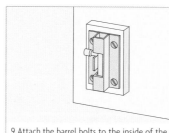
9 Attach the barrel bolts to the inside of the cupboard doors by screwing through 10–12 mm spacer blocks.

alternative might be to use the bottom shelf of the cupboard as a plane storage shelf by adding a small batten as a lip and covering the shelf with waxed self-adhesive baize.

13 To determine the best layout for your tools, lie the cupboard flat with its doors open (you will need to support the doors so that they are level) and arrange the tools in groups of similar types, such as measuring and marking tools, saws, hammers, chisels and so on. When you are happy with the layout, attach the hooks, racks or clips for the tools. Many people find it useful to paint the box and its doors, then trace around the shapes of the tools

HINTS

- Mount a hook and eye fastening at the point where the doors touch the wall when open, thus securing them in the open position. This gives ready access to the tools while you work.
- Return each tool to its place when you are not using it to reduce the risk of misplacing tools in the middle of a project.

so that it can easily be seen where a tool belongs or if one is missing. A row of clear jars that can be attached by their screw-on lids to the underside of the shelf is another useful addition.

The shelves provide handy storage for small loose items such as pencils, screws and nails.

PLANE RACK

This rack can be fixed to almost any vertical surface—a wall, the end of a workbench or a cupboard—and will keep your planes conveniently at hand. The shelves will fit planes up to 450 mm long (a No. 6).

CUTTING OUT THE PIECES

1 On a piece of 16 mm MDF, mark out the dimensions of the back board and use a handsaw to cut it out. Cut on the waste side of your pencil marks and plane the edges straight and smooth. The rounded top corners are optional, but give a nice finish. Use a jar lid or round template to trace the shape, cutting away the waste with a saw and smoothing with a file.

1 The round corners are created by using a compass or curved template such as a jar lid to trace the shape.

2 Mark out and cut the three shelves to the sizes indicated in the materials list and plane the edges smooth and square. The rounded corners are optional, and are created using the same template as for the back board.

3 Take the timber battens for the lipping and mark off three 420 mm lengths, allowing a few millimetres space for the saw cut in between each length. Cut each piece to length with a handsaw, then simply round

MATERIALS*

PART	MATERIAL	FINISHED LENGTH	WIDTH	NO.
Back board	16 mm MDF	500 mm	420 mm	1
Bottom shelf	16 mm MDF	500 mm	90 mm	1
Upper shelf	16 mm MDF	500 mm	70 mm	2
Lipping	31 x 19 mm solid timber PAR		420 mm	3

Other: Sixteen 30 mm x No. 8 chipboard screws; nine 20 mm x 1 mm panel pins; PVA adhesive; adhesive-backed baize; furniture wax.

* Finished size: 420 x 500 mm and 120 mm deep. Timber sizes given are nominal. For timber types and sizes see page 112.

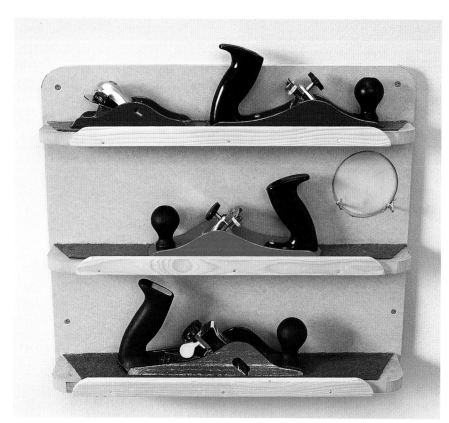

This simple plane storage rack can be mounted on a wall or cabinet. In addition to the planes, it has space for a traditional home-made waxing tin to lubricate the sole plates of the planes before use.

TOOLS

- Builder's square and pencil
- Tape measure
- Handsaw
- Smoothing plane
- Second-cut file
- Portable electric drill
- Drill bits: 4 mm, countersink, masonry bit (if required)
- Two 100 mm G-cramps
- Scissors
- Hammer
- Dust mask
- Safety glasses
- Hearing protection

the top corners off with a second-cut file—it is not necessary to use a template for these small curves.

ADDING THE SHELVES

4 On the back face of the back board, 8 mm up from the lower edge, mark a line parallel to that edge. Mark four screw holes along this line, the first 15 mm from the side edge, then at 140 mm intervals. Drill and countersink the holes with a 4 mm drill bit suitable for the 30 mm x No. 8 chipboard screws.

5 To position the other shelves, measure up 160 mm from the first line and mark and drill countersunk screw holes as for the bottom shelf. Measure 160 mm from this line and

repeat the process. Note: the top shelf will be 80 mm from the top edge of the back board. This should accommodate a low-angle plane and a No. 3 smoothing plane.

6 On the front face of the rack, measure 160 and 320 mm from the bottom edge and

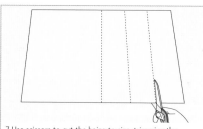

7 Use scissors to cut the baize to size, trimming the corners to shape after it has been applied to the shelves.

mark the positions of the shelves, 8 mm below the pilot holes for the screws. Drill pilot holes in the back edge of each shelf to correspond with the positions of the pilot holes in the back board. Apply adhesive to the back edges of the shelves, clamp them in place with their bottom faces aligned with the base of the back panel and the marked lines, and screw them in place using 30 mm x No. 8 chipboard screws.

FINISHING

7 Using scissors, cut three lengths of adhesive-backed baize 450 mm long and

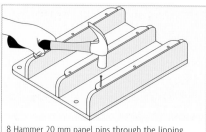

8 Hammer 20 mm panel pins through the lipping battens to secure them to the front of the shelves.

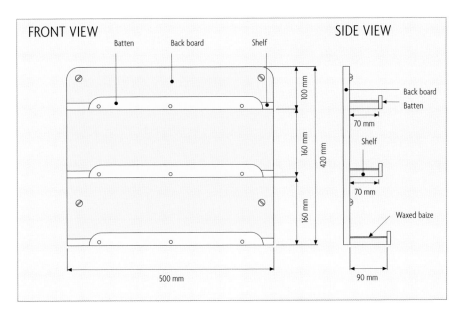

FRONT VIEW — Batten, Back board, Shelf

SIDE VIEW — Back board, Batten, Shelf, Waxed baize

100 mm, 160 mm, 420 mm, 160 mm, 500 mm

70 mm, 70 mm, 90 mm

70 mm wide. Peel off the backing paper and apply it to the top face of each shelf. Trim the baize at the front corners with scissors, and very lightly wax the baize using furniture wax. The waxed baize is intended to keep the sole plates from rusting, and

the minuscule amount of wax that adheres to the sole will help the plane glide over your work.

8 Centre the wooden battens on the front of each shelf and ensure that the bottom edge

of the batten is flush with the bottom of the shelf. Use three 20 mm x 1 mm panel pins to secure the batten to the front of each shelf. This will prevent the planes falling off the rack.

9 To hang the plane rack on a wall or the side of your workbench, drill four countersunk screw holes through the back board. Position a screw approximately 25 mm from each top corner and the other two screws approximately halfway between the bottom shelf and the second shelf. If you are attaching the rack to a storage cupboard or folding board made of MDF or similar, 30 mm x No. 8 chipboard screws will be sufficient. If hanging the rack directly on a wall, use fasteners suitable for the wall construction and alter the position of the screw holes if necessary (see page 72).

CHISEL AND SCREWDRIVER RACKS

These simple racks can be fastened to almost any vertical surface so that your hand tools are always close by and safely stored.

CHISEL RACK

1 Mark out all pieces of the chisel rack to the sizes described in the materials list on a piece of 16 mm MDF, remembering to leave a 3 or 4 mm cutting space between the pieces. Cut out the pieces using a handsaw. Rounding the corners of the 550 x 44 mm rack top is optional.

2 On the rack top, use a marking gauge to scribe a line 25 mm in from the front edge and parallel to it. Starting 50 mm in from one end of the rack top, mark off 45 mm

sections by drawing a line with a pencil and square across the top face. Where the lines intersect, drill holes with a 10, 12 or 15 mm drill bit to fit your chisel shanks.

3 From the sides of each drilled hole to the front edge of the rack, use a square and pencil to mark two parallel lines approximately 8–12 mm apart. Cut along these lines with a handsaw and discard the waste.

4 On the back face of the back board, mark a line 8 mm from the top edge and parallel

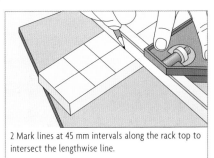

2 Mark lines at 45 mm intervals along the rack top to intersect the lengthwise line.

to it. Mark five evenly spaced screw holes along this line. On each side of the back board, 8 mm in from the edge, mark two

Chisels and other sharp-edged tools should not be loosely stored together, to prevent damage to the tools' edges and the user's hands. These two simple projects, mounted on a wall or workbench, can be an effective storage solution.

TOOLS

- Tape measure
- Builder's square and pencil
- Handsaw
- Marking gauge
- Portable electric drill
- Twist drills: 4 mm, 10 mm, 12 mm, 15 mm, countersink bit
- Two 100 mm G-cramps
- Screwdriver (cross-head)
- Dust mask
- Safety glasses
- Hearing protection

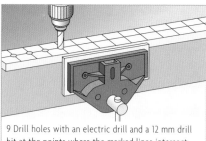

9 Drill holes with an electric drill and a 12 mm drill bit at the points where the marked lines intersect.

38 mm x No. 8 chipboard screws. Repeat the gluing, clamping and screwing process for the two side pieces.

6 Mark a screw hole in each end of the front face of the safety cover. Locate this hole 8 mm in from the edge and halfway (30 mm) from the top and bottom edges. Drill and countersink the holes. Apply adhesive to the lower front edges of the side pieces and clamp the safety cover in place. Insert the screws.

7 To hang the rack, drill and countersink two holes in the back panel. Chipboard screws will be fine if you are attaching the rack to an MDF storage cupboard or other cupboard.

screw holes approximately 40 mm from the top and bottom edges. With a 4 mm twist drill, drill pilot holes and countersink them.

5 Spread adhesive on the back edge of the top, clamp it at right angles to the top of the back board, drill pilot holes and insert the

If you are hanging the rack on a wall, select the appropriate fasteners (see page 72).

SCREWDRIVER RACK

8 Take the 400 x 32 mm piece of MDF and slightly round the two front corners if desired. This size rack holds up to thirteen screwdrivers but can be made to hold more by increasing the length appropriately. Allow an extra 30 mm per screwdriver.

9 Using a marking gauge, scribe a line 12 mm from the front edge and parallel to it. Use a square and pencil to mark transverse lines across the piece 20 mm from one end, then at 30 mm increments. Where the lines intersect, use a 12 mm drill bit to drill holes through the rack.

10 The rack can be simply mounted on the wall by drilling two screw holes through the front edge and countersinking them. Position them between the second and third holes from each end of the rack (65 mm from each end). Use 50 mm x No. 8 chipboard screws to fasten the rack to a wall or vertical surface.

MATERIALS*

PART	MATERIAL	FINISHED LENGTH	WIDTH	NO.
Chisel rack back board	16 mm MDF	550 mm	150 mm	1
Chisel rack top	16 mm MDF	550 mm	45 mm	1
Chisel rack side piece	16 mm MDF	120 mm	30 mm	2
Chisel rack safety cover	16 mm MDF	550 mm	60 mm	1
Screwdriver rack	16 mm MDF	400 mm	32 mm	1

Other: Fifteen 38 mm x No. 8 chipboard screws for chisel rack; two 50 mm x No. 8 chipboard screws for screwdriver rack; PVA adhesive.

* Finished size: Chisel rack: 550 x 150 mm and 62 mm deep; Screwdriver rack: 400 mm long and 32 mm deep.

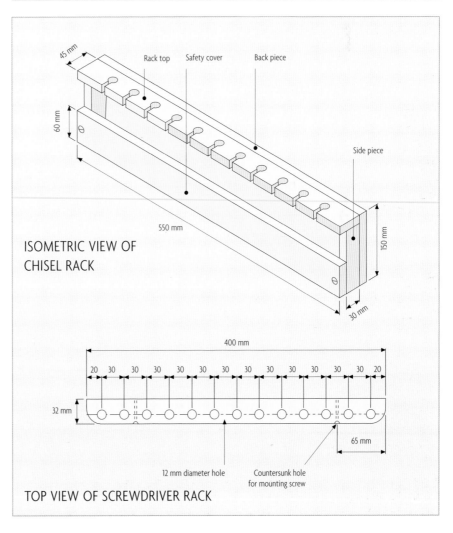

ISOMETRIC VIEW OF CHISEL RACK

Rack top   Safety cover   Back piece
45 mm
60 mm
Side piece
550 mm
150 mm
30 mm

TOP VIEW OF SCREWDRIVER RACK

400 mm
20 30 30 30 30 30 30 30 30 30 30 30 20
32 mm
65 mm
12 mm diameter hole   Countersunk hole for mounting screw

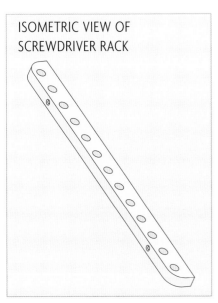

ISOMETRIC VIEW OF SCREWDRIVER RACK

indoor

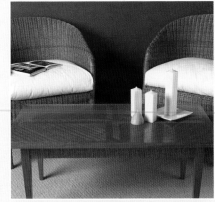

STORAGE

SHELVING

BOOKCASES

CHESTS AND BOXES

COFFEE TABLES

PLAYHOUSES AND DOLL'S HOUSES

contents

storage

storage

MODULAR DISPLAY CABINET

Made up of four individual modular units joined together with dowels, this cabinet can be expanded or altered to suit your requirements. Some modules are cupboards with doors, others form open shelves.

MATERIALS*

PART	MATERIAL	LENGTH	WIDTH	NO.
Side	16 mm thick MDF	320 mm	250 mm	8
Bottoms	16 mm thick MDF	304 mm	245 mm	4
Rail	16 mm thick MDF	304 mm	226 mm	2
Top	16 mm thick MDF	337 mm	250 mm	1
Shelf	16 mm thick MDF	304 mm	245 mm	1
Door	16 mm thick MDF	302 mm	302 mm	2
Back	16 mm thick MDF	320 mm	325 mm	3
Top back	16 mm thick MDF	320 mm	325 mm	1

Other: 2 m of 8 mm dowelling; PVA adhesive; four 110-degree fully concealed cabinet hinges and mounting plates (make sure they are the type that allow the door to be placed inside the cupboard); two handles; eighteen 20 mm flat-head nails; finish of choice.

* For this project you will need one 2400 x 1200 mm sheet of MDF board. Finished size of cabinet (four units): 1296 mm high; 336 mm wide; 250 mm deep. Each unit is 320 mm high without top. For a note on MDF see page 86.

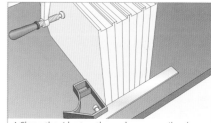
4 Clamp the sides together and use a pencil and square to mark a line for the positions of the dowels.

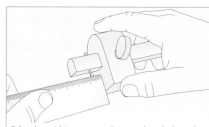
5 Set the marking gauge to 8 mm and mark along the edges to find the centre position for the dowel holes.

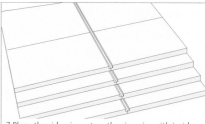
7 Place the side pieces together in pairs with inside face up. Mark a line across the centre for the shelf.

PREPARING COMPONENTS

1 Lay the sheet of material across a safe working platform. Mark out the rip cuts (250 mm apart) along the length of the board using a pencil and a straight edge. Set up a fence to guide the saw along the cut. It is best to cut the strip a fraction oversize to allow for planing and final sizing at a later stage. Mark out the cross-cuts after you rip cut each length.

2 With the length firmly secured to the work surface, mark out the cross-cuts using a combination square and pencil. If you are using a portable circular saw, you can mark out and cut as you go.

3 Select the side pieces and place a small cross on what will become the back edge. Using a saw or router with a rebating bit in it, cut the rebates 5 mm wide and 11 mm deep. Cut rebates on the back edges.

4 Cramp the sides together in pairs with the front edges flush and the rebates together. With a pencil and square, mark out the position of the dowels, on the top and bottom edges, 50 mm in from the front and 55 mm in from the back. Measure carefully, as the dowel holes must be positioned accurately.

5 Set the marking gauge to 8 mm as shown in the illustration and mark along each edge to find the centre position at which to drill. Drill the holes to a minimum of 10 mm.

Measure 10 mm along the drill bit and place a piece of masking tape there to act as a depth guide when drilling.

6 Take the shelf and rails and clamp them together with their back edges flush. Mark and drill them as for the side pieces, but drill the holes to a depth of 30 mm.

TOOLS

- Combination square
- Straight edge
- Pencil
- Portable circular saw
- Portable electric router (optional)
- Chisel: 25 mm
- Two 400 mm quick-release cramps
- Two sash cramps
- Marking gauge
- Portable electric drill
- Drill bits: 5 mm, 8 mm, 35 mm forstner type
- Smoothing plane
- Hammer
- Screwdriver (cross-head or slotted)
- Dust mask
- Safety glasses
- Hearing protection

7 Take the side pieces of the units with centre shelf or rails and drill dowel holes to correspond to those in the shelf and rails. Clamp the side pieces together in pairs with the inside face up and the rebated edges together. Mark a line across the centre for the shelf.

ASSEMBLING COMPONENTS

8 With all the holes drilled, check to see all the parts fit together with faces and edges flush. Some of the dowel positions may need to be adjusted by slicing small amounts off the edges of the dowel. When you are satisfied that all parts fit together accurately, decide whether the doors will hang on the left or right side. Place a small mark on the side chosen and take the units apart.

The units are made in such a way that they may be stacked up in any configuration. Each has a bottom panel, and a top panel is added only to the topmost unit. The units can also be placed side by side to enlarge the cabinet.

FRONT ELEVATION

16 mm

320 mm

127 mm

127 mm

320 mm

320 mm

320 mm

Side

336 mm

SECTION THROUGH SIDE

Top — Rail
— Door

Bottom

Shelf

Bottom

Bottom Rail

Bottom

250 mm

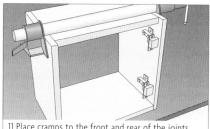

11 Place cramps to the front and rear of the joints and a temporary spreader across the open end.

9 Take the sides requiring hinges, and using the template provided with the hinges mark the position of the hinge-mounting plates. Be sure to read the mounting instructions very carefully before installing the fittings. It is easier to do this now than when the cupboards are assembled. Fix on the hinge-mounting plates and then remove them: they will be fixed back after assembly and painting.

10 Organize the components so that they are in sets, that is with sides, bottom and shelves or top, if applicable, together. Make sure you have a wet rag handy to help remove any excess adhesive that may be squeezed out during clamping. Apply adhesive to the holes and use a pencil to spread it around the hole and remove some of the excess. Add a small bead of adhesive to the edge of the shelves and rails. Spread it with your finger to cover the entire edge.

11 Place the dowels in the holes and gently tap them in with a hammer. Bring the corresponding pieces together and push them into place. If they are a little tight, tap them gently using a hammer and block. Place the cramps to the front and rear of the joints to hold the assembly together while the adhesive sets (about 30 minutes). It is wise to use timber blocks between your work and the cramps to prevent any damage to the work. Check that the units are square by checking the diagonal measurements

Back

Rail

Side

Side

Bottom

Door

EXPLODED VIEW OF CUPBOARD

FITTING CABINET HINGES

1 Turn the cupboard on its side so that the hinging side is down. Mark a centre line from the mounting plate position to the edge. Bring the door into contact with this closing edge, ensuring it has clearance top and bottom.

2 Transfer the centre line position to the door and square the line in about 30 mm from the edge. Mark the drill centres for the mounting plates on these lines, 21 mm in from the closing edge. Take the forstner bit and the drill, and drill the holes 13.5 mm deep. Don't go too deep.

3 Attach the hinges to the doors using the screws supplied or $^5/_8$ inch x No. 5 screws. Ensure the hinge arm is at right angles to the door edge and attach the door. It is rare for the doors to fit perfectly when you first put them on, so some adjustments will probably be necessary.

2 Mark out the drill centres for the mounting plates on the doors, 21 mm from the closing edge.

to see that they are the same. Adjusting the positions of the cramps slightly can help to square up the unit. Wipe off excess adhesive before it sets, using the wet rag and a chisel to get into the tight corners. Repeat this process for all four modules. If the joints are still loose because of poorly fitting dowels you can place a 40 mm panel pin into the joint, punching the nail heads below the surface and filling the holes with filler. Place a temporary spreader across the open end of the three-sided unit to ensure it dries square. Leave the units to dry.

ADDING THE DOORS

12 Take up the doors and check to see that they fit neatly into the cupboard openings. Adjust them with a smoothing plane if necessary. Fit the hinges (see box above).

FINISHING

13 Check that the backs fit the cupboards and, if necessary, plane them to fit.

14 Take the doors off the cupboards and prepare all the parts for painting. (It is easier to paint this unit with doors and backs off.) Finish the unit as desired (see page 87).

15 Nail the backs on the units as indicated in the diagram opposite, using 20 mm flat-head nails. Note the finished position of the backs.

16 Put the hinges back on the doors and the mounting plates back on the units. Hang and adjust the doors. Fit handles to the doors or touch catches if desired.

SHELVES WITH STORAGE BOXES

These handy little boxes not only look great but provide excellent storage space. The hand holes in the ends of each box make it easy to slide them in and out, and the shelf unit is conveniently at standard table height.

CUTTING OUT

1 Using a pencil and measuring tape, mark out all the parts on the MDF sheet, allowing enough clearance between each piece for the cut.

2 Cut out the pieces using either a panel or circular saw. Trim your pieces to size using

a smoothing plane or, for a better finish, use a router. Use a square to check for accuracy on all edges and faces. Use a soft pencil to number or label each part on the inside face.

CUTTING HOUSING JOINTS

3 Take the unit ends and decide which of them will be the left-hand end and which the

right-hand end. On the inside face of each piece, measure up 66 mm from the bottom and mark a line parallel to the bottom edge with a pencil. This line indicates the position where the kicker will be located.

4 Measure up 16 mm (the thickness of the sheet material) from the first pencil line and

TOOLS

- Soft pencil
- Tape measure
- Panel or circular saw
- Tenon saw
- Hole saw: 30 mm (optional)
- Smoothing plane
- Chisel
- Marking gauge (optional)
- Straight edge
- Large square
- Electric router (optional)
- Router bits: 16 mm straight, 10 mm straight and 6 mm rounding
- Electric sander (optional)
- Cork sanding block
- Hammer
- Nail punch
- Portable electric drill
- Screwdriver (cross-head)
- Chisel: 25 mm (optional)
- Portable circular saw (optional)
- Dust mask, safety glasses and hearing protection

draw another parallel line representing the bottom of the unit. Then measure the distance to the top and divide by two in order to determine the position of the shelf. Mark this position with a parallel line. To set out the housing joint for the shelf, measure 8 mm either side of this line, drawing a parallel line each time.

5 Lay one marked-out end piece on a flat surface and place the divider beside it so the top edges are aligned. Using a large square, transfer the set-out lines for the shelf from the end piece to the division. Turn the

Bright colours make this storage unit ideal for a child's bedroom, but painted in more subtle shades it would look just as useful anywhere in the house.

MATERIALS*

PART	MATERIAL	LENGTH	WIDTH	NO.
Unit top	16 mm MDF	790 mm	400 mm	2
Unit end	16 mm MDF	734 mm	380 mm	2
Unit divider	16 mm MDF	657 mm	380 mm	1
Unit bottom	16 mm MDF	728 mm	380 mm	1
Unit shelf	16 mm MDF	361 mm	380 mm	2
Kicker	16 mm MDF	718 mm	66 mm	1
Unit back	6 mm MDF	744 mm	688 mm	1
Box front/back	10 mm MDF	350 mm	250 mm	8
Box side	10 mm MDF	340 mm	250 mm	8
Box bottom	6 mm MDF	340 mm	340 mm	4

Other: 50 mm lost-head nails; 30 mm lost-head nails; 20 mm flat-head nails; six 50 mm x No. 8 cross-head screws; six 25 mm x No. 8 cross-head screws; four 75 mm x No. 8 cross-head screws; abrasive paper: three sheets each of 120 grit and 180 grit; PVA adhesive; craft adhesive; wood filler; 10 x 120 cm piece of felt; finish of choice.

* One sheet of each thickness of MDF will make this project. For a note on MDF see box on page 86. Finished size: 766 mm high, 790 mm wide, 400 mm deep.

Boxes are 250 mm high, 350 mm wide and 350 mm deep.

division over and repeat on the other side. If you don't have a large square, use a tape measure and straight edge.

6 Lay the unit bottom on a flat surface with the inside face upward and measure the length. Divide this by two to find the centre; square a line across the face. Measure 8 mm either side and draw two parallel lines to mark the housing joint.

7 Cut out the housing joints using a tenon saw and chisel, or a router and 16 mm straight bit (see box on page 118).

ASSEMBLING THE SHELVES

8 Lay the two end pieces side by side on a flat surface, and check that one is for the left end and one for the right. On the bottom of each piece, measure back 20 mm from the front edge and square a line up to the bottom of the housing for the position of the kicker.

9 Using your jigsaw or panel saw, remove this 66 x 20 mm corner from the end pieces by cutting along the line and bottom edge of the housing.

10 Round off the front and end edges of the two top pieces, using a plane and abrasive paper or a router with a 6 mm rounding bit inserted. Don't round the back edge.

11 Smooth all edges and faces with 120 grit abrasive paper.

12 To attach the shelf, first apply PVA adhesive to the housing joints on one end

piece. On a flat surface, stand this side and one shelf on their back edges. Bring the shelf into the glued joint, ensuring it fits snugly on the bottom of the housing and that the front edges are flush. At least 40 mm in from the front and back edges, skew a 30 mm lost-head nail through the bottom of the shelf into the housing at an angle so that the nail will not come through the outside. Punch the nail below the surface. Repeat this process when attaching the bottom to the end piece, ensuring that the housing joint for the divider is facing upwards.

13 Apply adhesive to the housing joint on the bottom piece and the divider. Place the divider into the housing and then fit the shelf into the housing in the divider, ensuring all joints fit well. Using 50 mm lost-head nails, nail through the bottom into the end of the divider. Nail through the shelf housing in the divider into the end of the shelf. Glue and skew-nail, with 30 mm lost-head nails, the remaining shelf and end in the correct position.

14 Stand the unit upright and lay one top piece on the unit with a 20 mm overhang on each end and the front. Check the divider and end pieces are parallel. Drill through the top into the ends and divider; secure the top to each piece with 50 mm x No. 8 screws. Lay the second top piece over the first, ensuring it lines up on all edges. Secure the two tops together by drilling and screwing from underneath using 25 mm x No. 8 screws. We used three across the front and three across the back approximately 25 mm in from each upright piece.

15 To attach the kicker to the unit, drill four 4 mm holes through the bottom edge of the kicker, one approximately

FRONT ELEVATION

Hand hole

Divider

Top

20 mm overhang
front and sides

End

Slide-out
storage box

Housing joint

Housing joint

766 mm

66 mm

750 mm

SECTION THROUGH SIDE

Back

Slide-out storage box

Shelf

HOUSING JOINT

Housing
5 mm deep

End

Shelf

Bottom

Kicker

380 mm

50 mm from each end and two evenly
spaced between. Lay the unit on its back
and place the kicker in position, 5 mm
back from the front edge of the side
pieces. Fix with 75 mm screws. Glue and
nail a small block of scrap timber 50 mm
long to the ends behind the kicker for
added strength.

16 Lay the unit down on its face on a flat
surface. Measure and check the diagonals
to ensure that the unit is square. Place the
back in position and fix it to all edges of the
unit, including the divider and shelves, using
20 mm flat-head nails set approximately
40–50 mm apart.

CUTTING THE MATERIAL

If you don't want to cut the material yourself,
or you don't have the tools to do this, you
may take advantage of the cut-to-size service
offered by some companies. Check your local
telephone directory for fibreboard suppliers
who offer this service.

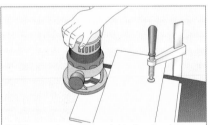

17 Using a router (or saw and chisel), cut a rebate
5 mm deep and 10 mm wide into both ends.

CUTTING OUT THE BOXES

17 Select the front and back pieces for
the boxes. Using a router with 10 mm
straight bit, or a circular or tenon saw
and chisel, cut a rebate 5 mm deep and
10 mm wide into the inside face of both
short edges.

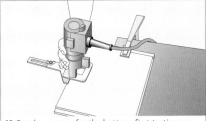
18 Cut the grooves for the bottom, first testing on a piece of scrap and checking the fit.

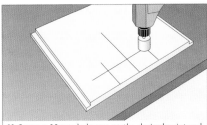
19 Centre a 30 mm hole saw on the desired point and drill through the piece to start the hand hole.

BOX BOTTOM

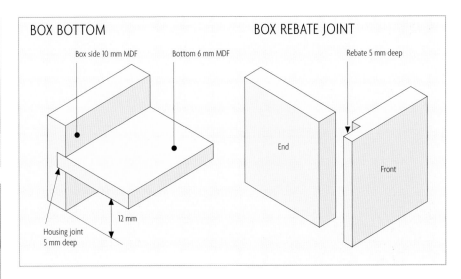

Box side 10 mm MDF

Bottom 6 mm MDF

12 mm

Housing joint
5 mm deep

BOX REBATE JOINT

Rebate 5 mm deep

End

Front

24 Felt is glued to the base of the box sides to act as runners.

18 Cut the grooves to hold the bottom 5 mm deep on the inside faces of all the front, back and side pieces. If using a router insert a 6 mm bit and set the guide fence 12 mm from the edge of the cutter.

19 To make the hand holes, select one front piece and mark the centre on the top edge. Measure 50 mm to the left of this point and square a line across the face. Repeat this to the right of the centre point. Measure 40 mm down the face on these lines and mark. Centre a 30 mm hole saw on each point and drill through, or use an electric drill with HSS bit. Join the holes together with lines at the top and bottom edge to create a long oval shape. Cut along this line with the jigsaw. Smooth the edges of the hole with abrasive paper. Repeat for all front and back pieces.

ASSEMBLING THE BOXES

20 Each box consists of two sides, a front, a back and a bottom. Using one side and a front, apply adhesive to the rebate joint and assemble the joint by placing the side piece

into the rebate. Using 30 mm lost-head nails, nail through the side piece into the rebate joint, ensuring the grooves line up so the bottom will fit easily.

21 Repeat this process and attach the back to the remaining side. Select one half of the box and fit the bottom into the groove. Apply adhesive to the rebate joints and attach the remaining half of the box. Nail the rebate joints together.

22 Punch all nails to ensure that the joints fit tightly. Before the adhesive sets, check that the box is square by measuring the diagonals. If necessary, apply light pressure to the longer diagonal until it is square. Fill all nail holes with filler and sand the edges using 120 grit abrasive paper, ensuring that all joints are flush.

FINISHING

23 Apply the finish of your choice (see box on page 87). Leave to dry.

24 Use craft adhesive to glue 10 mm wide strips of felt to the base of the box sides. This will help the boxes slide easily and protect the shelf.

TIMBER

SOFTWOOD OR HARDWOOD?

Timber is classified as either softwood or hardwood, but this classification depends not on the relative hardness or density of the timber, but on the type of tree it comes from. For example, balsa, a softish timber used to make model aeroplanes and other lightweight models, is actually a hardwood. Hardwoods are mostly from deciduous trees that lose their leaves in winter; softwoods are from conifers with needle-like leaves.

For most of the projects in this book you can choose either a softwood or a hardwood. The main determining factors will be cost, availability and suitability for the particular project.

TIMBER CONDITIONS

Timber is sold in three conditions:
- sawn or rough-sawn: brought to a specific (nominal) size by bandsaw
- planed, either planed all round (PAR), planed on two sides (P2S) or double planed (DP)
- moulded: dressed to a specific profile for architraves, window sills, skirting boards etc.

Planed timber is sold using the same nominal dimensions as sawn timber, for example 100 x 50 mm, but the surfaces have all been machined down to a flat, even width and thickness so that the '100 x 50 mm' timber is actually 91 x 41 mm. The chart at right shows the actual sizes for seasoned timber; those for unseasoned timber such as radiata pine will vary, especially for timbers larger than 100 x 50 mm.

Moulded timbers are also ordered by their nominal sizes. Their finished sizes will generally compare with those given in the chart for planed timber, but check them carefully at the timber yard as there will be many variations.

Timber is now sold in stock lengths, beginning at 1.8 m and increasing by 300 mm to 2.1 m, 2.4 m and so on. Short lengths and offcuts are also usually available.

Sawn (nominal) size (mm)	Size after planing (mm)
10	6
13	9
16	12
19	15
25	19
31	23
38	30
50	41
75	66
100	91
125	115
150	138
175	160
200	185
225	210
250	231
300	281

BOXES WITH LIDS AND CASTORS

These boxes are simple to make and provide a practical storage option. The front, back and sides are held together with rebated joints, and the bottoms are fitted into a groove.

CUTTING THE MATERIAL

1 Mark out all the parts on the material, ensuring each part is there and on the right thickness of board. Allow enough clearance between each piece to cut and straighten.

2 Cut out the pieces using either a panel saw or jigsaw. If preferred, use a circular saw, with a straight edge to ensure the cuts remain straight. Trim the pieces to size with a smoothing plane or a router, using a straight edge to guide the router. Use the square to check that all edges and faces are square.

3 Take one front piece and measure up 40 mm from the bottom edge. Mark a parallel line the full length of the material. This is where the bottom of the box will

3 To make the groove for the bottom using a router, set the fence guide to 40 mm and cut the full length.

indoor

TOOLS

- Tape measure
- Pencil
- Panel saw
- Jigsaw
- Tenon saw
- Hole saw: 30 mm (optional)
- Portable circular saw (optional)
- Straight edge
- Smoothing plane
- Electric router (optional)
- Router bit: 10 mm straight and 6 mm rounding
- Chisel: 25 mm
- Square
- Marking gauge (optional)
- Hammer
- Nail punch
- Cork sanding block
- Portable electric drill
- Drill bits: 3 mm high-speed steel (HSS) bit
- Screwdriver (to suit castors)
- Dust mask
- Safety glasses
- Hearing protection

MATERIALS*

PART	MATERIAL	LENGTH	WIDTH	NO.
Front/back	16 mm MDF	350 mm	250 mm	8
Side	16 mm MDF	600 mm	250 mm	8
Bottom	9 mm MDF	600 mm	338 mm	4
Lid	9 mm MDF	600 mm	338 mm	4
Locating batten	12 x 12 mm timber		326 mm	8

Other: Abrasive paper: three sheets each of 120 grit and 180 grit, and two sheets of 220 grit; PVA adhesive; 30 mm lost-head nails; finish of choice; four 50 mm castors per box; 12 mm x No. 6 screws.

* One sheet of each thickness of board will make four boxes 270 mm high, 350 mm wide and 612 mm deep. The size of these boxes may need to be adjusted to fit under your particular bed. For a note on MDF see page 86.

be inserted, allowing 10 mm clearance off the floor for the castor (adjust this distance if you are using castors other than 50 mm). Using a saw and chisel or a router with 10 mm bit (see box on page 120), cut a 10 mm deep groove the full length of the material. Fit one of the bottom pieces into this groove and ensure that it fits neatly. Complete the bottom groove on the inside face of all the front, back and side pieces.

4 On the front and back pieces cut rebates in the inside face (the same side as the groove) of both ends. Make the rebates 10 mm deep and 16 mm wide and cut them using the router, or a circular saw or tenon saw and chisel.

5 Select the lids and round all four corners and the top edges to a 6 mm radius, using

4 Cut a rebate 10 mm deep by 16 mm wide in both ends of the inside face of the front and back pieces.

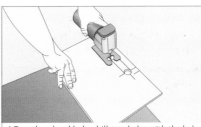

6 To make a hand hole, drill two holes with the hole saw and join them together with the jigsaw.

the smoothing plane and 220 grit abrasive paper, or the router with a 6 mm rounding-over bit inserted.

MAKING HAND HOLES

6 To make a hand hole, select the front piece of one box and mark the centre on the top edge. Measure 50 mm to the left of this point and square a line across the face. Repeat this to the right of the centre point. Measure 40 mm down the face on these lines and place a mark. Centre the 30 mm hole saw on each of these points and drill through the piece (or use an electric drill with high-speed bit). Join the drill holes by drawing lines across at the top and bottom edges, creating a long oval shape. Cut along the lines with the jigsaw. Smooth the edges of the hole with abrasive paper. Make a hole in each front piece and each lid, positioning the holes in the lids in the same way.

ASSEMBLING THE BOX

7 Take one side and a front, apply adhesive to the rebate joint and assemble the joint by placing the side piece into the rebate. Using 30 mm lost-head nails, nail through the side piece into the rebate joint, ensuring that the grooves in both pieces are lined up so that the bottom will fit easily.

8 Repeat this process to attach the back to the remaining side. Select one half of the box and fit the bottom into the groove. Apply adhesive to the rebate joints and attach the remaining half of the box. Nail the rebate joints together.

9 Punch all nails to ensure that the joints fit tightly. Before the adhesive sets, check that the box is square by measuring the diagonals. If necessary, apply light pressure to the longer diagonal until it is square.

MAKING THE LID

10 Take two 12 x 12 mm battens per lid and glue and nail them to the underside of each lid, 12 mm in from the front and back edges respectively and carefully positioned so they finish 12 mm in from the sides. The battens should fit neatly inside the box when the lid is in position to prevent it sliding off.

FINISHING

11 Wearing a dust mask, sand all edges well using 120 grit abrasive paper. Apply the finish of your choice (see box on page 87).

12 On the underside of the box, accurately measure in 40 mm from each side at the corner. Mark this with a pencil and carefully drill a 3 mm pilot hole. This will be the outside corner of the castor mounting plate and allow sufficient room for the castor wheel to swivel. Attach the castor with a 12 mm x No. 6 screw, ensuring the plate is parallel to the outside edge of the box. Drill the remaining pilot holes and fix the screws. Fix the remaining castors in the same manner.

These practical and smart storage boxes will have plenty of use as they slide in and out under the bed. Without the castors, they could be stacked for more permanent storage.

ASSEMBLY

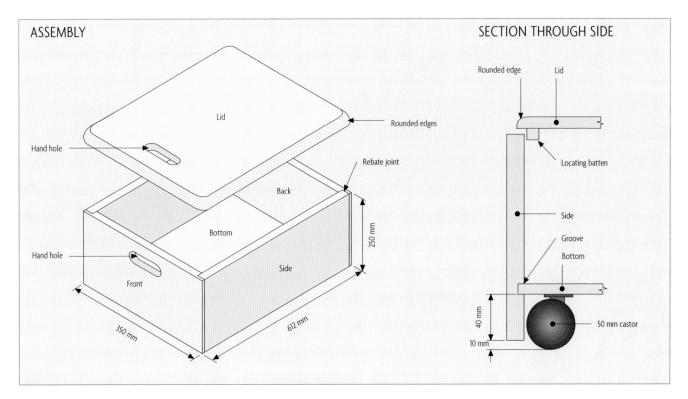

Lid

Hand hole

Rounded edges

Back

Rebate joint

Bottom

250 mm

Hand hole

Side

Front

350 mm

612 mm

SECTION THROUGH SIDE

Rounded edge

Lid

Locating batten

Side

Groove

Bottom

40 mm

10 mm

50 mm castor

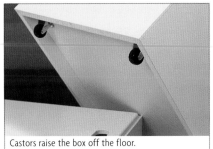

Castors raise the box off the floor.

POWER TOOLS

- Power tools can be used to make some of the heavier work in these projects much easier, but they are not essential. All the projects can be made using only traditional hand tools if you prefer or if you don't have access to the power tool specified.
- When using power tools, always wear safety goggles, hearing protection and a dust mask.

PLATE RACK

Racks made of dowelling and dowelled joints are the basis of this wall-mounted plate rack, which can be used to dry and store up to twenty-four plates.

PREPARING RAILS AND DOWELS

1 Measure all the parts and cut them to length.

2 Take the three rails. Choose the best face of each, and mark a centre line along this face with a combination square. On one rail (this will be the centre rail) mark a centre line on the next face around (not the opposite face). Mark the left-hand end of each piece to ensure they remain correctly oriented. Decide which rail will be the front rail and which the back rail, and mark them. Starting from the end that is marked, measure 30 mm increments along each centre line. Each rail should have twenty-three holes.

2 Use a combination square to mark a centre line down each rail, and then mark off 30 mm increments along it.

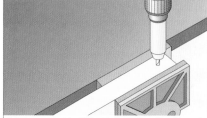

3 Using an electric drill with 8 mm dowelling bit and a depth gauge, drill the holes for the dowels.

Made from light oak with a gloss varnish finish, this plate rack makes an elegant addition to the kitchen.

3 Use a scribe or point marker to indent each mark (this will help to position the drill accurately). Using an electric drill with an 8 mm dowelling bit, carefully bore all the holes to a depth of 10 mm, using a depth gauge (see box on page 118). Keep checking as the depth gauge can move quite easily. It's very important to keep the drill straight. Use a drill press if you have one available, as it will ensure the holes are straight.

4 Sand the lengths of dowel with 150 grit abrasive paper before you cut them. Cut twenty-three lengths of dowel 205 mm long and twenty-three 225 mm long. The best way to do this is to bundle the five lengths of dowel tightly together, securing them with thick rubber bands. Measure and mark the distance to be cut and slide the rubber band just behind the mark; use a jigsaw or fine handsaw to cut the lengths. Remove the sharp edges from the ends, either with the

belt sander or hand-held abrasive paper (100 grit), to help the dowels fit into the holes.

5 Sand the three rails with 150 grit abrasive paper and take the sharp corners off the long edges with a plane or cork block. Leave the ends square. Dust off the dowels and rails, paying particular attention to the holes in the rails. Blow them out if necessary to remove all the dust.

ASSEMBLING THE RACK

6 Using a small stick shaped to suit the hole, put a small amount of adhesive in the holes of the back rail and the corresponding row of holes in the centre rail. Place dowels in the holes on one rail and, using a rubber mallet, hammer them in enough to hold them in the holes. With all the dowels pointing up, bring the opposing rail down onto the dowels, work them into the holes and tap with the rubber mallet. Keep working the dowels in as you tap until all the dowels are in the holes.

TOOLS

- Pencil
- Tape
- Steel rule (600 mm)
- Combination square
- Tenon saw
- Jigsaw
- Scribe/point marker
- Electric drill
- Drill bit: 5 mm high-speed steel (HSS)
- Countersink bit
- Drill press (optional)
- Belt sander (optional)
- Cork sanding block
- Rubber mallet
- Plane (block or smoother)
- Four G-cramps
- Two sash cramps
- Scraper
- Dust mask
- Safety glasses
- Hearing protection

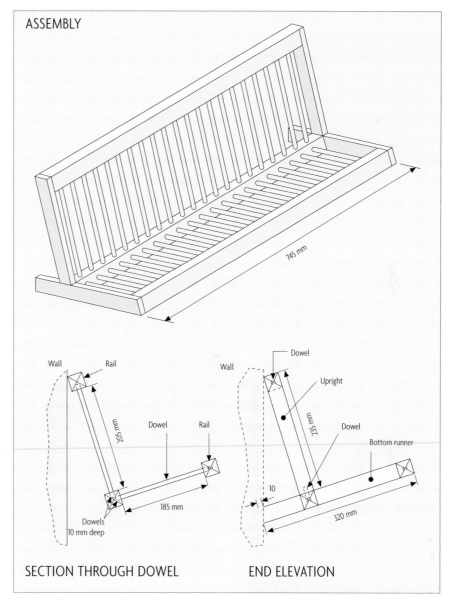

ASSEMBLY

745 mm

SECTION THROUGH DOWEL

Wall · Rail · 205 mm · Dowel · Rail · 185 mm · Dowels 10 mm deep

END ELEVATION

Dowel · Wall · Upright · 235 mm · Dowel · Bottom runner · 10 · 320 mm

7 Use a sash cramp at each end and two G-cramps in the middle to pull the two rails together and prevent bowing. It's very important to check for parallel, and using a square, make sure the dowels are square to the rails. Clean up any excess adhesive with a scraper and warm, damp rag: there shouldn't be too much oozing out. When the adhesive is dry, remove the cramps and repeat the process on the other side.

8 Take the two bottom runners. On the end that will butt up to the wall, measure in 10 mm from the end and mark across the

top of the runner. Cut an angle from the mark to the bottom corner.

9 Drill an 8 mm hole in the end of each rail to a depth of 30 mm. Put the centre markers from the dowel jointing kit into the holes and transfer the marks to the two bottom runners. Drill an 8 mm hole on that point, to a depth of 10 mm. Check the fit.

10 Hold the upright in position on the bottom runner and against the back rail, and mark off its length.

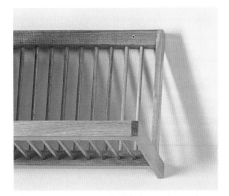

The bottom runners hold the rack out from the wall at an angle.

10 Hold the timber for the uprights in position on the runners and mark the required length. Cut the uprights to length. Drill a hole 10 mm deep in the bottom runner, in the centre of where the upright meets it. Using the centre marker in this hole, position the upright and transfer the mark. Remove the centre marker and, placing it in the hole in the end of the back rail, position the upright to transfer the mark. Drill the holes to 10 mm deep.

11 Check the fit of the pieces before pulling them apart. Cut the dowels to 18 mm (always cut the dowel a couple of millimetres shorter than the depth of both holes added together). Apply the adhesive. Insert the dowels. Clamp using sash cramps, and clean off excess adhesive.

MAKING A DEPTH GAUGE

You can make a depth gauge from a piece of dowel. Once the drill bit is in the drill, measure the length of the bit and subtract the depth of the hole.

Cut a piece of dowel to this length, place it in the vice and bore an 8 mm hole right through. Remove the bulk of the timber at one end, making it look like a pencil with the drill as the lead.

MAKING JOINTS

Joining timbers and board materials is a basic requirement for carpentry, and the most effective joints are rebates and housing joints. The quickest and most accurate way to make them is with a router. However, if you don't have a router, these joints can be made using other tools.

The joints were originally made using hand tools, some of which were very specialized. For example, rebate planes were used to make rebates. They can still be found, but they can be expensive for such a specialized tool.

Housing joints can be made with a tenon or circular saw and a chisel.
1 Mark out the position of the joints on the material. Continue the markings down the edges only as deep as the joint will be. Trace over the lines with a knife.
2 If you are using a circular saw, set the depth of the joint accurately on the saw, and clamp a batten across the board to guide the saw through the joint.
3 Saw across the face of the material, being careful to cut on the waste side of the line.
4 Use the appropriate-sized chisel to remove the waste until the bottom of the housing is flat and to the correct depth.

Rebates can be made using a tenon or circular saw to make a cut on each edge, and then cleaned up with a chisel.

MATERIALS*

PART	MATERIAL	LENGTH	NO.
Rail	38 x 38 mm timber PAR	720 mm	3
Bottom runner	38 x 19 mm timber PAR	320 mm	2
Upright	38 x 19 mm timber PAR	240 mm	2

Other: Five 2.4 m lengths of 8 mm dowelling; abrasive paper: 100, 120 and 150 grit; medium and coarse sanding belts (optional); PVA adhesive (or two-part adhesive for a stronger job); 8 mm dowel-jointing kit; finish of choice; two 75–100 mm x No. 10 screws.

* Finished size: 745 mm long and 320 mm deep. For a note on timber types and sizes see page 112. Timber sizes given are nominal.

FINISHING

12 Sand all the glued joins. If you are using a belt sander, use a medium- to fine-grade belt. Keep the belt sander level, otherwise it will dig in on the edge and cause damage to the rack. With an orbital sander continue through the 100, 120 and 150 grit paper on the rails and runners. Hand sand all the dowels, and apply the finish of your choice.

13 To fasten the rack to a concrete or brick wall, first drill a hole approximately 100 mm in from each end of the back rail, with a 5 mm HSS drill bit. Use 100 or 75 mm x No. 10 screws, and countersink to suit the screw head. On a stud (timber) wall you must first find the studs to fasten into. This will determine the positions of the holes for the screws.

CUPBOARD WITH TWO DOORS

This basic cupboard has two doors and stands on a plinth. The doors can be filled with cane, metal or timber to vary the appearance, and the units can be placed side by side to create a larger storage unit.

MAKING THE CUPBOARD

1 Mark out the parts on the sheet of chipboard, using a square to check that each part is square. Carefully cut them out.

2 Take the two side pieces and on the inside face of each mark the position of the kicker (50 mm up from the end) and then make another mark 16 mm above it for the housing for the bottom of the cupboard. Measure up 275 mm from the second line and draw a line for the bottom of the shelf, and then draw one 16 mm higher for the top of the shelf. (If you want the shelf higher or lower, adjust the housing accordingly.) Draw a line 16 mm down from the top edge for the top. When measuring for position, remember to measure from the same side of the board every time. This will compensate for any irregularities in the shape of the board.

3 Using a saw and chisel, or a router (see page 120), cut the grooves for the housing joints 6 mm deep. There will be three grooves in each side, for the top, shelf and bottom.

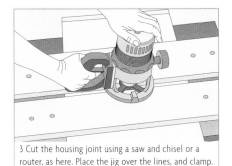

3 Cut the housing joint using a saw and chisel or a router, as here. Place the jig over the lines, and clamp.

The wicker used in the door panels gives this cupboard an individual appearance, but plywood or perforated tin could be used just as effectively.

TOOLS

- Square
- Pencil
- Tape measure
- Tenon saw
- Panel saw or circular saw
- Chisel
- Electric router (optional)
- Router bits: 16 mm straight, 10 mm straight
- Portable electric drill
- Drill bits (including ones for fixing hinges)
- Countersink bit
- Screwdriver
- Hammer
- Nail punch
- Cramps
- Plane
- Cork sanding block
- Dust mask
- Safety glasses
- Hearing protection

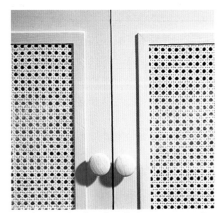

Beading is glued and nailed on to cover the edge of the wicker.

USING A ROUTER

- Always read the manufacturer's instructions before attempting to operate the router.
- Always use cramps or a vice to hold the work securely so that you have two hands free to operate the router. A fence or batten can also be used to help guide the router.
- Always do a test cut on a scrap piece of material to check the router setting before cutting into the components. This will prevent mistakes and improve the quality of your work.
- Wear safety glasses for all routing operations, as well as hearing protection and a dust mask.
- When cutting straight grooves and slots, use the guide fence supplied or clamp a straight piece of timber to the work and run the baseplate of the router firmly along it. Check the positioning carefully before making the cut.
- Set the router to depth. Run the router across the piece, moving it back and forth so as to remove all the waste.

4 To accommodate the back, make 6 mm rebates in the back edges of the sides, top and bottom. Make sure the rebate is in the lower part of the top and upper part of the bottom.

5 Drill three holes in each groove, one in the centre and one 50–75 mm from each end. Be careful not to drill too close to the edge or the board may split. Countersink these holes from the outside, and then screw the top, the shelf and the bottom to one of the side pieces so that they are flush with the front edge. Repeat the process for the other side.

6 Test the fit of the kicker in place below the bottom and inset 50 mm from the front edge. If the unit wobbles, plane a little from the bottom edge of the kicker. Drill two holes through one side of the unit, 58 mm in from the front, and 12 mm and 38 mm up from the bottom. Repeat on the other side. Countersink the holes on the outside and screw on the kicker.

7 Fit the back in place. If it does not fit square, push the unit into shape until it does. Run adhesive around the rebates and along the back edge of the shelf.

Place the back in position, and nail.

MAKING DOOR FRAMES

8 The stiles and rails of the doors are fixed together with pairs of dowels. On the inside edge at the top of each stile, mark the width of the rail. Locate the centre point between this marked line and the top: the dowel holes will be made halfway above and below the centre point (see diagram right). Repeat at the bottom of each stile. If desired, use a piece of tin or strong cardboard to make a template of the end of the rail and indicate the dowel positions, and use it to mark both stiles and rails.

9 Drill the dowel holes, taking care not to make them too deep or too shallow. Too deep, and the dowels may not hold the pieces together; too shallow, and they will not meet.

10 Spread adhesive evenly over the dowels and work some into each hole. Insert the dowels into the holes in the rails.

11 Spread more adhesive over the end grain of the rails, insert the dowels into the stiles and clamp the pieces together.

indoor

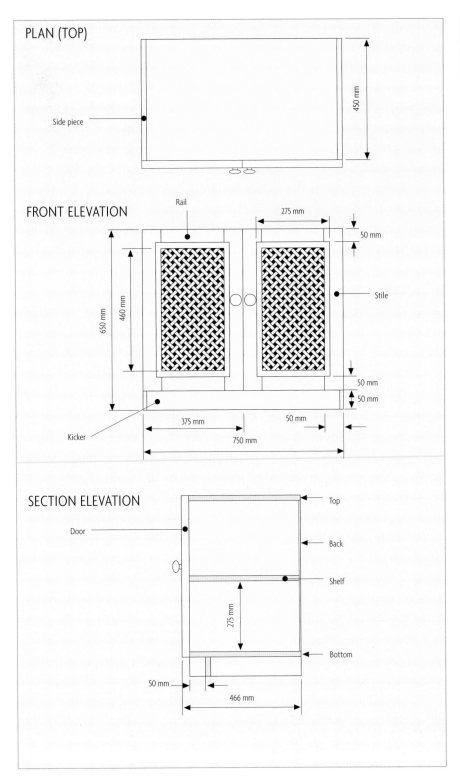

PLAN (TOP)

Side piece

450 mm

FRONT ELEVATION

Rail

275 mm

50 mm

Stile

650 mm

460 mm

50 mm

50 mm

Kicker

375 mm

50 mm

750 mm

SECTION ELEVATION

Door

Top

Back

Shelf

275 mm

Bottom

50 mm

466 mm

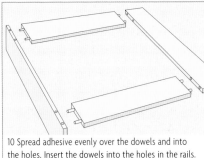

10 Spread adhesive evenly over the dowels and into the holes. Insert the dowels into the holes in the rails.

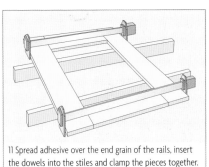

11 Spread adhesive over the end grain of the rails, insert the dowels into the stiles and clamp the pieces together.

Leave the adhesive to dry as in the manufacturer's specifications. Once the adhesive is set, remove the cramps, plane the joints level and sand the door faces.

12 In the back of the door drill all the holes needed for the hinges (this cannot be done when the cover beading has been fixed to the front). Follow the instructions on the hinge packaging when locating and making the holes.

FINISHING
13 Cut the cover beads to length with 45-degree mitres at each corner.

14 Soak the wicker in water for at least an hour, until it has expanded. Give it a shake and hang it up for about 5 minutes. While it is still wet, cut it to size (375 x 600 mm —it needs to be at least 50 mm larger all around than the opening so that you can grasp it to pull it tight). Glue it in

MATERIALS*

PART	MATERIAL	LENGTH	WIDTH	NO.
Top, bottom	16 mm edged chipboard	730 mm	450 mm	2
Shelf	16 mm edged chipboard	730 mm	444 mm	1
Side piece	16 mm edged chipboard	650 mm	450 mm	2
Back	6 mm plywood	730 mm	580 mm	1
Kicker	16 mm chipboard	718 mm	50 mm	1
Door stile	75 x 19 mm timber	605 mm		4
Door rail	75 x 19 mm timber	235 mm		4

Other: Chipboard screws; PVA adhesive; nails; one packet dowels; 19 mm flat beading; wicker; panel pins; four cabinet hinges; two handles; finish of choice.

* This cupboard was made with chipboard, but medium-density fibreboard (MDF) could be used. One sheet of chipboard will be sufficient to make this project. Finished size: 655 mm high (including plinth), 750 mm long and 450 mm deep. Timber sizes given are nominal (see page 112).

HINT

To keep track of which face of a piece is which, mark the 'best face' (the one that will be on the outside of the unit) and the 'best edge' (the one that will be seen most). Always measure from this edge (so the mark is not cut off).

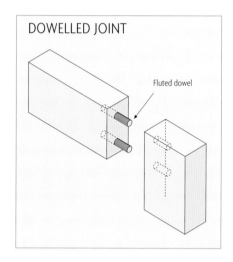

DOWELLED JOINT

Fluted dowel

---

position. Use staples or small panel pins to fix it in place. Cut off excess wicker.

15 Glue the beading around the edge of the stiles and rails to cover the edges of the wicker, and nail it into place. Punch the heads beneath the surface and fill the holes. Fill the gap around the outside of the beading with a water-based latex filler.

16 Fix on the hinges (see box on page 107). Make sure the doors are evenly placed and that they close and open smoothly.

17 Apply the finish of your choice (see box on page 87). Leave the cupboard to dry completely. Fix on the door knobs of your choice.

WINE RACKS – STORING WINE

Storage conditions are important if wine is to be kept for any length of time as the conditions affect how the wine ages. Put your wine rack in the best possible place in your home and you'll know you are doing all you can for your wine.

WHERE TO PUT YOUR WINE RACK

Most households do not have, or need, a special wine cellar but it is still worth paying attention to how your wine is stored and where you place your wine rack. If you always drink the wine within a few weeks of purchasing it, a small rack can be placed anywhere that isn't too hot or in bright light, but if you tend to keep even some of your bottles longer it is worth trying to achieve the best storage conditions you can.

Most homes have a few areas that will provide reasonable wine storage conditions. Possible spots include the area under the stairs, a hall cupboard, an unused fireplace or a basement. Rooms that have a fluctuating temperature, such as kitchens, are not suitable.

Table wines and ports should be stored lying down so that the cork remains moist. Only wines with metal caps are stored upright.

indoor

HOW WINE AGES

Each wine is meant to be drunk at a certain age, when its flavour will be fullest. Wine that hasn't reached this stage or is past its best will inevitably be a disappointment.

The conditions in which wine is stored affect how quickly it will age. Ageing should progress at a certain rate. If the storage conditions are not right, the wine will age too quickly, but premature ageing doesn't mean the wine is ready to drink sooner—it ruins it—and keeping a wine chilled below the optimum temperature just prevents it ageing properly and reaching its potential.

TEMPERATURE

Temperature is the most important factor when storing wine. A cool, stable temperature of 10–12 degrees centigrade is best, although most wines can be stored between 5 and 18 degrees. It is most damaging if the temperature fluctuates rapidly, as this causes the wine to expand and contract.

Even wines meant to be drunk chilled should not be kept in the refrigerator for more than a few days.

LIGHT

Light can increase the ageing process in wine and so wine should be kept in a dark place. Certainly avoid bright light, and don't store wine close to a window. Wine in light-coloured bottles is most affected, and sparkling wines are more susceptible than others.

As well as storing your wine safely and neatly, an attractive wine rack can enhance the appearance of your home.

HUMIDITY

Moderate humidity is best for storing wine, for although the humidity will not affect the wine itself, too little (below about 50 per cent) will dry out the cork. High humidity is less damaging to the wine, but it can cause the labels to rot and make it impossible to identify your wines.

VIBRATION

Some wine authorities believe wines are affected by vibration and so should be stored where they will not be disturbed or subjected to vibrations such as those caused by passing road traffic, low-flying planes or even very loud noises.

ODOURS

Wine can absorb odours through the cork so don't store it in a place where there are strong odours or food that may ferment.

WINE PILLAR

This pillar holds sixteen bottles but it could be made taller to hold more. The stiles are joined to rails with wedged mortise and tenon joints and screwed to a flat base.

This bottle rack fits neatly against a wall or in a corner. Made from figured myrtle and finished with clear acrylic lacquer, it provides an interesting storage option for a modern setting.

PREPARING THE STILES

1 Check the timber carefully for visual defects and straightness. Select a best face and mark it. Use the combination square to square a line across the face of the 125 x 25 mm timber close to one end and then all round. Measure and mark off the two stiles, leaving 5 mm between each piece for saw cuts. Measure and mark off the two rails. Square the lines all around the timber and trace over the lines with a utility knife and combination square.

2 Using the combination square and pencil, mark a line down the centre of the face on the stiles. Following the diagram on page 126, measure and mark out on this line the positions of the bottle holes so that they are 120 mm apart and 60 mm from the ends of the stiles.

3 Place a scrap piece of material under the stile so that you achieve a neat finish on both sides and, using the 32 mm spade bit, drill the holes at a slight angle downwards (about 10 degrees). Drill one stile as a left-hand piece and one as a right-hand one. Using a drill press with a tilting base will ensure that the angle of the holes is consistent.

4 With a tenon saw cut all the pieces slightly overlength and plane the end grain back to the knife lines. Plane from both edges towards the centre to avoid chipping out the sides of the timber.

SETTING OUT THE MORTISES

5 On the face side of the stiles measure 110.5 mm up from the bottom and down

TOOLS

- Combination square
- Tape measure and pencil
- Utility knife or marking knife
- Tenon saw
- Panel saw
- Coping saw or electric jigsaw
- Electric drill
- Drill bits: 3 mm, 5 mm, countersink, 16 mm spade bit, 32 mm spade bit
- Drill press (optional)
- Smoothing plane
- Marking gauge
- Chisel: 18 mm
- G-cramps
- Electric sander or sanding cork block
- Electric router with 6 mm round-over bit (optional)
- Screwdriver
- Hammer

MATERIALS*

PART	MATERIAL	LENGTH	NO.
Stile	125 x 25 mm solid timber PAR	980 mm	2
Rail	125 x 25 mm solid timber PAR	140 mm	2
Base	150 x 25 mm solid timber PAR	500 mm	1

Other: Abrasive paper: one sheet each of 120 grit, 180 grit and 240 grit; six 50 mm x No. 8 countersunk screws; PVA woodworking adhesive; wood putty; finish of choice.

* Finished size: 500 x 138 mm (base) and 1000 mm high. Timber sizes given are nominal. For timber types and sizes see page 112.

from the top, and square a line across the face at these points. Use the rails to mark off the thickness of the material, working towards the centre of the stiles. Square the lines across the face, down the edge and over onto the opposite side.

6 On the face side measure out from the centre line 45 mm each way and draw vertical lines between the marks made in step 5. These lines should be 90 mm apart. Measure in from these vertical lines 12.5 mm and set the marking gauge to this mark. Measure in a further 19 mm towards the centre and mark vertical lines to form 19 x 19 mm squares. Repeat on the back of the stiles.

7 Find the centre of each square by marking the diagonals and use the 16 mm spade bit to

drill holes right through the timber. Be sure to use a backing board when drilling.

8 Use the 18 mm chisel to square down the sides of the holes, working to the lines. Chisel down half the depth of the hole, then turn the stile over and chisel out the remaining waste from the reverse side.

MAKING THE TENONS

9 To determine the exact width of the rails, check the distance between the outer faces of the mortises and add 25 mm (it should total 90 mm; see diagram on page 126). Set the combination square to this width and transfer the width to the rail material. Use the panel saw to bring the material close to width, and smooth the edges back to the lines with the smoothing plane.

10 Hold the rails to the mortises and mark off the size of each tenon on the end of each rail. Number the tenons and corresponding holes in case the sizes vary. Find the middle across the face of each rail, measure out 50 mm each way from the middle and square lines across the face, edges and reverse side to indicate the depth of the tenons. These lines should be 100 mm apart. Set a marking gauge to the marks on the ends and square lines over the ends and across the faces only to these lines. You

should now have two tenons marked out on each end of the two rails. Mark the waste to be removed with a cross. Use the combination square and utility knife to trace over the lines where the material will be removed.

11 Set a rail end up in a vice, or clamp it to a suitable work surface and use the tenon saw to cut down to the 100 mm marks on the waste side of the line. Use the coping saw or jigsaw to remove the bulk of the waste from between the tenons. Clamp the material to a suitable work surface. Using the 18 mm chisel remove the remaining waste back to the knife lines, chiselling down halfway and then turning the material over and chiselling down from the other side. Cut away the end waste pieces. Check the fit of the tenons and adjust until you achieve a sliding fit.

12 Use the tenon saw to make a diagonal cut across the end of each tenon, stopping 1–2 mm short of the depth. The tenons should protrude through the stiles by about a millimetre. From scrap material cut eight narrow wedges that can be driven neatly into the end of the tenons. Measure them so they fit the width of the diagonal cuts.

13 Dry-fit the tenons in the mortises without the wedges or adhesive.

FRONT VIEW

100 mm

120 mm

Rail

Stile

Stile

Rail

120 mm

Base

SIDE VIEW

100 mm

60 mm

120 mm

120 mm

120 mm

120 mm

120 mm

120 mm

120 mm

60 mm

TOP VIEW

500 mm

138 mm

BASE

118 mm

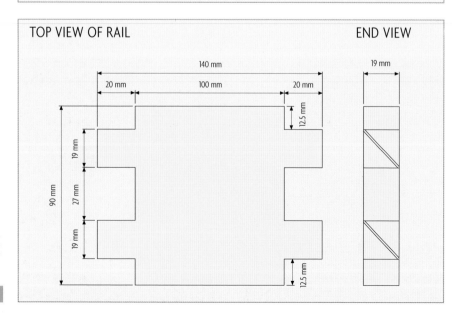

TOP VIEW OF RAIL

140 mm

20 mm

100 mm

20 mm

12.5 mm

90 mm

27 mm

19 mm

19 mm

19 mm

12.5 mm

END VIEW

19 mm

ADDING THE BASE

14 Use the tenon saw to cut the base piece to length and the smoothing plane to smooth the ends square. Measure along the length to find the centre. Measure out 59 mm each way and square lines across the face of the base (the lines should be 118 mm apart). Find the centre of each line and measure out from the centre 45 mm each way. These are the centres for the six screws that will hold the stiles to the base. Use a 5 mm bit to drill clearance holes for the screws at these points. On the underside use a countersink bit to countersink each hole.

15 Dry-assemble the stiles and rails. Stand the assembly bottom up and align the base on the stiles. Use a 3 mm bit to drill pilot holes for the screws. Insert the screws. Remove the screws, pull the assembly apart and sand all the surfaces well with 120 grit abrasive paper.

TO FINISH

16 Round over all exposed corners using a router with a 6 mm round-over bit and ball-bearing guide wheel, or a smoothing plane (planing the end grain first and then rounding the edges). Hold the plane diagonally to the end grain with the toe of the plane away from the timber. If preferred, you can leave the corners and edges square.

17 Fill any holes or chips with matching wood filler. Allow to dry and then sand all the components well with 180 grit abrasive paper.

18 Reassemble the unit, making sure that the face sides are to the outside and that the holes are angled downwards. Use a little PVA adhesive on each tenon. Fix the base into position with 50 mm x No. 8 screws and a little adhesive. Clean off any excess adhesive with a wet rag and chisel.

19 Place a smear of adhesive on each wedge and hammer them into place. Don't hammer the wedges in too hard, as you may split the timber. If the tenons are still sloppy, use some scrap material to make fine wedges that can be packed around the sides of the tenons to tighten them up. Use a chisel to pare off the excess wedges and a smoothing plane to flush the tenons back to the stiles.

20 Give the unit a final sand using 240 grit abrasive paper and apply your choice of finish.

FINISHING THE WINE RACKS

If burn marks appeared on the timber when you were using a router, clean them off with a cabinet scraper, and then sand all surfaces with 120 grit abrasive paper followed by 180 grit. To sand inside curves, wrap the paper around a piece of 25 mm dowel. Make sure you sand in the direction of the grain, and always wear a dust mask when sanding. Clean off the dust with a brush.

For the best result apply the finish with a spray gun and compressor, which can be hired. If you don't want to go to this expense, a foam roller will give a good finish. When it is dry, sand again with 240 grit abrasive paper. Clean off the dust with a moist cloth and apply the second coat. For a top-quality finish, apply a third coat.

PIGEONHOLE RACK

The shelves and divisions of this rack are slotted together with halving joints to form a strong structure. It holds forty-eight bottles and weighs over 84 kg when fully loaded. Fix it carefully to the wall (it is not recommended for metal-framed walls).

PREPARING COMPONENTS

1 Cut and plane the pieces to size (see box on page 131). Apply edging tape with an iron, using clean paper between the iron and veneer to prevent scorching. Apply tape to both short ends of the end pieces, one long edge of each shelf and each division, and both long edges of the back. File off any excess strip.

2 Mark out and cut the jigs for routing the halving joints in the shelves and divisions (see diagram on page 130). The centre to centre measurements are 123 mm (to make 110 mm openings for the bottles). The slots are 118 mm long and 13 mm wide (the thickness of the board). Modify the jig to suit your router. Use a piece of scrap material to test the jigs before routing the divisions and shelves.

3 Use the jigs and router to cut the slots in the shelves, working from the front edge of the shelf. Then cut the slots in the divisions,

MATERIALS*

PART	MATERIAL	LENGTH	WIDTH	NO.
Top/bottom	17 mm VPB (see page 131)	1020 mm	226 mm	2
End	17 mm VPB	806 mm	243 mm	2
Back	17 mm VPB	1040 mm	806 mm	1
Shelf	13 mm VPB	1019 mm	222 mm	5
Division	13 mm VPB	749 mm	222 mm	7
Vertical lipping	50 x 25 mm timber PAR	807 mm		2
Horizontal lipping	50 x 25 mm timber PAR	1053 mm		2
Subframe stile	50 x 25 mm timber PAR	1020 mm		2
Subframe rail	50 x 25 mm timber PAR	142 mm		5
Ledger	50 x 25 mm timber PAR	1053 mm		1

Other: 12 m iron-on edge tape to match particleboard; masking tape; twelve 50 mm long 8 mm diameter dowels; eighteen 40 mm particleboard screws; two 75 mm x No. 10 screws for ledger; thirty 25 mm panel pins; PVA woodworking adhesive; abrasive paper: two sheets each of 120 grit, 180 grit and 240 grit; wall fastenings; finish of choice.

* Finished size: 1054 x 260 mm and 807 mm high. Timber sizes given are nominal (see page 112). The sizes given above are cutting sizes; allowances have been made for edge tape. You will need one 2400 x 1200 mm sheet each of 17 mm and 13 mm veneered particleboard (VPB).

This neat rack was made from brush box-veneered particleboard with matching solid timber for the lippings; it was given a clear lacquer finish.

TOOLS

- Tape measure and pencil
- Circular saw or panel saw
- Tenon saw
- Smoothing plane or jack plane
- Utility knife or marking knife
- Old iron
- Smoothing file
- Portable electric router
- Straight cutting router bits: 13 mm, 18 mm
- Marking gauge
- Combination square
- Electric drill
- Drill bits: 3 mm, 5 mm, 8 mm, countersink
- Dowelling jig (optional)
- Two 1350 mm sash cramps
- Three 300 mm G-cramps or quick-release cramps
- Screwdriver (cross-head or slotted)
- Mitre box
- Orbital sander or cork sanding block
- Spirit level

working from the back edge. Apply a strip of masking tape over each area where the slots will be cut to prevent the edge veneer chipping out. Replace any damaged edge strips.

4 Take the end panels and cut rebates for the back in one long side. The recess should be 10 mm deep and as wide as the back panel is thick. Check the thickness of the board you are using, as it can vary slightly. The back should finish flush with the edge of the end panels. If you are using a router, test the set-up on scrap first and place masking tape over the edge to prevent chipping.

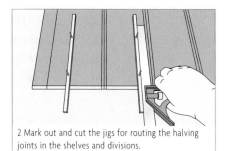

2 Mark out and cut the jigs for routing the halving joints in the shelves and divisions.

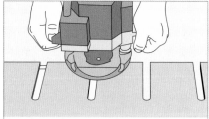

3 Use the jig and router to cut slots in the shelves from the front edge and in the divisions from the back edge.

indoor

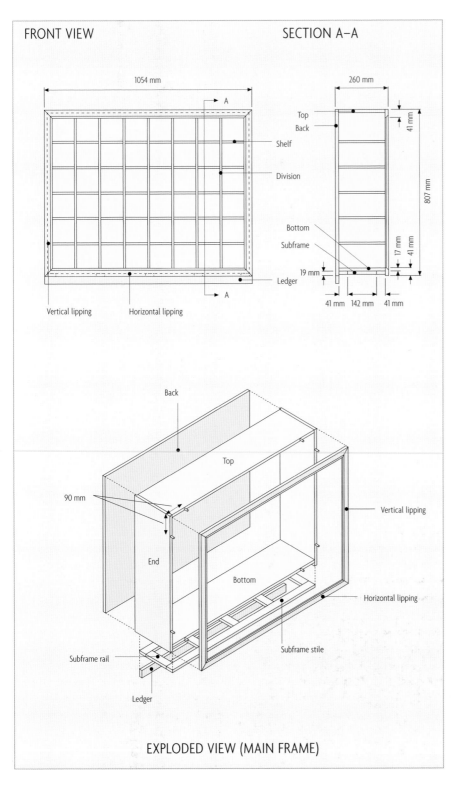

FRONT VIEW

1054 mm

A

Shelf

Division

Bottom
Subframe

Ledger

Vertical lipping   Horizontal lipping

SECTION A–A

260 mm

41 mm

Top
Back

807 mm

17 mm   41 mm

19 mm

41 mm   142 mm   41 mm

EXPLODED VIEW (MAIN FRAME)

Back

Top

90 mm

End

Bottom

Subframe rail

Ledger

Vertical lipping

Horizontal lipping

Subframe stile

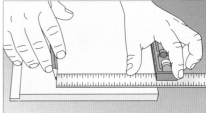

5 Use a combination square to mark the positions for the three dowel holes along the gauged line.

6 Working from the outer face of the top and bottom, square lines across the edge for the dowel positions.

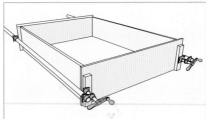

7 Dry-fit together all the parts, using sash cramps to hold the unit together while you fit the back.

5 On the end panels use a marking gauge to mark out the positions for the dowels to fix the top and bottom. Position them 8 mm down from the top edge and 33 mm up from the bottom edge. Make sure they are set as a pair. Mark the distances from the front edge with a combination square. The first hole will be 30 mm in from the front edge, the second 110 mm and the third 190 mm. Use an 8 mm drill bit with masking tape around it as a depth indicator and drill the dowel holes 13 mm deep.

6 Establish the front of the top and bottom and mark out corresponding dowel holes on the short edges, continuing the lines over the

JIGS FOR ROUTING SHELVES AND DIVISIONS

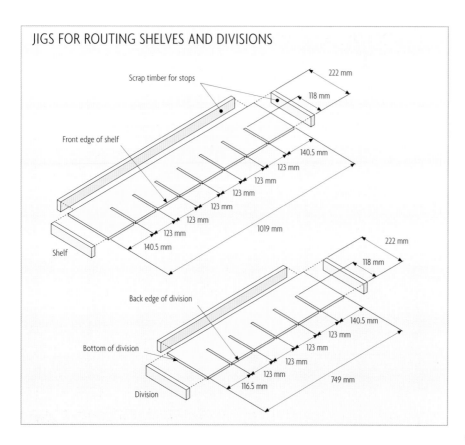

Scrap timber for stops

Front edge of shelf

222 mm

118 mm

140.5 mm

123 mm

123 mm

123 mm

123 mm

123 mm

123 mm

140.5 mm

1019 mm

Shelf

Back edge of division

222 mm

118 mm

140.5 mm

123 mm

123 mm

123 mm

123 mm

116.5 mm

749 mm

Bottom of division

Division

outer face. Working from the outer face of the top and bottom, and using a marking gauge set at 8 mm, mark square lines across the edge. Set up the dowelling jig and test it on a scrap piece of material before drilling the holes in the top and bottom panels.

7 Dry-fit together all the parts so far. Make sure the unit is square by measuring the diagonals. Use two sash cramps to hold the unit together while you fit the back to the unit using 40 mm particleboard screws. Drill 5 mm clearance holes and use the 3 mm bit to make pilot holes for the screws. Use four screws evenly spaced down each side and five screws across both top and bottom.

8 Turn the unit upside down on a pair of padded sticks or old piece of carpet to

protect the veneer. Cut the subframe stiles to fit between the ends. Glue and nail them in place using adhesive only on the face that comes in contact with the bottom. Cut five rails to fit between the stiles. Glue and nail them in place using 25 mm panel pins. This frame will prevent the bottom shelf bowing when the unit is loaded with wine.

THE LIPPINGS

9 With the cramps still in place, turn the unit face up. Measure in from each corner 90 mm along the front edges. Square a line across the edges and over onto the inside face. Set a marking gauge from the outside faces of the unit to mark a centre line for the dowels for the lippings. On the bottom panel work from the inside face as the lipping is to finish flush with the inside of the frame. Drill the dowel holes 26 mm deep.

10 Mark and cut the side lippings 10 mm overlength. Hold it in place and mark the dowel positions on each. Drill holes 14 mm deep. Check the fit of each piece and adjust.

11 Take one lipping and mark the mitre joints, allowing 0.5 mm more at each end. Use a combination square and utility knife to score the lines. Cut them with a saw and mitre box. Glue and clamp the piece to the appropriate edge. Use three 300 mm cramps to get good pressure, and insert scrap material as protection from the cramps. If preferred, use 40 mm nails to fasten the lippings but punch and fill the holes before sanding and final finishing. Use a smoothing plane if necessary to clean up the faces of the mitre joints.

12 Mark off the mitre lengths on the two adjoining lippings and cut them to length. If the adjoining mitres are slightly open, shave down the dowels with a sharp chisel to get a good fit. When the first lipping is dry, glue and clamp the second in place. Don't apply adhesive to the ends of the mitres at this stage. For the best results cut and fit one lipping at a time: mitre joints tend to creep open if you cut and fit them all at once.

13 Determine the fastening points needed to fix the unit to the wall. If it is a framed wall, the position of the fastenings will be determined by the wall studs. Measure out the positions carefully so that they will not be covered by the shelves and divisions. Use at least four screws to hold the unit to the wall with a minimum of two more fasteners in the ledger. Drill the appropriate size holes through the unit back.

14 Allow the lippings to dry thoroughly before removing the sash cramps. Take the unit apart. Remove the dowels and sand the lippings flush with the sides (or use a cabinet scraper, which is faster and safer). Use 120 grit and then 180 grit abrasive paper in an orbital sander to sand all the parts. Give a final sand by hand using 240 grit paper in the direction of the grain. Apply finish to all components (see box on page 127).

FINAL ASSEMBLY

15 Lay the end pieces face side down on a clean, dust-free, padded surface. Place a small amount of adhesive in the dowel holes and use a pencil to spread it around. Insert the dowels. Apply adhesive to the dowel holes in the top and bottom, spread a bead of adhesive onto the adjoining edges and assemble the frame. Lay the unit face down (you will need a helper for this) and use the sash cramps to clamp it together. Check the diagonals for square. Clean off excess adhesive with a damp cloth.

16 Assemble the shelves and divisions (see diagram above right) and lift them into the frame. Apply adhesive to the rebate and fasten the back in place. Clean away any excess adhesive with a damp cloth. Leave the unit in the cramps overnight.

INSTALLATION

17 Fasten the ledger to the wall so it will sit below the unit, using a spirit level to make sure it is level. For timber-framed walls fix it into the studs with 75 mm x No. 10 screws.

18 Have a helper hold the unit flat against the wall and insert two fasteners through the back near the top of the unit.

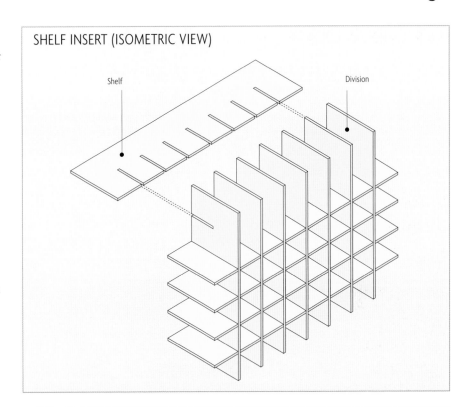

SHELF INSERT (ISOMETRIC VIEW)

Shelf

Division

USING VENEERED PARTICLEBOARD (VPB)

If you haven't previously worked with VPB, practise on offcuts before beginning the project.

When you cut VPB across the grain, one side is liable to chip out. If you use a panel saw or table saw without a scribing blade the under face of the board will chip out, while if you use a circular saw the upper surface will chip out. You can reduce chipping by cutting the veneer fibre with a utility knife before you make the cut. Fixing a length of masking tape across the area to be cut will also help.

Save time and effort by having major parts cut and edged by the supplier (check the telephone directory for one who will do this). Take offcuts away to use later. Buy 1 m of spare edge strip to repair any damage.

Veneered products are prone to scratching, so cover the work surface with old sheets or carpet, and rest the work on timbers wrapped in fabric.

BUTLER'S TRAY

This trolley doubles as a storage rack for wine and a serving surface. Ideal for entertaining, it is fitted with castors so it can be moved to the desired location. It holds twenty-four bottles.

TOOLS

- Tape measure and pencil
- Circular or panel saw
- Tenon saw
- Smoothing plane
- Jack plane
- Utility knife or marking knife
- Two 900 mm sash cramps
- Three 300 mm G-cramps or quick-release clamps
- Electric router and 13 mm or larger straight-cutting bit
- Combination square
- Electric drill
- Drill bits: 30 mm spade bit, 3 mm, 5 mm, 8 mm, countersink
- Marking gauge
- Dowelling jig
- Bench hook
- Chisel: 12 mm
- Short-handled screwdriver (cross-head or slotted)
- Cork sanding block or portable electric sander
- Hammer

Silky oak was the timber used for this very useful trolley. The rails are dowelled to the legs, while the shelves are held in triangular mortises.

THE RAILS

1 Take the timber for the rails and select and mark the best faces. Cut it into 1050 mm lengths. If necessary, use a jack plane to straighten and square the edges. Clamp the material down and cut a rebate 13.5 mm deep and 13 mm wide along both edges.

2 Beginning 2 mm from one end, mark off the rails along each piece leaving 5 mm between each for the saw cut. Square the lines right around the material and trace over them using the combination square and utility knife.

3 Setting a marking gauge to half the width of the material, gauge a line down the length of all rail pieces on the face side. Use a circular saw with a rip guide or fence to cut along the centre line. Then use the tenon saw, with a bench hook to steady the material, to cut the rails to length. You should have four front rails, four back rails and eight side rails.

4 Set the marking gauge to 50 mm and gauge lines along the length of the rails, making sure the butt of the gauge is against the rebated side. Use the jack plane to smooth the edges down to the 50 mm marks. Don't plane beyond the gauge lines.

5 Take two front rails and clamp them together face side up and top edges together. On the face side measure and mark 69 mm from one end along the join, then 90 mm seven times with 69 mm left at the end. Clamp the material down with scrap timber underneath and use a 30 mm spade bit in the electric drill to bore the eight holes. Take a third front rail and a scrap piece of material the same thickness and clamp them together. Repeat as for the two rails.

THE LEGS

6 Cut the legs to length with a tenon saw and smooth the ends by careful planing with a smoothing plane.

7 Hold the legs with the top ends up so that only the face sides can be seen, and with a pencil draw a square on the ends and number each leg. Lay them down with the bottom ends flush and the inside faces exposed. Use a G-cramp to hold the legs together while marking out the dowel holes. Measure 73 mm up from the bottom, then 15 mm, then 198 mm, 15 mm, 198 mm, 15 mm until you have the dowel positions for four rails (see diagram at right). You should have 23 mm left over. Square the marks across all four legs. Undo the cramps, turn the legs over so the other inner face is exposed, and square the marks over these faces. Set a marking gauge to 20.5 mm or

MATERIALS*

PART	MATERIAL	LENGTH	WIDTH	NO.
Leg	50 x 50 mm solid timber PAR	750 mm		4
Front/back rail	125 x 25 mm solid timber PAR	768 mm		4**
Side rail	125 x 25 mm solid timber PAR	268 mm		4**
Shelf	13 mm VPB	816 mm	316 mm	4

Other: Sixty-four 50 mm long 8 mm diameter timber dowels; sixteen 30 mm particle-board screws; sixteen 25 mm x No. 6 screws; abrasive paper: one sheet each of 120 grit, 180 grit and 240 grit; PVA woodworking adhesive; four small brass castors.

* Finished size: 850 x 350 mm and 750 mm high without castors. Timber sizes given are nominal. For timber sizes and conditions see page 112. You will need one sheet of 13 mm veneered particleboard (VPB) for this project.

** Pieces will be cut in half.

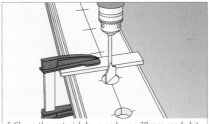

5 Clamp the material down and use a 30 mm spade bit to bore the eight holes required for the bottle necks.

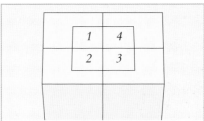

7 Hold the legs with the top ends up, and with a pencil draw a square on the ends and number each leg.

DOWEL POSITIONS FOR EACH LEG

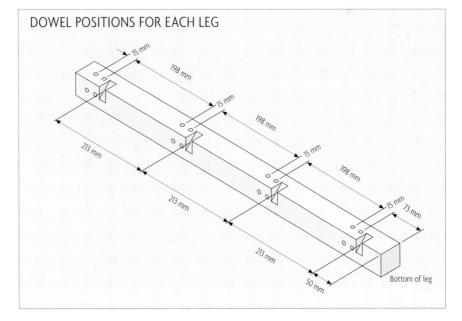

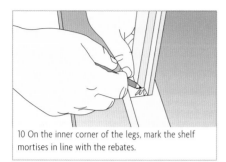

10 On the inner corner of the legs, mark the shelf mortises in line with the rebates.

half the thickness of the legs and mark the dowel centres.

8 Take the four front rails and tape them together with rebates facing the same way and bottom edges aligned. On the ends, measure in from the bottom 23 mm and then 15 mm. Square the lines right across all ends. Repeat for the back and side rails in sets of four. Set the marking gauge to half the thickness of the rails and gauge a line on the end of each rail for the dowel centres.

9 Set the dowelling jig on the end of one rail from the face side to align with the first dowel hole. With an 8 mm bit drill the holes 30 mm deep in the end of the rail. Repeat for all rails. Then set the dowelling jig to bore 22 mm deep holes in the legs.

10 Dry-assemble the frame, starting with the two end frames. Set the completed frame bottom up so that access to the rebates is easiest. On the inner corner of the legs, mark the depth and thickness of the shelf mortises in line with the rebates (see diagram opposite). Then use a square to square the lines across the faces of the material.

11 Take the frame apart. Use a combination square and utility knife to cut across the grain at the marked lines for the mortise. Hold a leg firmly in a bench hook and cut to the depth marked, cutting on the waste side of the lines.

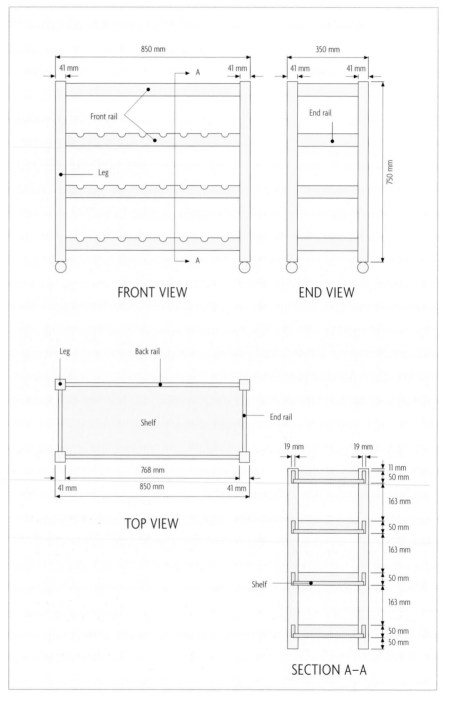

FRONT VIEW

END VIEW

TOP VIEW

SECTION A–A

Clamp the leg in a vice or to a bench and remove the waste from the shelf mortise with a 12 mm chisel. Repeat for each leg.

THE SHELVES

12 To cut the shelves, lay the particleboard across a pair of trestles and mark off 316 mm

LEG JOINT DETAIL

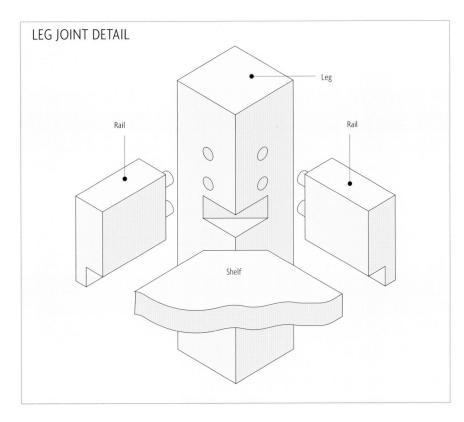

Leg

Rail

Rail

Shelf

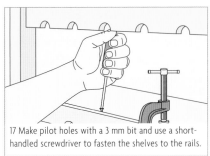

17 Make pilot holes with a 3 mm bit and use a short-handled screwdriver to fasten the shelves to the rails.

from the edge. Clamp a straight edge on the sheet and use a circular saw to make a rip cut to this width. Cut a second piece the same width. Check the panels and, if necessary, smooth back to the lines with a jack plane. Lay the two panels on top of each other. Mark off the length of the first shelf from one end and the second shelf from the opposite end. Hold the straight edge across the boards with two cramps. Check the cramp is square to the edge of the material, and score the line with a utility knife. Check the shelves are all the same size and are square by measuring the diagonals. Clean them up to the correct size with a jack plane.

13 On the underside of the shelves measure in from each end 200 mm and 7 mm from each long edge. At these points drill 5 mm clearance holes for the screws that will fix

the shelves to the rebates in the rails. Use a countersink bit to countersink the holes so the screw heads will sit flush or just below the surface of the shelf.

14 From each corner measure 25 mm along each edge and mark off the diagonal cut with the combination square. Trace over the marks with a utility knife and cut off the corners.

15 Dry-assemble the frame again, this time inserting the shelves. Make any adjustments needed. Take the unit apart and sand all parts well with 120 grit and 180 grit abrasive paper.

ASSEMBLY

16 Adjust the two 900 mm sash cramps to take the end frames, allowing for the open joints and scrap material to be placed at

each end. Apply adhesive to the holes in the legs and spread the adhesive around the hole. Insert dowels in the holes and use a hammer to drive them in carefully. Apply adhesive to the corresponding holes in the end rails and assemble the two end frames. Place them in the cramps with newspaper under them to catch any drips of adhesive. Tighten the cramps until the joints are tight. Clean off any excess adhesive as you work with a wet rag and chisel. Check the diagonal measurements to make sure the frames are square. If they are not, adjust them by offsetting one or both of the cramps. Check the frames are not twisted horizontally. If so, packing under one end of the cramps can help alleviate some of the problem. Leave the frames to dry overnight.

17 Assemble the rest of the frame in the same way. Use a cramp to pull the shelf to each rail. Make pilot holes with a 3 mm bit and fasten the shelves to the rails with 25 mm x No. 6 screws.

18 Fit the castors to the bottom of the legs and test them. Give the unit a final sand and clean off all dust. Apply the finish, not forgetting the underside of the shelves.

This contemporary rack is made from particleboard with sapele mahogany veneer and a clear acrylic finish. The lippings are matching solid timber. Several racks could be placed side by side for large-scale storage.

SHELF RACK

Perfect for storing large quantities of wine, this unit is solid and compact. It has fourteen shelves, each of which holds up to eight bottles. The shelves are housed into the sides and are finished with solid timber lippings.

PREPARATION

1 Lay one sheet of particleboard across the saw trestles and, with the tape and square, mark out the pieces. See the box on page 131 before using veneered boards. If you are going to use a circular saw, fix a long straight edge to the sheet with G-cramps to help guide the saw. Do a test cut on scrap material and cut the material slightly oversize to compensate for chip out. Use an electric plane to bring the panels close to their correct width, then finish with a jack plane. Cut the panels, making the long cuts first.

2 Use an old iron to fix the edge tape to the front edges of the side panels, and a smoothing file to remove excess tape, running the file along the edge with a scissor action. Remove any remaining sharp edges with a sanding cork and 120 grit abrasive paper.

3 Cut a rebate 18 mm wide and 12 mm deep along the back edge of the side panels. If you are using a router, test the cut on a piece of scrap material first. If you only have a small router make two passes to achieve the correct depth.

THE SHELF HOUSINGS

4 Lay the side panels side by side with the face edges together and the inside faces up, and align the bottom edges carefully. Measure up from the bottom edge 12 mm and 30 mm and square lines across both panels. This is the position of the bottom shelf. Cut the housing 18 mm wide and 6 mm deep. Set a fence to guide the router when making the cut, and check

the settings of the router and the fence to ensure the cut is the correct depth and the fence is set square to the edges. Make the cut from the front edge to the rebate.

5 The gap between each shelf is 102 mm. Measure out the shelf positions accurately and clamp the fence into position for each housing. You can make a jig similar to the one on page 130, and this will allow you to repeat the housings exactly, but it must be made very accurately. The top will finish 12 mm down from the top of the side panels.

6 Sand all components with 120 grit abrasive paper. Then sand all the parts with 180 grit

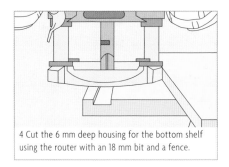

4 Cut the 6 mm deep housing for the bottom shelf using the router with an 18 mm bit and a fence.

HINT

Always use a fence to help guide the circular saw on long cuts, and always check that the fence is set square to the face edge.

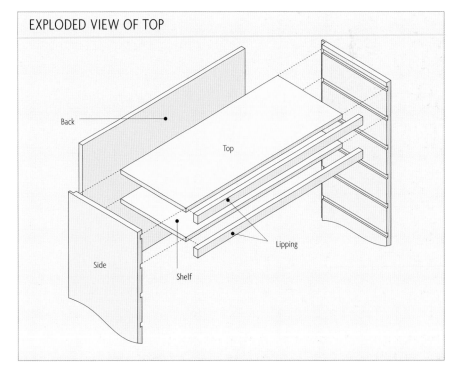

EXPLODED VIEW OF TOP

Back

Top

Lipping

Side

Shelf

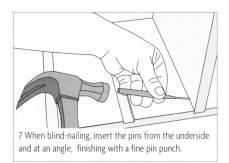

7 When blind-nailing, insert the pins from the underside and at an angle, finishing with a fine pin punch.

paper. Remove the sanding dust and apply the finish of your choice to all the components (see box on page 127). Allow each piece to completely dry before turning it over and coating the other side.

ASSEMBLY

7 Lay one side panel on a padded surface and apply a little PVA adhesive to the top housing and to the edge of the top panel. Place the top in position, making sure it is flush both back and front. Working from the upper face, use two 25 mm panel pins to blind-nail the shelf in place. To do this insert the pins at an acute angle. This can be difficult, so start the nailing with a hammer and finish it with a fine pin punch. Take care not to put a nail through the side. Repeat for each shelf but work from underneath.

8 Apply adhesive to the housings on the other side panel and a little on the end of each shelf. Put the side panel in position on the shelves and get some help to turn the unit on its back. Take care the joints don't come apart. Apply sash cramps to the unit, making sure all the joints are closed up, and use padding to protect the finish. Secret nail the shelves to the side panel. Remove the cramps. Turn the unit face down on the padding, apply the sash cramps to this side and blind-nail the back of the shelves to the side panels.

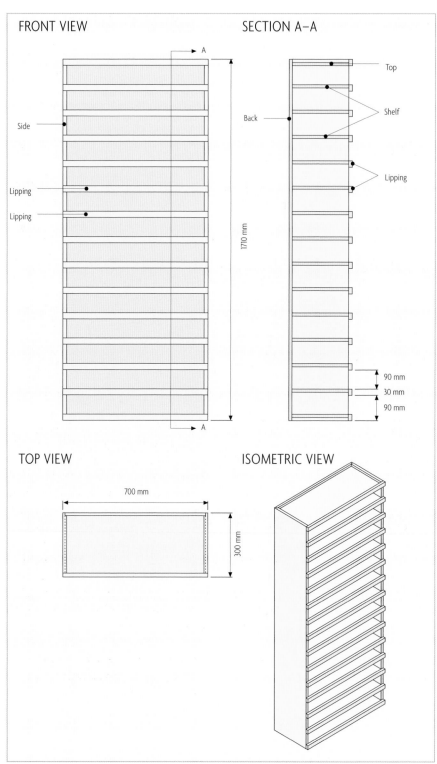

MATERIALS*

PART	MATERIAL	LENGTH	WIDTH	NO.
Side	18 mm VPB	1710 mm	280 mm	2
Shelf/top	18 mm VPB	676 mm	262 mm	15
Back panel	18 mm VPB	1710 mm	687 mm	1
Lipping	38 x 25 mm solid timber PAR	701 mm		15

Other: 3.6 m iron-on edge tape to match veneered particleboard; abrasive paper: two sheets each of 120 grit, 180 grit and 240 grit; matching coloured wax filler; PVA woodworking adhesive; sixty 25 mm panel pins; forty-five 40 mm panel pins; fifteen 35 mm particleboard screws; finish of choice.

* Finished size: 700 x 300 mm and 1710 mm high. Timber sizes given are nominal. For timber sizes and conditions see page 112. Three sheets of 18 mm thick 2400 x 1200 mm veneered particleboard (VPB) were used, but you could substitute 13 mm or even 6 mm board for the back, although this will require some modification of the rebates.

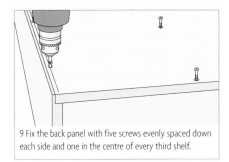

9 Fix the back panel with five screws evenly spaced down each side and one in the centre of every third shelf.

9 Check that the unit is square by measuring the diagonals, and adjust if necessary. Mark the centre line of the top and every third shelf on the back edge of the side panels. Set the back panel in place and use a 5 mm bit to drill clearance holes for the screws into the side panels. Use five screws evenly spaced down each side and one screw in the centre of the top and every third shelf. Countersink the holes and use a 3 mm drill bit to make pilot holes for the screws. Insert 35 mm particleboard screws.

THE LIPPINGS

10 Measure the length required for each lipping: it should be 700 mm. On the solid timber mark off the required lengths plus 1 mm. Leave a 5 mm gap between each for saw cuts. Use a combination square to square the lines all around the timber and trace over the lines with a utility knife. Use a bench hook to support the timber while you cut it to length with a tenon saw. Check the fit of the pieces and sand the end grain until it fits the width of the unit.

11 Sand all lippings well with 120 grit and then 180 grit abrasive paper. Apply two coats of finish to the surfaces that will be visible.

12 Apply adhesive to the front of the shelves and use three 40 mm panel pins to secure a lipping flush with the top face of each shelf. You can make a pilot hole in the lippings by cutting the head off a nail and using it in an electric drill.

13 Punch the nail heads below the surface with the pin punch and fill the remaining holes with wax filler.

TOOLS

- Tape measure and pencil
- Combination square
- Two G-cramps or quick-release clamps
- Two 900 mm sash cramps
- Utility knife or marking knife
- Portable circular saw or panel saw
- Tenon saw
- Smoothing plane or jack plane
- Old iron
- Smoothing file
- Cork sanding block
- Electric sander (optional)
- Portable electric router and 18 mm straight cutting bit
- Cabinet scraper
- Hammer
- Fine nail punch or pin punch
- Electric drill
- Drill bits: 3 mm, 5 mm, countersink
- Screwdriver (cross-head or slotted)
- Dust mask
- Hearing protection
- Safety goggles

IRON-ON EDGE TAPE

Iron-on edge tape can sometimes be purchased in 2.4 m strips, but is generally sold in 20 or 50 m rolls. Always buy extra to replace tape damaged during construction.

LADDER RACK

Dowels fitted into frames form the basic structure of this wine rack, which will hold over 90 bottles. Accurate cutting of the many pieces will result in a sturdy, attractive structure.

CUTTING COMPONENTS

1 Take the timber for four stiles, set a marking gauge to 29 mm and mark lines from one end of the timber to the other. Trim the lengths to size, using a tenon saw or a circular saw with rip guide set to the same width. Use a jack plane to smooth the rough sawn edges back to the line. The other stiles are 41 mm wide.

2 Cut all the stiles to length with the tenon saw and mitre box or a drop saw. If you are going to use a tenon saw and bench hook, use the combination square and utility knife to score the lines around the timber faces and edges.

3 Cut the front and back rails to 856 mm in the same way and then cut the end rails.

4 Cut the dowels. You can cut several pieces of dowel at the same time if you bind them together with masking tape.

PREPARING THE RAILS

5 Take four front/back rails and clamp them together edge to edge with the ends flush and square to each other. Measure in 53 mm from one end and then measure off sixteen 50 mm intervals. There should be 53 mm left

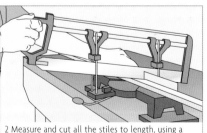

2 Measure and cut all the stiles to length, using a tenon saw and mitre box or a drop saw as here.

at the other end. Square the lines across all four rails. Repeat this step until all the rails have been marked out. Set a marking gauge and gauge a line down the middle of the inner face of each rail so the dowel positions are marked. Alternatively, you can make a drilling jig from a scrap piece of same-size material that sits over the rails. This way you only have to mark out the positions once accurately. It also helps to put fences and stops of scrap timber or plywood on each end and side of the jig.

6 Use a 10 mm drill bit to make 11 mm deep holes on the inner faces of the rails at the

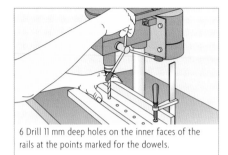

6 Drill 11 mm deep holes on the inner faces of the rails at the points marked for the dowels.

points marked. A piece of masking tape around the bit can act as a depth guide.

7 Sand all the components well with 120 grit abrasive paper and then 180 grit, removing the sharp edges.

PREPARING THE FRAMES AND CORNERS

8 Take one front rail and an end rail. Attach an end rail flush with each end of the front rail. Use a little PVA adhesive in the joint and two 40 mm panel pins to hold the front rail to the end rails. Apply a little adhesive to each dowel hole and insert the dowels.

8 Apply adhesive to the dowels and to the dowel holes in the back rail and insert the dowels into the back rail.

MATERIALS*

PART	MATERIAL	LENGTH	NO.
Stile	50 x 16 mm solid timber PAR	1441 mm	10
Front/back rail	50 x 25 mm solid timber PAR	856 mm	22
End rail	50 x 25 mm solid timber PAR	208 mm	22
Dowel	10 mm diameter timber dowel	230 mm	176

Other: Masking tape; abrasive paper: one sheet each of 120 grit, 180 grit and 240 grit; PVA woodworking adhesive; eighty-eight 40 mm panel pins; twenty 30 mm panel pins; 30 mm particleboard screws.

* Finished size: 880 x 270 mm and 1441 mm high. Timber sizes given are nominal. For timber sizes and conditions see page 112.

indoor

TOOLS

- Marking gauge
- Tape measure and pencil
- Combination square
- Circular saw
- Tenon saw
- Drop saw/mitre saw (optional)
- Smoothing plane
- Utility knife or marking knife
- Bench hook
- Hammer
- Dowelling jig (optional)
- Electric drill
- Drill bits: 3 mm, 10 mm, countersink
- Drill press (optional)
- G-cramps or quick-release clamps
- Screwdriver (cross-head or slotted), battery-operated if possible
- Electric sander or cork sanding block

Apply a little adhesive to the ends of the end rails and the dowel holes in the back rail, and align the dowels and the back rail. If the rails want to stay apart, use a 300 mm G-cramp or a quick-release clamp to add some pressure. Repeat for all eleven shelves. Make sure all the shelves are square (measure the diagonals and adjust if necessary).

9 While the shelves are drying, assemble the corners using one 41 mm wide stile and one 29 mm wide stile for each corner (see detail diagram on page 142). Apply adhesive and use five 30 mm panel pins to fix each corner. Set them aside to dry.

10 Apply the finish to the shelves and other components. (It is easier to do this before they are assembled.)

This simple rack was made from kauri pine and given a distressed finish, which was then coated with wax and buffed to a soft sheen.

FRONT VIEW

880 mm

Front rail

140 mm

END VIEW

270 mm

Stile

Stile

End rail

1441 mm

TOP VIEW

Back rail

Dowel

Stile

End rail

DETAIL

Front rail

Dowel

CORNER DETAIL

End rail

29 mm

41 mm

Front rail

Stile

FINAL ASSEMBLY

11 Make two spacers 250 x 99 mm. Place a rear corner on a suitable work surface, apply a little adhesive and align the top shelf with the top of the corner. Clamp it in place and use a 3 mm drill bit to make a pilot hole for the 30 mm screw through the frame and into the corner. If you are using a hard timber, drill a clearance hole. Insert the screw into the frame and tighten it until the head is flush with the timber surface. Repeat for the opposite rear corner. Use the spacer to position the next shelf, and continue until all the shelves have been fixed into position on the two back corners.

12 Measure along the ends of the top and bottom shelves and mark the centre of each. Align the middle of a centre stile with these marks. Clamp it in position. Ensure that the top frame is square in both directions, and fix the centre stile to the top shelf and then to the bottom shelf. Use the spacer to ensure the next frame is accurately positioned and fix it in place using 30 mm screws. Repeat the process until all the shelves have been fastened on one side and then fasten the centre stile to the opposite side of the shelves.

13 Apply a little adhesive to the shelves where the front corners will be attached. Check the shelves for square, clamp the corners into position and fasten the top and bottom shelves. Turn the unit face down and

11 Fix the top and bottom shelves to the rear corners, aligning the top shelves with the ends of the stiles.

indoor

SHELF

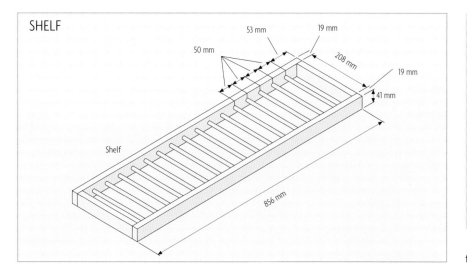

53 mm

50 mm

19 mm

208 mm

19 mm

41 mm

Shelf

856 mm

USING A DROP SAW

In this project there are 230 pieces, many of which are the same size. A drop saw will make the cutting much easier, and you are advised to hire one for a day if you don't already have one.

To improve the quality and accuracy of your cutting you can set up the drop saw with a piece of scrap material below the piece and a fence behind it to reduce the chipping out of the timber. The scrap can be held in place with masking tape.

fasten all the shelves using the spacer. The screw heads will be less noticeable if you fix the shelves from the underside.

14 Leave the unit to dry overnight, then touch up any areas that may have been damaged during assembly.

Two stiles form each of the corners into which the shelves are fixed.

shelving

shelving

SHELVING

Whether you use them for display or storage, shelves make a useful addition to most rooms. The commercial kits and modular systems available may not always be suitable, and these simple designs can be modified to suit any style or purpose.

SHELF SUPPORTS

When deciding on the support for your shelf, you need to consider the appearance you want and the weight it will have to hold.

- Shelves are most often supported on brackets of wood or metal. Depending on the spacing of the brackets and the thickness of the shelving material, such shelves can support even heavy weights.

- Shelves can be supported on a back batten fixed to the wall, or on side ones attached to uprights or the sides of an alcove. Use both for a really strong shelf.

- Bookcases and other shelf units that will support a fair weight are often constructed using housed joints. Butt joints are easier to construct, but they will not support as much weight.

Before placing any heavy items on your shelves, make sure they are strong enough to support the weight.

MAXIMUM SHELF SPANS*

MATERIAL	THICKNESS	MAXIMUM SPAN
Solid timber (PAR)	19 mm	750 mm
	30 mm	1000 mm
	41 mm	1250 mm
Particleboard/MDF	16–18 mm	600 mm
	25 mm	800 mm
	33 mm	1000 mm
Glass	6 mm	600 mm
	10 mm	1000 mm

* For shelves supported on brackets at each end with no rear batten. Some sagging may occur if excessive weight is placed on the shelf.

- Cantilevered shelves are attractive but cannot support any great weight.

SHELF SPANS

If you want a shelf of any length, you need to consider the spacing between supports (the span). The table above gives a guide to possible spans. There is no hard and fast rule as the span is dependent on the shelf material, the methods used to construct and support it, and the weight you will put on it. Always err on the side of caution: you don't want your shelf to collapse.

WALL FIXINGS

There are so many building materials and methods used today it can often be difficult to decide on the best method of fixing a shelf to a particular wall. First, find out exactly which methods have been used to build your house and then consult your local

hardware supplier. Among the more common fastenings are:

- Wall plug, a hollow plastic tube that expands inside the hole when the right size screw is inserted. It is suitable for fixing most shelves to masonry walls but not for lightweight concrete, or timber- or metal-framed walls. It is not suitable for heavy loads.

- Wall mate, a cast piece of metal with a coarse thread and self-drilling tip. It is used only for light objects. Once it is inserted in the wall, a screw is placed in its hollow shaft and then screwed tight. Use it in plasterboard and lightweight concrete, but not solid masonry.

- Nylon toggle, a toggle with wings that fold back to hold the item securely to the wall.

indoor

Only suitable for holding light weights, it is mostly used for hollow walls where no frame member can be found. Drill a hole in the wall, insert the fitting and fix a screw into the hollow end. The wings fold back to hold the item securely to the wall.

- Spring toggle, a toggle useful for medium-weight fixing if no framing member can

be found, as long as the wall lining is suitable (fibre cement sheeting, timber or plywood).

- Nylon anchor, a device used for medium-weight fixing to masonry. It has an expanding nylon sleeve and a drive pin or screw. Drill a suitable sized hole, insert the anchor in the shelf and align it with the

hole. Drive the nail or screw home. The screw pin is easily removed; the drive pin is more difficult to remove.

- Secret fixings. Steel rods fixed into the back of the shelf and the wall.

SHELF FIXED WITH HIDDEN RODS

These elegant shelves are fixed to the wall with steel rods and have no visible support. They are strong enough to carry a vase of flowers or a row of pictures, but they should not be used for heavy items or they will sag.

MAKING THE FRAME

1 The shelf is fixed to the wall with steel support rods, and their spacing is determined by the type of wall to which you are fixing the shelf. Decide exactly where the shelf is to go and the type of wall.

- For masonry walls the rods should be spaced 450 mm apart: locate one rod in the centre and then measure 450 mm either side to determine the positions of the other rods.

- In timber-frame construction studs are usually spaced between 450 mm and 600 mm apart. Locate the stud centres (see box on page 162). If the studs are at

MATERIALS FOR TWO SHELVES*

PART	MATERIAL	LENGTH	NO.
Stile	25 x 25 mm pine PAR	1190 mm	4
Rail	25 x 25 mm pine PAR	243 mm	10
Lipping (side)	38 x 25 mm maple or other hardwood PAR	300 mm	4
Lipping (front)	38 x 25 mm maple or other hardwood PAR	1228 mm	2
Rod	$\frac{3}{8}$ inch diameter threaded steel rod	360 mm	6
Panel	4 mm plywood	1200 x 281 mm	4

Other: Twelve $\frac{3}{8}$ inch nuts; PVA adhesive; masking tape; eighteen 40 mm nails; wood filler; abrasive paper: two sheets of 120 grit; finish of choice.

* Finished width 300 mm, length 1225 mm (see step 1 above if you want to adjust the length). Timber sizes given are nominal (see page 112).

2 Cut the stile and rail material, cutting all pieces the same length at once so that they correspond exactly.

600 mm centres, only two supports can be used. Space them evenly as shown in the diagram on page 150. If studs are positioned at 400 or 450 mm centres, locate the centre rod and then measure out.

- This shelving is not suitable for use with metal-frame wall construction.

2 Select your material, choosing timber that is straight and without any twists so that the shelf will remain straight. Cut the stile and rail material to the given lengths. Cut all pieces the same length at once.

3 Take the stiles and mark the positions for the steel support rods. Drill the holes using

Hidden steel rods project into the wall to support these neat display shelves.

TOOLS

- Tape measure
- Pencil
- Panel saw
- Tenon saw
- Portable power drill
- Drill bit: 9.5 mm
- Solid domestic paper stapler
- Old paintbrush (optional)
- G-cramps or similar
- Boards for clamping
- Electric router (optional)
- Smoothing plane
- Mitre box or mitre saw
- Hammer
- Nail punch
- Electric sander or sanding cork
- Spirit level

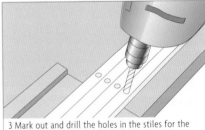

3 Mark out and drill the holes in the stiles for the steel support rods, using the 9.5 mm drill bit.

the 9.5 mm drill bit. Also mark where the rails will butt up against the stiles (see page 150).

4 Butt the rails against the stiles in the positions marked and staple them together. The staples will hold the frame together well enough for you to locate it neatly on the plywood during the gluing process. Make sure the frames are square and will remain that way.

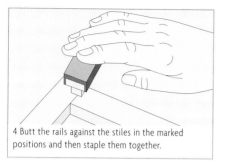

4 Butt the rails against the stiles in the marked positions and then staple them together.

5 Insert the rods into the frame, so that the nuts are firm and the rod is 3 mm in from the front of the frame.

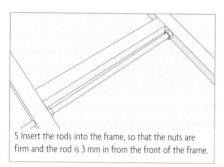

6 Spread a good quantity of adhesive across the frame and locate the frame on the plywood.

COMPLETING THE SHELF

5 Insert the rods into the holes in the frame, using nuts against the inner sides of the stiles. Make sure the nuts are firm but not tight and the end of the rod is inset approximately 3 mm from the front edge of the frame. The nuts will prevent the shelves being pulled off the rod by accident and will ensure maximum support right across the shelves.

6 Spread a good quantity of adhesive across the bottom of the frame. An old paintbrush will help spread it effectively while keeping your hands clean. Place the frame on the

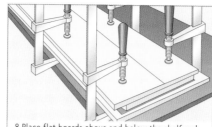

8 Place flat boards above and below the shelf and apply G-cramps or stack plenty of weight on top.

bottom panel. Make sure the back edges of the frame and panel are aligned and use a piece of masking tape to keep them in place—you won't be able to straighten the back edge later, as the steel rods will be in the way. The panel should project slightly on all other sides: it will be trimmed after the adhesive has dried.

7 Glue scrap pieces of 25 x 25 mm timber inside the frame area to prevent the panel sinking down between the rails. Spread adhesive on the top of the frame. Lay the top panel on the frame and align the back edge as before. If you are making more than one shelf, place the shelves one on top of the other with a layer of newspaper between to prevent them sticking together.

8 Place the shelf or shelves on a flat board and place another on top of them to prevent damage when they are clamped and to ensure even distribution of pressure over the plywood and frames. If you have them, use G-cramps, but otherwise stack plenty of weight on top. Check that the frame and panels are perfectly aligned and wipe off any excess adhesive with a damp cloth. Leave to dry overnight.

9 While the adhesive is drying, prepare the edge lippings, which are used to hide the edges of the frames and plywood panels. They also give extra strength to the shelf. Plane the lipping timber to a finished size of

28 x 19 mm and cut the pieces to slightly overlength to allow for the mitres: the side lippings have a mitre on one end only and the front lipping has mitres on both ends.

10 Remove the shelf from the cramps and check that the panels have stuck successfully to the frame. If not, apply more adhesive and clamp the shelf a second time. If all is well, trim the excess plywood from the frame, using a router with a trimming bit, or clean up the edges with the smoothing plane. Use a smoothing plane to ensure the edges are flat and straight.

11 Hold the front lipping to the front edge of the shelf and mark the inside mitres onto the lipping. Cut the mitres. Apply the two side lippings using two 40 mm nails and a good smear of adhesive. Make sure the mitres are well aligned with the corners of the shelf and the lipping is flush with the top of the shelf (or it can project just over as it can be planed flush later if necessary).

12 Fix the front lipping onto the shelves using five 40 mm nails and some adhesive. If you prefer not to nail on the lippings, they can be attached using long cramps. Do not use tape, as this does not give a strong joint and can result in gaps between the lippings and shelves.

13 Use a smoothing plane to flush up the lipping with the top and bottom of the shelf, taking care not to gouge the surface

HINT

Place a little construction adhesive in the holes and along the metal rods to prevent them being pulled out accidentally.

of the plywood. Offsetting the plane blade slightly with the lateral adjustment lever will help prevent gouging. Punch the nail holes and fill any gaps with wood filler. Sand the shelf smooth using 120 grit abrasive paper.

FINISHING AND INSTALLATION

14 Finish the shelf as desired (see box below).

15 Measure up from the floor to the height where you want the top of the shelf, and use a spirit level to strike a level line. Measure down from the line half the thickness of the shelf, line up the support rods with this line and mark the positions.

16 Drill the appropriate number of holes into the wall. Make sure the holes go square into the wall or at a slight downward angle so the shelves are level or slightly pitched up. This will help counteract any sag and stop items falling off the shelf, particularly if your house is subject to vibration from traffic outside or heavy feet inside.

FINISHING YOUR PROJECT

- If painting your shelf, use two coats, sanding between each with 180 grit abrasive paper. Use a primer undercoat first to choke the timber grain and make it easier to sand. On MDF don't sand the faces too hard as this makes them furry, but work hard on the edges. Use a good-quality wood filler to stop up bruises or holes visible before finishing.
- If you intend to use stain or clear lacquer, remove all excess adhesive first or the stain will not penetrate through into the timber, and there will be white blotches.

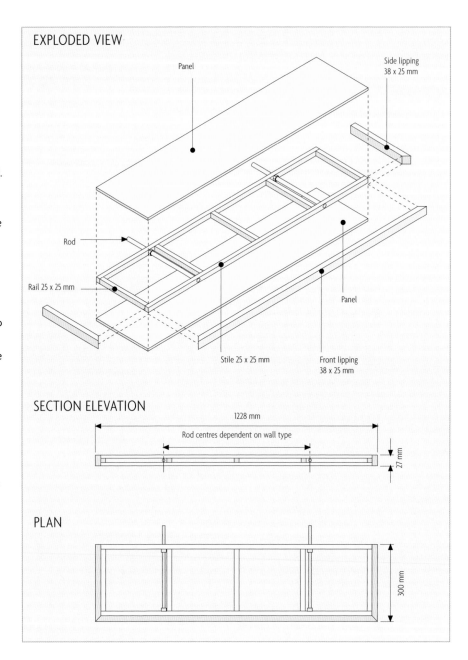

EXPLODED VIEW

Panel

Side lipping 38 x 25 mm

Rod

Rail 25 x 25 mm

Panel

Stile 25 x 25 mm

Front lipping 38 x 25 mm

SECTION ELEVATION

1228 mm

Rod centres dependent on wall type

27 mm

PLAN

300 mm

SLATTED SHELF

This shelf with parallel slats is supported on two end brackets and has a rod fixed from bracket to bracket. It is useful in the kitchen or in the hallway, and can easily be made longer by adding more brackets as necessary.

1 Plane the materials to the required width and thicknesses, and clean up with a smoothing plane.

CUTTING OUT

1 Select your material carefully, making certain it is free from twisting and other defects as far as possible. Plane the materials to the required width and thicknesses by sawing and cleaning up with a smoothing plane. Be sure to remove any machine marks as this will help enhance the final appearance.

2 Mark the required lengths for the vertical and horizontal pieces, and use a square and pencil to mark the lines all the way around the timbers. Also mark off the lengths on the slats. Use a utility or razor knife to cut the fibres around the pencil lines before you start sawing, then cut the pieces to the required lengths carefully. Ensure you keep to the waste side of your pencil lines when cutting, as timbers can be planed back if necessary but not lengthened.

3 Using the combination square, mark out and cut the brace pieces. The longest edge is to the outside and is 353 mm long.

4 Mark out the centre of the brace pieces where the dowel will be inserted. Drill the holes for the dowels using the correct size bit to a depth of 10 mm.

The dowel rail is an optional feature of this classic slatted shelf.

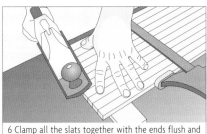

6 Clamp all the slats together with the ends flush and plane the chamfer across all pieces at the same time.

8 Glue and nail the vertical and horizontal pieces together, using the 40 mm nails.

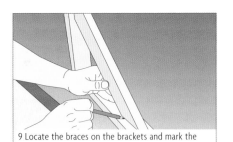

9 Locate the braces on the brackets and mark the inside and outside positions of the joints.

MATERIALS*

PART	MATERIAL	LENGTH	NO.
Vertical	50 x 25 mm mahogany or other hardwood PAR	300 mm	2
Horizontal	50 x 25 mm mahogany or other hardwood PAR	320 mm	2
Brace	50 x 25 mm mahogany or other hardwood PAR	353 mm	2
Rod	12 mm diameter timber dowelling	600 mm	1
Slat	25 x 25 mm mahogany or other hardwood PAR	680 mm	11

Other: PVA adhesive; 40 mm nails; four 50 mm x No. 10 countersunk brass wood screws; twenty-two 30 mm x No. 8 countersunk brass wood screws; abrasive paper: 180 and 240 grit; wall fixings (see step 15); finish of choice.

* Finished width 320 mm, length 640 mm. Timber sizes given are nominal. For timber types and timber sizes, see page 112.

5 Bring all the components to their exact lengths. Place the common components together in the vice and plane the end grain back to the marking knife lines. To help prevent the end grain breaking out, use a backing block of the same material located just a millimetre or so below the marking knife lines. Remember that your plane needs to be razor-sharp and set quite fine to achieve a good result.

6 Clamp all the slats together with the ends flush, and plane the chamfer across one edge of all the ends at the same time. Turn them over and repeat the process until all the ends

have been chamfered all round. One end of the vertical and horizontal pieces can be chamfered similarly, but only on the short sides and one long side.

ASSEMBLY

7 Sand all the components. If you are going to stain the shelf it is a good idea to stain the components now, as some places will be difficult to get at once the shelf is assembled.

8 Glue and nail the vertical and horizontal pieces together using 40 mm nails so the chamfered ends are at the bottom of the verticals and the front of the horizontals.

9 Locate the braces on the brackets as shown in the diagram opposite, and mark the inside and outside positions of the joints on both verticals and horizontals. Mark the centre line of the joints and measure from the inside of the brace joint 15 mm along the

centre line to locate the position for the screw fastening. Drill 5 mm holes and countersink for the screws on the external faces. Align the braces in the brackets and screw, and glue them into position using the 50 mm x No. 10 screws.

10 Check the wall to determine the type of construction used, as this will affect the spacing of the brackets. For masonry construction, space the brackets at 600 mm centres; for timber-frame construction, the positions will be determined by the spacing of the studs (usually somewhere between 400 mm and 600 mm). To find the studs, use one of the methods in the box on page 162. Having determined the positions of the brackets, make any necessary adjustment to the length of the rod.

11 Clamp all the slats together and mark out the stud centre distances evenly across all slats. Mark off a line slightly to one side of

indoor

TOOLS

- Tenon saw
- Smoothing plane
- Square
- Pencil
- Tape measure
- Utility or razor knife
- Combination square
- Mitre box or mitre saw
- Electric drill
- Drill bits: 5 mm, 3 mm
- Vice
- Cramp
- Hammer
- Sanding cork (or portable electric sander)
- Countersink bit
- Screwdriver (cross-head or slotted)
- Spirit level

the centre line so that the slat screws will not interfere with the brace-fixing screws. Drill 5 mm holes in each slat and countersink them for neatness.

12 Start fixing the slats by aligning the first one with the front edge of one bracket. Slip in the rod, bring in the next bracket and fasten the slat to it with a 30 mm x No. 8 screw. Next, use a 10 mm spacer to position the next slat and each subsequent slat. Ensure that the brackets remain square to the slats and that the slat ends are lined up.

FINISHING AND INSTALLATION

13 The shelf will require a minimum of two coats of whichever finish you have chosen, either varnish over the stain already applied or paint. A brush will do the job, but it will be

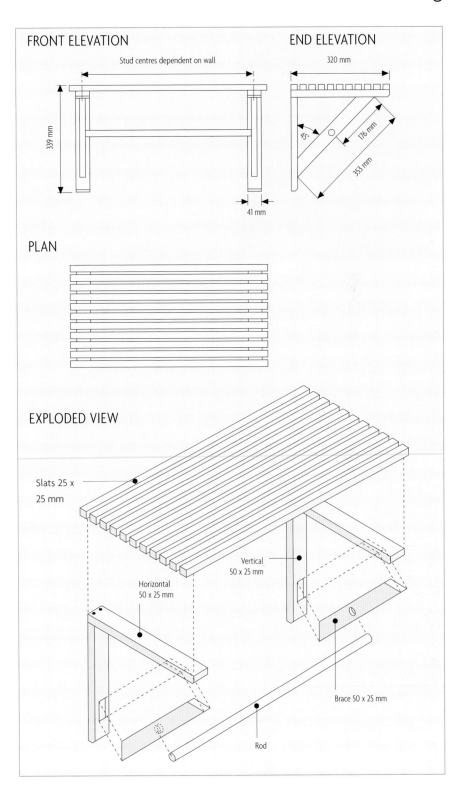

FRONT ELEVATION

Stud centres dependent on wall

339 mm

41 mm

END ELEVATION

320 mm

45°

176 mm

353 mm

PLAN

EXPLODED VIEW

Slats 25 x 25 mm

Vertical 50 x 25 mm

Horizontal 50 x 25 mm

Brace 50 x 25 mm

Rod

Slatted shelves are traditionally used in the kitchen, bathroom or hallway.

HINT

Always make sure your cutting tools are very sharp before you begin work. Sharp tools will not only make work easier, they will allow you to make the cuts much more precisely.

14 Drill two 5 mm holes in each bracket for fixing. They will be less noticeable on the inside of the brace. Don't forget to countersink them.

15 Position the shelf on the wall and drill a pilot hole into the wall. The size will depend on the fastening you use and the wall construction. For masonry walls you should use 75 x 6.5 mm nylon anchors, 75 mm x No. 10 countersunk screws with appropriate wall plugs or 75 mm x 6.5 mm countersunk expansion bolts. For framed walls 75 mm x No. 10 countersunk wood screws should be used. Fix in one fastening first, then bring the shelf to the level

Braced brackets are used to firmly fix the shelf to the wall.

position, checking with a spirit level. Drill the wall and fix the second fastening. Test that the shelf is level and make any adjustments before securing it with the final fastenings.

very difficult to reach some places, and so it is recommended that you use a spray can. A final preparatory sand with 180 grit abrasive paper will be fine, but use 240 grit between coats. See the box on page 150 for finishing tips.

SHELF WITH LIP

This simple shelf is perfect for displaying plates or other small items, and yet is very easy to make. The shelf proper rests on a back batten, and attached to the front of it is a lip to prevent the objects slipping forward.

MAKING THE SHELF

1 Using the straight slots of a mitre box to keep the saw square, cut all three pieces of timber to exactly 1500 mm long.

2 Take the wall support and the lip, and mark on the face of the timber the positions for the screws that will attach them to the shelf (see diagram on page 156). On the wall support, mark positions 10 mm down from the top edge. Place them 50 mm in from each end and approximately 200 mm apart. On

the lip, mark positions 15 mm down from the top edge, 50 mm from each end and 200 mm apart. Using the 5 mm drill bit, drill holes through each piece of timber on the marks.

3 Using the 120 grit abrasive paper wrapped around the cork block, sand all the timber, removing pencil marks and blemishes. Dust off.

4 Lay the shelf piece front edge down on the workbench and position the wall

support flush with the top edge of the shelf. Placing a nail through the holes in the support, mark the screw positions onto the shelf. Remove the wall support. Using the 3 mm drill bit, drill holes on the marks to about 30 mm deep. Wipe clean, and apply adhesive along the edge. Reposition the wall support, and then screw the shelf and support together. Wipe off any excess adhesive.

5 Turn the shelf over so the support is lying on the bench. Repeat to attach the lip to the

The lip on this shelf projects upward just enough to hold a plate or picture frame in place. It won't obscure your view of them.

2 On the lip mark the positions for the screws that will hold it to the shelf. Drill the holes.

5 Attach the lip to the shelf, positioning it so that it projects 6 mm above the shelf.

6 Countersink the screw holes and then fill them with wood filler for an even surface.

TOOLS

- Mitre box
- Tenon saw
- Pencil
- Tape measure
- Fold-out rule
- Electric drill
- Drill bits: 3 mm, 5 mm
- Countersink
- Screwdriver (or screwdriver bit for drill)
- Filler knife
- Cork sanding block
- Spirit level

(If fixing to a masonry wall, you will also need a hammer drill and masonry drill bit to suit.)

shelf, positioning the lip so its top is 6 mm higher than the shelf (see diagram on page 156).

6 Countersink the screws on the lip so they are just below the surface. Fill the countersunk screw holes with wood filler. When it is dry, sand the surface with 120 grit abrasive paper around a sanding block. Change to 150 grit and sand the whole piece.

7 Dust off well and apply the desired finish (see box on page 150).

FIXING IN POSITION

8 Drill holes in the wall support, as close to the underside of the shelf as possible. The spacing of the holes and the method of drilling will be determined by your wall. If you have a masonry wall, space the holes 400 mm apart. On a stud partition wall (usually a plasterboard surface), find the timber studs to drill into—they will be 400–600 mm apart (see box on page 162). Once you have found the studs, measure and mark the corresponding positions onto the

The lip is attached to the shelf so that it projects both above and below.

support, close to the under side of the shelf. Drill holes on the marks, using the 5 mm drill bit, and countersink the holes so the screw heads will be below the surface.

9 Hold the shelf in position (you may need help) and sit the spirit level on the shelf. Using a nail (or the drill and 3 mm drill bit), mark the wall through the holes. Remove the shelf. For a masonry wall, use a masonry drill and drill holes 40 mm deep. Insert plastic plugs into the holes and cut them flush with the wall (a chisel is best for this). For a stud partition wall, use the 3 mm drill bit and drill holes about 30 mm deep on the marks. Screw the shelf in place; countersink the screw heads.

10 Fill in over the screw heads with wood filler and allow it to dry. Sand lightly and touch up the finish.

MATERIALS*

PART	MATERIAL	LENGTH	NO.
Wall support	100 x 19 mm pine PAR	1500 mm	1
Shelf	75 x 25 mm pine PAR	1500 mm	1
Lip	50 x 25 mm pine PAR	1500 mm	1

Other: Twenty 40 mm x No. 8 screws; PVA adhesive; water-based wood filler; abrasive paper: one sheet of 120 grit and two sheets of 150 grit; wall plugs or individual plastic plugs (if mounting on masonry wall); finish of choice.

* Finished width behind lip 77 mm; length 1500 mm. The length can be adjusted to suit your location. Timber sizes given are nominal. For timber types and timber sizes, see page 112.

SHELF ASSEMBLY

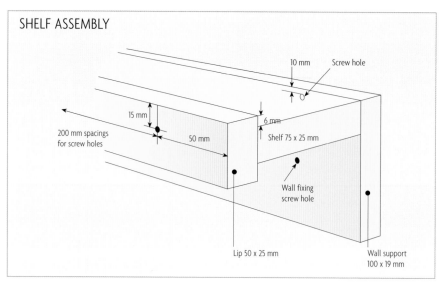

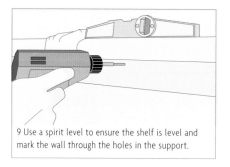

9 Use a spirit level to ensure the shelf is level and mark the wall through the holes in the support.

WALL-MOUNTED SHELF UNIT

A small unit of open shelves can hold spices and other kitchen items, a collection of miniatures or even rows of tiny plants.

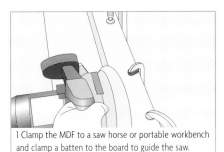
1 Clamp the MDF to a saw horse or portable workbench and clamp a batten to the board to guide the saw.

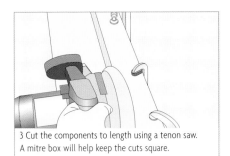
3 Cut the components to length using a tenon saw. A mitre box will help keep the cuts square.

Housed joints hold the shelves on this simple unit. It has no back, and the wall behind can be painted to emphasize this or to match the shelves.

CUTTING COMPONENTS

1 Clamp the MDF to a bench. Clamp a batten to the board to guide the saw straight along the cut. Cut three 118 mm wide strips.

2 Hold the strips together in a vice or portable workbench so that the edges are flush. Plane the edges so that they are straight and free from cut marks. Remove them from the vice and use the combination square (set it at 115 mm) to mark along the face the finished width of the strips. Don't mark near the edge you have just planed. Bring all three strips together again with their planed edges flush, and put them back in the vice and plane the strips together down to 115 mm.

3 Using the rule, pencil and combination square, set out the length of the components along the three strips, leaving 3–5 mm between each part to allow for saw cuts. Take the pencil lines around all sides of the material. Trace along the pencil lines with a utility knife to cut the top fibres. Use the tenon saw to cut parts to the marked length.

4 Take the matching parts and hold them together in a vice, making sure the marking knife lines match up. Use the smoothing plane to square up the ends of the parts and to bring them to the correct lengths. Repeat this process for all the pairs of parts.

MATERIALS*

PART	MATERIAL	LENGTH	WIDTH	NO.
End	12 mm MDF	490 mm	115 mm	2
Top/bottom	12 mm MDF	400 mm	115 mm	2
Shelf	12 mm MDF	384 mm	115 mm	2

Other: One packet 30 mm panel pins; PVA adhesive; filler; wall fixings; finish of choice.

* Finished height of unit 498 mm; width 400 mm; depth of shelves 115 mm.

TOOLS

- Straight edge
- Portable circular saw
- Vice or portable workbench
- Plane
- Combination square
- Pencil
- Utility knife
- Tenon saw
- Electric router
- 12 mm straight cutting bit or smaller
- Hammer
- Nail punch
- Filler knife

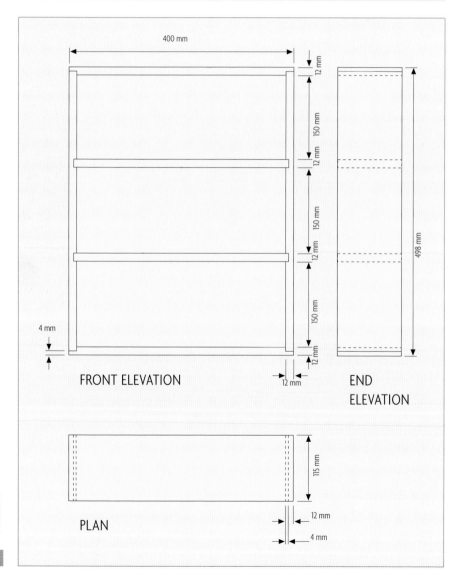

FRONT ELEVATION

END ELEVATION

PLAN

5 Using a pencil and combination square, mark out the positions for the rebates on the top and bottom pieces. They will be 12 mm wide and 8 mm deep. Make sure they are in the bottom of the top piece and the top of the bottom piece. Then mark out the housings for the shelves on the inside face of the side pieces. To do this measure up 162 mm from the end of the piece and draw a line across. Then measure up 12 mm for the top of the housing. The second housing is 150 mm further up. The housings are 4 mm deep.

6 The rebates and housings can be cut with the tenon saw and a chisel, but are more easily made with a router. Set the router cutter to a depth of 8 mm and the fence to about 8 mm for the width of the cut. Make the first pass over the cutter with a scrap piece of material, and make any adjustments to the depth of the cut at this time. Cut the rebates in the top and bottom pieces. Adjust the fence for the second pass of the material over the cutter to the full width of the cut at 12 mm. Be sure to make a test cut on a scrap piece of material first. Check to see that the rebates will fit neatly.

7 For the housing cuts, set the fence 158 mm away from the closest cutting edge of the router cutter and reduce the depth of cut to 4 mm. Make a test cut in a scrap of material. If you are using a full 12 mm cutter, check the fit of the material in the housing joint. When satisfied with the depth and position of the housing, make the cuts in the side pieces. Work from each end as the spacings are equal. If the cutter is smaller than 12 mm,

adjust the fence to make the groove 12 mm wide. Use a test piece to check your adjustments, and then cut the housing joints.

ASSEMBLY

8 Test that all the parts fit together accurately; make any adjustments. When you are satisfied, pull the components apart and apply adhesive to the housing joints. Assemble the joints and join them together using 30 mm panel pins. Apply adhesive to both faces of the rebate joints; bring together with the rest of the unit. Nail together through the sides with 30 mm panel pins.

9 Punch and fill all the nail holes and rub back the wood filler when it has dried. Apply the finish of your choice (see box on page 150).

10 Fix to the wall with eye-screws and hollow wall anchors or small masonry fasteners.

FREE-STANDING SHELF UNIT

Recycled fence palings are used to make this shelf unit, but any timber would serve as well. The shelves are made independently and bolted to the slats.

PREPARING THE TIMBER

1 Lay out the palings and remove the nails. Carefully select the best palings, that is, the straightest pieces with a uniform thickness. You will need about thirty-five palings altogether.

2 Take the framing material and mark off and cut the lengths required. Mark across the face and down the edges with the square and pencil to ensure that you have a squared line to follow when cutting. Always cut on the waste side of the pencil line. Hold the combination square against the timber to provide a guide for the saw to run against. If you are not completely proficient with a circular saw, use a mitre saw or tenon saw and bench hook.

3 The palings will generally be rotten at the bottom and fairly good at the top. Stack two or three on top of each other and square them off near the top. When all are cut

MATERIALS**

PART	MATERIAL	LENGTH	NO.
Side/back slat	old fence palings*	1500 mm	16
Shelf slat	old fence palings*	768 mm	16
Frame stile	50 x 25 mm rough-sawn hardwood	767 mm	8
Frame rail	50 x 25 mm rough-sawn hardwood	320 mm	12
Plinth rail	50 x 25 mm rough-sawn hardwood	298 mm	4
Plinth face	old fence paling	768 mm	1

Other: Abrasive paper: ten sheets each of 60 and 120 grit; PVA adhesive; 60 mm lost-head nails; 30 mm flat-head nails; four plastic scouring pads; clean rags; Danish teak wax or finish of your choice; eighty-four $2\frac{1}{4}$ inch square-neck mushroom-head bolts and washers.

* Old palings are well seasoned and should remain dimensionally stable. You will need, however, to adjust the width and depth of the unit to suit your palings. If desired, 95 mm wide hardwood slats can be used instead.

** Finished height of unit 1500 mm; width 795 mm; depth of shelves 378 mm. Timber sizes given are nominal. For timber types and sizes, see page 112.

This attractive shelf unit is a perfect way to re-use palings or other old timber. Palings are nailed to the shelf frames as well as providing the side and back timber, and the whole is finished with teak oil.

TOOLS

- Hammer
- Combination square
- Measuring tape
- Pencil
- Handsaw or circular saw
- Safety glasses
- Gloves
- Dust mask
- Mitre saw or tenon saw and mitre box
- Bench hook
- Electric sander
- Smoothing plane
- Portable electric drill
- Drill bit: 6.5 mm
- Wire wheel for electric drill
- Four G-cramps
- 11 mm socket and socket wrench

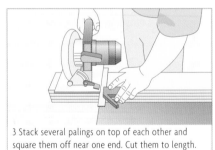

3 Stack several palings on top of each other and square them off near one end. Cut them to length.

square at one end, mark and cut them to 1500 mm in length. Trim the tops with angled cuts as shown in the diagram opposite. Don't be too fussy with the angle and size as a slight unevenness will add to the rustic appeal.

4 Cut the shelf slats, using the technique described in step 2.

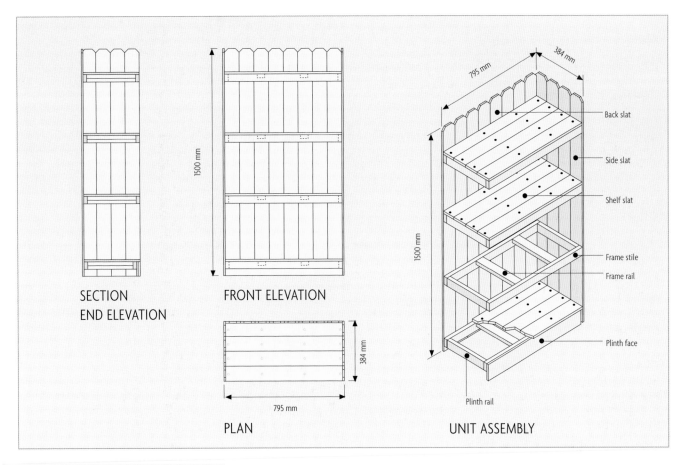

SECTION
END ELEVATION

FRONT ELEVATION

PLAN

UNIT ASSEMBLY

Back slat

Side slat

Shelf slat

Frame stile

Frame rail

Plinth face

Plinth rail

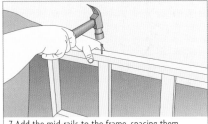

7 Add the mid-rails to the frame, spacing them evenly and making sure they are flush with the top.

5 Using 60 grit abrasive paper, sand all the components. Plane the top edges only of the frame material to give a straight edge. Plane a light 2 mm chamfer on the edges of the frame members.

ASSEMBLING THE FRAMES

6 Take a frame rail and place it in the vice with one end facing up. Spread a little PVA adhesive on the end grain and rub it in with your finger. Then place adhesive on the end of the timber. This ensures a stronger joint. Take a stile and start a 60 mm nail into the face of the timber, near the end. Locate the stile on the rail so that the ends are flush and the planed edges are aligned accurately. Hammer in the nail and adjust the fit. Hammer a second nail into the joint and then repeat this process for the other end. Check that the frames are square by measuring the diagonal distance across the frames from corner to corner. When these measurements are the same, the frame is square.

7 Add the mid-rails to the frame. They should be spaced evenly, but the exact position is not essential as long as the faces are flush with the top of the frame.

8 Construct two more shelf frames and the plinth frame, which uses the shorter rails.

ASSEMBLING THE SHELVES

9 While the adhesive is drying on the frames, scrub and sand the palings. Wear safety glasses and gloves, and if possible use a wire wheel fitted to a portable drill to scrub all along each paling, both sides and edges, paying attention to the areas where most rot and decay have occurred. A plain wire brush can be used, but the process will be more laborious and take longer. When all slats have been wire-brushed, sand them using 60 grit abrasive paper. Be sure to sand

The angled cuts on top of the palings look more rustic if they are a little irregular.

FINDING STUDS IN A TIMBER-FRAME WALL

In order to fix a shelf to a timber-frame wall, you will need to locate the studs. This can be done in several ways.

- Use a stud finder (joist and batten detector). This is a battery-operated instrument designed to locate studs. It is available from most hardware stores.
- Tap gently on the wall and listen for the solid sound.
- Use a nail at shelf height to locate the studs.
- Look for nail marks in the plasterwork, as they may indicate the stud positions.
- Climb into the roof cavity and find the tops of the studs. Then measure their distance apart and the distance from the corner.

the edges well to remove splinters and sand along the grain, not across it. For a smooth finish go over each piece again using 120 grit abrasive paper. Brush off the sanding dust with a soft brush.

10 Check the adhesive is dry. Take the plinth frame (it is narrower), and using PVA adhesive and the 30 mm flat-head nails, nail on the front plinth, making sure the top edge is flush with the top of the frame.

11 Apply a generous quantity of adhesive to the area on the plinth frame where the front slat is to be fixed, and lay the slat on the frame so that it overhangs the plinth facing by no more than 10 mm. Check that it is flush with or just slightly over the end of the frame and nail it off with flat-head nails. Apply some more adhesive to the frame,

position the next slat and nail it off, ensuring that the ends line up. Repeat this process for a third slat. Leave the fourth slat for now: it will be too wide to fit and will have to be cut down to size.

12 Fix three slats to each of the shelf frames in the same way, setting them flush with the front face of the frame.

13 Place the fourth slats in position on the frames and mark the necessary width right along their length. Clamp them to a suitable work surface and cut them to width. Nail the final slats in position.

PREPARING THE SIDE AND BACK SLATS

14 Take one side slat and measure 60 mm up from the bottom. From this mark measure a further three 400 mm increments for the positions of the other shelves. Mark a line down the centre of the slat to locate the four positions for drilling the holes. Place a 6.5 mm drill bit in the drill and drill these positions.

15 Use the first slat as a template for drilling the remaining slats. Stack two or three slats together with the template on top. Clamp them together and drill right through the stack at the appropriate positions.

16 Apply the finish to all the side slats and shelves (access to these surfaces will be difficult later). We used Danish teak wax to give a rustic appearance as it makes the grain stand out. Rub it well into the grain of the timber using a scouring pad and a circular motion. This will pick up any small splinters that the sanding missed, so wear appropriate gloves. Use a dry, clean cloth to wipe off all the excess wax. The bolt heads were painted matt black. They were pushed through a sheet of corrugated cardboard, leaving only the heads exposed, and spray-painted.

ASSEMBLY

17 Clear a space for assembly. You may need another pair of hands at this stage. Take the base shelf and stand it on its end. Take the first side slat and position it so it is flush with the bottom edge of the plinth and the front edge of the shelf slat. Use a cramp to hold it in position. Take the remaining shelves and clamp them flush with the edge of the slat in their correct positions, making sure the bolts will go

ALTERNATIVE FINISHES FOR A NATURAL LOOK

- Natural beeswax. This is very popular, but it requires hard rubbing and uses a lot of wax.
- Teak oil. Use several coats to achieve a good finish.
- Matt lacquer. Use a couple of spray coats of lacquer.

indoor

through the middle of the shelf frames and there is clearance for a socket spanner. The bolt holes into the plinth will have to be angled back a little to clear the framework, but this will not affect the final appearance. Place 2 1/4 inch bolts into the holes, slip on the washers and nuts and do them up, finger-tight only at this stage.

18 Take the next slat and line it up with the bottom of the first slat. Using a combination square laying along the front edge, check the new slat is square to the last slat and the plinth is sitting square to the front edge of the first slat. Repeat the squaring check at each shelf position and clamp the pieces in place. Drill the holes and place bolts into them. Repeat this for the other two slats. Do not trim off the overhang. Tighten up the bolts.

19 Place down a groundsheet and turn the unit over. Place the first slat on the other side, flush with the plinth and shelves as described in step 11. Check that the distance between the shelves is the same on both sides and clamp the slat into position. Drill the holes and insert the bolts. Fix the other slats to the side.

20 Lie the unit on its face and add the back slats. Work from both sides to the centre, so that if the palings do not fit evenly, the two centre ones can be trimmed down to fit. This looks better than having a narrow paling at one end. Drill the bolt holes, angling them towards the bottom of the unit to avoid bolts fouling slightly on the framing members. Insert the bolts. Stand the unit up, place the washers and nuts on the bolts and tighten the bolts.

21 A second application of teak wax can now be made.

CANTILEVERED GLASS SHELF

Brilliantly simple in concept, this glass shelf cantilevered from a timber rail is very easy to make. It will look equally at home as a display shelf in the living room or in the bathroom.

MAKING THE RAIL

1 Use a rule to mark out the length on the timber. Square the lines all around with the combination square; score them with a knife and square to prevent the fibres breaking out. Cut the timber to length, making sure you keep to the waste side of the line and that the cut is square.

2 Mark out the position of the groove and bevels on one end of the length; double-check to see that the marking-out is accurate. Use a combination square to transfer the groove marks along the face of the timber to the opposite end of the material, and then set out the groove and bevels again on the other end.

3 Set up the fences on the table saw or router for cutting the groove. Check that the depth of cut is going to be accurate. Use an offcut or scrap piece of material to check the adjustments before you make any cuts in the good piece. Put on your safety glasses, hearing protection and dust mask. Now make the first cut. Keep your fingers away from the blade and use a push stick to hold and push the timber through the last part of the cut. Because a saw blade is narrower than the width of the groove required, adjust the fence for the second cut. Use the same piece of scrap stock to check your adjustments and check that a 6 mm piece of glass will fit in

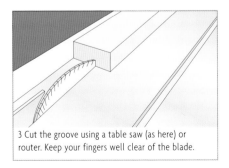

3 Cut the groove using a table saw (as here) or router. Keep your fingers well clear of the blade.

MATERIALS*

- 600 mm length of 100 x 50 mm timber PAR
- 600 x 120 mm piece of 6 mm thick glass (see box on page 168)
- Abrasive paper: 180 grit
- Two 35 mm x No. 6 countersunk screws
- Clear silicone sealant

* Finished length 600 mm; width 130 mm. Timber sizes given are nominal (see box on page 112).

the groove. The glass should fit neatly in the groove, not too tightly and not loosely at all. Run the second cut. Finally, check that the groove is clean and the glass fits neatly.

The glass shelf was purchased cut to size and with polished edges for safety.

4 Make sure the saw blade has completely stopped before you tilt the saw over to 45 degrees. Cut the wider bevel first. Adjust the fence on the saw to 40 mm, and check the set-up by holding the timber up to the blade. Make the first bevel cut. Now set up for the second bevel cut the same way, but reduce the depth of the cut so that the blade cuts into only one side of the groove. When you are satisfied with the set-up, cut the second bevel.

5 Place the bevelled stock into a vice, being careful not to damage the edges, and plane the bevelled faces to remove any saw marks.

FINISHING AND INSTALLATION

6 Decide where the shelf is to go and determine the type of wall construction used. If it is a timber stud wall, determine the distance apart of the studs from centre to centre and transfer the dimension to the back of the rail. The markings should be in line with the groove, as the fastenings will be placed in the groove. At these positions drill 5 mm holes through the support and check that the heads of the fastenings fit into the groove. If not, the heads may be filed down slightly to fit.

7 Using the sanding cork and 180 grit abrasive paper, sand the bevels smooth. Finish the shelf as desired (see box on page 150), but consider where you'll put it. It could go in a bathroom, even a shower recess, but would need to be sealed, groove and all, with a paint that is waterproof and has a fungus guard additive.

8 Using a spirit level at the height required, draw a level line on the wall. Hold the rail

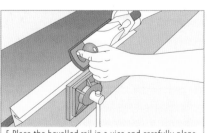

5 Place the bevelled rail in a vice and carefully plane the edges to remove the saw marks.

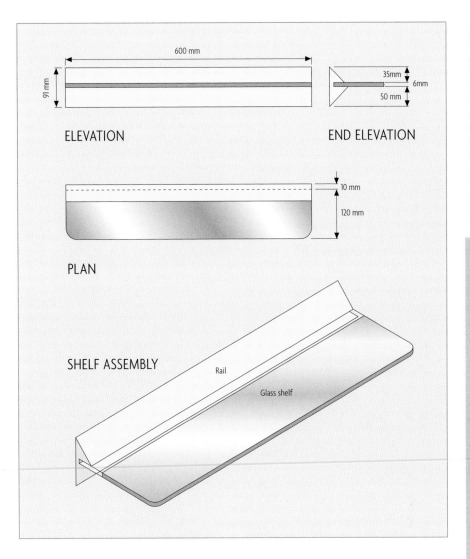

600 mm

91 mm

ELEVATION

35mm
6mm
50 mm

END ELEVATION

10 mm

120 mm

PLAN

SHELF ASSEMBLY

Rail

Glass shelf

PLANING THE BEVELS

Mark the planing angles on the end of the timber. Place the timber in a vice or clamp it down so that you can plane the angle on one edge. At first have enough blade out to take a fair amount off in one pass. Check the angle regularly. As planing becomes more difficult, reduce the amount of blade exposed. Turn the piece around and plane the bevel on the opposite edge.

TOOLS

- Tape measure or fold-out rule
- Pencil
- Combination square
- Utility or marking knife
- Sliding table saw*
- Safety glasses
- Hearing protection
- Dust mask
- Vice
- Smoothing plane
- Portable power drill
- Drill bit: 5 mm
- Sanding cork
- Screwdriver (cross-head or slotted)
- Sealant gun

* Optional. If you don't have a sliding table saw, you can achieve the same results using a circular saw, set up under a bench in a similar way using fences and stops to cut the groove and bevel the faces.

Alternatively, a router can be used to cut the groove and a hand plane to bevel the faces. See the box above if you are using these alternative tools.

up to the line and place a nail in the fixing holes to mark the position for the pilot holes. If the wall is difficult to mark with a nail, transfer the marks with a pencil and rule. Drill the appropriate size of hole and insert the fastenings.

9 Place the shelf in the groove and mark on the shelf the depth that it penetrates the support. Remove the shelf and place masking tape on the outside of these marks. Also mask around the groove. This will make it easier to remove excess silicone. Now place a fine bead of clear silicone sealant in the groove and push the shelf into the groove, adjusting the fit. Immediately remove any excess silicone sealant with your finger, taking care not to spread it on other areas. Then remove all the tape immediately, before the silicone has a chance to set.

10 Leave the shelf for twenty-four hours to allow the silicone sealant to dry before placing anything on it.

GLASS SHELVES ACROSS WINDOW

These glass shelves are fitted into timber brackets, which can be fixed across a window or any alcove. The length of the shelves can be varied to fit, but you will need to adjust the glass thickness and the width of the brackets accordingly.

MAKING THE BRACKETS

1 Make a cardboard template for the bracket, using the elevation diagram at right as a guide but adjusting it to fit your situation. In particular, the width of the bracket should be at least one-third the depth of the shelf, and it should be even wider if heavy items are to be placed on the shelf. If necessary the brackets can protrude beyond the reveal and architrave. Use the pair of compasses to form the curved section but don't make the curve too tight or you will have difficulty manoeuvring the jigsaw around it. Take a pair of scissors and cut out the template.

2 Using the template, mark out the bracket shape on the timber. Remember the brackets will be in pairs, so turn the template over and mark out the reverse pattern. Repeat for as many shelves as you are making. Leave 3 mm between each bracket as an allowance for saw cuts. Place an 'x' on the face of each bracket near what will be the top to guide you as you mark them out.

3 From the top of each bracket mark down a distance of 20 mm to establish the top of

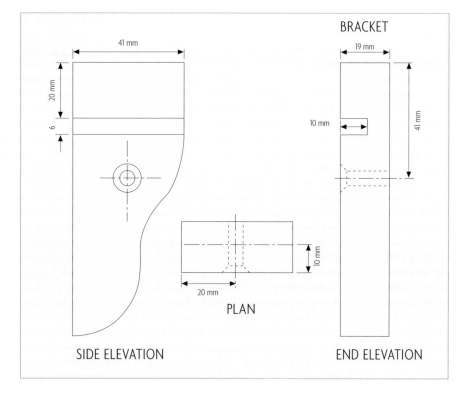

SIDE ELEVATION

PLAN

BRACKET

END ELEVATION

the groove for the glass shelf. From this mark square a line across the face and down each edge a distance of 10 mm (the depth of the groove). From this last line, mark off the thickness of the glass shelf you intend to use (either 6 mm, 10 mm or 12 mm). Square

the line across the face and down each edge a distance of 10 mm.

4 Using a utility knife and the combination square, go over the lines of the groove, marking across the faces and 10 mm down the sides. Also cut the line for the top of the bracket, marking both faces and both edges. These knife cuts will prevent the grain of the timber fibres from breaking out during cutting.

5 If you have a bench stop or hook, use it to support the material while you cut the grooves to the correct depth. If not, clamp your piece of material down to a surface

2 Use the cardboard template to mark out the bracket shape on the timber, reversing it for the opposite face.

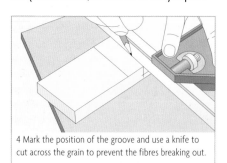

4 Mark the position of the groove and use a knife to cut across the grain to prevent the fibres breaking out.

TOOLS

- Pencil
- Pair of compasses
- Scissors
- Tape measure
- Combination square
- Utility knife (razor knife)
- G-cramp
- Tenon saw
- Hammer or mallet
- 6 mm chisel (bevelled-edge or mortise type)
- Jigsaw or coping saw
- Vice
- Smoothing plane
- Sanding cork or block
- Spirit level

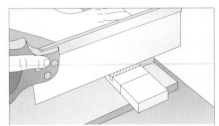

5 Saw down the sides of the groove to a depth of 10 mm, sawing on the waste side of the line.

suitable for cutting on. Cut the grooves, using the tenon saw, cutting on the waste side of the line so that the groove does not end up too wide. This is especially important when glass shelves are to be placed in the groove, as they need to fit neatly for safety's sake.

6 Clamp the material to the work surface now if it is not there already. Take up the 6 mm chisel and, with bevelled side up, line it up with the 10 mm mark on the edge of

Glass shelves turn this window into a mini conservatory. It's an ideal use of the centre panel, which doesn't open.

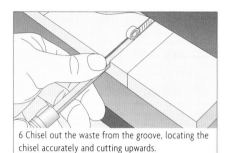

6 Chisel out the waste from the groove, locating the chisel accurately and cutting upwards.

the material and strike the chisel with a hammer or mallet. Cut upwards towards the centre of the material. Turn the material around and repeat the process from the opposite edge. Continue to remove the waste material, levelling out the bottom of the groove as you go. Check for level by placing the edge of the chisel in the bottom of the groove and seeing if it rocks. If it does, more material may need to be removed from the centre of the groove until the chisel sits steady in the groove.

7 Check you have marked the pieces out in pairs. Use the jigsaw or coping saw to cut out the bracket shapes, working slowly and staying on the waste side of the lines. Keep the tool moving in a single cut and try to complete each bracket in one go. Trim the tops square with a jigsaw. Keep to the waste side of the line.

8 Match the brackets up in pairs (grooves and tops together) and check that the grooves line up and that the tops line up at the utility knife marks. Hold them together using masking tape. Place them in a vice and plane the tops flush and down to the knife lines. Avoid chipping out with the plane by using a backing block. (If you don't have a vice and plane, use a sanding block to sand out the jigsaw marks across the flat tops.) With the pieces still together, sand the curved edges with 80 grit abrasive paper to get rid of the saw marks and then with

You can vary the length of the shelves, but you'll need to adjust the width of the brackets as well as the thickness of the glass.

120 grit paper to prepare the pieces for painting. Repeat this process with each pair. When working on the curved surfaces, use a short piece of dowelling with abrasive paper wrapped around it.

INSTALLATION

9 Use a spirit level to check the sill is level. Measure up from the sill, making allowance if it isn't level, and locate the positions for the brackets on the reveal linings, as shown in the diagram opposite. Hold the bracket in position and fix it in

MATERIALS*

- Cardboard
- 25 mm thick timber PAR (50 mm, 75 mm, 100 mm or 125 mm wide)
- Glass for shelves (see box below)
- Masking tape
- Abrasive paper: one sheet each of 80, 120 and 180 grit
- Six 40 mm panel pins
- Paintable silicone

* For three shelves. For timber types and sizes, see page 112.

GLASS SHELVES

The thickness of glass necessary for these shelves depends on the length of the shelves.

- Up to a length of 600 mm the glass should be a minimum of 6 mm thick, between 600 mm and 1 m it should be 10 mm thick and between 1.0 and 1.2 m it should be 12 mm thick. If the shelf is over 1.2 m long you will need to insert a central support.
- It is best not to try to cut the glass, but to purchase the shelves already cut to size and shape, and with the edges smoothed.

MAKING JOINTS

Joining timbers and board materials is a basic requirement when making shelves, and the most effective joints are rebates and housing joints. The quickest and most accurate way to make them is with a router, but they can be made with specialized tools such as a rebate plane, or with a tenon or circular saw and chisel.

1 Mark out the position of the joints on the timber. Continue the markings down the edges only as deep as the joint will be. Trace over the lines with a knife.

2 If using a circular saw, set the depth of the joint accurately on the saw, and clamp a fence across the board to guide the saw.

3 Saw across the face of the piece on the waste side of the line.

4 Use the appropriate sized chisel to remove the waste until the bottom of the housing is flat and to the correct depth.

indoor

SHELF ASSEMBLY

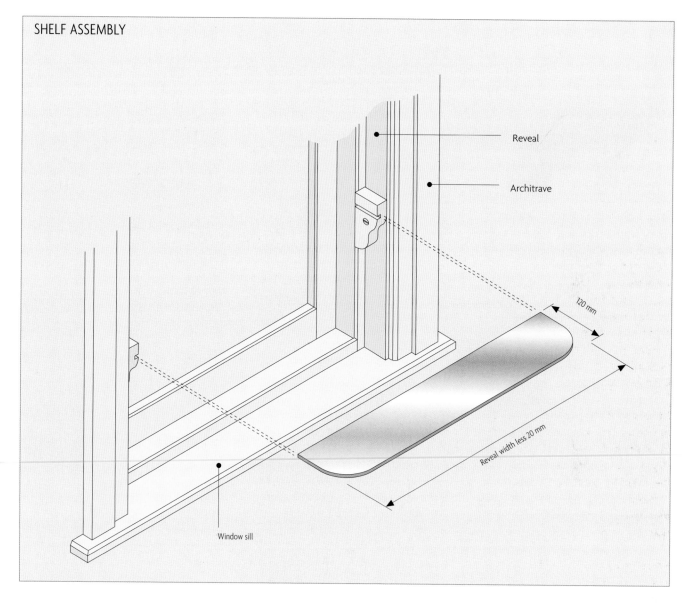

Reveal

Architrave

120 mm

Reveal width less 20 mm

Window sill

with a 40 mm panel pin. Locate the matching bracket on the opposite side and fix it. Check with a spirit level that the two brackets are level and make any adjustments necessary. Fix the brackets to the reveal using 40 mm panel pins. If you prefer, the brackets can be fixed to the reveal linings with 40 mm screws and wall plugs as appropriate. Mark out the position of the screw holes as indicated

and drill them using a 5 mm drill bit while the brackets are still fastened together. Countersink the screw holes.

10 Test the shelves for fit and adjust the groove depth if necessary. Remove the shelves and finish the brackets to match the reveal.

11 Place a very small amount of paintable

silicone in the groove. This will keep the shelf in place if the fit is a little sloppy and prevent accidents. Slide in the shelves.

PICTURE RAIL SHELF

This narrow shelf runs right around the room above the doors and windows, resting on a series of wooden brackets that can be shaped to match the style of the room.

MEASURING UP

1 Measure the room accurately to determine the length of timber required for the shelving, and then calculate the number of brackets you will need. The brackets should be spaced no more than 1000 mm apart, and so first divide each wall length by 1000 and then go up to the next full number. Thus, if the wall is 3300 mm long, divide 3300 by 1000 to arrive at 3.33, or four brackets.

2 Locate bracket positions on the wall.

- For masonry walls, locate the first and last brackets. The first bracket will be 250 mm away from the adjoining wall and the last will end 250 mm from the opposite wall. Deduct this 500 mm from the wall length: 3300 − 500 = 2800 mm. This is the space into which you will fit the other brackets. Then divide the 2800 mm by the number of spaces between the remaining brackets, that is, the number of brackets (two), plus one. In this example it is three spaces, so 2800 ÷ 3 = 933. The remaining brackets will, therefore, be spaced at 933 mm centres.

- On timber-framed walls the spacing of the brackets is determined by the position of the studs, and you need to determine the centre of each stud. Normally there is a stud at each end of the wall as the sheeting material is attached to it. This stud is generally 50 mm thick, so allowing for the sheeting material on the adjoining wall the centre of these studs should be about 15 mm away from the adjoining wall. Locate the intervening studs (see box on page 162) and use a fine nail to penetrate the sheeting material to locate each stud centre precisely. Do this in an area that will be covered by the shelving to save patching later. (Note that there will be a stud on either side of each window and door to support the frames.) If the studs are close to 450 mm apart, you will need to fix a bracket only at every second stud. As the shelving is not very heavy and will not be carrying a lot of weight, hollow wall anchors can also be used for fixing points where there is no stud.

MAKING THE BRACKETS

3 Make a cardboard template of the bracket shape (see pattern on page 172), using a compass and combination square. Cut out the template and set it out on the bracket material. Transfer the pattern to the timber.

4 Clamp the bracket material to a suitable work surface and cut out the rough shape with a jigsaw. Be sure to wear safety glasses, keep the electric lead out of the way and always cut on the waste side of the line.

5 Clean up the surfaces. Without expensive machinery it is not easy to clean up curved surfaces cut with a jigsaw, but one way is to clamp several brackets together and use coarse grades of abrasive paper around a sanding block to remove the saw marks on the external curves. Then wrap a small piece of abrasive paper around a dowel rod and use it to smooth out the marks on the inside curves.

TOOLS

- Tape measure
- Compass set
- Combination square
- Scissors
- Pencil
- Cramp
- Jigsaw
- Sanding block
- Portable electric drill
- Drill bits: 5 mm drill bit and countersink; 3 mm masonry bit
- Tenon saw or panel saw
- Portable electric sander
- Straight edge
- Spirit level
- Screwdriver (cross-head or slotted)

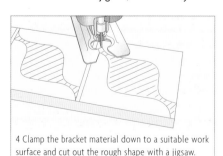

4 Clamp the bracket material down to a suitable work surface and cut out the rough shape with a jigsaw.

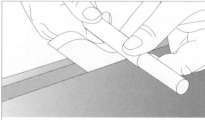

5 To clean up the inside curves of the bracket, wrap a small piece of abrasive paper around a dowel rod.

indoor

The perfect way to display a collection of small objects, this easy-to-erect shelf also keeps them out of harm's way.

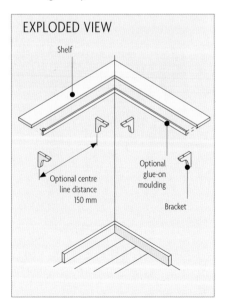

6 Mark out the screw holes on the brackets and drill the holes. With a countersink bit countersink the holes.

6 Make the screw holes. If you have one, use a pedestal drill with attached fences and stops to keep the holes consistent. Otherwise, keep the brackets clamped together and mark out the hole positions across all the brackets at the same time, using a combination square and pencil to get them in line. Using a drill with a 5 mm bit, drill the holes as marked. Replace the bit with a countersink bit and countersink the holes.

MAKING THE SHELVES

7 If you want the front edge of the shelf shaped, cut it with a router (remember to mitre the corners) or buy lengths of glue-on moulding from your local hardware store and attach them, making allowances for them on the adjoining shelf lengths. Cut the shelves to their final length and mitre the ends that will fit together in the corners.

8 Having cut the shelves to length, hold them in position and check whether or not they fit neatly against the wall. The walls may be bowed one way or the other, which will leave unsightly gaps between the wall and the shelf. If the gaps are too large (more than 5 mm), you will need to plane the boards to fit neatly against the wall.

FINISHING AND INSTALLATION

9 When you are satisfied with the fit, take shelves and brackets and give a final sand. Finish as desired (see box on page 150).

MATERIALS*

- 125 x 25 mm maple or pine PAR (for brackets**)
- 150 x 25 mm maple or pine PAR (for the shelf)
- Small sheet of stiff cardboard for template
- Abrasive paper: two sheets of 120 grit and one sheet of 60 grit
- 2 inch x No. 8 countersunk wood screws (one per bracket)
- 1½ inch x No. 8 countersunk wood screws (one per bracket)
- Construction adhesive for fixing brackets to wall
- Masonry fasteners or hollow wall anchors to suit
- Finish of choice

* Finished width of shelf: 140 mm. Timber sizes given are nominal (see page 112).

** For each pair of brackets you will need 150 mm of 125 x 25 mm PAR solid timber. See step 1 to determine how many you will need.

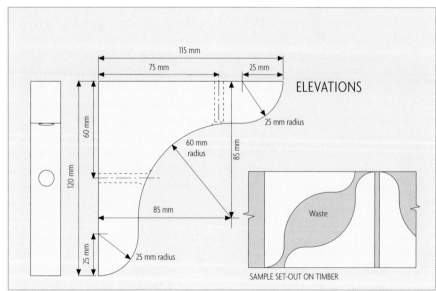

EXPLODED VIEW

Shelf

Optional centre line distance 150 mm

Optional glue-on moulding

Bracket

ELEVATIONS

115 mm
75 mm
25 mm
60 mm
120 mm
85 mm
60 mm radius
25 mm radius
85 mm
25 mm
25 mm radius

Waste

SAMPLE SET-OUT ON TIMBER

10 Strike a level line around the room at the height at which the brackets will finish (you will probably need a friend to help). At one corner mark this height and raise a straight edge to the position. Use the spirit level to check that the straight edge is level and, with a pencil, mark a line on the wall.

11 Mark the centre line positions of the corner brackets and all the other brackets (see step 2). Take up the drill and appropriate drill bits and attach the brackets to the wall with the 2 inch x No. 8 countersunk wood screws, placing a small drop of construction adhesive to the back of each before fixing them to the wall. Stretch a string line across the front edge of the brackets to see they all line up. Make the necessary adjustments to get them in line.

12 Lay the shelves on the brackets and secure them from below using 1¹⁄₂ inch x No. 8 screws. A bit of construction adhesive on top of the brackets helps to hold the shelf in place. Fill gaps with a gap filler and touch up any marks on the finish.

HINT

When marking the shelf height around the room, it may be faster to use a water level and chalk line. This method can be carried out by one person, and it can often be more accurate than using a spirit level.

A shelf can be as much a decoration as the objects that are put on it.

bookcases

bookcases

PLANNING YOUR BOOKCASE

Bookcases do not have to be plain and uninspiring in order to be functional. They can be attractive pieces of furniture in their own right, as well as practical, versatile storage and display units.

Plan your bookcase design carefully. This will help you to maximize available storage and ensure that shelves are sufficiently sturdy for your purposes.

PLANNING

When planning extra shelving to hold your book collection, take into account the number of books, their sizes, and whether there is a need for easy access and/or protective storage.

If space is at a premium, remember that you may be able to construct built-in shelves that wrap around doors or windows.

WEIGHT LOAD

A major consideration in building a bookcase is the weight that the shelf or shelves will have to support—which, in the case of even a small collection of paperbacks, is quite substantial. The weight load will affect your choice of materials, construction methods, the thickness of shelves, the width of shelf spans and the types of joints or brackets you will use to support the shelves. Bookcases are often built using housed joints, as these support more weight than other kinds of joints.

For wider bookcases the spacing between the supports (spans) is very important, and again depends on the weight load as well as the type of timber or board used. Thicker timbers will obviously bear more books compared with lightweight boards. For units made of lightweight materials such as chipboard or particleboard, a plywood or hardwood back will provide extra strength.

Wall-mounted bookshelves will be under particular stress and must be fixed securely. The fixing method depends on whether your home is of solid masonry or frame construction, and on the weight load.

POSITIONING SHELVES

You can use adjustable or fixed shelving, or both. If you have large 'coffee table' books, or you want to display ornaments as well as books, adjustable shelving would allow you to adjust shelf heights to suit.

Fixed shelves are usually stronger than adjustable shelves. Position some fixed shelves far enough apart to accommodate your tallest books, allowing a few centimetres clearance above the height of the books so they are easy to remove and return.

Shelves should be deep enough that books don't sit right on (or over) the edge, but not so deep that books are pushed to the back of the unit, making them difficult to retrieve.

Taller, deeper shelves should be positioned towards the bottom of the bookcase, to provide stability and easy access to the

indoor

back of the shelves. It is much easier to lift heavier or more frequently used books from the lower and centre shelves than from the shelves at the top of the unit, which could be reserved for rarely handled or valuable items.

CARING FOR YOUR BOOKS

Books should be stored upright rather than on their sides, which can scuff the covers. If you have a valuable collection, place the shelves for those books away from direct sunlight and neon lighting.

Make sure you don't pack your books too tightly together. To avoid too much wear and tear on a book, remove it by grasping it on either side of the spine, rather than using a finger to tease it out of the shelf by the top of the spine.

SIMPLE SHELVES WITH BRACKETS

These easy-to-make timber shelves are supported by brackets that can be left as solid timber pieces or decorated with diamond-shaped cut-outs. Moulded edges provide a professional finish.

CUTTING THE PARTS

1 Lay the timber on a workbench, and mark out the parts with a tape measure and square. Check that the pieces are square and straight.

2 Wearing safety glasses, cut out the parts using a panel saw or a circular saw, then lightly plane the pieces. Label the pieces on the inside face for easy identification, and mark the face side and edge. Use a square to check for accuracy on all edges and faces.

SHAPING AND JOINING SHELVES AND FIXING RAILS

3 After you have cut them to length, check the two shelves and two fixing rails to make sure that the face edges are square and parallel.

4 Mark along each shelf with a marking gauge set to the thickness of the fixing rail (19 mm), then cut a rebate 13 mm deep using a rebate plane or a router. If you are using a router, attach a fence and an 18 mm straight cutter. Move along the back edge of the shelf piece, taking out 5 mm at a time (see box on page 180 for information about using a router). Leave at least 6 mm at the top of the rebate.

MATERIALS*

PART	MATERIAL	FINISHED LENGTH	NO.
Shelf	250 x 25 mm timber PAR	2100 mm	2
Back fixing rail	100 x 25 mm timber PAR	2100 mm	2
Bracket	250 x 25 mm timber PAR	300 mm	6

Other: Thirty 50 mm x No. 6 cross-head countersunk screws; wall fixings (see step 17); PVA adhesive; cloths; abrasive paper: four sheets of 180 grit and three sheets of 240 grit; clear lacquer or finish of your choice.

* For two shelves. Finished size: 319 mm high (base of bracket to top of shelf); 2100 mm long; 238 mm deep. For timber sizes and styles see page 112. Timber sizes given are nominal.

5 Take the 2100 mm back fixing rail and mark the centre. On the back of the rail, mark 50 mm in from either end of the rail. Starting and finishing at the marked 50 mm positions, measure and mark eight 250 mm wide spacings. Using a marking gauge, measure and mark 7 mm down from the top edge to the lines you have just drawn. Where the lines cross, drill a 4 mm hole right through. Countersink all the holes.

6 Put the two shelves on your workbench and carefully cut the moulded edges with a router, using a bevel cutter shape. Mould the underside of each shelf on the two short end edges first, then on the long front edge.

7 Set the fixing rail in the rebate on the shelf, face side out. Mark the depth of the rebate on to the rail. Cut mouldings on the ends of the rail, up to the pencil marks, and on the bottom edge of the rail.

8 Sand all the moulded edges to a smooth finish with 180 grit abrasive paper. Join the back fixing rail to the shelf to check the fit, apply adhesive to the rebate and clamp the fixing rail to the shelf with G-cramps. Drill 3 mm pilot holes, then screw the fixing rail to the shelf. Wipe off excess adhesive with a damp cloth and leave to dry.

Although these shelves are designed to hold books, they could also be adapted for use as kitchen storage or general display shelving. Figured ash timber was used to build the shelves shown here.

TOOLS

- Tape measure and pencil
- Combination square
- Pair of safety glasses
- Dust mask
- Hearing protection
- Panel saw or circular saw
- Electric jigsaw or coping saw
- Tenon saw
- Smoothing plane or jack plane
- Rebate plane
- Electric router
- Router bit: 45-degree bevel cutter
- Chisel: 25 mm
- Six G-cramps
- Electric drill
- Drill bits: 3 mm, 4 mm, 5 mm, 8 mm, 10 mm countersink
- Utility knife
- Cork sanding block
- Flat file
- Screwdriver (cross-head)
- Spirit level

MAKING THE BRACKETS

9 Cut the six bracket pieces to 300 mm long and 220 mm wide, and mark out a top and a face edge.

10 Make the cut-out before marking out the basic bracket (see diagram on page 180). Working from the top 220 mm side, measure straight down 130 mm and draw a horizontal line parallel to the top. Then, from the back 300 mm side, measure straight across 100 mm and draw a vertical line parallel to the side. Measuring from the centre, where the lines cross come up and mark 30 mm, then mark down 30 mm, across 30 mm and back 30 mm to form a diamond.

11 Use an 8 mm drill bit to drill on the inside of the four points of the diamond, and then cut out the rest of the shape with a jigsaw or a coping saw. Clean up the edges of the cut-out with a file, then mould the edges of the diamond.

12 Now mark the basic bracket shape (see diagram on page 180). Starting at the top of a 300 mm side, measure 70 mm straight down along the edge and mark the position. Working from what will be the bottom edge of the bracket, measure 70 mm straight across along the edge and mark. With a combination square and pencil, draw a straight line joining the two marks. Trace over the lines with a utility knife and cut out the shape with a panel saw or circular saw.

13 Mark out the back of the bracket for a cut-out to accommodate the moulded edge

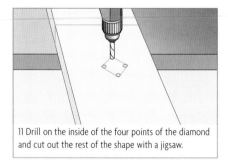

11 Drill on the inside of the four points of the diamond and cut out the rest of the shape with a jigsaw.

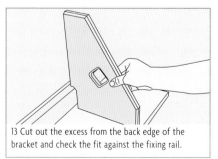

13 Cut out the excess from the back edge of the bracket and check the fit against the fixing rail.

SHELF PLANS

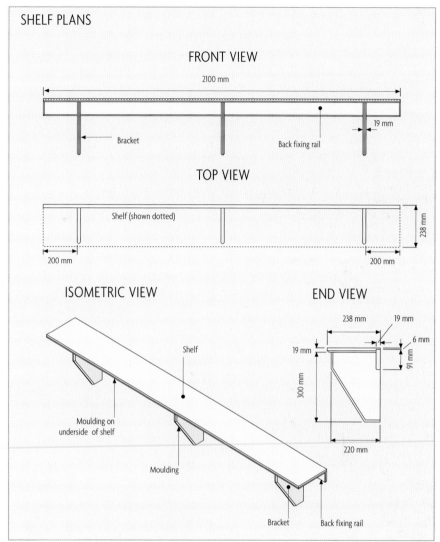

FRONT VIEW
2100 mm
Bracket
Back fixing rail
19 mm

TOP VIEW
Shelf (shown dotted)
200 mm
200 mm
238 mm

ISOMETRIC VIEW
Shelf
Moulding on underside of shelf
Moulding
Bracket
Back fixing rail

END VIEW
238 mm
19 mm
6 mm
19 mm
91 mm
300 mm
220 mm

of the fixing rail. Place each shelf on the bench and sit the bracket on the shelf. Position the bracket against the rail, then use a square to mark a straight line across the back edge of the bracket at 90 degrees. Place the bracket back on the bench. Set up the marking gauge at 19 mm, and mark downwards to indicate the area to be cut out. Cut out the excess from the back edge of the bracket and check the fit against the fixing rail. Sand with 180 grit abrasive paper.

14 Rout a moulding along the three outside edges of the bracket. Don't cut too deeply. Don't shape the edge that fits to the wall and the shelf.

ASSEMBLING BRACKETS AND SHELVES

15 Lay each shelf down on the workbench with the fixing rail facing up, and mark the positions where you will attach the brackets. Find the centre of the rail and mark a vertical line with your square, then measure 210 mm

USING A ROUTER

- Use cramps or a vice to secure the work.

- Always do a test cut on a scrap piece to check the router settings.

- Wear safety glasses, hearing protection and a dust mask.

- When cutting straight grooves and slots, use the supplied guide fence or clamp a straight piece of timber to the work and run the baseplate of the router firmly along it. Set the router to depth and run it back and forth along the piece to remove all waste.

- Don't cut to the required size the first time. Always make two or three passes with the router.

- If the router sticks, wipe along the fence with soap or candle wax.

- If your router skips and leaves a dent, fill the dent with a plastic filler that sets hard, or an epoxy filler, and run the groove again.

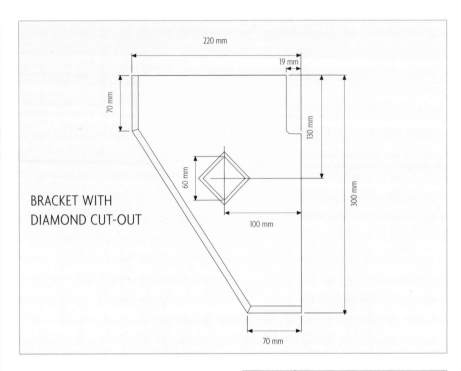

BRACKET WITH DIAMOND CUT-OUT

in from either end and again mark vertical lines. Measure 20 mm and 60 mm down these lines and mark horizontal lines across, to find the centre position for the screw holes. Where the lines cross, drill 4 mm holes, then countersink.

16 Sand all parts with 180 grit abrasive paper, then with 220 grit. Apply adhesive to the top and back edges of the brackets and the shelves where the brackets will be attached. Cramp the pieces together. Remove excess adhesive with a damp cloth. Fasten the shelves and brackets with 50 mm x No. 6 countersunk cross-head screws.

INSTALLING THE SHELVES

17 How you fit the walls to the shelves will depend on the wall construction. For

masonry walls, use at least four 50 mm x No. 10 countersunk screws with wall plugs of the appropriate size. Nylon anchors are an alternative. If very heavy objects will be placed on the shelves, use 75 x 6.5 mm expansion bolts. For timber-framed walls, you will need to locate the studs behind the lining to determine the spacings; you should use 50 mm x No. 10 countersunk screws at the least.

18 Fix one fastening first, then bring the shelf to the level position, checking using a spirit level. Drill the wall and fix the second fastening. Test that each shelf is level and adjust before securing with the final fastenings.

The edges of the cut-outs are decorated with mouldings.

CHILD'S BOOKCASE

This whimsical 'boatshed' style MDF bookcase, with decorative trim on the shelves and roof, is perfect for a child's room. It lends itself to a brightly coloured paint scheme.

CUTTING OUT

1 Lay the MDF sheet on a bench and mark out the parts with a tape measure and combination square.

2 Wearing safety glasses and a dust mask, cut out the parts with a panel saw or circular saw. Use a smoothing plane or jack plane to smooth the edges and bring all parts to their finished size, checking that you are planing square. Label all pieces on the inside face to identify them. A timber merchant may be able to cut the MDF to size for you.

MAKING FRONT APRONS

3 Pencil a half-pattern for the front shelf aprons in freehand on the 400 mm long plywood (or use a ruler and compass). Only draw a half-pattern—it will be traced on to one half of the apron, then repeated in mirror image on the other half. Cut out the template with a jigsaw or coping saw. Clean it up with a file.

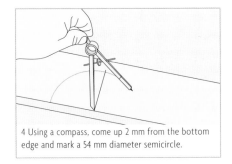

4 Using a compass, come up 2 mm from the bottom edge and mark a 54 mm diameter semicircle.

4 Take one of the 764 x 54 mm front aprons and mark a centre line with a combination square. Using a compass at the centre line, come up 2 mm from the bottom edge and mark a 54 mm diameter semicircle.

The decorative patterns on the shelf and roof aprons were marked on the MDF sheet by means of re-usable plywood templates. The designs for the patterns can be drawn freehand or marked out using a ruler and a compass.

TOOLS

- Tape measure or rule
- Combination square
- Builder's square
- Pencil
- Pair of safety glasses
- Dust mask
- Hearing protection
- Smoothing plane or jack plane
- Jigsaw or coping saw
- Tenon saw
- Panel saw or circular saw
- Four G-cramps
- Hammer
- Electric drill
- Drill bits: 3 mm, 5 mm, 10 mm countersink
- Electric router
- Router bit: 12 mm twin-flute flush cutter
- File
- Cork sanding block
- Screwdriver (cross-head)
- Filler knife
- Compass (optional)

MATERIALS*

PART	MATERIAL	LENGTH	WIDTH	NO.
End panel	18 mm MDF	1200 mm	400 mm	2
Top panel	18 mm MDF	764 mm	400 mm	1
Shelf	18 mm MDF	764 mm	400 mm	4
Front apron for upper, centre and lower shelves	18 mm MDF	764 mm	54 mm	3
Front apron for bottom shelf**	18 mm MDF	764 mm	80 mm	2
Roof apron	18 mm MDF	563 mm	70 mm	2
Roof panel	18 mm MDF	600 mm	400 mm	2
Back*	4 mm MDF	1550 mm	796 mm	1
Template for front aprons	3 mm plywood	400 mm	54 mm	1
Template for roof aprons	3 mm plywood	600 mm	70 mm	1

Other: Sixty 25 mm flat-head nails; twenty 10 mm panel pins; eight 28 mm x No. 8 countersunk screws; twenty 32 mm x No. 8 countersunk screws; thirty-two 40 mm x No. 8 countersunk screws; PVA adhesive; cloths; abrasive paper: two sheets of 120 grit and four sheets of 180 grit; plastic filler; paint of your choice.

* Finished size: 1625 mm high; 850 mm wide; 400 mm deep.

** One for front (to be shaped), one for back (not shaped).

* To be cut at assembly stage.

5 Place the template on the front apron piece, aligning it with the centre line. Trace the shape, then flip the template over and trace the shape on the other side of the centre line. Remove the template. Fix the apron on to the bench with G-cramps and cut out the rough shape with a jigsaw or coping saw, cutting on the waste side of the line and leaving 3–5 mm excess. Fasten the template back on to the apron with 10 mm brad nails.

6 Clamp the apron and attached template to the bench. Using a jigsaw or coping saw, or a router with a 12 mm flush cutter, cut around the template (see page 180 for information on routers). Remove the template. File the curved profile to remove rough edges and sand with 120 grit abrasive paper. This piece is the template for the remaining front aprons, including the 80 mm wide bottom apron. Repeat the cutting-out process for all front aprons.

ASSEMBLING THE SHELVES

7 Take the shelves and measure and mark 50 mm in from either end and 10 mm in from the front edge. Drill and countersink 5 mm holes. Mark three equally spaced screw positions between the 50 mm marks (see the diagram on page 183) and drill and countersink 5 mm holes.

8 Apply adhesive to the top edge of one front apron and clamp it to the shelf, ensuring the ends are flush and the front of the apron is set back 2 mm. Drill 3 mm pilot holes and use 32 mm x No. 8 countersunk screws to secure the apron. Remove excess adhesive with a damp cloth and repeat the process for all the aprons.

9 Take the end panels and mark out the position of the top panel and the shelves on inside and outside faces. Lay the shelves on

FRONT VIEW

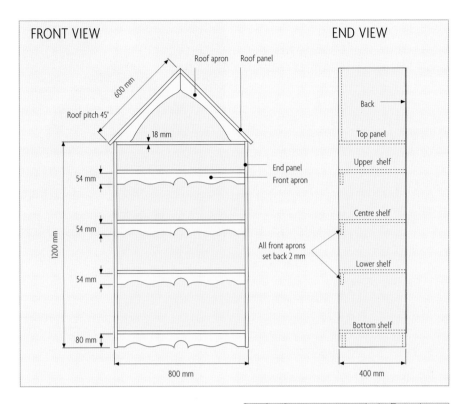

Roof apron Roof panel

600 mm

Roof pitch 45°

18 mm

54 mm

54 mm

54 mm

80 mm

1200 mm

End panel
Front apron

All front aprons
set back 2 mm

800 mm

END VIEW

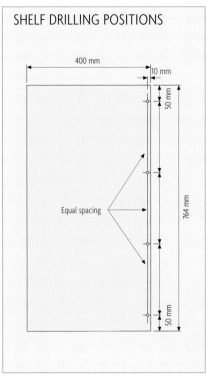

Back

Top panel

Upper shelf

Centre shelf

Lower shelf

Bottom shelf

400 mm

SHELF DRILLING POSITIONS

400 mm

10 mm

50 mm

764 mm

50 mm

Equal spacing

the bench at right angles to one end panel. Drill 5 mm holes in the end panels, and then countersink so the screw heads finish 1–2 mm below the surface. Spread adhesive where the top panel and shelves will join the end panel, and fasten the pieces with 40 mm x No. 8 countersunk screws. Repeat for the other end panel. Remove excess adhesive. Fill screw holes with plastic filler, leave to dry, and sand with 120 grit abrasive paper.

MITRING THE ROOF PIECES

10 Place the two roof pieces on the bench and mitre the top joining ends. Use a combination square to mark each 45-degree mitre, then square a line across each side. Cut the angle with a circular saw or panel saw, or simply plane the mitre, then check the fit and if necessary adjust by planing.

11 Take one roof piece and on the mitred edge mark a screw position 50 mm in from

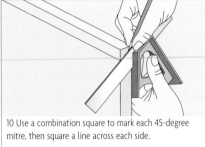

10 Use a combination square to mark each 45-degree mitre, then square a line across each side.

each end and 10 mm back from the mitred edge. Mark another screw position halfway between the two 50 mm marks. Drill 5 mm clearance holes and then countersink 10 mm. On the other mitred edge of the roof, mark

a screw position 125 mm in from each end and 10 mm back from the facing edge. Drill 5 mm screw holes and countersink as before.

12 Place the roof pieces together to drill 3 mm pilot holes. Glue the mitred ends, hold them together, and fasten with 40 mm x No. 8 countersunk screws.

MAKING THE ROOF APRONS

13 Draw an arched shape as a pattern for the roof aprons (this time draw a complete pattern). As for the front aprons, make a template for the roof aprons and cut and rout to shape.

TIMBER-CUTTING SERVICES

If your workshop is small or if you want to save time, you can have board materials for your project cut to size professionally. Ask when you buy your boards if the timber merchant has a cut-to-size service. The modern machinery used by such services will give a high-quality finish that would be impossible to achieve in most home workshops.

14 Place the aprons on the bench. Use a square to mark a 45-degree angle on the ends to be joined, and cut out the mitres.

15 Lay the roof on its back edge, with the facing edge up towards you. For each side, mark three screw positions 10 mm in from the facing edge, the first 100 mm in from the top mitred end, the other two at intervals of 220 mm. Drill 5 mm holes and countersink as before.

16 Glue and clamp the apron pieces to the roof assembly, flush with the front. Drill 3 mm pilot holes into the aprons and use 32 mm x No. 8 countersunk screws to secure the aprons. Ensure the screw heads are below the surface before filling them with plastic filler. Leave to dry, then sand with 120 grit abrasive paper.

ASSEMBLING THE UNIT

17 Align the roof assembly on the base unit. Measure and mark out three screw positions on each roof panel, then drill 5 mm clearance holes at these positions through the roof panels. Countersink the screw holes in preparation for filling them. Use a 3 mm bit to make pilot holes for the screws.

18 Using 28 mm x No. 8 countersunk screws, fasten the assembled roof to the base unit. Fill the screw holes with plastic filler, and leave to dry. When the filler has dried, sand it flush with 120 grit abrasive paper.

19 Lay the unit face down. Place the back piece into position to check the fit, then pencil in a cutting line. Using a panel saw, cut the back to size, planing off any rough edges. Fasten with 25 mm flat-head nails.

Mitred joints are used to fasten the basic roof panels as well as the shaped roof aprons.

20 Sand the entire unit with 180 grit abrasive paper. Undercoat it and paint in the colour of your choice.

BUILT-IN SHELVING

These shelves allow you to maximize storage space in an awkwardly shaped spot. Instructions are given for units of equal width, but the specifications can easily be adapted—the example opposite features two top units, one on either side of a window.

PREPARATION

1 Measure the area to find the exact lengths of timber required.

2 If you retain skirting boards and architraves, the units must be fastened to fixing blocks screwed to the skirtings and wall. If you want to remove a skirting, start at an external corner or join in the skirting. Lever the board out with a chisel until you can fit a crowbar behind it to prise it from the wall (a timber block between bar and wall will protect the wall). On hollow walls, lever against the wall frame. Remove any nails and patch the plaster. To remove an architrave, drive a chisel into the joint between the architrave and jamb (do not chisel between the wall lining and architrave). Place scrap timber between the chisel and jamb, and lever off the architrave. Remove or drive in any nails, sand the jamb edge and fill the holes.

CUTTING OUT

3 Lay the chipboard and timber on a bench, and mark out the parts with a tape measure and square, checking that they are square and straight.

4 Cut the parts with a panel saw or circular saw, then lightly plane the timber pieces. Check edges and faces for accuracy.

5 Glue matching veneer edging to any raw chipboard facing edges (see step 3 on page 193 for instructions). A timber merchant may also be able to cut and edge the pieces.

KICKER ASSEMBLY

6 Lay the kicker front and back panels side by side. Mark 18 mm in from either end of both panels, and square a line across (see diagram on page 187). Mark the panel into five sections of equal width between the marked 18 mm positions. On each division, drill 5 mm holes, 25 mm in from the front and back edges.

7 Align the rails with the lines on the front and back panels and drill 3 mm pilot holes in each rail end. Fix the rails to the panels with 40 mm x No. 8 countersunk screws.

8 Check the kicker is level using a spirit level. Fasten to fixing blocks screwed along the skirting board.

9 Attach the kicker face, which should be 18 mm thick x 100 mm wide, from inside the kicker. Drill 5 mm holes and fasten with 28 mm x No. 8 countersunk screws.

BASE UNIT ASSEMBLY

10 Sand all remaining components, starting with 180 grit abrasive paper and finishing with 240 grit.

11 Place base unit top and bottom panels edge to edge, best faces up. Mark 18 mm in from either end of both panels. Square a line across and divide each panel into five sections as in step 6. On each division drill two 5 mm holes 30 mm in from the front and back edges, and a central hole, then countersink. Make a drilling template from scrap chipboard for positioning the adjustable shelf pins. The holes can be 30–50 mm apart.

12 Place the left-hand end panel and bottom panel on the bench, face edges up. Glue the joining end of the end panel and align it flush with the end of the bottom panel. Drill 3 mm pilot holes and fasten with 40 mm x No. 8 countersunk screws. Repeat this step for the opposite end.

13 Make a spacer block to suit the divider spacings. Put the spacer hard against the end. Glue the end of the divider and fasten as in step 12. Repeat to attach all dividers to the bottom panel. Turn the unit upright and fasten the top in the same way. Remove excess adhesive.

This versatile shelving arrangement comprises a generous number of adjustable shelves and a feature shelf of contrasting cedar. The kicker and decorative top are made of solid silver ash.

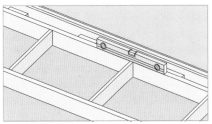

8 Check the kicker is level, then fasten it to fixing blocks screwed along the skirting board.

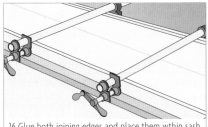

16 Glue both joining edges and place them wthin sash cramps, then immediately remove excess adhesive.

MATERIALS*

PART	MATERIAL	FINISHED LENGTH	WIDTH	NO.
Kicker front/back panel	18 mm veneered chipboard	2630 mm	100 mm	2
Kicker rail/end panel	18 mm veneered chipboard	250 mm	100 mm	6
Kicker face	125 x 25 mm light timber PAR	2710 mm		1
Base unit feature shelf*	200 x 50 mm dark timber PAR	2730 mm		1
Base unit top/bottom panel**	18 mm veneered chipboard	2630 mm	316 mm	2
Base unit divider/end panel**	18 mm veneered chipboard	668 mm	316 mm	6
Base unit fill pieces	18 mm veneered chipboard	668 mm	40 mm	2
Base unit back**	12 mm veneered chipboard	668 mm	1053 mm	2
Base unit back**	12 mm veneered chipboard	668 mm	523 mm	1
Base unit shelf*	18 mm veneered chipboard	502 mm	315 mm	5
Top unit top panel**	18 mm veneered chipboard	2594 mm	210 mm	1
Top unit divider**	18 mm veneered chipboard	1892 mm	210 mm	4
Top unit end panel **	18 mm veneered chipboard	1892 mm	215 mm	2
Top unit fill pieces	18 mm veneered chipboard	1910 mm	40 mm	2
Top unit back**	12 mm veneered chipboard	1910 mm	1053 mm	2
Top unit back**	12 mm veneered chipboard	1910 mm	523 mm	1
Top unit shelf**	18 mm veneered chipboard	502 mm	214 mm	30
Decorative top	250 x 50 mm light timber PAR	2730 mm		1

Other: Twenty 50 mm x No. 8 countersunk screws; eighty 40 mm x No. 8 countersunk screws; twenty 28 mm x No. 8 countersunk screws; 5 mm shelf supports; abrasive paper: two sheets of 120 grit, ten sheets of 180 grit and six sheets of 240 grit; PVA adhesive; cloths; clear lacquer.

* Overall finished size of units: 2740 mm high; 2710 mm wide. Top unit is 235 mm deep with decorative top; base unit is 350 mm deep with feature shelf. Timber sizes given are nominal. For timber types and sizes see page 112.

** With one long edge of matching pre-glued edging.

* Made from two pieces of edge-jointed timber.

** Back pieces to be joined.

14 Place the unit on the bench, face up. Sand all edges—if available, use an orbital sander over all surfaces for a smooth finish. Check the backs are square. After sanding, lay the backs on the unit, face side down: the two large backs should be to the outside, the narrow back should be positioned between them. The back panels should join over a divider. Drill 3 mm pilot holes 250 mm apart all around the back edge of the unit and the back pieces. Stagger the screw holes over the dividers. Drill 5 mm holes and countersink, then attach the back using 28 mm x No. 8 countersunk screws.

15 Apply clear lacquer to the unit before installation. Cut two fill pieces the height of the base unit and plane to the width of the gap between the wall and the unit. With a coping saw, make a cut-out to fit around the skirting board. Use adhesive, and two 40 mm nails inserted from inside the base unit, to fasten the pieces. Punch in and fill the nail heads, sand back, then touch up with lacquer.

FEATURE SHELF ASSEMBLY
16 Take the two timber feature shelf pieces and plane and join them, straight and square. The finished shelf should be 36 mm thick x 350 mm wide. Glue joining edges, hold together with sash cramps, then remove excess adhesive. Ensure the top joints are flush, and leave to dry.

TOOLS

- Tape measure or rule
- Combination square
- Pencil
- Pair of safety glasses
- Dust mask
- Hearing protection
- Panel saw or portable circular saw
- Coping saw
- Smoothing plane, jack plane or power plane
- Chisel: 25 mm
- Crowbar (optional)
- Portable electric drill
- Drill bits: 3 mm, 5 mm countersink
- Screwdriver
- Spirit level
- Six G-cramps
- Eight 600 mm sash cramps
- Electric router (optional)
- Router bit: 19 mm bullnose cutter
- Spokeshave (optional)
- Millsaw file
- Old iron
- Cork sanding block
- Orbital sander (optional)

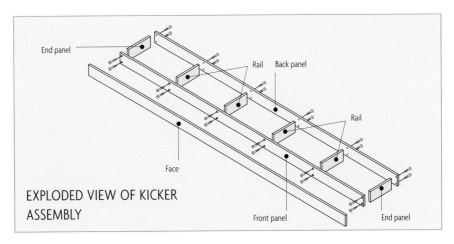

EXPLODED VIEW OF KICKER ASSEMBLY

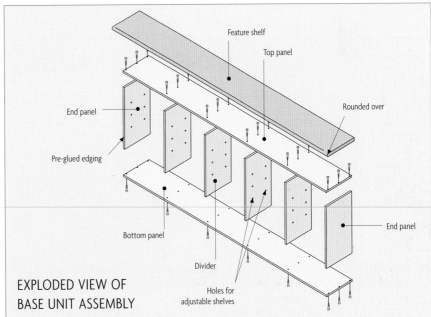

EXPLODED VIEW OF BASE UNIT ASSEMBLY

17 Use a plane, spokeshave or roundover bit in a router to round-over the front edge of the shelf.

18 Sand the shelf with 240 grit abrasive paper, apply matching filler and finish with clear lacquer.

TOP UNIT ASSEMBLY
19 Take the top unit end panels and dividers, and mark adjustable shelf positions. Drill 5 mm holes for the shelves, 35 mm in from the front and back edges, starting 40 mm up from the bottom of the panels.

20 The feature shelf acts as the bottom panel for the top unit. Set out the placement of dividers and end panels from a squared line across the bottom of the shelf. From this centre line measure half the division distance each side of centre, then 18 mm, then the full division distance, until all the spaces have been marked. Fit the feature shelf to the wall very carefully at the front of each end and to 150 mm back from the front edge. Beyond that will be hidden by the top unit filler pieces.

21 Mark 18 mm in from each end of the top panel. Square a line across and divide each panel into five sections as in step 6. On each divider, drill 5 mm holes 40 mm in from both the front and back edges.

FRONT VIEW

40 mm

2710 mm wall to wall

504 mm | 504 mm | 504 mm | 504 mm | 504 mm

40 mm

36 mm

Decorative top
(20 mm overhang)

18 mm

18 mm

Adjustable shelves

Fill piece

1910 mm

2750 mm

Feature shelf
(20 mm overhang)

36 mm

Fill piece

Adjustable shelf

704 mm

Divider

Divider

Kicker
(20 mm set-back)

Note: Preglued veneer edging is attached
to all 18 mm chipboard facing edges.

100 mm

EXPLODED VIEW OF TOP UNIT ASSEMBLY

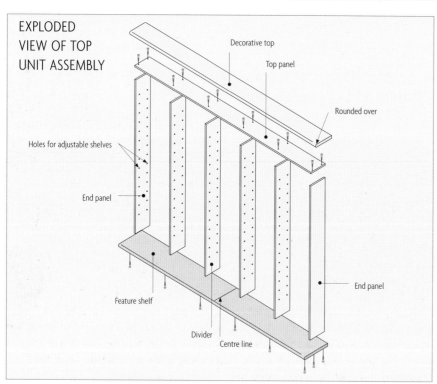

Decorative top

Top panel

Rounded over

Holes for adjustable shelves

End panel

End panel

Feature shelf

Divider

Centre line

22 Lay the left-hand end panel and top panel on their back edges. Glue joining edges, clamp in position, and fasten with 40 mm x No. 8 countersunk screws. Do the same to fix dividers and the other end panel to the top panel. Align the feature shelf and dividers and fasten with two 60 mm x No. 8 countersunk screws at each divider.

TOP UNIT INSTALLATION

23 Slide the top unit into position on base unit. Fasten it with 28 mm x No. 8 countersunk screws, screwing through the top panel of the base unit into the feature shelf. Use a 5 mm clearance hole and countersink the screw holes so the screws finish flush.

24 Measure the gap between the wall and the unit on the sides, bottom, middle and top. Mark the measurements on the faces of the fill pieces and use a straight edge to join the marks. Plane down to the line and fit the fill pieces to the gaps. Fasten to the wall.

25 The finished decorative top should be 36 mm thick x 235 mm wide. Round over the front edge of the top, then cut it to the correct length. Use 50 mm x No. 8 countersunk screws to fasten it to the top of the unit from above.

26 Carefully fill holes and repair any damage. Sand all parts, including adjustable shelves, with 240 grit abrasive paper, and finish with lacquer.

27 Place shelf supports in the prepared holes and insert the shelves.

indoor

SMALL TURNTABLE BOOKCASE

This ingenious unit is ideal for storing paperbacks and other small books. It is mounted on a swivelling base, providing access from all four sides.

CUTTING OUT

1 To save time, get a timber supplier to plane the timber on all faces.

2 Lay the 175 x 25 mm timber on the bench and measure, mark and cut two pieces 920 mm long. These will be edge-jointed to make a wide board, from which the top, base and long divider will later be cut.

3 Mark best faces. Check each piece is straight and square with a combination square. Ensure joining edges can be clamped up tightly—adjust with a smoothing plane or jack plane. Hold the two lengths edge to edge with the ends flush. Mark the lengths of the top, base and the long divider, allowing space for saw cuts and cleaning up. Square the lines around all faces of each piece.

4 With a marking gauge mark a centre line down the middle of each joining edge. Clamp the boards face sides together so the length lines align. Find the centre of each component along the edge. Measure 100 mm each side of centre and square the lines across and over edges and faces. Mark six dowel holes on each edge.

5 Use a dowelling jig and 6 mm drill bit to bore 16 mm deep dowel holes.

6 Place the boards in two loosened sash cramps. Use a pencil to spread PVA adhesive in the dowel holes and across the face edges, and to remove any excess adhesive. Insert 6 x 30 mm dowels in the holes in one board and gently hammer in. Position the dowels against the holes in the opposite board, then

The top and base of this bookcase are made from two pieces of timber joined almost invisibly by a dowelled joint. A strip of dark teak inlay makes an effective contrast with the rock maple used for the rest of the unit.

TOOLS

- Tape measure or steel rule
- Combination square
- Marking gauge
- Pencil
- Pair of safety glasses
- Dust mask
- Hearing protection
- Smoothing plane or jack plane
- Panel saw or circular saw
- Tenon saw
- Mitre saw (optional)
- Electric jigsaw or coping saw
- Mitre box (optional)
- Dowelling jig with 6 mm bush
- Electric router
- Router bit: 19 mm straight
- Electric drill
- Drill bits: 3 mm, 4 mm, 6 mm, countersink
- Chisel: 16 mm, bevelled edges
- Utility knife
- Four 600 mm sash cramps
- Six G-cramps
- Cork sanding block or timber 19 mm thick x 110 long x 70 mm wide
- Hammer or mallet
- Screwdriver
- Vice
- Flat-bottomed spokeshave
- Compass

MATERIALS*

PART	MATERIAL	FINISHED LENGTH	NO.
Top**	175 x 25 mm light timber PAR	300 mm	2
Top lipping*	38 x 25 mm light timber PAR	1500 mm	1
Inlay*	7 x 25 mm dark timber PAR	1500 mm	1
Long divider**	175 x 25 mm light timber PAR	280 mm	2
Short dividers	175 x 25 mm light timber PAR	280 mm	2
Vertical supports	25 x 25 mm light timber PAR	270 mm	4
Base**	175 x 25 mm light timber PAR	300 mm	2
Base lipping*	75 x 25 mm light timber PAR	1500 mm	1
Turntable base	18 mm MDF	295 x 295 mm	2

Other: Fourteen 6 x 30 mm dowels for exterior supports; PVA adhesive; cloths; scrap board 16 mm thick, 400 mm long, 120 mm wide; abrasive paper: three sheets of 120 grit, three sheets of 180 grit and two sheets of 240 grit; eight 12 mm x No. 8 pan-head self-tapping screws; one 'lazy susan' swivel; finish of your choice.

* Finished size: 357 mm high; 352 mm wide. For timber types and sizes see page 112. Timber sizes given are nominal.

**To be cut from two edge-jointed timber pieces.

* To be mitred into four pieces.

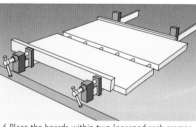
6 Place the boards within two loosened sash cramps. Insert dowels, then push the boards together.

push the boards together. If necessary, tap them with a hammer and block. Tighten the cramps, then attach two extra sash cramps. Remove excess adhesive with a damp cloth. When dry, check for twist, bowing or cupping. Plane to adjust them.

MAKING THE TOP AND BASE

7 Cut out the 300 x 300 x 19 mm top and base pieces from the joined piece. Use a square and utility knife to cut cross-grain fibres, then cut the lengths to size with a panel saw. Plane edges and ends square and straight. Plane the end grain from each side towards the centre to form a 'hill', then plane the hill flat.

8 Place the top piece best face down. Find the centre and mark a line square to one side. Measure out 9.5 mm either side of centre and mark a line. Turn the board through 90 degrees and do the same again.

9 If routing the through housings, clamp a 400 x 120 x 16 mm fence to the top piece (see page 180 for notes on using a router). Attach a 19 mm bit, set to cut 5 mm deep. Set up the router on the marks and cut right through them, running the baseplate along the fence. Repeat steps 8 and 9 for the base piece.

MAKING THE DIVIDERS

10 The timber for the long divider should measure 280 x 300 x 19 mm. Use a ruler to measure in 150 mm from one end and mark a line straight across to the opposite side. Measure out 9.5 mm from either side of this line and mark lines down to the opposite end. Turn the divider over and repeat the

indoor

MAKING THE LONG DIVIDER

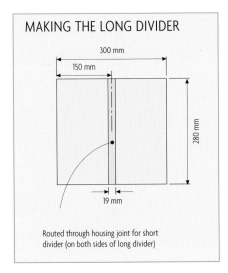

300 mm

150 mm

280 mm

19 mm

Routed through housing joint for short
divider (on both sides of long divider)

TOP VIEW

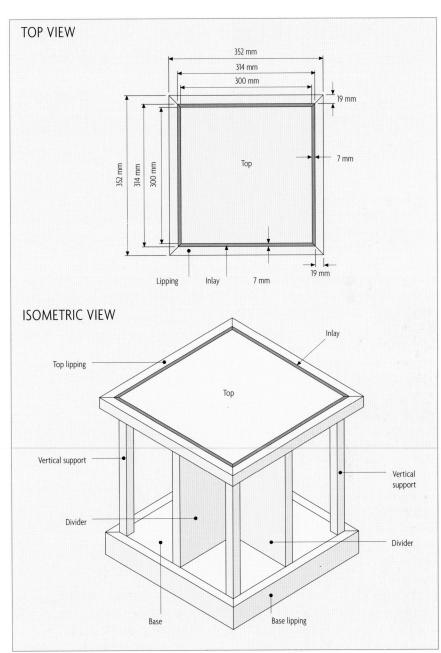

352 mm

314 mm

300 mm

19 mm

352 mm

314 mm

300 mm

Top

7 mm

19 mm

Lipping   Inlay   7 mm

POSITION OF DIVIDERS

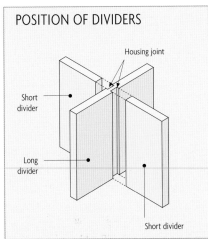

Housing joint

Short
divider

Long
divider

Short divider

ISOMETRIC VIEW

Inlay

Top lipping

Top

Vertical support

Vertical
support

Divider

Divider

Base

Base lipping

process. Using a router with a 19 mm cutter,
or a tenon saw and chisel, cut a through
housing 5 mm deep. Turn the divider over
and repeat the process.

11 The two short dividers must measure
280 x 146 x 19 mm. Check that the long and
short dividers fit together and in the top and
base piece housing joints. Flush the divider
edges to the top and base pieces, and
number each joint correspondingly.

MAKING THE BASE LIPPING
12 Mark a 45-degree line at one end of the

base lipping and measure along 300 mm
from the inside edge. Mark a 45-degree line
at the measurement. Square a line across
each side, allowing 5 mm for saw cuts. Score
the mitre lines with a utility knife. Mark
three more mitred sections the same way.

13 Use a mitre box and fine-toothed saw to
cut the mitres. Position the four lengths
together and adjust the fit by planing.

14 Glue the joining edges of the mitred
lipping to the base. Attach lippings to

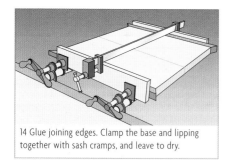

14 Glue joining edges. Clamp the base and lipping together with sash cramps, and leave to dry.

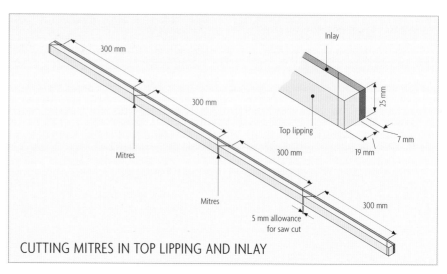

CUTTING MITRES IN TOP LIPPING AND INLAY

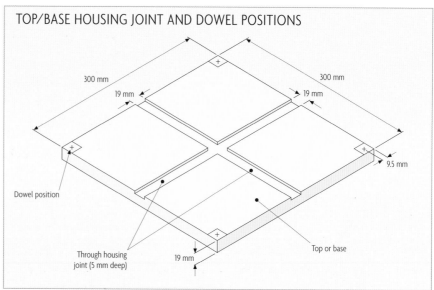

TOP/BASE HOUSING JOINT AND DOWEL POSITIONS

opposite base edges first. Clamp the base and lippings together with sash cramps, remove excess adhesive, and leave to dry. Then fit the remaining two lippings.

MAKING THE INLAY AND TOP LIPPING

15 Take the inlay strip, which should be 19 mm wide and 7 mm thick, and glue it to the top lipping. Clamp the inlay and lipping together with G-cramps, remove any excess adhesive, and allow to dry.

16 Mitre the joined lipping and inlay into four pieces using the process described in steps 12 and 13 (see diagram top right).

17 Plane the mitre edges, then glue one mitred piece to one edge of the top piece. Clamp with sash cramps and leave to dry. Repeat for each mitred piece. Sand or plane the lippings flush with the base and top.

FINAL ASSEMBLY

18 Take the top and base pieces and mark dowel positions for the vertical supports. Set a marking gauge to 9.5 mm and mark a line from each corner of the top of the base piece (see diagram below right). Repeat this marking process for the underside of the top piece. Drill 6 mm holes to a depth of 12 mm at the point where the marked lines intersect at each corner.

19 For each support, use a marking gauge set at 9.5 mm to find and mark the centre of the end faces. With a dowelling jig and a drill and twist bit, bore 6 mm holes 22 mm deep at the centre of each support.

20 Sand all parts with 120, 180 and 240 grit abrasive paper. Glue the dowel holes in the supports and tap in dowels. Next, glue the base piece housing joints. Insert the long divider and two short dividers, which have been glued along the bottom edges. Apply adhesive to the base piece dowel holes and insert vertical supports and their dowels. Take the top piece and glue the dowel holes and housing joints as you did for the base. Insert the glued dividers into the housing joints—the short dividers slot into the housings in the long divider. Fix the dowelled supports into the dowel holes. Clamp with four sash cramps, clean off excess adhesive and leave to dry overnight.

indoor

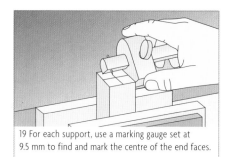

19 For each support, use a marking gauge set at 9.5 mm to find and mark the centre of the end faces.

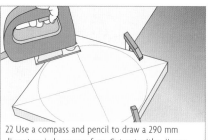

22 Use a compass and pencil to draw a 290 mm diameter circle on one face. Cut out with a jigsaw.

Supports are fastened with dowels, and dividers are held in place by through housing joints.

21 Finely sand the unit with 180 grit abrasive paper and finish with 240 grit abrasive paper. Apply your chosen finish.

MAKING THE SWIVEL BASE
22 Glue and cramp the MDF pieces together. When dry, mark the centre and use a compass and pencil to draw a 290 mm diameter circle on one face. Wearing a dust mask and safety glasses, cut out the circle

with a jigsaw or coping saw. Clean up the edges using 120 grit abrasive paper or a flat-bottomed spokeshave.

23 Fit the 'lazy susan' between the bookcase and swivel base following the manufacturer's instructions. 'Lazy susan' swivels come in many sizes. For best results use one no larger in diameter than 300 mm and no smaller than 200 mm.

MODULAR UNITS WITH OPTIONAL DOORS

These sleek units can be used as open shelving, or two glass doors can be attached to each unit. This project provides an opportunity to perfect a variety of important basic techniques.

CUTTING OUT
1 Select timber with minimal defects. Lay the chipboard and timber on a workbench, and with a tape measure and square mark out the parts, checking they are square and straight.

2 Wearing safety glasses, cut the parts with a panel saw or circular saw, then lightly plane the timber. Use a square to check accuracy on all edges and faces. Label the pieces, and mark the face side and edges. A timber merchant may be able to cut the pieces and attach veneer edging.

3 Fix matching veneer edging to the raw chipboard edges as specified. Use an old iron

at a hot setting. Hold the chipboard on its edge and position the veneer, adhesive side down. Move the iron back and forth along the veneer, pressing it down ahead of the iron with a cork block. Clean up overhanging edge tape with a round file, then sand the edges and arris with 120 grit abrasive paper.

PREPARING END PANELS
4 Lay out the end panels in pairs (using best faces for the outer sides). Cut a rebate 15 mm deep and 5 mm wide along the back inside edge of each panel, using a rebate plane or a router. If using the router, fit a fence and an 18 mm straight cutter (see page 180 for notes on using a router). The

plywood back will be secured within this rebate at a later stage.

5 Before routing, build a jig (see diagram on page 197).

6 Mark the positions of the housing joints on the end panels. Leave 60 mm between the top of the end panel and the top joint, and 60 mm between the base of the panel and the bottom joint. The central joint should be an equal distance between the top and bottom joints.

7 Rout the joints. Slide each end panel into the jig and clamp with a G-cramp.

Without doors each unit is an easily accessible bookcase; with doors it becomes a secure display cabinet for your most valuable and beautiful books. The doors are made of solid silver ash, and the basic unit is veneered in matching timber.

TOOLS

- Steel rule: 150 mm or 300 mm
- Tape measure
- Combination square
- Pencil
- Pair of safety glasses
- Dust mask
- Hearing protection
- Panel saw or circular saw
- Tenon saw
- Utility knife
- Vice
- Rebate plane
- Smoothing plane or jack plane
- Electric router
- Router bit: 18 mm straight
- Four G-cramps
- Six 800 mm sash cramps
- Marking gauge
- Mortise gauge
- Chisel: 16 mm, bevelled edges; 25 mm
- Smoothing file
- Round file
- Old iron
- Cork sanding block
- Belt sander (optional)
- Electric drill
- Drill bit: 3 mm, 5 mm, 6 mm, 10 mm countersink, 32 mm forstner
- Dowelling jig with 6 mm bush
- Dowel stick (optional)
- Hammer
- Nail punch

MATERIALS*

PART	MATERIAL	LENGTH	WIDTH	NO.
End panel**	25 mm veneered chipboard	2100 mm	395 mm	6
Top/bottom/centre panel**	25 mm veneered chipboard	510 mm	390 mm	9
Adjustable shelf**	25 mm veneered chipboard	498 mm	370 mm	12
Back	4 mm veneered chipboard	1980 mm	531 mm	3
Top rail and base kicker	25 mm veneered chipboard	500 mm	60 mm	6
Timber cleat (horizontal)	19 x 19 mm timber PAR	458 mm		6
Timber cleat (vertical)	19 x 19 mm timber PAR	59 mm		12
Door stile*	70 x 20 mm timber	951 mm		12
Door rail*	70 x 20 mm timber	378 mm		12
Door bead (vertical)*	9 x 9 mm timber	833 mm		12
Door bead (horizontal)*	9 x 9 mm timber	361 mm		12

Other (for three units): 150 x 25 mm flat-head nails (units and doors); four 5 mm supports for each shelf; twenty 8 mm brass sleeves for each shelf; twelve concealed hinges with 16 mm cranking; thirty 30 mm x No. 8 countersunk cross-head screws; eighty 15 mm panel pins; forty-eight 32 mm long x 6 mm diameter timber dowels; six sheets of pre-cut clear glass 829 mm long x 376 mm wide x 3 mm thick; abrasive paper: nine sheets of 180 grit and five sheets of 220 grit; finish of your choice; handles of your choice.

For the jig: one piece 16 mm MDF 1800 x 850 mm; two pieces 12 mm MDF 1800 x 90 mm (with long edges laminated); one piece 16 mm MDF 850 x 120 mm (with long edges laminated); two 14 mm blocks 120 x 90 mm.

* Quantity of materials based on building three units. Finished size of single unit: 2100 mm high; 550 mm wide; 396 mm deep. For timber types and sizes see page 112. Timber sizes given here are nominal unless otherwise indicated.

** With one long edge of matching timber veneer pre-glued edging.

* Finished size.

Attach an 18 mm straight cutter set to cut 5 mm deep. Rout a 25 mm wide groove, leaving 10 mm uncut on the front edge. Make two passes for a width of 25 mm.

8 Mark and drill holes for adjustable shelves in the end panels. Bore 8 mm deep holes 60 mm in from front and back edges, 32 mm apart.

PREPARING FIXED PANELS

9 Take one of the top fixed panels. On each end use a marking gauge set at 5 mm to mark a line right across the facing edge and in 15 mm on either side. Repeat for the other fixed panels.

10 Hold the top panel in a vice and use a tenon saw to cut out a 5 mm rebate as shown in the diagram on page 197. Repeat for the other fixed panels.

ASSEMBLING THE UNIT

11 Sand all the unit components with 180 grit abrasive paper.

12 Lay both end panels on the bench and glue the housing joints. Place the fixed panels into position, hold with sash cramps, then clean off excess adhesive and leave to dry.

13 Check that the back fits in the end panel rebates, cutting the back board to

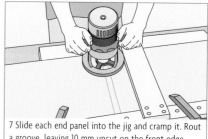

7 Slide each end panel into the jig and cramp it. Rout a groove, leaving 10 mm uncut on the front edge.

adjust the size if necessary. Fix using 25 mm flat-head nails.

ATTACHING THE RAIL, KICKER AND CLEATS

14 Lay the unit on its back on the bench, ready for the top rail, kicker and cleats.

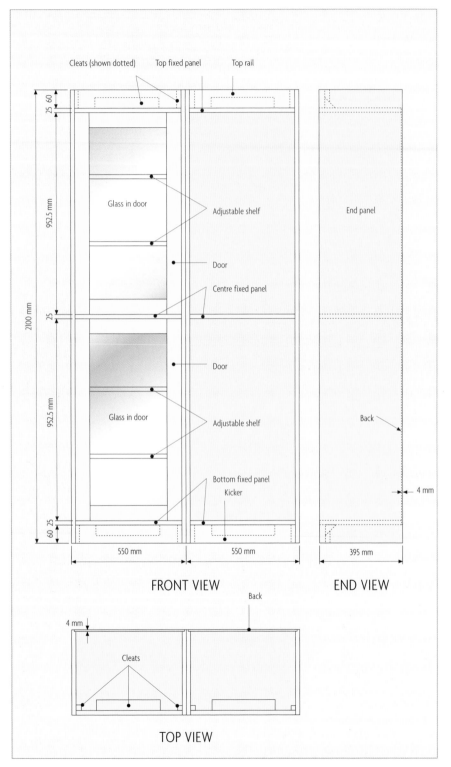

Cleats (shown dotted)   Top fixed panel   Top rail

25 60

952.5 mm

Glass in door

Adjustable shelf

2100 mm

25

Door

Centre fixed panel

952.5 mm

Door

Glass in door

Adjustable shelf

Bottom fixed panel
Kicker

60 25

550 mm   550 mm

End panel

Back

4 mm

395 mm

FRONT VIEW   **END VIEW**

Back

4 mm

Cleats

TOP VIEW

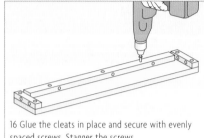

16 Glue the cleats in place and secure with evenly spaced screws. Stagger the screws.

15 Place the top rail flat on its good face. On the back face, position a short vertical cleat at either end, flush with the edge. Attach the long horizontal cleat along the bottom edge between the two short cleats.

16 Glue the cleats in place. Secure the short cleats with two evenly spaced screws each way, and the long cleat with six screws. Stagger the screws so they don't run into one another. Bore 3 mm pilot holes through the cleats into the rail. Drill 5 mm holes in the cleats only and countersink. Insert 30 mm x No. 8 countersunk cross-head screws and tighten. Wipe off excess adhesive. Repeat the process for the kicker, but attach cleats at the top edge.

17 Glue the edges of the top rail and kickboard that will join the unit, and fix to the unit with sash clamps. Bore 3 mm pilot holes in the pieces at regular intervals, drill 5 mm holes, countersink, then insert 30 mm x No. 8 screws and tighten. Wipe off excess adhesive with a damp cloth. Apply the finish of your choice. Insert brass sleeves in the shelf holes, and insert shelves now if you are not adding doors.

MAKING DOWELLED JOINTS FOR THE DOORS

18 Use a rebate plane or a router for the following step. If using a router, set it up with an 18 mm bit to cut 14 mm deep and 10 mm wide. Clamp all stiles and rails to

indoor

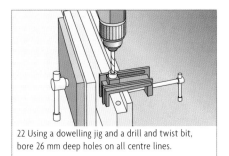

22 Using a dowelling jig and a drill and twist bit, bore 26 mm deep holes on all centre lines.

the bench with G-cramps and cut out one long edge along each piece. Glass panels will sit within these rebated edges.

19 Set the marking gauge to 10 mm and mark a line on the facing edge of the rails. Using a square and utility knife, score along the marked line.

20 Place each rail in a vice. On the front edge of the end that will meet the stile, cut a 10 x 6 mm rebate with a tenon saw and chisel, rebate plane or router (see diagram on page 198). Check the fit of each rebate. If routing, clamp all rails together with their ends flush, face side up (place scrap material on each side). Set the router to cut 6 mm deep. Maintain the same width of cut, or set up a fence and run the rebates on all rails at the same time.

21 Use a marking gauge, a pencil and a square to mark the dowel positions (see diagram on page 198). Working from the inside face of each stile, use the gauge set to 7 mm to mark a 60 mm long line down from the top. Repeat this process for the bottom of each stile, marking 60 mm up. Reset the gauge and then mark 20 mm in from both ends of each rail, then 20 mm and 50 mm from the top and bottom of the stiles.

22 Using a dowelling jig with a 6 mm bush and a power drill and twist bit, bore 26 mm deep holes on all centre lines.

STOPPED HOUSING JOINTS AND FIXED PANELS

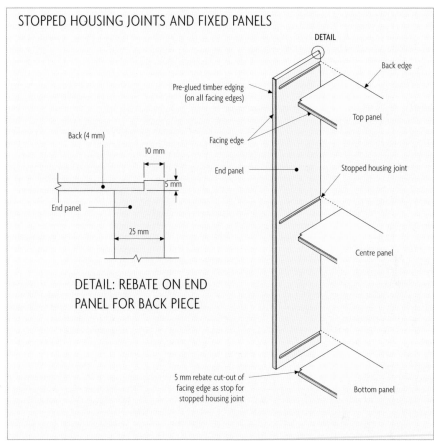

DETAIL: REBATE ON END PANEL FOR BACK PIECE

JIG ASSEMBLY

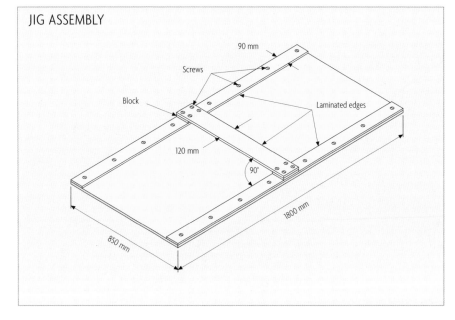

REBATE AND DOWELLED JOINT IN DOOR

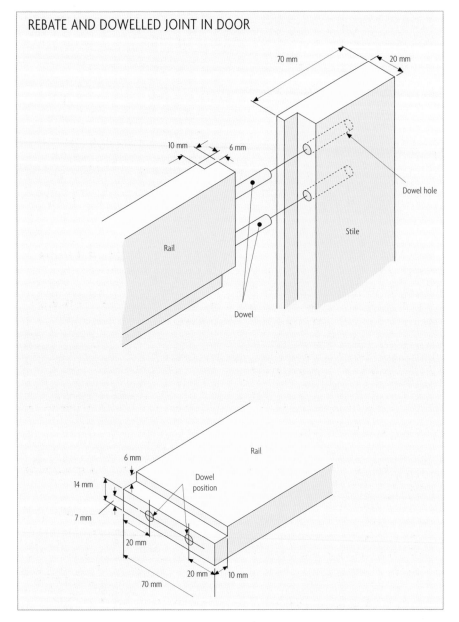

70 mm
20 mm
10 mm
6 mm
Dowel hole
Rail
Stile
Dowel

6 mm
Rail
14 mm
Dowel position
7 mm
20 mm
20 mm
10 mm
70 mm

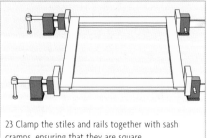

23 Clamp the stiles and rails together with sash cramps, ensuring that they are square.

23 Put adhesive in the dowel holes and spread some across the joint. Use a pencil to apply adhesive and to remove any excess. Insert dowels in the holes in the rails and gently tap them in with a hammer. Push the pieces together. Clamp stiles and rails together with sash cramps, ensuring they are square. Carefully clean off excess adhesive. Leave to dry completely.

ASSEMBLING THE DOORS

24 When dry, remove the cramps. Plane the joints level if necessary. Check the fit of each door, then sand with 180 grit abrasive paper and finish with 220 grit.

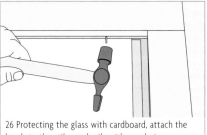

26 Protecting the glass with cardboard, attach the beads to the stiles and rails with panel pins.

MARKING TIMBER

After planing and checking for straightness, mark the face side and edge of timber pieces in pencil. These marks help you quickly identify pieces, and indicate that two adjacent pieces are square to each other. Always work from the face side and edge.

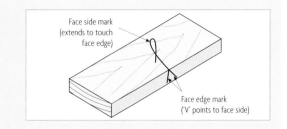

Face side mark (extends to touch face edge)

Face edge mark ('V' points to face side)

indoor

TIMBER CONDITIONS

Timber is sold in three conditions:

- sawn or rough-sawn: sawn to a specific (nominal) size
- planed, either planed all round (PAR), planed on two sides (P2S) or double planed (DP)
- moulded: planed to a specific profile for architraves, skirting boards and so on.

Planed timber is mostly sold using the same nominal dimensions as sawn timber, for example 100 x 50 mm, but the surfaces have all been machined to a flat, even width and thickness so the '100 x 50 mm' timber is actually 91 x 41 mm. The chart shows the actual sizes for seasoned timber; unseasoned timber such as radiata pine will vary in size.

Moulded timbers are also ordered by nominal sizes, but check them carefully, as there will be variations.

Sawn (nominal) size (mm)	Size after planing (mm)
19	15
25	19
38	30
50	41
75	66
100	91
125	115
150	138

25 Check the size of the rebated area and set the pre-cut glass panels into the rebate at the back of each door.

26 Protect the glass with cardboard and attach beads to the inside back edges of stiles and rails using panel pins (start with vertical beads). Punch the heads beneath the surface.

INSTALLING THE DOORS

27 Use concealed hinges to fit the door to the bookcase. Place the unit on its side with the hingeing side down, and mark a centre line from the mounting plate position to the edge. Follow the manufacturer's instructions for fitting the hinges. Ensure the hinge arm is at right angles to the door edge, and attach the door. Adjust as necessary.

28 Attach handles and apply the finish of your choice.

DIAMOND-SHAPED BOOKSHELVES

Timbers of contrasting colours are used for this piece of fine furniture. Skill in using a router is essential for making the dovetail splines that fasten the shelves and supports.

PREPARATION

1 Timber must be straight, square and defect-free. Season the timber by stacking it for a month in the room where the shelves will be installed. This reduces the chance of shrinkage.

2 For this project, get your timber merchant to supply the timber at the finished sizes in the Materials list. Draw a full-sized set-out on 4 mm MDF, setting the dovetail joints out on a centre line. The set-out should correspond to the thicknesses of your timber.

3 You must also make an accurate jig for cutting the dovetail joints and splines.

CUTTING OUT

4 Using a jack plane or smoothing plane, plane the diagonal supports and shelves to their finished width of 225 mm.

5 With a combination square and tape measure, mark the lengths of the shelves and diagonal supports. Leave 5–10 mm space between the pieces for saw cuts. Check the dimensions against the set-out, then continue the lines over the edges and across the back face of the timber.

6 Score the lines with a utility knife. Cut the pieces to length and smooth the ends.

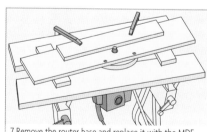

7 Remove the router base and replace it with the MDF. Set the router in a suitable workbench or vice.

MACHINING DOVETAIL HOUSINGS

7 Make a central hole in 12 mm MDF for the dovetail cutter. Remove the router base and replace it with the MDF. Set the router in a suitable workbench or vice.

All components were laid out on an MDF set-out at final assembly to help in piecing together the correct diamond shape. Shelves and fixing rails are made of silver ash, supports and dovetails of Western cedar.

8 Clamp an 18 mm MDF fence to the router base. Set the router to cut a 5 mm deep dovetail housing exactly in the centre of the end of the board. Run dovetails on the eight diagonal supports.

MAKING THE END LIPPINGS

9 Take the 41 x 24 mm timber and cut it into four 1050 mm lengths. With a protractor, set a sliding bevel to 35 degrees. Use the bevel to set the base of a power saw to this angle.

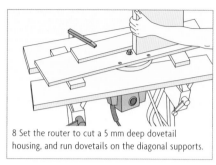

8 Set the router to cut a 5 mm deep dovetail housing, and run dovetails on the diagonal supports.

10 With a marking gauge or square, mark a line 35 mm along one face of a length. Clamp the piece to the bench. Set the rip guide on the saw to cut the angle slightly overwidth, then cut. Repeat for all four lengths.

11 Clamp one length in a vice, edge up. Plane the angle back to the marked line. Repeat for all lengths.

12 With a marking gauge, make a line down the centre of the bevelled edge and over the ends of each piece. Rout a dovetail groove down the square edge of each piece, then move the fence to cut the groove down the centre of the bevelled edge.

13 With a square, mark the lengths of the pieces to the same width as each diagonal support (225 mm). Score the lines with a utility knife and use a tenon saw to cut the pieces 1–2 mm overlength.

MAKING AND ATTACHING DOVETAIL SPLINES

14 Machine the 19 x 12 mm timber to a thickness of 10 mm, then cut it into eight 1050 mm lengths. Reset the router fence and cut a dovetail pitch on the 10 mm edge. Turn the timber over and rout the other side (see diagram Detail B on page 202).

15 Machine the matching dovetail joints on the opposite squared edge. Ensure you

TOOLS

- Rule: 300 mm and 1 m
- Tape measure
- Pencil
- Combination square
- Marking gauge
- Pair of safety glasses
- Dust mask
- Hearing protection
- Smoothing plane or jack plane
- Panel saw (optional)
- Portable circular saw
- Tenon saw
- Vice or suitable workbench
- Electric router
- Router bit: 15 mm dovetail
- Sliding bevel
- Protractor
- Electric drill
- Drill bit: 5 mm, 10 mm countersink
- Four G-cramps
- Six 600 mm sash cramps
- Round paintbrush: 12 mm
- Hammer
- Screwdriver
- Cork sanding block
- Utility knife

MATERIALS*

PART	MATERIAL	LENGTH	NO.
Centre shelf	225 x 24 mm light timber	1200 mm	1
Upper and lower shelf	225 x 24 mm light timber	800 mm	2
Top shelf and base	225 x 24 mm light timber	400 mm	2
Fixing rail**	31 x 19 mm light timber	3000 mm	1
Diagonal support	225 x 24 mm dark timber	278 mm	8
End lipping**	41 x 24 mm dark timber	4200 mm	1
Slip dovetail**	19 x 12 mm dark timber	4200 mm	2
Base for set-out	4 mm MDF	1200 x 1200 mm	1

Other: Ten 40 mm x No. 8 cross-head screws; wall fixings (see steps 24 and 25); PVA adhesive; cloths; abrasive paper: six sheets of 180 grit and four sheets of 220 grit; clear lacquer or finish of your choice.

For the jig table: One piece of 12 mm MDF 350 mm long x 180 mm wide.

For the jig fence: One piece of 18 mm MDF 350 mm long x 50 mm wide.

* Finished size: 1200 mm high; 1200 mm wide; 225 mm deep. Finished timber sizes are given here. For timber types and timber sizes, see box on page 199.

** To be cut later into the required number of pieces.

achieve a good slide fit by gradually reducing the width with a number of passes over the router.

16 Cut thirty-two dovetail splines, each 227 mm long. Using a paintbrush, glue all dovetail grooves in the diagonal supports and the matching end lippings. Insert a dovetail spline in each diagonal support joint, attach the lippings, then clamp. The ends of the lippings and dovetail splines will overhang the supports at each end. Remove excess adhesive with a damp rag, then leave to dry. Don't put dovetail splines in the angled edge of the lippings at this stage.

MAKING THE SHELVES

17 Measure and mark the length of each shelf directly from your set-out. Square the lines across each face and over the edges. Score the lines with a utility knife and cut the shelves to length with a panel or power saw.

18 Position each shelf on the set-out. Use a square to mark the centre-line position of each dovetail joint across the appropriate face.

19 Clamp the top shelf and base to your bench, with centre lines aligned. Set up a fence parallel to one of the centre-line marks, set at the correct distance. With your router cutter centred on the centre line, machine 5 mm deep cuts. Repeat for the remaining shelves.

20 Check the fit of all pieces, then disassemble them. Plane lipping and dovetail spline overhangs so they are flush with the diagonal supports. Sand all parts with 220 grit abrasive paper, then 180 grit. Clean up the rough-sawn ends of each shelf.

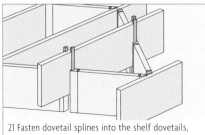

21 Fasten dovetail splines into the shelf dovetails, then fix the shelf into the support dovetails.

FINAL ASSEMBLY AND INSTALLATION

21 Assemble the unit on the set-out. Take the top shelf and glue the two shelf dovetails and both ends of two dovetail splines. Next, glue the angled-edge dovetails in the diagonal supports. Fasten dovetail splines into the shelf dovetails, then fix the shelf into the diagonal support dovetails. Repeat for all shelves.

22 Cut the 3000 mm length of light timber to make four fixing rails. Set up a sliding bevel at 35 degrees and cut the ends of the rails at this angle with a tenon saw, to fit flush against the inside edge of the supports.

23 Lay the unit front-side down and attach the rails to the shelves (see diagram at right). Drill 5 mm holes and countersink, then fasten the rails with 40 mm x No. 8 cross-head screws. Finish the unit with clear lacquer.

24 To fix the unit to a framed wall, find the stud centres and mark them on the wall at the required height. Support the unit at this height (you may need help), and transfer the wall marks to the fixing rail. Drill and countersink a 5 mm clearance hole, then drill a 3 mm pilot hole. Attach the unit on one side first, with a 75 x No. 10 countersunk screw. Check the level with a spirit level, then drill and screw at the other end.

25 For a masonry wall, use a similar method and the same size screws. You will also need to use a wall plug in the hole, into which you can fasten the screw.

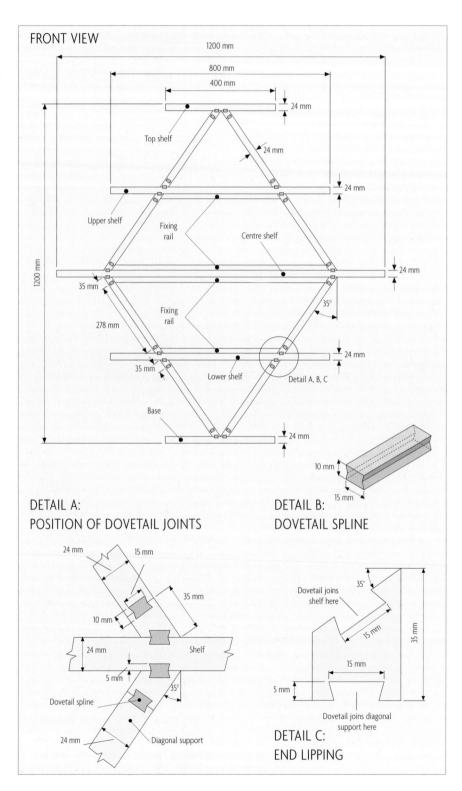

FRONT VIEW

1200 mm
800 mm
400 mm
24 mm
Top shelf
24 mm
24 mm
Upper shelf
Fixing rail
Centre shelf
1200 mm
24 mm
35 mm
35°
278 mm
Fixing rail
35 mm
24 mm
Lower shelf
Detail A, B, C
Base
24 mm

10 mm
15 mm

DETAIL A:
POSITION OF DOVETAIL JOINTS

24 mm   15 mm
35 mm
10 mm
24 mm   Shelf
5 mm
35°
Dovetail spline
24 mm   Diagonal support

DETAIL B:
DOVETAIL SPLINE

35°
Dovetail joins shelf here
15 mm
35 mm
15 mm
5 mm
Dovetail joins diagonal support here

DETAIL C:
END LIPPING

indoor

BOOKCASE WITH PULL-OUT DESK

One of these two joined units contains a writing desk, which pulls out and rises to the level of the shelf proper by means of an ingenious system of pins and grooves. This project requires experience in using a router.

CUTTING OUT

1 Lay the MDF (medium-density fibreboard) on a bench. Mark out the parts with a tape measure and square.

2 Wearing safety glasses and a dust mask, cut parts slightly oversize with a panel saw or circular saw. Trim edges back with a router. A timber supplier could cut the MDF to size.

MAKING THE HOUSINGS AND REBATE

3 Use a guide fence clamped to the face of the boards, or make a router jig with the threaded rod and nuts.

4 Attach it to the router, 82 mm away from the 18 mm cutter, and set the cutter depth to 6 mm. Take one of the end panels and rout the first stopped housing for the shelves, stopping 10 mm in from the front edge. Repeat this process on all the end panels. Turn the fence over and set the distance to 300 mm. Do not change the cutter depth. Ensure that the fence fits neatly into the first housing and that it slides easily. Start from the back edge and rout to the front edge, repeating the process to make the right number of cuts on the right-hand end panels. Swap the fence to the other side of the router for the left-hand ends.

5 Now rebate the back edges. Pair off the end panels, and on the inside face use a pencil to mark the back edges with a cross. Replace the jig with the normal fence and set the router to cut to a depth of 12.5 mm

This unit is more than a simple bookcase—with its pull-out desk it also serves as a small office or library area. The decorative mouldings shown here are made from chamfered and fluted maple, but moulded skirtings can also be used.

MATERIALS*

PART	MATERIAL	LENGTH	WIDTH	NO.
End panel	18 mm MDF	2000 mm	300 mm	4
Shelf	18 mm MDF	775 mm	296 mm	11
Rail	18 mm MDF	764 mm	82 mm	4
Shelf (sliding)	18 mm MDF	760 mm	200 mm	1
Back	4 mm MDF	1836 mm	787 mm	2
Side moulding	50 x 25 mm softwood PAR	319 mm		3
Front moulding (top)**	50 x 25 mm softwood PAR	1639 mm		1
Front moulding (bottom)**	50 x 25 mm softwood PAR	838 mm		1
Loper*	50 x 25 mm hardwood PAR	600 mm		1
Glue block	50 x 50 mm softwood PAR	200 mm		12

Other: PVA adhesive; cloths; sixteen 40 mm long x 8 mm diameter timber dowels; abrasive paper: three sheets of 120 grit and three sheets of 180 grit; four 40 mm x No. 8 countersunk screws; eighteen 30 mm x No. 6 countersunk screws; 30 mm panel pins; two 50 x 6 mm coach bolts with washers and wing nuts; sixteen 30 mm lost-head nails; 25 mm flat-head nails; four 12 x 5 mm diameter steel guide pins; finish of your choice.

For the jig: Two lengths of threaded rod 600 mm long and four nuts to suit.

* Finished size of each unit: 2000 mm high; 800 mm wide without moulding; the shelves are 295 mm deep. When opened out the desk-shelf is approximately 500 mm deep. For timber types and timber sizes see page 199. Timber sizes given here are nominal.

** Commercial moulding 100 x 25 mm (finished size 91 x 19 mm) can be used instead of timber.

* To be cut later to make two lopers.

7 Mark the angled cut and fence positions. With the fence on the right, push the router away from you.

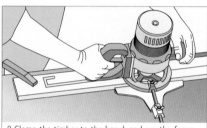
8 Clamp the timber to the bench and run the fence along one edge. Rout the long grooves.

4 Turn the fence over and set the distance to 300 mm. Start from the back edge and rout to the front.

and to a width of 4.5 mm. Rout rebates on the inside back edge of the end panels.

ROUTING THE DESK TRACK AND SHELF STOPS

6 Before routing the sliding track for the desk with a 5 mm straight cutter, carefully set the grooves out on the end panels (see diagram Detail A on page 207). Take a pair of ends and measure the distance from the cutting edge of the router bit to the outer edge of the router base. Set the bit to cut 9 mm deep. Clamp on a piece of offcut as a fence the measured distance away from the marked groove position.

7 Use a square to mark the positions of the angled cut and the fence. With the fence on the right, push the router away from you. Drill 5 mm holes for the guide pins now.

8 Take the 600 x 50 x 25 mm timber and set out the grooves as shown in diagram Detail B on page 207, working from each end so that the grooves form a pair. Clamp the timber to the bench and run the fence along one edge. Rout the two long grooves. To cut the short grooves parallel to the long ones, re-attach the fence to the router and set the distances before cutting.

9 Cut the piece in half to separate the lopers and line up the two end grooves with a square. Clamp the pieces with a length of offcut as a fence, and rout the groove. Place the lopers with faces together in a vice and plane the edges to the bevel indicated. Drill and counterbore two screw holes on each loper (see diagram on page 207) and two 5 mm holes for the guide pins.

10 Clamp the shelves together, all ends square and flush. Rout stops 19 mm deep and 6 mm wide.

FIXING THE RAILS

11 Rails are placed at the top front edges of both units, the bottom front of the large

TOOLS

- Tape measure
- Combination square
- Pencil
- Pair of safety glasses
- Dust mask
- Hearing protection
- Tenon saw
- Panel saw or circular saw
- Jigsaw
- Electric router
- Router bit: 5 mm and 18 mm straight
- Six G-cramps
- Six 900 mm sash cramps
- Vice
- Electric drill
- Drill bits: 8 mm, 5 mm, 3 mm, countersink
- Plane
- Dowelling jig (optional)
- Small paintbrush (optional)
- Screwdriver (cross-head or slotted)
- Half-round wood rasp or half-round file
- Hammer
- Cork sanding block
- Straight edge

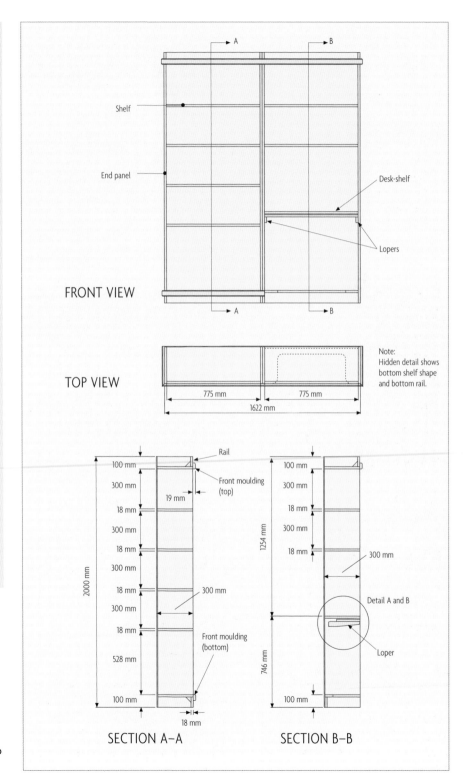

FRONT VIEW

TOP VIEW

Note:
Hidden detail shows
bottom shelf shape
and bottom rail.

SECTION A–A

SECTION B–B

unit and the bottom back of the desk unit. Mark out dowel hole positions on the rails, 20 mm in from the top and bottom and in the centre of the rail end. Use a square to mark corresponding hole positions on the end panel. Place the rails together in a vice, with all ends flush. Use a dowelling jig and a drill and twist bit to bore 8 mm x 31 mm deep holes in the rail ends. Drill 11 mm deep holes in the end panels.

A system of pins in routed slots allows the desk to pull out and lift up to the level of the shelf behind.

ASSEMBLING THE UNIT

12 Use a paintbrush to glue the housing grooves on one end first. Spread adhesive into the dowel holes. Insert dowels, rails and shelves and tap them in. Glue the other end panel and locate it on the assembled parts.

13 Nail or screw the unit together or clamp it overnight. If the housing joints are a little loose, they should be nailed and glued. If very loose, they should be screwed using a 40 mm countersunk screw with a clearance hole and pilot hole 50 mm back from the front edge and 50 mm from the back edge. If the unit is nailed or screwed you can work on it half an hour after gluing, but you will have to fill the heads and sand

back at a later stage. Apply glue blocks behind the rails.

14 Measure from the inside face of each end panel 100 mm along the bottom shelf. Square a line from front to back at this point.

15 With a marking gauge, mark a line parallel to the back edge and 60 mm in. Set a compass to 40 mm and inscribe the curved corners of the cut-out onto the bottom shelf. Use a jigsaw to remove the waste. Clean up the rough saw marks with a half-round wood rasp or file, finishing the curves with 120 grit abrasive paper.

16 Check that the backs fit, but do not fix them on. To temporarily keep the units square, tack an offcut of backing material diagonally across the corners and place shrinkage plates across the bottom of each end panel.

17 For a trim, use chamfered and fluted timber or a moulded skirting. Mark out the mitres with a square, cut them, then cut the mouldings to length. Clamp them to the unit and fix to the sides with adhesive and 30 mm panel pins, first checking they are square to the face edges (or fasten from inside the rail, using 30 mm x No. 6 countersunk screws). To fix the bottom front moulding, place it over the mitred side piece and mark the length at the opposite end. It should overlap the front edge of the other unit 18 mm. Cut to length and fit. Don't fix the top moulding yet.

18 Lay the large unit on its side. Put the desk unit on its side on top of the large unit and align the front and top edges. Drill two 6.5 mm holes through both end panels where they won't be seen, 150–200 mm

indoor

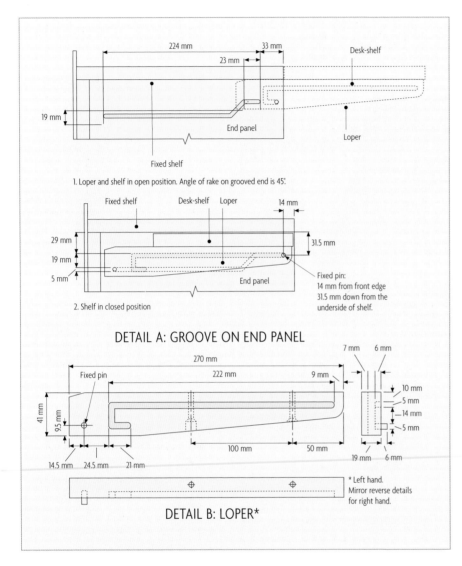

1. Loper and shelf in open position. Angle of rake on grooved end is 45°.

29 mm
19 mm
5 mm

2. Shelf in closed position

Fixed pin:
14 mm from front edge
31.5 mm down from the
underside of shelf.

DETAIL A: GROOVE ON END PANEL

270 mm
222 mm
9 mm
Fixed pin
41 mm
9.5 mm
14.5 mm 24.5 mm 21 mm
100 mm 50 mm
7 mm 6 mm
10 mm
5 mm
14 mm
5 mm
19 mm 6 mm

DETAIL B: LOPER*

* Left hand.
Mirror reverse details
for right hand.

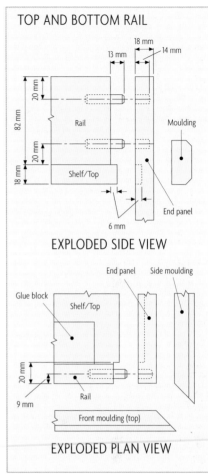

TOP AND BOTTOM RAIL

18 mm
13 mm 14 mm
82 mm
20 mm
20 mm
18 mm
Rail
Moulding
Shelf/Top
End panel
6 mm

EXPLODED SIDE VIEW

End panel Side moulding
Glue block
Shelf/Top
20 mm
9 mm
Rail
Front moulding (top)

EXPLODED PLAN VIEW

apart. They will take two 50 x 6 mm coach bolts with washers and nuts. Drill and countersink four 4 mm holes for four 30 mm x No. 6 screws further down the end. Place two holes below the second shelf, one each near front and back edges, and two above the bottom shelf (these two must be accessible after assembly).

FINISHING
19 Thoroughly sand all components. Sand the edges with 120 grit paper, finishing with 180 grit. Do not sand the MDF faces. Finish as desired.

20 Lay the units face down on padded bearers to protect the faces. Remove the braces. Mark the shelf centre-line positions on the back edge so you can locate them when the back is in place. Position the back flush with the top edge and fasten with 25 mm flat-head nails. Use a straight edge and pencil to draw a line across the back where the shelves will be

nailed, then nail them down. Repeat for the other unit.

21 Turn the desk unit upside down. Drop in the shelf and bring it to within 1 mm of the front edge. Ensure the gaps on each side are equal and lightly clamp it in position. Insert guide pins in the ends and lopers. Position the lopers flush with the front edge and sides of the shelf, and attach with 40 mm x No. 8 countersunk screws.

22 Stand the shelf unit in position, align the desk unit and fasten with nuts, bolts and screws. Glue and nail the top front moulding in place.

chests and boxes

chests and boxes

JEWELLERY BOX WITH BEADING

This beautiful box with a gabled lid and fine beading is a project for experienced woodworkers. It is made as one piece, and the lid is then cut to ensure a perfect fit.

This jewellery box was made from sycamore, a warm honey-coloured wood, with rich rosewood used for the contrasting beading and feet. The fine brass hinges and a jewellery box hasp are evocative of times past.

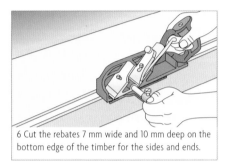

6 Cut the rebates 7 mm wide and 10 mm deep on the bottom edge of the timber for the sides and ends.

PREPARING THE BOX

1 Have the 16 mm timber planed to 10 mm thick when you buy it. Take this timber, mark a face side and plane a face edge straight and square. Don't reduce the width to less than 130 mm.

2 Roughly cut one 700 mm long piece of timber for the sides and one 360 mm long piece for the ends.

3 Mark out and plane the side timber to no less than 107 mm wide. Set out the sides and ends as per the diagrams opposite, making sure that the sides are going to match up with the ends. Remember that the box is made as one piece and the lid is cut later.

4 Mark the mitre lines across the edges of the sides and ends, and trace over the lines with a utility knife to cut the cross-grain fibres. Place each panel in a vice and cut the mitres with a tenon saw. If the saw is not wide enough, turn over the panel and cut from the other edge. Plane back the mitres to the lines using a smoothing plane. Repeat for each mitre and check the fit of the joints.

TOOLS

- Smoothing plane or jack plane
- Rebate plane (or router and rebate bit)
- Hammer
- Chisel: 6 mm, 25 mm
- Tenon saw
- Dovetail saw
- Jigsaw (or tilting blade table saw)
- Coping saw
- Tape measure or folding rule
- Combination square and pencil
- Utility knife
- Set of jeweller's screwdrivers
- Sliding bevel
- Cork sanding block
- Set square, compass set and scissors
- Cabinet scraper
- Rat-tail file and flat file
- Cramps: frame, quick-release

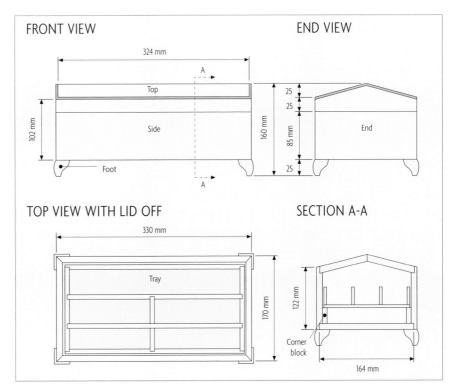

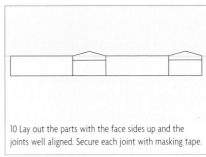

10 Lay out the parts with the face sides up and the joints well aligned. Secure each joint with masking tape.

5 Cut the gable on the top edges of the ends with a tenon saw, and plane back to the lines where the beading will be fixed.

6 Clamp each side piece firmly to a work surface and cut rebates on the top edges 7 mm wide and 5 mm deep. Repeat for the end pieces, cutting the rebates 7 mm wide and 7 mm deep. Cut rebates 7 mm wide and 10 mm deep on the bottom edges of the sides and ends. Check all the corners meet exactly and number the joints. You can use a rebate plane to cut the rebates, or use a router with a rebating bit.

7 Take the 100 x 16 mm timber and cut two 340 mm boards for the bottom. Plane an edge of each board straight and make sure the face sides are flush. Put adhesive on the

joining edges, bring the boards together and apply two 300 mm quick-release cramps. Put the panel aside to dry.

8 Cut two 340 mm pieces from the 100 x 16 mm timber for the top. Work out the edge angle where the boards join the sides. Set a sliding bevel to that angle. Mark the angle on the board edges and plane the angle, checking the fit often. Sand the inside faces of all panels.

ASSEMBLING THE BOX

9 Remove the cramps from the bottom. Check the face side is flush. Plane a long edge square with a smoothing plane. Square one end and trace over the line with a utility knife. Plane the end square.

10 Lay out the parts with the face sides up and the joints well aligned. Secure each joint with a piece of masking tape on the outside

from top to bottom and three shorter pieces at 90 degrees to the first. Assemble the box into its upright form and check that it is square.

11 Mark the size of the box frame on the bottom and make sure it is square. Cut the bottom with a tenon saw and plane to finished size. On it, draw a line 4 mm in from all edges and mark the screw positions: on the sides 85 mm in from the ends and on the ends, centrally across the width. Drill the

MATERIALS*

PART	MATERIAL	LENGTH	NO.
Box side	150 x 16 mm timber P2S	330 mm	2
Box end	150 x 16 mm timber P2S	170 mm	2
Box bottom	100 x 16 mm timber PAR	324 mm	2
Box top	100 x 16 mm timber PAR	324 mm	2
Beading (side)	38 x 25 mm timber PAR	330 mm	2
Beading (end)	38 x 25 mm timber PAR	90 mm	4
Foot	38 x 25 mm timber PAR	25 mm	8
Corner block	125 x 10 mm timber P2S	30 mm	4
Tray side	125 x 10 mm timber P2S	307 mm	2
Tray end	125 x 10 mm timber P2S	143 mm	2
Tray division (long)	125 x 10 mm timber P2S	299 mm	2
Tray division (cross)	125 x 10 mm timber P2S	92 mm	1
Tray bottom	125 x 10 mm timber P2S	303 mm	2

Other: PVA adhesive; 25 mm wide masking tape; epoxy resin adhesive; six 20 mm x No. 4 countersunk wood screws (cross-head or slotted); eight 15 mm panel pins; eight 12 mm x No. 0 countersunk brass wood screws (cross-head or slotted); abrasive paper: one sheet of 120 grit, two sheets each of 180 grit, 240 grit and 600 grit wet-and-dry; 000 grade steel wool; two 25 mm brass butt hinges; jewellery box hasp, staple and fixings; lacquer.

* Timber sizes are nominal. For timber types and sizes, see page 199. Finished dimensions (without feet): length 330 mm; width 170 mm; height 135 mm.

FOOT PATTERN

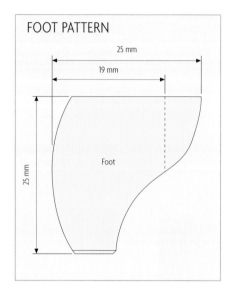

3 mm pilot holes and countersink the holes. Check the fit and adjust if necessary.

12 Put adhesive in the mitres of the sides and ends, and join the parts. Use masking tape to secure the final joint and apply a frame cramp. Make sure the rebates finish flush. Turn the box over, prop it up with scrap material, and put the bottom in position, but do not attach it at this stage.

FITTING THE TOP

13 Mark the length of the two top pieces. Trace over the lines with a utility knife and cut with a tenon saw. Plane back the pieces to the lines, working from the ends towards the centre to avoid chipping out the end grain.

14 Set a sliding bevel to the angle required for joining the top boards to the sides. Hold the pieces in position and mark the width. Set a marking gauge to the width and draw lines on both pieces. Plane to width and the correct bevel angle, checking the fit frequently to ensure a perfect join.

15 The inside face of each board has to be bevelled at 90 degrees to the angle on the

PATTERN FOR ENDS

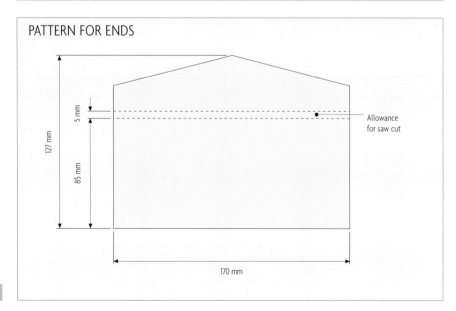

TOOLS

- Jack plane and smoothing plane
- Coping saw or electric jigsaw
- Dowelling jig
- Tenon saw or portable circular saw
- Electric orbital sander
- Combination square and pencil
- Carpenter's square (roofing square)
- Utility knife
- Marking gauge
- Drill bits: 8 mm and 8 mm plug cutter, 5 mm, 3 mm, countersink
- Screwdriver (cross-head or slotted)
- Hammer
- Three 900 mm sash cramps
- One G-cramp
- Flat-bottom spokeshave
- Mitre saw (optional)

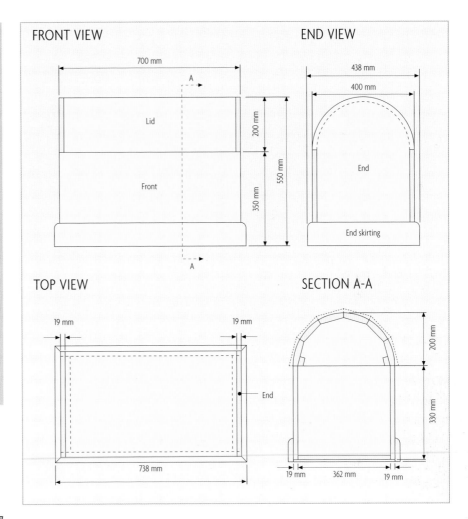

5 Put each board in a vice, set the dowelling jig from the face side and drill the dowel holes 26 mm deep. Use a piece of masking tape on the drill bit as a depth guide.

6 Organize the boards into panels and, working on one panel at a time, spread adhesive on the joining edge of one board and in the holes. Tap in the dowels with a hammer. Spread adhesive on the edge of the next board and bring the boards together. Put scrap timber between the boards and the sash cramps and tighten the cramps. If you overtighten the cramps, the boards will buckle. Place a third cramp over the top of the panel with a block under it to keep the panel flat. Tighten the cramps and clean off any excess adhesive. Join the boards for each panel.

7 When the front, back and bottom are dry, straighten a long edge on each. Mark the

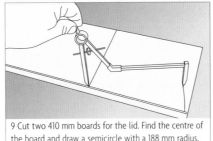

9 Cut two 410 mm boards for the lid. Find the centre of the board and draw a semicircle with a 188 mm radius.

length of each panel and square lines across. Trace over the lines with a utility knife and cut the panel to length. If using a circular saw, clamp a straight edge to the board to guide the saw.

8 Mark the width of the front, back and bottom, and cut each panel slightly over-width. Straighten and square the edges with a jack plane. Put the panels aside, but keep the offcuts for the hinge rails.

MAKING THE LID

9 Cut two 410 mm boards for the lid ends. Find the centre of the board width and square a line across. Use a compass to draw a semicircle with a 188 mm radius. Working from the centre line, use a 60/30 set square to mark angle points on the radius line (see diagram on page 219). Draw lines from the central point to each point and join the

MATERIALS*

PART	MATERIAL	FINISHED LENGTH	NO.
Front	200 x 25 mm timber PAR	700 mm	2
Back	200 x 25 mm timber PAR	700 mm	2
End	200 x 25 mm timber PAR	400 mm	6
Bottom	200 x 25 mm timber PAR	662 mm	2
Lid	125 x 25 mm timber PAR	659 mm	6
Lid ends	225 x 25 mm timber PAR	400 mm	2
Hinge rail	225 x 25 mm timber offcuts	621 mm	2
Skirting (side)	100 x 25 mm timber PAR	738 mm	2
Skirting (end)	100 x 25 mm timber PAR	438 mm	2

Other: PVA adhesive; abrasive paper: two sheets each of 100 grit and 320 grit, three sheets of 180 grit; forty 40 mm x No. 8 countersunk wood screws; ten 30 mm x No. 8 countersunk wood screws; two 20 mm x No. 6 round-head screws with washers; 30 mm pins; twenty-four timber plugs or alternatives (if using 10 mm plugs, change drill bit to suit); two strap hinges with fixings; one hasp and staple with fixings; 300 mm fine chain; two box handles; twenty-eight 50 x 8 mm timber dowels; lacquer; teak oil; 000 grade steel wool.

* Timber sizes given are nominal. For timber types and sizes, see page 199.
  Finished dimensions: length 738 mm; width 438 mm; height 550 mm.

points. Draw parallel lines 19 mm outside the lid shape lines for the timber thickness.

10 Temporarily nail the lid ends together with 30 mm pins. Use a jigsaw to roughly cut them to shape, and plane both pieces back to size with a smoothing plane.

11 On the 125 x 25 mm timber, mark the lengths for the lid boards, leaving a 5 mm gap between each one. Cut out each board with a

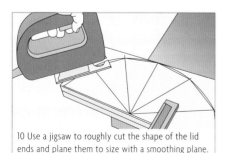
10 Use a jigsaw to roughly cut the shape of the lid ends and plane them to size with a smoothing plane.

tenon saw and leave them all slightly over-length at this stage. Set a sliding bevel to 75 degrees, mark the angle on the joining edges of the boards and continue the lines over the edges. Place each board in a vice and carefully bevel one edge with a plane. Don't bevel both edges yet.

12 Using the lid ends, mark the inner width of each board and gauge a line down the length of the board. Referring to step 11, plane the bevel on the other joining edge of each board, but do not plane the two top boards to width until they are fitted.

13 Measure in 10 mm from the end lines of each board and square lines across. Find the centre of the width and mark the screw position on the line. Drill 8 mm plug holes 6 mm deep. Change to a 5 mm drill bit and drill the boards right through.

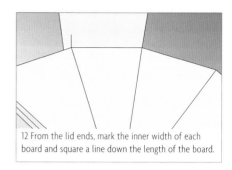
12 From the lid ends, mark the inner width of each board and square a line down the length of the board.

14 Take one lid end and put adhesive on the lowest section on either side. Attach the boards with screws. Then attach these boards to the other lid end. Make sure the lid ends line up with the end marks on the boards and the bevelled edges match the angles on the lid ends. Clean off any excess adhesive. Dry-fit the next boards on either side and make adjustments before attaching them in the same manner. Plane the top two boards to fit exactly before attaching them. Make sure all screws are below the surface of the boards. If there are gaps because the boards are too narrow, plane them down from the underside to get a better fit.

SHAPING THE END PANELS

15 Plane the bottom of the end panels straight and square. On each panel, square a line up the centre. From the bottom, measure 340 mm and square a line across. On this line, draw a semicircle with a radius of 200 mm. Below the line, measure in 19 mm from each side, square a line to the bottom, around the edge and back up the other side. Trace over the straight lines with a utility knife.

16 Carefully cut the curved top with a jigsaw. Then cut the indented sides. Plane back the edges to the knife lines using a smoothing plane. Use a sharp chisel to pare back the corners.

ASSEMBLING THE CHEST

17 At each end of the front panel, mark a

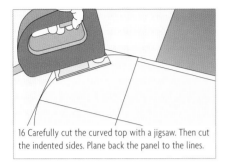

16 Carefully cut the curved top with a jigsaw. Then cut the indented sides. Plane back the panel to the lines.

VIEW OF LID WEB AND COOPER CONSTRUCTION

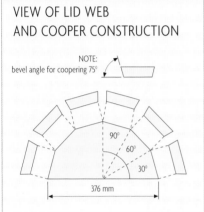

NOTE:
bevel angle for coopering 75°

90°
60°
30°
376 mm

ASSEMBLY

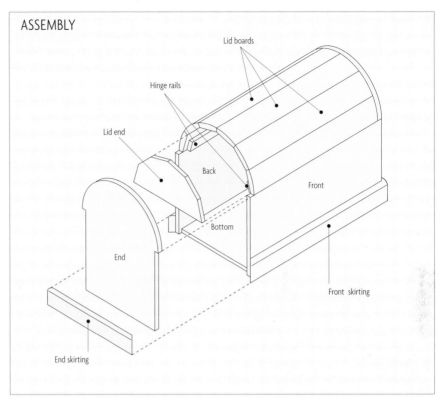

Lid boards

Hinge rails

Lid end

Back

Front

Bottom

End

Front skirting

End skirting

screw hole 50 mm from the top, then three more holes 80 mm apart, the last being 50 mm from the bottom. Find the centre of the bottom edge, mark two screw holes 250 mm on either side of it, then measure out another 250 mm for two more holes. Repeat for the back. On the ends, find the centre of the bottom edge and mark two screw holes 125 mm on either side of it. Check the panels and holes line up exactly and make any adjustments. Drill 8 mm plug holes, 6 mm deep. Change to a 5 mm drill bit and drill the holes right through.

18 Put adhesive on the end of the bottom and bring the end panel into contact with it. Align the panels. Drill 3 mm holes in the bottom and attach the end with 40 mm screws. Clean off the excess adhesive. Then attach the other end and the front and back. Make sure the panels are square. Plane

the front and back to the ends flush with a smoothing plane.

ATTACHING THE SKIRTING

19 Take the skirting timber, hold it against the chest front and mark the length on the skirting, including the mitres. Draw mitres on the edges and across both faces. Trace the lines with a knife before cutting with a tenon saw. Repeat for all skirting. Check the mitres match, and plane if necessary. Use a smoothing plane to round over the top edges.

20 Draw a line 35 mm up from the bottom edge around the entire box. On the front and back, find the centre and measure out 250 mm on either side for the screw holes. On the ends, mark the centre. Drill the 5 mm screw holes and countersink the holes on the inside of the box.

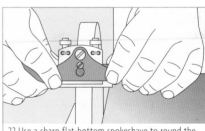

22 Use a sharp flat-bottom spokeshave to round the ends of the box back to the lines.

21 Lay the box on its side and draw a line 80 mm up from the bottom on the ends. Apply adhesive to the box and attach the skirting, lining up the top edge with the 80 mm line. Fix the skirting with 30 mm wood screws and repeat for all skirting.

FITTING THE LID

22 Use a sharp spokeshave to round the ends of the box to the lines. Work from the top of the curve down the sides, not upwards, as the spokeshave will dig in. Then plane the ends of the lid boards flush with the lid ends and check the lid fits between the ends of the box.

23 Cut the hinge rails from the offcuts, glue them to the inside bottom edges of the lid and clamp into place. Plane the rails flush once the adhesive has set.

24 Sit the lid in position and copy the shape of the chest ends on the lid ends. Remove the lid and secure it to a work surface by nailing cleats around it. Plane the lid to a round shape, following the grain, and check the fit often. Finish with an electric sander and 100 grit abrasive paper. Flat spots can be removed by sanding across the grain, but you must finish by sanding with the grain.

FINISHING THE BOX

25 Bend one leaf of each strap hinge to match the curved shape of the top. Attach the

hinges on the back, 90 mm in from each end and at 90 degrees to the hingeing edge. Attach the hasp and staple or use a similar latch. Mark the position of the chest handles below the curved top of the ends to prevent the internal fixings from catching on the lid ends and attach the handles. Using two 20 mm x

No. 6 roundhead screws with washers, attach one end of the chain inside the box on the centre line of the lid end, about 100 mm up from the bottom edge. Fix the other end of the chain to the inside face of the chest end, about 30 mm below the face edge height.

26 Finish the screw holes with plugs made

from 8 mm dowel or by using an 8 mm plug cutter to make your own. Try to match the grain of the chest if you have made plugs from the same timber. Use a smoothing plane to flush the plugs to the surface of the chest after they have been glued in and the adhesive has set.

27 Remove the fittings and the lid. Fill any holes or gaps with wood filler, and steam out bruises in the timber with a damp cloth and hot iron. Sand the chest inside and out, finishing by hand. Apply two coats of lacquer. Use 000 grade steel wool to rub two coats of teak oil into the grain.

BLANKET BOX

Dovetai joints and fine timber ensure this classic blanket box will be a joy to make as well as a useful addition to the household's storage facilities. The boards in each panel are joined with dowels. This is a project for an experienced worker.

MAKING THE PANELS

1 Have the timber cut to its rough size and planed on two faces. Lay the boards on a work surface and select the face sides. Match the boards as best you can for colour and grain pattern. The sides, ends, top and bottom are each composed of three boards. Once the boards are matched, use chalk or crayon to place an arrow-shaped mark over the face of the boards and label each panel. Do not use pencil, as it is harder to remove.

2 Using the jack plane, plane the rough-sawn edges of the boards so they are

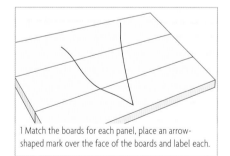

1 Match the boards for each panel, place an arrow-shaped mark over the face of the boards and label each.

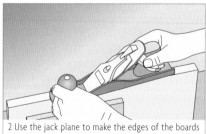

2 Use the jack plane to make the edges of the boards straight and square and remove any marks.

straight and square. Use a combination square to check that the edges are square. Also check the quality of the joints by laying the boards flat and pushing the edges

together, all the time looking for gaps.

3 Take the top and centre boards from one panel. Place them with their joining

TOOLS

- Chalk or crayon
- Tape measure and pencil
- Jack plane
- Combination square and builder's roofing square
- Vice
- Marking gauge
- Dowelling jig
- Electric drill
- Utility knife
- Drill bits: 3 mm, 5 mm, 8 mm, 10 mm
- Hammer or wooden mallet
- Six 1200 mm sash cramps
- Two G-cramps
- Panel saw, portable circular saw or table saw
- Dovetail saw or tenon saw
- Coping saw or jigsaw
- Straight edge
- Sliding bevel
- Bevelled-edge chisels: 25 mm and 12 mm
- Electric router (optional)
- Router bits: 12 mm straight cutting bit (for rebates); 6 mm round-over bit
- Cork sanding block or electric sander
- Mitre box

This blanket box was made from Tasmanian blackwood, the edge beads were stained black, and the box finished with clear lacquer finish. Wrought-iron handles and the tortoiseshell-style escutcheon plate provided finishing touches.

edges and ends flush and back-to-back in a vice. Find the centre of the edges and, using a square and pencil, square a line across both edges. Mark out dowel centres at 150 mm each side of the centre mark. The end panels will need three dowels and the sides, top and bottom five. Set up a marking gauge to the centre of the boards' thickness and draw a line for the dowel centres.

4 Replace the top board with the bottom board of the panel, flush the joining edges of the centre board and bottom board, and mark the dowel centres as described above. Repeat this process until all the dowel centres have been marked out.

5 Set up each board in the vice and use the dowelling jig and 8 mm bit to drill each dowel hole to a depth of 26 mm. Clean

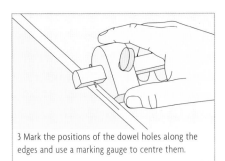

3 Mark the positions of the dowel holes along the edges and use a marking gauge to centre them.

MATERIALS*

PART	MATERIAL	LENGTH	NO.
Side	150 x 25 mm timber P2S	790 mm	6
End	150 x 25 mm timber P2S	440 mm	6
Top	150 x 25 mm timber P2S	770 mm	3
Bottom	150 x 25 mm timber P2S	778 mm	3
Front trim	10 x 10 mm timber	790 mm	2
End trim	10 x 10 mm timber	440 mm	2

Other: Thirty-two 50 x 8 mm diameter timber dowels; PVA adhesive; twelve 40 mm x No. 8 countersunk screws; 15 mm x No. 5 countersunk screws; 30 mm panel pins; three 75 x 20 mm brass butt hinges (for cabinets); box lock (cut type with parrot-beak type catch); escutcheon plate (key hole plate); length of fine chain; two trunk handles; 25 mm wide masking tape; clear lacquer.

* Finished dimensions: length 790 mm; width 440 mm; height 420 mm.

7 Use the builder's roofing square and a straight edge to square up the panels.

around each hole to remove any torn grain, which can hold the panels apart slightly and reduce the strength of the joint. Place a small amount of adhesive into each hole and use a pencil to spread it around the perimeter. This will also help to get rid of any excess adhesive. Place a bead of adhesive along the joining edges of the board and spread it to ensure maximum coverage of the joint. Insert the dowels in the holes and hammer them home just enough so that a little adhesive is expressed from around the dowel. Bring the two boards together, tapping them using a hammer and block to protect the edges of the timber from damage. Turn the boards over and repeat the process to attach the third board.

6 Place the panel into the sash cramps with the face side up, and tighten the screws to bring the joint completely together. Wipe off any excess adhesive with a clean rag. It should be possible to fit two panels into each pair of sash cramps. If the panels begin to buckle under the pressure of clamping, reduce the pressure slightly and place some weights on top of the panels, or alternatively

place a third sash cramp across the top of the panel to keep it level. Leave the panels in the cramps overnight to dry.

7 Bring the side and end panels to the correct sizes. Plane one edge of the panel straight and square. From this straight edge mark out carefully the width and length of the panel using the roofing square to form the ends and a straight edge for the other long edge of the panels. Score the pencil lines across the end grain of the faces and edges with a utility knife to prevent any grain breakout when you are cutting the material. Plane from each edge towards the centre to avoid chipping the edges. Use a circular saw and straight edge or a table saw to bring the panels close to their finished sizes. Place each pair of panels in the vice together and plane the edges flush. Make sure the panels are square.

JOINING SIDES AND ENDS

8 Now set out the dovetails (see pages 226–227). Use a sharp pencil and do not cut anything until you are completely sure that the set-out is correct. Don't forget to mark

the waste areas clearly and check by holding the parts together that all the marked waste areas on one piece will be filled by a corresponding pin on the joining piece. Mark the cross-grain lines with a utility knife to prevent chipping out.

9 Use a tenon saw or dovetail saw to cut down the sides of the tail sockets. Keep to the waste side of the line. Next use a jigsaw or coping saw to remove the bulk of the waste from the tail sockets. Clamp the material to a work surface, making sure the tail sockets are supported by the bench. Place the cutting edge of the 25 mm bevelled-edge chisel neatly in the line made by the utility knife. Angle the chisel slightly so you undercut the joint and, with the aid of a hammer or mallet, chisel down to about half the thickness of the timber. Chisel out all the tail sockets on the same side, and then turn the panel over and repeat the cut from the opposite side. Use the 25 mm chisel to pare down the sides of the tail sockets to remove most of the saw-cut marks.

10 Take one side panel and lay it on a flat surface. Stand one end panel on the side panel as if you were joining them together. Align the joints and trace around the tail sockets with a sharp pencil to give you the exact shape for the pin sockets, as they may be slightly different from what you marked out originally. Do this for all the dovetail

indoor

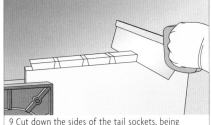

9 Cut down the sides of the tail sockets, being careful to keep to the waste side of the line.

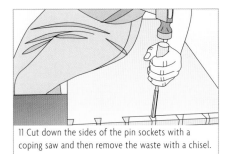

11 Cut down the sides of the pin sockets with a coping saw and then remove the waste with a chisel.

joints. Place the side panel in the vice and cut down the sides of the pin sockets as for the tail sockets with the tenon saw or dovetail saw, keeping to the waste side of the line and following the lines you have just made. Do not go past the knife marks.

11 Remove the waste from the pin sockets with a coping saw, taking care not to go past the knife lines. Lay the end panel down on the work surface as you did the side panel, and chisel out the waste. Test the fitting of the joints. Make any adjustments necessary. Only a highly skilled tradesperson will get the joints to fit perfectly without the need for some adjustment. Tap the joints gently together using a hammer or mallet and a block of wood to protect the faces of the timber from damage. If the half-pin joints are too tight the timber may split along the grain, so take great care.

12 Take the components apart and apply adhesive to the internal faces of the joints.

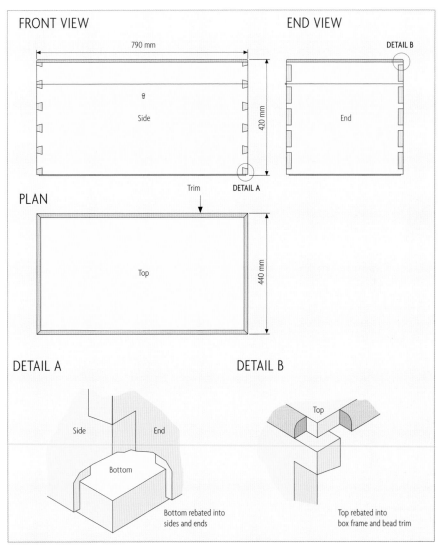

FRONT VIEW

790 mm

420 mm

Side

Trim

DETAIL A

END VIEW

DETAIL B

End

PLAN

440 mm

Top

DETAIL A

Side   End

Bottom

Bottom rebated into
sides and ends

DETAIL B

Top

Top rebated into
box frame and bead trim

Bring the joints together again with the mallet and block of wood. Once all the joints are together, apply a light pressure with the sash cramps to bring them fully together. Use timber blocks to protect the face of the timber, but keep the blocks back from the joints so they pull up tight. Wipe off excess adhesive with a wet rag. Check the box frame is square by measuring the diagonals. Stand the box frame to one side and allow the adhesive to dry for twenty-four hours.

ADDING TOP AND BOTTOM

13 While the box frame is drying, prepare the top panel following the method described in step 7, bringing it to 780 mm in length, which is 10 mm longer than its finished size. Measure the inside dimensions of the box frame and transfer them to the underside of the top, where there will be a rebate to allow the top to sit down over the frame.

14 Clamp the top face down to a suitable work surface. Using a router and rebating bit,

EXPLODED VIEW

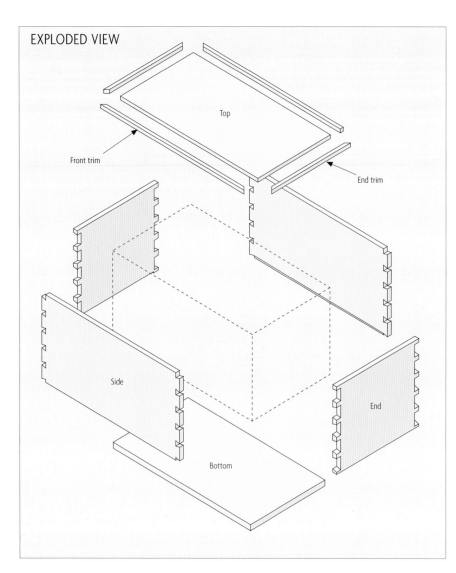

Front trim

Top

End trim

Side

End

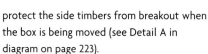

Bottom

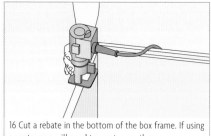

16 Cut a rebate in the bottom of the box frame. If using a router you will need to run two or three passes.

following wheel will run around the inside perimeter of the box. If you don't have a following wheel, run a fence along the outer perimeter of the box but the direction of feed for the router will have to be reversed and it will have to be lowered carefully over the edge of the box to avoid mishaps. You must be very careful to ensure the cutter stops near the end of the box and does not pass through the end of it. With the rebates cut, square out the rounded corners using a 25 mm chisel and hammer.

17 Check that the top and bottom edges of the frame sides are flush at the joints. If they are not flush use a smoothing plane to flush them off. Use a good bead of adhesive in the rebate for the bottom panel. Place the bottom in the rebate, insert the 40 mm x No. 8 screws and drive them into position just below the surface. Use a wet rag to clean off any excess adhesive.

18 Place a bead of adhesive in the rebate of the top and spread it evenly across both faces of the joint. With a wet rag, clean off any excess adhesive running down the inside face of the box. Lay the top in position and hold it down with sash cramps. While it is in the cramps, insert 30 mm panel pins through the sides and into the top to secure the joint. The pins should be located 8 mm down from the top edge and angled slightly to go into the top. Leave the unit overnight to dry.

cut a rebate in the underside of the top 9 mm deep and back to the inside dimension lines marked out in step 13. Be sure to cut across the end grain first.

15 Bring the bottom to its exact size as described in step 7. On the underside, drill four 5 mm screw holes 9 mm in from each side edge, and two 5 mm screw holes 9 mm in from each end edge. Countersink the holes. When the bottom is fixed it should sit 2 mm below the bottom edges of the box to

protect the side timbers from breakout when the box is being moved (see Detail A in diagram on page 223).

16 Cut a rebate in the bottom of the box frame for the bottom of the box. If using a router, make two or three passes as the amount of material to be removed is quite large. Set the cutter depth to 17 mm and, if you have one, a following-wheel width of cut to 4 mm (gradually increase this width until you have a rebate width of 13 mm). The

indoor

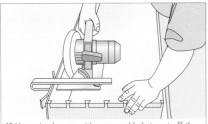

19 Use a circular saw with a narrow blade to cut off the lid. Attach a straight edge or rip guide to the saw.

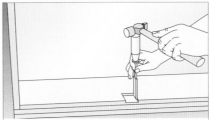

22 Lay the box with the front face down on a work surface and mark out the mortise for the lock.

MAKING THE LID

19 Use a combination square to mark the line where the lid will be cut off. Draw the line around the entire outside of the box. The saw cut should pass through the centre of the first pin (see diagram on page 223). Use a portable circular saw with a narrow blade to make the cut and use a straight edge or a rip guide attached to the saw to guide the saw along the cutting line.

20 Plane the closing edges of the lid and the box so that they are smooth and even, and check that they fit neatly together. Take a brass butt hinge, hold it on the back edge of the box flush with one end and mark the position one hinge length in from the end. Move the hinge to this mark and mark off the length of the hinge. Do this at both ends of the hinging edge. The centre hinge should be evenly spaced between the two outer hinges. Hold the lid up against the box in the open position and transfer the hinge marks to the lid. Square the lines across the edge using a combination square. Set the combination square to half the width of the open hinge and mark off the width of the hinge mortise. Use a utility knife to cut across the end grain of the hinge mortise, and then use a chisel or router to remove the waste to a depth equal to the thickness of the hinge leaf. Use the screws provided or 15 mm x No. 5 countersunk screws to fix the hinges into position.

FINISHING

21 To fit the lock, mark a centre line on the top edge at the front of the box and transfer the line using a square and pencil across the edge and down the inner and outer faces. Measure the position of the keyhole and transfer these measurements to the centre line on the face. Double-check the position of the keyhole, and select an appropriate size of drill bit to drill the keyhole. The size of the bit will be determined by the type of keyhole plate or escutcheon.

22 Lay the box with the front face down on a work surface and continue to mark out the mortise for the lock. It is best to hold the lock flush to the top edge and trace around the perimeter of the lock with a sharp pencil and across the grain with a utility knife. The keyholes of some locks are off-centre, so check before setting this lock out.

23 Fit the lid to the box and make any adjustments necessary to ensure a good fit. Mark the position of the striker plate of the lock on the lid and attach it. Now fit the escutcheon plate to the front of the box.

24 Fit a piece of fine chain to the inside of the lid to run between the lid and the main frame to prevent the lid opening back too far and bursting the hinges and dovetails.

25 Cut a rebate around the edge of the top. If using a router, set the fence at 10 mm depth of cut and 10 mm width of cut. Cut across the ends first and then along the sides. Dress up some scrap material on one face and one edge to 11 x 11 mm. Hold it in the rebate and mark the inside corners of the rebates. Cut the mitres with a tenon saw and mitre box if you have one. Use a utility knife to mark the mitres on the trim pieces and cut.

26 Run a bead of adhesive in the rebate, place the trim in position and fasten it with masking tape. When the adhesive has set, plane the excess trim flush with the sides and top of the lid. Place a 6 mm round-over bit in the router and round over the top edges of the lid.

27 Fit the handles to the two ends of the box, placing them in the centre and a little towards the top. Then remove the handles, lock and hinge, and use an orbital sander with 120 grit abrasive paper to sand the entire box inside and out. Clean out the sanding dust from the box using a vaccuum cleaner.

28 Finish the box with clear lacquer, or as desired, and make sure you seal the inside faces as well. Refit the hardware to the box.

CUTTING REBATES WITH A ROUTER

When using a router with a straight cutting bit to make the rebates, use a backing piece to prevent chipping out the top and bottom edges when the bit comes through. For the best results, don't cut the full depth of the rebate the first time. Take off half the amount required in the first pass, adjust the router and finish the rebate to the correct depth in the second pass.

MAKING DOVETAIL JOINTS

1 Decide which component will have the tails and which the pins. Mark them clearly.

2 Calculate the pin size and the number of pins. Pins and half pins* should be two-thirds the thickness of the material; the width of the tails should be about three to four times the thickness of the material. As our material is 19 mm thick:

pin width = 19 x $^2/_3$ = 12 mm (approx.)

tail width = 3 x 19 = 60 mm (approx.)

or = 4 x 19 = 80 mm (approx.)

To work out the number of tails, divide the width of the material (410 mm) by 60 or 80:

410 ÷ 60 = 6.8, say 7 tails or

410 ÷ 80 = 5.1, say 5 tails.

We will use 5 tails.

3 Take the component that is to have the pins, and set out half pins (12 mm wide) at either end. Using a combination square and pencil, mark a centre line down each half pin.

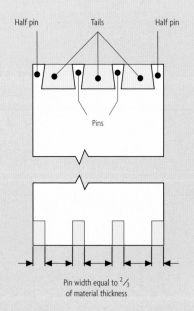

Half pin   Tails   Half pin

Pins

Pin width equal to $^2/_3$ of material thickness

4 Take a rule and set it diagonally across the component. Move it until it is positioned with one number on each of the half-pin centre lines. Divide the distance by the number of tails required (in this example, 3).

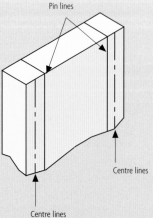

Pin lines

Centre lines

Centre lines

5 Mark these points: they will be the centre-line positions for the full pins. Use a square to transfer them to the end of the component, measure 6 mm each side to indicate the full pins and square the lines down the face.

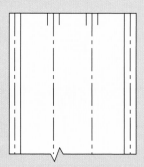

6 Set up a pitch of 1:6 or 1:8 on the pin material.

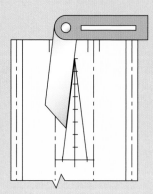

7 Set up a sliding bevel to these pitch angles and mark the angle across the end grain.

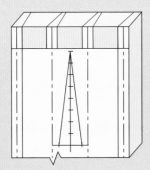

8 Mark the thickness of the adjoining stock across the end of each piece where the joint is to be formed.

9 Use the sliding bevel to mark the pitch of the pins. Mark out the tail sockets as waste. Transfer these marks to the opposite side of the material. Use a utility knife to cut the fibres across at the tail sockets only. Remove the waste in the tail sockets.

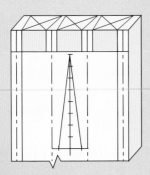

10 Stand the pin piece on its end on top of the tail piece flush with the end as shown. With a sharp pencil, trace around the pins. Now transfer the marks to the opposite side of the tail piece. Mark the pin-socket waste and use a utility knife to cut across the grain of the pin socket on both sides and edges of the material and remove the waste.

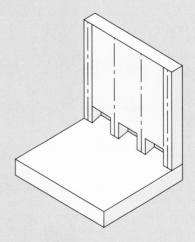

* Half pins are angled on one side only. They are the same width as the pins.

Mark the positions of the tails by drawing around the pins with a knife.

The simple dovetail joint can be an attractive feature on wooden boxes.

WINDOW SEAT WITH MOULDED FRONT

This window seat with decorative moulding has been made to fit into a bay window, but you can alter it to suit your window dimensions and shape. It has a large capacity for storage, with a hinged lid for convenient access.

CUTTING THE PIECES

1 Measure your window and adjust the measurements and side angles to suit. Lay the MDF on trestles. Mark out the main parts using the rule, carpenter's square and pencil. Draw the longest pieces near the edges so they can be cut first. Mark all edges to be mitred with a cross. Make sure the parts are square. Leave 5 mm between them for saw cuts.

2 Clamp a straight edge to the board to guide the circular saw and cut the parts to width. Don't cut the mitres.

3 Mark the mitre ends on the bottom and cut at 45 degrees using a circular saw. Measure the width of the mitred end and make sure that it matches the width of the side.

4 On the 489 mm wide board, square a line across one end and cut a mitre. Mark the width of the side and cut the panel. Repeat for the other side. On each side panel, draw a line 37 mm from the bottom edge and mark the screw holes, 80 mm from each end and one in the centre. Drill and countersink the 5 mm holes. Attach the sides to the bottom using 40 mm chipboard screws. Plane the sides flush with the bottom at the front and back.

5 Place the box frame face down and measure the length of the back. Mark the length on the back panel, including the mitres, and cut the panel a millimetre oversize. Draw lines 11 mm in from either end and mark three screw holes 60 mm from the top and the bottom, and one in the centre. Carefully drill the holes at an angle of 45 degrees.

Whether made to fit a bay window or used as a bench box to sit below a conventional window, this seat will be a practical addition to your home. The decorative moulding can be painted to contrast.

MATERIALS*

PART	MATERIAL	LENGTH	WIDTH	NO.
Top (left, right)	16 mm MDF	435 mm	405 mm	2
Lid	16 mm MDF	1327 mm	405 mm	1
Front	16 mm MDF	2104 mm	489 mm	1
Side	16 mm MDF	516 mm	489 mm	2
Back	16 mm MDF	1366 mm	489 mm	1
Bottom	16 mm MDF	2026 mm	353 mm	1
Front skirting	16 mm MDF	2162 mm	90 mm	1
Side skirting	16 mm MDF	545 mm	90 mm	2
Front glue block	16 mm MDF	443 mm	40 mm	2
Rear glue block	16 mm MDF	443 mm	60 mm	2
Stiffening rail	16 mm MDF	1321 mm	70 mm	1
Front frame (centre)	19 mm moulding	982 mm	40 mm	2
Front frame (verticals)	19 mm moulding	279 mm	40 mm	6
Front frame (sides)	19 mm moulding	380 mm	40 mm	4
Front panel (centre)	16 mm MDF	740 mm	90 mm	1
Front panel (sides)	16 mm MDF	138 mm	90 mm	2
Cleat (rear)	16 mm MDF	1200 mm	29 mm	1
Cleat (front)	16 mm MDF	900 mm	29 mm	2

Other: Three 75 mm butt hinges (semi-recessed); forty-five 25 mm x No. 6 countersunk screws (cross-head or slotted); skirting; six 15 mm x No. 6 countersunk screws (cross-head or slotted); thirty-four 40 mm chipboard screws; sixteen 40 mm nails; panel pins: twenty-eight 30 mm and six 25 mm; PVA adhesive; abrasive paper: two sheets of 180 grit and one sheet each of 120 and 240 grit; MDF sealer undercoat; paint; two-part plastic filler; wood filler.

* Finished dimensions: length 2197 mm; width 421 mm; height 505 mm. Don't pre-cut the components to their exact lengths until you need them.

TOOLS

- Portable circular saw
- Electric drill
- Tenon saw
- Screwdriver (cross-head or slotted)
- Folding rule or tape measure
- Combination square
- Two quick-release F-clamps
- Filler knife and nail punch
- Hammer
- Jack plane and smoothing plane
- Bench hook and straight edge
- Utility knife
- Mitre saw or mitre box
- Set of trestles (optional)
- Orbital electric sander (optional)
- Drill bits: 5 mm, 3 mm, 2 mm, countersink
- Carpenter's square

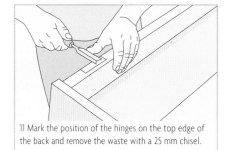

11 Mark the position of the hinges on the top edge of the back and remove the waste with a 25 mm chisel.

6 Draw a line 37 mm from the bottom edge along the back panel and mark the five screw holes, 100 mm in from each end, then 250 mm in, and one in the centre. Drill the 5 mm pilot holes. Apply adhesive to the edges, position the back on the box frame and attach using 40 mm chipboard screws. Cut out the front panel and attach it. Plane all the joints flush with a smoothing plane.

7 Cut four glue blocks and mitre one long edge of each. Plane the mitred edge and glue the blocks in place.

8 Cut the stiffening rail and mitre one end. Hold the rail in place and mark off the length. Cut the other mitre. Attach with eight 25 mm x No. 6 screws and PVA adhesive and clamp in place. Make sure it is flush with the top of the back panel.

9 Turn the box on its back. Cut the three cleats, clamp them in place and attach them with adhesive and three 25 mm x No. 6 screws in each front cleat and four screws in the rear one. Turn the box upright. Insert two evenly spaced screws through the bottom into each front cleat, and three screws into the rear cleat.

FITTING THE LID

10 Mark and cut out the top panels so they overhang 20 mm at the sides and front. Draw

FRONT VIEW

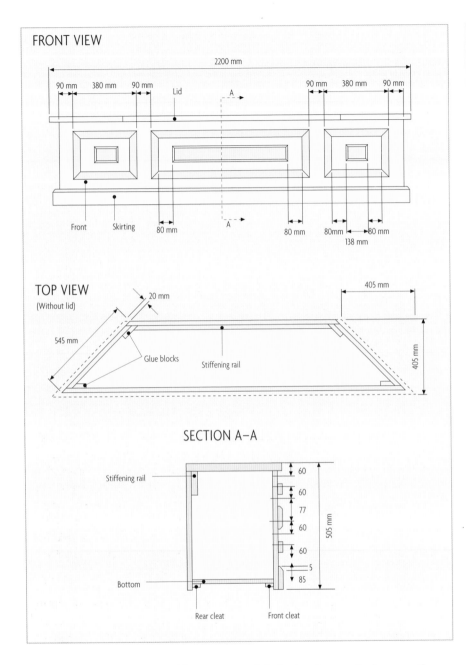

2200 mm

90 mm · 380 mm · 90 mm · Lid · A · 90 mm · 380 mm · 90 mm

Front · Skirting · 80 mm · A · 80 mm · 80mm · 80 mm · 138 mm

TOP VIEW
(Without lid)

20 mm · 405 mm · 545 mm · 405 mm · Glue blocks · Stiffening rail

SECTION A–A

Stiffening rail · 60 · 60 · 77 · 60 · 505 mm · 60 · 5 · 85 · Bottom · Rear cleat · Front cleat

The decorative moulding can be painted to contrast the box.

attach the lid with one screw per hinge. Stand the box upright and check the fit before inserting the remaining screws.

FINISHING THE BOX

12 From the MDF offcuts, cut the side skirting overlength. Cut a mitre at one end, hold the skirting in place, and mark and cut the other mitre. Attach the side skirting using PVA adhesive and three 25 mm x No. 6 screws from the inside of the box, making sure the front of the mitre is flush with the front of the box and the screws are countersunk. (Only attach the skirting temporarily if you plan to bevel the edges.) Mark and cut the front skirting and attach it from the inside of the box using five screws evenly spaced. If required, remove the skirting and bevel or round over the top edge and corners. Sand with 120 grit abrasive paper.

13 Lay the box on its back and mark out the size and position of the moulding. Cut out the vertical frame parts (a mitre box or mitre saw will help) and attach to the box with 30 mm panel pins and PVA adhesive. Make sure all parts are parallel to each other. From

a line 28 mm in from the side and front edges of each top. Attach the tops to the sides and front with 40 mm nails and adhesive.

11 Position two hinges one hinge length in from either end of the lid, and the third in the middle. Mark the hinges on the top edge

of the back and square the lines over the edge. Mark the width of the leaf on the back and remove the waste with a 25 mm chisel. Position the hinges, drill the 2 mm holes, and attach with 25 mm x No. 6 screws. Place the box on its back on scrap 19 mm material and align the lid. Drill 2 mm holes in the lid and

indoor

EXPLODED VIEW

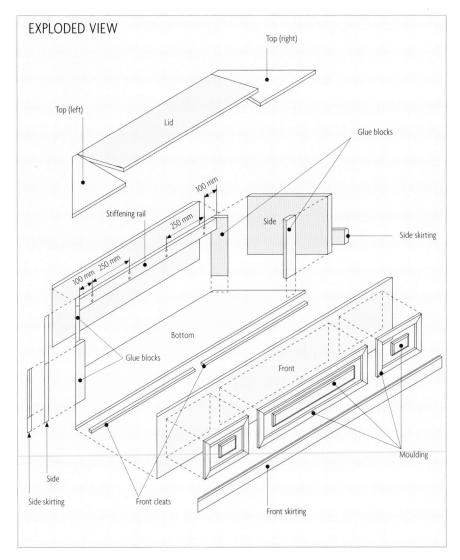

Top (left)

Top (right)

Lid

Stiffening rail

100 mm

250 mm

100 mm 250 mm

Side

Side skirting

Glue blocks

Bottom

Glue blocks

Front

Side

Side skirting

Front cleats

Front skirting

Moulding

CORNER DETAILS

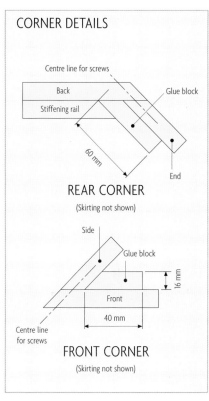

Centre line for screws

Back

Glue block

Stiffening rail

60 mm

End

REAR CORNER
(Skirting not shown)

Side

Glue block

16 mm

Front

40 mm

Centre line
for screws

FRONT CORNER
(Skirting not shown)

coat it. Use 120 grit abrasive paper to sand back the exposed edges of the board to a smooth finish. Don't sand the surface of the MDF as it tends to 'fur up' after the paint has been applied if sanded too heavily. Apply one coat of MDF sealer, paying particular attention to the edges. When the sealer is dry, use 180 grit abrasive paper to sand it back to a smooth finish.

15 Apply the first coat of paint, allow to dry and sand back with 240 grit abrasive paper. Then apply the second coat. If you need to, sand the box again with 240 grit abrasive before applying a third coat of paint.

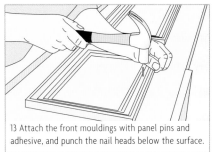

13 Attach the front mouldings with panel pins and adhesive, and punch the nail heads below the surface.

the vertical parts, mark the length of the horizontal pieces. Cut the mitres and attach

the horizontal frame parts. Cut the centre panels from the 16 mm MDF and attach them using the 25 mm panel pins and adhesive. Punch the nail heads and fill holes with wood filler.

14 Use two-part epoxy filler to fill all the holes. Punch the nail heads below the surface of the box. This is very important as steel reacts with acrylic paint and will show through as a brown spot on the surface of the paint, no matter how many times you

MINIATURE TREASURE BOX

The construction of this beautiful treasure box is based on neat mitre joints and rebates. Contrasting timber is used for the frames and beading, and a feature panel on the lid completes the elegant and simple design.

PREPARATION

1 Plane the 100 x 16 mm timber to 91 x 12 mm. Cut two pieces 280 mm long for the bottom. Place adhesive on one long edge of each and clamp together with quick-release clamps. Make sure the face sides are flush. Wipe off excess adhesive with a wet rag. Put the panel aside to dry.

2 For the sides and ends, straighten a long edge of the remaining 91 x 12 mm timber with a jack plane, select a face side and mark it. Mark the width using a marking gauge and plane the timber to finished width.

3 Measure and mark the length of the sides and ends, leaving a 5 mm allowance for the saw cuts. Square the lines with a combination square and pencil. Trace over the lines with a utility knife to cut the cross-grain fibres. Clamp the board or use a bench hook to hold it steady and cut the parts slightly overlength on the waste side of the lines.

4 Place the end pieces face sides together in a vice or against a bench hook, and plane one end square and back to the knife lines. Turn the pieces over and plane the other end

back to the lines. Use a sharp, fine-set plane and plane from each edge of the piece towards the centre so that you don't chip out the end grain.

5 Place the sides face down and draw lines 12 mm in from the knife lines for the rebates. Continue the lines over the edges 8 mm for the depth. Set a marking gauge to 8 mm, draw a line from the inside across the ends of the sides and to the

12 mm lines or place an end piece on the edge of the side and mark the rebate width from the end panel. This allows for size or dressing variations. Trace over the lines with a utility knife and cut the shoulder lines of the rebate to depth using a tenon saw. Place the side in the vice and pare down the rebate using a 25 mm bevelled-edge chisel. Clamp the side to a work surface and finish off the rebates. Repeat for all side rebates.

MATERIALS*

PART	MATERIAL	FINISHED LENGTH	NO.
Side	100 x 16 mm timber PAR	280 mm	2
End	100 x 16 mm timber PAR	152 mm	2
Bottom	100 x 16 mm timber PAR	272 mm	2
Top frame (side)	125 x 25 mm timber PAR	300 mm	2
Top frame (end)	125 x 25 mm timber PAR	200 mm	2
Top panel	100 x 25 mm timber PAR	192 mm	1
Beading (side)	125 x 25 mm timber PAR	198 mm	2
Beading (end)	125 x 25 mm timber PAR	100 mm	2
Lid rail (side)	125 x 25 mm timber PAR	256 mm	2
Lid rail (end)	125 x 25 mm timber PAR	137 mm	2
Bottom frame (side)	100 x 25 mm timber PAR	320 mm	2
Bottom frame (end)	100 x 25 mm timber PAR	200 mm	2

Other: PVA adhesive; six 25 mm x No. 6 countersunk steel wood screws (cross-head or slotted); six 20 mm x No. 5 countersunk steel wood screws (cross-head or slotted); ten 15 mm panel pins; clear lacquer; wood filler (to match timber colour); 00 grade steel wool; abrasive paper: one sheet of 180 grit, one sheet of 240 grit and one sheet of 600 grit wet-and-dry.

* Timber sizes given are nominal, see page 199. For this project, you will need: 1500 x 100 x 16 mm timber PAR (main box); 1800 x 125 x 25 mm timber PAR (frames, beading); 300 x 100 x 25 mm timber (top panel). Finished dimensions of box: length 320 mm; width 200 mm; height 131 mm.

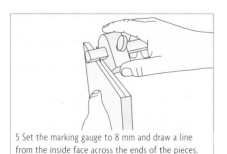

5 Set the marking gauge to 8 mm and draw a line from the inside face across the ends of the pieces.

6 Cut the rebates on the bottom edges of the sides and ends to a width of 12 mm and depth of 8 mm using a rebate plane or a router.

7 Plane the face of the bottom panel flush with a smoothing plane if necessary. Plane one long edge of the bottom straight and square. Use a marking gauge or combination square to mark the width on the face side. Cut on the waste side of the lines with a panel saw or circular saw and plane the bottom panel to width. Mark off the 272 mm panel length, square the lines across, and trace over the lines with a utility knife. Cut the panel to length, and plane the edges to the knife lines with a smoothing plane.

ASSEMBLING THE BOX

8 Practise fitting the joints and check the box is square by measuring the diagonals. Check the bottom fits and make any adjustments. Sand all inside faces with 180 grit abrasive paper.

9 On the outer face of the bottom panel, draw a line 6 mm from the edges. Mark drilling positions on the sides 80 mm in from the ends and centrally across the width on the ends. Drill 4 mm screw holes, angling them to the outside, and countersink the holes.

10 Apply adhesive to the adjoining rebates on the side and end pieces and spread it evenly with your finger. With their bottom edges facing up, bring the sides and ends together. Place a quick-release clamp at each end and one from end to end, using scrap material between the clamps and the panels to protect the timber. Place the bottom panel in the rebates and square up the box. Drill 2 mm pilot holes in the box through the bottom. Insert six 20 mm x No. 5 screws. Place the box aside to dry.

The main body of this box was made in rock maple; padauk was used for the contrasting frames and beading, and the top panel is a lovely piece of bird's eye maple. The box is finished with three coats of clear, semi-gloss lacquer.

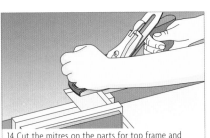

13 Mark the bevel of the top face, clamp the timber over the edge of a work surface and plane the bevel.

THE TOP FRAME

11 Take the 125 x 25 mm timber and plane it down to 115 x 19 mm. Cut a piece 1100 mm long. Using a marking gauge set to 66 mm, mark a line on both faces of the piece. Cut slightly overwidth using a panel saw or circular saw with a ripping guide, and plane to width with a jack plane.

12 Cut a rebate 16 mm wide and 12 mm deep on the inner edge of the top face of this piece.

13 From the bottom face, draw a line 5 mm along the outer edges to mark the bevel of the top face. Fasten the timber over the edge of a work surface and plane the bevel.

14 Mark the length of the frame ends and sides on the outer edge. Use a combination square to draw mitres on the bottom face and return the lines over the edges. Mark the mitres in the rebates. Mark the joint across the bevelled face with a straight edge. Trace over the lines with a knife. Use a tenon saw

MAKING MITRES

A mitre joint can be hard to cut, but mitre saws, electric drop saws and combination mitre saws can make the task easier. Mitres cut by hand will need to be planed back for a perfect fit. Use a bench hook with a fence set at 45 degrees as a guide for the plane.

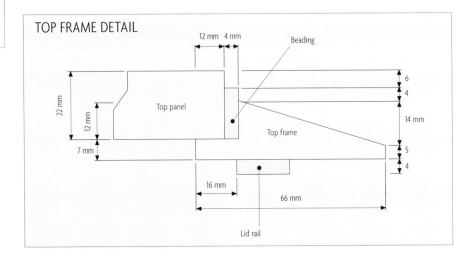

TOP FRAME DETAIL

to cut the mitres and plane back to the lines, regularly checking the joint fit.

15 Place some adhesive on the adjoining mitres and rub it in well. Apply a little more adhesive to the mitres and bring the parts together in a frame cramp. Make sure all the joint faces are flush, and remove any excess adhesive with a wet rag.

THE BOTTOM FRAME

16 Take the offcut timber from the top frame and plane a face side and a long edge

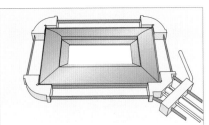

15 Place some adhesive in the adjoining mitres and bring the top frame together in a frame cramp.

straight and flat. Using a marking gauge, draw a line 38 mm in from the edge along the length of the timber and plane to width with a jack plane. Gauge a 12 mm line around the edges and plane the piece to thickness. Mark off the length of the sides and ends, allowing space for mitres and saw cuts. Repeat the method described in steps 14 and 15 to join and finish the bottom frame.

MAKING THE BEADING

17 From the remaining frame timber, rip cut three strips 5–6 mm thick with a circular saw or panel saw and finish to 16 x 4 mm with a jack plane. Plane the fourth strip to 19 x 4 mm for the frame rails that will be used under the lid to locate it.

18 Hold beading in place and mark the lengths. Mark the mitres on the ends and square the lines across the face sides. Trace over the lines with a utility knife and cut the

14 Cut the mitres on the parts for top frame and plane the mitres back to the knife lines.

mitres with a tenon saw. If necessary, trim the mitres carefully with a 25 mm chisel.

FITTING THE TOP PANEL

19 Take the rough-sawn timber for the top panel and plane a face side and edge with a plane. Set a marking gauge to 22 mm, draw lines along all the edges and plane the panel to thickness. Select the portion of timber to be used by moving the top frame over the face side and trace the position with a pencil. Cut the panel to a rough size with a tenon saw. Plane one side and end square. With the beading in place, use the frame to mark the exact size of the top panel. Square the lines across the face of the top panel and over the edges. Plane the panel to length and width, planing a slight bevel on the edges as this will help with locating the fit.

20 Apply adhesive to the adjoining edges of the beading and place them in the rebates. Apply adhesive to the rebate, spread it evenly across the bottom and sides, and clamp the top panel in place.

ASSEMBLING THE BOX

21 Round over or mould the top outside edge of the bottom frame with careful planing and sanding or by using a round-over bit in a router.

22 Place the box open end down and position the bottom frame evenly over the box base so that the overhang is equal on all sides. Mark the position and set out the screw positions following the diagram on page 236. Drill 4 mm pilot holes in the bottom frame and countersink the holes. Place the frame in position and drill 2 mm pilot holes in the box for the screws. Insert the six 25 mm x No. 6 screws and tighten them.

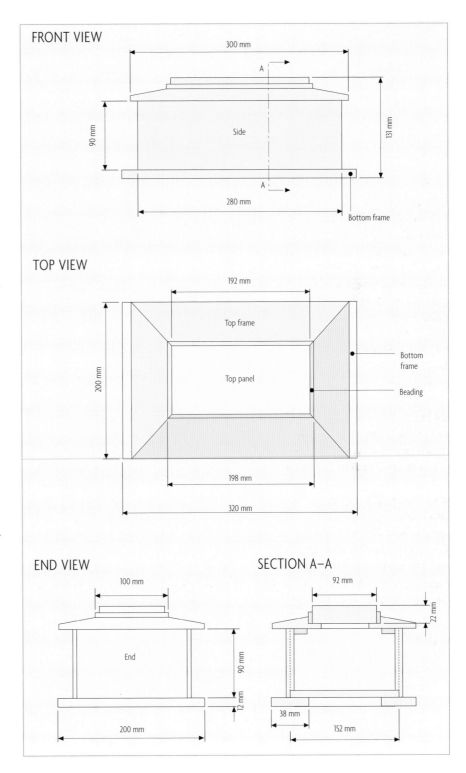

TOOLS

- Tape measure
- Jack plane or smoothing plane
- Marking gauge
- Utility or marking knife
- Tenon saw
- Panel saw or portable circular saw
- Chisel: 25 mm bevelled-edge
- Combination square and pencil
- Rebate plane or router with a 12 mm straight cutting bit
- Electric drill
- Drill bit: 4 mm, countersink
- Mitre box and mitre square (optional)
- Frame cramps
- Three quick-release cramps: 300 mm
- Cork sanding block or electric sander
- Screwdriver (cross-head or slotted)
- Fine nail punch and cabinet scraper

23 Measure the opening of the box, reduce the size by 2 mm all around and draw a rectangle of this size on the underside of the lid to position the lid rails. Take the 19 x 4 mm strip and mark the length of the lid rails, including mitres for the corners. Trace the lines with a utility knife before cutting the rails with a tenon saw. Fix the rails in place with 15 mm panel pins, and

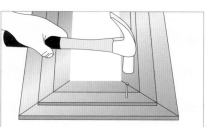

23 Fix the lid rails into place using 15 mm panel pins, and punch the pins below the surface of the timber.

punch the pins below the surface of the timber.

FINISHING

24 Remove the bottom frame from the box and sand all faces carefully with 180 grit abrasive paper. Use a damp rag to lightly dampen the surface of the timber after the first sanding and allow it to dry before sanding all over with 240 grit paper. Use a cabinet scraper to remove any blemishes, bruises and scratches. An iron and wet rag can be used to steam out small scratches and dents. Fill gaps with appropriate wood filler. Do not use wood glue and dust, as the adhesive can stain the timber and show under the lacquer.

25 Apply a semi-gloss clear lacquer to finish the box. You may also use a water-based acrylic lacquer, but you must use an acrylic thinner to extend its drying time in hot weather as this will give you a better finish. Make sure you follow the manufacturer's instructions and use a good-quality paintbrush. Apply a coat of lacquer to all the

inside surfaces and leave to dry. Sand back with 240 grit abrasive paper and apply a second coat. Finish the inside faces before lacquering the outside. For a super-smooth surface finish on the outside, sand the surface well with 600 grit wet-and-dry abrasive paper, then with 00 grade steel wool. Dust well before applying the third coat of lacquer.

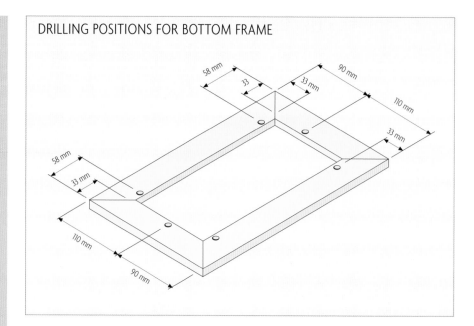

DRILLING POSITIONS FOR BOTTOM FRAME

58 mm
33
33 mm
90 mm
110 mm
33 mm
58 mm
33 mm
110 mm
90 mm

SEWING CHEST WITH UPHOLSTERED LID

This versatile chest has a tray attached with a hinge and pivot bars, and a front panel that folds down for easy access. Once the pieces are cut to size, this project is quick and easy to assemble.

PREPARATION

1 Mark the main chest parts on the 16 mm MDF using a tape measure, pencil and a straight edge for the larger pieces and a combination square and pencil for the smaller ones. Leave a 5 mm space between each piece for the saw cuts. Check the pieces are square by measuring the diagonals. With a straight edge clamped to the board, cut the parts a little oversize and use a smoothing plane to bring them to finished sizes. Plane the edges straight and square.

2 Set out the screw holes using a combination square to draw lines 8 mm in from the edge along the ends and bottom of the back panel and along the bottom of the side. On the bottom of the back, mark screw holes 70 mm in from either end, then 186 mm. On the sides of the back, mark a screw hole 50 mm from the top edge, then mark two more holes 85 mm apart. On the bottom of the end panels, mark the screw holes 50 mm in from both ends, then 113.5 mm. Drill the 5 mm holes and countersink them. On the bottom panel, draw lines 21 mm in from the back and sides to mark the positions of the back feet. For the front feet, draw lines 21 mm in from the sides and 35 mm in from the front. Drill 3 mm pilot holes for the feet.

ASSEMBLING THE CHEST

3 Attach the ends to the bottom with PVA adhesive and 40 mm chipboard screws. If you nail the joint together first to make attaching the ends easier, punch the nails below the surface and fill the holes when finishing. Then attach the back panel to the ends and bottom.

You can make this chest a much easier project by having the materials cut to size when you purchase them. The upholstery work is easily done at home, but you may choose to have the fabric fitted by a professional upholsterer.

5 Turn the chest upside down, centre the hinge and attach with enough screws to hold the front temporarily.

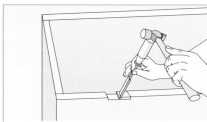

6 Mark the position of the support cleats on the chest ends and attach the cleats with screws and adhesive.

8 Cut the hinge recess on the box with a tenon saw and remove the waste with a 25 mm chisel.

4 On the front edge of both sides, mark a dowel position 40 mm from the top edge and in the centre of the edge. Drill an 8 mm hole to a depth of 30 mm. Insert the dowels with adhesive. Mark two matching holes on the inner face of the front flap and drill them to a depth of 10 mm. Check the front will sit flush.

5 Turn the chest upside down with the front in position. Open the piano hinge and lay the hinge across the bottom of the chest and front flap. Centre the knuckle over the joint. Drill 2 mm holes for the 15 mm x No. 4 screws. Insert only enough screws to hold the front in place temporarily.

6 On the sides, draw a line 79 mm from the top to mark the position of the support

EXPLODED VIEW OF TRAY

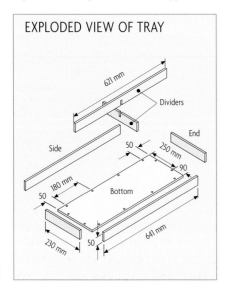

621 mm

Dividers

Side

End

50

250 mm

90

180 mm

50

Bottom

230 mm

50

641 mm

cleats. Fold the front down and measure 7 mm in from the front edge of the sides to position the front of the cleats. Mark and cut the cleats from 25 x 25 mm timber. Drill two 5 mm pilot holes in each cleat, 50 mm from either end. Countersink the holes. Attach with 30 mm x No. 8 screws and adhesive.

7 Attach the ball feet using four 40 mm x No. 8 screws and a little PVA adhesive.

8 On the top edge of the back, measure in 75 mm from the sides and square a line across the edge. Hold a hinge in place, mark the length and square another line across. Continue the lines a few millimetres down the outside back. Set a marking gauge to slightly less than the thickness of a hinge knuckle (no more than 1 mm) and draw a line on the outside back between the two hinge lines. Cut the hinge recess on the inside of the lines with a tenon saw and remove the waste with a 25 mm chisel. Attach the hinges so the leaf is flush with the inside back and the hinge knuckle is set a few millimetres away from the chest.

MAKING THE TRAY

9 Mark the tray parts on the 10 mm MDF and check that they are square. Using a circular saw with a ripping guide or straight edge, cut the 50 mm strips and the bottom panel a little oversize. Use a smoothing

plane to bring the parts to the finished width and remove the saw marks.

10 Cut the tray parts to length on the waste side of the lines using a tenon saw. Square the ends on the smaller pieces with a smoothing plane. The bottom can be left a little oversize until it is fitted.

11 Following the diagram opposite, set out the halving joints on the dividers. Cut down the sides of the halving joint with a tenon saw and use either a 10 mm chisel or a coping saw to remove the waste.

12 Join the parts of the tray frame with 30 mm panel pins and adhesive. Make sure the joints are flush on the top and bottom and at the sides, and nail a piece of timber diagonally across the frame to keep it square while the adhesive sets. Punch the heads of the panel pins below the surface. When the adhesive is dry, fit the dividers inside the tray and make adjustments if necessary. Check the dividers are square before attaching them with panel pins and adhesive.

13 Bring the tray bottom to size with a smoothing plane and check that it is square. Mark the screw holes 5 mm in from the edges (see diagram left). Drill the 4 mm pilot holes, turn the bottom over and countersink the holes. Remove the brace from the frame and attach the bottom to

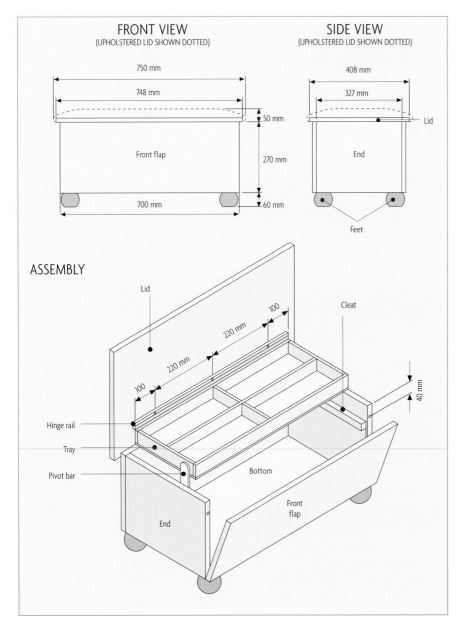

FRONT VIEW
(UPHOLSTERED LID SHOWN DOTTED)

750 mm
748 mm
50 mm
Front flap
270 mm
700 mm
60 mm

SIDE VIEW
(UPHOLSTERED LID SHOWN DOTTED)

408 mm
327 mm
Lid
End
Feet

ASSEMBLY

Lid
100
220 mm
220 mm
100
Cleat
40 mm
Hinge rail
Tray
Bottom
Pivot bar
End
Front flap

TOOLS

- Portable circular saw
- Hacksaw
- Smooth file
- Chisels: 25 mm, 10 mm
- Screwdriver (cross-head or slotted)
- Smoothing plane
- Electric drill
- Drill bits: 2 mm, 3 mm, 5 mm, 8 mm, countersink
- Hammer
- Quick-release F-cramps
- Tape measure or fold-out rule
- Combination square and pencil
- Scissors
- Paintbrush
- Marking gauge
- Filler knife and nail punch
- Coping saw (optional)

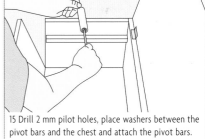

15 Drill 2 mm pilot holes, place washers between the pivot bars and the chest and attach the pivot bars.

one edge with 20 mm x No. 6 screws. Square the tray sides with the bottom and attach the remaining sides.

14 Place the hinge rail face up on a work surface. Open the piano hinge flat and place one leaf on the rail so the hinge knuckle is in line with the edge of the rail and centrally

located in length. Drill 2 mm pilot holes in the hinge rail and attach the hinge with a few 15 mm x No. 4 screws. Hold the hinge rail against the tray. Place the loose leaf of the hinge on the tray so that the leaf edge is flush with the inside of the tray. Mark and drill the 2 mm holes in the edge of the tray and attach the rail. Drill three 5 mm holes in

the face of the hinge rail (see diagram above left) and countersink the holes.

15 Cut two pivot bars from the scrap 10 mm MDF. Round over the ends with a coping saw or tenon saw and smoothing plane, and sand back the rough edges. Mark the positions of the two 3 mm pilot holes 93 mm apart on each pivot bar, and centred across the width

The box lid opens to reveal a tray attached by a hinge and pivot bars.

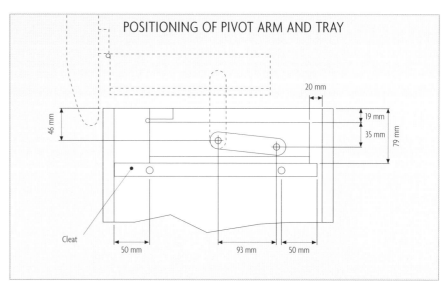

POSITIONING OF PIVOT ARM AND TRAY

of the bar. Drill and countersink the holes. Following the diagram at right, mark the screw position for attaching the pivot bars to the sides of the chest. Drill 2 mm pilot holes, place washers between the pivot bars and the chest, and fasten the pivot bars using the 25 mm x No. 6 countersunk screws. Tighten the screws, then loosen them a little so the bars move freely.

ASSEMBLING THE CHEST

16 Position the lid on the chest so there is a 25 mm overhang on all sides. Copy the position of the hinges on the chest to the lid, paying careful attention when tracing around the hinge knuckles. Lay the lid on a work surface and align it with the hingeing edge of the chest. Attach the hinges to the lid. Turn the chest upright and check the lid opens correctly to an angle greater than 90 degrees. Make adjustments to the lid if necessary.

17 Open the lid and lay some 10 mm scrap material across the box from front to back. Sit the tray on the scrap material. Mark the position where the hinge rail will be fixed to the lid. Drill the 3 mm pilot holes into the lid. Fold the hinge rail down and apply

indoor

MATERIALS*

PART	MATERIAL	LENGTH	WIDTH	NO.
Lid	16 mm MDF	748 mm	408 mm	1
Front flap	16 mm MDF	700 mm	270 mm	1
End	16 mm MDF	327 mm	270 mm	2
Back	16 mm MDF	700 mm	270 mm	1
Bottom	16 mm MDF	667 mm	327 mm	1
Tray side	10 mm MDF	641 mm	50 mm	2
Tray end	10 mm MDF	230 mm	50 mm	2
Tray divider	10 mm MDF	621 mm	50 mm	1
Tray divider	10 mm MDF	230 mm	50 mm	1
Tray bottom	10 mm MDF	641 mm	250 mm	1
Pivot bar	10 mm MDF	118 mm	25 mm	2
Hinge rail	10 mm MDF	640 mm	35 mm	1
Cleat	25 x 25 mm PAR	320 mm	19 mm	2

Other: PVA adhesive; sixty 15 mm x No. 4 countersunk wood screws (cross-head or slotted); sixteen 40 mm chipboard screws; two 25 mm x No. 6 countersunk screws; two 20 mm x No. 6 countersunk wood screws and four washers; seven 30 mm x No. 8 countersunk wood screws; sixteen 30 mm panel pins; twelve 20 mm x No. 6 wood screws; two 38 x 8 mm timber dowels; four timber ball feet, 60 x 75 mm in diameter; contact adhesive; two-part epoxy wood filler; abrasive paper: 180 grit and 240 grit; 1.5 m piano hinge; two 50 mm butt hinges and screws; one gripper catch and fixings (or magnetic catch); 750 x 410 mm foam; upholstery tacks (or staple gun with 10 mm staples); 900 x 550 mm fabric (allow for pattern); 2.4 m braiding.

*   Finished dimensions for this chest are: length 750 mm; width 408 mm; height 380 mm.

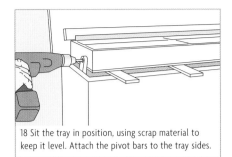

18 Sit the tray in position, using scrap material to keep it level. Attach the pivot bars to the tray sides.

adhesive. Fasten the hinge rail to the lid with the 30 mm x No. 8 screws.

18 Raise the pivot bars up vertically, placing the washers between the tray and bars. Insert the 20 mm x No. 6 screws and fasten the pivot bars. Remove the scrap material and test the closing of the lid. Some adjustment may be required if the screws catch on the box sides. Countersink the washers and screws if necessary.

UPHOLSTERING THE LID
19 Remove the lid from the box and sand and paint the underside before upholstering.

Plane all the edges and corners of the lid so they are rounded both on top and below. Glue the foam to the top of the lid using contact adhesive.

20 If you have chosen a patterned fabric, centre the pattern on the lid. Put the fabric on a clean surface and place the lid on top. Pull the fabric over one long edge and attach the fabric to the centre of the edge with upholstery tacks or staples. Working outwards from the centre, continue to attach the fabric. Gently stretch the fabric towards the sides as you go and keep the pattern straight. Leave the corners open at this stage so that you can fold the corner pleats later. Stand the lid on its edge and slide your hand across the fabric to help pull down the edges of the foam and smooth the fabric over the shoulders of the lid. Attach the fabric to the opposite edge in the same manner. Use the same technique to pull the fabric over the side edges and attach it. To fold the corner pleats, tuck one fabric edge under

the other and pleat the fabric at the corner. Practise pleating the corners a few times until you have a good finish and then staple or tack the pleats into place. Use adhesive to attach a piece of braiding over the edge of the fabric to hide the tacks or staples.

FINISHING THE CHEST
21 Mix a small amount of two-part plastic filler according to the manufacturer's instructions and use a filler knife to fill the screw holes. Sand the chest with 180 grit abrasive paper, paying particular attention to the edges. Paint the chest with an MDF sealer both inside and out. Allow to dry and sand the box and tray using 240 grit abrasive paper. Apply two coats of paint, sanding lightly with 240 grit abrasive paper between coats.

22 Fit a gripper catch or a magnetic catch to the inside face of the front flap following the manufacturer's instructions, and reassemble the box.

PAINTED TOY BOX ON CASTORS

This painted toy box with curved edges is a quick weekend project. It is made from MDF and decorated with a simple stencil motif. Swivel castors make it very easy to move around.

PREPARING THE BOARDS
1 Using a tape measure, combination square and straight edge, mark the parts on the MDF, leaving a 5 mm allowance for saw cuts. Check the parts are square.

2 Cut the parts on the waste side of the lines, using a circular saw and a straight edge clamped to the board. Pin the matching pieces together with panel pins, and plane the edges straight and square back to the lines.

SHAPING THE TOP EDGE
3 Square a line down the centre of the face side. On the cardboard, draw a 350 x 64 mm rectangle (make sure it is squared) and inside it draw a curved shape to be used as a half template. Cut out the template. Line up the template with the centre line of the sides. Trace the template, flip it over and trace the shape on the other side.

4 Keeping the sides pinned, cut the top edges with a jigsaw. Use spokeshaves or a

sanding block and 100 grit abrasive paper to smooth the curved top. Draw a line 18 mm in

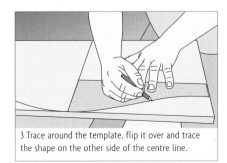

3 Trace around the template, flip it over and trace the shape on the other side of the centre line.

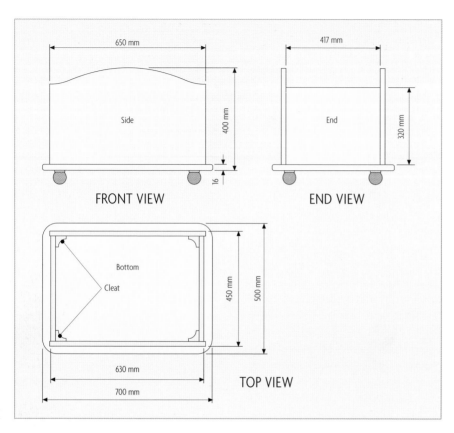

FRONT VIEW

650 mm

400 mm

16

Side

END VIEW

417 mm

320 mm

End

TOP VIEW

Bottom

Cleat

450 mm

500 mm

630 mm

700 mm

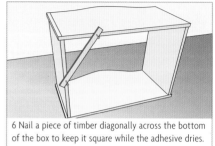

6 Nail a piece of timber diagonally across the bottom of the box to keep it square while the adhesive dries.

and attach the second side in the same manner. Keep the bottom edges flush.

6 Nail a piece of timber diagonally across the bottom of the box to keep it square while the adhesive sets.

7 Use a round object to draw the round corners on the bottom panel. Cut the corners with a coping saw or jigsaw, and smooth them over with a flat-bottom spokeshave or a sanding block and abrasive paper.

8 Draw lines 33 mm in from the sides of the bottom for the screws. Mark a screw hole 350 mm in from the end and measure out 250 mm either side of it for two more screws. Draw lines 43 mm in from the ends and mark a screw hole in the centre. Drill 5 mm holes and countersink.

from either end and continue the lines over the edges. Take the pinned pieces apart.

ASSEMBLING THE BOX

5 Start three nails evenly spaced on the 18 mm

line. Put adhesive on the edge of an end panel. Apply a little more adhesive and line up the joint, making sure the guideline matches the centre of the edge of the end. Drive the nails in. Attach the other end. Turn the box around

9 Remove the brace and place the frame with the bottom edge facing up. Prop it into position. Align the bottom panel and make 3 mm pilot holes in the bottom edge of the frame. Attach the bottom panel to the frame with 40 mm chipboard screws. Turn the box right way up.

10 Cut the four cleats, sand the exposed ends and glue the cleats in place. Use masking tape to hold them while the adhesive dries.

11 Place the box face down on a work surface and draw a guideline 50 mm in from the

MATERIALS*

PART	MATERIAL	LENGTH	WIDTH	NO.
Bottom	16 mm MDF	700 mm	500 mm	1
Side	16 mm MDF	650 mm	384 mm	2
End	16 mm MDF	417 mm	320 mm	2
Cleat	25 mm scotia moulding	319 mm		4

Other: PVA adhesive; four small swivel castors; eight 40 mm chipboard screws; sixteen 15 mm x No. 6 countersunk screws (cross-head or slotted); twenty 40 mm panel pins; abrasive paper: one sheet each of 100 grit and 240 grit; 400 x 120 mm cardboard; acrylic-based paint; MDF sealer undercoat; wood filler.

* Finished dimensions: length 700 mm; width 500 mm; height 416 mm.

TOOLS

- Smoothing plane
- Portable circular saw
- Tape measure and straight edge
- Combination square and pencil
- Hammer
- Spokeshaves: round-bottom and flat-bottom
- Electric drill
- Drill bits: 2 mm, 3 mm, 5 mm, countersink
- Utility knife and scissors
- Cork sanding block or electric sander
- Screwdriver (cross-head or slotted)

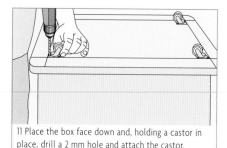

11 Place the box face down and, holding a castor in place, drill a 2 mm hole and attach the castor.

edges of the bottom. Hold a castor in place, drill a 2 mm pilot hole and attach the castor with 15 mm x No. 6 screws. Repeat for each castor.

FINISHING

12 Apply one coat of an MDF undercoat and at least two coats of paint. Sand lightly between coats with 240 grit abrasive paper. Choose your own design and decorate the box.

This movable box on castors has many uses, but is especially handy for storing toys. The design is very adaptable—alter the height or size of the box to suit your needs—and the box can be decorated in various ways.

coffee tables

coffee tables

COFFEE TABLE BASICS

Coffee tables can be made in many forms, from contemporary to traditional, from simple to more elaborate. Most of the ones in this book can be made using basic joinery techniques.

It is the special features such as these turned legs that give real character to a coffee table, and it matters very little whether they are new or recycled.

- If the top panel is made from boards, use quarter-sawn boards as they help keep the panel flat and reduce the risk of splitting.
- When selecting timber, check it is straight by sighting down one long edge. Check it is flat across the width and not twisted along the length.

Timber is a renewable resource, but much of the replanting uses fast-growing conifers such as radiata pine rather than hardwoods. For a coffee table with real character, try using recycled timber. Not only does this save cutting new timber, but it is more dimensionally stable as it has had more time to be seasoned, and the quality is often superior as more care was taken in the past when grading timber. The trees were generally a lot older, too, and so they developed more heartwood, which is more resistant to insect attack.

SIZES OF COFFEE TABLES

A coffee table is usually 400–500 mm high, depending on the seating with which it will be used. For example, with traditional upright chairs the height should be at the upper end of the range, but with low lounge chairs it should be at the lower end.

The length and width also vary, depending on the size of the room and the position of the table, and you will need to allow space to move around the table. It's a good idea to allow 400–500 mm of leg room between the table and the seating.

SELECTING TIMBER

A coffee table is a prominent piece of furniture. Choose the timber for it carefully

so the table contributes to the overall character of the room. Dark timbers such as mahogany or walnut highlight brass or other metal insets, while timbers with elaborate patterns add interest to a plain design.

The material you buy will help determine the quality of the table, so take care when selecting it.

- When ordering timber have it planed to the finished thickness and width. This saves time, and timber yards usually have better equipment than you would and so can do it more accurately. Do insist that the quality is up to furniture standard.
- For a really attractive table always choose a furniture-grade timber with few knots and other visible defects.

FINISHING YOUR TABLE

Your first concern when choosing a finish for your coffee table will be for it to fit in with the rest of your furniture, and this will decide whether it should be painted or receive a more natural finish. The top of a table will, however, be subject to a lot of wear and possible spills, so give it a good, hard-wearing finish. (If you are varnishing, a polyurethane varnish is preferable.) A few coats of lacquer is often a good idea.

First sand the table with 180 grit abrasive paper. Remove blemishes or bruises by placing a wet rag over them and pressing with a hot iron. Fill gaps or holes with wood filler and allow it to dry before sanding off with 180 grit paper. Wipe over with a damp cloth and then sand again with 240 grit paper.

If you are using a resinous timber with lots of knots and veins, such as the various types of pine, seal the timber to prevent the resins bleeding through. Then apply the finish of your choice. When painting, use an undercoat

and two coats of top coat, sanding back between coats with 240 grit paper.

BEFORE YOU START
When you have chosen the table you want to make, read through the instructions to gain

an idea of what is involved. If you have not had a lot of woodworking experience you can then practise the techniques required, and particularly how to make the relevant joints on scrap material before beginning on the actual table.

SIMPLE TABLE WITH INSET TOP

This square coffee table is simple to make and yet looks neat and smart. The frame is held together with dowel joints, and the top boards are fixed to cleats screwed to the frame.

THE LEGS AND RAILS
1 Use a tape and pencil to mark out the legs on the timber, leaving a 5 mm space between each for saw cuts. With a combination square and pencil, square the lines around all four faces of the timber. Check the legs are 60 mm square and all the same length and trace over the lines with a knife to cut the surface fibres.

2 Using a bench hook or G-cramp hold the timber steady on a work surface. Use a tenon saw to cut the legs to length. Be sure to cut on the waste side of the lines. Hold the legs together and check they are the same length. Take a smoothing plane and plane the bottoms of the legs back to the line (the tops can be planed after the frame is assembled). Set the plane finely to reduce the risk of chipping, and plane down only to the lines. Use a square to check that the end grain is square in both directions.

3 In the same way mark out and cut the rails to 630 mm. Bring them to the same length by planing the end grain with a finely set smoothing plane. Continually check that the ends remain square. When planing the end grain use a circular motion so the edges aren't chipped out.

To achieve this brilliant finish the table was given two coats of acrylic paint and then two coats of clear satin acrylic lacquer.

MAKING THE JOINTS
4 Take the legs and select the two best surfaces for the outer faces. The other two

will be joined to the rails. Lay the legs down on a work surface with a joining face up and use a combination square to align the tops.

MATERIALS*

PART	MATERIAL	FINISHED LENGTH	NO.
Top	100 x 25 mm timber PAR**	630 mm	7
Leg	75 x 75 mm timber PAR	420 mm	4
Rail	75 x 75 mm timber PAR	630 mm	4
Cleat (long)	25 x 25 mm timber PAR	629 mm	2
Cleat (short)	25 x 25 mm timber PAR	590 mm	2

Other: PVA adhesive; newspaper and rag; twenty-four 50 mm long 10 mm diameter timber dowels; twenty 30 mm x No. 8 countersunk wood screws; abrasive paper: two sheets each of 120 and 180 grit; finish of choice.

* Finished size: top 805 mm square; height 420 mm. Timber sizes given are nominal. For timber types and sizes see page 199.

** Recycled tongue and groove floorboards are ideal. They are usually 90 mm wide, but check carefully as you may need to adjust the measurements of the table if your boards are a different width.

TOOLS

- Tape measure or rule
- Combination square and pencil
- Utility knife
- Marking gauge
- G-cramp
- Panel saw
- Two 900 mm sash cramps
- Tenon saw or portable circular saw
- Smoothing plane
- Jack plane
- Dowelling jig
- Electric drill
- Drill bits: 3 mm, 5 mm, 10 mm, countersink
- Hammer or mallet
- Screwdriver (cross-head or slotted)
- Cork sanding block

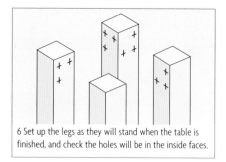

6 Set up the legs as they will stand when the table is finished, and check the holes will be in the inside faces.

8 Use a dowelling jig and 10 mm bit to bore the holes for the dowels, first in the legs and then in the rails.

9 Check that all the leg and rail joints fit tightly and square, and make any adjustments necessary.

Measure down from the top line of one leg 60 mm and square a line across all legs. Turn them over so the other joining faces are up, and repeat.

5 Measure down from the top of the legs 15 mm and a further 30 mm. Square these lines across the joining faces of the legs.

6 Use a marking gauge set to 15 mm to mark a line on both sides of the joining faces from the top of the leg to just short of the 60 mm line. You now have four crosses on each joining face. Three will be used for dowels: the two outside positions and one of the inside ones (the inner holes will be staggered

so the dowels can be inserted without hitting each other). See diagram opposite. Cross out the fourth hole and set up the legs as they will be in the table to check the holes are in the right faces.

7 Number each joining face and each end of the rails to match. Use the gauge to mark out matching positions on the end of each rail.

8 Use a dowelling jig and 10 mm bit to bore the dowel holes 26 mm deep. Drill the holes in the legs first, then the ones in the rails.

ASSEMBLING THE FRAME

9 Check all the joints fit tightly and square

,and adjust them if necessary. Pull the frame apart and set up each leg with a connecting rail. Set up the sash cramps to the right size. Have scrap timber handy to place between the frame and the cramps to prevent the timber being stained, and a wet rag to clean off excess adhesive. Cover the bench with newspaper. Place PVA adhesive in the holes. Spread it around the hole and spread the excess over the face of the joint. On the end of the rails rub the adhesive in well with

13 Using 30 mm x No. 8 wood screws fix the cleats to the rails, flush with the marked line.

your finger and spread more over the end. Insert the dowels in the holes in the legs and tap them home gently. Fit the rail in place and push the joint together. Place the joined pieces in the cramps; leave to dry for about two hours.

10 Place adhesive in the remaining holes and complete the frame. Check the frame is square by measuring the diagonals, and not twisted by sighting over the top to see that the rails are all level. Adjust the cramps if necessary before the adhesive sets. Placing the cramps off-centre can often correct out-of-square frames and eliminate twist. Clean off all excess adhesive with the damp rag and leave the frame to dry overnight.

11 Using a tape and tenon saw, mark out and cut the cleats, two 629 mm long and two 590 mm long. Measure in 60 mm from each end, and also place a mark at the centre of each. These are the drilling positions for fixing the cleats to the frames. Use a 5 mm bit to drill the screw holes in the cleats. Countersink the holes with a countersink bit.

12 Remove the frame from the cramps. Set a marking gauge to the thickness of the top pieces. Working from the top face of the rails, mark a line around the inside of the frame.

13 Take one long cleat and spread adhesive on the face that will be against the rail.

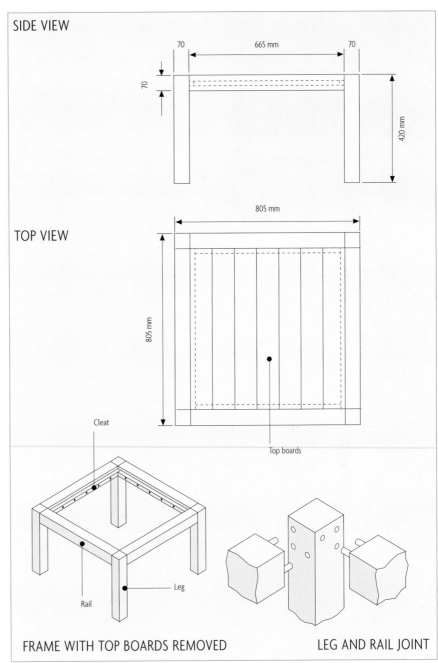

SIDE VIEW

TOP VIEW

Cleat

Top boards

FRAME WITH TOP BOARDS REMOVED

Leg

Rail

LEG AND RAIL JOINT

Holding the cleat in position with its top at the marked line, bore pilot holes with a 3 mm bit through the cleat for the screws. Using 30 mm x No. 8 wood screws fix the cleat to the rail, flush with the marked line.

Repeat for the second long cleat, fastening it to the side opposite the first. Check that the top pieces will be flush with the top of the rail by holding an offcut of the top pieces in position. Finally fit the remaining two cleats.

The legs and rails are the same size and form a neat frame for the boards of the top.

ADDING THE TOP

14 Measure the frame to check the precise length of the top pieces. With a tape measure, combination square and pencil, mark off and cut them. Allow 5 mm between each for saw cuts. Trace across the top surface of the lines with a knife. Use a panel saw or circular saw to cut the pieces, leaving them a little long. Clamp all the pieces together and check they form a panel 630 mm wide. If using tongue and groove

floorboards, remove the tongue from the outside board with a jack plane, taking care not to reduce the width of the board.

15 Starting with the piece with the tongue removed, use a finely set smoothing plane to plane each piece to length, working from each side of the end towards the centre. Make a slight bevel to the underside. Check regularly with a square that you are planing square to the edge. Repeat this process for each board.

16 Fit all the pieces in the top and turn the table upside down. To fix the end of each board, use a 5 mm bit to drill a clearance hole through the cleat at the centre of the

board. Avoid the screws holding the cleat to the rails. On the other two edges drill holes for three screws. Make a 3 mm pilot hole in each board to help with the screw fixing. Insert the screws and fasten on the top panel.

FINISHING

17 Turn the table over and use a smoothing plane to smooth the tops of the legs flush with the rails and all other joints. Take care to plane in the direction of the grain where possible.

18 Use 120 grit abrasive paper and then 180 grit to sand the table all over. Apply the finish of your choice (see pages 246–247).

MARKING OUT DOWEL HOLES

Both sets of dowel holes can be marked out separately, or you can use dowel 'points' to transfer the marks from one component to the other. These points are metal inserts that have a centre pin moulded into the surface. Mark out and drill the holes in one component (here, the leg) and insert the points in the holes. Then bring the second component (the rail) into contact with the first, align it and push it onto the points. The centre pin on the point will mark the end of the rail in the correct position for the dowel hole.

SMART TABLE WITH SHELF

A coffee table with a shelf serves a double purpose, as it can be used to store magazines and newspapers. The top and shelf are fixed to the legs with dowels in diagonally cut mortises.

MAKING WEDGE CRAMPS

1 Cut the 75 x 50 mm hardwood into four pieces 1100 mm long. The offcuts will be used later for wedges. Turn the lengths on edge and use a G-cramp to hold them together. Along the edge mark two points 560 mm apart (the finished width of top and shelf, plus 80 mm so the wedges and cramping block can be placed in position). Drill 1/8 inch holes 40 mm deep at each of the marked positions.

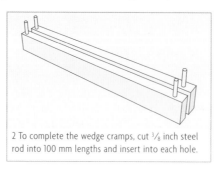

2 To complete the wedge cramps, cut 1/8 inch steel rod into 100 mm lengths and insert into each hole.

2 Use a hacksaw to cut the steel rod into

100 mm lengths and insert a piece into each hole. If you want to make the cramp variable in length, drill extra holes—40 mm increments should give you a flexible system.

3 From the timber offcuts cut wedges 25 mm thick at one end.

PREPARING THE TOP AND SHELF

4 The material for the top should be planed to 115 x 19 mm. Cut eight 900 mm lengths,

TOOLS

- Panel saw or portable circular saw
- Tenon saw
- Tape measure or rule
- Square and pencil
- Four G-cramps
- Four 1200 mm sash cramps or frame cramps
- Electric drill
- Drill bits: 10 mm, 3/8 inch
- Dowelling jig
- Hacksaw
- Jack plane
- Smoothing plane
- Hammer or mallet
- Utility knife
- Marking gauge
- Vice
- Chisel: 16 mm bevelled-edge
- Cork sanding block or electric sander
- Side cutters or pincers

This table was made from white oak and for a contemporary look was finished with acrylic semi-gloss lacquer over a white liming stain.

four for the top and four for the shelf. Shuffle the pieces until you are satisfied with the grain pattern and colour for both panels. Place a chalk arrowhead across the face of the boards as a face mark and indication of their position.

5 Use a square to check the edges are straight and square with the face so that the boards fit together neatly. Poorly fitting edges weaken the joint, and if the joints are not square the panels will not lay flat in the cramps and will be bowed. Use a jack plane to smooth and straighten the edges.

6 Apply adhesive to the joining edges, spreading it across the entire join with your

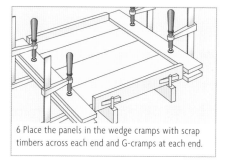

6 Place the panels in the wedge cramps with scrap timbers across each end and G-cramps at each end.

finger. Place the panels in the wedge cramps with newspaper between the cramp and panel to prevent them sticking together. Put scrap timbers across each end, on top and on the bottom with newspaper between. Place two cramps at each end to hold the timbers

flush. Place the wedges into the end of the cramps and gently tap them tight. If necessary protect the boards by interposing a block of wood, and use a mallet to tap the boards down flush. Use a wet rag to remove any adhesive from the surface of the panels. Leave to dry.

THE LEGS

7 Take the timber for the legs and mark out four legs 450 mm long. Leave a small gap between each for saw cuts. Cut across the grain with a knife and cut to length. Lightly plane each leg with a smoothing plane to remove any marks. Hold the legs together and mark and number the two inside faces on each.

MATERIALS*

PART	MATERIAL	FINISHED LENGTH	NO.
Top/shelf	125 x 25 mm timber PAR	860 mm	8
Leg	50 x 50 mm timber PAR	450 mm	4

Other: Chalk; PVA adhesive; newspaper and rag; eight 20 mm panel pins; abrasive paper: two sheets each of 120 grit and 180 grit; eight 38 mm long 10 mm diameter timber dowels; finish of choice.

For cramps: 600 mm length of ⅜ inch steel rod (may be threaded); four pieces 75 x 50 mm hardwood 1500 mm long (makes four, two for each panel).

* Finished size: top 900 x 480 mm; height 450 mm. Timber sizes given are nominal. For timber types and sizes see page 199.

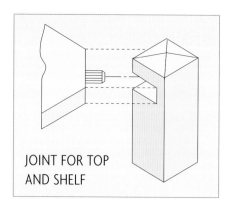

JOINT FOR TOP AND SHELF

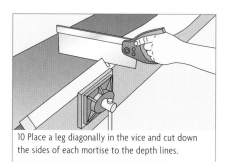

10 Place a leg diagonally in the vice and cut down the sides of each mortise to the depth lines.

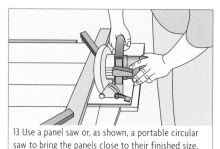

13 Use a panel saw or, as shown, a portable circular saw to bring the panels close to their finished size.

8 On one inside face of each leg measure down 12 mm from the top and up 150 mm from the bottom, and square marks across the face and the adjoining inside face. Measure the thickness of the two panels. Measure down from the marks the thickness of the panels and square marks across the two faces to indicate the levels of the diagonal mortises.

9 Set a marking gauge to 30 mm and, working from the inside corner, mark the depth of the mortise on both inside faces between the two sets of lines (see diagram above right). Use a knife to cut across the grain of the mortise only to the depth of the mortise and no further.

10 Place a leg diagonally in a vice and cut down the sides of each mortise to the depth

lines only. Keep to the waste side of the lines. Place a third saw cut in the centre of the mortise to help clear the waste. Using a chisel and hammer or mallet, remove the waste, starting at the top and working down carefully to the depth line. Trim out the last bit using only your hand on the chisel. Use the edge of the chisel to check that the bottom of the mortise is straight. Repeat for each leg.

11 Mark down 3 mm from the top of each leg and square the line right around the leg. Then mark diagonal lines across the top. Place a leg in the vice, top end up, and use the smoothing plane to form the crown by planing down at an angle from the centre to the 3 mm mark. Be careful not to split the end. If you prefer, use a coarse abrasive paper to sand the crown to shape. Repeat for the other legs.

COMPLETING THE TOP AND SHELF

12 When the top and shelf have dried overnight, remove them from the cramps and, if necessary, use a smoothing plane to level off the joints. Sand both panels with 120 grit abrasive paper. Check the mortises are the correct thickness, and make any adjustments to them.

13 Use a jack plane to plane one edge of the top panel straight and square. From this edge mark out the size of the top. Trace over the cross-grain lines with a knife. Use a panel saw, or a portable circular saw and a straight edge, to bring it close to its finished size. (If you are using a circular saw, be sure to work with the underside of the panel up to prevent the top surface being chipped.) Repeat for the shelf.

14 Use a jack plane to plane the end grain of the panels to their exact length, working from the sides towards the centre. Avoid planing over the edges so they don't chip out. Plane the boards to width. Plane both together to ensure they finish the same size.

15 On each panel measure 30 mm from each corner along each edge and draw a line diagonally across the corner. Use a tenon saw to remove the corners, and finish the cuts back to the lines with a smoothing plane.

indoor

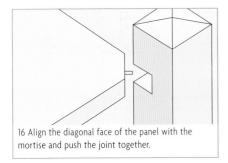

16 Align the diagonal face of the panel with the mortise and push the joint together.

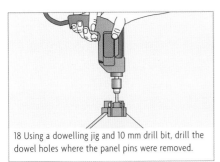

18 Using a dowelling jig and 10 mm drill bit, drill the dowel holes where the panel pins were removed.

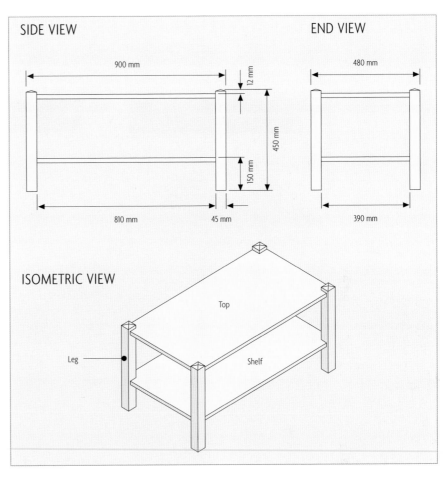

SIDE VIEW

900 mm

12 mm

450 mm

150 mm

810 mm

45 mm

END VIEW

480 mm

390 mm

ISOMETRIC VIEW

Top

Leg

Shelf

Don't plane beyond the line. Check the panels and legs fit together neatly.

ASSEMBLY

16 Use a marking gauge set to half the thickness of the panel and mark a line across each diagonal corner. Find the centre of the diagonal face and insert a 20 mm panel pin at this point. Use side cutters or pincers to cut the head off the pin, leaving about 3 mm of the pin exposed. Align a leg and the top panel and push the joint together carefully. Ensure the pin has marked the inside face of the mortise where the dowel hole will be drilled. Number all joints so no confusion occurs during final assembly. Repeat for all leg joints. Pull the joints apart and remove the pins.

17 Sand all the parts well with 120 grit abrasive paper and then 180 grit, especially the end grain.

18 Using a dowelling jig and 10 mm bit, drill dowel holes 22 mm deep where the panel pins

were removed from the top and shelf. Place each leg diagonally in the vice and drill 17 mm deep dowel holes, keeping the drill straight.

19 Apply adhesive to the dowel holes in the top and shelf and spread it around the hole with a pencil. Insert the dowels carefully so as not to split the timber, and remove any excess adhesive with a wet rag. Apply adhesive to the holes in the legs and spread it well within the hole and the mortise. Fit one leg to the shelf and top at a time, tapping the pieces together with a mallet and protecting the timber with scrap timber.

20 Apply the wedge cramps diagonally across the table to pull it together. Drill

a new set of holes in the cramps so they fit properly. Alternatively, use frame cramps.

FINISHING

21 Apply the finish of your choice (see pages 246–247).

FRAME CRAMPS

Special frame cramps are available from specialist tool suppliers, or you can make them yourself. Tie strong cord around the table at the level of the top and shelf. Leave the loop a little slack, insert a length of dowel and twist it to pull the cord tight. Use packing pieces at each corner to prevent the cord cutting into the legs.

BOX-LIKE TABLE WITH BRASS BRACKETS

This simple box-like table consists of five panels made up of boards dowelled together. The panels are screwed to cleats, and the brass brackets are merely decorative.

Beautifully patterned oak was chosen for this table. A coat of shellac and two coats of water-based acrylic lacquer emphasize the silky patterning.

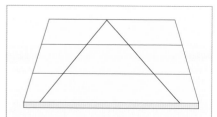

1 Place the four boards side by side as they will be joined, and draw an arrowhead across the face.

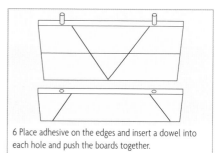

6 Place adhesive on the edges and insert a dowel into each hole and push the boards together.

CUTTING THE BOARDS

1 Take one length of 150 x 25 mm timber and, for the top, mark off four 900 mm lengths. Leave 5 mm cutting space between each. Square the lines across the face and down the edges. Place the lengths side by side and shuffle them until you are satisfied with the match. If there are gaps in the joints, straighten the edges and plane them square with a jack plane. Use a piece of chalk or pencil to place an arrowhead across the face of the four boards.

2 Repeat for the side and end panels, making the side pieces 900 mm long and the end pieces 500 mm.

JOINING THE BOARDS

3 Take the four top boards. Set a marking gauge to 9.5 mm and mark a line along all the joining edges. Along the edge of an outer board mark the centre. From there measure out 125 mm towards each end; square lines across the edge. Return the lines slightly over the face. Then measure a further 250 mm and repeat the process. These are the four dowel centres. Repeat for all joining edges. Lay the pieces out and check all the dowel positions line up accurately. If necessary, adjust them now.

4 Mark out the dowel centres for the side panels in the same way. The end panels have two dowels 300 mm apart: mark out 150 mm from the centre in both directions.

5 With a dowelling jig and 10 mm bit bore the dowel holes 26 mm deep.

6 Set up sash cramps and cover the surface with newspaper to catch any drips. Cover the bars on the cramps with paper to prevent the adhesive and metal reacting and staining the timber. Take one board and place

indoor

MATERIALS*

PART	MATERIAL	FINISHED LENGTH	NO.
Top	150 x 25 mm timber PAR	874 mm	4
End	150 x 25 mm timber PAR	462 mm	6
Side	150 x 25 mm timber PAR	880 mm	6
Side cleat	19 x 19 mm timber PAR	350 mm	4
Long cleat	19 x 19 mm timber PAR	840 mm	2
End cleat	19 x 19 mm timber PAR	420 mm	2

Other: Chalk; newspaper and rag; PVA adhesive; thirty-six 50 mm long 10 mm diameter timber dowels; fifty-two 30 mm x No. 8 countersunk wood screws; sixteen $\frac{1}{2}$ inch x No. 8 countersunk steel screws (cross-head or slotted); sixteen $\frac{1}{2}$ inch x No. 8 countersunk brass screws (slotted); 300 mm length of 50 x 50 mm brass angle; masking tape; abrasive paper: three sheets of 120 grit and two sheets each of 180 grit and 240 grit; finish of choice.

* Finished size: top 880 x 500 mm; height 390 mm. Timber sizes given are nominal. For timber types and sizes see page 199.

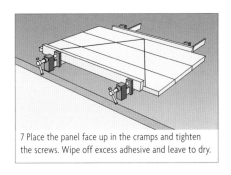

7 Place the panel face up in the cramps and tighten the screws. Wipe off excess adhesive and leave to dry.

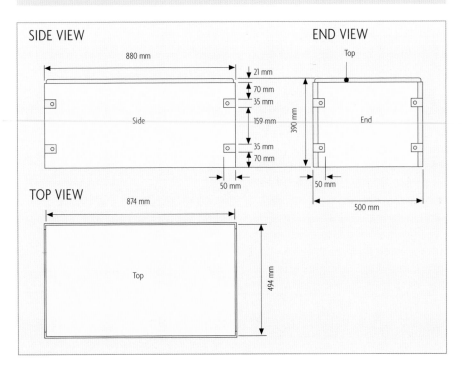

SIDE VIEW

880 mm

Side

874 mm

TOP VIEW

Top

494 mm

END VIEW

Top

21 mm
70 mm
35 mm
159 mm
35 mm
70 mm
50 mm

390 mm

End

50 mm

500 mm

adhesive along the edge and a bit in each hole. Spread it around the hole and force out any excess. Spread adhesive across the whole face of the joint and insert dowels in the

holes. Spread adhesive on the next piece in the same way and push the pieces together. Repeat until all the top boards have been glued and joined.

7 Place the panel face up in the cramps and tighten the screws. Wipe off excess adhesive with a wet rag. The panel may spring up, so place weight on it to keep it flat. Leave it to dry for at least two hours. Repeat for the side and end panels.

PREPARING THE BRACKETS

8 While waiting for the panels to dry, take the brass angle and use a combination square and metal scribe to mark out eight 35 mm brackets. Leave a gap between each for cuts. Using a G-cramp, hold the angle down and use a hacksaw to cut the brackets to length. Hold each bracket steady in a vice or G-cramp, and file the edges square using a round file.

9 Cover each bracket with masking tape and mark the centre of each face. Clamp the bracket in a vice or to a bench and use a 5 mm bit to bore screw holes. The masking tape will help prevent the drill bit slipping. Countersink the holes so that the heads of the screws finish just below the surface of the brackets.

MAKING THE PANELS

10 Use a smoothing plane to plane all the top joints flush. Place the top panel in a vice and use a jack plane to plane one long edge straight and square. Along this edge mark the centre, and from there mark out the length of the top panel: 437.5 mm each side of the centre for 875 mm. Square lines across both ends and down the edges. Use a knife to

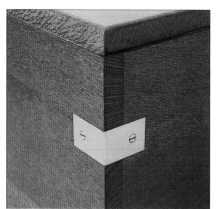

The brass angles and screw heads were given two coats of metal lacquer to prevent tarnishing.

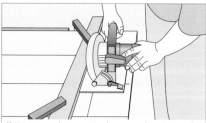

11 Using a panel saw or circular saw and cutting on the waste side of the lines, cut the ends of the panels.

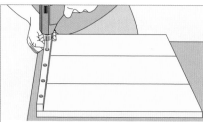

13 Drill pilot holes through the cleats into the panel, insert the 30 mm x No. 8 screws and tighten.

TOOLS

- Tape measure or rule
- Combination square and pencil
- Marking gauge
- Panel saw or portable circular saw
- Jack plane
- Smoothing plane
- Dowelling jig
- Electric drill
- Drill bits: 3 mm, 5 mm, 10 mm, countersink
- Two 900 mm sash cramps
- G-cramp
- Metal scribe (or anything to scratch metal)
- Fine-toothed hacksaw
- Round file
- Vice
- Utility knife
- Chisel: 38 mm bevelled-edge
- Screwdriver (slotted)
- Router or laminate trimmer with round-over bit (optional)

trace across the lines and square down the edges. Repeat for the side and end panels. The sides are 880 mm long and the end panels are 462 mm long.

11 Starting from the first straight edge, mark out the width of the panels. The side and end panels are 371 mm wide and the top panel is 494 mm wide. Using a panel saw or portable circular saw, cut the ends of the panels and use a smoothing plane to bring them to length. Check often that you are not going past the lines. Plane from the outside of the panel towards the centre to prevent chipping out the side edges. Cut the panels to width the same way.

ASSEMBLY

12 Cut the cleats to length. The two 840 mm cleats will have four screws in each direction, and the others will have three in each direction. Space the screws evenly and stagger them so they do not run into each other. Use a 5 mm bit to bore the holes and countersink for the screw heads.

13 Take one end panel and position a 350 mm cleat along the side edge, 2 mm from the bottom and 0.5 mm in from the edge. Place adhesive on the face of the cleat and fix it in

place. Repeat for the other side edge. With a 3 mm bit drill pilot holes through the cleats into the panel. Insert 30 mm x No. 8 screws and tighten. Wipe off excess adhesive. Repeat for the other end panel.

14 Take one end and two sides, place adhesive on the face of each cleat and fit on the side panels. Use a sash cramp to hold them together. Ensure the top and face of each joint are flush, and bore pilot holes with the 3 mm bit through the cleat to the side. Insert the screws and wipe off excess adhesive. Fit on the other end.

15 In the same way, fix two 840 mm cleats to the inside of the sides, along the top edge. Then fix the 420 mm cleats to the top edges of the ends. Check that the box is square.

16 Use a smoothing plane, or a router or laminate trimmer, to round over the top edge of the top panel. Round over the end grain first and then the long edges. Turn the panel face down on a clean surface. Place

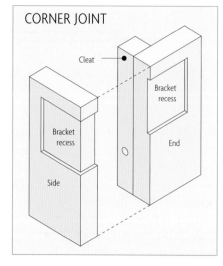

CORNER JOINT

Cleat

Bracket recess

Bracket recess

End

Side

adhesive around the top edge of the box and the cleats. Turn the box over and align it on the top panel. Use the 3 mm bit to bore pilot holes for the screws through the cleats. Insert the screws. With a plane or orbital sander make the joints flush.

FITTING THE BRACKETS

17 Turn the box on its side and measure 70 mm down from the top and 70 mm up from the bottom for the top of the top bracket and the bottom of the bottom bracket. Square the lines 50 mm around the corners. Repeat for the four corners.

18 Hold a bracket on the bottom line so it just covers the line. Trace around it with a sharp pencil. Repeat for the other leg of the

PLANING

Be sure to plane both ways across the ends of components or the frame will end up out of square and with unsightly gaps. When planing the end grain of any timber use a backing block set just below the marks to avoid breaking out the end grain or, alternatively, plane from both directions towards the centre.

bracket, and then for the other brackets. Trace over the cross-grain lines using a knife and combination square.

19 Set a marking gauge to the thickness of the brackets. Run the gauge between one set of bracket marks on the side of the box.

With the box well supported, use a 38 mm chisel to remove the waste to the depth indicated. Check that the bracket fits the recess. Repeat for the other leg and the other brackets.

20 Fit the brackets in the recesses. Use a 3 mm bit to bore pilot holes through the brackets into the box. Insert the steel screws to cut the thread and so that the brass screws won't be damaged.

FINISHING

21 Remove the screws and brackets from the box. Sand off all the sharp corners and apply the finish (see pages 246–247). Replace the brackets using brass screws.

ELEGANT TABLE WITH PARQUET TOP

A beautiful parquet top and tapered legs characterize this elegant coffee table. The parquet and rail facings are of plywood, and the frame is held together with barefaced tenon joints.

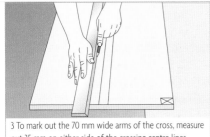

3 To mark out the 70 mm wide arms of the cross, measure out 35 mm on either side of the crossing centre lines.

PREPARING THE TOP

1 Use a square, pencil and tape to mark out the top on the chipboard. Cut it to 940 x 490 mm, using a portable circular saw with a straight edge to guide it. If using a panel saw, cut the top slightly oversize and plane it to size.

2 Mark out the plywood backing for the top 10 mm oversize with the grain running

lengthwise. At the same time mark out the facings for the rails, also 10 mm oversize but with the grain running cross-wise. Use a knife to cut through the top layer of veneer and then cut the pieces using a panel saw (ensure the face side is up to reduce splintering) or a circular saw (in this case place the face side down).

3 Take the chipboard piece and with a straight edge mark out two lines crossing in the centre (see diagram on page 260). Measure 35 mm either side of the lines and draw lines parallel to them to form a 70 mm wide cross. Draw in a small cross in the centre. At the end of each arm of the main cross use a combination square to make a triangle by marking 45-degree lines from the edges to the centre line.

CUTTING THE PARQUETRY

4 Make a 430 x 205 mm rectangular cardboard template. Using a combination square as a guide, set it on the plywood sheet at 45 degrees to the grain and close to a corner. Trace around the template. Move the template and square along the edge, leave 5 mm and draw another rectangle. Repeat twice more.

5 Trace over the lines with a knife and cut out the rectangles. Clamp them together end up in a vice with one long edge flush. Plane a short edge square and straight.

6 Using a square and pencil, mark out on the left-over plywood eight strips 35 mm wide and 500 mm long, diagonally to the grain. Do not add the mitre ends. Trace over the

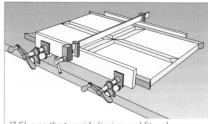

17 Glue on the two side lippings and fit sash cramps to hold them firmly while the adhesive dries.

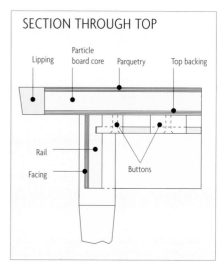

SECTION THROUGH TOP

Lipping Particle board core Parquetry Top backing

Rail

Facing Buttons

The beautiful inlaid top was made from hardwood-faced plywood and was French-polished. A coat of water-based clear varnish was added to protect it.

lines with a knife and cut the strips slightly oversize. Clamp them in a vice with the edges flush; plane the edges straight. Turn them over and plane the opposite edges so the strips are 35 mm wide. Check that the strips fit the marks on the top panel.

7 Use the square to mark 45-degree mitre cuts on one end of each strip so the strips will fit together at the centre. The mitre angle should run in the same direction as the timber grain. Use a block plane to plane the mitres so that they fit together.

8 On each strip mark off the exact length and then mark the mitre at the outer end, again in the same direction as the grain. Cut

the pieces, use masking tape to hold them together in the cross shape and place on the top panel. Fix them in place with masking tape over the ends and check the fit of the corner rectangles. Adjust them if necessary, using a block plane and planing with a slight angle to the underside of the piece. Tape each piece in position.

9 Cut and fit the triangular pieces at the ends in the same way.

ASSEMBLING THE TOP

10 Spread a thin layer of contact adhesive on the bottom of the chipboard panel and the ply backing. Allow it to dry. (When the gloss goes off, test by touching the panel lightly

with the back of your hand. If it is still tacky it is not dry enough.) Place a second thin coat on the ply backing. Allow to dry.

11 Bring the ply panel into contact with the chipboard, first lowering one short edge of the ply to the board with a small overhang. Hammer the ply into place, using scrap timber to protect the ply from the hammer. Work from the centre to the edges to remove air bubbles. Plane off any overhang.

12 Turn the main panel face up and the parquetry panel face down. Sand lightly with 120 grit abrasive paper. Wipe clean. Number each part of the parquetry and the corresponding positions on the chipboard. Carefully remove the tape and reassemble the pattern face down.

MATERIALS*

PART	MATERIAL	FINISHED LENGTH	WIDTH	NO.
Top	16 mm thick chipboard	940 mm	490 mm	1
End rail	16 mm thick chipboard	354 mm	80 mm	2
Side rail	16 mm thick chipboard	804 mm	80 mm	2
End rail facing	4 mm plywood	330 mm	80 mm	2
Side rail facing	4 mm plywood	780 mm	80 mm	2
Top backing	4 mm plywood	940 mm	490 mm	1
Leg	50 x 50 mm timber PAR	392 mm		4
End lipping	38 x 38 mm timber PAR	550 mm		2
Side lipping	38 x 38 mm timber PAR	1000 mm		2
Button	50 x 25 mm timber PAR	45 mm		10

Other: Extra plywood for parquetry; cardboard; masking tape; newspaper and rag; 1 litre liquid contact adhesive; abrasive paper: two sheets each of 120 grit, 180 grit and 240 grit; lacquer thinner or mineral turpentine; PVA adhesive; ten 40 mm x No. 8 countersunk screws (cross-head or slotted); finish of choice.

* Finished size: top 1000 x 550 mm; height 420 mm. You will need one 1200 x 900 mm sheet of chipboard and one 2400 x 1200 mm sheet of plywood. Timber sizes given are nominal. For timber types and sizes see page 199.

Strips of plywood are used to create this elegant parquet pattern.

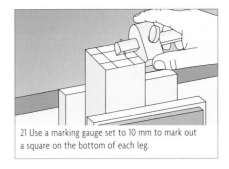

21 Use a marking gauge set to 10 mm to mark out a square on the bottom of each leg.

13 Take one ply corner piece and fix it to the face of the chipboard as described in steps 10 and 11. Then fix on the adjoining pieces, ensuring all joints meet up neatly. Repeat until the panel is complete.

14 Plane the overhanging material and remove excess adhesive from the top with a lacquer thinner or mineral turpentine. Lacquer thinner works best, but mineral turpentine fumes are less harmful and less volatile. Do not flood the surface, as this may affect the bond strength of the adhesive.

ADDING THE LIPPINGS

15 Cut two pieces of lipping timber to 1010 mm and two to 560 mm. Using the square, mark a 45-degree mitre across the top face close to one end on each long piece. Square the lines down each edge and return them to the other side. Number each piece corresponding to an edge of the top panel.

16 Hold one long lipping to the corresponding side edge of the panel with the mitre mark to a corner, and use a square and pencil to mark the mitre on the top face of the other end. Transfer the marks over the edges and join them up. Use a knife to cut the cross-grain fibres along the lines. Use a tenon saw to cut the mitres and a block plane to clean up the face of the mitres if necessary. Repeat for the other side lipping.

17 Using PVA adhesive, glue on the side lippings. Hold them in place with masking tape and fit sash cramps to hold them firmly while the adhesive dries. Place blocks between the cramps and sides. Allow to dry.

18 Mark out and cut the mitres on the end lippings in the same way and apply them to the panel.

19 Lay the top panel face down on a clean work surface and pencil a mark 6 mm in from the outside edge. Run the line around the entire bottom face of the lippings.

20 Place the panel in a vice and work from each end towards the centre to plane a bevel on one end lipping. Plane from each end towards the centre. Repeat for all lippings.

THE LEGS

21 Mark out and cut the leg timber into four pieces 392 mm long. Set a marking gauge to 10 mm and mark out a square on the bottom of each. From the top of each leg measure down 100 mm; square a line around all faces. Using a straight edge mark out the 10 mm taper from this line to the bottom on two opposite faces of the legs.

22 Set one leg in the vice and use a smoothing plane to plane the taper on one

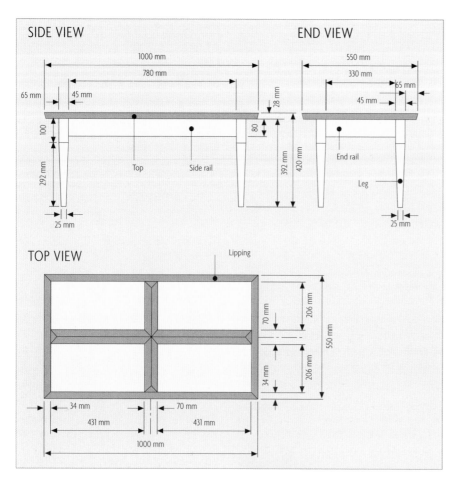

SIDE VIEW

END VIEW

1000 mm
780 mm
65 mm
45 mm
100
292 mm
25 mm
Top
Side rail
28 mm
80

550 mm
330 mm
65 mm
45 mm
392 mm
420 mm
End rail
Leg
25 mm

TOP VIEW

Lipping

70 mm
206 mm
34 mm
206 mm
550 mm
34 mm
431 mm
70 mm
431 mm
1000 mm

TOOLS

- Tape measure or rule
- Combination square and pencil
- Portable circular saw or panel saw
- Jigsaw (optional)
- Tenon saw
- Smoothing plane or jack plane
- Block plane
- Utility knife
- Vice
- 1 inch paintbrush or spreader for adhesive
- Hammer or mallet
- Two 1200 mm sash cramps
- Two G-cramps
- Marking gauge
- Chisel: 6 mm mortise, 25 mm bevelled-edge
- Plough plane or electric router with 6 mm straight cutter
- Rebate plane
- Electric drill
- Drill bits: 3 mm, 5 mm
- Screwdriver (cross-head or slotted)

face; turn the leg over and repeat. Mark the taper on the remaining two faces and plane them. Repeat for all legs. Remove the sharp edge on the bottom of the legs.

23 Hold the four legs together with the tops up; number each. Draw a line around near the top to mark the two joining faces of each (see step 13 illustration, page 263). From the top of each measure 80 mm and square a line around the joining faces. Set a gauge to 9 mm and work from the outer faces to mark a line from the top of the leg down a joining face to the 80 mm line. Return it over the top of the leg. Repeat on all joining faces. Set the gauge to 15 mm and repeat, then set it to 12 mm and mark the depth of the

27 Use a tenon saw to cut down the sides of the mortise at an angle and then use a chisel to remove the waste.

barefaced mortise across the top of the leg.

THE RAILS

24 Set the square to 80 mm and mark a line parallel to a long edge of the unused chipboard. Cut off the strip. Repeat twice until you have enough for the rails.

25 Measure two long rails 804 mm long and two end rails 354 mm long. Using a tenon saw cut them to length, cutting on the waste side of the line. Measure 12 mm from each end on each rail and square a line across the inside face for the tenon shoulder lines. Check the distance between the lines is 780 mm on the side rails and 330 mm on the end rails.

26 Square the lines 10 mm across the edges. Set a marking gauge to 6 mm and, working from the outside face, mark the tenon across each end and down the edge to the 12 mm line.

indoor

LEG AND RAIL JOINT

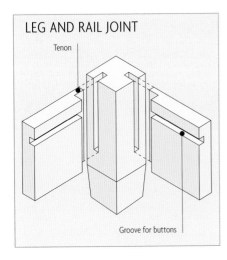

Tenon

Groove for buttons

27 Clamp a leg to a work surface with a joining face up. With a tenon saw cut down the sides of the 12 mm deep mortise at an angle, and remove the waste with the 6 mm chisel. Repeat for the mortises on all legs.

28 Mark a groove around the inside face of each rail 13 mm down from the top edge, 6 mm wide and 7 mm deep. Clamp a rail to a bench with a G-cramp and use a plough plane or router to cut the groove. Repeat for all rails.

29 Use a tenon saw to cut the shoulders of the tenons on the rails to a depth of 10 mm, leaving 6 mm on. Set one rail in a vice vertically and remove the waste with a tenon saw or the 25 mm chisel, leaving the tenon projecting. Check the fit of the first joint before cutting the remaining tenons. Adjust your technique if necessary.

ASSEMBLING THE FRAME

30 Set up the sash cramps, cover the bench with newspaper to catch any drips, and have handy a wet rag and scrap timber.

31 Take two legs and a rail for one end frame. Place PVA adhesive in each groove, spread it around and then over the tenon. Assemble the joints and adjust them so the top edge

of the rail and top of the leg are flush. Place the frame in the cramps, check it isn't twisted, and allow to dry. Repeat for the other end frame.

32 In the same way complete the frame. When it is clamped, check by sighting over the rails that it is not twisted and sits flat on the floor.

33 Take the ply strips for the rails and use a block plane to plane one end square. Hold the planed end in position on a rail, and mark the required length. Plane it to fit neatly between the legs. Repeat for all the rails. Number each strip.

34 Sand in the leg joints with 180 grit abrasive paper. Using contact adhesive, glue the strips to the rails, following the process in steps 10 and 11, but use hand pressure only. When bringing the strip and rail into contact, check the straight edge of the plywood is aligned with the bottom edge of the rail. The top can be planed flush later. Don't get adhesive on the legs.

ADDING THE TOP

35 Take the material for the buttons and on one edge cut a rebate 13 mm wide and 6 mm deep. Cut the piece up into ten buttons 45 mm long. In each drill a 5 mm screw hole through the centre of the flat face. Check the buttons fit the groove in the rails and don't project beyond the rail top.

36 Sand the top and frame by hand using 180 grit abrasive paper—take care not to sand through the face veneer, which can be very thin. Sand only in the direction of the grain, and take care on the edges.

37 Lay the top face down on a protected surface and centre the frame on top. Insert the buttons, three on each side and two at

BUTTON FIXING FOR TOP

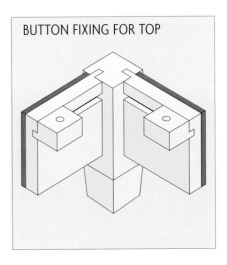

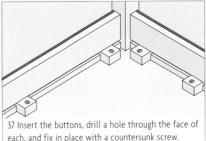

37 Insert the buttons, drill a hole through the face of each, and fix in place with a countersunk screw.

each end. Use a 3 mm bit to bore pilot holes into the top through the buttons—don't drill through the top. Fix each button with a 40 mm x No. 8 countersunk screw.

FINISHING

38 Give the table a final sand using 240 grit abrasive paper, and apply the finish of your choice (see pages 246–247).

CLASSIC TABLE WITH DRAWER

This coffee table with a drawer set into the side rail is for experienced woodworkers. It has a neat bevelled edge and tapering legs. Dowelled joints hold the frame together.

Made from pine, this table was given an aged appearance with two coats of orange shellac, one of thinned-down bituminous paint and finally two of a clear acrylic varnish with satin finish.

THE TOP PANEL

1 For the top panel cut four pieces 1030 mm long. Lay the boards out for the best arrangement of colour and grain. Place any timber defects on the bottom. Using chalk, place an arrowhead across the boards as a face mark and position marker. Plane the edges straight so the joints fit neatly.

2 Set up the sash cramps and have scrap blocks handy to insert between them and the work to protect the edges. Spread newspaper over the work surface, and have a wet rag handy to clean off excess adhesive. Spread adhesive over one edge of the first board and lay it in the cramps. Repeat for each board, joining them as planned. Place the scrap blocks in the cramps, and tighten the screws just enough to hold the material. To get the ends of the boards flush and prevent them buckling up under pressure, place timbers across each end, one on top and one on the

bottom and hold them in place with G-cramps. Use paper to prevent the blocks sticking to the top. Lay the assembly on a level surface. Using a timber scrap to protect the boards, gently tap the joints flush with a mallet. Tighten the screws on the sash cramps. Leave to dry.

MAKING THE LIPPINGS

3 Cut the lippings 20 mm overlength to allow for the mitre cuts. Choose a top side. Place face marks on this side and the outside edge.

4 For the bevel, set the marking gauge to 7 mm and mark a line along the outside edge from the top side. From the outside edge measure in 37 mm and draw a line along the top side. Plane the bevel on this side.

5 Clamp the lippings to the bench with the inner edge just overhanging and use a rebate plane or router to cut a rebate 9 mm wide and 10 mm deep in the inside edge (see diagram on page 265).

6 On the underside of the pieces mark out their length (1120 mm for the side ones, 580 mm for the end ones). Working from the outside edges, use a square and pencil to

6 With a knife trace over the mitres on the lippings, taking care on the bevelled side as it is not a true mitre.

indoor

MATERIALS*

PART	MATERIAL	FINISHED LENGTH	NO.
Top panel	125 x 25 mm timber PAR	1006 mm	4
End lipping	75 x 25 mm timber PAR	580 mm	2
Side lipping	75 x 25 mm timber PAR	1120 mm	2
Leg	75 x 50 mm timber PAR	451 mm	4
End rail	150 x 25 mm timber PAR	418 mm	2
Side rail	150 x 25 mm timber PAR	878 mm	2
Drawer front/back	100 x 25 mm timber PAR	360 mm	2
Drawer side	100 x 25 mm timber PAR	388 mm	2
Drawer runner	50 x 25 mm timber PAR	466 mm	2
Drawer bottom	4 mm thick MDF or plywood	390 x 340 mm	1
Fixing cleat (short)	25 x 25 mm timber PAR	200 mm	4
Fixing cleat (long)	25 x 25 mm timber PAR	350 mm	2

Other: Chalk; newspaper and rag; PVA adhesive; abrasive paper: two sheets each of 120 grit, 180 grit and 240 grit; twenty-four 50 mm long 10 mm diameter timber dowels; eight 40 mm panel pins; eight 25 mm panel pins; twenty-four 30 mm x No. 8 countersunk wood screws; four 40 mm x No. 8 countersunk wood screws; finish of choice; handle for drawer.

* Finished size: top 1120 x 580 mm; height 470 mm. Timber sizes given are nominal. For timber types and sizes see page 199.

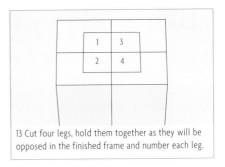

13 Cut four legs, hold them together as they will be opposed in the finished frame and number each leg.

mark the mitres across the underside, up the edges and across the top side. The line across the bevelled side is not a true mitre so mark it carefully. Trace over the lines with a knife. Use a bench hook or G-cramp to hold the material steady, and cut the pieces slightly overlength. Place them in a vice and plane back to the lines. Check the fit of the mitres.

7 Place adhesive on the mitre joints and rub it in well. Add more and bring the two pieces together face down on the bench. Hold the joint together and staple across it to hold it while the adhesive sets. Set the frame on a flat surface and leave it to dry.

COMPLETING THE TOP

8 Take the top panel and plane the surface flat, planing diagonally and then in the direction of the grain.

9 Plane a straight face edge on the panel. Check the size of the frame and, measuring from the face edge, mark out the panel to fit into the rebate in the frame. Trace over the cross-grain lines with a knife. Place the top in a vice with the end grain up and plane down to the line, planing from one side towards the centre, then from the other and then from the centre towards the outer edges. Repeat for the other end, checking the fit.

10 Use a panel saw to cut the panel close to its width, and then plane it to fit.

11 Lay the panel face down on a work surface and cut a 9 x 9 mm rebate on the underside,

first on the short edges and then the long edges. Check the size of the rebate often.

12 Apply adhesive to the rebates on the panel and frame, and fit the top into the frame. Clamp it up as in step 2 and allow to dry.

THE LEGS

13 Cut four legs 451 mm long. Hold them together as they will be in the table and mark the joining sides and edges. Number each leg.

14 On the inside edge of each leg measure down 150 mm from the top and square a line across the edge for the start of the taper. Turn the leg over with outer side up and, at the bottom, measure in 33 mm from the outside edge. Square a line across the bottom to the other side and join the lines of the taper. Check the taper is on the inside edge. Place the leg in a vice and plane the taper.

15 Set a gauge to 19.5 mm and, working from the outside faces, mark a line down from the top on the inside face and edge for 130 mm, the centre line for the rail dowels. Clamp the legs together with their tops flush and the inside faces exposed. From the top, measure down along the line 25 mm for the first dowel position and then 44 mm for the next two. Use a square to transfer the marks across all four legs and around to the inside faces.

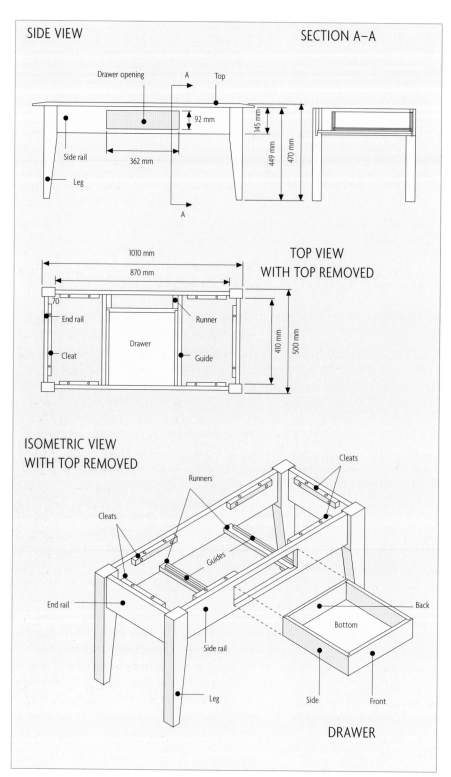

SIDE VIEW

SECTION A–A

Drawer opening
A
Top
Top
92 mm
145 mm
449 mm
470 mm
Side rail
362 mm
Leg
A

TOP VIEW
WITH TOP REMOVED

1010 mm
870 mm
70
End rail
Runner
Cleat
Drawer
Guide
410 mm
500 mm

ISOMETRIC VIEW
WITH TOP REMOVED

Cleats
Runners
Cleats
Guides
End rail
Back
Bottom
Side rail
Leg
Side
Front

DRAWER

TOOLS

- Tape measure or rule
- Combination square and pencil
- Panel saw or portable circular saw
- Tenon saw
- Jigsaw or coping saw
- Smoothing plane
- Two 1200 mm sash cramps
- Four G-cramps
- Hammer or mallet
- Marking gauge
- Rebate plane or router and 12 mm rebating bit
- Mitre square (optional)
- Vice
- Stapler
- Electric sander
- Belt sander (optional)
- Utility knife
- Chisels: 10 mm bevelled-edge, 25 mm bevelled-edge
- Electric drill
- Drill bits: 3 mm, 5 mm, 9.5 mm
- Dowelling jig
- Cork sanding block
- Plough plane with 5 mm blade or router with 5 mm straight cutting bit

THE RAILS

16 Mark out two rails at 878 mm and two at 418 mm. Across the outer side trace over the lines with a knife. Use a tenon saw to cut the rails on the waste side of the lines. If the pairs of rails are not exactly the same size the frame will end up out of square, so put the rails in a vice together. Plane them back to the lines, planing towards the centre. Check that the ends are square in both directions.

indoor

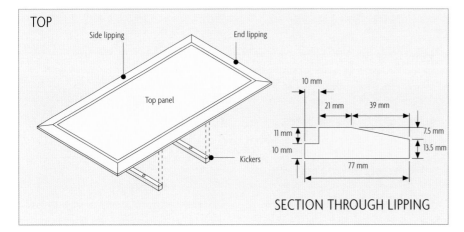

TOP

Side lipping   End lipping

Top panel

Kickers

SECTION THROUGH LIPPING

10 mm

21 mm   39 mm

11 mm

10 mm

7.5 mm

13.5 mm

77 mm

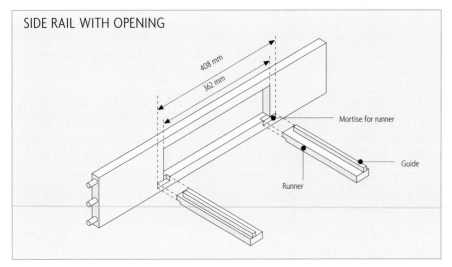

SIDE RAIL WITH OPENING

408 mm

362 mm

Mortise for runner

Guide

Runner

17 Set the marking gauge to 9.5 mm and mark centre lines down the ends of all rails. Choose a top edge for each rail and place a face mark on it and the outside face. Keeping the rails together as pairs with outside faces together, mark out the dowel positions on the ends. Number the ends to correspond to the legs.

18 Lay the long rails face down on the bench. Measure in 237 mm from each end, near the bottom edge, and then a further 41 mm. Square the marks across the inside face for about 50 mm. Set up a marking gauge to 25 mm and, working from the bottom edge, mark a line along the inside face between the two sets of marks. Reset the gauge to 13 mm and repeat. These are for the mortises for the drawer runners. The recess should be 41 x 12 mm (see diagram above).

19 Clamp one long rail to the bench and use a 10 mm chisel to remove the waste from a mortise to a depth of 12 mm. Repeat for the other three mortises.

20 Take one long rail and mark out the opening on the inside face. Make the bottom of the opening level with the top of the runner mortise. Measure up 88 mm for the top; the opening is 362 mm long, with each

end at the centre of a mortise. Using a 9.5 mm bit, bore a hole on the inner corner of the opening and use a jigsaw, with a straight edge as a guide, or a coping saw to cut out the area. Use a 25 mm chisel to square the corners. Lightly sand the edges.

ASSEMBLING THE FRAME

21 With a dowelling jig fixed to the end of a rail, drill the 10 mm dowel holes 26 mm deep. Repeat for all the dowel holes in rails and legs.

22 Check all parts of the frame fit together, inserting a couple of dowels into the end of each rail, but make sure you can remove them easily—you may need to sand them slightly. Use sash cramps to dry-assemble the end frames; then insert the front and back rails. Make sure the numbered joints are correctly aligned. Check the frame for square and twist. All the legs should sit on the ground.

23 Cut the runners to their exact length of 466 mm. Mark in 12 mm from one end and square a line across the face and down each edge for a shoulder line for the barefaced tenon. Turn the assembled frame upside down on the bench and check the joints are tight. Hold the runner in position with the shoulder line in line with the inner face of the back rail and mark where it crosses the inner face of the front rail. Both shoulder lines for the tenons are now marked. Transfer the shoulder lines to the other runner. Transfer the lines down the edges. Set a marking gauge to 7 mm and mark the rebate for the tenon along the edge and across the end of each runner.

24 Score across the grain of the cut line with a knife. Use a bench hook or G-cramp to hold the runners steady while you cut down the shoulder lines of the tenon to 7 mm. Then cut down the side of the tenon or chisel out the waste with a 25 mm chisel.

25 Pull the frame apart and check that the runners fit in the mortises. At the front rail they should finish flush with the bottom of the drawer opening. Adjust the fit if necessary.

26 To assemble the end frames spread adhesive around the dowel holes. Insert the dowels carefully, using a mallet to tap them in gently. Bring the legs and end rails together and leave them to dry. Add the front and back rails, inserting the drawer runners at the same time. Make sure the rails are the right way up.

27 Take scrap timber from the top and cut two 10 x 10 mm drawer guides 430 mm long, and two 26 x 19 mm kickers 430 mm long. The kickers must be 26 mm wide.

MAKING THE DRAWER
28 Check the height of the opening in the front rail and set a marking gauge to the height minus 2 mm: it should be 86 mm. Plane the top edge of the drawer material straight and square and mark a line along the face, across the end and back along the inside face. Set the material in a vice, and plane to the gauge line.

29 To make the groove for the bottom, use a router with 5 mm bit or a plough plane with 5 mm blade. Cut the groove on the inside face of the material 5 mm wide and 10 mm deep, 10 mm up from the bottom edge, but leave 360 mm ungrooved for the back.

30 Mark out the drawer parts along the material (the back is ungrooved), leaving room for saw cuts. Square the lines around all faces and trace over the lines with a knife. Check the lengths—the sides are 388 mm, the front 360 mm and the back should be trimmed to 359 mm (a difference of 1 mm).

31 On the inside face of the back and front mark in 19 mm from each end. Square lines across the face and the top and bottom edges to a depth of 12 mm. These are for the shoulders of the rebate joints. Set a marking gauge to 12 mm and, working from the inside face, mark a line across the end of each piece and over the edges down to the shoulder lines. Trace over the cross-grain lines with a knife. Use a tenon saw to cut out the rebate.

32 Cut the drawer bottom to size and adjust the fit of the pieces. The bottom will hold the joints slightly apart if it is too big. Take the drawer apart and sand all the internal faces.

33 Apply adhesive to each joint and nail the joints together, using 40 mm panel pins through the sides. Wipe off excess adhesive with a wet rag, check the drawer for square and adjust it if necessary. Allow it to dry.

ASSEMBLING THE TABLE
34 Sand the frame and top, using 120 grit abrasive paper, removing all pencil marks and sharp edges. Wipe away the dust and prepare the parts for finishing (see pages 246–247).

35 Cut the cleats to length. Using a 5 mm bit, drill holes in each 40 mm in from each end through one face and 50 mm in from the ends of the adjoining face (see diagram on page 264). Fix them to the top of the inside of the rails using adhesive and 30 mm countersunk screws.

36 Fit the kickers to the top 380 mm from each end, using two 40 mm screws placed 30 mm in from each end along the 19 mm wide side. Do not use adhesive, as they may need to be replaced should they wear out.

37 Place the frame right way up on the bench and insert the drawer into its opening. Locate the front flush with the front rail and, using a pencil, trace lines along the runners flush with the drawer sides and mark the depth of the

31 On the inside face of the drawer back and front mark out the rebates, 19 mm from each end.

drawer on the runners. Remove the drawer and locate the guides on the runners so they line up with the outside of the lines. Use adhesive and 25 mm panel pins to fasten the guides in place. Try the drawer again. You may need to plane the drawer sides down a little so the drawer runs smoothly. If it is sticking, rub candle wax or soap on the runners.

38 Lay the top face down on the bench with an old blanket under it. Centre the frame on it. Use a 3 mm bit to bore pilot holes into the top through the cleats and fix on the top using 30 mm x No. 8 screws.

39 Turn the table up and try the fit of the drawer again. A light plane on the bottom edge will ease any sticking on the kickers.

FINISHING
40 Apply the finish of your choice. Fit a handle to the centre of the drawer front.

A drawer is not difficult to make as long as your measurements and cutting are accurate.

TRADITIONAL TABLE WITH TURNED LEGS

The turned legs and moulded edge of this coffee table give it a traditional look. The frame is joined by mortises and barefaced tenons, and is strengthened with corner blocks.

THE TOP

1 Cut the four top pieces to length. Check the faces and edges are square and parallel, and the boards are uniformly thick.

2 Lay the boards out as they will be joined. Square and straighten the edges with a plane. Use chalk to draw an arrowhead across them as a face mark and to keep them in order. Use a marking gauge to mark a centre line along each joining edge for the dowels.

3 Place the boards on top of each other and use a G-cramp to hold them together with the joining edges exposed. Find the centre of the length and square a line across the edges for the centre dowel. From there measure and mark 225 mm and 450 mm in each direction. Square these lines across. Turn the boards; repeat for the other edges.

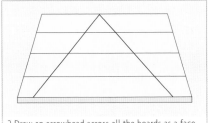

2 Draw an arrowhead across all the boards as a face mark and to keep the boards in the correct order.

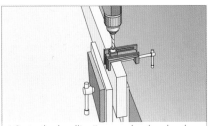

4 Centre the dowelling jig over a dowel mark and use a 10 mm bit to drill the hole 26 mm deep.

The finish used on this table is in keeping with its classic appearance. The pine was given a coat of orange shellac and two coats of clear lacquer.

4 Centre the dowelling jig over one dowel mark. Use a 10 mm bit to drill a hole 26 mm deep. Wrap an elastic band or masking tape around the bit as a depth guide. Repeat for all holes.

5 Set up the sash cramps. Use two on the bottom and one over the top. Have scrap timber handy to place between the cramps and the boards (the adhesive and cramps could react and stain the timber). Cover the bench with newspaper to catch any drips.

6 Spread adhesive around each hole on the first edge. Spread any excess over the edge of the board and insert the dowels. Apply adhesive to the joining edge and push the boards together. Repeat until all boards are joined. Place the top in the cramps face side up. Tighten the screws until excess adhesive is squeezed out and the joints appear tight. If the boards start to buckle, use packing between the top cramp and the panel to keep it flat. Allow it to dry.

MATERIALS*

PART	MATERIAL	FINISHED LENGTH	NO.
Top	150 x 38 mm timber PAR	1000 mm	4
Leg	75 x 75 mm timber PAR	360 mm	4
End rail	75 x 25 mm timber PAR	368 mm	2
Side rail	75 x 25 mm timber PAR	758 mm	2

Other: Chalk; PVA adhesive; newspaper and rag; fifteen 50 mm long 10 mm diameter timber dowels; twelve 40 mm x No. 6 countersunk wood screws; ten 50 mm x No. 8 countersunk wood screws; abrasive paper: two sheets each of 120 grit and 180 grit; finish of choice.

* Finished size: top 1000 x 550 mm; height 390 mm. Timber sizes given are nominal. For timber types and sizes see page 199.

11 Chisel out the waste, starting with a vertical cut and then chopping back towards the bottom.

THE LEGS

7 Take the leg material and mark off the length of each leg. Square the lines around all sides of the timber. Trace over them with a knife. Use a bench hook or cramp to hold the timber steady and a tenon saw to cut the legs on the waste side of the line.

8 Turn the legs on a lathe, or take them and a plan of the turning you want to a wood-turner (check your local telephone directory or a woodworking magazine).

9 Hold the legs together and mark a square across the ends to identify the outer and inner faces to which the rails will be attached. Number each leg (see step 13 illustration, page 263).

10 Measure 66 mm down from the top of each leg on one inner face and mark it for the bottom of the rail and mortise. With a square and pencil, continue this mark around the other inside face for the other mortise. Set a marking gauge to 14 mm and, working from the outer face, mark a line from the top to the 66 mm mark. Continue it 25 mm across the top for the top of the mortise. Set the gauge to 27 mm and from the same face mark a line from the top of the leg parallel to the 14 mm line. Continue it 25 mm across the top of the leg for the inside face of the mortise. Set the gauge to 25 mm and,

working from the inside face, mark the depth of the mortise across the top of the leg. Trace across the bottom of the mortise line with a knife, only between the gauge lines.

11 Clamp one leg in a vice and cut down the sides of a mortise with a tenon saw. Chop out the waste with a 12 mm chisel. Start with a vertical cut 2 mm from the bottom of the mortise, lay the bevelled side down at an angle between the two gauge lines and chop back towards the bottom. Repeat for all mortises. Straighten the sides of the mortise with a 25 mm chisel and make them a consistent 13 mm wide.

MAKING THE FRAME

12 Mark out the side rails to length. Square the lines around all sides of the rails and cut with a tenon saw.

13 On the inside face of each rail measure in 25 mm from the end and square a shoulder line across the face and 6 mm down the edges. Match the rails with the legs and number each joint. Set up a marking gauge to the width of a mortise. Working from the outside face, mark the width of the mortise across the end of the rail and down each edge to the 25 mm mark, to form a

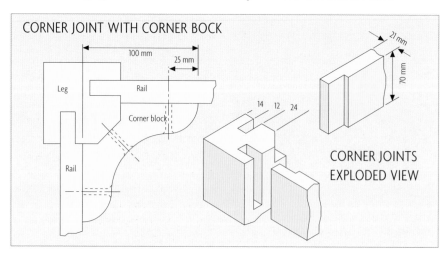

CORNER JOINT WITH CORNER BOCK

Leg · Rail · Corner block · Rail

100 mm · 25 mm · 21 mm · 70 mm · 14 · 12 · 24

CORNER JOINTS EXPLODED VIEW

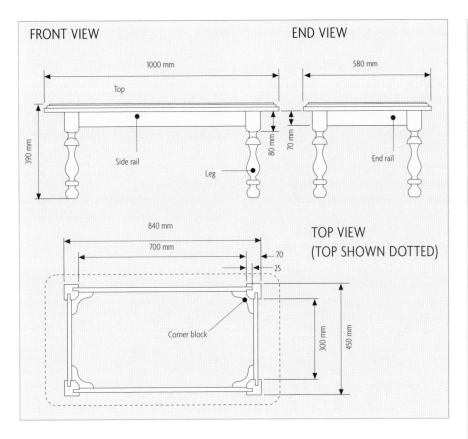

FRONT VIEW

1000 mm

Top

390 mm

Side rail

Leg

END VIEW

580 mm

80 mm

70 mm

End rail

840 mm

700 mm

70

25

TOP VIEW
(TOP SHOWN DOTTED)

Corner block

300 mm

450 mm

TOOLS

- Combination square and pencil
- Tape measure or rule
- Marking gauge
- Panel saw
- Tenon saw
- Smoothing plane or jack plane
- Three 1200 mm sash cramps
- G-cramp
- Dowelling jig
- Electric drill
- Drill bits: 3 mm, 5 mm, 10 mm, countersink
- Utility knife
- Woodturning lathe for legs (optional)
- Vice
- Chisels: 12 mm mortise or bevelled-edge, 25 mm bevelled-edge
- Compass
- Coping saw or electric jigsaw
- Spokeshave (optional)
- Ogee bit for router (optional)
- Electric router with 12 mm straight cutting bit (optional)
- Cork sanding block
- Screwdriver (cross-head or slotted)

barefaced tenon. Repeat for all tenons. Check the distance between the shoulder lines is 708 mm on the side rails and 318 mm on the end rails. Trace over the cross-grain lines with a knife.

14 Place a rail end up in a vice. Cut down the shoulder line with a tenon saw. Check the fit of each tenon, adjusting by trimming the inside edge of the tenon with a chisel.

14 Check the fit of the tenon in each mortise and, if necessary, trim the inside edge of the tenon.

15 On top of each leg measure in from the inside corner 20 mm. Mark a line diagonally across the corner; square it 19 mm down each inside face. At the inside corner measure 19 mm from the top and square lines across from point to point. Trace over the end-grain lines with a knife. Place the leg end up in a vice and cut down the diagonal line with a tenon saw. Turn the leg over and cut out the corner; clean up with the chisel.

16 Make the corner blocks from scrap pieces 19 mm thick. Make up a full-size pattern (see diagram on page 268). Use a compass and square to mark out the blocks and cut out with a coping saw or jigsaw. Sand rough edges and mark out holes for the screws. Use a 5 mm bit to drill the holes and countersink them.

17 Lay out sash cramps and have scraps of timber and a wet rag handy. Assemble the end frames. Use a brush to spread adhesive in the mortise and over the end of the tenon. Assemble the joints and place the end frames in the cramps. Check the legs and rails are square and the joint fits before adhesive sets.

18 Reorganize the cramps on the floor and follow the same process to insert the side rails. Clean off excess adhesive with the rag, and check the frame is square and without twist. If it is out of square, adjust the position of the cramps and tighten them. Leave to dry overnight.

19 Take the corner blocks and use a 3 mm drill bit to make pilot holes in the rails and legs. Spread adhesive on the joining faces and screw in place, using 40 mm x No. 6 screws.

ADDING THE TOP
20 Set a marking gauge to 9 mm, and mark a line along the top edge of each rail. Measure in 50 mm from each joint and square a line across. Find the centre of each side rail and square a line across. With a 5 mm bit, drill down through the rails for the fixing positions for the top. Turn the frame

over. With a 10 mm bit counterbore the holes to 40 mm.

21 Take the top and dress one side edge straight and square. From this edge square a line across one end. Use a knife to carefully trace over the lines and then plane back to the line. Mark 1000 mm from the planed end. Square the second end across, trace over the lines with the knife, and plane the end square and straight. Mark out the width from the dressed side edge, and plane the opposite edge straight and square.

22 To round the corners trace around a tin or glass. Cut the waste away with a coping saw or jigsaw, and finish with a plane and sanding block, or spokeshave. Complete

the top edge with a router or round over the edge with a plane or spokeshave.

23 Lay the top face down and centre the frame on it. Use a 3 mm bit to drill pilot holes through the counterbored holes into the top. Screw in 50 mm screws. Be careful they don't come through the top.

FINISHING
24 Take the top and frame apart and hand sand all parts well. Apply the finish (see pages 246–247). Reassemble.

SOPHISTICATED TABLE WITH GLASS TOP

The glass top of this elegant coffee table sits in the rebated edge of a timber frame, which is joined by tongued mitre joints. The end frames have neat bridle joints and decorative brass rods.

PREPARING THE TIMBER
1 Take the material and check that it has no defects. Use a smoothing plane to remove any machine marks, but be careful not to reduce the width and thickness too much: one pass with the plane should be enough. Use a combination square to check that the material is all square and straight.

2 Place face marks on the best face and edge. Mark off the end stiles and rails, leaving 5 mm between each. Use the square and pencil to square the lines around all faces of the material. Hold the parts to a bench with a G-cramp and, with a tenon saw, cut them slightly overlength.

MAKING BRIDLE JOINTS
3 Lay the end rails down side by side with the lines aligned. Lay a stile face down across the top of the rails so the stile just covers the line, and mark the width of the stile on the rails; repeat at the bottom of the rails. Repeat the whole process, laying a rail on the stiles. These are the shoulder lines for the bridle joints. Check they are 238 mm apart on the stiles and 408 mm on the rails. Adjust if necessary. Label the rails and stiles clearly, as mortises will be cut on the stiles and tenons in the rails.

4 Set a marking gauge to 10 mm. Working from both faces, mark lines from the shoulder line over the end and down to the

line on the other edge. Repeat on both ends of each rail and stile. Put a cross on the waste sections at each joint (the two outer bits of the rails and the centre bit of the stiles).

5 Take the rails and use a knife and square to cut the surface fibres at the shoulder lines

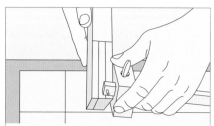
4 Mark lines from the shoulder line over the end and down to the shoulder line on the other edge.

This table was made from maple and was given a light walnut stain followed by three coats of satin-finish lacquer. The glass top has polished edges and was cut to fit after the table was assembled.

and around the edges as far as the gauge lines. In the same way cut the waste lines on the mortise section of the stiles.

6 Clamp a stile in a vice edge up. Use a 10 mm bit to bore a hole through it near the inner end of the mortise. Drill halfway, and then turn the timber over and drill from the other side. Repeat on all stiles.

7 Turn the stile end up in the vice and use a tenon saw to cut down the sides of the mortise on the waste side of the lines. Use the 10 mm chisel to remove the waste and level the bottom of the mortise. Repeat the process for all mortises.

8 With a G-cramp, hold a rail face down on the bench. Use a tenon saw to make a series

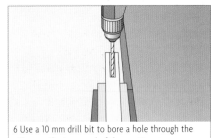

6 Use a 10 mm drill bit to bore a hole through the stile near the inner end of the mortise.

MATERIALS*

PART	MATERIAL	FINISHED LENGTH	NO.
End stile	100 x 38 mm timber PAR	420 mm	4
End rail	100 x 38 mm timber PAR	590 mm	4
Long rail	100 x 38 mm timber PAR	940 mm	2
Short rail	100 x 38 mm timber PAR	570 mm	2

Other: PVA adhesive; newspaper and rag; four 300 mm long brass rods 6 mm in diameter; abrasive paper: three sheets of 120 grit and two sheets each of 180 grit and 240 grit; ten 50 mm long 10 mm diameter timber dowels; 6 mm thick glass top with polished edges (777 x 406 mm, but check the size required when the table is finished); finish of choice.

* Finished size: top 1000 x 590 mm; height 420 mm. Timber sizes given are nominal. For timber types and sizes see page 199.

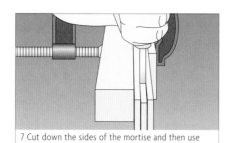
7 Cut down the sides of the mortise and then use a 10 mm chisel to remove the remaining waste.

of cuts about 10 mm apart along the waste piece up to the shoulder lines. Cut down only to the gauge line, stopping on the waste side of the line. Use the 30 mm chisel to remove the waste by chiselling from the side at an angle up towards the face. Repeat for the other face. Test the fit in the mortise, trimming the side of the tenon until you have a neat fit. Then trim down the

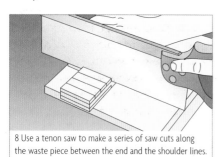
8 Use a tenon saw to make a series of saw cuts along the waste piece between the end and the shoulder lines.

shoulders until they are squared back to the knife lines. Repeat for all the tenons.

ASSEMBLING END FRAMES

9 Dry-assemble the end frames with the face marks out and the edge marks to the inside. On the rails measure 136 mm from each shoulder and square a mark across the inner edge. The holes for the brass rods are set off-centre so the rods can cross. Set up a marking gauge to 12 mm and work from the outside face of one rail to place a small mark at the drilling position for one rod. Repeat for the other hole, but work from the inside face. Then mark the holes in the opposite rail, making sure they correspond diagonally. Place a straight edge across the frame on the diagonal marks and set up a sliding bevel to 60 degrees. Take the frame apart and set one rail in a vice with inner edge up. Using a 6 mm bit and sliding bevel to guide the angle of the drill, make a hole 15 mm deep. Repeat for all holes, and for the other end frame. Insert the rods.

10 Spread newspaper to collect any drips. Take the components and place PVA adhesive on the tenon; spread it over the sides of the joint. Spread adhesive around

9 Line the drill up with the hole, and use the sliding bevel to guide the angle of the drill.

the mortise. Bring the parts together. Use sash cramps to pull the joints tight, one across the rails and one across the stiles. Put scrap blocks between the cramps and the frame to protect the edges. With a wet rag remove excess adhesive. Leave to dry for two hours.

PREPARING THE TOP RAILS

11 Take the remaining timber and use a square and pencil to mark a mitre line across the face 15 mm in from one end. Square the lines down the edges and across the opposite face so they meet. From the longest point mark off 940 mm. Use the square to mark the opposite mitre across the face and around the material. Allow 10 mm between each piece, and repeat this step for the other long rail and for the two short rails, which will be 570 mm long.

12 Between each piece square a line across the face of the material and down the edges. Use a tenon saw to cut the pieces off square to this rough mark. Do not cut on the mitre lines.

13 Set a marking gauge to 20 mm. On the long rails only, work from the inside edge to mark a line from the mitre line to the end of the material over the end and back to the mitre line. Use the gauge to mark a point on the mitre line 20 mm in from the outer edge. Square a line from the 20 mm point on the mitre line to the other

indoor

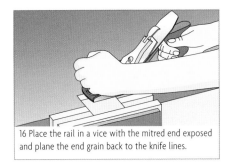

16 Place the rail in a vice with the mitred end exposed and plane the end grain back to the knife lines.

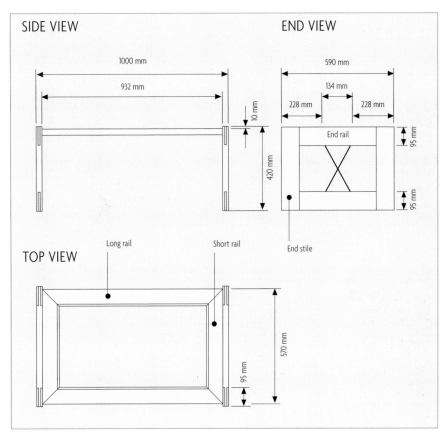

SIDE VIEW

1000 mm

932 mm

10 mm

420 mm

END VIEW

590 mm

134 mm

228 mm 228 mm

End rail

95 mm

95 mm

End stile

TOP VIEW

Long rail Short rail

570 mm

95 mm

20 mm line. On the face of the rail you should now have a tenon projecting from the mitre (see diagram on page 275).

14 Set the marking gauge to 10 mm. Holding the butt of the gauge against the face on the inside edge, mark a line from the mitre line to the end and across the end. Do this from both faces. This gives you the thickness of the tenon. Mark the waste pieces with a cross on all faces.

15 Use a knife and square to cut across the face and edges at the mitre lines on all pieces.

16 Hold a short rail in a vice. Use a tenon saw to cut the mitres on the ends, cutting on the waste side of the line. Place it edgewise in the vice with the mitred end exposed and plane the end grain back to the knife lines. Plane only in the direction of the mitre, have a fine set on the blade and ensure the cutting edge is parallel with the plane's sole. Repeat for each end of both short rails.

17 With the gauge set to 10 mm, mark lines 10 mm in from each face across the mitre face. Set the gauge to 20 mm and from the edges mark across the mitred edge between the two gauge lines. Put a cross on the area in the centre, the recess for the tenon. Repeat for all the mortises.

MAKING THE TOP JOINTS

18 Set the long rail in a vice with the mitre line parallel to the floor but close to the vice jaws. Use a tenon saw to cut down the sides of the tenon on the waste side of the lines. Cut down to just short of the mitre lines. Place the rail perpendicularly in the vice and cut down the 20 mm gauge line on the inside of the rail. Turn the inside edge of the rail up and cut the end of the tenon down to just short of the mitre line.

19 Hold the material to the bench with a G-cramp and use the tenon saw to cut down the mitre lines to the tenon lines (10 mm) on both faces of the rails. Carefully cut these away, working on the waste side of the lines. Use the 12 mm chisel to clean back to the mitre lines and square the shoulders and

edges of the mitre. Repeat this step to cut the other three tenons.

20 Lay long and short rails together with joints aligned; trace around the tenon onto the face of the end rail as a guide for chiselling out the mortise. Clamp an end rail to the bench with a mitre up. Use an 8 mm chisel to remove the waste from the mortise. Start with the flat back of the chisel towards the inside end of the mortise and use a mallet or hammer to strike the chisel square down into the timber. Then chisel horizontally to remove a little waste. Continue until the mortise is cut. Check the tenon fits neatly in the recess. Repeat for all the mortises.

21 Clamp one long rail to the work surface and cut a rebate 6 mm deep and 10 mm

Bridle joints hold the end frames, with their decorative rods, together.

wide in the inside edge (this will hold the glass top). Repeat for the other long rail and the two short rails. Use a rebate plane, a router or laminate trimmer.

ASSEMBLING THE TOP FRAME

22 Dry-assemble the top frame, setting up the sash cramps as you go. Check the joints and make any adjustments. Use one sash cramp to pull the short rails into the long rails, and one at each end to pull the long rails into the short rails.

23 Take the frame apart, cover the work surface with newspaper and use an old paintbrush to apply adhesive to the tenon, the mortise and the shoulders of the mitre. Reassemble the frame in the cramps, placing scrap blocks between the cramps and the

frame to prevent damage to the timber, and tighten the screws. Use a wet rag to remove excess adhesive. Check the frame for square, and make any adjustments by offsetting the cramps. Leave to dry for two hours.

ASSEMBLING THE TABLE

24 Place an end frame in the vice and plane the bridle joints down flush. Plane the end grain towards the centre of the frame. Turn the frame over and repeat. Repeat for the other end frame.

25 Set the marking gauge to 25 mm. Working from the top edge on the inside face of each end frame, mark a line, starting and stopping it 15 mm in from each end. Measure to the centre of the frame on

this line and square a mark across the line for the centre dowel. Measure out each side 125 mm and a further 125 mm and square lines across the gauged line. You now have five dowel centres. Use a 10 mm bit to bore the dowel holes 20 mm deep. Wrap a piece of tape around the bit as a depth guide.

26 Check the top is dry and remove it from the cramps. Set a marking gauge to 15 mm and, working from the top face, mark a line across each end. Square a line across the centre of the line. Measure out from the

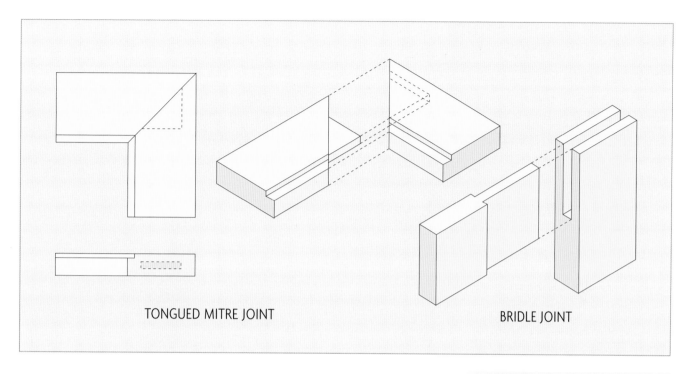

TONGUED MITRE JOINT

BRIDLE JOINT

centre mark 125 mm each way and a further 125 mm and square lines across. Check the dowel marks align with those on the end frames. If they don't, adjust the marks on the top. Use the 10 mm bit to drill holes into the top frame to a depth of 33 mm.

27 Check that the frames fit together neatly and make any adjustments. Take the frames apart. Protect the brass rods with newspaper, taping it at the ends. Sand the entire table with 120 grit abrasive paper. A sanding block will help you reach into the corners and

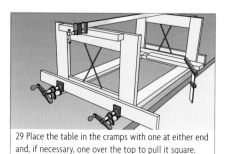

29 Place the table in the cramps with one at either end and, if necessary, one over the top to pull it square.

rebates. Use a sharp chisel to remove any adhesive that has set hard. Prepare the frames for finishing (see pages 246–247). If you need to stain the timber, do it now.

28 Spread adhesive around the dowel holes and on the joint faces. Insert the dowels in the holes and tap them in. Tap the three frames together with a hammer or mallet, protecting the surface with a block of wood.

29 Place the table in the cramps upside down. Use two cramps, one on each side of the end frames. Check the end frames are square to the top. If necessary, place a cramp over the top of the end frames to pull them parallel and square to the top. Leave the table to dry overnight.

FINISHING
30 Remove the table from the cramps and give it a final sanding with 240 grit abrasive paper round a sanding block. Apply your finish.

CUTTING MORTISES

- A mortise chisel cuts straighter than a bevelled-edge chisel.
- Chisel towards the centre from both sides to prevent chipping out the edges of the mortise.

31 Check the size of the rebated area and have glass cut to fit. Place the glass in the rebate.

playhouses and doll's houses

playhouses and doll's houses

BUILDING PLAYHOUSES AND DOLL'S HOUSES

Doll's houses and other play buildings are a delight to play with—and to build. The designs used here require only basic woodworking skills, but can be adapted to suit your expertise.

When finishing playhouses such as this farm or country house (above right), let your imagination run riot. They can be painted any colours you like.

ADAPTING THE DESIGNS

The projects in this book can be simplified as you prefer. For example, the doll's houses can be made without staircases, doors or windows and will still provide children with many hours of enjoyment, or you can add fireplaces and chimneys, balustrades or gardens.

Doll's houses are traditionally built at a scale of 1:12, and components for houses built to that scale can be purchased. They include window frames (complete with acrylic panes and opening sashes), door frames and doors, skirting boards, cornices and staircases with turned balusters. There are also wallpapers made to scale, and most doll's house furniture is made to suit these houses. Specialist suppliers (check your phone book) will provide catalogues.

SAFETY

Preschool children should not be left unsupervised while they are playing with these houses. Children always use items in ways that were never intended, so take all precautions to ensure the items are safe.

- Ensure nails are punched in and holes are filled, and remove sharp edges, against which a child could fall, with a sanding block and abrasive paper. If the medieval castle is intended for young children, you may prefer to omit the battlements.
- If younger children are likely to play with the structures, do not include in the furnishings small items that could be swallowed or cause choking. Also, make sure all small trim pieces are securely attached.

indoor

CITY HOUSE

This delightful front-opening doll's house has three storeys, and the front part of the roof lifts up to reveal an attic with dormer windows. At a scale of 1:12 it is the right size for traditional doll's house furniture.

TOOLS

- Tape measure and pencil
- Straight edge
- Combination square
- Handsaw
- Circular saw (optional)
- Jigsaw
- Smoothing plane
- Cork sanding block
- Cramp
- Utility knife
- Portable electric drill
- Drill bits: 1.6 mm, 2 mm, 10 mm
- Hammer
- Nail punch
- Mitre box
- Screwdriver
- Dust mask
- Safety glasses
- Hearing protection

The city house is a truly elegant abode but you could give it an individual touch by adding a chimney, or balustrades on the stairs. The sizes of the rooms can be adjusted as desired by moving the internal walls.

CUTTING OUT

1 Using the tape, square, pencil and straight edge, mark out the pieces on the MDF sheets, leaving 4 mm cutting space between each (see cutting diagrams on pages 281–282). Cut them out and label each piece.

2 Plane the edges to the finished size and smooth them with the sanding block and abrasive paper. Ensure that the edges are straight and square where required.

3 Create 45-degree bevels on the joining edges of the dormer roofs so that they will fit together neatly, and a 45-degree bevel on the base of the dormer front wall (see box on page 284).

4 Again using the tape, square, pencil and straight edge, mark out the positions of the windows, doors and stair openings. In one corner of each drill a 10 mm hole, insert the jigsaw blade and cut out the holes.

THE FLOORS

5 If you want to have a floorboard finish on the internal floors, mark the short side of each floor every 10 or 15 mm and then, using the straight edge as a guide, score the

MATERIALS*

PART	MATERIAL	FINISHED LENGTH	WIDTH	NO.
Back wall	9 mm MDF	880 mm	619 mm	1
Side wall	9 mm MDF	1065 mm	350 mm	2
Floor	9 mm MDF	600 mm	350 mm	4
Front wall	9 mm MDF	775 mm	309 mm	2
Base lipping	9 mm MDF	619 mm	50 mm	1
Top lipping	9 mm MDF	619 mm	50 mm	1
Internal wall	9 mm MDF	350 mm	254 mm	3
Attic wall	9 mm MDF	350 mm	225 mm	1
Roof (front)	9 mm MDF	619 mm	280 mm	1
Roof (back)	9 mm MDF	619 mm	270 mm	1
Dormer front wall	9 mm MDF	135 mm	100 mm	2
Dormer side wall	3 mm MDF	80 mm	80 mm	4
Dormer roof	3 mm MDF	155 mm	95 mm	4
Stair tread	30 x 19 mm timber	65 mm		42
Window internal stile	6 mm moulding	130 mm		10
Window internal rail	6 mm moulding	65 mm		10
Window external stile	6 x 6 mm timber	125 mm		10
Window external rail	6 x 6 mm timber	80 mm		10
Window external centre rail	6 x 6 mm timber	60 mm		5
Window pane	2 mm acrylic	130 mm	65 mm	5
Dormer internal stile	6 mm moulding	65 mm		4
Dormer internal rail	6 mm moulding	65 mm		4
Dormer external stile	6 x 6 mm timber	60 mm		4
Dormer external rail	6 x 6 mm timber	75 mm		4
Dormer pane	2 mm acrylic	65 mm	65 mm	2
Door	3 mm MDF	200 mm	80 mm	1
Door stile	3 mm MDF	200 mm	10 mm	4
Door rail	3 mm MDF	60 mm	10 mm	6
Doorway stile	6 x 6 mm timber	197 mm		2
Doorway rail	6 x 6 mm timber	97 mm		1

Other: Abrasive paper; PVA adhesive; 25 x 1.6 mm lost-head nails; six 50 mm long hinges and screws to match; filler; masking tape; 6 mm quadrant moulding for skirting boards; finish of choice.

* Finished size: 619 x 368 mm and 1075 mm high. The timber sizes given are actual sizes. MDF sheets used are 1220 x 2440 mm.

surface with the utility knife to make parallel lines. Sand the floor lightly to remove any raised edges.

6 Apply stain and clear finish (gloss or satin) to the floors to achieve the effect required and allow it to dry. Paint the under side of the three upper floors (the ceilings of the rooms below) as required.

ASSEMBLING THE HOUSE

7 Paint the internal walls and the inside of the outer walls and roof pieces as required. It will be more difficult to paint them once the house has been assembled.

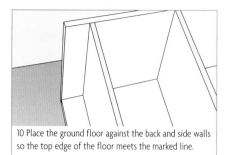

10 Place the ground floor against the back and side walls so the top edge of the floor meets the marked line.

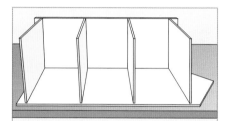

11 Using an internal wall as a spacer, tack the upper floors in place on the side wall.

8 Take the back wall of the house and the two side walls. Using the tape, square and pencil, mark a line on the inside of each 50 mm above the bottom. Place the walls on the workbench so that the side with the marked line is facing up.

9 Using the 1.6 mm bit, drill four holes down the left edge of the back wall, each one 5 mm in from the edge. Apply adhesive to the back edge of one side wall and fix it to the back wall. Nail through the drilled holes into the edge. Ensure that the side wall is flush with the edge of the back wall and that the base of the side wall is flush with the base of the back wall. As you assemble the house, punch the nails below the surface so that the holes can be filled before the final paint touch-up.

10 Take the ground floor and place it against the attached back and side walls so that the top edge of the floor meets the marked line. Fix it in place with adhesive and nails.

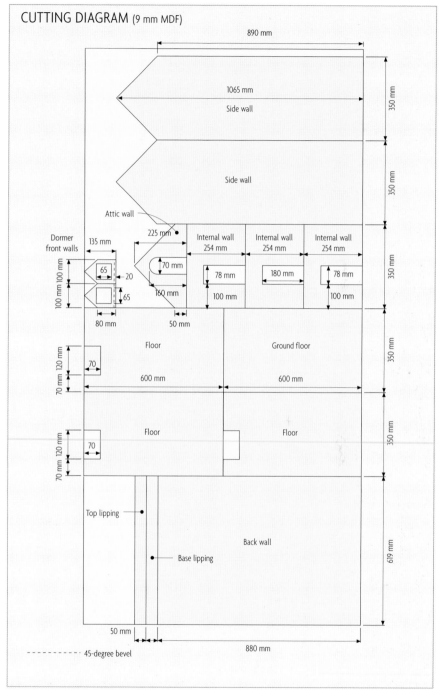

CUTTING DIAGRAM (9 mm MDF)

890 mm

1065 mm
Side wall

350 mm

Side wall

350 mm

Attic wall

Dormer front walls

135 mm 225 mm Internal wall 254 mm Internal wall 254 mm Internal wall 254 mm

350 mm

100 mm 100 mm 65 20 70 mm 78 mm 180 mm 78 mm
160 mm 100 mm 100 mm
65

80 mm 50 mm

Floor Ground floor

350 mm

70 mm 120 mm 70 600 mm 600 mm

Floor Floor

350 mm

70 mm 120 mm 70

Top lipping

Back wall

619 mm

Base lipping

50 mm

45-degree bevel 880 mm

11 Take an internal wall and place it on the ground floor, next to the side wall, and use it as a spacer for the location of the next floor. Tack this in place on the side wall and repeat for the next floor and the top floor.

CUTTING DIAGRAM (9 mm MDF)

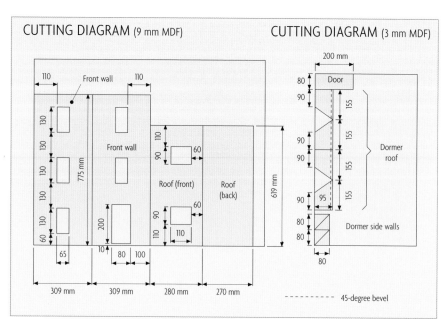

| 110 | Front wall | 110 |

130
130
130
130
60

775 mm

Front wall

200

110
90
110

Roof (front)

60
90
60
90

Roof (back)

619 mm

10
65
80 100

309 mm | 309 mm | 280 mm | 270 mm

CUTTING DIAGRAM (3 mm MDF)

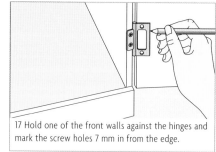

200 mm

80
Door
90

155

90
90

155

155

Dormer roof

90
95

155

80
80

Dormer side walls

80

- - - - - - - 45-degree bevel

17 Hold one of the front walls against the hinges and mark the screw holes 7 mm in from the edge.

17 Hold one of the front walls against the hinges and mark their location. The screw holes should be 7 mm in from the edge. Repeat with the other front wall.

18 Attach hinges to the back roof so they are centred 155 mm in from each end in the same way. Attach the front part of the roof to the hinges.

THE STAIRS

19 Take fourteen of the stair treads. On the top (wide face) of each tread mark a line across the centre 15 mm in from each long edge. Glue one tread on top of another, aligning the top tread with the line. Glue them together in pairs, then glue the pairs together and so on. Repeat to make two more sets of stairs. Apply your chosen finish to the stairs.

20 Position the stairs so that they sit on the floor near the front of the house and run back to the opening in the next floor. The back half of the top tread will be flat against the ceiling beyond the opening. Place adhesive under the bottom tread and on the back half of the top tread, and fix the stairs in place.

THE FRONT DOOR

21 Take the door and glue a stile to each side of the front so that the stile is flush with the edge of the door. Repeat on the back of the door.

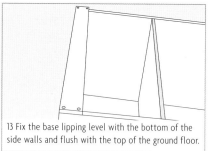

13 Fix the base lipping level with the bottom of the side walls and flush with the top of the ground floor.

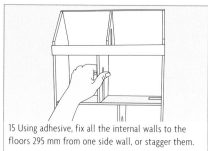

15 Using adhesive, fix all the internal walls to the floors 295 mm from one side wall, or stagger them.

12 Take the other side wall, ensure that the marked line is on the inside and locate the line along the top of the ground floor. The base of the side wall should be level with the base of the back wall and flush with the edge of the back wall. Again using the internal walls as spacers, locate the upper floors on the side wall. Glue and nail the wall and all floors in place.

13 Using adhesive and nails, fix the base lipping so it is level with the bottom of the side walls and flush with the top of the ground floor. Fix the top lipping so the bottom is level with the bottom of the top floor and the ends are flush with the side walls.

14 Stand the house up and glue and nail on the back part of the roof so that it is flush with the top of the gable and each side wall.

15 The internal walls can all be located 295 mm from one side wall to form a vertical line, or they can be staggered. Score the floor where they will go, sand lightly and then fix them in place with adhesive.

16 The hinges for the front walls are attached to the front edges of the side walls and are centred 80 mm from the bottom and top. Drill holes for the screws 4 mm in from the outside edge, using the 2 mm bit. Fix the hinges to the walls.

indoor

22 On both sides of the door place the rails at the top and bottom, and across the centre 55 mm from the bottom of the top rail. Cut the remaining stiles and fit them down the middle between the rails.

23 Plane the edges of the door to ensure that it fits in the doorway. Using abrasive paper, round off the edges down the hinged side of the door so that it will swing open easily. Paint the door.

24 The door is hinged on pins inserted into the top and bottom of the door opening. Working from the bottom edge of the front wall and using the 1.6 mm bit, drill a hole 5 mm in from the hinge side of the door opening and in the centre of the thickness of the MDF.

25 Place the door in the hole, flush with the face of the house, and drill a 10 mm deep hole into the door. Drill similar holes at the top of the door opening and the top of the door.

26 Cut the head off a nail and insert it as the top hinge, and then insert a nail through the bottom as the lower hinge, pushing it firmly into place.

27 Take the doorway stiles and rail and paint them. Fix the doorway stiles to the sides of the opening so that they slightly overlap the opening, and then fix the doorway rail across the top of the opening.

THE WINDOWS

28 Take the window internal stiles and rails and cut mitres on each end so that the pieces will fit into the openings cut for the windows. Paint the pieces as required and glue them in place, positioning them so that the acrylic for the window pane will sit flush with the outside of the house.

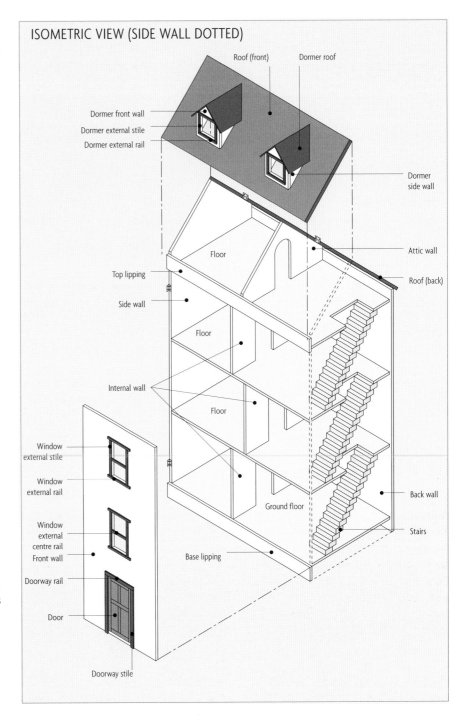

ISOMETRIC VIEW (SIDE WALL DOTTED)

Roof (front) · Dormer roof · Dormer front wall · Dormer external stile · Dormer external rail · Dormer side wall · Attic wall · Roof (back) · Floor · Top lipping · Side wall · Floor · Internal wall · Floor · Window external stile · Window external rail · Window external centre rail · Front wall · Doorway rail · Door · Ground floor · Base lipping · Back wall · Stairs · Doorway stile

29 Allow the adhesive to dry and use the filler to fill any small gaps that remain. Sand to a smooth finish and touch up the finish.

30 Paint the external stiles and rails. Place the acrylic pane in the first window and glue a base rail along the bottom of the window so that it covers the pane by about 3 mm. Glue the stiles to the sides of the window so that they are flush with the ends of the base rail and cover the pane by about 3 mm.

31 Install the top rail, again covering the window acrylic by 3 mm. Place adhesive on each end of the centre rail and place it across the centre of the window between the stiles. Repeat for each of the other windows.

THE DORMERS

32 Glue two dormer side walls to a dormer front wall so that they are flush with the sides of the front wall and the angle of the side wall forms a continuous line with the bevel on the base of the front wall. Repeat for the second dormer. Allow the adhesive to dry.

33 Paint the dormer side and front walls. Also paint the window stiles and rails. Let them dry.

34 Fit the stiles and rails and the window pane as in steps 26–29.

35 Lay the roof pieces side by side and place masking tape over the joint. Turn the pieces over and place adhesive in the joint. Place adhesive along the top edge of the front wall and side walls, and lift the roof into place. The tape will hold the roof together while the adhesive dries.

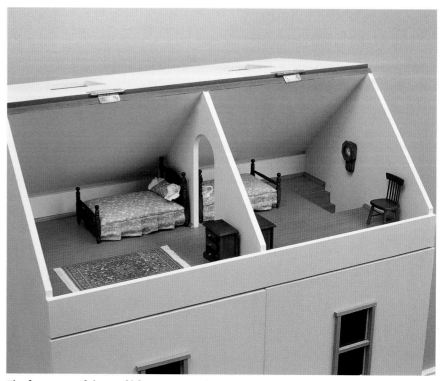

The front part of the roof lifts up to reveal two extra rooms in the attic.

36 Apply adhesive to the edges of the dormers and fix them in place on the roof.

TO FINISH

37 Punch and fill the nail holes. Paint the exterior of the house and touch up any paint as necessary.

38 Apply finish to the lengths of timber for the skirtings. Allow it to dry and then cut it into lengths to fit each room, with mitres where pieces will meet in the corners. Apply adhesive to the back of the pieces and glue them in place.

CREATING A BEVEL AT 45 DEGREES

To create a 45-degree bevel, measure down the face the same distance as the thickness of the MDF. Draw a line along the face and over the edges. On the edges, draw a line from that point to the corner. Clamp the board securely and use a plane to make the bevel. Check the fit of the pieces and adjust as necessary.

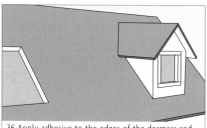

36 Apply adhesive to the edges of the dormers and then fix them in place on the roof.

MEDIEVAL CASTLE

This exciting castle has a stable and tower block, ramparts with staircase, and a drawbridge. The back is open for easy access to the tower and stable. The tower is completed as a separate unit and then located on the stable.

PREPARATION

1 Using the tape, square, pencil and straight edge, mark out the pieces on the MDF sheet, leaving about 4 mm cutting space between each (see diagram on page 287). Cut them out and label each piece.

2 Plane the pieces to their finished sizes and use the sanding block and abrasive paper to smooth the edges. Ensure that they are straight and square where required.

3 Again using the tape, square, pencil and straight edge, mark out the positions of the windows, doors, gate and stair opening. For the curved tops, see the box on page 289. Where necessary, use the 10 mm bit and drill a hole in a corner of the opening to fit the blade and use a jigsaw to cut out the holes. Put the piece cut from the gate aside, as it will form the drawbridge.

4 To give the walls an appearance of being made from stone, score the external faces in

The outer walls of this enchanting castle have been scored to give the impression of regular stone blocks, and then painted a creamy stone colour. The battlements are made separately and fixed on with adhesive.

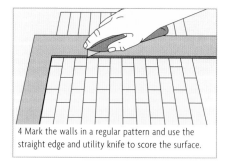

4 Mark the walls in a regular pattern and use the straight edge and utility knife to score the surface.

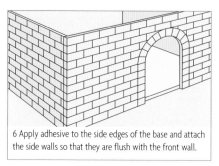

6 Apply adhesive to the side edges of the base and attach the side walls so that they are flush with the front wall.

MATERIALS*

PART	MATERIAL	FINISHED LENGTH	WIDTH	NO.
Base	9 mm MDF	800 mm	619 mm	1
Front wall	9 mm MDF	819 mm	300 mm	1
Side wall	9 mm MDF	619 mm	300 mm	2
Rear wall	9 mm MDF	241 mm	100 mm	2
Stable wall	9 mm MDF	800 mm	250 mm	1
Stable roof	9 mm MDF	800 mm	291 mm	1
Sub-base (front/back)	42 x 19 mm timber	819 mm		2
Sub-base (side)	42 x 19 mm timber	628 mm		2
Tower roof/floor	9 mm MDF	600 mm	291 mm	2
Tower front wall	9 mm MDF	619 mm	519 mm	1
Tower side wall	9 mm MDF	519 mm	291 mm	2
Tower internal wall	9 mm MDF	291 mm	250 mm	2
Stair tread	30 x 19 mm timber	50 mm		12
Rampart (front)	9 mm MDF	800 mm	100 mm	1
Rampart (side)	9 mm MDF	319 mm	100 mm	2
Rampart support	9 mm MDF	241 mm	90 mm	2
Battlement	9 mm MDF	50 mm	50 mm	34

Other: Abrasive paper; PVA adhesive; 25 x 1.6 mm lost-head nails; six 25 mm x No. 4 wood screws; four brass eyes; small-scale chain; filler; finish of choice.

*   Finished size: 819 x 628 mm and 847 mm high. Timber sizes are actual sizes. MDF sheets used are 1220 x 2440 mm.

a regular pattern. To do this, mark the short sides of the piece every 25 mm and then, using a straight edge to join the marks, score the surface with a utility knife. Mark the long sides every 50 mm and score between alternate pairs of lines. Add curved blocks over the gate. Sand lightly to remove raised edges.

5 Apply your chosen finish to the inside and outside of each piece.

ASSEMBLING THE CASTLE

6 Apply adhesive to the side edges of the base and attach the side walls so that they are flush with the front wall and the back edge of the base. Carefully drill locating holes with the 1.6 mm bit, and nail them in place. Always punch the heads below the surface and fill the holes with wood filler.

7 Using the mitre box and handsaw, cut the pieces for the sub-base to length with 45-degree mitres on each end. Place them

under the base so that they are flush with the edges of the base, and attach them with adhesive and nails. If you have pieces of timber left over, attach them under the floor as additional support.

8 Position the stable wall with its front edge 300 mm from the rear of the castle. Ensure that it is vertical, and then glue and nail it in place. Using the two rear walls as spacers, position the stable roof so that it sits flush with the top of the stable wall and is horizontal. Apply adhesive along the front and side edges of the roof, and fix it in place. Drill locating holes and nail through the side walls.

THE TOWER

9 Using adhesive and nails, attach the tower roof to the top of a tower side wall so that the top is flush with the top of the wall. Use a tower internal wall as a spacer, and attach the tower floor on the same side wall. Let the adhesive dry completely, and then attach the other tower side wall.

10 Apply adhesive and position the front wall of the tower over the roof, floor and side walls.

11 Insert the internal walls of the tower and glue them in place.

indoor

TOOLS

- Tape measure
- Straight edge
- Pencil
- Combination square
- Handsaw
- Circular saw (optional)
- Jigsaw
- Smoothing plane
- Cork sanding block
- Utility knife
- Mitre box
- Hammer
- Nail punch
- Screwdriver
- Portable electric drill
- Drill bit: 1.6 mm, 10 mm
- Dust mask
- Safety glasses
- Hearing protection

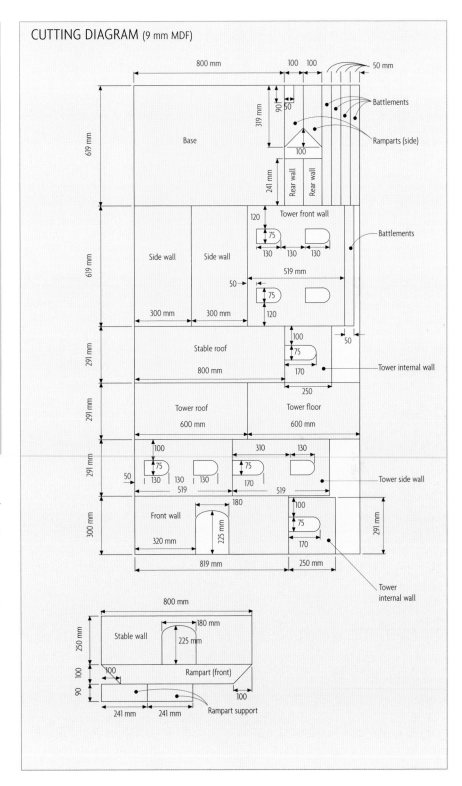

CUTTING DIAGRAM (9 mm MDF)

12 On the top of the stable roof measure and mark a line 90 mm from each side wall. Position the tower on the stable so that the sides of the tower are contained within the drawn lines and the front wall of the tower is sitting over the top of the stable wall to form a continuous vertical wall. Attach the tower with adhesive and screws up through the stable roof into the tower side walls.

THE BATTLEMENTS

13 The battlements are glued to the top of the castle and tower walls. Ensure that they are free from dust, and position the first battlement in the centre of the front wall and then the next two on the ends of the front wall. Calculate the positions of the

ISOMETRIC VIEW

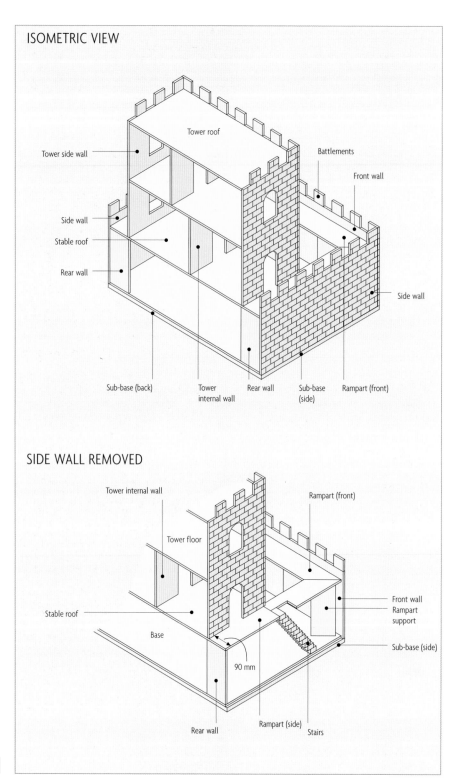

Tower roof

Tower side wall

Battlements

Front wall

Side wall

Stable roof

Rear wall

Side wall

Sub-base (back)

Tower internal wall

Rear wall

Sub-base (side)

Rampart (front)

SIDE WALL REMOVED

Tower internal wall

Rampart (front)

Tower floor

Stable roof

Base

90 mm

Front wall
Rampart support

Sub-base (side)

Rear wall

Rampart (side)

Stairs

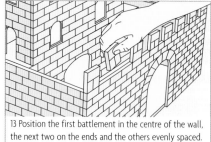

13 Position the first battlement in the centre of the wall, the next two on the ends and the others evenly spaced.

other battlements for the front and side walls so that they are spaced along the wall evenly.

14 On the tower, locate the first battlement in the centre of the front wall, the next two on the ends, and space out the rest evenly.

THE RAMPARTS

15 Using the two rampart supports as spacers, position the front rampart against the front wall. Fix it with adhesive and nails. Position and fix the side ramparts in the same way, flush with the stable roof. Fix the supports under the mitres.

16 Take the stair treads and mark a line down the centre of the flat side of each tread, that is 15 mm from a long edge. Glue one tread on top of another so that the front of the top tread lines up with the drawn line. You will find it easier if you glue them together in pairs, then the pairs together and so on.

17 Position the stairs with the bottom tread sitting on the base and the top tread flush with the top of the side rampart. Fix the stairs in place with adhesive below the bottom tread and on the back of the top tread.

THE DRAWBRIDGE

18 Take the drawbridge and ensure that it fits neatly into the opening in the front wall.

DRAWBRIDGE

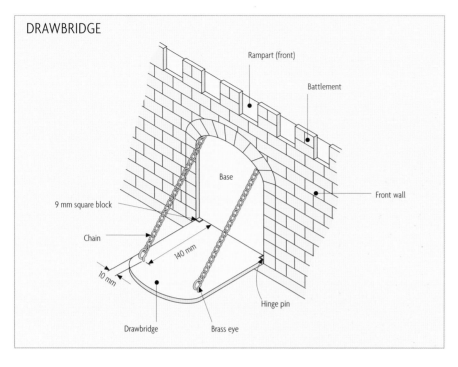

Rampart (front)

Battlement

Base

Front wall

9 mm square block

Chain

140 mm

10 mm

Drawbridge

Brass eye

Hinge pin

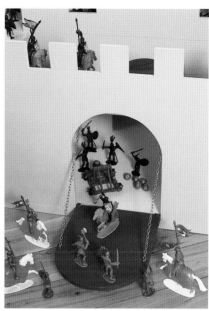

The drawbridge is supported by two chains fixed to the underside of the front rampart.

19 In the bottom edge of the drawbridge, cut a 10 mm square notch at each end. Using the 1.6 mm bit, drill a hole sideways into each notch, 5 mm up from the bottom of the drawbridge and 4.5 mm in from the front face.

20 From scraps of MDF or other timber make two 9 mm square blocks. Drill a hole into the centre of one side of each block.

21 Cut the heads from two 1.6 mm nails. Insert one nail into each hole in the bottom of the drawbridge and then into the corresponding block to create a pin hinge.

22 Finish the drawbridge and then glue the blocks into place in the corners of the gate opening.

23 Locate two brass eyes on the inside of the drawbridge, 140 mm up from the base of the drawbridge and 10 mm in from the side. Set the other two eyes under the front

rampart, 80 mm either side of the centre and 10 mm in from the edge. Connect the chain so that the drawbridge, when open, is supported by the chain and level with the floor of the castle.

TO FINISH

24 Insert the rear walls at the back of the stable and glue them in place.

25 Punch all nails below the surface, fill the holes with filler and finish painting the castle.

DRAWING A CURVE

To create curved tops on window or door openings, use a nail, string and pencil.

Hammer the nail into the centre of the proposed opening at the height where the curve begins. Tie onto it a piece of string and loop the string over the pencil, leaving a length equal to half the width of the opening. Then hold the string taut while drawing in the curve.

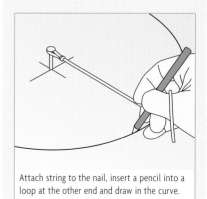

Attach string to the nail, insert a pencil into a loop at the other end and draw in the curve.

HOLIDAY HOUSE

This doll's house is at a larger scale than usual, suitable for dolls up to 300 mm tall. Open at the front, it has decks with safety railings on either side, and the upper floor is reached by an external staircase.

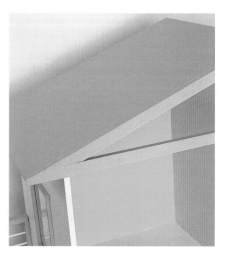

This bright and modern house will provide countless hours of fun. The large rooms allow furniture and dolls to be moved easily, and the open plan encourages play to spill out into the surrounding 'beach' or 'garden'.

PREPARATION

1 Using the tape, square, pencil and straight edge, mark out the pieces on the MDF sheet, leaving 4 mm cutting space between each (see diagram on page 292). Cut them out and label each piece.

2 Plane the edges to the finished size and use the sanding block and abrasive paper to smooth the edges.

3 Mark 19-degree bevels on the joining edges

of the roof pieces and on top of walls D and E. Clamp each piece securely, and use a smoothing plane to make the bevel.

4 Again using the tape, square, pencil and straight edge, mark out the positions of the windows, doors, stair opening and notches for the verandah posts. Cut them out using a handsaw. Use the chisel to remove the material from the post notches. For the windows, use a 10 mm bit to drill a hole in one corner and then cut out the opening using a jigsaw.

ASSEMBLING THE HOUSE

5 Take the ground floor piece and, on the back edge, mark the centre point (500 mm from each end). Find and mark the centre of the back wall. Apply adhesive to the back edge of the floor and position the back wall against it, matching the centre marks. Use the 1.6 mm bit to drill locating holes and nail through the wall into the floor. As you assemble the house,

MATERIALS*

PART	MATERIAL	FINISHED LENGTH	WIDTH	NO.
Floor	9 mm MDF	1000 mm	450 mm	2
Back wall	9 mm MDF	834 mm	720 mm	1
Wall (A–E)	9 mm MDF	350 mm	350 mm	5
Wall (F)	9 mm MDF	475 mm	350 mm	1
Roof	9 mm MDF	450 mm	360 mm	2
Base (front/rear)	42 x 19 mm timber	1000 mm		2
Base (side)	42 x 19 mm timber	450 mm		2
Stair tread	42 x 7 mm timber	55 mm		12
Stair string	42 x 7 mm timber	405 mm		2
Window internal stile	6 mm moulding	150 mm		6
Window internal rail	6 mm moulding	120 mm		6
Window external stile	6 x 6 mm timber	145 mm		6
Window external rail	6 x 6 mm timber	130 mm		6
Window pane	2 mm acrylic	150 mm	120 mm	3
Post	19 x 9 mm timber	470 mm		9
Handrail	19 x 9 mm timber	460 mm		2
Handrail (rear)	19 x 9 mm timber	140 mm		2
Rail A	4 mm dowel	215 mm		6
Rail B	4 mm dowel	125 mm		6
Rail C	4 mm dowel	60 mm		3
Rail D	4 mm dowel	160 mm		3
Rail E	4 mm dowel	205 mm		3
Pediment trim	19 x 9 mm timber	410 mm		2
Gable trim	19 x 9 mm timber	830 mm		1

Other: Abrasive paper; PVA adhesive; 25 x 1.6 mm lost-head nails; masking tape; extra
4 mm diameter dowel; filler; finish of choice.

*   Finished size: 1000 x 459 mm and 870 mm high. The timber sizes given are actual
    sizes. MDF sheets used are 1220 x 2440 mm.

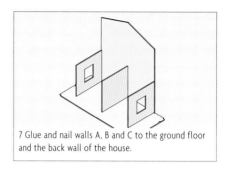

7 Glue and nail walls A, B and C to the ground floor
and the back wall of the house.

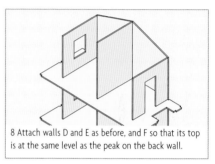

8 Attach walls D and E as before, and F so that its top
is at the same level as the peak on the back wall.

HINT

When fixing into the edge of MDF, always
drill a locating hole first to ensure the nail is
centred within the edge.

and E in the same manner as the ground
floor walls. Attach wall F so that its top is at
the same level as the peak on the back wall.
Allow the adhesive to dry.

9 Lay the house down with the front facing
up. Lay the two roof pieces with the
bevelled edges together and place masking
tape across the join to hold the peak
together when the roof is located on the
house. Put adhesive in the valley of the
bevels, along the top edge of the back and
along the bevels on top of walls D and E.
Place the roof onto the house and securely
nail it to the walls.

THE WINDOWS

10 Cut the internal window stiles and rails to
length with 45-degree mitres on the ends so

punch nails below the surface so the holes can
be filled before painting.

6 Take the base pieces and, using the mitre
box and handsaw, cut them to length with
mitre joints on each end. Using adhesive,
attach the pieces to the underside of the
ground floor, ensuring that the outer edges
are flush with the edges of the floor.

7 Glue and nail walls A, B and C to the
ground floor and the back of the house.
Walls A and B should be flush with the
edges of the back and C should be in the
centre of the back.

8 Allow the adhesive to dry, then glue and
nail the first floor to the top of walls A, B
and C and the back wall. Attach walls D

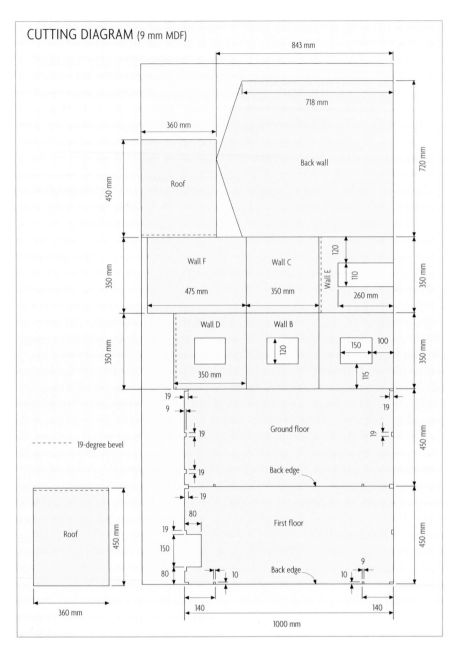

CUTTING DIAGRAM (9 mm MDF)

843 mm

718 mm

360 mm

720 mm

Back wall

Roof

450 mm

350 mm

Wall F

Wall C

Wall E

120

110

475 mm

350 mm

260 mm

350 mm

Wall D

Wall B

150

100

120

350 mm

350 mm

350 mm

115

19

19

9

19

Ground floor

19

450 mm

- - - - - 19-degree bevel

19

Back edge

19

80

Roof

First floor

450 mm

19

150

450 mm

80

10

Back edge

9

10

360 mm

140

140

1000 mm

TOOLS

- Tape measure
- Straight edge
- Pencil
- Combinaton square
- Handsaw
- Circular saw (optional)
- Jigsaw
- Smoothing plane
- Cork sanding block
- Sliding bevel and protractor
- Cramps
- Chisel
- Hammer
- Nail punch
- Mitre box
- Utility knife
- Portable electric drill
- Drill bits: 1.6 mm, 4 mm, 10 mm
- Dust mask, safety glasses and hearing protection

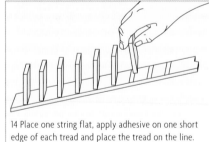

14 Place one string flat, apply adhesive on one short edge of each tread and place the tread on the line.

that the pieces will fit into the openings cut for the windows. Paint them and allow to dry. Glue them into the openings so that the acrylic panes will sit flush with the outside of the house. When the adhesive has dried, use the filler to fill any gaps that remain. Sand to a smooth finish and touch up the paint.

11 Paint the external stiles and rails. Allow to dry.

12 Take one acrylic window pane and place it in the opening. Glue an external rail along the bottom of the window so that it covers the pane by about 3 mm. Install the stiles vertically

so that the outside edge is flush with the end of the rail and they overlap the panel by 3 mm. Install the top rail in the same way.

THE STAIRS

13 Take one string and cut the angles on the ends (see diagram on page 293). Mark every

indoor

ISOMETRIC VIEW

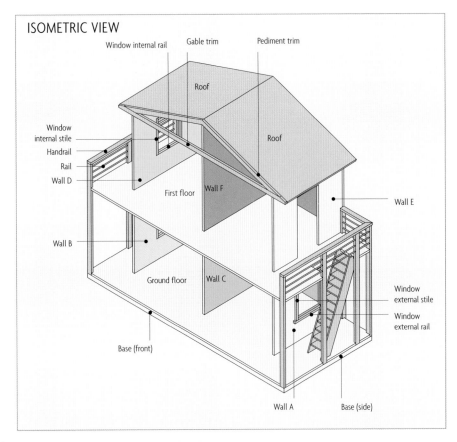

Window internal rail
Gable trim
Pediment trim
Roof
Window internal stile
Handrail
Rail
Wall D
Roof
First floor
Wall F
Wall E
Wall B
Ground floor
Wall C
Window external stile
Window external rail
Base (front)
Wall A
Base (side)

PAINTING

Always paint the pieces before assembling them, especially if more than one colour is being used. Otherwise it is hard not to smudge your work, especially on trim pieces and in tight corners.

STAIR STRING

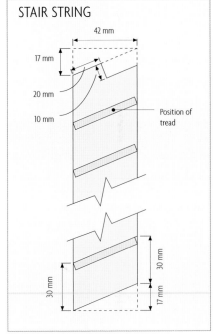

42 mm
17 mm
20 mm
10 mm
Position of tread
30 mm
30 mm
17 mm

30 mm up one side. Repeat on the other side, starting from the same end and then join the points to create evenly spaced lines. Repeat for the other string, but reverse the slopes.

14 Place one string flat with the side with the lines facing up. Apply adhesive on one short edge of each stair tread and locate the treads on the string so that the top of the tread is on the line. When the adhesive is dry, apply adhesive to the other short edge of the treads and locate them on the other string.

15 Apply your chosen finish to the stairs and put them aside to dry.

THE DECK RAILINGS

16 Take the posts and, using the 4 mm bit,

drill the required holes (see diagram on page 294). Six posts have holes in the wide face (two of them also in the narrow face), and three have holes in both narrow faces. Stand the posts in the recesses already cut for them, and ensure that each is in the correct location.

17 The posts are attached to the floors with dowels. Using the 4 mm bit, carefully drill a hole through the post into the edge of the MDF. Cut short pieces of dowel for the joints: you will need fourteen pieces about 15 mm long and four pieces about 24 mm long. Lay out the posts, dowels and the rails in their correct positions (see diagram on page 294).

18 Start assembling the railings at the back with posts 3 and 4 and three rails B. Place

adhesive in the holes in the posts and insert the rails. Work towards the front of the house, and then repeat for the other side. Stand the posts in place and check that the fit is good.

19 Mitre the joining ends of the handrails. Using the 1.6 mm bit, drill locating holes and nail the handrails to the tops of the posts.

20 Apply adequate adhesive to the rear of the posts where they will meet the MDF and in the holes, and fix the railings in place. Insert a small piece of dowel into each hole, gently tapping it into place with a hammer. When the adhesive has dried,

20 Using a hammer, gently tap a small piece of dowel into each hole and into the floor.

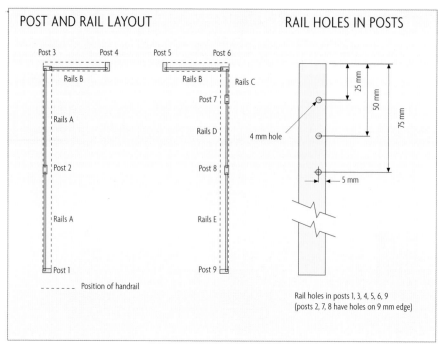

POST AND RAIL LAYOUT

RAIL HOLES IN POSTS

Post 3 Post 4 Post 5 Post 6

Rails B

Rails B

Rails C

Post 7

Rails A

Rails D

4 mm hole

25 mm

50 mm

75 mm

5 mm

Post 2

Post 8

Rails A

Rails E

Post 1

Post 9

Position of handrail

Rail holes in posts 1, 3, 4, 5, 6, 9
(posts 2, 7, 8 have holes on 9 mm edge)

trim off any protruding dowel with the utility knife.

TO FINISH

21 Insert the stairs into the opening and fix them in place with adhesive.

22 Position the gable and pediment trims, and cut them to create a neat fit where they join. Using the 1.6 mm bit, drill and nail the gable trim in place and then the pediment trims.

23 Fill the nail holes. Touch up the paint and finish the house as desired.

FUN FARM

A farm shed with loft is the basis of this toy farm, and it can be adapted to suit most farm uses. There is also a fenced yard to keep the animals safe.

CUTTING OUT

1 Using the tape, square, pencil and straight edge, mark out the pieces on the MDF sheet, leaving 4 mm cutting space between each (see diagram on page 297). Cut them out and label each piece.

2 Plane the pieces to the finished size and use the sanding block and abrasive paper to smooth the edges. Ensure that they are straight and square where required. Create a 45-degree bevel along the back edge of the loft (see page 284).

3 Mark out the notches for the beam on the side walls, those for the posts in the floor, and the positions of the windows. To make the curved top, see the box on page 289. Using the 10 mm bit, drill a hole in one corner of the windows and cut out the openings with the jigsaw.

4 Cut the pieces to form the rafters, the posts and the stays.

ASSEMBLING THE SHED

5 Apply adhesive to the back edge of the floor and position the back wall against it. Using the 1.6 mm bit, carefully drill locating holes and fix the wall with nails. Attach the side walls in the same way. As you work, punch the nails below the surface so that the holes can be filled before you paint.

6 Using the mitre box and handsaw, cut the base pieces to length with mitres on each end. Attach them to the underside of the floor so that they are flush with the front edge of the floor and the walls.

indoor

TOOLS

- Tape measure and pencil
- Straight edge
- Square
- Handsaw
- Circular saw (optional)
- Jigsaw
- Chisel
- Smoothing plane
- Cork sanding block
- Cramp
- Hammer
- Nail punch
- Mitre box
- Utility knife
- Portable electric drill
- Drill bits: 1.6 mm, 4 mm, 10 mm, 12.5 mm spade bit
- Dust mask
- Safety glasses
- Hearing protection

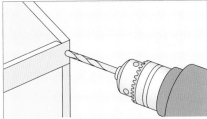

7 Fit the beam into the notches in the side walls and drill a hole through the beam into the edge of the side wall.

7 Fit the beam into the notches in the side walls. Using the 4 mm bit, drill a hole through each end of the beam into the edge of the side wall and insert a piece of 4 mm dowel. Remove the beam and paint it. Let it dry and re-attach it using adhesive and dowels. If the dowel is too

Construction of this colourful farm shed and yard is straightforward and does not require much experience in woodworking. Quite large animals will fit in the shed, and so it is perfect for younger children.

long, trim it with the utility knife once the adhesive has dried.

8 Attach the two front walls to the edge of the side walls and the floor so that they fit under the beam.

9 Place the loft in position with the bevelled side on top of the back wall. Attach it with adhesive, and nail through the side walls into the loft.

10 Paint the shed, inside and out—there will be little access to some of the corners once the rafters are in place. Also paint the rafters and posts.

FINISHING THE SHED

11 Apply adhesive and glue the two end rafters to the side walls, the underside of the loft and the back of the beam. The other three rafters can then be evenly spaced across the shed and glued to the underside of the loft and to the back of the beam.

12 Glue the two end posts in position against the front walls, and glue the centre post to the beam and the base. Ensure it is vertical. Glue the stays in place.

13 Attach the roof using adhesive and nails and aligning the front edge with the ridge.

14 Fill the nail holes with filler and finish painting the shed, as desired.

THE YARD

15 Cut the pieces to form the fence rails and posts.

16 Take the yard base and mark the positions of the posts (see diagram opposite). Using the 12.5 mm spade bit, drill the holes through the base.

MATERIALS*

PART	MATERIAL	FINISHED LENGTH	WIDTH	NO.
Floor	9 mm MDF	600 mm	300 mm	1
Back wall	9 mm MDF	600 mm	259 mm	1
Side wall	9 mm MDF	414 mm	309 mm	2
Front wall	9 mm MDF	231 mm	100 mm	2
Loft	9 mm MDF	600 mm	165 mm	1
Roof	9 mm MDF	619 mm	230 mm	1
Base (front/back)	19 x 9 mm timber	619 mm		2
Base (side)	19 x 9 mm timber	309 mm		2
Rafter	19 x 9 mm timber	291 mm		5
Beam	19 x 9 mm timber	619 mm		1
Post	19 x 9 mm timber	240 mm		3
Stay	19 x 9 mm timber	70 mm		4
Yard base	9 mm MDF	400 mm	300 mm	1
Yard sub-base A, B	19 x 9 mm timber	400 mm		2
Yard sub-base C, D	19 x 9 mm timber	300 mm		2
Yard post	12.5 mm dowel	110 mm		11
Yard rail A	4 mm dowel	75 mm		8
Yard rail B	4 mm dowel	120 mm		24
Yard rail C	4 mm dowel	130 mm		8

Other: Abrasive paper; PVA adhesive; 25 x 1.6 mm lost-head nails; 4 mm dowel; filler; finish of choice.

* Finished size of shed: 619 x 309 mm and 430 mm high. Timber sizes are actual sizes.

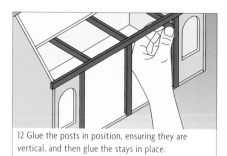

12 Glue the posts in position, ensuring they are vertical, and then glue the stays in place.

18 Drill holes in the posts to receive the rails, 10 mm, 35 mm, 60 mm and 85 mm from the top of the post.

17 Using the mitre box and handsaw, cut the pieces for the sub-base with a mitre on each end and glue them into place under the base. Paint the base as desired.

18 Using the 4 mm bit, drill the holes in the posts to receive the rails. The top hole should be 10 mm from the top of the post, the second 35 mm, the third 60 mm and the fourth 85 mm. In the five centre posts the holes are drilled straight through, in the four corner posts the holes are drilled halfway through with matching holes at right angles, and in the two gate posts the holes are drilled halfway through.

19 Paint or apply clear finish to the posts and rails.

20 Starting at one back corner of the base and using adhesive in each hole, insert a corner post. Into this post insert four rails and then insert the other ends of the rails into a centre post. Place the centre post into its hole. Repeat the process all the way around the yard.

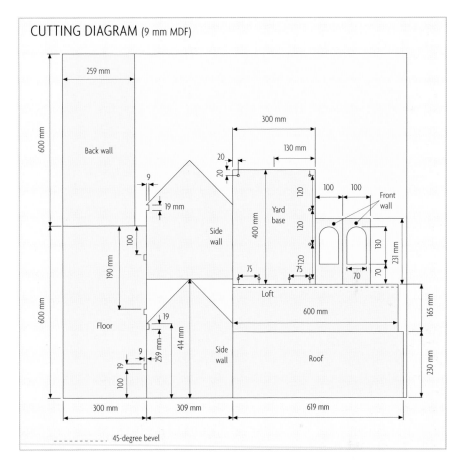

CUTTING DIAGRAM (9 mm MDF)

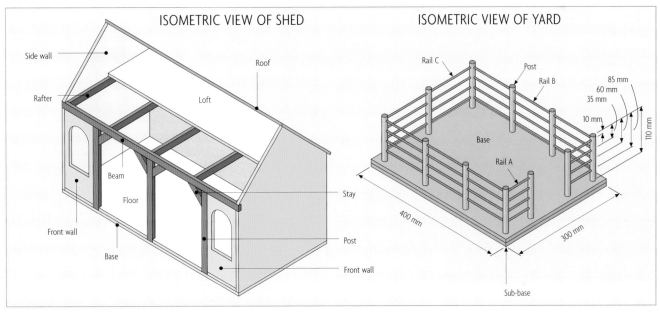

ISOMETRIC VIEW OF SHED

ISOMETRIC VIEW OF YARD

outdoor

contents

fences

fences

PLANNING YOUR FENCE

Fences are constructed for a variety of purposes, whether these be functional or decorative. These uses will have the greatest influence in determining the design or style of fence you choose.

A well-designed fence can provide the perfect finishing touch to your home. This gothic-shaped picket fence is painted in cream, blue and terracotta to complement the house.

CHOOSING A FENCE STYLE

When choosing the style of fence for your home, first consider these three points:

- Location of your property. Fences on a rural property are usually designed to maintain the feeling of openness; inner-city fences are designed for soundproofing and privacy; and suburban fences are often designed for aesthetic effect.
- Construction period or age of your property. The style of fence should complement the style of the house. A picket fence on a modern house would only look awkward.
- The function of the fence. A front fence enhances your property visually and prevents people and animals from entering your front garden. Side and rear fences are usually higher than those at the front, as privacy from neighbours is the main concern.

FENCES FOR DIFFERENT PURPOSES

You may also find that your fence is multi-functional, so consider the following purposes to help you identify your exact needs. Fences are constructed for:

- Security and safety. Many people build high brick or timber-panelled fences to give them a sense of security. Some areas of your property, such as swimming pools, will require specific types of fencing to make them safe, and these may be specified by building regulations.
- Good-neighbour fences. Some fences, such as basketweave or lattice fences, are designed to look the same on both sides; others, such as paling fences, have only

HOW A SOLID FENCE AFFECTS THE WIND

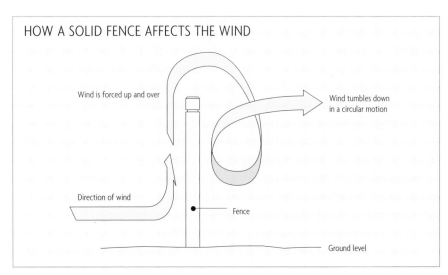

Wind is forced up and over

Wind tumbles down
in a circular motion

Direction of wind

Fence

Ground level

This fence is more decorative than functional, but it does keep animals out of the garden.

one 'good' side. If your neighbours are not keen about having the 'back' of the fence facing into their property, consider paling the fence on both sides or choose an alternative style.

- Soundproofing. Tall, closeboard or overlapped timber fences are good options for reducing noise levels. For maximum noise reduction, panel the fence on both sides of the rails. Plant a screen of tall, thick plants directly behind the fence to further absorb the noise and direct it upwards.
- Privacy. In cases where you need to screen a garden for privacy, consider alternatives that allow for the flow of air and sunlight. A basketweave or louvre fence would serve this purpose.
- Selective screening. The main purposes of selective screening, other than to provide privacy, are to provide shade and shelter

from the elements and protection or support for plants. For attaching plants such as climbers to a fence, lattice is the best choice. When screening plants or people from the elements, a louvre fence is appropriate, as it allows some flow of light and air without creating a feeling of enclosure.

- Landscape fencing. Landscape fencing needs to be constructed using the open-slatted, latticed or louvred styles to allow plants to grow around and through the fence. This way the fence will 'blend' into the garden.
- Animal enclosure. In a rural setting, fences need to be practical and sturdy. The post and rail fence used to contain horses is far kinder on livestock than a barbed wire fence.

WIND CONTROL

For homes in high-wind areas, a protective fence allows plant growth, prevents erosion and provides personal comfort.

By building a solid timber fence between your property and the wind, it may be possible to reduce constant or gusting wind blasts, but you could be creating new problems:

- You could restrict your view.
- Constant winds could cause the fence to lean.
- When moving air hits a solid object it goes up and over the object, eddying downwards in circles, causing greater discomfort and damage (see diagram above).

The solutions to these problems lie in selecting the correct type of timber fencing. A louvred or lattice fence helps to break down the force of the breeze, dispersing it through the slats or lattice. Where solid fences are preferred, positioning angled cappings on the top of the fence will help to redirect wind up and over the area to be protected, operating as a windfoil to prevent eddying.

REGULATIONS AND OBLIGATIONS

Before building a new fence or repairing an old one, it is important to find out any laws or building regulations that will affect it (although this is very unlikely in the case of timber fences). Laws covering fences are controlled by local planning authorities who work within the Town and Country Planning Act of 1990. Covenants placed on the title deeds of properties by the original developers may also restrict the height and

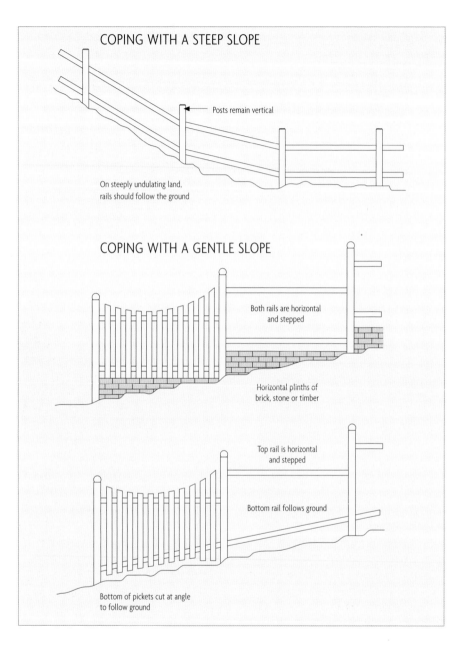

COPING WITH A STEEP SLOPE

Posts remain vertical

On steeply undulating land,
rails should follow the ground

COPING WITH A GENTLE SLOPE

Both rails are horizontal
and stepped

Horizontal plinths of
brick, stone or timber

Top rail is horizontal
and stepped

Bottom rail follows ground

Bottom of pickets cut at angle
to follow ground

When building on a gentle slope it is best to keep the rails horizontal and step the panels.

positioning of fences, particularly in the case of properties built since the 1970s as part of housing developments.

In general, fences up to two metres high are exempt from planning consent. Exceptions to this include:

• Where the fence will be within 20 m of a road.

• The style of a fence may be limited according to heritage and conservation requirements, such as for listed buildings..

Before building, it is a good idea to contact your local government authority and find out local rules and restrictions, if any.

Swimming pools are a special case and, in some areas, are covered by laws. They should be fenced separately from the home using a childproof fence. To be certain of the rules and restrictions, contact your local council before you install a pool.

Regulations for the construction of a dividing wall, as opposed to a timber fence, to separate adjoining properties may also be covered by law. They may, for example, state that landowners should share equally the cost of the construction of a 'sufficient' dividing wall. This means a wall that is sufficient to separate the adjoining land, such as a tall fence in a residential area. If one owner wants a division of better quality than 'sufficient', then that owner would be required to pay the extra cost. Obviously, for the sake of good neighbour relations, it is best to deal with this matter in a personal and friendly manner; some Building Control officers may be willing to act as a mutual contact in the case of a dispute.

To ensure your fence lasts for many years, keep the timber protected with a solid coat of paint and use preservative-treated timber to reduce the chance of attack by insects and mould.

If there are any disagreements regarding the boundary line, it may be a good idea to ask a surveyor to establish it for you.

For further information on building fences, contact your local Building Control officer. Information is also available from solicitors, local courts and the Land Registry.

COPING WITH A SLOPE

As part of your initial design work, you need to carefully examine the proposed line of the fence and calculate any variation in slope so that your design will be appropriate to the situation. This can be done by a surveyor or by the following method:

- String a level line between the two ends of the fence.
- Measure the distance to the ground from the line at each end or at various other points.
- The difference between each measured

point gives you the amount of fall in that section.

If possible, sketch a drawing to scale so you can clearly see the appearance of your proposed fence.

On steep slopes it is often better to run the rails parallel with the ground, but on a gradual slope, a stepped effect, keeping the rails horizontal, is more appropriate. To calculate the amount of step in each panel of fencing, divide the total fall by the number of panels in your design. If the step is too big, bring the posts closer together to increase the number of panels and decrease the height of the step.

FENCE MATERIALS

Timber fences can last from a few short years to more than 50 years, depending on their construction, treatment and the choice of materials. During their lifetime, timber fences

have to withstand the ravages of weather and attack by insects and fungus, therefore it is important to select appropriate materials for their construction (see box on page 310).

ORDERING TIMBER

Usually timber merchants carry timber with a minimum length of 1.8 m, and then in lengths increasing by 0.3 m (consider this when ordering posts and rails). Palings and pickets usually come in set lengths, so check the length you require. If you want to have the timber cut to size, it may cost you extra. Timber can be ordered as rough-sawn or planed all round (PAR). Timber that is PAR has had all four surfaces machine-planed to a smooth finish. This reduces the finished size of the timber but makes it easier to paint or stain.

When selecting timber, you should also consider your own level of experience and the tools you have. Softwoods, such as preservative-treated pines, are easier to work with than hardwoods.

PRESERVATIVE-TREATED TIMBER

Softwood of low durability, usually types of pine, can be treated with chemicals to transform it into a product of higher durability, resistant to attack by fungi, borers and termites. These preservative-treated softwoods are rated according to a hazard level system ranging from low—the least durable (and the least hazardous)—through to high. This rating is branded on the timber (see page 370).

The timber is treated with compounds of copper, chromium and arsenic, termed CCA. When using this material, wear gloves and dust masks when sawing. Any cut or sawn surface of this material will need resealing to ensure its effectiveness in resisting attack. Dispose of any offcuts by burying them. Don't burn them, as the smoke and ash are toxic.

MATERIALS FOR A QUALITY FENCE

The fences in this book use treated pine timber with a high-durability rating for the posts, and treated pine timber with an H3 rating for the rails. If you intend to use hardwood, select a timber with a very durable rating for posts and a durable rating for rails. Take the time to choose the right materials for your fence or, if necessary, consult your local timber or fencing supplier for advice.

COVERING BOARDS

These may take the form of pickets, palings, slats, boards or louvres, and should not come in contact with the ground. As a result, they can be constructed from moderately durable hardwoods, or from a preservative-treated pine with a medium-to-high rating. The durability rating of hardwoods and the hazard level of preservative-treated softwoods can be obtained from timber merchants.

POSTS

As fence posts are in contact with the ground, they are prone to attack by insects, fungus and moisture. Therefore, choose the most durable hardwood timbers or preservative-treated pine with a high-durability rating.

RAILS

As these are not in contact with the ground, they can be selected from any durable hardwoods or from preservative-treated pine with a medium-to-high rating.

FIXING MATERIALS

Like the timber, the materials to fix the timber together will be exposed to the elements—to the sun, rain and damp. Nails should be hot-dipped galvanized to ensure maximum resistance to corrosion and also to reduce marking of the timber from rust stains. Ordinary steel nails may corrode when in contact with CCA timber products (see page 309). Bolts, nuts, washers, coach screws or any other fixing device should also be hot-dipped galvanized to maximize the longevity of the fence.

FENCE BASICS

It doesn't matter what type of fence you decide to build; you will generally find that these basic steps will remain the same. For best results, careful planning and preparation are essential.

INITIAL PREPARATION

1 If building a boundary fence, discuss fence styles and sharing of costs with your neighbour. Check building regulations and establish the boundary line positions (see pages 307–308).

2 Examine the degree of slope and then decide on a design.

3 Calculate quantities, select and order the materials for the fence. Consult your timber merchant for advice, if needed.

4 Prepare the site by clearing debris or vegetation.

MATERIALS FOR LAYING OUT THE FENCE

PART	MATERIAL	LENGTH	QUANTITY
Stake	50 x 25 mm hardwood	2500 mm	minimum of 2
Brace	50 x 25 mm hardwood	1500 mm	2 per stake
Pegs	50 x 25 mm hardwood	400 mm	2 per stake, 1 per post

Other: Creosote or insect and fungus repellent, stain of your choice; nails.

5 Coat the below-ground part of any posts that have not been pretreated. Use an insect and fungus repellent, such as creosote.

6 Prime the timber with an initial stain or undercoat if you are intending to paint it.

LAYING OUT THE FENCE

7 Locate the beginning and end of the fence line, as well as positions where direction changes will occur. Take your time with this, as accuracy at this stage will save problems later.

outdoor

TOOLS

- Basic construction kit
  (see Post and rail fence, page 315)

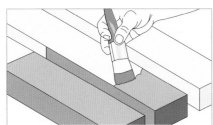

5 Treat the below-ground part of the fence posts using a brush and an insect and fungus repellent.

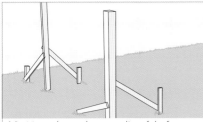

8 Position stakes on the correct line of the fence, usually 1 m away from the corners.

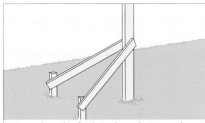

9 Brace the stakes firmly in place, placing wooden offcuts on both sides to hold the stakes vertically.

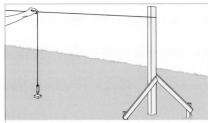

13 Drop a plumb bob at each marked point along the string, holding the plumb bob just above ground level.

A galvanized wire mesh and regular maintenance have enabled this fence to last for many years. The wire mesh creates a feeling of space in the garden, allowing you to 'borrow' the scenery from next door.

8 Position pointed stakes on the fence line but about 1 m beyond the corners (or the points where there is a change in direction). This allows you to continue the line over the corner and dig the holes without removing the stakes.

9 Brace the stakes firmly in position, placing wooden offcuts on both sides to hold the stake in a vertical position. Use a spirit level to check each stake is vertical.

10 Stretch a taut string line between the stakes. Check the string line for level using a spirit level and ascertain the degree of slope (see Coping with a slope, page 309).

11 Measure the distance between the stakes. Divide the distance so that the posts will be placed an equal distance apart along the length of the fence. Make the necessary adjustments if a gate is needed.

12 Stretch your tape along the taut string line and use a pen to mark the centre of each post location on the string line.

13 Drop a plumb bob at each mark, holding it just above ground level. This can also be done using a spirit level and straight edge.

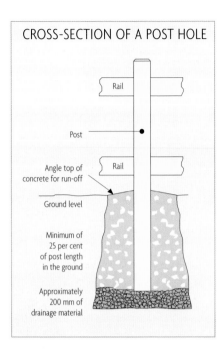

CROSS-SECTION OF A POST HOLE

Rail

Post

Angle top of
concrete for run-off

Ground level

Minimum of
25 per cent
of post length
in the ground

Approximately
200 mm of
drainage material

Rail

14 Drive a small peg into the ground at each plumb bob location. Your post locations have now been identified and marked.

DIGGING A POST HOLE

15 The type of soil into which you will be digging will influence your selection of tools, so examine your soil type.

- For sandy soil you may simply need a spade or long-handled shovel.
- For clay-based soil you may require either a manual or power-driven auger. If there are many holes to dig, hire a bobcat digger with an auger attachment for ease of excavation.
- For rocky locations you may need to use a jackhammer or even heavier machinery, such as a backhoe with a rock-breaking attachment.

16 Excavate the holes to a depth so that at least 25 per cent of the post's length will be in the ground. Increase the depth of the holes if they are for end posts or gate posts, or in areas that are windy or sandy.

HINT

An alternative method for laying out the fence on level sites is to lay the rails on the ground, overlapping the ends to locate the post positions.

For soils with poor drainage, increase the depth of the hole by approximately 200 mm and refill it with tightly packed gravel or other drainage material so that the posts will not be sitting in water for lengthy periods.

17 Excavate the holes to a diameter of between 200 mm and 300 mm, depending on the size of the post. Holes should be widest at the base, narrowing slightly at the surface to create a wedge-like effect (see diagram left). Use a steel tape measure to check that the holes are all the same depth. In very soft conditions, fix small cross-pieces to the below-ground section of the posts for added strength.

SETTING UP THE POSTS

18 Position the corner, gate or change-of-direction posts first. Check the centre position off the mark on the string line.

19 Set these posts to the required height. If the posts have been mortised or notched for rail attachment, cut the excess off the bottom only.

20 Use a spirit level to check the posts are vertical both ways; brace and fix with stakes. Fix a brace across the top of any gate posts to keep them the correct distance apart.

21 Set the posts in position with concrete, tamping the concrete down with a wood offcut. Angle the concrete away from the

PAINTING AND STAINING

After you have constructed your fence, it is worth the extra effort to finish the fence with a coat of paint or stain. This will enhance the appearance and increase the life of your fence, as it helps protect it from the elements. Here are a few hints to make the job of painting or staining your fence easier and to help you to achieve a quality finish.

- Use good-quality exterior gloss paint and good-quality brushes.
- Discuss paint selections carefully with your paint dealer as some darker colours will fade over time.
- Apply two coats of the final colour to get a good finish.
- As many paints have built-in primers, you may not need to undercoat before applying colour, but this is a personal choice.
- Use stain, rather than paint, on paling fences.
- Hardwood that has been creosoted is difficult to paint.
- Bevel the edges of the timber beforehand, as paint tends to run away from square edges.
- Pre-paint pickets and any areas that will be difficult to reach after construction is completed.

post to allow for water run-off. Use a spirit level to continually check the posts remain vertical while tamping the concrete.

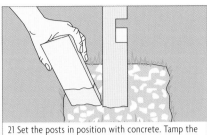

21 Set the posts in position with concrete. Tamp the concrete down with a wood offcut.

CONCRETING

Concrete can be delivered pre-mixed or it can be hand-mixed. It is generally better to hand-mix concrete if time is needed for plumbing and bracing the fence. Hand-mixing the concrete also allows time between setting corner and intermediate posts, particularly if the fence is on a sloping site or where post stepping is required. If all the posts are plumbed and braced in position, it is possible to have pre-mixed concrete delivered.

22 Set a string line from the finished heights of the corner, gate or change-of-direction posts.

23 Place intermediate posts and compare their height with the string line. If the posts are too long, cut the bottom of the post only, or deepen the hole. If the post is cut, treat the end of the timber again for protection.

24 For sloping sites, start at the bottom of the slope and work up, increasing the height from the previous post by the required amount. To calculate the amount of step, refer to Coping with a slope, page 309.

25 Following the process in step 21, position the intermediate posts in concrete and allow the concrete to set for two to three days.

ADDING THE RAILS

26 There are many ways to attach rails to posts. Your level of skill and the tools you have will determine the jointing technique selected. Two simple techniques are to:
- fix the rails flush to the posts by screwing or nailing them, with joints butted mid-line on the posts;
- use metal brackets to attach rails, with the rails butting squarely to the inside face of the posts.

Two more advanced techniques are to:
- cut mortises to provide a hole in the post for the rail to pass through;
- cut housings that allow the rails to be bedded into and flush with the line of the post.

If you select a mortise joint, it can be advantageous to add the rails before concreting the posts, as you may need to move the posts to fit the rails into the mortise.

If you want to use one of the more advanced techniques but lack the skill or equipment, ask your local timber supplier to house or mortise the posts for you.

27 For fences less than 1500 mm in height, two parallel rails will usually suffice, but if your fence height is 1500 mm or more, consider using three rails for added strength. Also for strength, the length of the rails should cover the distance of two panels or three posts. Stagger the rail joints on alternate posts. Remember to space the rails equally.

JOINTING TECHNIQUES

The jointing technique that you select will determine whether or not you can pre-set the fence posts in concrete (see step 26, Adding the rails).

The rails also have to fit together, either on or in the fence post, and there are three main jointing techniques that you can select from:
- angle or scarf joint
- square or butt joint
- lap or notch joint.

Within the mortise on a post, the rails usually have a scarf (angle) joint and are fixed with galvanized nails, coach screws or bolts.

For butt (square) joints that are housed or are on the outside of the fence posts, it is best to fix the rails with galvanized bolts or coach screws.

For lap (notch) joints fixed on the outside of posts, use galvanized bolts or coach screws.

JOINTS FOR RAILS

Angle or scarf

Square or butt

Lap or notch

POST AND RAIL FENCE

These fences are relatively inexpensive to build because there is not a great deal of timber involved in their construction. The posts are mortised, and the rails are joined using a scarf joint contained within the mortise.

The post tops can be prepared in a number of ways for appearance and weather protection. This fence has rounded tops, preventing water from sitting on top of the posts.

MATERIALS*

PART	DIMENSIONS	LENGTH
Posts	150 x 50 mm	1800 mm
Rails	100 x 50 mm	4800 mm

Other: Concrete; 75 x 3.5 mm twisted flat-head galvanized nails; felt-tipped pen; abrasive paper; string; paint or stain of choice.

* This fence has posts that are 1200 mm above ground and up to 600 mm below ground. It has two rails, set 400 mm apart, which are 4800 mm in length, allowing a panel width every 2400 mm.

FENCE BASICS

1 Make the initial preparations for the fence, and then lay out the fence referring to Fence basics on pages 310–313.

2 Dig the post holes for the fence. The dimensions of the holes need to be 300 x 200 mm with a depth of up to 600 mm, depending on soil type and conditions.

MORTISING A POST

3 Using the try square and pen, mark the position where the rail will pass through the post. The hole should be slightly bigger than the dimensions of the rail.

4 Drill out the four corners, staying just within the marked lines.

5 Place the jigsaw in one of the holes and cut from corner to corner along the marked lines.

6 Square up the corners with the jigsaw, and check that the rail will pass through the mortise.

7 Re-prime or re-seal any cut surfaces.

STOP-MORTISING A POST

8 End posts do not have to be mortised all the way through. They can be stopped halfway for better weathering and a neater finish if the end post is on display. Following step 3, use the try square and pen and mark the location of the holes.

9 Using a hammer and chisel, cut out the stop mortise to a depth of 20–25 mm. To make chiselling easier, drill holes in the corners and along the edges to the required depth.

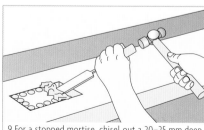

9 For a stopped mortise, chisel out a 20–25 mm deep hole. Pre-drilled holes make chiselling easier.

BASIC CONSTRUCTION KIT

- Steel measuring tape
- Pencil
- String line
- Spirit level
- Plumb bob
- Claw hammer
- Excavation equipment
- Hand and power saws
- Combination or try square
- Power drill and bits: twist and spade
- Jigsaw
- Chisels: 13 mm, 15 mm, 25 mm, 32 mm
- Wheelbarrow
- Two trestles
- Nail punch
- Socket spanner set
- G-cramps
- Permanent marker pen

ROUNDING THE POST TOPS

10 Measure 75 mm in from the side and 75 mm down from the top. Mark the location where both the points cross. Hammer a nail in this point.

11 Attach a string to the nail with a fixed loop and loop the string around a pen, 75 mm from the nail. Holding the string taut, draw a curved line around the top of the post.

12 Cut out the semicircular shape with a jigsaw. Sand smooth and re-seal any cut surfaces. The rounded tops will help the rain to run off the posts.

ADDING THE RAILS

13 As this fence has rails passing through mortised posts, it is easier to fit the rails into the posts before concreting the posts into position. For added strength, the rail lengths should cover the width of two panels and the joins should be on alternate posts.

Start with a 4800 mm rail at the top and

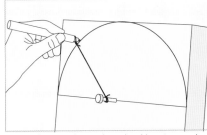

11 Attach a string line to the nail and loop it around a pen. Hold the string taut and draw a curved line.

a 2400 mm rail at the bottom. As the posts are mortised, a scarf joint (see page 313) is required to join the rails within the mortise.

CUTTING A SCARF JOINT

14 Measure 50 mm back from the end of the rail. Using a square, draw a line across the rail at this point.

15 Draw a diagonal line from the edge of the squared line to the corner at the end of the rail. Cut along the diagonal using a power saw or handsaw. Cut the other rail to match.

16 Fit the two rails together in the mortise. Nail across the scarf joint and into the post using a 75 x 3.5 mm twisted flat-head galvanized nail.

SETTING THE POSTS

17 With the rails in place, brace and stake the posts in a vertical position, following your string line.

18 Concrete the posts into position following the steps on pages 312–313. Leave the concrete to set before removing the braces. Finish the fence with a final coat of stain or paint.

HINT

It is difficult to mortise and round posts if using hardwood. If you plan to do this yourself, treated pine is recommended.

POST AND RAIL

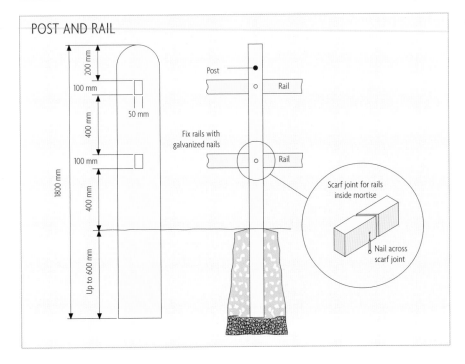

200 mm
100 mm
50 mm
400 mm
100 mm
400 mm
1800 mm
Up to 600 mm

Post
Rail
Rail

Fix rails with galvanized nails

Scarf joint for rails inside mortise

Nail across scarf joint

TRADITIONAL PALING FENCE

The paling fence has served for over a hundred years as the traditional fence for suburban homes, and it remains a popular choice today. The palings are fixed to one side of the fence so the rails are visible on the other.

The traditional paling fence is a popular and inexpensive fence that can easily be constructed by the home owner. It is usually either 1500 or 1800 mm in height and is constructed of hardwood or treated pine.

FENCE BASICS

1 Lay out the fence, following pages 310–312. When considering a slope, remember that the traditional paling fence is not stepped but follows the contour of the ground. The posts remain vertical, but the rails run parallel to the ground. The palings are stepped to a string line or angle cut at the top and/or bottom edge (see diagram opposite).

2 Dig the post holes, referring to page 312. The 90 x 90 mm end posts need a hole of at least 250 x 250 mm. If 120 x 45 mm rectangular posts are used, the hole will need to be at least 300 x 200 mm with a depth of between 500 and 750 mm, depending on soil type and conditions.

POST PREPARATION

3 Prior to setting up the posts, bevel the top edges of the posts using a plane.

4 Pre-cut and chisel out the housing for the two rails at 300 mm and 1100 mm down from the post tops. This is easier to do before setting the posts in concrete, as the posts can be laid in a horizontal position for cutting. Refer to the instructions for the Picket fence, pages 319–320.

ADDING THE POSTS, RAILS AND PALINGS

5 Set up the posts referring to the steps on pages 312–313. Concrete the posts into position.

6 Fix the rails using a scarf joint (see page 313) and 75 x 8 mm galvanized coach screws.

MATERIALS

PART	DIMENSIONS	LENGTH
Posts	90 x 90 mm	2100 mm
Rails	70 x 45 mm	4500 mm
Palings	100 x 10 mm	1500 mm

Other: Concrete; 75 x 8 mm galvanized coach screws; 40 x 2.5 mm twisted flat-head galvanized nails.

TOOLS

- Basic construction kit (see Post and rail fence, page 315)

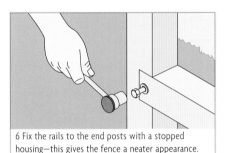

6 Fix the rails to the end posts with a stopped housing—this gives the fence a neater appearance.

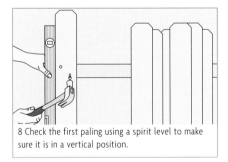

8 Check the first paling using a spirit level to make sure it is in a vertical position.

A stopped housing on end posts provides a neater finish. Re-seal any cut surfaces. Add the top rail first, stagger the joints and have the rails covering two panels.

7 Before attaching the palings to the fence, notch the corners off the top of each paling.

TRADITIONAL PALING

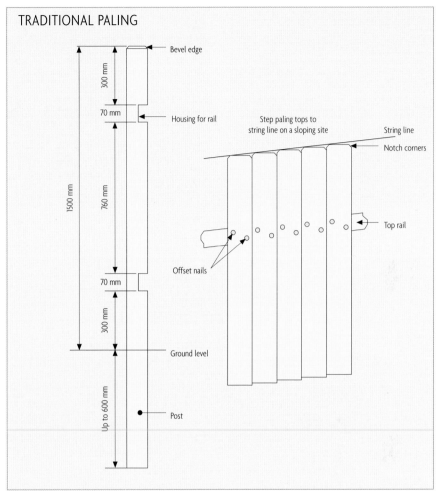

To do this, measure 15 mm across and down from each corner. Mark and draw a diagonal line across each corner. Cut the corner off with a circular saw or mitre saw. For speed, place five palings together and align them. Cut off the corners using the saw.

8 Check the first paling carefully with a spirit level to make sure it is in a vertical position as the other palings will follow a similar line. Set up a string line as a guide for the top of the palings. Fix the palings twice at each rail position using 40 x 2.5 mm flat-head twisted galvanized nails. Palings should be a minimum of 100 mm in width, so position

each nail approximately 25 mm in from each edge. Offset the nails to help avoid paling twist and rail split.

9 Nail the palings in small groups of five to eight, and then check with the spirit level again before proceeding any further.

10 Continue in this manner to complete the fence.

OTHER FIXINGS

Suggested alternatives for fixing palings to a sloping fence are:

- Attach the palings at an angle with the tops left unnotched. This will create a stepped effect.
- Attach palings at an angle with the tops cut square.
- Attach palings vertically after pre-cutting the tops to a point.

PREFABRICATED FENCE UNITS

An alternative to constructing your own timber fence is to purchase prefabricated fencing, available in a variety of styles and colours. These units are usually constructed of metal and range from precoloured profile sheets and tubular powder-coated pool fences, to PVC-coated wire mesh units.

Construction of these units can incorporate timber or metal posts and rails. Alternatively, you can purchase the appropriate metal posts and rails into which these units fit easily.

If you decide on this type of fencing, 'do-it-yourself' guidelines are available from the suppliers of the units.

PICKET FENCE

This Victorian-style picket fence is constructed using an acorn-topped picket. With such a variety of picket fence styles available, you should have no difficulty selecting one that enhances the architectural features of your home.

FENCE BASICS

1 Carry out the initial preparations for the fence (see page 310). Picket fences can have tops that are straight, stepped or a curved concave shape. If you construct a picket fence on a steep slope, the rails should follow the slope contour and the picket tops should be straight, also following the slope contour.

2 Calculate the distances for your panel width between the posts, considering the number of pickets and setting the distance so that the panel has an even number of pickets (this will give the curved panels a better visual balance).

The picket width is 70 mm, so allow half this width for each gap. This makes a total width for the picket, plus the gap, of 105 mm. You also need to allow an extra gap spacing of 35 mm as 20 pickets need 21 gaps (15 pickets need 16 gaps, and so on) to allow for the gap between the picket and the post. Therefore, the overall panel length for 20 pickets is 2135 mm:

20 pickets x 105 mm + 35 mm (extra gap) = 2135 mm

A variety of ready-cut pickets is available from timber merchants. Pickets are available in lengths of 900 mm, 1200 mm, 1500 mm and 1800 mm, with the first three being the most common sizes.

3 Lay out the fence and dig the post holes following pages 310–312. The 90 x 90 mm posts require a hole of at least 250 x 250 mm with a depth of 500–750 mm, depending on soil type and conditions.

POST PREPARATION

4 Place the post in a horizontal position and mark the location of the 10 mm bevel, the diamond cut-out, the groove, the rail positions and the plinth (see diagram on page 320).

5 Bevel the top edges of the posts using a plane.

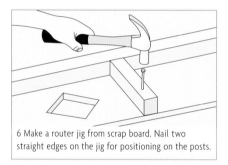

6 Make a router jig from scrap board. Nail two straight edges on the jig for positioning on the posts.

6 To rout out the decorative diamond shape, you will need to make up a router jig. This is made from scrap board. The diamond shape in the jig is a 57 x 57 mm square, creating diagonals of 80 mm. (It has been cut 3 mm larger all round than the finished pattern to allow for the distance between the collar and the cutter. Check your router operation manual, as this distance varies with different brands.) Position the diamond so it is 8 mm from the bevel, the marked location of the groove and the edges of the post. Nail two straight edges to the jig for positioning against the side and top of the post.

TOOLS

- Basic construction kit
  (see Post and rail fence, page 315)
- Router and bits

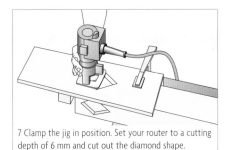

7 Clamp the jig in position. Set your router to a cutting depth of 6 mm and cut out the diamond shape.

7 Clamp the jig in position. Set the router to a cutting depth of 6 mm after allowing for the depth of the jig. Move the router back and forth to make sure all waste is removed from the recess.

8 To rout out the groove located 8 mm below the diamond, position a straight edge (allowing for the router's collar, as per step 6). Clamp the straight edge into position and cut out a 5 mm wide groove to a depth of 6 mm.

CUTTING THE HOUSING

9 To cut the housing, first determine the position of the two rails on the post, 400 mm and 1110 mm down from the top of the post.

10 Measure the dimensions of the rails and mark these on the post. The housing should be 90 mm wide and 35 mm deep.

POST CAPITALS

Instead of routing a shape on the top of the post, you may prefer to add on a capital that matches the style of the picket.

MATERIALS

PART	DIMENSIONS	LENGTH
Posts	90 x 90 mm	2100 mm
Rails	90 x 35 mm	4500 mm
Pickets (acorn) (20 per panel)	70 x 20 mm	1200 mm
Plinth	200 x 50 mm	2400 mm

Other: Scrap board for router jig; concrete; 40 x 2.5 mm and 75 x 3.75 mm twisted flat-head galvanized nails; 75 x 8 mm coach screws; felt-tipped pen; string line or light chain; paint or stain of choice.

This fence is constructed using acorn-shaped pickets fixed in curved, or scalloped, panels. The post tops have a diamond shape cut on each face between the bevelled top and the groove.

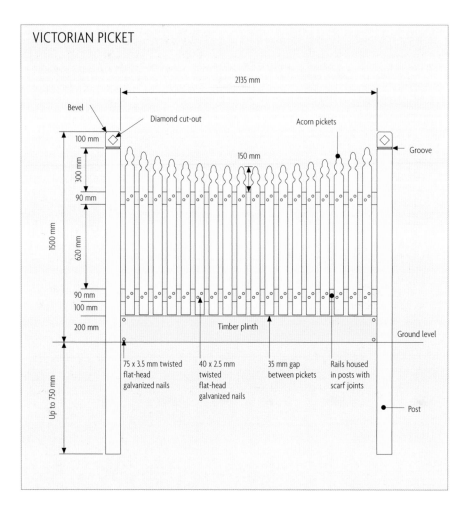

VICTORIAN PICKET

2135 mm

Bevel

Diamond cut-out

Acorn pickets

100 mm

150 mm

300 mm

90 mm

Groove

1500 mm

620 mm

90 mm

100 mm

200 mm

Timber plinth

Ground level

Up to 750 mm

75 x 3.5 mm twisted flat-head galvanized nails

40 x 2.5 mm twisted flat-head galvanized nails

35 mm gap between pickets

Rails housed in posts with scarf joints

Post

HINT

Rails 90 mm wide provide extra base width for the pickets, and this helps to prevent the pickets twisting. Rails should also be spaced as far apart as possible for the same reason.

PICKET	LENGTH FROM PLINTH TO STRING LINE
1	1200 mm
2	1170 mm
3	1145 mm
4	1120 mm
5	1100 mm
6	1085 mm
7	1075 mm
8	1065 mm
9	1055 mm
10	1050 mm

increased, a third rail should be added. Fix the plinth using either 75 x 3.75 mm twisted flat-head galvanized nails, or galvanized brackets and coach screws.

ADDING THE PICKETS

17 Mark the position of the pickets on the top rail and number them.

18 Pickets can be level, stepped or have a curved top, as used for this fence. Several methods can be used to obtain an even curve: string line, template or measurement. The easiest method of calculating the desired curve is to use the string-line method. Temporarily nail the two end and two centre pickets into position. For this fence, the end pickets are 1200 mm in height and the centre pickets are 1050 mm, creating a curve fall of 150 mm. The shortest picket must be positioned so the 'head and shoulders' stay above the top rail.

11 Use either a power saw or handsaw to cut out the housing joint. If you use a power saw, pre-set the cutting depth of the saw to 35 mm (or whatever the depth of your rail). Cut on the top and bottom marked lines for each rail first. Make some extra cuts inside these lines to make chiselling out easier.

12 Chisel out the housing joint and then check for depth by fitting a piece of rail timber into the joint. Adjust the depth of the housing, if necessary, so that the rail is contained flush within the post.

13 Repeat these steps with all the posts. Re-seal or re-prime any cut or planed surfaces.

SETTING UP THE POSTS

14 Set up the posts and concrete them in position, following the instructions on pages 312–313.

ADDING THE RAILS AND PLINTH

15 Add the 90 x 35 mm rails using a scarf joint and fix with one 75 x 8 mm galvanized coach screw.

16 A 200 x 50 mm wide plinth with a high-durability rating is positioned between the posts 100 mm below the bottom rail, and finishes at ground level. The plinth provides a base for the pickets. If a plinth is not used and the picket length is consequently

outdoor

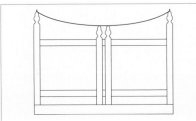

19 To create the picket curve, attach a string-line between two nails on the end pickets and let it drop.

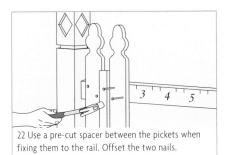

22 Use a pre-cut spacer between the pickets when fixing them to the rail. Offset the two nails.

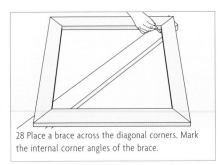

28 Place a brace across the diagonal corners. Mark the internal corner angles of the brace.

19 Hammer a small nail in the top of the two end pickets. Attach a string line or light chain between the two nails, letting it sag until it just touches the top of the two centre pickets. This will create a natural curve.

20 At each picket position measure the distance from the string line to the top of the plinth. In this example of a 20-picket panel, the heights of the pickets are given in the table opposite.

21 Cut the pickets to the correct lengths and number them in order. Write each number on the bottom of each picket.

22 Fix the pickets at the correct spacing with two 40 x 2.5 mm flat-head nails per picket. A spacer between the pickets makes this easier.

ADDING A GATE
The choice of gate is determined by its location.
- Side gates are located between the house and the boundary fence. They are usually 1800 mm high for privacy, but need to be at least 1000 mm wide if you want to get a wheelbarrow through.
- Front entrance gates usually blend with the existing fence and are located either on one side or in the middle of the fence, depending on the front door position. They open inwards and may be as narrow as 600 mm.
- Driveway gates also open on to the property and need sufficient ground clearance for the entire swing of the gate. They swing on 150 x 150 mm posts, or larger if the gates are tall and heavy. Consider double diagonal bracing for wide gates.

GATE CONSTRUCTION
23 Measure the distance between hinge post and latch post. Ensure they are equidistant both top and bottom.

24 Swing space is needed both sides of the gate, so allow for a 15–20 mm gap each side. Subtract these two spaces from the measurement between the posts. This gives the width of the gate.

25 Measure the height of the frame. This is usually set at the same spacing as the fence rails. Rail timber may also be used for gate framework.

26 Construct the frame using height and width measurements. Cut four frame pieces

To support the weight of the gate, angle the diagonal brace from the bottom hinge up to the latch.

TROUBLESHOOTING
If a problem is going to occur with a fence, it usually happens with the gate. To avoid problems, keep a few things in mind.
- Use adequate (100 x 100 mm) posts for front and side gates.
- Ensure that the one diagonal brace, fixed between the rails, angles from the bottom hinge up to the top edge where the latch is usually attached. This will support the weight of the gate.
- When you set your gate posts in concrete, the posts should be braced at the top to keep them parallel. This will make construction and fitting of the gate trouble-free, as everything will be square and vertical.

ALTERNATIVE
An alternative method of gate construction is to set the hinge post first, add the gate and then set the latch post.

to length, ensuring all the ends are square. Mitre the ends and fit together.

27 Place the frame on level ground. Measure the distance between the diagonal corners. Adjust the frame so that the distance is the same, making the frame square. Fix firmly, preferably with galvanized screws rather than nails, for strength.

28 Place a brace across the diagonal corners of the frame. Mark the internal corner angles at both ends of the brace with a pencil. Cut both ends, leaving the pencil lines so that the brace will fit securely in the frame. Fix the brace into the frame with screws.

29 Check the frame in the opening. The bottom of the diagonal brace must be angled from the bottom hinge up (see box on page 321). Mark the position of the hinges using the hinge as a template.

30 Fix the pickets and hinges to the gate frame. To fix the pickets, mark the picket and gap locations on the rails. Start on the outside edges and work to the centre. After fixing the two outer pickets at the correct height, nail a straight edge to the bottom of the pickets as your height guide. Use a spacer, cut to the correct width between pickets. Nail only to hold the pickets in position until you have checked the spacing alignment. To curve the top of the picket gate, refer to the instructions for the Picket fence, pages 320–321.

31 Reposition the gate; mark, drill and fix the hinges to the hinge post. Check the spacing and swing of the gate.

32 Mark, drill and fix your selected latch set. Select good-quality hinge and latch sets for durability.

FENCE REPAIR

TO REPAIR A DAMAGED POST

After prolonged exposure to moisture in the ground, the bottom section of posts may become damaged by rot or termite attack. To replace this lower portion of the post, carry out the following steps.

1 Remove the palings from the area to be repaired. Support the fence by bracing it.

2 Cut the damaged section of the post away. Dig out the old footing and the damaged post. (It is often difficult to remove posts from concrete footings.) Use levers and a fulcrum to ease the post out rather than digging a larger hole, which will require increased quantities of concrete to refill.

3 Prepare the new section of the post from creosoted hardwood or treated pine. Cut the new length to go into the ground.

4 Brace either side and put two galvanized bolts through the braces and old section of the post. Put two galvanized bolts through the braces and new section of the post. Concrete in position.

5 Replace the fence covering.

TO REPAIR DAMAGED RAILS

To replace an entire rail, remove the palings from the panel of the fence. To repair a section of rail, carry out the following steps.

1 Remove the palings from the area to be repaired.

2 Prepare a 200 mm long lap or notch joint to connect the new rail section to the existing section. Alternatively, use metal brackets or plates to connect the notched rails.

3 Fix into position using coach screws. Replace the palings.

4 Hold the new posts in place with bolts. Concrete in place.

BASKETWEAVE FENCE

The basketweave fence is a 'good-neighbour' type of fence as it is visually the same on both sides. The slats fit into grooves in the posts, and the basketweave effect is achieved by positioning the slats around vertical spacers.

TOOLS

- Basic construction kit
  (see Post and rail fence, page 315)
- Router and bits
- 32 mm hole-cutting bit

FENCE BASICS

1 Make the initial preparations and lay out the fence following the steps on pages 310–312. The basketweave fence looks best constructed on a level site; on a sloping site, slats may follow the contour of the ground, or they may be stepped.

2 The 90 x 90 mm posts require a hole of at least 250 x 250 mm with a depth of between 500 mm and 750 mm, depending on soil type and conditions.

POST PREPARATION

3 The posts need a groove down the centre line wide enough for the slats to sit in. To groove the posts, check that the tops of the posts are square. Fix the slats to the outside edges of the posts if a groove is not desired. (It is not necessary to bevel the post tops, as they are covered by a top rail.)

4 Lay the posts in a horizontal position to make routing easier. The end posts need a groove down the centre of one side; the intermediate posts need a groove on both sides. Set the router with a straight bit to suit the thickness of the slats. Run a groove down the centre of the post 12 mm deep, using the fence on the router as a guide. (You can also use a power saw or fix two straight

The woven nature of this fence creates areas of dark and light which change with the sun's movement.

edges to the posts to create a groove.) The groove needs to be 1500 mm long to accommodate ten slats.

PREPARING RAILS AND SLATS

5 The bottom and top rails need two holes drilled and chiselled out to contain the two round spacers (in this case, galvanized waterpipe) used for each panel. To do this,

mark the rail on the centre line at 630 mm and 1260 mm.

6 Using a power drill and a 32 mm hole-cutting bit, drill to a depth of 15 mm and then chisel out the waste. (If using square or rectangular spacers, chisel out the appropriate shaped hole.) Drill a 5 mm wide hole through the rail hole.

324

9 Position the bottom rail 1500 mm down from the top of the post and fix with a metal bracket.

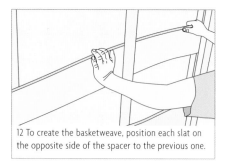

12 To create the basketweave, position each slat on the opposite side of the spacer to the previous one.

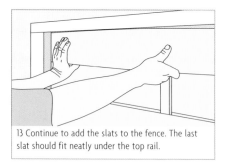

13 Continue to add the slats to the fence. The last slat should fit neatly under the top rail.

SPACERS

The woven pattern can be made tight or loose by varying the number of spacers in the fence. Spacers can be flat, round or square and made from either timber or metal. This fence uses galvanized waterpipe spacers for added strength.

MATERIALS*

PART	DIMENSIONS	LENGTH
Posts	90 x 90 mm	2100 mm
Rails	90 x 45 mm	4200 mm
Slats	150 x 10 mm	4200 mm
Spacers (galvanized waterpipe)	25 mm diameter	1530 mm

Other: Concrete; galvanized 90-degree brackets (two per panel); 75 x 3.5 mm galvanized flat-head twisted nails; 38 x 8 mm galvanized coach screws; paint or stain of choice.

* Treated pine is used for posts and rails, and larch or pine is used for the slats.

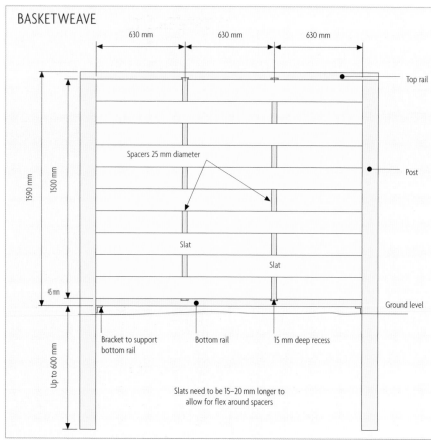

BASKETWEAVE

630 mm · 630 mm · 630 mm · Top rail · Spacers 25 mm diameter · Post · 1590 mm · 1500 mm · 45 mm · Slat · Slat · Ground level · Up to 600 mm · Bracket to support bottom rail · Bottom rail · 15 mm deep recess · Slats need to be 15–20 mm longer to allow for flex around spacers

7 The width of the slats will affect the visual appearance of your fence. The narrower the slat, the more weaving you will need to do; the more spacers you use, the tighter the weave will be. This fence uses larch or pine offcuts from larger timber sections that are 150 x 10 mm. Paint or stain the slats before constructing the fence.

8 The panel width between the posts is 1890 mm. Set the posts into position and then concrete. Leave to set for two days.

ADDING THE RAILS AND SLATS

9 Measure 1500 mm down from the top of the post, and position the bottom rail at this

outdoor

point. Fix with a metal bracket at each end using a 38 x 8 mm coach screw. Pre-drill the holes with a 6 mm drill bit.

10 Temporarily fix the top rail with 75 x 3.5 mm twisted flat-head galvanized nails. Do not drive the nails completely in at this stage.

11 Place the 1530 mm long spacers into the pre-cut holes between the rails as the top rail is being temporarily fixed.

12 Position the slats into the grooves in the posts. No fixing is needed at the spacers or posts if the slats are cut at the correct length. Each slat is positioned on the opposite side of the spacer to the previous one in order to create the basketweave pattern. The slats need to be 20 mm longer than the length of the panel to allow for the flex around the spacers.

13 Continue to add the slats. The last slat should fit neatly under the top rail. Complete the fixing of the top rail.

LOUVRE FENCE

A louvre fence allows the flow of air and light into the garden, and redirects breezes in the desired direction. The louvres are fixed into grooves in the rails. Before doing this, carefully consider the angle of the louvres in relation to prevailing breezes, screening or privacy, and the maintenance of a specific view.

FENCE BASICS

Louvre fences can be constructed with either vertical or horizontal louvres. Horizontal louvres provide greater privacy, but they may bow over time. Generally, louvre fences are constructed in short lengths and are useful for enclosing areas such as swimming or ornamental pools.

1 Make the initial preparations and lay out the fence following the steps on pages 310–312. Louvre fences look best when constructed on level sites.

2 Dig the post holes, referring to page 312. The posts will require a hole of at least 250 x 200 mm with a depth of between 500 and 750 mm, depending on soil type and condition.

POST PREPARATION

3 Bevel the side edges of the fence posts, using a plane or sander to remove squareness.

4 Check that the top of the post is square; re-cut if necessary.

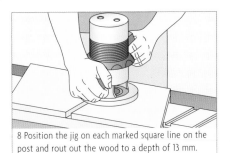

8 Position the jig on each marked square line on the post and rout out the wood to a depth of 13 mm.

5 For end posts, cut a 15 mm deep housing for the bottom rail to sit in, 1475 mm down from the top of the post. Intermediate posts will need the housing cut on both sides of the post.

RAIL PREPARATION

6 For this fence, the rails have been routed with grooves at 45 degrees to hold the louvres. Alternatively, use spacer blocks nailed along rails with the ends cut at the desired angle.

To rout out the grooves, make up a router jig from a piece of scrap board. The 45-degree groove needs to be cut 3 mm larger all round (18 mm) in the jig than the finished pattern (12 mm), to allow for the

TOOLS

- Basic construction kit (see Post and rail fence, page 315)
- Router and bits

distance between the collar and the cutter (see diagram on page 327). Check your router operation manual, as this varies with different brands.

7 Mark a square line across the rail every 120 mm. These lines are a guide for your jig placement for each groove. The first groove should start flush to the post to maintain privacy. Remember to allow 15 mm to recess the rail in the housing.

8 Before clamping the jig into position, nail two straight edges to the jig at the same width as the rail. Use a 12 mm straight bit and set the router to a cutting depth of 13 mm, after allowing for the depth of the jig. Move the router back and forth, ensuring that all waste is removed. If there is no collar on the router, set the jig further apart to allow the

The louvre fence has the advantage of maintaining privacy from one angle while making a view available from the opposite angle.

MATERIALS

PART	DIMENSIONS	LENGTH
Posts	100 x 75 mm	2400 mm
Rails	100 x 50 mm	2400 mm
Louvres	150 x 15 mm palings	1500 mm

Other: Concrete; 75 x 3.5 mm and 30 x 2 mm galvanized lost-head nails; scrap board for router jig; paint or stain of choice.

SETTING UP POSTS

9 The spacing on the posts is determined by the number of louvres. A rail length of 120 mm is needed for each louvre set at 45 degrees. Brace the posts in position.

ADDING THE RAILS AND LOUVRES

10 Add the bottom rails and fix them with two 75 x 3.5 mm lost-head nails angled through the rail and into the post. Pre-drill the holes to avoid splitting the hardwood. Fix the top rail temporarily in position.

11 Concrete the posts in position. Leave the concrete to set for two to three days.

The louvres in this fence are set at a 45-degree angle, but it is possible to set them at any angle. However, be aware that the more acute the angle, the wider the louvres will need to be.

HINT

Louvres should be a tight but sliding fit. If they are too tight, plane or chisel the top and bottom edges until the desired width is achieved.

baseplate to run against the jig. Move the jig to each square line and rout a total of 18 grooves. This will give you a distance between the posts of 2160 mm. Repeat the procedure of steps 6–8 to prepare the other bottom rails.

outdoor

REVERSING THE JIG

To prepare the top rails, pull the jig apart and reverse the angle. If you have a left-handed jig for the bottom rail, the top rail will need a right-handed jig. Following step 8, prepare the top rails with the reversed jig. As the top rails sit on top of the posts, allow extra length for a butt joint on the centre line of the intermediate post and for total coverage on end posts.

10 Add the rails and fix with nails angled through the rail into the post. Pre-drill holes to avoid splitting.

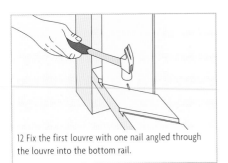

12 Fix the first louvre with one nail angled through the louvre into the bottom rail.

12 Paint or stain the louvres before fixing them into the rails. Slide the first louvre between the bottom and top rail and fix it in place with one 30 x 2 mm galvanized lost-head nail angled through the louvre and into the bottom and top rails. Pre-drill the wood to prevent it from splitting. Continue in this manner, working across the bottom of the panel in the one direction.

13 Firmly fix the top rail by nailing into the top of the posts using 75 x 3.5 mm galvanized lost-head nails. Again, pre-drill to avoid splitting the hardwood.

LOUVRE FENCE

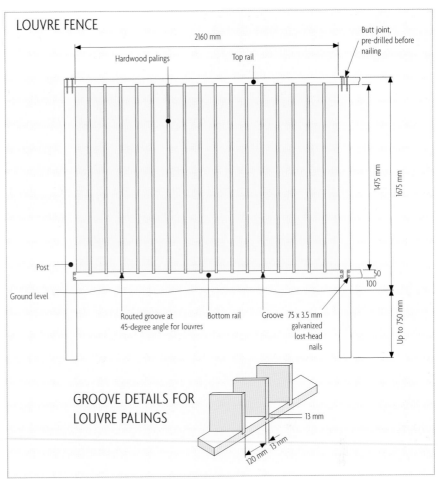

Hardwood palings · Top rail · Butt joint, pre-drilled before nailing · 2160 mm · Post · Ground level · Routed groove at 45-degree angle for louvres · Bottom rail · Groove · 75 x 3.5 mm galvanized lost-head nails · 1475 mm · 1675 mm · 50 · 100 · Up to 750 mm

GROOVE DETAILS FOR LOUVRE PALINGS

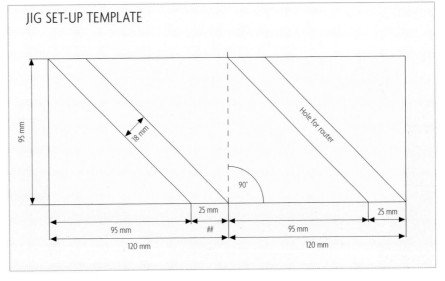

13 mm · 120 mm · 13 mm

JIG SET-UP TEMPLATE

95 mm · 18 mm · Hole for router · 90° · 25 mm · 25 mm · 95 mm · ## · 95 mm · 120 mm · 120 mm

decks

decks

PLANNING YOUR DECK

Careful planning and attention to the design before you start will make building your deck easier—and you'll end up with a deck that satisfies all your requirements.

A deck provides a comfortable area for outdoor living, whether it is attached to the house or built in a sheltered corner of the garden.

WHY BUILD A DECK?

A deck extends your living area, providing a level area outside where you can sit comfortably. It is also practical as it will:

- compensate for sloping land
- eliminate the problem of damp or shady areas where grass won't grow
- increase the value of your house.

THE SIZE

The size of your deck will depend on the area available, its proposed function and, of course, your budget.

You may want to use the deck as:

- a place for children to play
- an entertainment area
- a place for outdoor barbecuing
- a place to relax
- a bridge or walkway
- a surround for a pool, spa or children's sandpit.

A family of four to six people will generally need a deck approximately 12 m² to be comfortable. This will allow for a table and chairs but not a barbecue or plants. A safe estimate would be 2–2.5 m² per person.

THE LOCATION

The ideal location for a deck is on the southern side of the house where it will catch the summer sun. If this isn't possible, build it where it will be most useful. Note where shadows are cast on the ground as the sun moves through the sky from season to season. If necessary, add a screen or covered pergola to protect your deck from wind, rain or strong sun.

DECK TERMINOLOGY

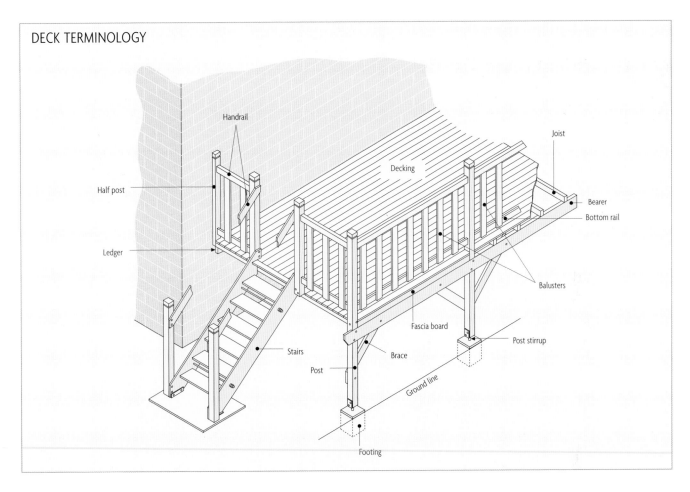

Handrail

Joist

Decking

Half post

Bearer

Bottom rail

Ledger

Balusters

Fascia board

Post stirrup

Stairs

Brace

Post

Ground line

Footing

Other points to consider are:
- proximity to the house, especially the kitchen or family room
- access to the garden
- views
- privacy (both your own and that of your neighbours).

TYPES OF DECKS

There are two main types of decks: attached and free-standing. An attached deck may be classified as a balcony, porch or patio. It is fixed to the building for stability by means of a ledger, and so offers easy access to the house and its facilities.

A free-standing deck is an independent structure that supports itself. Instead of a ledger it has another row of posts. It is usually set away from the house, but can be next to the house if you want to reduce the stress and load on the house and its footings. This type of deck is usually supported on brick piers or posts embedded in the ground. Posts supported in stirrups may be used, but they require additional bracing.

A free-standing deck can be built anywhere in the garden to take in a view, make better use of sloping land or surround a pool. It can be at ground level or raised, and it can be built in any shape, geometric or irregular. Walkways are essentially free-standing decks.

The basic elements of a deck are the same, whatever the type (see diagram above).

DESIGNING A DECK

Once you have determined the function, size and location of your project, lay some timber around to mock up a full-size outline of the proposed deck. If you do not have timber available, use rope or even a garden hose to represent the outline.

Test out the area by positioning the tables, chairs or barbecue that will be used on the deck. Can you move around them comfortably? Will there be sufficient room to enjoy your deck? If not, you may need to increase the size or change the shape. Keep in mind, however, that bigger is not always better. Too big a deck can overpower the house and garden.

Be creative with your design, but keep it

simple or it will be more difficult to build and will cost more. A split-level deck can make building a deck on a steep site much easier, as it reduces the overall height of the construction. It also helps the deck blend into the garden.

ACCESS

If you are attaching a deck to the house, consider how best to ensure a smooth traffic flow from house to deck. Draw a plan of the rooms affected by the deck and map the traffic flow. You may need to move a door or replace a window with a door (this should be done before the deck is built). A double-width door will allow the room inside to operate as an extension of the deck.

Decide whether you want stairs from the deck to the garden and where to locate them so they will provide a convenient entry.

ADDED FEATURES

Rocks or trees can be incorporated into the deck. Deciduous trees give shade in summer and let the sun in during winter. Just allow room for the tree to grow and move with the wind. Lay temporary decking boards that are removed as the tree grows.

Handrails and, perhaps, a pergola can be built as one with the deck by extending the posts up to the relevant height.

PREPARING PLANS

Once you have settled on a design, make some sketches of the deck with the dimensions on them. Discuss these with your local Building Control office before finalizing the project, to check whether there are restrictions. You may need to provide larger scale plans (with construction details) and obtain development and building approval before starting.

CHOOSING MATERIALS

Select the materials for your deck carefully, and it will be strong and last for many years. If timbers and hardware are not strong enough, the deck may actually be dangerous.

CHOOSING THE RIGHT TIMBER

The timber used for a deck will be exposed to all types of weather conditions and must be able to withstand them. With the increase in the numbers of wood-boring insects, it must also resist their attacks.

If you use unseasoned timber it will inevitably shrink, warp or bow. Most hardwood is only semi-seasoned when purchased, as fully seasoned hardwood is very difficult to work. Most treated timber, however, is seasoned.

When buying timber for your project, watch for faults such as bowing or twisting. Lightly bowed or twisted timber may be flattened or pulled straight while it is fixed in position, but badly affected timber may be unusable.

DURABILITY

Hardwoods have a high durability and can be used both in and out of the ground. However, it is recommended that any timber in direct contact with the ground be treated with a suitable preservative.

Any timber used in the ground will require a higher level of protection than that being used above the ground. There are various standards of rating durability against the elements and resistance to attack. Any hardwood placed in the ground must have a high-durability rating. Low-rated timber should not be used for weather-exposed structural members such as posts, bearers, joists or decking unless it has been pressure-treated.

PRESSURE-TREATED TIMBER

The most commonly used timbers for decks are pressure-treated softwoods such as varieties of pine. Preservative-treated softwoods are readily available from most timber merchants and are commonly treated with a compound of copper, chromium and arsenic, known as CCA. This gives the timber a characteristic green tone.

When using timber treated with CCA, wear gloves, goggles and a dust mask while sawing. Any cut or sawn surface of this material will need to be re-sealed to ensure it is effective in resisting attack. Dispose of any offcuts by burying them—do not burn them, as the smoke and ash created are toxic.

Commercially treated softwoods are available. These can be bought with a range of hazard levels from a low to a high level of treatment. Brush-on preservative should be applied to all sawn or shaped surfaces.

Some treated timber may be water repellent, but it will still weather, turning silvery grey over time. A decking oil or stain will counteract this though it will, in turn, require some maintenance.

Always take precautions when using treated timber:

- Always wear gloves when handling treated timber.
- Use a dust mask and goggles when machining, sawing or sanding.

outdoor

- Ensure there is good ventilation in the work area.
- Wash your hands and face before drinking or eating.
- Wash work clothes separately.
- Never use treated timber for heating or cooking, especially on barbecues.

STRESS GRADINGS

Timber is also stress-graded. The 'C' rating is followed by a number, which indicates the bending stress. The higher the number the greater the stress the timber can withstand. Normally, bearers and joists should not be less than C24; posts may be C24 or more if seasoned softwood. In the tables on pages 356–357, 'oak' is used as a shorthand for 'hardwood' for reasons of space.

SPECIFICATIONS FOR DECK TIMBERS

The timber sizes suggested here for use in the various parts of the deck (see the tables on pages 334–335) are a rough guide only. Consult your local Building Control office for details of the specifications required in your local area. Note that the standards for England and Wales are different from those in Scotland.

HARDWARE

Any deck is only as good as its fasteners, so make sure you always use good-quality fittings and fasteners that will stand the test of time without corroding.

Most fasteners and fittings are made from mild steel with a protective coating and, in most situations, hot-dipped galvanizing is the preferred coating. Stainless steel fasteners may be needed where there are high-corrosive conditions such as decks built around saltwater pools or those built in areas subject to sea spray. Other metals such as brass and copper may be appropriate in some conditions, depending on the preservative—check with your supplier.

Using good quality timbers with the appropriate durability and stress gradings will ensure your deck is strong and lasts for many years.

POST SIZES FOR DECKS

STRESS GRADE	POST SIZE*	MAXIMUM HEIGHT** SPACING BETWEEN EACH POST	
		1800 mm	3600 mm
C16 unseasoned softwood	100 x 100 mm	3000 mm	2000 mm
	125 x 125 mm	4500 mm	3200 mm
C24 seasoned softwood	100 mm diameter	1900 mm	1300 mm
	90 x 90 mm/125 mm diameter	2700 mm	1900 mm
	150 mm diameter	4800 mm	3400 mm
Hardwood or better seasoned softwood	70 x 70 mm/100 mm diameter	2400 mm	2400 mm
	90 x 90 mm/125 mm diameter	3000 mm	2400 mm
	150 mm diameter	4800 mm	3700 mm

* When using sawn timber, increase the section size to the next largest, for example if using 90 x 90 mm, order 100 x 100 mm.

** Maximum height is taken from finished ground level.

DECK BEARER SIZES (SINGLE SPAN)

STRESS GRADE	JOIST SPAN	SIZE OF BEARERS (mm) MAXIMUM BEARER SPAN		
		1800 mm	2400 mm	3000 mm
C16 seasoned softwood	1800 mm	120 x 70	170 x 70	240 x 70
	2400 mm	140 x 70	190 x 70	240 x 70
	3000 mm	170 x 70	240 x 70	
C20 seasoned softwood	1800 mm	120 x 70	170 x 70	190 x 70
	2400 mm	120 x 70	170 x 70	240 x 70
	3000 mm	140 x 70	190 x 70	240 x 70
C24 seasoned softwood	1800 mm	120 x 70	170 x 70	190 x 70
	2400 mm	120 x 70	170 x 70	240 x 70
	3000 mm	140 x 70	170 x 70	240 x 70
	3600 mm	140 x 70	190 x 70	240 x 70

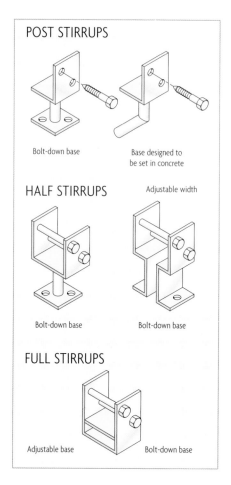

POST STIRRUPS

Bolt-down base

Base designed to be set in concrete

HALF STIRRUPS

Adjustable width

Bolt-down base

Bolt-down base

FULL STIRRUPS

Adjustable base

Bolt-down base

Machine or roundhead bolts hold structural members together more strongly than nails. Coach screws may be used where access is restricted to one side. Washers should be used on both ends of machine bolts and under the head of coach screws to prevent them pulling into the timber too far.

Masonry anchors may be required to fix ledgers to brick walls, or stirrups to footings. Use the appropriate size anchor—if the anchor is too short, the device may not hold tight; if it is too thin, it may snap when subjected to stress.

The decking itself is subject to constant movement as it expands and contracts according to the weather and as people walk over it. Galvanized nails with a spiral or twist shank are, accordingly, best for fixing it, as lost-head (bullet-head) plain-shank nails do not have as much holding power. Lost-head nails are satisfactory for the framework.

There are special decking screws available with countersunk heads but they are only needed under extreme conditions. A well-nailed deck will normally give long service.

Other metal timber connectors, such as

outdoor

nail plates, frame connectors and joist hangers, are made from galvanized steel. There are many different types of connectors, and they can be used for scores of different applications.

Post stirrups, or supports, and brackets (see diagram opposite) are hot-dipped galvanized by the manufacturer. If they are cut or drilled for any reason, reapply a protective coat of galvanized paint.

ESTIMATING MATERIALS

The plans of the deck that you have drawn up to submit to your local authority for approval will probably have to include detailed specifications and dimensions. These drawings will help when you come to estimate all the materials required for your deck. Mistakes at this stage can be costly, as timber is expensive.

Use the materials and tools lists on page 336 to make a checklist of all you'll need, deleting or adding to suit your deck. This will also help you cost the deck.

ORDERING MATERIALS

Most timber merchants will help you order the correct quantities, grades and species of timber for your project—just show them the plan.

Timber is sold in set lengths, starting at 1.8 m and increasing in multiples of 300 mm. A supplier cannot hold every length, and so you may need to combine lengths to avoid waste. For example, if 1.8 m joists are required and the supplier's lengths start at 2.4 m, there would be 600 mm of waste from each joist. However, the supplier may have 3.6 m lengths, in which case two joists could be obtained from each.

Decking may be purchased by the square or linear metre. Allow at least 10 per cent waste for cutting.

MAXIMUM JOIST SPAN (AND CANTILEVER) WITH JOISTS AT 450 mm CENTRES (mm)

UNSEASONED TIMBER	C16	C24	HARDWOOD
150 x 50 mm	2800 (800)	2900 (800)	3400 (900)
175 x 50 mm	3000 (800)	3600 (1000)	3900 (1100)
200 x 50 mm	3800 (1100)	4000 (1100)	4300 (1200)
225 x 50 mm	4200 (1200)	4300 (1200)	
250 x 50 mm	4500 (1300)	4700 (1400)	
275 x 50 mm	4900 (1400)	5100 (1500)	

SEASONED TIMBER	C16	C24	HARDWOOD
140 x 45 mm	2600 (700)	2600 (700)	3100 (900)
190 x 45 mm	3500 (900)	3700 (1000)	3900 (1100)

MAXIMUM JOIST SPAN (AND CANTILEVER) WITH JOISTS AT 600 mm CENTRES (mm)

UNSEASONED TIMBER	C16	C24	HARDWOOD
150 x 50 mm	2700 (700)	2800 (800)	3100 (900)
175 x 50 mm	3200 (900)	3300 (1000)	3600 (1000)
200 x 50 mm	3600 (1000)	3700 (1000)	4000 (1100)
225 x 50 mm	3900 (1100)	4000 (1200)	
250 x 50 mm	4200 (1200)	4400 (1300)	
275 x 50 mm	4500 (1300)	4700 (1400)	
300 x 50 mm	4900 (1400)	5000 (1400)	

SEASONED TIMBER	C16	C24	HARDWOOD
140 x 45 mm	2500 (600)	2500 (700)	2900 (900)
190 x 45 mm	3200 (900)	3500 (1000)	3600 (1000)

JOINT CONNECTORS

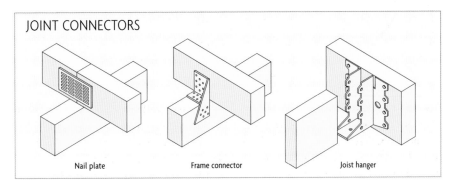

Nail plate　　　Frame connector　　　Joist hanger

TOOLS

- Builder's square
- Chalk line
- Chisels
- Circular saw
- Combination square
- Cramps
- Crowbar
- Electric drill and bits
- Electric plane
- Excavation machinery*
- Hammer
- Handsaw
- Nail punch
- Plumb bob
- Pneumatic nail gun and compressor*
- Post-hole shovel or auger*
- Shovel
- Spanner
- Spirit level
- String line
- Tape measure
- Water level

* Can be hired if necessary.

FASTENINGS

Round-head bolt   Machine bolt   Nut   Washer   Masonry anchor   Coach screw   Twisted-shank nail for decking   Lost-head nail for framing

STORING TIMBER

When timber is delivered to the job, keep it off the ground to prevent it being affected by moisture rising from the ground. Also keep it covered to protect it from rain. Moisture can cause it to warp or split. Keep the stack out of the way so it doesn't interfere with the smooth flow of the job.

MATERIALS CHECKLIST

TIMBER (SPECIFY TYPE AND SIZE)

- Posts (or steel posts or bricks for piers)
- Ledger
- Bearers
- Joists
- Decking
- Handrailing
- Balusters
- Stair strings
- Stair treads
- Fascia boards
- Bracing
- Temporary bracing or props

OTHER

- Concrete for footings
- Drainage pipes, gravel, weed mat, landscape fabric
- Flashing
- Galvanized post stirrups or brackets
- Galvanized bolts
- Capping (for brick piers)
- Galvanized bolts/coach screws with washers (for fixing bearer to post, ledger to wall, handrail to deck)
- Masonry anchors
- Lost-head galvanized nails: 100 x 3.75 mm, 75 x 3.5 mm for construction
- Twist-shank decking nails: 50 x 3.5 mm
- Framing brackets (joist hangers)
- Nail plates
- Tie rods for stairs
- Oil finishes or stains (primers, filler, finish coats)

GETTING STARTED

Before you begin building your deck you will need to prepare the site and set out the area for construction.

PREPARING THE SITE

If necessary, level the site, although the post heights can be adjusted to allow for uneven ground.

DRAINAGE

If you are building on clayey soil or the site is subjected to a lot of water, use a rubble drain to divert water away from the structure. It should connect to an absorption pit or stormwater pipe drained to the street, and should not direct water onto a neighbouring property.

To construct a rubble drain, dig a trench around the area, allowing for a slight fall to the stormwater pipe or pit. Dig the trench 50 mm deeper than the bottom of the footing. Place 75 mm of coarse gravel or river stone in the bottom of the trench. Lay a plastic agricultural drainage pipe (slotted PVC pipe, preferably with a fine nylon screen sock over it) on top and cover it with fine gravel. Cover this with a landscape fabric (weed mat) and a layer of soil.

WEED CONTROL

Ideally, remove the top layer of soil to ensure grass and weeds don't grow through the deck. The area can also be covered with a landscape fabric and 50 mm of medium gravel. This will also help to drain the surface.

THE LEDGER

When building an attached deck, first fix the ledger to the house, tying the frame of the deck to the building and its solid foundation. The ledger must be secured at the correct height, and it must be level. The height depends on whether the joists will be placed on top of it or against its face.

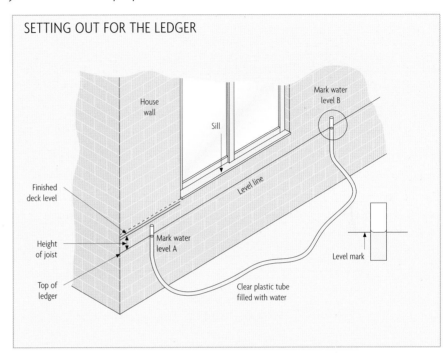

SETTING OUT FOR THE LEDGER

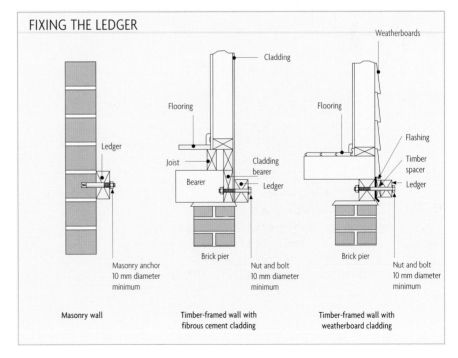

FIXING THE LEDGER

SETTING OUT A LINE FROM THE HOUSE

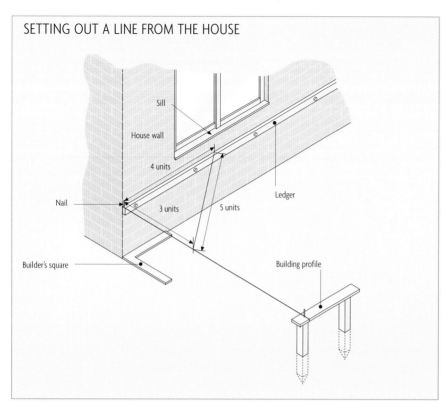

Sill

House wall

4 units

Nail

3 units   5 units

Builder's square

Ledger

Building profile

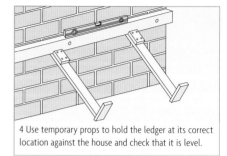

4 Use temporary props to hold the ledger at its correct location against the house and check that it is level.

FIXING THE LEDGER

1 Determine the height for the top of the ledger. Allow for the thickness of the decking (usually 22 mm) and the height of the joists, if applicable. The decking should lie 25 mm below any threshold, so that rainwater won't back up into the house. Use a spirit level and straight edge, or a water level and chalk line, to mark a line for the top of the ledger on the side of the house.

2 If the house has weatherboards, remove one or two to provide a flat surface for the ledger. Place flashing directly above the ledger to prevent water entering the house, and fit a timber spacer behind the ledger so the full width of the ledger will support the joists.

3 Use coach screws to attach the ledger to the house frame, or bolt it through to the bearer or joists. Drill holes through the ledger for the screws, directly below where each alternate deck joist will be.

4 Hold the ledger at its correct location against the house and check that it is level. Insert a pencil through the drilled holes and mark the wall. You may need a helper or temporary props to hold the work, as accuracy is important. Insert screws or bolts.

FINISHING THE SET-OUT

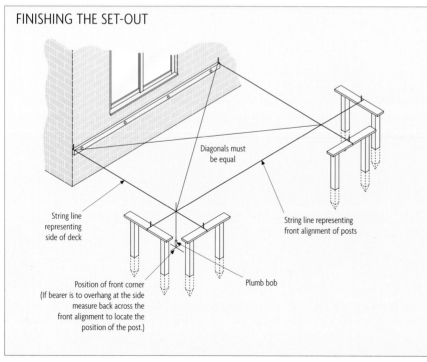

Diagonals must be equal

String line representing side of deck

String line representing front alignment of posts

Position of front corner (If bearer is to overhang at the side measure back across the front alignment to locate the position of the post.)

Plumb bob

outdoor

SETTING OUT AN ATTACHED DECK

5 Tack a nail into the top of the ledger at one end. Tie a string line to the nail and square this line off the house by placing a builder's square on the ground. At least one arm of the square must be level. This will give you a rough line for erecting the building profile. Measure out along this line 600 mm more than the required location of the posts.

6 Construct a building profile using pointed pegs and a horizontal cross-piece 600 mm long (see diagram opposite). The pegs must be strong enough to support the stretched string. If the deck is too high for the profile,

fix a temporary ledger (batten) to the wall while you are setting out. This should be about 300 mm above the ground, level and parallel to the ledger. Place the top of the profile in the same horizontal plane as the ledger. Remove the temporary string line.

7 Using the '3–4–5' method, square the string line off the house at the end of the ledger. Fix the string line to the profile at this position. Repeat at the other end of the ledger.

8 Erect profiles parallel to each string line and 600 mm outside them. Set up the string line for the posts by measuring the required distance from the house along the string lines. Stretch a third string line

across and tie it to the outside profiles.

9 Check the string lines are parallel and at the same slope, and measure the diagonals. If they are equal, the set-out is square. Adjust as required. Attach the string line to a small nail in the top of the profile; check again.

SETTING OUT A FREE-STANDING DECK

Free-standing decks have an extra row of posts and a bearer instead of a ledger. Drive in pegs at the corners on the high side of the area. Use a string line and level to bring them to a level plane. Set out the other sides as for the attached deck, using the level line instead of the ledger.

FOOTINGS AND POSTS

The footings and posts provide the basic support for the deck. The footings must be spaced correctly to make a strong structure, and the posts must be strong enough to bear the weight.

FOOTINGS

A footing (normally made of concrete) is placed in the ground to stabilize the deck structure. The footing must rest on solid ground capable of carrying the load of the deck safely without any undue movement. Depending on the type of soil at your site, the size of the footing will vary (consult your local Building Control office).

If you are using timber posts, the height of the concrete footing is not important, although the top should be approximately 50 mm above the ground and the surface graded away from the post or post support so that water doesn't well around the post. If a timber post is to be placed in the footing, 75 mm of coarse gravel (approximately 20 mm in diameter) should be placed in the bottom of the hole.

If the deck is to rest on brick piers the

footings usually finish below ground level. The precise height will depend on the pier, which must be an even number of brick courses and finish immediately below the bearer.

MAKING THE FOOTINGS

1 Set out the site (see pages 337–339). Use a permanent marker to mark the location of each post on the string line. The spacing for the posts will depend on the section, size and grade of timber used for the bearer (see table on page 334). The standard spacing is 1.8 m, although this may increase to 3.6 m. Using a plumb bob or spirit level, transfer these positions to the ground. This mark will represent the centre front alignment for each pier or post. Use a peg to indicate the centre of each post and remove the string line.

A metal stirrup supports this timber post, raising it and protecting it from rot and insect attack.

DIGGING IN SOFT SOIL

If you have sandy, soft soil that tends to fall into the hole as you dig, cut the top and bottom from a 23 litre drum. Place the drum in position and dig through the drum, pushing it into the excavation as you go. This drum may also be used as formwork when you are pouring the wet concrete for the footing.

To stop sandy soil falling into the hole as you dig, place a drum in position and dig through it.

Spread the handles to hold the soil, then lift it out and place the dirt far enough away from the excavation to avoid any falling back into the hole. (If there is a large number of holes, you can hire a powered post-hole auger, but be sure to obtain adequate instructions from the hire company.)

4 Construct a 100 mm high timber-form box and place it over the hole, centred on the post position. Fix it with pegs—you may need to brace it temporarily to hold it in the correct location. Paint the inside of the formwork with a little oil—this makes it easier to remove once the concrete has set.

5 The concrete mix should not be too wet. The consistency should be wet enough to pour, yet stiff enough to hold the post or stirrups until set. Pour the concrete mix into the form and ram it down well with a piece of timber to prevent air pockets, as they will hold water and can cause the post to rot or rust.

The light, airy look of this raised deck or verandah is achieved by continuing the deck posts up in one line to support the roof.

2 Determine the size of the footings (see table on page 342).

3 The bottom of the footing must rest on stable ground, so remove any tree roots.

Remove the top layer of dirt with a garden spade and use a post-hole shovel or auger to dig the footing holes. Hold the handles together and drive the blades into the ground a few times to break up the soil.

STIRRUP EMBEDDED IN FOOTING

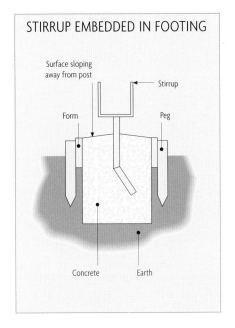

Surface sloping away from post

Stirrup

Form

Peg

Concrete

Earth

POST AND FOOTING TYPES

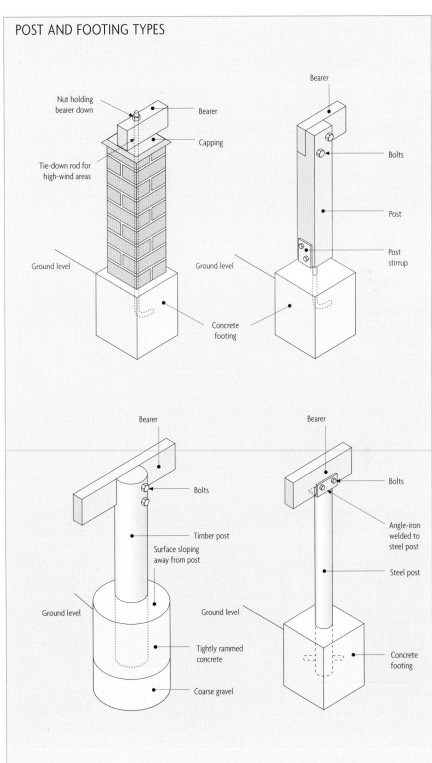

Nut holding bearer down

Bearer

Capping

Tie-down rod for high-wind areas

Ground level

Concrete footing

Bearer

Bolts

Post

Post stirrup

Ground level

Bearer

Bolts

Timber post

Surface sloping away from post

Ground level

Tightly rammed concrete

Coarse gravel

Bearer

Bolts

Angle-iron welded to steel post

Steel post

Ground level

Concrete footing

POSTS OR PIERS

Generally, decks are supported by posts, or by piers or columns. Timber or steel posts are the more common method of support, and they can be either round or square. Steel posts are embedded into the concrete footing, while timber posts may be placed in the footing or on post stirrups (supports). Posts may extend through the top of the deck to provide support for a handrail or even a pergola (roof).

Timber posts should have a C24 stress rating if they are hardwood and at least C24 if treated softwood (see pages 332–334). For suitable timber sizes see table on page 334. When softwood posts will be embedded in the ground, use timber with a high-durability rating (check with your local authority about conditions in your area). Ensure you place the trimmed end up so that it is above ground level and the end in the ground is the one fully treated by the supplier. You can use brush-on preservatives, but they do not have the same amount of penetration as pressure treatment.

FOOTINGS FOR BRACED DECKS*

AREA SUPPORTED BY EACH POST**	MINIMUM FOOTING SIZE
5 m²	300 x 300 mm; 600 mm deep
10 m²	600 x 600 mm; 600 mm deep
15 m²	600 x 600 mm; 600 mm deep
20 m²	750 x 750 mm; 600 mm deep

* Suitable for decks up to 3.6 m above ground on minimum soil-bearing pressure of 150 kPa, such as rock, sand or gravel of medium density, or moderately stiff clay.

** This can be calculated by multiplying the bearer span by the joist span.

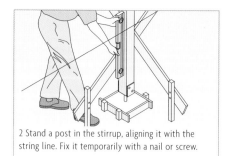

2 Stand a post in the stirrup, aligning it with the string line. Fix it temporarily with a nail or screw.

Piers or columns are normally made of brickwork or reinforced concrete poured into a form tube. For high-wind areas a tie-down rod must be placed in the columns and embedded into the footing during construction.

If necessary, packing such as fibrous cement sheets can be placed on top of the pier to get the precise height for the bearer. The external face of the pier should align with the string line. On top of each pier place a damp-proof course and, in areas where insects are a problem, capping. Brick piers and footings must comply with current building standards and codes.

For a narrow attached deck with ledger, only one bearer and one row of posts are required. For a free-standing deck you need a minimum of two bearers and two rows of posts. Extra bearers and rows of posts will have to be added to make a larger deck.

ERECTING THE POSTS

1 If stirrups are to be embedded in the footing, place them in the wet concrete, ensuring they are aligned with the string line. Use a level to check the alignment. Alternatively, embed a treated timber or steel post in the concrete. The posts may need to be temporarily braced in

HINT

Check with your local authorities for the location of underground services such as gas or water pipes, phone or electric cables. If you damage them you may not only have to pay the repair cost, but you may be placing yourself in danger.

position while the concrete is poured and setting. They must be perfectly vertical and in alignment, as there is no easy way to correct this once the concrete is set. Timber posts can be cut to height after the concrete has set. Steel posts must be set in the concrete at the correct height, as they cannot be cut later. The string line should line up with the position of the lower edge of the bearer or its housing. Allow the concrete footings to cure for approximately seven days before continuing.

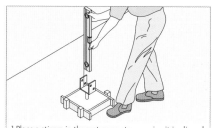

1 Place a stirrup in the wet concrete, ensuring it is aligned with the string line. Use a level to check alignment.

2 If you are using bolt-down stirrups, bolt them in place. Take one post and stand it in a stirrup in its correct alignment with the string line. It should be a little longer than the finished post to allow for fitting and levelling. Temporarily fix the post with one nail, or screw through the holes in the stirrup. This will hold the base of the post and leave the top free. Use a spirit level to check for vertical both ways and temporarily brace the post. Repeat this for the post at the opposite end and for any intermediate posts. Check and recheck that the posts are vertical and in alignment, and adjust them as required.

THE HORIZONTAL FRAMEWORK

A deck is a simple structure similar to the interior floor of a house. Bearers rest on the posts and joists on the bearers, thus making the horizontal framework for the deck.

TIMBER

Bearers and joists usually have a medium durability rating, and are of pressure-treated timber (see pages 332–335). They should have a stress rating of no less than C24 For suitable sizes, see tables on pages 334–335.

BEARERS

The bearers span from post to post. In the case of an attached deck, the decking boards and bearers usually run parallel to the house and the ledger, although if you want the decking boards to run at 90 degrees from the house, you can fix the bearers to the top of the ledger at the same angle.

Bearers can be fixed to the posts in a number of ways:

- They can be housed into the posts below the level line (see page 344).
- They can sit on top of the posts and be fixed with skew-nailing or, preferably, nail plates.
- Bearers can be bolted directly into the face of the post.

If desired, a pair of bearers can be used, one on either side of the post with solid blocking between. In this case smaller timber sections can be used, but take care to ensure that the top edges of both bearers are at the same level and alignment, or they will not support the joists properly.

DETERMINING THE BEARER HEIGHT

Take care in determining the bearer height and levels, as you don't want a twisted, uneven or out-of-level deck. Check again that the posts are aligned and plumb, and transfer a level mark from the top of the ledger to each post. For wider decks use

The ends of the joists here have been painted to match the bearer and bottom railing so that they create a decorative checked effect. A fascia board could have been used to conceal them.

ATTACHING BEARERS

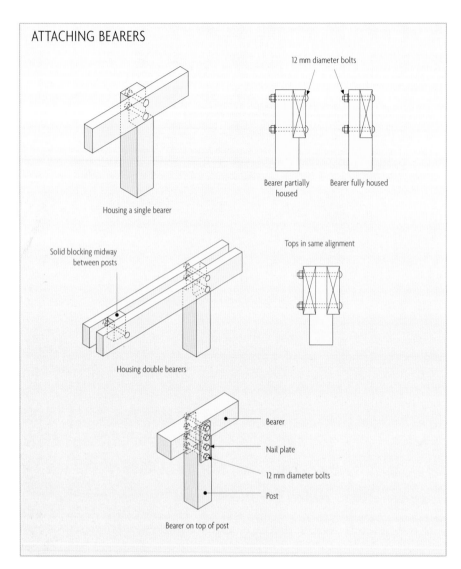

12 mm diameter bolts

Housing a single bearer

Bearer partially housed

Bearer fully housed

Solid blocking midway between posts

Tops in same alignment

Housing double bearers

Bearer

Nail plate

12 mm diameter bolts

Post

Bearer on top of post

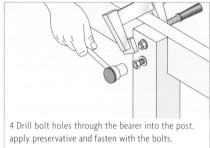

4 Drill bolt holes through the bearer into the post, apply preservative and fasten with the bolts.

ATTACHING THE BEARERS

1 If the posts are in stirrups, number each post and stirrup to match (the post heights may vary). Place a cross on the side of the post where the bearer is to be fitted. Remove the posts from the stirrups and lay each post on a set of trestles so that you can work on them easily.

2 The bearers are housed into the posts below the level line. From the line on each post measure down the height of the bearer. Square both lines across the face and down each side. Mark the depth of the housing: it is generally the thickness of the bearers or a maximum of two-thirds the thickness of the post. Cut the housings with a power saw. Clean them out with a chisel and check that they fit neatly.

3 Re-erect each post in its correct location and check it for alignment and plumb. Use braces to hold it in position. Fasten it to the stirrup with 10 mm bolts.

4 Place the bearer in position. Level it and secure it with a cramp. Use galvanized roundhead bolts (preferably two per post). Drill the bolt holes through the bearer into the post. The drill bit may not be long enough to go through the bearer and the post, so remove the bearer and continue to drill the holes all the way through. Apply a coat of preservative to both surfaces within the joint. Replace the bearer and fasten with the bolts.

a water level, but on narrower decks a straight edge and spirit level may be used. Rest the spirit level in the centre of the straight edge. With one end of the straight edge resting on top of the ledger, move the other up or down until the straight edge is level. Mark the edge bottom on the post.

• If the joists are to be fixed on top of the ledger and bearer, this will represent the top of the bearer. Transfer the mark onto all the corner posts. Pull a string line tightly from each corner post and mark the

bearer height on each intermediate post.
• If the joists are to be fixed at the height of the ledger but over the bearers, the bearer will need to be lower. Measure down the height of the joists from the original mark, and make a mark. Transfer this mark to all posts in the same way.

If bearers are not long enough and have to be joined end to end, the joint must be placed directly over a post and, in the case of double bearers, the joins should be staggered. Use a scarf joint for maximum strength.

HINT

Creosote is an excellent insect repellent and is used on the underside of decks or around the bottom of posts that are placed in the ground. Care must be exercised when using this product. Be sure to follow the manufacturer's instructions.

JOISTS

Joists span the width of the deck and are fixed to the bearer and ledger, or two bearers, in one of several ways:

- Joists may sit on top of the bearers, and be skew-nailed or fixed with a frame connector.
- Joists may sit against the face of the bearers and ledger. Use joist hangers for maximum strength.
- Joists may fit against the face of the ledger and over the bearers.

Other types of framing brackets may also be used. If you are using joist hangers, the ledger, bearers and joist should be the same size.

The joists may finish at or extend past the outside bearer. Allowing them to overhang the bearer will make the deck more attractive as the posts will be set back from the edge and be less noticeable, especially if they are camouflaged by plantings. The overhang must not exceed one-quarter of the joist span (see diagram on page 346).

Although joists are usually laid at right angles to bearers, this can vary, for example if you are laying decking boards in a pattern (see page 349).

ATTACHING JOISTS

1 Mark the spacings for each joist on top of the ledger and bearers by measuring along both from the same end. This will ensure the joists are parallel, even if the spacings between them are not even. The maximum recommended spacing will not always suit

This bearer is housed into the posts, which continue up to support the railing.

FIXING TO A ROUND POST

1 To house a bearer into a round post, first measure the thickness of the bearer back from the front edge. Then mark this thickness across the top of each post, measuring from the front. Pull a string line across the top of the row of posts to represent the back of the housing.

2 Draw a vertical line down each side of the post the height of the bearer. Use a square piece of cardboard as a guide, and mark a line around the post.

3 Cut the housing with a handsaw for safety, and remove the waste with a chisel.

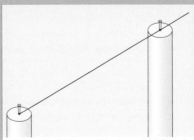

1 Measure the thickness of the bearer back from the front edge and pull a string line across the posts.

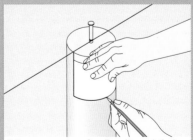

2 Use a square piece of cardboard to mark the line for the bottom of the housing around the post.

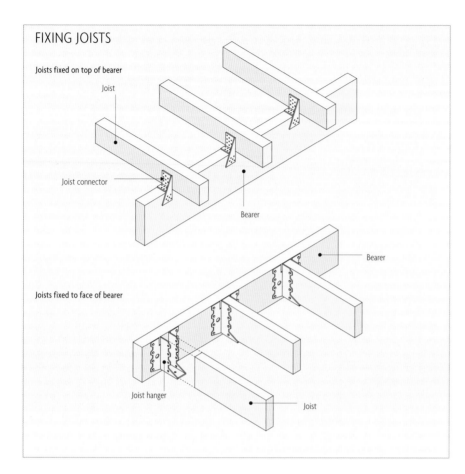

FIXING JOISTS

Joists fixed on top of bearer

Joist

Joist connector

Bearer

Bearer

Joists fixed to face of bearer

Joist hanger

Joist

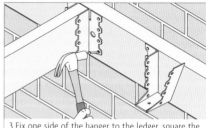

3 Fix one side of the hanger to the ledger, square the end of the joist, then fix the other side of the hanger.

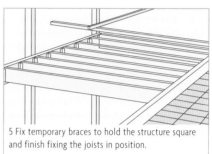

5 Fix temporary braces to hold the structure square and finish fixing the joists in position.

your deck, so you can adjust it and keep all the spacing the same or adjust the two end spaces only. Never exceed the maximum recommended spacing (see page 335).

2 Square the spacings down the face of the ledger and place a cross to mark the position of the joist. Using galvanized 30 x 2.8 mm clout nails or those recommended by the manufacturer, fix one side of the hanger to the ledger or bearer, positioning it so the joist and ledger are flush on top. Use an offcut of joist material to help position the hanger (this will be easier than manoeuvring a joist).

3 Square the ledger end of the two outside joists. Do not cut them to finished length

unless they are to fit between the ledger and the bearer. If they sit over the bearer, they are trimmed later. Apply a preservative and fit the joist in the hanger. Fix the other side of the hanger to the ledger, and then fix it to the joist. If the joists sit on top of the ledger, leave a 10 mm gap between the end of the joist and the wall.

4 Check that the posts are still plumb and aligned. Skew-nail the other end of the joist to the top of the bearer with one 75 x 3.5 mm galvanized nail, or temporarily fix a hanger in place.

5 Measure the diagonals of the structure for square and adjust as required. You may need a temporary brace to hold the

structure square. When you are satisfied, finish fixing the end joists and all the remaining joists, keeping any bows in the timber to the top.

6 If the joists overhang, mark the required length on each end joist and stretch a string line between them. Draw vertical lines down the sides of each joist to correspond with the string line, and cut all joists to length.

FINISHING THE FRAMEWORK

7 If desired, fix a fascia board over the ends of the joists to give the deck a neater finish. The board must be well secured if a handrail is to be attached to it.

8 Fix any necessary bracing (see box opposite). Once these braces are permanently fixed, any temporary bracing that was used to hold the structure square during construction may be removed.

outdoor

BRACING THE DECK

A deck that is securely fixed to a house, especially in a corner, will require only minimal bracing, if any. A deck higher than 1200 mm should have at least a pair of opposing braces. Decks higher than 1800 mm and wider than 2000 mm need a pair of opposing braces in both directions. Any deck built in a high-wind area or free-standing on stirrups should also be braced.

A simple 100 x 50 mm timber brace at 45 degrees (from post to bearer and secured with bolts) will be adequate in most situations. The brace angle may vary up to 5 degrees, but the bottom of the brace should not be lower than half the post height.

For free-standing decks, cross-bracing from the top of one post to the bottom of the next will provide better stability.

The bracing will not necessarily detract from the appearance of the deck, as it can be concealed with lattice, vertical or horizontal battens, or a trellis for a climbing vine. Fix the diagonal bracing under the joists with halving joints in the centre. Use 90 x 45 mm timbers and bolt them at each end with a 12 mm diameter bolt. Nail them to each joist.

ATTACHING A BRACE

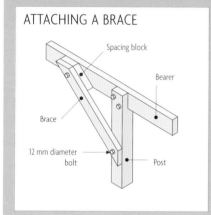

Spacing block

Bearer

Brace

12 mm diameter bolt

Post

CROSS-BRACING

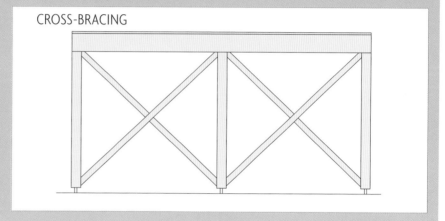

THE DECKING

The decking is the part of a deck most often seen, and so selection of the decking timber and accurate fixing are a crucial part of building a deck.

DECKING BOARDS
The decking boards are fixed on top of the joists parallel to the bearers. They must be spaced a little apart to allow water to pass through.

Decking boards come in various sizes, the two most common being machined from 100 x 25 mm or 75 x 25 mm timber. They are suitable for 450 mm joist spacings. Other sizes may be machined to order.

Decking is subjected to weather and traffic and so must be good-quality timber. Use either seasoned hardwood with medium durability or treated softwood with a medium or high rating. Decking should be free of structural defects, especially splits and knots. Boards that are cup-faced should be laid with the cup down to prevent anyone tripping on them.

Most timber suppliers will have a selection of decking boards, varying in durability, grading, shapes and, of course, price. Decking is usually purchased by the square or lineal metre; allow 10 per cent for wastage.

Don't use short lengths: the boards must span at least three joists. Fluted or skid-resistant boards are best, as they are attractive and make the gaps between boards less obvious. They should be used around pools.

The most commonly used decking profiles have rounded top edges that are splinter-free, more even to walk on and accept stain more readily.

DECKING PATTERNS
Decking is usually laid parallel to the house, but laying it at different angles can give a more interesting effect. This takes more time

Decking boards should be securely fixed and properly spaced to provide a safe and comfortable floor for a deck.

HINT

When using a nail as a spacer, drive it through a piece of thin timber to prevent it repeatedly falling between the boards. Use three spacers—one at each end and one where you are working.

1 Check the frame with a long straight edge and trim the tops of the joists with a power plane.

remove any bows that project too high. Check the frame with a long straight edge and trim the tops of the joists with a power plane.

2 Select the straightest decking board for a starter board which will determine the position of all the others. Allow the board to extend past the finished length (it will be trimmed later). The deck will look better if it has a 10–25 mm overhang on all outside edges (see diagram on page 350). To determine the placement of the starter board, subtract the overhang from the width of the board, for example, a board of 66 mm width with an overhang on the outside edge of 10 mm will have a starter width of 56 mm. Measure in 56 mm from the outside edge at both ends and stretch and snap a chalk line between these two points. This will provide a straight line to start on.

3 Secure the starter board in line with the chalk mark. Using twisted-shank nails (see page 336), nail from one end to the other, straightening the board as you go. Drive in

outdoor

and costs more, but the result will be well worth it.

If you are laying a pattern, the placement and direction of the joists will need to be worked out to accommodate it. To ensure a solid surface where decking is joined, use double joists. The joist spacing should be calculated in the direction in which the decking is to be laid, not square off the joists.

LAYING THE DECKING

1 Cut the tops of all the joists flush and

DECKING SPANS*

	THICKNESS	MAXIMUM JOIST SPACING
Hardwood	19 mm	500 mm
	25 mm	650 mm
Treated softwood	22 mm	450 mm

* Standard grade timbers. The spans for different designs are given in the diagram below.

DECKING PROFILES

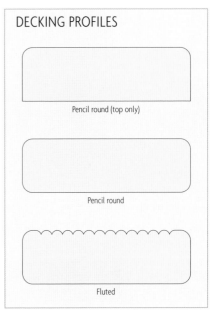

Pencil round (top only)

Pencil round

Fluted

DECKING PATTERNS

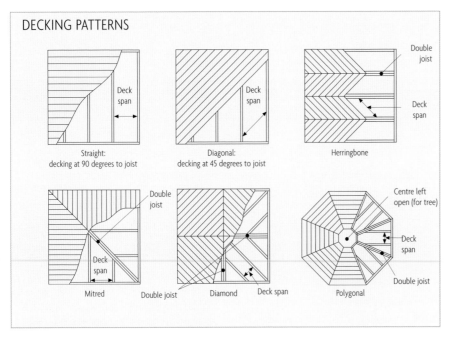

Straight:
decking at 90 degrees to joist

Diagonal:
decking at 45 degrees to joist

Herringbone

Double joist

Deck span

Deck span

Mitred

Double joist

Diamond

Deck span

Double joist

Polygonal

Centre left open (for tree)

Deck span

Double joist

Deck span

4 Scatter a number of boards on the joist at a time to provide a work platform. Position the next board against the starter board with its end extending past the finished length. It will be trimmed off later. Leave a small gap (3–4 mm) between the boards for drainage, and to allow dirt to fall through. (This gap may seem small, but the timber will shrink over time.) A nail can be used as a spacer to maintain the gap. Use a spacer at each end and one in close proximity to the joist the decking is being nailed to. Nail the boards down as for the starter board.

5 Straighten bowed decking boards as you work.

• If the board bows in, nail one end in place. Work along the board placing the spacer to create the required gap. At the bow, drive a chisel into the top of the joist and lever the board over to the spacer. Nail down. Continue this from joist to joist. Sight along the board to check for straightness.

• If the board is bowed out, secure each end with the correct spacing and place a spacer in the centre of the bow. Use

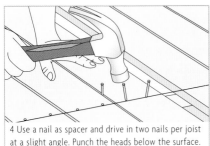

4 Use a nail as spacer and drive in two nails per joist at a slight angle. Punch the heads below the surface.

two nails per joist at a slight angle, and punch the heads below the surface.

• If there are handrail posts you may have to secure the starter board further in from

the edge to clear the posts. In this case, the starting position should match equal board widths and gaps from the outside. The decking can be cut in around the posts later.

• At the ends of boards drill pilot holes to prevent the boards splitting. Drill the pilot hole slightly smaller than the nail diameter. You may also need to drill holes through the decking if the timber is too dry and likely to split.

• To save time, you can use a pneumatic nail gun. Ensure the nails are suitable for use in the gun.

STARTER BOARD POSITION

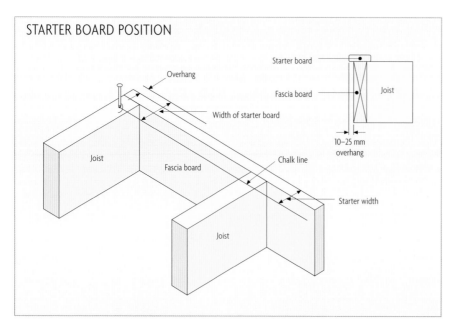

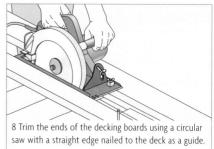

8 Trim the ends of the decking boards using a circular saw with a straight edge nailed to the deck as a guide.

FIXING DECKING

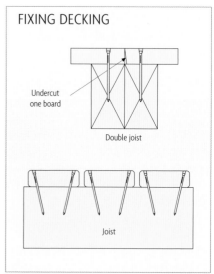

LAYING DECKING

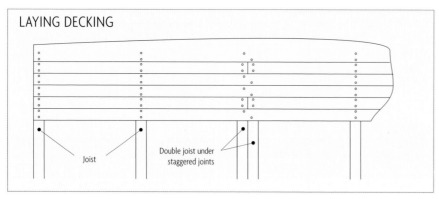

the chisel to lever the board over and nail. Repeat this on both sides of each joist. Sight the board for straightness and continue the process as required.

6 Regularly check the decking for parallel, especially the remaining spacing. Measure at each end and in the centre. If the spacing is not parallel, adjust the gaps over the next few boards and check again. To avoid ending up with uneven boards or spacing, carefully check your measurements on the last 900 mm or so, and open or close the remaining gaps slightly to make

any adjustment as required.

7 Stagger joins, and if possible support them on double joists. To obtain a tight fit one of the ends can be undercut slightly.

TRIMMING DECKING ENDS

8 Mark the overhang at each end of the deck, that is on the first and last boards. Measure the distance from the blade of your circular saw to the outside edge of the baseplate. Mark this distance in from the overhang position and secure a straight edge as a guide for the saw to run against. Sight along the

guide and straighten it if required by nailing at regular intervals. Alternatively, spring a chalk line between the two overhang points and cut along this line. However, this method does require greater accuracy in use of the saw.

9 Place the circular saw against the straight edge and trim the overhang. Round over the trimmed ends with a hand plane or router. Sand the boards if required.

HINT

Add a coat of preservative or stain before the boards are nailed down. It's also a good idea to apply a coat to the tops of joists and other hard-to-reach spots.

outdoor

DECK STAIRS

Whether the deck is attached or free-standing, it will in most cases need stairs for access to the garden and perhaps between levels. A basic open stair is all that is needed.

DESIGNING DECK STAIRS

Stairs for a deck should not be elaborate, as fine detailing can trap moisture and cause rot. Use a concrete pad or footings under the strings to keep them above the ground and away from moisture.

A comfortable width for a stair is about 900 mm, and it shouldn't be less than 760 mm. If it is wider than 900 mm it will require a string (centre carriage piece) for support.

The string tops can be fixed by one of two methods (see page 353):

- cutting hooks in the end of the string to sit on the joist or decking
- cutting the end to fit against the face of the joist and holding it in place with a ledger or angle brackets.

PARTS OF THE STAIRS

- Strings. These are the main support for the stairs. There is one on each side spanning from the deck to the ground. The treads are attached to them. Strings may have a sawtooth shape or a straight top. The timber used should be as straight as possible and free from any defects.
- Treads. These are the steps. To create a horizontal surface to walk on they are attached to strings on both sides, either the top of sawtoothed strings or the face of the strings. They can be housed into the string or secured to them on timber cleats or steel brackets (see page 354). Two pieces of timber laid side by side to obtain the required tread width are better than one wide piece, as wider pieces are more prone to distortion when exposed to the weather. The nosing is the front of the tread. The going is the clear tread width.

Stairs are essential to provide easy access to the garden from any deck apart from those right on ground level.

STAIR TERMINOLOGY

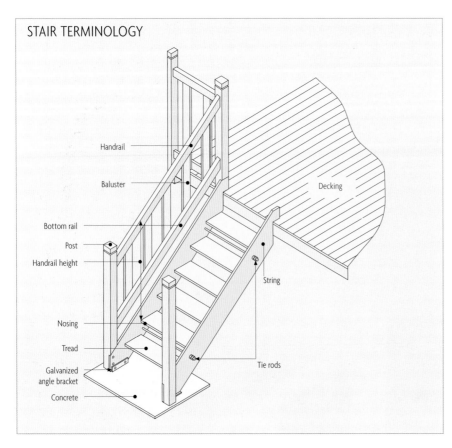

Handrail

Baluster

Decking

Bottom rail

Post

Handrail height

String

Nosing

Tread

Galvanized angle bracket

Concrete

Tie rods

STAIR CALCULATIONS

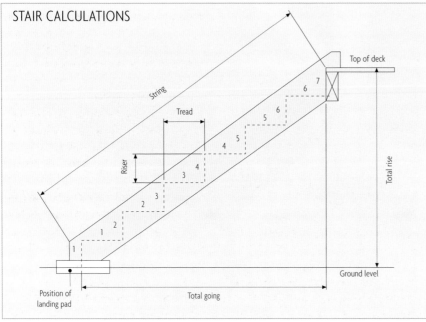

Top of deck

String

Tread

Riser

Total rise

Ground level

Position of landing pad

Total going

- Riser. This is the vertical distance between the top of one tread and the top of the next (the height of each step). Internal stairs may have a riser board placed between the treads but this is not common on external stairs. The total 'rise' is the effective height of all the risers added together.

Your local Building Control office will have regulations for building stairs and these will ensure that you construct a comfortable and safe stairway. Some of the regulations in the Building Regulations (1991) (Part 1) include:

- All the rise measurements in the stairway must be the same and measure between 115 mm and 220.
- Treads must have a clear width of between 220 and 355 mm.
- The relation between tread and risers must be such that:

2R + G = between 550 and 700 mm
(where R = riser and G = going
or clear tread width)

The code also states that a stair over 60 cm in height or more than five risers must have a handrail not less than 90 cm high.

MEASURING UP

1 To determine the rise and going of your stairs, measure the distance from the top of the decking to the ground. Be sure the measurement is taken plumb from the top and not at an angle. For example, the distance might be 1200 mm.

2 Divide this measurement by 175 mm (average riser height), then round it to the nearest whole number, for example 1200 divided by 175 = 6.86 or 7 risers. Now divide 1200 by 7 to find the finished riser height (171 mm).

3 To check that this riser height is acceptable, decide on a going (275 mm is

FIXING THE STAIRS

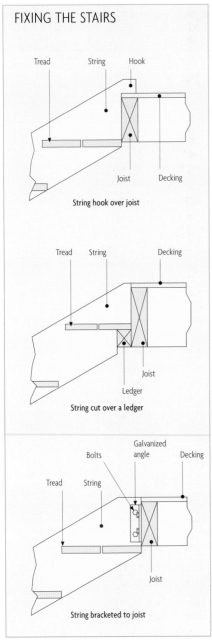

String hook over joist

String cut over a ledger

String bracketed to joist

STAIR SET-OUT

Top of stair

Hook

Plumb riser cut

Riser line

Pitch board

Top line
of tree

Tread thickness

90°

Tread
Pitch board

Ground line
foot cut

Bottom of stair
Margin line

Left-hand string
(reverse for right-hand one)

rise (see the diagram on page 352). The formula is $a^2 + b^2 = c^2$, where a is the total going, b is the total rise and c is the length of the stringer. In our example, $1650^2 + 1200^2$ = the length squared (2040.221^2). The length of the string is, therefore, rounded off to 2040 mm.

CONSTRUCTING THE LANDING PAD

6 Set out the pad. The position is determined by measuring out horizontally from the face of the deck the total going of the stair (for example, 1650 mm). The pad will need to be a little closer to the deck (about 300 mm) so the strings rest on it. It should be a little wider than both strings, extend in front of the strings (so that you can step on it) and be about 100 mm deep.

7 Excavate and make up a form in the area for the pad. Pour the concrete and leave it to set for at least 48 hours. Galvanized angle brackets to hold the strings may be cast in the pad or bolted on later.

8 Use a straight edge and level to determine the new rise height from the top of the pad. Divide the height by the number of risers (7) to find the finished height of each.

MARKING OUT THE STAIRS

9 Decide on the type of stair you want and cut a 'pitch board' template from plywood or thick cardboard, to represent one riser and one tread.

10 Cut two strings from 300 x 50 mm timber, cutting them longer than the calculation to allow for plumb cuts and hooks at the top and a level foot at the bottom (see above left). Place the two strings side by side. Mark a margin line on the face parallel to the top edge (not required if a sawtooth shape is being used).

average) and use the 2R + G formula: (2 x 171) + 275 = 617 mm, which fits the formula.

4 There is one less tread than risers (the top of the deck is not considered a tread). Therefore, in our example there would be

6 treads. The total going would be 6 x 275 = 1650 mm.

5 The length of the string is the hypotenuse of a right-angled triangle where the other two sides are the total going and the total

STAIR CONSTRUCTION METHODS

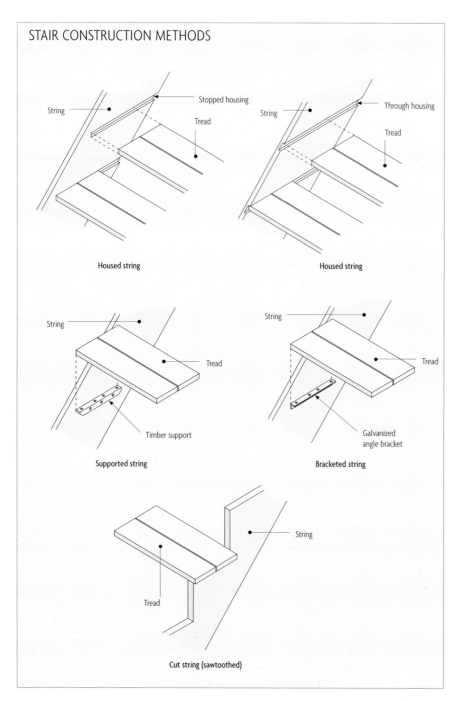

Housed string

Housed string

Supported string

Bracketed string

Cut string (sawtoothed)

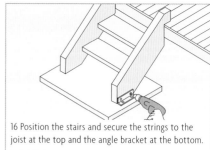

16 Position the stairs and secure the strings to the joist at the top and the angle bracket at the bottom.

12 Cut the housings in the strings to receive the treads with a power saw or router, and clean out with a chisel. Alternatively, fix brackets or cleats to the face of the strings, or cut the top of each string in a sawtooth shape.

13 Cut the end of the string as required, ensuring you have a pair (one left-hand and one right-hand).

14 Cut the treads to length. Check the fit in each housing and adjust as required. Slightly round or bevel each long edge with a hand plane. Apply a water repellent or stain to housings and end grains.

15 Stairs with more than four treads may be very heavy to manoeuvre, so fix only the top and bottom treads with 75 x 3.75 mm galvanized lost-head nails or screws. The remaining treads will be fixed later.

16 Position the stairs and secure the strings to the joist at the top and the angle bracket at the bottom. The rest of the treads may now be fixed.

17 If the stairs are not directly against a wall, place a number of threaded tie rods across the stairs directly under the treads at 1350 mm centres maximum. Use washers and nuts on both sides of each string to hold the rods in place.

11 Start about 50 mm in from one end of the string and trace around the template, moving it along the margin line for each tread and riser. Turn the template over and repeat on the other string. At the top, mark a hook if required. Mark the thickness of the treads.

DECK FURNITURE

Outdoor furniture can help you make the most of your deck. There is a large variety of ready-made timber furniture available, and you can choose timbers that match your decking material or purchase it without a finish so you can apply the one that matches your deck.

Benches can also be built as part of the deck structure. They can be fixed directly to the joist below the decking or attached to the posts around the edge of the deck (as in the diagram below). However, seating attached to the edge of the deck is not a substitute for a handrail and balustrades, and the handrail should be higher behind a bench so that anyone (especially children) standing on it does not fall over the edge.

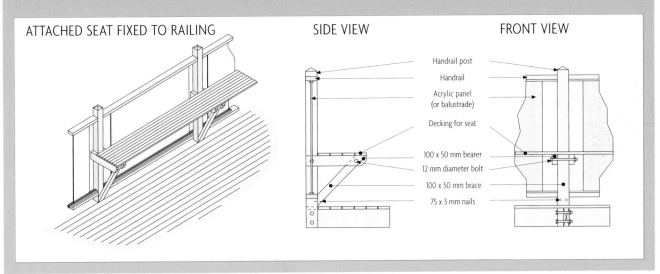

ATTACHED SEAT FIXED TO RAILING

SIDE VIEW

FRONT VIEW

- Handrail post
- Handrail
- Acrylic panel (or balustrade)
- Decking for seat
- 100 x 50 mm bearer
- 12 mm diameter bolt
- 100 x 50 mm brace
- 75 x 3 mm nails

HANDRAILS

Handrailing can transform a plain-looking deck into an architectural masterpiece. It should, however, blend in with its surroundings, as it will be the first part of the deck that people notice.

HANDRAIL REGULATIONS

In the interests of safety, any handrail must be securely fixed and built to current regulations. Check with your local authority, which will have regulations similar to these:

- Stairs over 600 mm or five risers high must have a handrail 900 mm or more above the front edge of the tread.
- Floors (decking) more than 600 mm above ground or floor level must have a handrail at least 900 mm high.
- Floors more than 3 m above ground or floor level must have a handrail at least 1 m high.

- The maximum span for handrails varies according to the size of the timber used and whether there is a balustrade (see tables on pages 356–357).
- The maximum space between balusters must not exceed 100 mm.
- Handrails are required on both sides of stairs and ramps when these are over 1 m wide.

THE STRUCTURE

There are many handrail designs, but all must have firmly secured posts and top rails. A bottom rail and balusters usually give extra support.

In some deck designs the posts extend from the footing through the decking to support the handrail. This is by far the strongest method. Otherwise, handrail posts must be fixed to the joists. The tables on pages 356–357 give the maximum permissible handrail spans and, therefore, the spacings for the posts. Note that for reasons of space in those tables, 'oak' is used as a shorthand for 'hardwood'.

Timber for handrail posts should not be

A securely fixed handrail is essential for any deck more than 600 mm above the ground in order to prevent accidents. Here, lattice infill is used to give an attractive finish with an outdoor feel.

MAXIMUM HANDRAIL SPANS (NO BALUSTRADE)

TIMBER (mm)	MAX. SPAN (mm)		
	C16	C24	OAK
170 x 25			1000
190 x 25		900	1000
70 x 35		900	1000
90 x 35	900	1000	1200
120 x 35	1100	1200	1400
140 x 35	1200	1300	1500
170 x 35	1300	1400	1600
190 x 35	1400	1500	1700
220 x 35	1500	1600	1900
240 x 35	1600	1700	2000
70 x 45	1200	1300	1500
90 x 45	1400	1500	1700
120 x 45	1600	1700	2000
140 x 45	1800	1900	2200
170 x 45	1900	2100	2300
190 x 45	2100	2200	2400
220 x 45	2200	2300	2500
240 x 45	2200	2300	2500
65 x 65	2100	2200	2400
70 x 70	2300	2400	2600
90 x 70	2500	2600	2800

smaller than 70 x 70 mm or 90 x 45 mm, with a stress rating of C24. House the bottom of the post over the joist and secure it at the base with two 10 mm diameter bolts. Use a level to keep them plumb.

Handrails and bottom rails may be fixed to the face of the posts or housed into the sides and secured with galvanized nails or screws.

Balustrades are fitted between the handrail and deck or bottom rail to form a safety screen and decoration.

The handrail should blend in with its surroundings and meet the requirements of the building regulations. Some common designs are shown opposite.

CONSTRUCTING A HANDRAIL

The handrail and balustrade are installed after the decking and stairs have been fixed.

1 Mark a level line on one end post to represent the top edge of the handrail. Transfer it to the other end post with

MAXIMUM HANDRAIL SPANS (WITH BALUSTRADE*)

TIMBER (mm)	MAX. SPAN (mm)		
	C16	C24	OAK
70 x 35	1700	1800	2100
90 x 35	2300	2400	2600
120 x 35	2900	3000	3300
140 x 35	3200	3400	3700
170 x 35	3400	3600	4000
190 x 35	3600	3800	
70 x 45	1900	2100	2300
90 x 45	2500	2600	2800
120 x 45	3100	3200	3500
140 x 45	3500	3600	3900
170 x 45	4000		
190 x 45	4000		

* Provide vertical support at 900 mm centres maximum.

HANDRAIL TERMINOLOGY

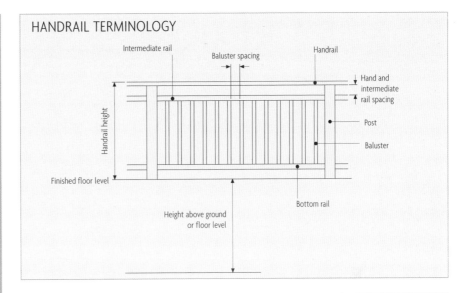

HANDRAIL DESIGNS

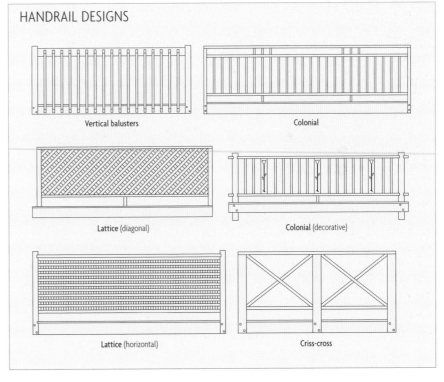

Vertical balusters

Colonial

Lattice (diagonal)

Colonial (decorative)

Lattice (horizontal)

Criss-cross

a water level. Snap a chalk line between to transfer the height onto any intermediate posts. Trim the posts to height (this may be above or below the line depending on your design). Locate the position for the bottom rail (if required) by measuring down from the top set-out line. Square these lines across the sides of the posts and mark a 10 mm deep housing at each location to receive the rails. With some designs the rails are simply screwed or bolted to the face of the posts and corners are either mitred or overlapped.

2 Apply a coat of preservative (stain or paint) and nail or screw the rails into their housing (see the diagram on page 358). Shaped handrail is best secured to the posts with pipe dowels and two screws from underneath to prevent the rail twisting. To prevent the bottom rail bowing down over a large span, a blocking piece is placed between it and the deck.

3 Space the balusters evenly along the railing with 100 mm maximum between them. To calculate the spacings, add the width of one baluster (say, 40 mm) to 100 mm:

40 + 100 = 140 mm

Divide the distance between the posts (say, 2000 mm) by this and round the result up to a whole number:

2000 divided by 140 = 14.28, rounded to 15 balusters

outdoor

FIXING HANDRAILS

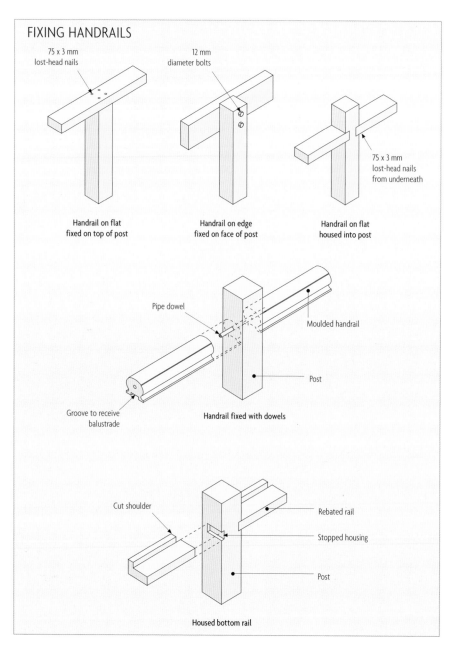

75 x 3 mm
lost-head nails

Handrail on flat
fixed on top of post

12 mm
diameter bolts

Handrail on edge
fixed on face of post

75 x 3 mm
lost-head nails
from underneath

Handrail on flat
housed into post

Pipe dowel

Moulded handrail

Post

Groove to receive
balustrade

Handrail fixed with dowels

Cut shoulder

Rebated rail

Stopped housing

Post

Housed bottom rail

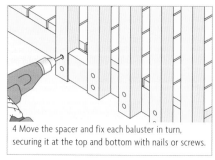

4 Move the spacer and fix each baluster in turn,
securing it at the top and bottom with nails or screws.

into any grooves or rebates on the rails.
Before fixing, check for plumb. Secure at top
and bottom with nails. Continue to move the
spacer and fix each baluster in turn. Once you
are about halfway, check the gap to ensure
your spacings are correct. Adjust as required.

FIXING HANDRAIL POSTS

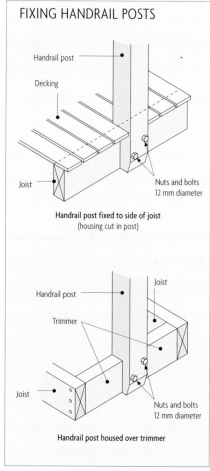

Handrail post

Decking

Joist

Nuts and bolts
12 mm diameter

Handrail post fixed to side of joist
(housing cut in post)

Joist

Handrail post

Trimmer

Joist

Nuts and bolts
12 mm diameter

Handrail post housed over trimmer

Multiply the result by the width of
one baluster:

15 x 40 = 600 mm

Subtract the result from the distance
between the posts: 2000 − 500 = 1400 mm
Divide by the number of spacings required
(15, one more than the number of balusters):

1400 divided by 15 = 96 mm, which is the
required spacing

4 Cut a piece of timber to this width to
act as a spacer. Place the first baluster in
position with the spacer between the
baluster and the handrail post, ensuring it fits

FINISHING THE DECK

Decks are exposed to the weather and so need to be given a protective finish so that the timber lasts longer and the structure remains in good condition.

PROTECTING TIMBER

The surface of all exterior timber will eventually become weathered and discoloured, and might even split or crack. Rot and mildew are more serious effects of weathering. To help counteract it, apply a water repellent and a finish coat of oil or paint.

- Most water repellents provide limited protection and need to be applied every six months or so. The repellent penetrates the surface of the timber without altering its natural colour, although pigments may be added. Other additives, such as ultraviolet stabilizers, insecticides and fungicides, can be incorporated for greater protection.

- Specially formulated decking stains or oils can be used for a natural look or to change the colour of the timber. Both stains and oils provide protection for up to three years, or even longer depending on the conditions. They are easy to apply and maintain, and don't peel, crack or blister like some paints do. Stains will perform better when the surface has had a primer coat of water repellent.

- Any paint used should be specially formulated for external timberwork: ordinary house paint will not withstand the constant exposure to the weather. Paint manufacturers make special paint for decking.

A finished deck will need a good, protective finish in order to withstand the elements of nature.

METHOD

1 Make sure the timber is dry, or the finish may blister or crack. To test, splash a handful of water across the boards. If the water is absorbed by the timber within a few minutes, the timber is dry. However, if the water remains on the surface for some time, the timber is wet and needs time to dry out before finishing. This could take up to a week or more.

2 If the timber has discoloured patches, remove them by sanding or washing the timber down with a timber bleach. To eliminate minor defects such as marks, splintering or rough surfaces, lightly sand the surface and then ensure it is free of dust or oil before finishing. Pressure-treated timber may have powdery deposits on the surface. Remove them by lightly washing the surface with mild soap and water.

3 Using a paint brush or roller, apply the finish, keeping an even amount on the surface and working the edges so that they remain wet to avoid a streaky or patchy appearance.

OCTAGONAL FREE-STANDING DECK

This octagonal split-level deck is attractive and useful. It rests on brick piers and is built around a tree. A step is incorporated on one low side and a storage box/seat on another side.

This free-standing octagonal deck was built to cover an area below a large tree where grass would not grow. It is now a pleasant place to sit in summer.

SETTING OUT

1 Set out the basic square shape as described on pages 338–339. For an octagon with sides 1.8 m long, start with a square with sides 4350 mm long. Make use of any slope as shown in the diagram on page 362. To locate the footing positions for the octagon, measure the diagonals and divide by 2 to find x. From each corner of the square, measure x distance along each side to find eight points *a*. Join point *a* to point *a* across each corner to form the octagon. To check the set-out, measure the distances from *a* to *a* around the octagon. If your set-out is correct, they should all be equal.

2 The size of deck will determine the number of footings required (see Bearer sizes on page 334). Each side of this octagon is 1.8 m and so it will require footings at each corner and one in the centre (see diagram on page 362). Add footings at corners of the original square where you want a step or storage box/seat.

3 Build footings and brick piers (see pages 339–342) with a lower pier for the step. Align them to the string line and add damp-proofing and capping.

OUTER FRAME

4 If you are incorporating a step, place 150 x 50 mm joists on the appropriate piers (see diagram opposite, top right). Use halving joints to join them and secure with nail plates. Keep each joist in line with the string line, checking with a spirit level. Check the corner for square and secure a temporary brace across the joists. Mark in from each corner the position of the

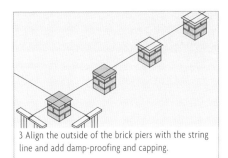

3 Align the outside of the brick piers with the string line and add damp-proofing and capping.

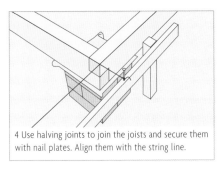

4 Use halving joints to join the joists and secure them with nail plates. Align them with the string line.

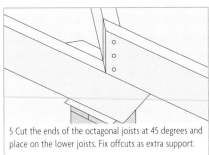

5 Cut the ends of the octagonal joists at 45 degrees and place on the lower joists. Fix offcuts as extra support.

OCTAGONAL DECK LAYOUT

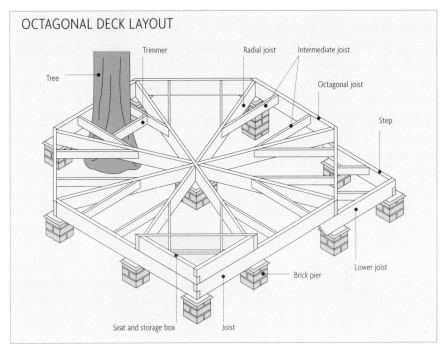

Tree — Trimmer — Radial joist — Intermediate joist — Octagonal joist — Step — Lower joist — Brick pier — Joist — Seat and storage box

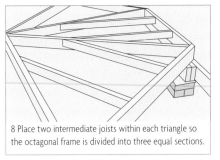

8 Place two intermediate joists within each triangle so the octagonal frame is divided into three equal sections.

11 Nail battens to each side of each radial joist to provide extra stability for the decking boards.

octagonal side. Cut an octagonal joist to length with the ends cut at 45 degrees. Place on the lower joists and fix at either end.

5 Cut the other joists the same way and lay them on the piers to form the octagon. If you are adding the seat at one corner, extend the joists there and join them with a halving joint. Take offcuts from the joists and fix them to the lower joists where there are two layers (at step and seat) as extra support.

INNER FRAMEWORK

6 Radial joists provide stability. Cut one joist to span from one corner of the octagon to

the other, passing over the centre pier. Bevel-cut both ends to fit into the octagonal frame. Fix the joist in position with 75 x 3.75 mm galvanized lost-head nails.

7 Measure along this joist and mark the centre. Cut six joists to span from the other corners of the octagon to the centre line. Bevel-cut the ends to fit; fix with 75 mm galvanized nails.

8 Place two intermediate joists within each triangle so the joist of the octagonal frame is divided into three equal sections. Fix them

to the octagonal frame with joist hangers. Bevel-cut the other ends and nail them to the radial joists.

9 Fix two intermediate joists in the step in the same way.

10 If necessary, fix trimmers between the joists to create an opening around a tree.

11 Nail 50 x 50 mm battens to each side of each radial joist to increase the surface width. This will provide extra stability for the decking boards.

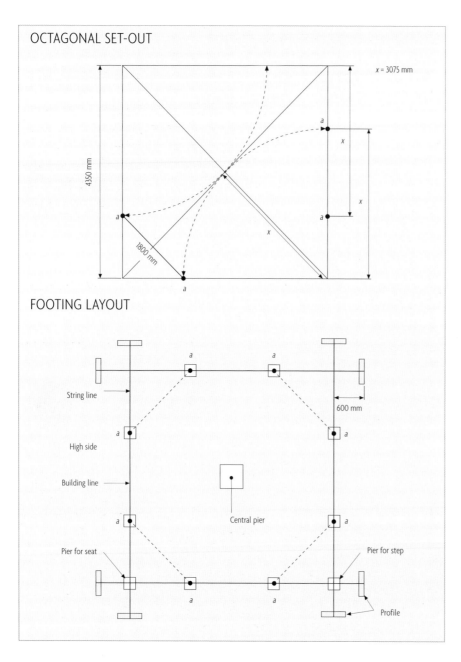

OCTAGONAL SET-OUT

x = 3075 mm

4350 mm

1800 mm

FOOTING LAYOUT

String line

High side

Building line

600 mm

Central pier

Pier for seat

Pier for step

Profile

a

MATERIALS

Concrete

Bricks and mortar

Damp-proof course

Capping

150 x 50 mm frame and radial joists

100 x 50 mm intermediate joists

50 x 50 mm battens

65 mm decking boards

Timber for temporary braces

Nail plates

75 mm galvanized nails

25 mm galvanized clout nails

Twisted-shank galvanized decking nails

so you can trim it later. Nail it to the intermediate joists, making sure that it aligns with the string line.

14 Scatter several boards loosely across the joists to determine the most appropriate ones to use. Cut lengths to fit the triangle as you work towards the centre. These boards will also provide a work platform. Fix each board, leaving a small gap between them (see page 349). Continue fixing boards until you reach the centre. Check the decking is parallel and straight.

15 Fix a straight edge across the face of the decking so that the trimmed ends of the boards align with the centre of the radial joists. This will act as a guide for the power saw. Cut the boards to shape. Repeat on the other side of the triangle.

16 Trim one end of the starter board for the next triangle at 22.5 degrees. Fix it in place as before with a 25 mm overhang. Trim the ends of several more boards at the same angle and fix them in place, keeping the ends aligned with the boards of the previous

12 Use a straight edge to check that the top edges of all joists are flush at each joint and straight. Use a power plane to correct high spots or bowing.

LAYING THE DECKING

13 On two adjacent radial joists, mark 40 mm in from the outside edge and stretch a string line between these points. This is the position of the starter board, allowing for a 25 mm overhang. Choose a straight decking board, slightly longer than the octagonal joist. Secure the board at one end, leaving enough board projecting

outdoor

TOOLS

See the basic tool kit on page 336.

section. Continue moving towards the centre, checking as you go. Repeat this procedure for the remaining sections and finish either side of the final section (the section with the tree if you are incorporating one into your deck).

17 If you are incorporating a tree, fix boards in the same way until you reach a suitable distance from the trunk (allowing the tree room to move and grow). Move to the other side of the tree. Starting at the first full

board away from the trunk, continue fixing boards towards the centre. Fill in the gap either side of the tree, ensuring the space around the tree is maintained.

FINISHING

18 Fix fascia boards made from decking around the perimeter of the deck. Mitre the corners.

19 Fit decking boards to the step and storage box, cutting them at 45 degrees on each end. Begin at the octagonal joist and work to the corner. Use decking boards to construct a lift-off lid for the box.

20 Add a protective finish to ensure the deck stands up to weathering.

The storage box has a lift-off lid that rests on the intermediate joists.

POOL DECKS

Decks can make ideal surrounds for swimming pools, as they ensure a non-slip surface that is comfortable and not too hot to walk on, even on the hottest day.

BUILDING A POOL DECK

If you have an above-ground pool or a pool that has been constructed on a sloping site, a timber deck is an ideal way of providing access to the water. A pool deck is constructed in the same way as any deck, but there are a few extra points to consider:

- Prepare the ground below the deck so water will drain away. One way is to lay landscape fabric on the ground and cover it with river pebbles.
- Leave a small gap between the decking boards to allow water to drain away and prevent 'ponding' on the surface.
- As the deck will be subjected to splashes, as well as rain, it should be built with timber that has been treated with a water repellent.
- For decks around saltwater pools all fittings should be of stainless steel or hot-dipped galvanized metal.

The blue and white colour scheme used on the balustrade here cleverly reflects the poolside ambience.

pergolas

pergolas

PLANNING YOUR PERGOLA

A pergola creates fresh opportunities for enjoying outdoor space, encouraging you to utilize your garden and appreciate its views. Pergolas are usually designed to blend with existing buildings and enlarge the living area of the home.

WHAT IS A PERGOLA?

In general terms, a pergola is any horizontal trellis or framework supported on posts to form a covered walkway. The noun 'pergola' owes its origin to the Latin noun *pergula* (meaning a projection or roof) and the verb *pergere* (to go forward).

Polycarbonate or metal sheeting, wooden shingles or battens, awning cloth, ceramic roof tiles or even leafy climbing plants can be added to provide various degrees of overhead protection from sun and rain for people using the structure. Full or half walls of timber lattice, wooden railings or foliage (either evergreen or deciduous) can be installed to increase privacy and screen out unwanted sun and wind, and many pergolas are erected above a wooden deck or an area of paving.

STARTING OUT

For many pergola builders, timber is the material of choice: it is readily available, relatively inexpensive and easy to use.

When planning a project, there are a few factors to consider.

- Take full advantage of the sunlight by positioning your pergola where it will catch the summer sun. If this isn't possible, build it where it will be most useful.
- Note the angle of the shadows cast by existing structures or trees as the sun moves through the sky at various times of the year and see how this will affect the pergola.
- Compensate for the site's exposure to prevailing winds or poor weather. A covered pergola can provide shelter from

Position your pergola to extend a living area or create a new setting for alfresco dining or relaxation. This combined pergola and deck opens off the kitchen to provide easy access for catering purposes, and doubles as a walkway to the garden.

wind and rain if a sturdy screen is erected on the 'bad weather' side.

- Add louvred or lattice screens to restrict unsightly views and enhance privacy without compromising the through-flow of air.

PARTS OF A PERGOLA

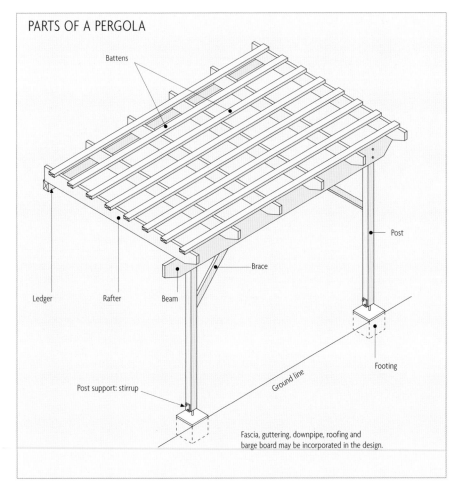

Battens

Post

Brace

Ledger

Rafter

Beam

Post support: stirrup

Footing

Ground line

Fascia, guttering, downpipe, roofing and
barge board may be incorporated in the design.

HINT

When timber is delivered to your site, stack it
well clear of the surrounding soil (preferably
on strips of scrap wood) to prevent moisture
rising from the ground. Always cover the pile
with a tarpaulin to keep it dry in wet weather,
as moisture absorption can cause warping
and splitting. Choose the intended position
of your stack carefully to avoid interfering
with the smooth flow of traffic around the
site once work begins, and ensure it does
not encroach on a driveway or other access
route required for the delivery of ready-mix
concrete or other heavy materials.

WORKING WITH NATURE

Large rocks or trees which at first appear to
be in the way of your proposed pergola can
be incorporated as important parts of the
overall effect. Do not attempt to remove
these so-called 'obstacles'; rather, use them to
advantage by building around them. Aim to be
both flexible and creative with your design,
and add extra interest by incorporating
unexpected angles and natural features.

CHOOSING A STYLE

There are two main types of pergola:
attached and free-standing.

- Attached pergolas are fixed to a building
  for stability. An attached pergola, situated
  directly outside a house (often at the
  back), is more useful than the free-
  standing one, as it offers users access to
  amenities such as a kitchen and bathroom.
- Free-standing pergolas are usually set
  away from the house and stabilized with
  additional bracing.

  Other variations include gazebos, arbours
  and walkways.

PREPARING PLANS

Sketch your chosen design, showing the
relevant dimensions.

- Determine the finished size of your
  pergola according to the area available
  and its intended use, working within
  your financial budget. Plan your project
  to meet individual needs. Do you require
  an all-weather play area for children, an
  entertainment venue for small or large
  groups, an outdoor cooking or barbecue
  setting, or simply a spot for quiet
  relaxation, either alone or with a
  few friends?
- The outward appearance of your proposed
  structure is equally important. Will it
  blend with its surroundings and complement
  existing buildings? Is it accessible to users?
  Once you have identified its intended use

and determined the desired size of your
project, mock up a full-sized plan using
lengths of timber laid out flat on the ground.
Alternatively, use a pliable length of rope or
even a long garden hose to represent the
pergola's outline. Test the practicality of the
layout by positioning tables, chairs, lounges,
barbecues and other items of furniture
within the makeshift border. With these in
place, is it possible for users to move around
in comfort? Is there sufficient room in which
to enjoy your pergola? If the answer is 'no',
consider increasing its size or changing the
shape. Make yourself aware of the full range
of options in the early days of the design
phase, well before construction begins.

Present these sketches to your local Building Control office for detailed discussion before finalizing your project. In many places it is necessary to obtain a written building-approval permit from the council before starting work, particularly if your property is in a Conservation area. Detailed information on submitting building-approval requests is available from council offices in most cities and towns. The applicant may also be required to supply (usually three) sets of plans and any specifications. These must provide a plan view, a side and end elevation view showing the necessary dimensions, and a cross-section view (drawn to a larger scale) setting out construction details.

To reduce the likelihood of making costly and wasteful errors, refer to the detailed drawings when calculating quantities and timber lengths and ordering materials for the project, and again at all stages during construction.

SITE PREPARATION

Once the design and location of your pergola are set, it is time to begin preparing the site. Concrete footings must be bedded firmly in the ground. If the soil is clayey or subject to a lot of water, consider creating a rubble drain to divert run-off away from the structure. Any drain must be attached to either an absorption pit or a stormwater pipe that drains to the street – not onto your neighbour's property.

Level the site, if necessary, before construction begins. If excavating more than approximately 300 mm, seek advice on installing a retaining wall. Consult your local Building Control office before commencing work, as this type of wall can be expensive to create.

Pergolas come in many shapes and sizes, and are often purpose-built to suit unusual space constraints. With its segmented and slatted ceiling, this square-sided gazebo-style design throws partial shade onto an outdoor table and chairs.

An attractive gable in the centre of the roof is an eye-catching addition to this attached pergola.

HINT

Many home building projects are never even started because the available site seems unsuitable for its intended use. If preparation for your pergola involves the removal or deposit of large amounts of soil or gravel, hire an operator with a machine, such as an excavator, to do the heavy work for you, saving time and energy. This applies equally to concreting, another daunting prospect for many weekend builders. When laying a slab, consider ordering a bulk delivery of ready-mix concrete from a reputable local contractor to reduce the workload and ensure your project remains achievable.

outdoor

BASIC MATERIALS

Exposure to weather and insect attack threatens many pergolas. By selecting the appropriate grade and treatment for timber, and ensuring it is seasoned correctly before construction begins, it is possible to guard against premature damage.

Although much smaller than the standard verandah-style pergola, this flat-roofed frame is a stylish addition to an entrance way. As a support for climbing plants, it can be used to provide light all-weather protection at the door.

outdoor

CHOOSING TIMBER

Any timber used in a pergola faces exposure to all types of weather and can be subject to attack by insects. It must be able to withstand the test of time.

Many hardwoods have high durability and can be used both in and above the ground. (Any timber intended for direct contact with soil must be treated with a suitable preservative. Ask the advice of an expert at your local timber yard or hardware store, and always follow the manufacturer's instructions when applying the recommended number of coats.)

Hardwoods are extremely heavy and difficult to handle, and are not recommended for use in overhead structures. They are best suited for use as posts.

More commonly used in pergola building are pressure-treated softwoods such as the many types of pine. Such softwoods are available from most timber merchants.

PRESSURE TREATMENT

Pressure-treated softwoods are protected by a timber preservative: a compound of copper, chromium and arsenic known as CCA. This compound produces a green tone on treated timber.

Light organic solvent preservative (LOSP), which is available from some hardware suppliers, is much less permanent than CCA. Timber treated in this way should be given a protective coating to prolong its life and is not suitable for use in the ground.

Any timber that is to be buried beneath the surface requires a higher level of protection than that demanded above soil level. Durability is rated in classes from low to high, with high-rated timber being the most hardy and resistant to attack. If using hardwood in the ground, choose this type for durability.

Hardwoods and treated softwoods are available in a range of hazard levels. In this

case, the finished timber is rated from 1 to 5, number 5 softwood containing the highest concentration of treatment chemicals (see Treated timber hazard levels table above).

When embedding posts in the ground, position the trimmed (and therefore untreated) ends uppermost. Although brush-

on preservatives can be used, they do not penetrate as effectively as does pressure treatment. All sawn or shaped surfaces must be retreated.

Although some treated timbers repel water, weathering turns them silvery-grey in colour over time. Applying a suitable

TREATED TIMBER HAZARD LEVELS

CLASS	USE
1	Internal, dry conditions only (borer-immunised) for furniture, panelling, framing and joinery
2	Internal, dry conditions only (protection from a slight risk of termite attack) for furniture, panelling, framing and joinery
3	Exterior, weather-exposed, above-ground timber (moderate termite attack and decay protection) for posts in stirrups, rafters, pergolas, garden furniture, fencing lattice and above-ground playground equipment, both public and private Level 3 may be used in-ground in specific locations (check with your local Building Control office) or for landscaping and above-water wharf components
4	As for 3, particularly in ground-contact situations (resistant to fungal and severe termite attack) for foundation stumps, crib walls and foundation piling in freshwater
5	Used specifically in marine conditions where floating on or immersed in saltwater (seek advice on local areas and specific hazards)

TIMBER STRESS GRADINGS

SPECIES	AVAILABILITY	STRESS GRADING
Radiata and other plantation pines	Seasoned	C24
Hardwood (oak)	Unseasoned	D30
	Seasoned	D40
Hardwood (other)	Unseasoned	D40
	Seasoned	D50
Cypress	Unseasoned	C16
Oregon (or Douglas fir) from North America	Unseasoned	C16
	Seasoned	C24
Unidentified hardwood or softwood	Unseasoned	C16
Spruce, pine or fir (SPF)	Seasoned	C24
Fir	Seasoned	C18

POST AND FOOTING TYPES

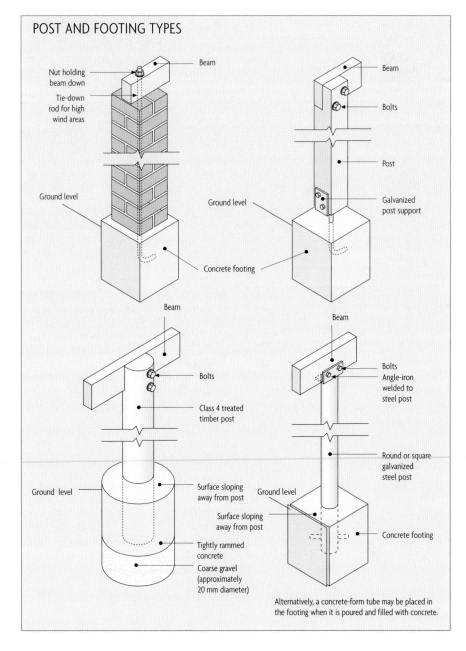

Nut holding beam down
Tie-down rod for high wind areas
Beam
Ground level
Concrete footing

Beam
Bolts
Post
Galvanized post support
Ground level

Beam
Bolts
Class 4 treated timber post
Ground level
Surface sloping away from post
Tightly rammed concrete
Coarse gravel (approximately 20 mm diameter)

Beam
Bolts
Angle-iron welded to steel post
Round or square galvanized steel post
Ground level
Surface sloping away from post
Concrete footing

Alternatively, a concrete-form tube may be placed in the footing when it is poured and filled with concrete.

oil or stain can counteract this. Maintain applied finishes as recommended by the product's manufacturer.

Precautions

When working with treated timber, follow these basic precautions:

- Wear a dust mask and goggles when machining, sawing or sanding.
- Provide good ventilation in your work area.
- Wear gloves when handling timber (but not when using power tools).
- Wash your hands and face before drinking or eating.
- Wash your work clothes as a separate load.
- Never burn treated timber for heating or cooking, not even in outdoor barbecues.

STRESS GRADING

Individual C or D ratings (also known as stress gradings) are applied to timber offered on the market. In labelling, the letter is followed by a number that indicates the bending stress of the particular piece. The higher the rating, the greater the stress the timber can withstand. Timber for load-bearing posts can go up to D70 in hardwood, and C24 or greater may be needed in treated softwood. Neither beams nor rafters should be made from timber graded less than C16.

SEASONING

Using unseasoned timber in a project inevitably results in shrinking, warping or bowing as it dries, particularly in varieties of hardwood. Most hardwood is semi-seasoned when purchased as sawn timber for construction, making it easier to use. Generally, treated timber sold is seasoned.

When buying timber for your project, watch for faults such as bowing or twisting. Lightly bowed or twisted timber can usually be pulled straight as it is fixed firmly into position, but badly disfigured pieces are often unusable and must be discarded.

PARTS OF A PERGOLA

Each pergola—whether free-standing or attached to another structure (such as a house)—consists of a series of standard parts.

Footings

A footing (which is normally poured from concrete into a temporary timber form box and allowed to harden in position) is placed in the ground to stabilize the structure. Footings must rest on a solid, compacted base that is capable of bearing the full load of the finished pergola safely without allowing any undue movement.

Piers and columns

The piers and columns on which the wooden posts rest are normally built of brick or constructed from reinforced concrete poured into a form tube. In high-wind areas, a tie-down rod must be placed into each pier or column and embedded in the footing during construction.

As an alternative to traditional timber or metal posts, support the roof frame directly on brick columns constructed to the full height of the beam. Secure the beam with an iron hoop strap embedded in the brickwork and nailed to the timber. As a variation, construct a shorter column, finish it with a capping of tiles or sandstone and fix a concrete column or timber post to the top to extend it to the desired height.

Brick piers, columns and footings must comply with building standards and codes as set down by your local Building Control office.

Timber posts

Set round or square timber posts in concrete footings, or place them on top, secured in galvanized metal stirrups. Concrete each stirrup into the footing as it is being poured, or bolt it with masonry anchors to the surface once it has set.

Steel posts

Embed steel posts of round or square section in a concrete footing, or bolt them down with masonry anchors. If using raw steel posts, protect them from corrosion by applying a galvanized coating. Drill a drainage hole near the bottom of each post to allow excess water to escape.

Fascia

A fascia board fixed over the ends of the rafters creates an attractive finish and provides a secure backing for the guttering.

Ledger

In an attached pergola, a piece of timber known as the ledger is fixed to the wall of the house at the same height as the beam. The ledger acts as a second beam, tying the frame to the building and its solid foundation.

Beams

The overhead structure of a pergola consists of a frame of beams spanning the distance between the posts. The beams of an attached pergola should run parallel to the house.

Rafter

Each rafter spans the width of the pergola and is fixed from the beam to the ledger.

Battens

The roof covering is fixed to battens fastened on top of and at right angles to the rafters, parallel to the beam (and ledger when one is used).

Bracing

To help stabilize a pergola and prevent it swaying once completed, place angled timber or steel braces at appropriate points.

CHOOSING HARDWARE

Any pergola is only as strong as its fasteners and should be built using good-quality hardware that will not corrode. Generally, galvanized steel is the most durable material for fasteners and fittings that will be exposed to the weather.

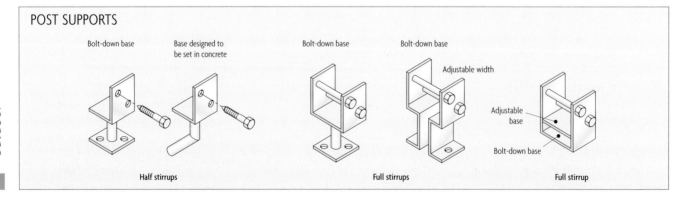

POST SUPPORTS

Bolt-down base | Base designed to be set in concrete | Bolt-down base | Bolt-down base | Adjustable width | Adjustable base | Bolt-down base

Half stirrups | Full stirrups | Full stirrup

outdoor

Choose quality galvanized metal bolts, masonry anchors, joist hangers and roofing screws for an attached pergola such as this. Ensure any cut edges or drill holes are sealed to prevent corrosion.

MACHINE OR CUP-HEAD BOLTS

Use machine or cup-head bolts to hold structural members together in a bond far stronger than that provided by nails. Coach screws are useful in situations where access for the builder is available from only one side of the project. Use washers under the heads of coach screws and on both ends of machine nuts and bolts to prevent them pulling too far into the timber when under extreme pressure.

MASONRY ANCHORS

Masonry anchors can be used to fix ledgers to brick walls and metal post stirrups to footings. Choose an appropriately sized anchor. If the anchor is too short for its intended use, the device may not hold tightly; if it is too thin, it may snap when subjected to load.

LOST-HEAD NAILS

Galvanized lost-head nails are used to secure joints. Choose nails with a spiral or twisted shank for fixing into softwoods.

ROOFING SCREWS

Special roofing screws are available in varieties ranging from stainless steel to hot-dipped galvanized metal, all with neoprene washers.

STIRRUPS AND BRACKETS

Post stirrups or supports and brackets are hot-dip galvanized by the manufacturer. If these are cut or drilled, apply a fresh coating of galvanized paint to protect the exposed surface.

OTHER HARDWARE

When choosing other metal timber connectors, nail plates and joist hangers, select those made from galvanized steel. Hardware and DIY stores stock a wide variety of connectors for many applications.

COVERINGS AND TRIMS

Timber battens, lattice, awning cloth, sheeting: the variety of modern roofing materials suitable for pergola projects is broad. A roof covering should suit the general architectural style of the structure and its surrounds as well as its intended use.

ROOFING

Once the main structure is complete, either stop working altogether or prepare to add your choice of roof covering: timber battens, lattice, awning cloth or, to create a completely weatherproof area, polycarbonate, fibreglass or metal sheeting. Fix roof covering according to the manufacturer's instructions.

Timber battens

Battens vary in size from 50 x 25 mm to more than 100 x 50 mm. The bigger battens generally look best on large pergolas, so keep the batten size in proportion to the job. You will find 70 x 35 mm treated pine suits most designs.

Fix the battens either flat or on edge at a 90-degree angle to the rafters (see Attaching battens diagram opposite). Space battens laid flat from 100 mm to 200 mm apart. The more closely the battens are positioned, the more shade is created, so adjust them to suit your needs. Battens fixed on edge should be spaced further apart (for example, at intervals of up to 300 mm).

Fix the battens securely to provide a sound base for the addition of roof covering should you decide later to make your pergola into an all-weather outdoor area. Skew-nail two 75 x 3.5 mm galvanized lost-head nails through each batten into the top of the rafter.

Lattice

Secure lattice directly to the tops of rafters with galvanized lost-head nails. This form of roof covering is ideal as a support for climbing plants or for providing filtered shade. Paint it, if desired, in coordinating colours to blend with the house.

Shadecloth

Shadecloth is available in a range of colours to suit many decors, ranging from shades of green and blue to pink or brown.

Most manufacturers supply shadecloth in 30 per cent, 50 per cent and 70 per cent grades of shade (70 per cent coverage providing the heaviest protection from the sun). Shadecloth can be either woven or knitted, with the latter requiring edge treatment to prevent it fraying. Sew a hem on the cut edge or sandwich the cloth between the batten and a rafter. Fix all edges of the cloth to either battens or rafters for a long-lasting result.

Polycarbonate/fibreglass sheeting

Fibreglass roofing lets in light but gives a distorted view through the fibre reinforcement within each sheet. A popular contemporary choice is polycarbonate, which is free of fibres and therefore provides a clear outlook. Both types are available in a range of profiles and colours. Some filter out ultraviolet rays and are not recommended as coverings for plants. Ask at your local nursery or garden centre for advice.

Before securing fibreglass or polycarbonate sheeting, drill a clearance hole through the sheet to allow for expansion and contraction.

Fix it to the battens and install flashing and guttering in the same way as when using metal sheeting. To fix the sheets in place, use screws with neoprene washers. While self-drilling screws can be used on metal, they

sometimes crack or split fibreglass or polycarbonate sheeting and so are not suitable for such roofs.

Metal sheeting

A metal roof cuts out the sun completely and is available in a choice of colours, the underside of which is usually an off-white shade.

To relieve the creaking noise caused by movement of the roofing as temperatures change, place foam rafter tape on top of the battens.

Fix solid roof coverings to a 70 x 35 mm batten skew-nailed to the top of the rafters at a spacing recommended by the manufacturer (generally around 1 m apart).

Seal the gap between the house and the pergola with a shaped flashing. Use barge capping to finish the ends neatly, and install

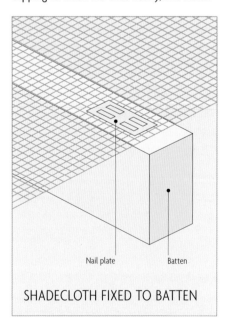

Nail plate   Batten

SHADECLOTH FIXED TO BATTEN

guttering with a downpipe to direct water run-off away from the structure.

FINISHING TOUCHES

To help your pergola blend with the existing style of your house, try to choose appropriate finishing touches.

Shaped posts

Turned posts can be purchased in a variety of shapes and sizes, but these ready-made decorative options can prove expensive.

Transform plain square timber posts into distinctive features by cutting flutes or grooves in the faces and rounding off the square corners. Run these machine-routed trims the full height of the post or stop short of both ends.

Dado moulds

To add interest to your pergola, fix shaped wooden or plastic mouldings, painted in a coordinating colour and mitre-joined at the corners, around each post approximately one-quarter of the way down from the top.

Brackets

Adding shaped brackets between the post and the beam is an easy way of giving your pergola an early-20th-century look.

Arches

Place curved arches under the beams or in the ends of the gables to draw attention to an entry.

Drops and finials

Drops added under the ends of beams and finials positioned on the tops of gables are eye-catching and can be painted to match or contrast with the body of the structure.

Privacy screens

Louvred or wooden lattice screens fixed between pairs of pergola posts increase

privacy for the occupants, give added protection from the prevailing weather and create a feature wall. These screens also provide excellent support for climbing plants.

PLANTS

Hanging baskets and potted and climbing plants add life and colour to a pergola. Seek your local nursery expert's advice on the most appropriate deciduous or evergreen plants.

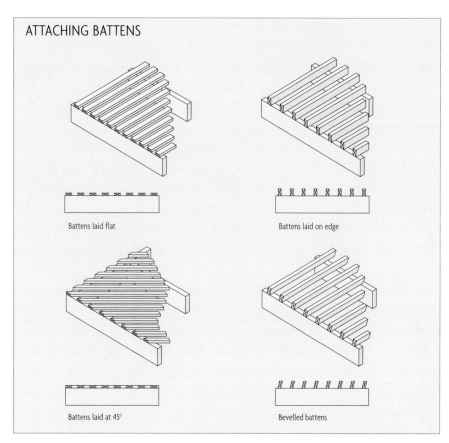

ATTACHING BATTENS

Battens laid flat

Battens laid on edge

Battens laid at 45°

Bevelled battens

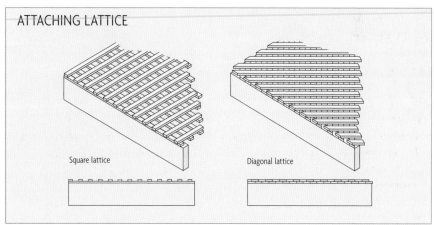

ATTACHING LATTICE

Square lattice

Diagonal lattice

A gable let into the centre of the roof interrupts a potentially uninteresting expanse of polycarbonate sheeting. The covering in this case is ideal, casting light shade onto the house wall and protecting the furniture from sun and rain.

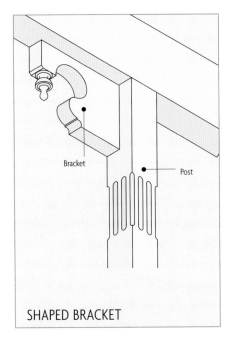

SHAPED BRACKET

Bracket

Post

SHAPED WOODEN POST
WITH DADO MOULD

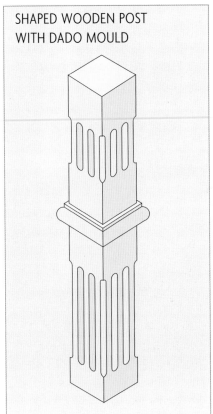

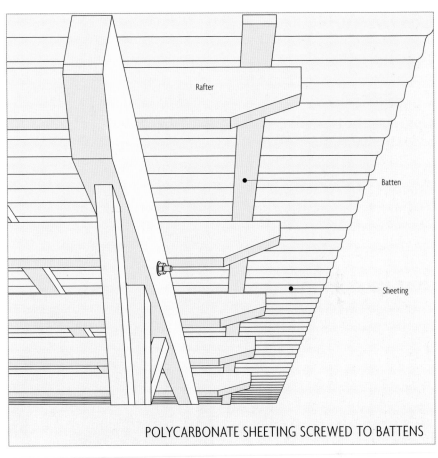

Rafter

Batten

Sheeting

POLYCARBONATE SHEETING SCREWED TO BATTENS

ARCH WITH DROP AND FINIAL

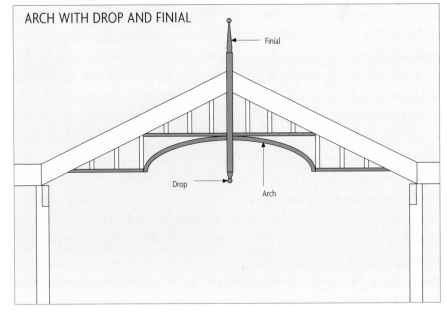

Finial

Drop

Arch

ESTIMATING AND ORDERING

Estimating the quantity of material required for each project is relatively simple using approved building plans as a guide. All calculations should be checked thoroughly with reference to a detailed list of components to ensure nothing is overlooked.

CALCULATING QUANTITIES

Working with your building plans as a guide, it is possible to estimate—not 'guesstimate'—the quantity of each material or item of hardware required for your pergola.

Set up a materials list to ensure all the supplies and preliminaries are considered. Alternatively, simply work from the example provided (opposite page), ticking off each component in turn or expanding the model to create a chart with third and fourth columns headed 'quantity' and 'cost'. Working through a formal planning process on paper helps cost a project accurately to prevent initial overspending on unnecessary supplies that end up going to waste.

Refer to this list to ensure all essential aspects of the job are covered. Delete or add specific items as required to suit your particular circumstances.

Most timber merchants will assist you to order the correct quantities, grades and species of timber for your project if you show them your building plan.

When preparing a cutting guide, consider various options before selecting your timber length. For example, if your project requires two 1800 mm lengths of timber but this is not available, do not buy 2400 mm pieces, as 600 mm will be wasted from each. Instead, select a single 3600 mm length and cut it in half.

If you need numerous concrete footings to stabilize your pergola, or if a solid slab is required, you can order pre-mixed concrete to be delivered in bulk. This will save you from the heavy task of mixing your own. Check that clear vehicular access for the truck is available directly to your site.

Work from an accurate builder's plan when preparing a materials list for a large attached pergola such as this. Careful planning eliminates wastage, minimizes cost and ensures adequate supplies are available as needed.

outdoor

MATERIALS CHECKLIST

MATERIAL	DESCRIPTION
PRELIMINARY PLANS	
Drawings/specifications	Planning permission if necessary; application form
Council fees	
FOOTINGS	
Formwork	
Excavation	Machinery hire or sub-contract
Concrete	Bag or ready-mix pump for difficult sites
Stirrups	Embedded or bolt-on
Drainage	Pipes, gravel
TIMBER	
Posts	Size, grade, type, length
Ledgers & beams	
Rafters & battens	
Fascia & barges	
Trimmers & bracing	
Props	Temporary bracing or props
Screens/screen frame or channel	Lattice, louvres
HARDWARE	
Galvanized post stirrups or brackets	One per post
Galvanized bolts or coach screws with washers	One per stirrup or bracket for attaching beam to post, ledger or wall
Masonry anchors	For attaching stirrups and ledgers to bricks or masonry
Roof covering	Corrugated iron, shadecloth, polycarbonate, fibreglass
Roofing screws, neoprene washers	For attaching roofing to battens
Flashing/guttering and accessories	
Downpipes	
Galvanized nails	Lost-head with plain or twist shanks, 75 x 3.5 mm for construction
Connectors	30 x 2.8 mm flat-head joist hangers, nail plates, cyclone straps
MISCELLANEOUS	
Paint	Stains, primers, filler and finish
Equipment hire	Power tools, compressor, nail gun, post-hole auger
Labour	
Landscaping	Retaining walls, plants, pavers, concrete
Incidental services	Delivery, waste disposal
TOTAL COST	

BASIC TOOLS

- Handsaw
- Power saw
- Jigsaw
- Hammer and nail punch
- 25 mm chisel
- Builder's square/combination square/sliding bevel
- Tape measure
- Marking gauge
- Power drill with assorted bits
- Spanner (in size to suit nuts)
- String line
- Shovel/spade/mattock
- Post-hole auger
- Spirit level and water level
- Cramps
- Hand plane
- Router (optional)

HINT

Before beginning any form of excavation at your site, contact the relevant local authorities to request plans of underground pipes and cables running across your land. Make sure you consult your gas, water, electricity and telecommunications suppliers. Damaging these utilities not only exposes the home builder to the possibility of extreme physical danger but usually results in costly repair bills.

CHOOSING TOOLS

When assembling a basic building kit, choose good-quality tools designed to last for years. For best results, always buy recognized brands, and consult your local hardware stockist if you require additional advice.

When using power tools, always follow the instructions issued by the manufacturer.

Work in a well-lit area and ensure adequate ventilation is provided. Wear protective equipment to guard against eye damage and possible hearing loss.

Store your tools carefully in a secure, dry place. Using a tool rack or lockable box helps protect them from incidental damage and allows you to see the range clearly. Alternatively, leave each tool in its original storage box.

BUILDING TECHNIQUES

Most pergolas are attached directly to a house, increasing the stability of the structure and extending living space. Rafters are fixed to a wall-mounted ledger or attached to the fascia to avoid obstructing window or door openings directly under the eaves.

CHOOSING A METHOD

Usually, the connection of a pergola to a house is via a ledger bolted to an exterior wall. Rafters sit on top of the ledger or are fixed to the face with the aid of joist hangers.

Alternatively, fix the rafters directly to the fascia, either with or without a ledger. The latter method is preferred where the tops of any window or door openings are directly under the eaves. A major advantage of this is the increased height of the finished pergola.

FIXING THE LEDGER

Fixing the ledger and rafters securely is important, as the structure must be able to withstand pressures from storms or wind, particularly if roofing is added. Attach the ledger directly to the face of brickwork with masonry anchors, or fix it to a wall frame or fascia and rafter ends with coach screws. If the house is clad with weatherboards, remove a section to create a flat, even surface to accept the ledger. Place flashing directly above it to prevent water entering the house and causing damage.

When determining the height of a ledger—particularly if it is to be attached to a wall under the eaves—consider whether rafters, battens or roof coverings will be added

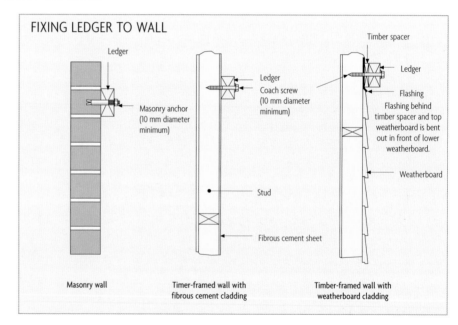

FIXING LEDGER TO WALL

Ledger

Masonry anchor (10 mm diameter minimum)

Masonry wall

Ledger

Coach screw (10 mm diameter minimum)

Stud

Fibrous cement sheet

Timer-framed wall with fibrous cement cladding

Timber spacer

Ledger

Flashing

Flashing behind timber spacer and top weatherboard is bent out in front of lower weatherboard.

Weatherboard

Timber-framed wall with weatherboard cladding

above it, and leave room for them.

Where possible, position fastenings directly below alternate rafters on the pergola. Use an extra set of hands or temporary props to hold the work together during this process, as accuracy is important.

CONSTRUCTING BUILDING PROFILES

Use profiles to set out the string lines for your project. Construct building profiles with

pointed pegs and a horizontal cross-piece approximately 600 mm long. Ensure the pegs are strong enough to be driven deep into the ground to support the tightly stretched string lines. Make sure the tops of the pegs are on a common horizontal plane.

INSTALLING FOOTINGS AND POSTS

Support the aerial structure on brick piers, concrete or steel columns or timber posts.

outdoor

Anchor the supports to the ground on concrete footings.

The spacing of the footings depends on the section size and grade of timber used for the beam. The size is influenced by the soil type and the style of post supporting the structure. The bottom of each footing must rest on stable ground, so remove tree roots and other obstacles.

Borrow or hire a post-hole auger to dig the footing holes or, for larger jobs, hire a powered post-hole auger. (Obtain operating instructions from the hire company.) To use a post-hole auger, hold the handles together and drive the blades into the ground several times to break up the packed soil. Spread the handles to hold the earth, then lift it out and dump the dirt far enough away from the excavation to prevent a cave-in.

When working with sandy soils that tend to fall into the hole as you dig, remove the top and bottom from a 23 litre drum. Place the drum in position and dig through it, pushing the tube further into the excavation as you work. Leave the drum in place to act as a makeshift formwork when pouring wet concrete for the footing.

Alternatively, place a 100 mm high timber box over the hole. Centre the timber formwork and brace it temporarily to ensure it remains in place.

If you choose to install timber posts, the precise height of the footing is not important. Aim to have the footings levelled off at approximately 50 mm above the ground with the surrounding soil graded away to prevent water pooling around the posts. (The tops of brick piers, on the other hand, must be below the beam at a level that accommodates an even number of brick courses, so the footing usually finishes below the ground.)

Mix the concrete until it is smooth enough to be poured yet stiff enough to hold the posts or stirrups upright while it sets.

Not all pergolas are additions to existing homes. This example, supported on sturdy concrete pillars, was incorporated into the original design. The eight rafters run horizontally from a ledger fixed to the brickwork under the eaves.

Pour the mix into the form and use a piece of timber to ram it down well to prevent the formation of unwanted air pockets, known as 'honeycombing'. Honeycomb holds water, often causing posts and fittings to rot or rust.

Embed the stirrups, if required, in the wet concrete, aligning them carefully with the string lines. (Fasten bolt-down stirrups in position after the concrete has been left to set for approximately seven days.)

If using treated timber or steel posts,

brace them temporarily while the concrete is poured and allowed to harden. Ensure the posts are perfectly plumb and in alignment, as there is no easy way to correct inaccuracies once the concrete is dry.

ATTACHING THE BEAM

To attach a beam to timber posts, cut a housing in the top of each post. Bolt the beam into position, securing it with two 12 mm diameter bolts. Make the housings no deeper than two-thirds the thickness of the post. Cut the housings with a power saw and clean them out with a chisel.

As an option, place beams on both sides of each post and block solidly in between. This enables smaller timber sections to be used. Keep both top edges in level alignment.

To create a housing in a round post, first measure the thickness of the beams on the tops and stretch a taut string line from one post to the next. The string line represents the back of the housing. Plumb a line down each side of the post and use a square piece of cardboard as a guide when marking the proposed height of the beam. For safety's sake, use a handsaw to make the cross-cut for the housing and work carefully with a chisel to remove the waste.

Position the end joint of each beam directly over a post, and stagger them. For maximum strength, use a scarf joint when joining beams end to end. Alternatively, fix the beam to the top of a post.

If you choose to install a waterproof roof covering, ensure you provide a 1:40 fall to allow rainwater to run off. Direct run-off water along guttering to a downpipe.

ATTACHING RAFTERS

Rafters can sit on top of or against the face of a ledger and beam, or against the face of the ledger and over the beam. Where rafters fit against the face of a ledger and/or beam,

use a joist hanger to strengthen the join.

Providing a rafter overhang of up to 600 mm beyond the beam reduces emphasis on the posts, which appear to be set back

from the edge.

When using joist hangers, ensure the ledger and rafter are of equal size. Use an offcut of rafter material when positioning

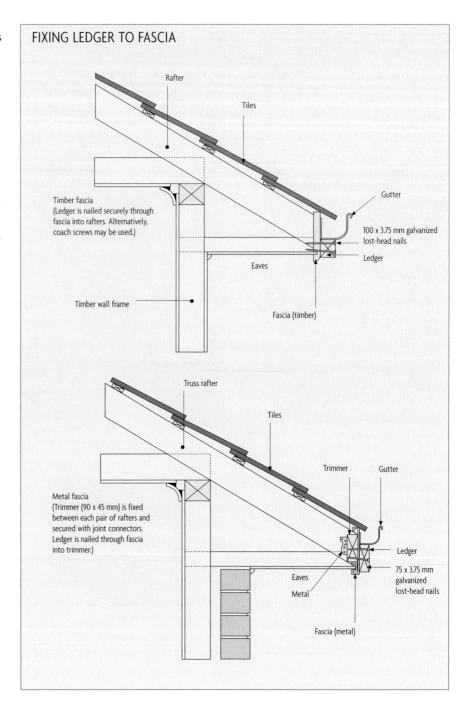

FIXING LEDGER TO FASCIA

Rafter

Tiles

Timber fascia
(Ledger is nailed securely through fascia into rafters. Alternatively, coach screws may be used.)

Gutter

100 x 3.75 mm galvanized lost-head nails

Eaves

Ledger

Timber wall frame

Fascia (timber)

Truss rafter

Tiles

Metal fascia
(Trimmer (90 x 45 mm) is fixed between each pair of rafters and secured with joint connectors. Ledger is nailed through fascia into trimmer.)

Trimmer

Gutter

Ledger

75 x 3.75 mm galvanized lost-head nails

Eaves

Metal

Fascia (metal)

outdoor

FITTING THE POST

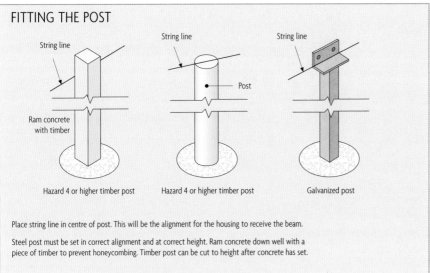

String line

String line

String line

Ram concrete with timber

Post

Hazard 4 or higher timber post

Hazard 4 or higher timber post

Galvanized post

Place string line in centre of post. This will be the alignment for the housing to receive the beam.

Steel post must be set in correct alignment and at correct height. Ram concrete down well with a piece of timber to prevent honeycombing. Timber post can be cut to height after concrete has set.

CUTTING HOUSING IN A ROUND POST

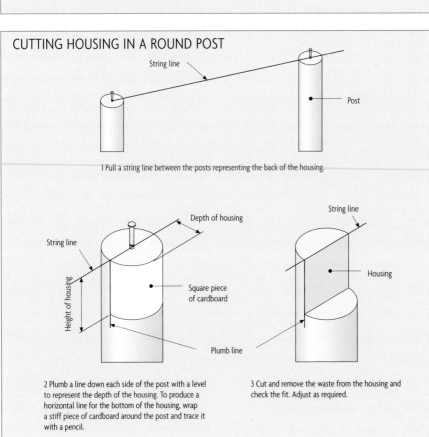

String line

Post

1 Pull a string line between the posts representing the back of the housing.

Depth of housing

String line

String line

Height of housing

Square piece of cardboard

Housing

Plumb line

2 Plumb a line down each side of the post with a level to represent the depth of the housing. To produce a horizontal line for the bottom of the housing, wrap a stiff piece of cardboard around the post and trace it with a pencil.

3 Cut and remove the waste from the housing and check the fit. Adjust as required.

RAFTER AND BEAM POSITIONS

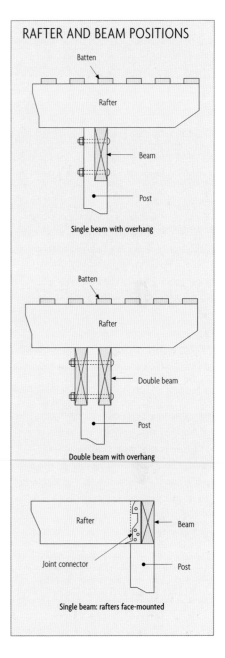

Batten

Rafter

Beam

Post

Single beam with overhang

Batten

Rafter

Double beam

Post

Double beam with overhang

Rafter

Beam

Joint connector

Post

Single beam: rafters face-mounted

the hanger. Fix one side to the ledger with galvanized 30 x 2.8 mm clout nails (or an alternative recommended by the manufacturer). Allow a 10 mm gap between the wall and the end of any rafter fixed to the top of a ledger. If the rafters sit over a beam, square the ledger end of the two end

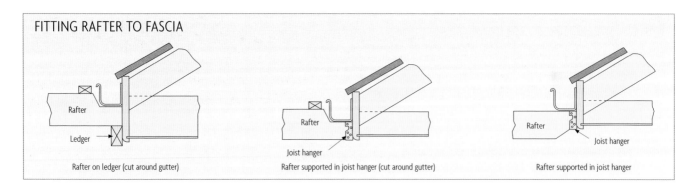

FITTING RAFTER TO FASCIA

Rafter on ledger (cut around gutter)

Rafter supported in joist hanger (cut around gutter)

Rafter supported in joist hanger

rafters on the outside. Shape these ends if necessary (if they must fit neatly under the guttering). Measure the finished distance from the house to the outside edge of the beam, and add the width of the desired overhang. Shape the ends of the rafters to suit the design, ensuring any bows in the timber are placed to the top.

If the rafters are to fit between the ledger and the beam, cut them to the finished length. Apply a preservative and fit the ledger end of each rafter into its hanger. Fix the opposite side of each hanger to the ledger, then attach the hanger to the rafter.

Check that the posts are plumb and aligned. Skew-nail the other end of the rafter to the top of the beam, using a 75 x 3.5 mm galvanized nail. Strengthen the joint with galvanized steel joint connectors.

Measure the diagonals for square, and adjust them if necessary. Use a temporary brace, if desired, to hold the structure square. Complete the fixing of the two end rafters.

Cut the intermediate rafters to length, shaping the ends if required. Fix the intermediate rafters in place following the steps described above.

BRACING THE PERGOLA

The use of bracing need not detract from the appearance of a pergola. Conceal bracing behind lattice, battens or a trellis for a climbing vine. To create an early-20th-century look, purchase pre-cut timber brackets from your local supplier.

A pergola fixed securely to a house (particularly in a corner) requires only minimal bracing. Fit an attached pergola with a pair of opposing braces running parallel to the house on each post. A simple 90 x 35 mm timber brace running at a 45-degree angle from the post to the beam is adequate in most situations. The angle can be allowed to vary slightly (by approximately 5 degrees).

Fix diagonal bracing to the tops of the rafters. Create halving joints in the centre, bolt each end with a 12 mm diameter bolt, and nail the bracing to the rafter, or use a steel angle-framing brace in place of timber.

Once the braces are fixed permanently, remove any temporary bracing used to hold the structure during construction.

Fit pergolas in high-wind areas and free-standing models on stirrups with both types of braces: from post to beam and on top of the rafters.

ATTACHED PERGOLA

The most common pergolas are those attached to the fascia board of a house. This simple rectangular, flat-roofed pergola—measuring 3300 x 3900 mm—is fixed to the fascia by a ledger and supported by timber posts with bolt-down stirrups.

PREPARATION

1 Using council-approved building plans, estimate the quantities required and order your materials (see Calculating quantities, pages 378–379). Specific requirements for this project are listed on page 386.

2 With the timber laid out on the ground, apply one or two coats of the paint or stain of your desired colour before construction begins. Be prepared to touch up later around the joints and on the cut ends.

FIXING THE LEDGER

3 Determine the length of the ledger by

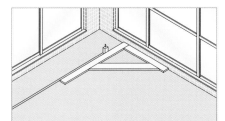

7 To ensure the set-out is square, place a builder's square on the ground against the house wall and the peg.

TOOLS

• Basic tool kit (see page 379)

marking the outside face of each end rafter directly onto the fascia.

4 Place trimmers behind the metal fascia to create a solid surface. Slide the bottom row of roof tiles up to gain access. Measure and cut a trimmer to fit between each pair of rafters. Nail through the rafters into the ends of each trimmer with two 75 mm lost-head nails. Fix a joint connector behind the trimmer and onto the side of the rafter for added strength. Replace the tiles.

5 Cut the ledger to length and fix it to the fascia with lost-head nails driven through the fascia board.

DETERMINING THE POST POSITIONS

6 Using a plumb bob, plumb a line from each end of the ledger to the ground. Drive temporary pegs into the ground at these points, then replumb to the top of each peg. Drive nails at these positions, leaving them protruding slightly from the pegs. Tie a string line to each nail.

7 To ensure your set-out is as close as possible to square, place a builder's square on the ground against the house wall and the

Attached to the house, this flat-roofed pergola extends the occupants' living space well into the garden. A ledger fixed to a trimmer behind the fascia supports the rafters, and posts in galvanized metal stirrups hold the beam.

MATERIALS*

PART	TIMBER	LENGTH	NO.
Post	90 x 90 mm treated pine (C24)	2400 mm	2
Beam	190 x 45 mm treated pine (C24)	3900 mm	1
Rafter	140 x 45 mm treated pine (C24)	3300 mm	7
Batten	70 x 35 mm treated pine (C24)	3900 mm	5
Ledger	70 x 45 mm treated pine (C24)	3900 mm	1
Trimmer	90 x 45 mm treated pine (C24)	3900 mm	1
Bracing	90 x 35 mm treated pine (C24)	2400 mm	1
Form box	90 x 19 mm offcuts	300 mm	8

Other: Two 40 kg bags of concrete; two galvanized stirrup post supports; eight 125 x 12 mm galvanized cup-head nuts and bolts with washers; twenty-one galvanized joint connectors (to suit); seven 90 x 45 mm galvanized joist hangers; 5 kg of 75 x 3.75 mm galvanized lost-head nails; four 75 x 10 mm galvanized masonry anchors; five 3300 mm sheets of 760 mm cover corrugated polycarbonate sheeting; one hundred 75 mm galvanized roofing screws with washers; 20 m roll of 25 mm rafter tape; timber preservative; stain or paint, primer and undercoat.

* Finished size: 3300 x 3900 mm. The timber lengths given are for a project similar to that pictured on page 385. Adapt these requirements to suit your needs.

FITTING A TRIMMER BEHIND METAL FASCIA

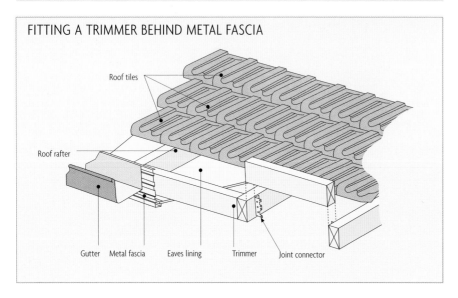

Roof tiles

Roof rafter

Gutter   Metal fascia   Eaves lining   Trimmer   Joint connector

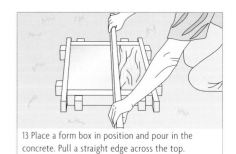

13 Place a form box in position and pour in the concrete. Pull a straight edge across the top.

8 From the original pegs under the ledger, pull a separate string line to the second set of profiles, passing over the temporary corner pegs and intersecting the first line.

9 Check the set-out for parallel and carefully measure the diagonals for square. Adjust the string lines.

10 The posts are set 300 mm in from the outside rafters. Measure this distance along the string line parallel to the house, and mark the required footing holes with temporary pegs.

POURING THE FOOTINGS

11 Once the set-out has been checked, tack a nail beside the string line into the top of each profile. These nails represent the permanent positions of the string lines and are used later as anchors for the string. Situate the footings so they extend beyond this line. Ensure the post will sit in the centre of each footing.

12 Place a 300 x 300 mm form box in the required position under the string line. Scratch the outline of the box on the ground to mark the location of the footing. Remove the string lines and box and dig the 300 x 300 mm footings to 450 mm deep.

13 Place the form box in position, ensuring it is level, and pour in the concrete. Pull a straight edge across the top. Allow the

peg. From the top of the peg, measure out the required distance for the posts, then sight back along the edge of the square. Place temporary corner pegs in the ground at these points.

Erect two profiles about 600 mm outside each corner peg. Pull a string line parallel to the house to represent the outside face of the posts and beam, passing over the tops of the temporary corner pegs.

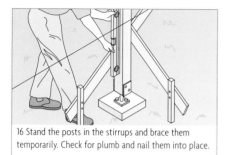

16 Stand the posts in the stirrups and brace them temporarily. Check for plumb and nail them into place.

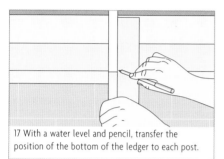

17 With a water level and pencil, transfer the position of the bottom of the ledger to each post.

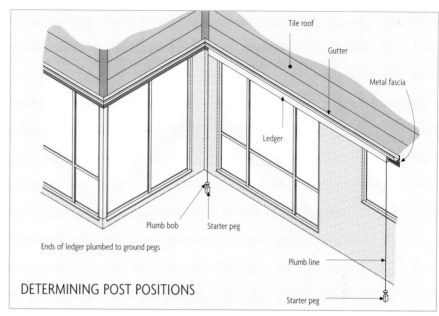

Tile roof

Gutter

Metal fascia

Ledger

Plumb bob

Starter peg

Ends of ledger plumbed to ground pegs

Plumb line

Starter peg

DETERMINING POST POSITIONS

concrete to set, remove the form box, and fill around the hole with soil.

14 Replace the string lines, securing them to the nails in the tops of the profiles. Using a spirit level, plumb a line down from the string line to the top of each footing and place a mark on the concrete to represent the outside face of each post.

ERECTING THE POSTS

15 Cut a length of post material long enough to reach from the top of the footing to the string lines. Secure it temporarily with nails in a stirrup. Position this on top of each footing, with the outside face of the post plumb with the string line. Mark the bolt holes at the top of each footing and drill with a tungsten-tipped masonry drill bit. Make each hole deeper than the length of the fastener. Bolt the stirrups down with masonry anchors.

16 Stand the posts in the metal stirrups and brace them. Check for plumb. Nail the post temporarily into the stirrup.

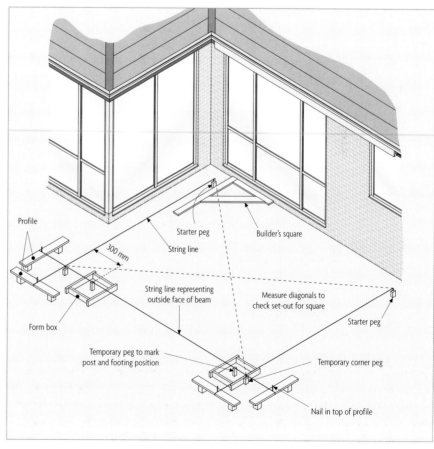

Profile

Starter peg

Builder's square

String line

300 mm

String line representing outside face of beam

Measure diagonals to check set-out for square

Starter peg

Form box

Temporary peg to mark post and footing position

Temporary corner peg

Nail in top of profile

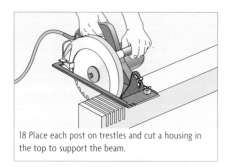

18 Place each post on trestles and cut a housing in the top to support the beam.

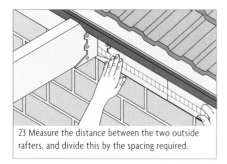

23 Measure the distance between the two outside rafters, and divide this by the spacing required.

ATTACHING THE BEAM

17 With a water level and pencil, transfer the position of the bottom of the ledger to each post to represent the top of the beam.

18 As heights sometimes vary, number each post and corresponding stirrup to allow for easy reassembly. Mark crosses on the sides where the beam will be housed. Remove each post from its stirrup and place it on trestles. Cut a housing in the top of each post to support the beam.

19 Re-erect the posts and brace them, checking for plumb.

20 The beam overhangs the posts by 450 mm and has a 45-degree splay cut on its bottom edge. Trim and shape the beam. Dress with a hand plane. Place the beam in its housings and clamp it into position. Drill two holes through the beam and posts and insert 12 mm diameter cup-head bolts with nuts.

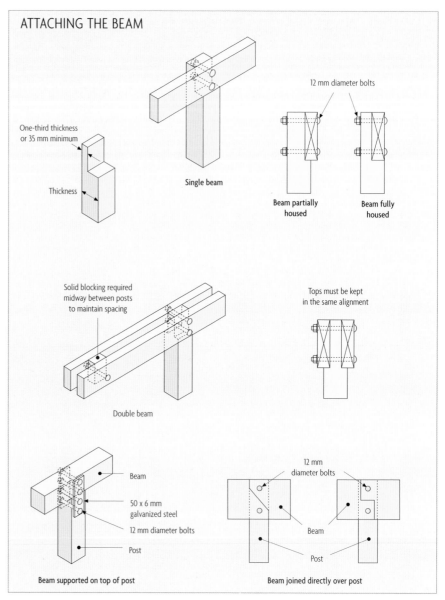

ATTACHING THE BEAM

One-third thickness or 35 mm minimum

Thickness

Single beam

12 mm diameter bolts

Beam partially housed

Beam fully housed

Solid blocking required midway between posts to maintain spacing

Double beam

Tops must be kept in the same alignment

Beam

50 x 6 mm galvanized steel

12 mm diameter bolts

Post

Beam supported on top of post

12 mm diameter bolts

Beam

Post

Beam joined directly over post

ATTACHING THE RAFTERS

21 The rafters, with a 30-degree splay and a 450 mm overhang, are cut around the guttering of the house. Position the end rafters 300 mm outside the corner posts.

22 Ensure any bows face towards the top of the pergola. Cut the rafters to length, then shape them. Secure one side of the

joist hanger to the ledger and insert the rafter. Attach the remaining side to the ledger and secure the rafter to the hanger. Skew-nail the remaining end to the top of the beam with 75 x 3.5 mm lost-head nails.

23 Measure the distance between the two outside rafters and divide this by the spacing

outdoor

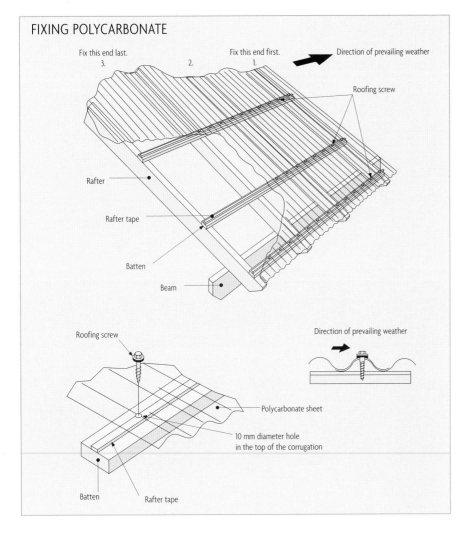

FIXING POLYCARBONATE

Fix this end last.
3.

2.

Fix this end first.
1.

Direction of prevailing weather

Roofing screw

Rafter

Rafter tape

Batten

Beam

Roofing screw

Direction of prevailing weather

Polycarbonate sheet

10 mm diameter hole
in the top of the corrugation

Batten

Rafter tape

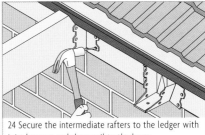

24 Secure the intermediate rafters to the ledger with joist hangers and skew-nail to the beam.

28 In this project, three intermediate battens are used to support the polycarbonate roofing sheets. Determine their spacing by dividing the distance between the outside battens by the number of intermediate battens. Place the battens approximately 900 mm apart, and fix them to the rafters with lost-head nails.

ATTACHING THE POLYCARBONATE

29 To minimize noise caused by the expansion and contraction of polycarbonate sheeting, place rafter tape on top of each batten before fixing the roofing in place.

30 Using a panel saw, cut the polycarbonate sheeting to length, allowing an overhang of 25 mm on the house side and 100 mm past the outside batten.

required. This project uses five intermediate rafters positioned 650 mm apart.

24 Mark the rafter positions on the ledger and the top edge of the beam. Cut and shape the intermediate rafters. Secure them with joist hangers and skew-nail as described for the outside rafters.

BRACING THE BEAM
25 Trim four 450 mm braces at a 45-degree angle on each end to fit under the beam and against the post. Nail through the edge of the brace into the beam and post, using

75 mm galvanized lost-head nails. Skew-nail through each face of the brace into the beam and post. Remove any makeshift bracing.

ATTACHING THE BATTENS
26 Cut the ends of the battens flush with the faces of the outside rafters. Fix the first batten at a 90-degree angle, 25 mm out from the guttering. Use two 75 mm galvanized lost-head nails driven through the top of each rafter.

27 Position the outside batten 75 mm in from the ends of the rafters and fix it securely.

31 Determine the direction of the prevailing winds and lay the sheets to prevent wind or rain blowing under the overlaps. Position the first sheet flush with the ends of the battens.
.

32 Working one sheet at a time, drill a 10 mm hole through the top of the first corrugation in line with the centre of the batten. Secure the sheeting with a roofing screw. Ensure the screw passes through the centre of the hole and is square to the top of the batten. Use only normal pressure when tightening the screws, as overtightening can distort or crack the sheet and restrict necessary movement.

33 Drill through the top of every second corrugation, and screw the roofing sheet to the batten.

and screw it to the batten, leaving room to overlap the next sheet.

34 Place the second sheet in position with an overlap of one-and-a-half corrugations. Drill through both sheets and screw them down. Measure periodically to check for square and adjust the sheeting as necessary. Continue to work across the roof until the polycarbonate sheeting is fully fastened.

35 Fit any flashing, capping or guttering as required.

33 Adjust the sheet to ensure it is square. Drill a hole in the other end and secure that too, then continue fixing the edge. Drill through the top of every second corrugation

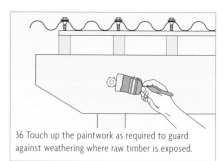

36 Touch up the paintwork as required to guard against weathering where raw timber is exposed.

FINISHING
36 Touch up the paintwork to guard against weathering.

GABLED PERGOLA

This gabled pergola measures 3300 x 6600 mm. The outside is supported on timber posts and incorporates collar ties for stability. The roof covering is polycarbonate sheeting, with guttering and a downpipe attached to the beam.

ESTIMATING YOUR MATERIALS
1 Use council-approved plans when ordering supplies for this project (see Calculating quantities, pages 378–379).

PREPARATION
2 Follow the steps described for the attached pergola (see Fixing the ledger, Determining the post positions, Pouring the footings, Erecting the posts and Attaching the beam, pages 384–388).

CREATING THE GABLE
3 With the ledger and beam in place and the posts braced temporarily, measure the distance between the ledger and beam. This measurement is the width of the pergola, which when finished has a central ridge board at the apex with equal rafters running down both sides.

Pitched roofs are constructed at an angle of between 22½ degrees and 30 degrees.

This roof is pitched at 26½ degrees, which means the rise equals one-quarter of the span.

4 Divide the distance between the ledger and the beam by two and subtract half the ridge thickness. This figure is the horizontal span of the rafter. (Span ÷ 2) – half ridge thickness
= (3300 mm ÷ 2) – 25mm
= 1650 mm – 25 mm = 1625 mm

5 To calculate the rise, divide that figure by two.
1625 mm ÷ 2 = 812.5 mm (813 mm rounded off)

MARKING OUT THE RAFTER
6 To gauge the length of each rafter, use a builder's square and rafter buttons to set up a pitch template. Calculate this as the horizontal span of the rafter divided by (say) five. 1625 mm ÷ 5 = 325 mm

TOOLS
- Basic tool kit (see page 379)

7 Set one button 325 mm along the blade of the builder's square. Set the other rafter button half this measurement (162.5 mm) along the stock of the square.

8 Trace the pitch template along the straightest rafter piece six times. Cut the rafter on the first and last lines made by the stock of the square (see the Marking out the rafter diagram, on page 392). Cut one rafter, then lay it on another and trace the outline. Keep any bows to the top. On a third length of timber, trace the rafter outline again, but do not cut it out. Position the first two rafters to check carefully for fit, making adjustments as required. Transfer any corrections onto the third rafter.

ERECTING THE GABLE

9 Cut the ridge board to length at 6600 mm. To check your angles and sizes, lay a pair of rafters flat on the ground with an offcut of ridge material between them. Measure the span distance at the ends of the rafters to ensure its accuracy.

10 Cut the ledger end of the rafter to fit around the guttering. Make straight cuts with a power saw or, for a neater fit, shape the cuts with a template and jigsaw. Make a template for the shape of the gutter from a piece of scrap ply or other material. Trace this onto the bottom end of one rafter and cut around it carefully with a jigsaw.

ATTACHING THE RAFTERS

11 Choose one end of the pergola as a starting point. You will need two ladders and a second person to help you when attempting this step. While one person stands on a ladder and holds the ridge end of the rafter and a scrap of ridge in place, the other should secure the ledger end by skew-nailing through the face into the ledger with two 75 x 3.75 mm galvanized lost-head nails. Repeat this process on the beam side, nailing the scrap piece of ridge temporarily between the rafters to maintain the required angle. Do not drive this nail in too far, as it must be removed once the ridge is in place. Check for fit and adjust the third rafter as required.

12 Cut the third rafter to length. This becomes the template for the rest of the rafters. Ensuring all bows will be at the top of the rafters, mark out the remaining rafters. As sawn timber can vary in width by as much as 5 mm or more, keep the tops in alignment so any variations are underneath. Cut the rafters to length. Shape half the rafters to fit around the gutter. Use the ply guttering template when tracing the outline onto the ledger ends of these rafters, then

Before erecting a pitched roof such as this, remember that additional rainfall running off the pergola might overwhelm the existing gutter and downpipe. Make sure you have access for clearing fallen debris from the gutter.

MARKING OUT THE RAFTER

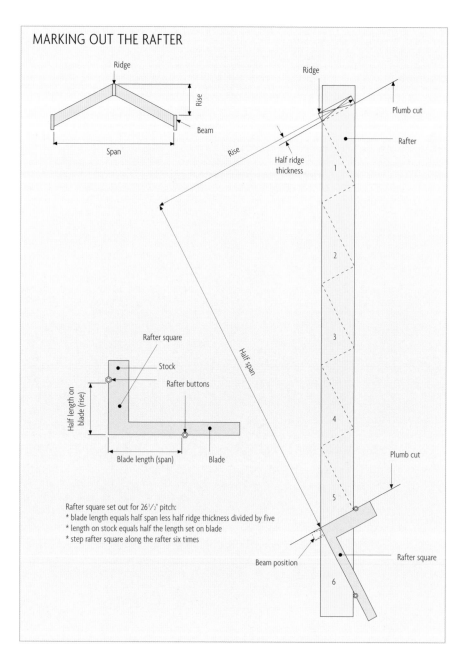

Ridge

Rise

Beam

Span

Rise

Ridge

Plumb cut

Half ridge thickness

Rafter

1

2

3

4

5

6

Half span

Plumb cut

Beam position

Rafter square

Rafter square

Stock

Rafter buttons

Half length on blade (rise)

Blade length (span)

Blade

Rafter square set out for 26¹/₂° pitch:
* blade length equals half span less half ridge thickness divided by five
* length on stock equals half the length set on blade
* step rafter square along the rafter six times

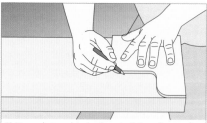

12 Use a ply template to shape half the rafters to fit around the roof gutter on the house.

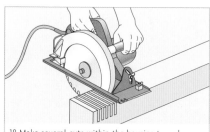

18 Make several cuts within the housing to make chiselling easy. Chisel the waste away from the sides.

rafter into the ridge. Sight across one end of the pergola, ensuring the end of the beam, the ridge and the ledger are in alignment. Fix temporary bracing to maintain this position.

FIXING THE INTERMEDIATE RAFTERS

14 Measuring from one end of the pergola, mark even spacings on the ledger, ridge and beam. Fix the rafters in pairs of one ledger rafter and one beam rafter to prevent the ridge and beam bowing, and skew-nail into position.

POSITIONING COLLAR TIES

15 Install collar ties two-thirds of the way down alternate pairs of rafters (see Creating the gable diagram opposite). Measure each rafter from the top of the ridge to the top of the beam. Mark the two-thirds point, calculated by multiplying the rafter length by two-thirds. In this case, each rafter measures 1817 mm.

1817 mm x 0.667 = 1211.939 mm (1212 mm rounded off)

outdoor

cut with a jigsaw. Position another pair of rafters at the opposite end of the pergola, and fix as described above.

FIXING THE RIDGE

13 Have some temporary braces on hand to steady the ridge while you work. With one

person at either end of the ridge, lift it up into position between the rafters, pushing the scrap ridge material through the top. Ensure the rafters are flush with the top and ends of the ridge. Check the ridge for level and fix it permanently in place by skew-nailing through the top and sides of each

Position the bottom of the collar tie on the mark and clamp it in place. Check for level and adjust as required. Mark the rafter angle with a pencil on the face of the collar tie. Remove it and cut the angle with a power saw. Reposition and clamp it, checking for level. Drill a 12 mm hole through the collar tie and rafter and secure it with a cup-head bolt, nut and washer at each end.

FIXING THE BATTENS

16 Let the battens in or nail them to the tops of the rafters. In this example, the battens are let in with a power saw and chisel. To determine the positions and ensure they are straight, use a string line. On one side of the pergola, mark 100 mm from the bottom on both end rafters. Place a nail in the top of each rafter at this point and pull a string line between them. Using a square, mark the top of each rafter, along the string line. This identifies the bottom edge of the batten. Use an offcut of batten material to gauge the width of the housing (about 75 mm) in each rafter and mark it with a pencil.

17 Fix the ridge capping to the top batten. As the capping used here is 300 mm wide, measure 150 mm down each side from the centre of the ridge. The bottom edge of the batten rests here. As described above, use a string line and batten offcut to mark the housings. Place the intermediate battens evenly between the top and bottom battens and set them out in the same manner. Repeat on the other side of the roof.

CUTTING THE HOUSINGS

18 Set a power saw to a depth to suit the battens. (In this case, 50 mm is appropriate.) Make several cuts in the housing to make chiselling easy. Chisel the waste away from both sides and level the bottom of each housing. Use the batten offcut to check for fit and adjust as required.

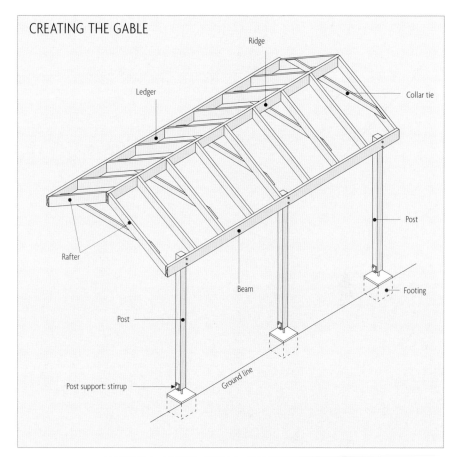

CREATING THE GABLE

Ridge

Ledger

Collar tie

Rafter

Post

Beam

Footing

Post

Ground line

Post support: stirrup

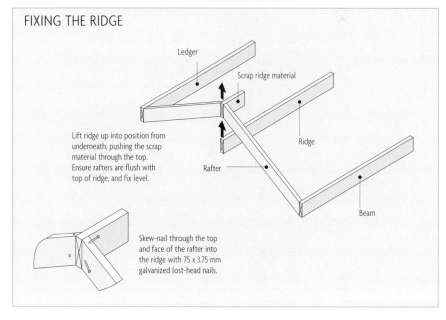

FIXING THE RIDGE

Ledger

Scrap ridge material

Ridge

Lift ridge up into position from underneath, pushing the scrap material through the top. Ensure rafters are flush with top of ridge, and fix level.

Rafter

Beam

Skew-nail through the top and face of the rafter into the ridge with 75 x 3.75 mm galvanized lost-head nails.

MATERIALS*

PART	TIMBER	LENGTH	NO.
Post	100 x 100 mm sawn pine (C24)	2400 mm	3
Beam	200 x 50 mm sawn pine (C24)	6600 mm	1
Rafter	150 x 50 mm sawn pine (C24)	2100 mm	24
Batten	75 x 50 mm sawn pine (C24)	6600 mm	8
Ledger	150 x 50 mm sawn pine (C24)	6600 mm	1
Ridge	150 x 50 mm sawn pine (C24)	6600 mm	1
Collar tie	150 x 50 mm sawn pine (C24	2100 mm	6
Collar tie	75 x 50 mm batten sawn pine	2100 mm	1
Form box	90 x 19 mm offcuts	300 mm	12
Bottom rail	70 x 45 mm treated pine (C24)	2100 mm	1
Baluster	45 x 45 mm treated pine (C24)	900 mm	5
Finial	70 x 70 mm treated pine (C24)	1200 mm	1
Bracket	150 x 50 mm sawn pine (C24) offcuts	450 mm	2

Other: Three 40 kg bags of concrete; three galvanized stirrup post supports; twenty-four 125 x 12 mm galvanized cup-head nuts and bolts with washers; 10 kg of 75 x 3.75 mm galvanized lost-head nails; six 75 x 10 mm galvanized masonry anchors; eighteen 2100 mm sheets of 760 mm cover corrugated polycarbonate sheeting; two hundred 75 mm galvanized roofing screws with washers; 40 m roll of 25 mm rafter tape; four 2100 mm lengths of 150 x 75 mm steel barge capping; 3600 mm length of 300 mm steel ridge capping; clear silicone sealant; paint, primer and undercoat.

* Finished size: 3300 x 6600 mm. The timber lengths given are for the project pictured on page 391. Adapt these requirements to suit your own needs.

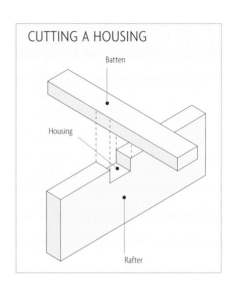

CUTTING A HOUSING

Batten

Housing

Rafter

19 Cut the battens to length and position them in the housings. Secure each batten with two 75 x 3.75 mm galvanized lost-head nails driven from the batten into the rafter.

ATTACHING THE ROOF

20 The roof covering for this pergola is basically the same as that described for the attached structure (see Attaching the polycarbonate, pages 389–390), and it is fixed in a similar manner. However, this pergola has the addition of metal barge and ridge capping, so do not secure the outside edges of the end sheets and the ridge ends of all sheets until the cappings are in place. Fill the gable end nearest the house with polycarbonate laid vertically to provide additional weatherproofing. The polycarbonate sheeting hangs down into the gutter by 25 mm. Provide a flat base for its attachment by ensuring the thickness of the collar ties on the end pair of rafters increases by the thickness of a rafter. To do this, place a batten on the face of the collar tie between the rafters. All temporary bracing can now be removed.

FIXING THE METAL CAPPINGS

21 Cut barge capping to cover the gap between the polycarbonate and the rafter faces at each end. Shape the lower end to fit around the guttering and against the ledger. Cut the other end plumb 5 mm longer than the centre line of the ridge. On the opposite side of the barge capping, create a plumb cut at each end to match the ridge and beam.

22 Position the capping over the polycarbonate sheeting and push firmly against the face of the rafters. Drill through the top face and the polycarbonate, and secure both to the battens with roofing screws. Do not fix to the ridge batten until the ridge capping is in place.

23 Place the second capping over the face and secure it in the same manner. Seal the overlapping join with clear silicone. Position ridge capping on top of the ridge and drill through it, then screw firmly through the polycarbonate into the ridge batten. Use two pieces to make up the required length. Fix the first capping flush with the outside face of the barge capping. Cut the second piece of ridge capping to length, allowing a 100 mm overlap. Seal the overlapping join with clear silicone and fix as before.

GABLE DECORATION

24 The bottom rail supports the balusters and brackets. Position it midway down the end of the gable. Bevel the ends to match the angle of the rafters. Before securing the

outdoor

bottom rail, check it for level. Fix it in place with two 75 mm lost-head nails driven into the bottom of each rafter end.

25 Fix a 150 mm offcut of batten vertically to the face of the end collar tie as a flat backing for the finial. Position the finial over the face of the gable end so the square section protrudes an equal distance above the ridge and below the bottom rail. Check the finial for plumb, and clamp it into position. Secure the finial to the ridge, collar-tie block and bottom rail. Use two 75 mm lost-head nails at each joint.

26 To determine the spacing between the balusters, measure the distance between the finial and the end of the bottom rail and divide it by the number of spaces required. This pergola project uses five balusters on each side of the finial, so divide the distance in this case by six. Working from the centre towards the outside, place a baluster on the bottom rail and hold it in position against the rafter. Check for plumb using a spirit level and scribe a mark on the back to match the angle of the rafter. Cut the baluster to length. Using 75 mm lost-head nails, fix it into position by nailing through the bottom rail into the baluster and skew-nailing through the top of the baluster into the rafter. Measure the distance to the next baluster and repeat.

27 For a more attractive look below the bottom rail, shape brackets from offcuts of rafter material and nail them in place.

FINISHING

28 Place guttering on the beam to divert rainwater away from the pergola. Add a downpipe connected to a stormwater drain.

29 Complete the paintwork as desired. This pergola is finished with two coats of external acrylic paint in contrasting colours.

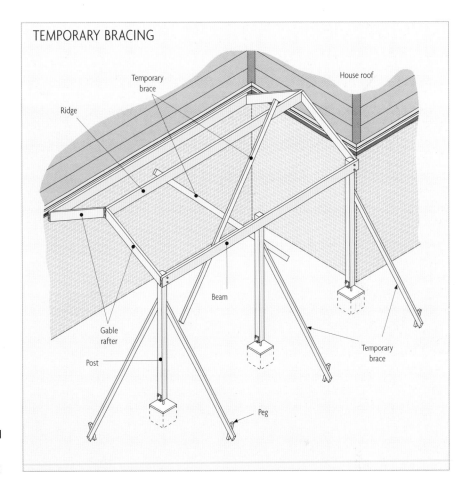

TEMPORARY BRACING

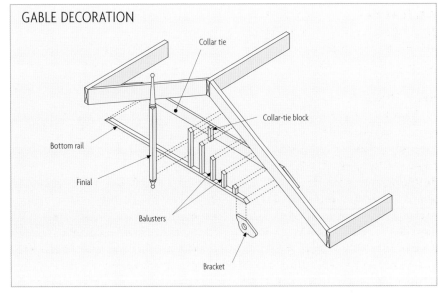

GABLE DECORATION

FREE-STANDING WALKWAY

This versatile design can be an arbour to support climbing plants, a grand garden entrance, an entertaining area or even a carport. It is supported on treated pine posts embedded in concrete and covered by lattice.

Clothed in wisteria and climbing roses, this simple wooden structure is perfectly at home in its garden setting. Supported by four posts, it is quick to build, with four rafters resting on parallel beams.

ESTIMATING YOUR MATERIALS

1 Using council-approved plans as a reference, estimate your material requirements and place the order (see Calculating quantities, pages 378–379).

PAINTING THE TIMBER

2 Remember to apply one or two coats of paint or stain in your desired colour before beginning to construct the pergola. It is easier to paint loose pieces of timber on the ground than when the structure is standing upright. Once the assembly is complete, you can touch up the joints and around the cut ends.

PREPARATION

3 Determine a building line for the front of the walkway. Lay a piece of timber across the path to represent the starting line. The path in this project measures 600 mm wide and has a 300 mm allowance for the post positions at each side. To determine the front positions, measure 300 mm to each side of the path on the building line. Place wooden pegs temporarily in the ground at these points to represent the outside faces of the posts. Just outside each peg, erect a building profile across the corner, at an angle of approximately 45 degrees. Insert a nail in the top of each profile and stretch a string line between the two, securing it to create a building line.

HINT

Protect timber from insect and water damage by applying a coat of preservative to all joints prior to fixing.

TOOLS

- Basic tool kit (see page 379)

MATERIALS*

PART	TIMBER	LENGTH	NO.
Post	90 x 90 mm treated pine (C24)	3000 mm	4
Beam	140 x 45 mm treated pine (C24)	3000 mm	2
Rafter	140 x 45 mm treated pine (C24)	2100 mm	4

Other: Eight 125 x 12 mm galvanized cup-head nuts and bolts with washers; 2 kg of 75 x 3.75 mm galvanized lost-head nails; stain or paint, primer and undercoat; approximately two buckets of coarse gravel; concrete; timber preservative; lattice (optional).

* Finished size: 2400 x 1200 mm (footprint) by 2100 mm high. The timber lengths given above are for the project pictured opposite. Adapt these requirements to suit your own needs.

4 Place a spirit level on top of the temporary corner pegs and plumb to the string line. Wrap masking tape around the string, then draw with a pencil onto the taped section where the plumb line crosses to create a clearly visible mark.

5 From the temporary corner pegs, measure 2400 mm along the path and drive in a second set of corner pegs. Erect another pair of profiles as described previously. Pull a string line down one side of the path, making sure it passes over the masking tape mark. Drive in an additional nail and secure the string line. Repeat this step on the other side of the path. Measure the distance between the string lines at two points to ensure they are parallel, adjusting them as required.

6 Working from the second set of temporary corner pegs, plumb up to the string line and mark it clearly. Stretch another string line across the path from one profile to the other, passing over the two marks. Measure the diagonals between the intersecting string lines to check that they are equal and that, therefore, the project is square. Once the set-out is correct, remove the string lines to provide easy access while digging the footings.

DIGGING THE FOOTINGS

7 As the string line represents the outside face of the post, the footing must extend beyond this line. The post sits in the centre of each footing. Scratch the outline of the footing on the ground to mark the position of the hole, and dig each footing 300 x 300 mm and to a depth of 550 mm.

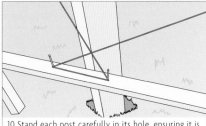
10 Stand each post carefully in its hole, ensuring it is vertical and in line with the intersecting string lines.

11 Brace each post temporarily with timber offcuts and, using a spirit level, recheck for vertical.

8 Add a 100 mm layer of coarse gravel to the bottom of each hole to aid drainage, particularly in areas with heavy clay-based soil.

9 Replace the string lines and secure them tightly to the nails in the tops of the profiles.

ERECTING POSTS

10 Stand each post carefully in its hole, ensuring it is plumb and in line with the intersecting string lines. Work with posts slightly longer than required, trimming any excess away later.

11 Brace the posts temporarily and recheck for plumb. Mix cement and sharp sand with water to form concrete to the consistency of stiff paste, then pour it into the hole. Ram the wet concrete down well to remove any air bubbles trapped in the mixture and

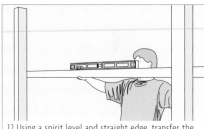
12 Using a spirit level and straight edge, transfer the position of the beam to the remaining three posts.

ensure the post is held firmly. Before beginning construction, allow the concrete to set for at least seven days and up to a fortnight.

FIXING THE BEAMS

12 In this project, the beams run parallel to the path at a height of 2100 mm. Beginning with those—if any—that stand on slightly higher ground, measure up from the bottom

When designing a free-standing pergola as a companion to an existing structure (such as this house), consider its overall dimensions. To create a pleasing scene, make sure its scale is in keeping with that of the original building.

of each post and square a line around all four sides. Use a spirit level, a straight edge and a pencil to transfer the beam marks to the remaining three posts.

13 Place a single cross on the side of each post where a beam will be housed. On the outside of each post, using a power saw and chisel, cut out and neaten a 140 x 45 mm housing just below the beam line to support the beam.

14 Plan for the beam to overhang the posts by 300 mm at either end. Cut a stepped splay on the bottom edge. Cut the beam to length and shape it, removing any sharp edges by dressing with a hand plane. Place the beam in its housings and hold it in position with cramps. Drill holes through the beam and posts and secure them with two 12 mm diameter roundhead nuts and bolts.

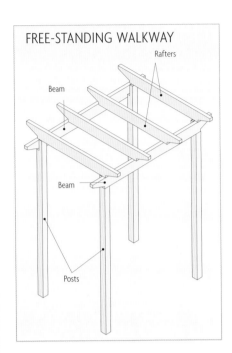

FREE-STANDING WALKWAY
Rafters
Beam
Beam
Posts

HINT

Use stainless steel fasteners and fittings in highly corrosive conditions (such as in areas with spray from saltwater).

FIXING THE RAFTERS

15 On each rafter, create a stepped splay and a 300 mm overhang to match those of the beam. Place the end rafters in line with the posts and space the two intermediate rafters evenly. Skew-nail each to the top of the beam with 75 x 3.75 mm galvanized lost-head nails.

FINISHING

16 Remove the temporary bracing and touch up the timber with your choice of paint or stain. This pergola is finished with two coats of white exterior acrylic paint.

17 Add a sheet of white-painted lattice to the roof, if desired.

outdoor

SHINGLE-ROOFED WALKWAY

This small covered walkway, constructed from sawn pine timber, is designed to mirror—and therefore complement—the general architectural style of a two-storey house.

Here, special touches include panels of square lattice on the front and back and a gabled shingle roof.

The structure rests on individual concrete footings and is bolted securely in place with galvanized metal stirrups. Diagonal bracing with metal rods adds stability to the sides.

Follow the general construction advice provided for the flat-roofed Free-standing walkway (see pages 396–398), then refer to the instructions on pages 390–395 for tips on designing and installing a gabled roof. Lay tiles and finish the roof with a length of metal ridge capping.

A shingle roof and coral and green paintwork echo the style of the house behind this walkway. Mounted on four concrete footings, this small pergola is finished with pairs of carved wooden brackets and a finial at the front.

barbecues

barbecues

TYPES OF BARBECUE

There are many different types of barbecue and several different types of fuel. Before you start building a barbecue, consider which types will best suit your home and lifestyle.

CHOOSING A BARBECUE

A built barbecue can become a feature in the garden landscape and an integral part of your outdoor lifestyle. It will, however, require considerable time and effort spent on construction, so be sure you will use it often enough to justify your work. You don't want to create a 'white elephant' that is never used. In some cases a portable or mobile unit may suit your lifestyle better.

Here are some points to consider:

- For any barbecue you will need a level site and, preferably, one close to the house, but for a built barbecue it will have to be large enough for the structure and for the cook and helpers to move safely around it.
- The area where you entertain may not be suited to a built barbecue (it may be a deck or tiled patio), so you may have to settle for a portable or mobile unit.
- You will need to have time and basic bricklaying or stone-working skills to build the barbecue, or be prepared to pay someone to do it.
- If you usually barbecue for only a couple of people, it may be a waste of fuel to use a large, built structure.
- Likewise, if you have many of your barbecues away from home, you may find a portable barbecue more useful.
- You will probably find the cost of a built barbecue is similar to that of an equivalent mobile type.

A built barbecue has the advantage that you can incorporate any number or size of preparation areas to suit your style of cooking and entertaining.

BUILT BARBECUES

Built barbecues can be constructed for use with solid fuel or with a drop-in gas cooktop similar to those used in mobile barbecues. If you have plenty of wood on hand, fuel costs are nil. The costs of building a barbecue increase in proportion to the size and detail of the construction as well as with the choice of fuel.

PORTABLE AND MOBILE UNITS

Portable barbecues (those smaller types that can be packed up and put away or taken on picnics) and mobile barbecues (trolley types that can be moved to suit the weather or for storage) have become increasingly popular. They include electric barbecues, hibachi and kamado units, and kettle barbecues.

However, these portable units are not very efficient when you are entertaining a large crowd, and they often need to be stored or protected from the elements. They vary from simple types to elaborate structures incorporating hoods, thermostats and side burners.

FUEL TYPES

Barbecues can be fired by a number of fuels. Those commonly used are solid fuels—such as wood, charcoal or heat beads—or gas or electricity.

Solid fuels

Solid fuels produce smoke, flames and smells that help create an 'outdoor' atmosphere. For some this is the essence of true barbecuing.

- Many people enjoy wood-fired barbecues for their traditional appeal, but you need time to collect the wood and kindling and get the fire going: wood is not a fuel for the cook in a hurry. Cooking is done over hot coals, so patience is needed as the flames heat the hotplate and then subside to provide a stable plate temperature. Using firelighters, which are cubes of compressed kerosene, makes it easier to start a fire as they burn longer than paper. The smoke generated by wood-fired

ADAPTING A CONVENTIONAL BARBECUE TO GAS

If you have a barbecue designed for solid fuel such as wood but find it is no longer practical, you can convert the existing firebox to accommodate a gas unit.

INSTALLING GAS BURNERS BENEATH THE EXISTING HOTPLATE

1 Measure the width and depth of the firebox beneath the hotplate. Purchase a drop-in burner unit to fit. These units come in a frame with from two to five gas burners, each with its own control knob. The unit dimensions will vary with different makes, but the figures in the table below will act as a guide. You will also need to purchase a gas bottle, regulator and hose.

2 The recommended spacing between the burners and the hotplate is 75 mm. This ensures adequate flame contact and heating of the cooking area. There are various ways of supporting the burner framework so that it is at the correct height.

• Position bricks or concrete blocks at either side of the firebox and set the framework on them.

• Determine the correct height on the walls either side of the firebox and fix metal angles to the walls using steel bolts.

• Position flat lintel or rods of steel at the correct height across the front and rear of the firebox.

INSTALLING A COMPLETE NEW UNIT

Mobile gas barbecue units can be purchased without the trolley and placed into the firebox area. Measure the width and depth of the existing firebox and purchase a unit to fit. Remember that a unit with a roasting hood will need adequate space at the rear of the firebox so the hood can open fully.

As the unit will be exposed to all weather conditions, select one that has been finished completely in vitreous enamel or stainless steel. If possible, choose a unit with a cover that will protect the plate when the barbecue is not in use.

TYPICAL DROP-IN UNITS*

NO. OF BURNERS	LENGTH REQUIRED	DEPTH REQUIRED
2	430 mm	490 mm
3	610 mm	490 mm
4	760 mm	490 mm
5	960 mm	490 mm

* Precise measurements will vary. Check before you purchase a unit.

barbecues can be a problem, especially if the wind is changeable. In some areas, council regulations prohibit open fires, and during summer there may be fire bans. However, if there is an adequate supply available, a wood-fired barbecue will give years of maintenance-free enjoyment.

• Charcoal is the residue of partially burnt wood. It fires quickly and provides ample heat for the barbecue. Lighting is easy if small pyramids of charcoal are built over a firelighter. Once alight, the charcoal can be spread out. It gives off little smoke and adds to the aroma. Charcoal is available widely.

• Heat beads are basically compressed charcoal and tend to burn longer. They can be lit in the same manner as charcoal, although some brands have been soaked in kerosene and are easier to light. However, they do not lose the kerosene smell after lighting.

Gas

Gas is a clean and efficient form of heat supply, enabling accurate temperature control at the turn of a knob. Plate temperature is reached quickly and can be controlled throughout the cooking process. If you have town gas supplied for heating and cooking, you may be able to have a line and connection made for the barbecue but this must be done by a CORGI-registered gasfitter. It is more common to use a gas bottle, which gives you greater freedom in siting the barbecue. Do ensure you have an adequate supply of bottled gas before you start cooking as there's nothing worse than running out when you are halfway through. Hot rocks (pieces of volcanic rock) are sometimes placed in a tray between the burner and the hotplate or grill to spread the heat.

Electricity

Like gas, electricity is clean, efficient and provides excellent temperature control. Electric barbecues for domestic use are, however, limited in size as plug-in household power supply has a maximum below the power required. Electricity can, therefore, be used to fuel only small units.

Smoking chips

Smoking chips can be burnt with the barbecue to add flavour to the food being cooked. Popular flavours include hickory or mesquite.

DESIGNING A BARBECUE

A built barbecue becomes a permanent part of the garden. It is worthwhile spending time to plan it carefully so that you get the result you want.

FACTORS TO CONSIDER

If you have decided that a built barbecue will suit you best, you will now have to decide on a design. This will depend on how much space you have, the type of fuel and whether you need preparation areas and storage for wood, or gas bottles. You will also need to consider whether to include a chimney, either real or decorative, and any other structures such as seating, planter boxes, walls or pergolas. Finally, consider how much you can afford to spend.

MATERIALS

The materials that you choose for your barbecue will depend on the style of your home, the formality or informality of your garden design, your budget and, of course, the availability of the materials.

Brick barbecues are the most common because of their ease of construction and their ability to tie the house and garden landscape together. If the barbecue is sited close to the house and the house is brick, you will need to choose bricks that match it. If this is not necessary, you should select bricks that will be able to withstand the heat of the barbecue, particularly if it is wood-fired. Avoid the softer, calcium-silicate bricks and choose well-burnt, dry-pressed bricks if possible. Your local brick supplier will be able to advise you.

Stone barbecues are also popular in areas where local rock and sandstone can be easily purchased. Rock lends itself to a natural, rustic setting and is an ideal choice for wood-fired, informal designs. Choose carefully, however, as river boulders and limestone can 'explode' when subjected to great heat. Sandstone is a softer, more

Sandstone blocks are used to decorative effect for the corners of this elegant natural gas barbecue, while brick walls form the sides and a cross-wall to support the slab below the gas unit. Sandstone is also used for the top.

porous stone and allows for shaping and facing. This makes it a popular choice in more formal and traditional settings. It can be purchased in regular geometric shapes in either block or slab form. Sandstone is also available in split, irregular forms.

DIMENSIONS

The dimensions to be considered include not only the overall length, width and height of the

unit, but also those of the surface areas that will be used for cooking and preparation. You will also need to consider the space required for the firebox or gas unit, and storage for wood, gas bottles and other accessories.

If you are working in brick or cut stone, design the barbecue to suit full brick or block dimensions. This will make laying easier and you will avoid unnecessary cutting. Brick sizes vary quite considerably, but a standard brick

BRICK MEASUREMENTS*

NUMBER OF BRICKS	LENGTH (mm)	HEIGHT (mm)
1	230	86
2	470	172
3	710	258
4	950	343
5	1190	429
6	1430	515
7	1670	600
8	1910	686
9	2150	772
10	2390	857
11	2630	943
12	2870	1029
13	3110	1115
14	3350	1200
15	3590	1286

* Including allowance for 10 mm joints. To include half a brick, add 120 mm to the length.

size is 230 mm long x 110 mm wide x 76 mm high. The table above gives the numbers of bricks necessary to make up various lengths or heights. If your bricks are a different size, adjust the measurements to suit.

HOTPLATE

The size of the area required for cooking depends on the number of people to be fed. An average sized cooking plate of 930 x 600 mm caters for 12–15 people. If you usually cook for smaller numbers, reduce the plate size to 690 x 600 mm, and then if you occasionally need extra space, you can bring out or hire a portable barbecue to supplement it.

When deciding on a plate size, ensure it will suit the brickwork dimensions. The two plate sizes given here will fit inside standard brickwork with a 10 mm gap all round for

expansion. The plate can be cut to any size needed.

The steel plate should not be too thin, or it will buckle over time. A good thickness is 6–8 mm. If the barbecue plate is larger than normal, increase the thickness or have steel rods welded onto the underside to prevent it bending or buckling.

PREPARATION AREA

Whether or not you incorporate preparation areas in the built unit, you will need to allow somewhere to place food and utensils during cooking. Most barbecue designs include a preparation area next to the hotplate on one or both sides. The size of this area can vary according to your needs and the space available. If the area is going to be used to store and prepare food before cooking as well as to serve guests, an area twice the size of the hotplate would be useful. If your barbecue setting includes a table where the cooked food, salads and utensils can be served, then a smaller preparation area would suffice.

When designing the preparation area, include an appropriate finish so that it will be easy to clean. Surfaces such as concrete and stone attract dirt and grease over time and would be better finished with wipe-clean surfaces such as ceramic tiles, sealed terracotta or slate.

WORKING HEIGHT

You should also consider the height of the preparation and cooking areas to avoid discomfort while cooking. An average height is between 850 and 950 mm, but if the main cook is particularly tall or short, you should adjust the height to suit. Ten courses of brickwork will give a height of 857 mm, while eleven courses will give 943 mm.

STORAGE

Including preparation areas in your design often creates space for storage below. These

storage areas can be left open to the weather or closed with doors. Shelves can be installed for utensils or equipment, or the space can be used to store wood or gas bottles. By providing covered storage for wood, you will ensure a dry supply of fuel in all weathers.

With gas-fired units, it is safer to store the gas bottle away from the burners and out of the weather. A small opening can be left in the brick jointing during construction so that the gas line can be connected to the burners. Incorporate this into your planning and design stage, or drill out a hole later. If doors are to be added to these areas, allow adequate ventilation in case of gas leakage. A gap at the top and bottom will allow air to circulate while protecting the area from the weather.

These areas are ideal for storing such things as the barbecue tools, perhaps hung on hooks on the backs of the doors, cleaning materials for the preparation areas, hot rocks or charcoal, smoking chips, dry matches, ignition gun or even small garden tools and implements.

LOCATION

Deciding where to locate your barbecue can often be the most difficult part of building it. To get full use from your barbecue you need to locate it somewhere that is comfortable and convenient for cooking and entertaining.

Build the barbecue close to the house where you will have easy access to food, drinks and utensils. If you have an outdoor living area, perhaps with a pergola or patio, it will naturally form part of that. A barbecue placed apart from the living area isolates the cook from the guests and is less likely to be used. If you have to build the barbecue any distance from the house, plan paths or walkways to link them.

The choice of location will also be influenced by the prevailing weather conditions, as using the barbecue will be more comfortable if it is not exposed to strong winds, direct sunlight or excessive shade. You may also require some privacy from your neighbours. If you are planning a large structure or want to remove trees, you should check with your local council before beginning work.

You may find it helpful to sketch a plan of your house and yard on paper (preferably to scale). On a separate piece of paper draw your proposed barbecue area to scale and cut it out. This cut-out can then be moved around the yard plan until you find the best location.

SURROUNDING AREA

Any outdoor entertainment area, whether large or small, needs to be level, hard-wearing and without drainage problems. If you have a sloping site, consider terracing or constructing a deck.

The size of the overall barbecue area will be determined by the amount of space available, the number of people you want to accommodate and your budget, but you should always include enough room for the cook to work unhindered and for the guests to be served comfortably.

If you don't plan to have a barbecue very often and don't intend to have large parties, a small paved area or deck may be sufficient. On the other hand, if you plan to use the barbecue for large-scale entertaining, it may be worthwhile creating a more elaborate area with roofing, lighting, storage and preparation areas, seating and screening.

SURFACE MATERIAL

Select the surfacing material for the area carefully to provide an easy-care, comfortable and durable surround for the barbecue. Your choice will depend on the style of the house and landscaping, and your choice of material for the barbecue itself. For example, a barbecue constructed of sandstone blocks will often look best when it is surrounded by matching sandstone flagging.

Popular materials for surfacing the area around a barbecue include:

- brick pavers of clay or concrete
- house bricks
- concrete (either plain, stencilled or stamped)
- exposed aggregate
- slate
- tiles (terracotta or concrete)
- sandstone
- timber decking.

If you use terracotta or slate, be aware that they provide a non-slip surface only if they are unsealed, but they are then likely to absorb grease from the barbecue.

Sandstone is porous and will show stains and discolour over time. It can be sealed, but you will need to check the manufacturer's instructions on a variety of sealants to select the best one for your paving. Lawn is not a good choice for a barbecue surround, as it tends to wear and remain wet underfoot. Loose materials such as gravel should also be avoided, as they can be unstable. This is a decided disadvantage when you are carrying plates of food.

SHELTER

The barbecue area may need some protection from the weather, and the amount will depend on how exposed it is to wind and sun.

When looking at alternatives, consider the probable cost, ease of construction (and your level of skill) and how each will complement your existing house and garden landscape. The most important consideration is to create a functional, and yet comfortable, outdoor area.

Some possible structures are:
- roofing attached to the house
- a separate cabana-type structure
- a pergola or other open timber framework which can be covered with light material such as lattice, shadecloth, overlapping fibreglass or metal sheeting
- a trellis structure, perhaps used with a pergola to support climbing plants such as ornamental grape

COSTS

The costs involved in the construction of a barbecue area depend on how elaborate it is. You will probably find that the cost of the barbecue itself will be minimal within the overall project budget.

Some of the features to include in your costing are:
- the barbecue itself
- retaining walls or screens
- paving or other surfacing
- any shade structure
- seating
- a lighting and power supply.

- a screen or hedge of plants.

There are also less permanent means of shelter, such as umbrellas. You may also be able to take advantage of existing shelter such as trees, parts of the building, fences or walls, thus reducing your costs.

LIGHTING

If you plan to use the barbecue area in the evenings, you will need adequate lighting. Family and friends will want to see what they are eating, and the cook will need to see what is being cooked. At the barbecue itself, a light directly overhead or directed onto the cooking area from the side is best. Fluorescent lighting casts fewer shadows, but an overhead spotlight onto the cooking and preparation surfaces will suffice.

Within the barbecue area, more subtle lighting can be used to create atmosphere and to highlight garden or landscaping features. Fixed permanent lighting must be installed by a qualified electrician, or you may choose to use movable garden lighting or portable floodlights, which can be run from a nearby power source.

Whatever you choose, it is important to decide about lighting during the planning stage so that electrical conduits can be run beneath any paving or concrete.

BRICKWORK BASICS

Most built barbecues are constructed from bricks. Basic bricklaying is not difficult, but it does require some practice to achieve a neat result.

Neat, accurate bricklaying is essential if you are to have a barbecue that looks attractive as well as adding to the amenities of your home.

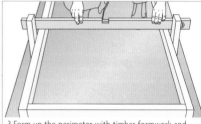

3 Form up the perimeter with timber formwork and check it for square and level before fixing it in position.

SETTING OUT THE SLAB

1 Mark out the area for the concrete slab, ensuring the corners are at 90 degrees. Check them with a builder's square or use the 3–4–5 method (see box on page 410). When the area has been laid out, check the corners are at right angles by measuring the two diagonals: if they are the same length, the area has been correctly laid out.

2 Excavate the area to a depth of 100 mm, removing grass and any other vegetation.

3 Form up the perimeter with timber formwork that will hold the concrete in position until it has hardened. For the formwork use long, straight pieces of timber held in place with a few pegs around the outside. Check the formwork for square and level before fixing it in position with nails

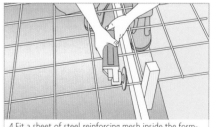

4 Fit a sheet of steel reinforcing mesh inside the formwork, ensuring a 50 mm clearance around the edges.

outdoor

TOOLS FOR BRICKLAYING

- Measuring tape
- String line
- Spirit level
- Builder's square
- Spade
- Hammer
- Steel mesh cutters or angle grinder
- Shovel
- Wheelbarrow
- Wooden float
- 75 mm edger
- Green masonry pencil
- Mortar board
- Bricklaying trowel
- Gauge rods (if needed)
- Corner blocks
- Club hammer and bolster
- Scutch hammer
- Jointing tool (optional)
- Small brush
- Sponge and bucket

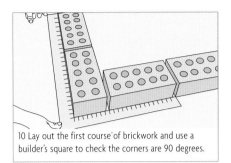

10 Lay out the first course of brickwork and use a builder's square to check the corners are 90 degrees.

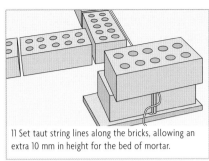

11 Set taut string lines along the bricks, allowing an extra 10 mm in height for the bed of mortar.

and more pegs. Build in a slight cross-fall to make it easier to hose down the slab once it is in use.

4 Lay a sheet of steel reinforcing mesh inside the formwork, making sure there is a 50 mm clearance around the edges. The mesh will increase the strength of the concrete and prevent it cracking at a later time. Support the mesh on bar chairs to lift it to the centre of the slab.

THE CONCRETE

5 Prepare the concrete.
- If you are hand-mixing the concrete, a mix of four parts coarse aggregate (gravel), two parts fine aggregate (sand) and one part cement (4:2:1) is sufficient. You will probably find 10 mm sized aggregate easiest to work. Mix these dry materials together with a shovel, form a well in the centre and then pour enough water into the well to achieve an even consistency.
- Ready-mixed concrete is delivered in quantities that increase by 1.2 m³: for example, standard quantities include 1.2m³, 2.4m³ etc. The required product description is 15–20 newtons.

6 Pour the concrete into the formwork, using a spade or shovel to spread it out. Keep the concrete level as you go, and make sure that it is packed firmly under the steel reinforcing mesh.

7 Screed the concrete off by moving a piece of timber in a sawing motion across the top of the formwork. Use a hammer to tap along the side edge of the formwork to help settle the concrete edge and to prevent honeycombing (air pockets).

8 Use a wooden float to cream up the surface and pack the concrete at the edges hard. Then use an edger to roughly edge the slab and push the stones down.

9 Allow the concrete to dry to a point where only the surface is still workable. Refinish the surface and edge. Allow the concrete to cure, keeping it damp, for two to three days.

THE BRICKWORK

10 Using a straight edge as a guide, lay out the first course of brickwork. Allow for 10 mm joints between the bricks. Use a builder's square to check the corners are at 90 degrees and measure the internal diagonal distance from corner to corner. The measurement should be the same both ways. Use a masonry pencil to mark the concrete along both sides of the brickwork, making guidelines to use later when laying the bricks.

11 Set taut string lines, allowing an extra 10 mm in height for the bed of mortar. Remove the bricks.

12 Unless you are an experienced bricklayer, construct gauge rods (see box on page 410). Stand them vertically at each corner of the layout, fixing them in position with braces and pegs. Use a spirit level to make sure they are vertical both ways. As you work upwards, attach a string line for each course at the indicated mark.

13 Prepare a mortar mix. As bricks in a barbecue are affected by variations in temperature and should be able to expand and contract, use a mix ratio that is not too strong. Six parts sand, one part cement and one part lime (6:1:1) is ideal. You can also add a plasticizer to make the mix more workable. Mix the dry materials together thoroughly, perhaps in a

CONSTRUCTING A GAUGE ROD

Construct a gauge rod by placing a length of timber vertically against an existing 'quality' brick wall. Mark on the timber the location of the top of each brick course for the number of courses needed for your barbecue. Use a square to draw each mark around all sides of the gauge rod. Alternatively, look at the height dimensions of brickwork provided on page 406 and transfer these onto the gauge rod.

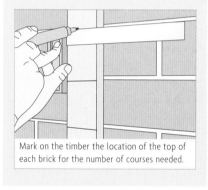

Mark on the timber the location of the top of each brick for the number of courses needed.

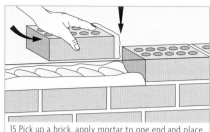

15 Pick up a brick, apply mortar to one end and place it on the bed of mortar, against the last brick laid.

17 As you build use the spirit level to check that the walls are vertical and the courses are aligned.

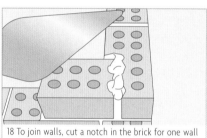

18 To join walls, cut a notch in the brick for one wall and remove one-quarter of a brick for the other wall.

THE 3–4–5 METHOD

From the corner point measure down one side 300 mm and down the other 400 mm (or you can use any multiples of these numbers, for example, 3 m and 4 m or 600 mm and 800 mm). The hypotenuse (or diagonal) should equal 500 mm (or the appropriate multiple) if you have made a right-angle triangle.

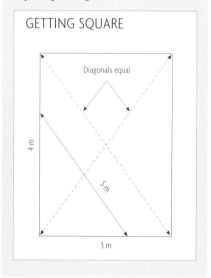

GETTING SQUARE

Diagonals equal

4 m

5 m

3 m

wheelbarrow, and then add enough water to make a pliable mix with a consistency a bit like toothpaste. Mortar is useful for only about one and a half hours, so don't mix too much at once.

14 Transfer the mortar to a mortar board. To keep it soft and pliable you will have to continually work it backwards and forwards across the board with a trowel.

15 Spread the mix between the guide lines and lay the first course of bricks to the set string lines. On the trowel, pick up enough mortar to lay two bricks. Spread it on the slab (or existing brick course) at an even thickness of 15–20 mm. Pick up a brick, apply mortar to one end and position it on the bed of mortar, butting up to the last brick laid. Use the trowel to tap the

brick into place so that the joints are a consistent thickness of 10 mm, and then remove excess mortar. Check that the course is level with a spirit level, and adjust by tamping if necessary.

16 Always lay the corners first and then fill in the wall between them. Lay the bricks so that the joints are staggered. To do this you will need to cut some bricks in half. Place a bolster at the appropriate place on the brick and hit it firmly with a club hammer. A scutch hammer can be used to chip off small pieces.

17 As you build, use the spirit level to check

that the walls are vertical and the steps are aligned.

18 To tie spur walls into the main wall, cut a notch halfway across and along the brick for the main wall and remove one-quarter of a brick for the spur wall. (Or use brick ties.)

19 Clean excess mortar off the bricks before it dries. Next day, wash the wall with water and a stiff brush. If necessary, wait several days and use a solution of one part hydrochloric acid to twenty parts water to clean the brickwork. Always add the acid to the water and wear protective goggles and gloves.

MAKING A GOOD FIRE

If you are going to use solid fuel in your barbecue, you need to plan the firebox carefully to ensure you have a fire that burns well.

Fire needs fuel and oxygen, and the secret of a good fire is to get plenty of air to it. If the fuel is set on a grate, air can be drawn up from underneath and then into the flue and up the chimney. A chimney helps produce a good draught, which is why one is often incorporated into a barbecue.

The fire will stop burning when it runs out of fuel or when the air supply is cut off. Having some method of controlling the air supply, therefore, gives you greater control over the fire. The Rustic-style barbecue below has a door across the firebox.

The opening to the flue should be two or three courses high, and the top should be level with the hotplate so that smoke is drawn up the chimney. If the opening is too small, smoke will build up and flow out the front of the barbecue.

A metal damper is used to open and close off each half of the chimney in this barbecue.

RUSTIC-STYLE BARBECUE

This barbecue doesn't have a chimney, but the firebox has a door to control airflow and burn rate. The structure is full of unusual features and will challenge more adventurous do-it-yourselfers.

DESIGN

This barbecue is fired with wood, giving a smoked taste to the food as there is no chimney. The firebox does, however, have an adjustable door to control the airflow and burn rate of the fire. Beneath the firebox and tiled preparation areas are storage areas. The left-hand preparation area contains a sink with tap.

The cooking area has a grill for chargrilling, and aluminium strips can be placed over the bars to control the flames, or a removable hotplate can be placed on it. The two centre arms are built higher to support a rotisserie. This has two height settings and is driven by an electric motor.

LAYING OUT

1 Mark out the 4000 x 1000 mm area for the concrete slab. Excavate to a depth of 100 mm, removing grass and other vegetation from the area. Position 50 mm

PVC pipe to carry waste from the sink. It should project at least 200 mm above the slab level for ease of connection later. Lay the concrete slab (see pages 408–409).

2 Following the bricklaying instructions on pages 408–410 and the set-out diagram on page 414, set out and lay the base course.

THE BRICKWORK

3 Construct the two end arms and corners to eight courses.

4 Set string lines back and front and use them as guidelines to lay the rear wall and centre arms. When course 4 is completed, erect braces (343 mm high) against the inside faces of the inner arms to carry the overhang of brickwork in course 5. To do this, position bricks on edge one above the other against each end of the arm and lay a piece of timber on top. Lay course 5 so that the inner

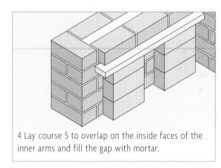

4 Lay course 5 to overlap on the inside faces of the inner arms and fill the gap with mortar.

row (except the front brick) overlaps the timber support by 50 mm. Fill the gap between the rows with mortar. The subsequent courses are set back but will hold the overhang in place. The bracing can be removed when the brickwork is dry. This overhang will be used to support the firebox slab. Complete the brickwork to course 8.

5 Construct timber formwork to contain the firebox slab. Cut a piece of fibre cement sheeting to fit exactly into the base of the

outdoor

Built from dry-pressed bricks laid in a rustic style, this unusual barbecue includes an area for chargrilling, a removable hotplate and a rotisserie unit, as well as a sink with running water and ample storage space.

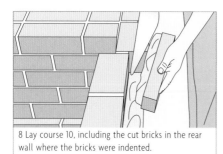

8 Lay course 10, including the cut bricks in the rear wall where the bricks were indented.

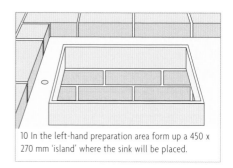

10 In the left-hand preparation area form up a 450 x 270 mm 'island' where the sink will be placed.

opening. Brace it in position to prevent it flexing under the weight of the concrete. Fix a 100 x 50 mm piece of timber across the front. Add steel mesh and concrete.

6 Position timber braces 686 mm high, as in step 4, on either side of the side bays (that is, the inner faces of the end arms and the outer faces of the inner arms). These will carry overhangs of brickwork in course 9 to support the preparation slabs. Position the six steel lintels across the front openings with two in each section, one behind the other. These will carry two rows of brickwork two courses high.

7 Lay course 9, overlapping the bricks on each side of the side bays as in step 4 and laying a double row of brickwork across the lintels.

8 Lay course 10 on the end arms, but lay only the outside row so as to accommodate the slab. In the cooking bay set timber braces in position at the sides and back to support brick overhangs in course 10. This three-sided overhang of 50 mm will support the grill frame. Cut three bricks lengthwise to

40 mm to fit in the back wall where the course 10 bricks will be indented.

9 Complete course 10, but the front wall in the side bays is only a single brick thick to allow for the slabs.

10 Construct the timber formwork to contain the concrete preparation slabs. Cut pieces of

TOOLS

- Bricklaying tools (see page 409)
- Angle grinder with masonry blade for cutting tiles
- Circular saw or tenon saw
- Jigsaw
- Drill with timber and masonry bits
- Screwdriver
- Cork sanding block
- Router (optional)
- Welding equipment

MATERIALS*

Concrete for base slab: 0.4 m³ ready-mixed, or cement, sand and 10 mm aggregate

100 x 50 mm timber for formwork

Timber pegs and nails

Steel reinforcing mesh: 3900 x 900 mm, 900 x 790 mm, 900 x 680 mm and pieces for around sink

Bar chairs

Portland cement, bricklayers sand, lime and plasticizer for mortar

660 bricks

Concrete for firebox and preparation slabs: 0.26 m³

5 mm thick fibre cement sheeting: 950 x 840 mm and two 950 x 730 mm

Capping pavers for central arms

1.8 m² tiles and grout

Six steel lintels 1100 x 90 x 8 mm

Sink 450 x 370 mm

Water tap plus 12 mm copper pipe and fittings

2000 x 50 mm PVC drainage pipe and fittings

Rotisserie unit including motor, skewer and 300 mm of notched angle iron

Two 230 mm lengths of 12 mm galvanized water pipe

Twelve grill bars 150 x 600 mm to cover a 930 x 610 mm area in two metal frames

Hotplate with handles 690 x 480 x 8 mm

Aluminium drop-down draft door 150 x 940 mm

3 mm aluminium strip 940 x 60 mm

Two hinges and sixteen pop rivets for firebox door flap

20 x 20 mm angle iron for fire grate and hotplate

Silicone for waterproofing sink

* Finished size: 3830 x 950 mm; height at centre arms 1372 mm (based on brick dimensions of 230 x 110 x 76 mm).

For materials for doors see page 415.

---

fibre cement sheeting to fit exactly into the base of the two openings and brace them. In the left-hand bay form up a 450 x 270 mm 'island' where the sink will go (adjust the size to fit your sink). Mark and then cut out the opening with a jigsaw. Form up the four sides of the opening with 100 x 50 mm timber, and nail into position.

11 Drill a 15 mm hole in the rear wall of the brickwork for a 12 mm copper water pipe to pass through. Position the copper pipe through the wall and the proposed slab.

12 Place steel reinforcing mesh in each formed up area. Mix and pour the concrete. Finish the slabs with a wooden float to produce a rough textured surface that will provide better adhesion for the tiles. Allow to cure for two to three days before stripping off the formwork.

13 Complete the two end arms and back wall, laying the final course 12 header style. Complete the two centre arms and centre

back wall to a height of fifteen courses, halfway back in each arm inserting a 230 mm length of water pipe in the joint above course 13 for the rotisserie. Add a capping of pavers to the centre arms and back.

FINISHING THE UNIT

14 Tile the surface of the two preparation areas and the front of the cooking area to make them easy to clean.

15 Have a plumber install the sink and tap. When seating the sink on the tiles, run a bead of silicone around the edge for waterproofing.

16 Using 20 x 20 mm angle iron construct a framework 930 mm long x 610 mm wide for the fire grate. Prepare mitred corners and weld them together. Place 6 x 150 mm grates across the framework and cover them with chicken-wire mesh to form a grate. Place bricks on edge at either side of the firebox slab, and rest the grate on them.

17 To construct a drop-down door for the firebox, take a 940 x 60 mm strip of aluminium and pop-rivet two hinges to it 20 mm from each end. Then rivet a 940 x 150 mm piece of aluminium to the hinges to create the 'flap' or door.

18 On the 60 mm wide strip, mark and drill two 5 mm holes in the centre and 300 mm from each end. Position the strip in front of the firebox slab. Mark the position of the holes with a pencil. Remove the strip and drill two holes into the face of the slab with a masonry bit. Plug them with plastic lugs. Screw the aluminium strip, with the 'flap' attached, to the front of the slab. Fix a latch with notches on one side of the flap to allow it to be adjusted.

19 Using 20 x 20 mm angle iron, construct a second framework 930 mm long x 610 mm

ISOMETRIC VIEW

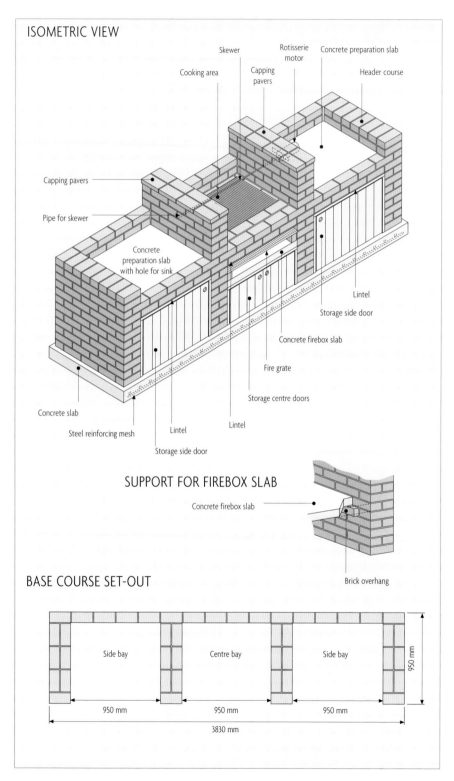

Skewer

Rotisserie motor

Concrete preparation slab

Cooking area

Capping pavers

Header course

Capping pavers

Pipe for skewer

Concrete preparation slab with hole for sink

Lintel

Storage side door

Concrete firebox slab

Fire grate

Storage centre doors

Concrete slab

Steel reinforcing mesh

Lintel

Lintel

Storage side door

SUPPORT FOR FIREBOX SLAB

Concrete firebox slab

Brick overhang

BASE COURSE SET-OUT

Side bay

Centre bay

Side bay

950 mm

950 mm

950 mm

950 mm

3830 mm

outdoor

wide for the cooking plate, again with welded mitred corners. Sit the framework on the brick ledges in the cooking area and insert 6 x 150 mm grates across the frame to form a grill. Sit the hotplate on top of these 'grill bars'.

20 Mark the position for the bracket that will hold the rotisserie motor. This is on the outside of the right-hand centre arm, with the centre of the drive shaft exactly over the hole formed by the galvanized pipe so that the removable skewer will pass through the hole and slot exactly into the drive mechanism. Drill holes and fix the bracket into position with steel bolts. Again use steel bolts to fix the notched support angle to the brickwork on the inside of the arm so it provides support for the skewer.

ADDING THE DOORS

21 Cut the outer jambs and header for the side storage areas, adjusting the lengths to fit your barbecue. Butt the header on top of the two jambs and nail them together. Position the frame in the opening.

22 Cut the inner jambs and header. Cut a 15 mm deep corner housing in each end of the header. Glue and nail the jambs to the header. Position the second frame 15 mm inside the first to create a rebate for the door. Glue and nail the two frames together.

23 Recess the jambs 10 mm from the front of the brickwork. Drill two 8 mm holes through each double jamb, and mark the points on the brickwork. Remove the framework and drill into the brickwork with a masonry bit. Plug the holes with timber or plastic plugs, and fix the frame in place with 50 mm x No. 8 screws. Nail a catch plate to the inner edge of the frame on the side where the door catch will be fixed.

24 Fit a framework to the centre storage area in the same way, but omit the catch plate. In the barbecue shown on page 412, the jambs were inset further and made thicker to accommodate the unusual hinges.

25 The side doors are 614 mm high by 824 mm long, and the centre doors each 364 mm high by 410 mm long. Measure the openings in your barbecue, allow for a 3 mm gap all round and adjust the door sizes as necessary. Cut the shiplap panelling slightly longer than will be required. Then cut the top, bottom and side rails to length.

26 Butt-joint the rails together with the bottom rail flush with the bottom of the side rails and the top rail 50 mm down from the top. Glue and nail them together. Using 30 x 2 mm lost-head nails, fix the panelling to the framework. Punch in the nails and fill the holes with filler. Square up the ends of the panelling, and trim it to the correct length.

27 Fix the hinges, latches and handles to the doors.

MATERIALS FOR DOORS*

PART	MATERIAL	LENGTH	NO.
Outer jamb (side area)	75 x 38 mm WRC	650 mm	4
Outer header (side area)	75 x 38 mm WRC	950 mm	2
Inner jamb (side area)	75 x 38 mm WRC	635 mm	4
Inner header (side area)	75 x 38 mm WRC	890 mm	2
Outer jamb (centre area)	75 x 38 mm WRC	400 mm	2
Outer header (centre area)	75 x 38 mm WRC	950 mm	1
Inner jamb (centre area)	75 x 38 mm WRC	385 mm	2
Inner header (centre area)	75 x 38 mm WRC	890 mm	1
Catch plate (side area)	50 x 16 mm WRC	620 mm	2
Side rail (side door)	75 x 50 mm WRC	614 mm	4
Top/bottom rail (side door)	75 x 50 mm WRC	692 mm	4
Side rail (centre door)	75 x 50 mm WRC	364 mm	4
Top/bottom rail (centre door)	75 x 50 mm WRC	278 mm	4
Panelling (side door)	110 x 10 mm shiplap	614 mm	16
Panelling (centre door)	110 x 10 mm shiplap	364 mm	8

Other: 30 x 2 mm galvanized lost-head nails; 50 mm x No. 8 screws; twelve timber fixing plugs; twelve 90 x 10 mm screws; eight door hinges; four bolts or latches; four handles; abrasive paper; filler; finish of choice.

* Western red cedar (WRC) is used for all frame components. Timber sizes given are nominal (see page 199). Adjust the lengths to fit your structure.

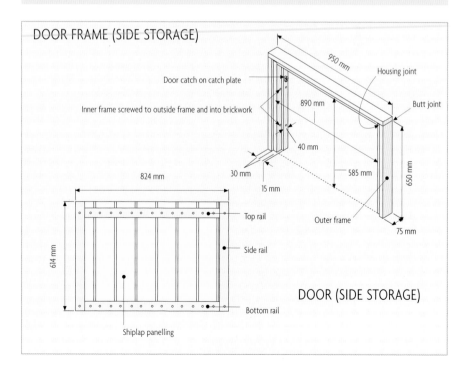

DOOR FRAME (SIDE STORAGE)

Door catch on catch plate
Inner frame screwed to outside frame and into brickwork
950 mm
Housing joint
Butt joint
890 mm
40 mm
30 mm
15 mm
585 mm
650 mm
Outer frame
75 mm

824 mm
614 mm
Top rail
Side rail
Bottom rail
Shiplap panelling

DOOR (SIDE STORAGE)

BARBECUE WITH DECORATIVE CHIMNEY

This neat gas-fired barbecue incorporates a non-functional chimney but requires only basic bricklaying skills. The storage area is topped with slate and closed with timber doors.

THE DESIGN

This barbecue is built with extruded bricks and ironed joints to accommodate gas burners that are fuelled by natural gas. There is a non-functional chimney, included for decorative effect, and a storage space below the cooking area is closed with double timber doors. The firebox is paved with slate. A custom-made stainless steel cover is placed over the gas burners when they are not in use.

BRICKLAYING

1 Mark out and prepare the 1650 x 800 mm area for the concrete slab and the 600 x 400 mm slab area for the chimney (see pages 408–409).

2 Following the bricklaying instructions on pages 409–410 and the set-out diagram on page 418, lay three courses, which includes the front, sides, back and chimney, tying in the chimney at the third course (and every third course thereafter).

3 Lay the next six courses for the sides, back and chimney, but not the front, as you need to create the opening for the storage area. At the end of the ninth course, place the 1200 mm lintel across the opening at the front to create a header above the doorway. Lay course number 10, including across the front.

4 Lay the next three courses, but again leave the front open to create the firebox.

5 Construct the remaining fifteen courses of the chimney. To create a flue opening, leave out courses 14 and 15 at the front of the chimney and place the 500 mm lintel across

MATERIALS*

Concrete for slab: 0.2 m³ ready-mixed, or cement, sand and 10 mm aggregate
100 x 50 mm timber for formwork
Timber pegs and nails
Steel reinforcing mesh: 1500 x 700 mm
Tie wire
Portland cement, bricklayers sand, lime and plasticizer for mortar
400 bricks (extruded bricks were used for the barbecue shown opposite)
25 paving bricks
Flat steel lintel 1200 x 90 x 8 mm
Flat steel lintel 500 x 90 x 8 mm
Five pieces of slate 300 x 110 mm
Stainless steel cover lid
Five-burner gas unit
Natural gas fuel line, stopcock and pressure regulator
Two 450 mm lengths of steel angle to support gas unit
Four 50 mm steel bolts

* Finished size: 1550 x 710 mm without chimney; height of arms 1175 mm; chimney 590 x 350 mm and 2400 mm high (based on brick measurements of 230 x 110 x 76 mm). For door materials see below.

MATERIALS FOR DOORS*

PART	MATERIAL	LENGTH	WIDTH	NO.
Jamb	100 x 38 mm WRC	515 mm		2
Door stile	100 x 38 mm WRC	530 mm		4
Door rail	150 x 38 mm WRC	520 mm		4
Door panel	6 mm waterproof plywood	255 mm	340 mm	2

Other: Epoxy adhesive; abrasive paper; 3 m of beading; four plastic plugs; 25 x 1 mm panel pins; 50 mm x No. 8 screws; four hinges and screws; two latches and screws; two handles; finish of choice.

* Western red cedar (WRC) is used for all timber components. Timber sizes given are nominal (see box on page 199). Adjust the lengths to suit your structure.

TOOLS

- Bricklaying tools (see page 409)
- Circular saw
- Drill and drill bits
- Screwdriver
- Cork sanding block
- Router (optional)
- Chisels
- Tenon saw
- Sash cramps

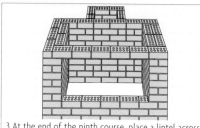

3 At the end of the ninth course, place a lintel across the opening and lay course number 10.

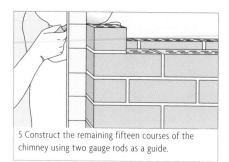

5 Construct the remaining fifteen courses of the chimney using two gauge rods as a guide.

the opening. You will find it easier when laying the upper courses of the chimney if you brace two gauge rods in place and follow them rather than string lines. Constantly check with a spirit level as you work to make sure that the chimney is vertical.

6 To cap the holes in the top of the extruded bricks, use brick pavers as the final

On either side of this barbecue a brick wall with two arms supports a slatted seat that can double as a preparation area. The surrounding area is surfaced with clay pavers laid in a herringbone pattern.

ISOMETRIC VIEW

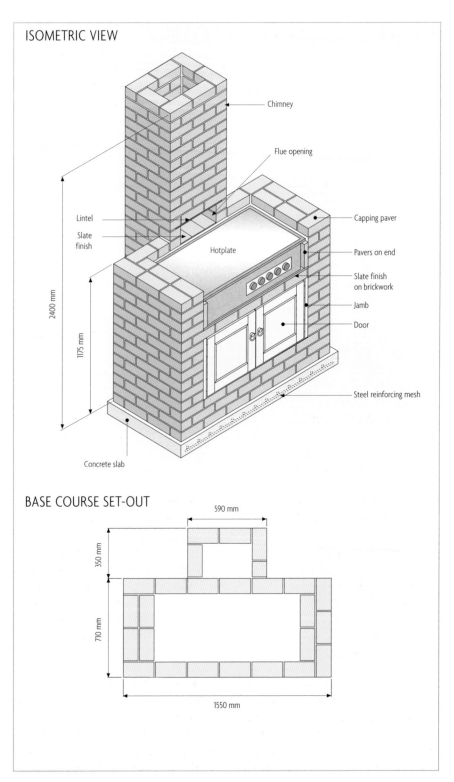

Chimney

Flue opening

Lintel

Slate finish

Hotplate

2400 mm

1175 mm

Capping paver

Pavers on end

Slate finish on brickwork

Jamb

Door

Steel reinforcing mesh

Concrete slab

BASE COURSE SET-OUT

590 mm

350 mm

710 mm

1550 mm

MORTISE AND TENON JOINT FOR DOOR

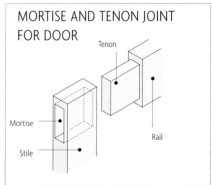

Tenon

Mortise

Stile

Rail

course on the unit. Alternatively, you can fill the holes with mortar or cover them with tiles or slate.

7 Using steel bolts, fix a 450 mm length of steel angle to each side of the firebox to support the gas unit. The precise positioning of the angle will depend on the size of your gas unit. In this barbecue the angle was positioned 230 mm below the bottom of the flue opening and waterproof adhesive was used to glue paving bricks onto each piece of steel angle, to provide extra support for the gas unit.

8 To cap the holes in the extruded bricks above the storage area and at the base of the flue, mortar pieces of slate in place.

ADDING THE DOORS

9 Cut the jambs to length and fix them to each side of the opening by drilling holes in the brickwork. Plug the holes with plastic plugs before fixing the jambs with screws.

10 Measure the width of the opening inside the frame, subtract 10 mm to allow a 3 mm gap between the doors and the jambs. Measure the height of the opening, subtract 6 mm to allow a 3 mm gap top and bottom. Divide the width by 2 to find the size of each door.

outdoor

11 Cut four stiles 20 mm longer than the height. Cut two top and two bottom rails 20 mm longer than the width. Mark the overall height on the stiles.

12 Prepare mortise and tenon joints with tenons on the ends of the rails and mortises through the stiles inside the height marks. Cut them with a tenon saw and chisel. Glue the joints together with epoxy adhesive and hold them tight with sash cramps. Check them for square, and adjust as required. Leave to dry. Saw off the protruding tenon.

13 Sand the frame. Cut a 10 mm wide and 12 mm deep rebate around the inside face with a router, and square the corners with a chisel.

14 Cut and fit the door panels into the rebates. Cover the join on the outside face with beading. Nail it in position with 25 x 1 mm panel pins. Cut the stiles flush with the rails and plane the doors to fit (allowing a 3 mm clearance all round).

15 Fit hinges to each door. Fit handles and latches; attach the doors.

TO FINISH

16 Install the gas burner unit into the firebox area by sitting it on the paving bricks or directly onto the steel angle. Connect the gas and light the barbecue.

17 Make a protective stainless steel lid to cover the gas burners as well as the firebox area or have one made to your specifications at an engineering, sheet metal or air-conditioning workshop. The cover should have a reasonable pitch so that water will run off it.

PIT BARBECUE

This is a version of the traditional campfire. The fire is contained within a brick pit set in a mosaic-paved square. Food is cooked on a campfire unit that fits into a pipe in the base of the pit.

DESIGN

The fire is contained within a pit that is constructed from bricks laid in a circle to create a 'well', capped with pool coping stones to form a neat edge. The pit is set within a square of pavers with mosaic infill.

The food is cooked on a steel plate that is supported on a steel pole. This also holds a separate grill and a hook for a billycan. All can be rotated around the pole and over the fire as required. Once the cooking is completed, the pole can be lifted out, the fire stoked and the guests can enjoy a contained open fire.

Before beginning this project, check with your local council about the use of open fires outdoors.

CREATING THE PIT

1 Decide how to drain the pit so it doesn't fill with water. If the base is above other points in the yard, run a pipe from the base to a low spot. If you have sandy soil, make holes in the slab for water to soak through, or you can make a lid for the pit.

2 Drive a peg into the centre of the pit area. Hammer a nail into the top of the peg with 20 mm protruding. Loop string around the nail, stretch it taut for 650 mm, loop it around a stick and scribe a circle on the soil.

3 Excavate the circle to a depth of 450 mm, keeping the sides vertical. With a club hammer drive 300 mm of galvanized pipe into the centre of the excavated hole. It should be slightly larger than the barbecue pole, which needs a firm but loose fit so that it can be withdrawn when not required. Check the fit before concreting the base slab. Make sure the top of the pipe is exactly 100 mm above ground level, the same as the top of the concrete. This pipe can also provide drainage in sandy soils.

4 Lay steel reinforcing mesh over a peg and use a taut string and permanent marking pen to scribe a circle with 600 mm radius on the mesh. Cut the circle with steel mesh cutters or an angle grinder. Position the mesh on bar

TOOLS

- Bricklaying tools (see page 409)
- Hacksaw for cutting galvanized pipe

chairs in the base of the pit and make sure that it is clear of the centre pipe.

5 Concrete the base slab (see section on concrete on page 409), finishing the concrete just below the top of the pipe. Check pipe is vertical. Angle the slab slightly towards the sides where the drainage outlets will be. Allow to cure for two to three days.

BRICKWORK

6 Using a taut string and a green masonry pencil, scribe a 450 mm radius circle onto the base slab. Using this as a guide, lay out the first course of brickwork (see section on bricklaying on pages 409–410). Insert drainage pipe between the bricks, stopping at the scribed line. Excavate any necessary trenches and complete laying the pipe.

7 Mix the mortar and lay the bricks. Wide vertical joints will be created in the back of the circle, but they can be filled with mortar. Alternatively, you can cut all the bricks in half. Laying halves around a circle makes jointing easier. Lay four courses of bricks to complete the pit. Allow to dry.

8 Backfill to the top of three courses with a porous material such as aggregate or sand for good drainage.

THE SURROUND

9 Form up the surrounding square with timber formwork with its top 15 mm below the top of the bricks to ensure that run-off is away from the pit. Peg and nail the formwork into position, and then check for square by measuring the diagonals. If it is square, the diagonals should be the same. Position four strips of steel mesh, 200 x 1450 mm, in the corners to give the slab strength.

10 Pour the concrete so it is level with the top of the formwork. Finish the surface with a wood float.

The pit barbecue is bordered by an expanse of basketweave-patterned paving so that people can gather around while the cooking is in progress.

outdoor

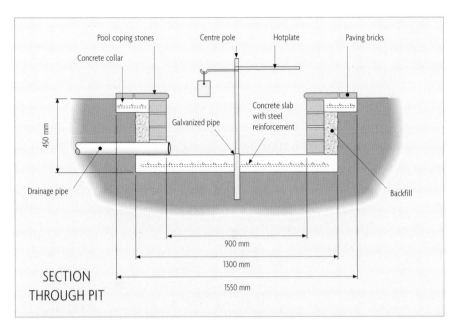

SECTION THROUGH PIT

Labels on diagram: Pool coping stones, Concrete collar, Centre pole, Hotplate, Paving bricks, Concrete slab with steel reinforcement, Galvanized pipe, Drainage pipe, Backfill

Dimensions: 450 mm, 900 mm, 1300 mm, 1550 mm

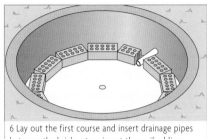

6 Lay out the first course and insert drainage pipes between the bricks, stopping at the scribed line.

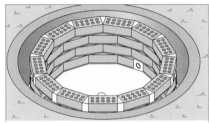

7 Lay four courses of bricks, filling the wide joints in the back of the circle with mortar.

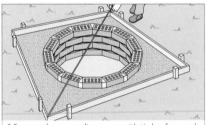

9 Form up the surrounding square with timber formwork and check for square by measuring the diagonals.

MATERIALS*

Concrete for base slab: 0.16 m³ ready-mixed, or cement, sand and 10 mm aggregate

Concrete for top collar 0.2 m³

Steel reinforcing mesh: 600 x 600 mm and four pieces 1450 x 200 mm

Bar chairs

Portland cement, bricklayers sand, lime and plasticizer for mortar

60 bricks

25 pool coping stones

50 paving bricks

Packing sand for backfilling the wall and beneath the paving

Aggregate for drainage

Permanent marking pen and green masonry pencil

Galvanized pipe 300 mm long to seat hotplate pole neatly

Pole, grill and hotplate plus hook and billycan

50 mm galvanized pipe for drainage

Timber formwork, pegs and nails for top collar slab

* Finished size: 1550 mm diameter and 350 mm deep.

13 To create the mosaic design in the corners, break up several paving bricks with a club hammer. Spread mortar in each corner. Position the pieces and tamp them down to the correct level with a straight edge held against the coping stones and the pavers. This ensures the correct slope.

14 After the mosaic pieces have set in the base mortar, grout the joints with a 6:1 sand:cement mortar mix. Sponge-clean the surface of the coping stones, pavers and mosaic pieces. Allow to dry.

11 Position the coping stones around the pit, adjusting the spacing to fit whole stones if possible. Scribe a line at the back of the copers as a laying guide. Remove the stones, mix mortar to provide a bed and lay them.

12 Set up string lines around the edge of the outside square. Spread a mortar bed and mortar the joints of the pavers as they are laid. Allow the coping stones and the pavers to dry.

STONE BARBECUE

This brilliant barbecue with central hotplate is built from shaped sandstone blocks. The construction is not difficult, but cutting the stones to shape is very time-consuming.

TOOLS

- Bricklaying tools (see page 409)
- Mobile wet saw and 300 mm masonry blade
- Sliding bevel
- Jigsaw
- Carborundum stone

DESIGN

Although the curved design of this structure requires careful stone cutting, the operation of the actual barbecue is simple. The central hotplate has an area of 930 x 700 mm, originally heated by a wood fire. Both the hotplate and plate for the firebox base are removable. A functioning chimney opens into the firebox immediately below the hotplate. The walls and chimney, which is tapered to reflect the curve of the wall, are constructed of rock-faced sandstone blocks that have been hand-cut and faced.

The barbecue has two curved wings, which enclose a court with sandstone flagging laid in a stretcher pattern. The ends of the two wings and the two centre walls are faced with blocks to give a buttress finish. The tops of these wings and the curved walls are capped with overhanging slabs of sandstone.

SETTING OUT

1 Lay the 3600 mm length of timber on the ground for the front of the barbecue. Drive in pegs either side of it to fix it in position. Hammer a 100 mm nail into the exact centre of the timber, so that it projects 50 mm.

2 In the 2000 mm length of timber drill a 5 mm diameter hole, 100 mm from one end. Locate and mark two positions 1300 and 1700 mm from the drill hole. At each mark hammer a 100 mm nail through the timber.

3 Place the hole over the centre nail of the fixed length of timber and rotate the 2000 mm timber in a semicircle so that the protruding nails scratch lines in the ground to indicate the front and back of the footings respectively. Leave the fixed board in position.

4 Excavate 300 mm deep trenches for the footings: the 400 mm wide curved wall plus 300 x 1100 mm at the back for the chimney and 700 x 300 mm for each of the centre arms (see diagram on page 425). Lay the trench mesh. To bend the straight mesh around the curve, cut it in several places, kink it around the curve and re-tie it. Fill the trenches with concrete and set for two to three days.

5 Take the nails out of the 2000 mm timber and mark two new locations at 1400 and 1600 mm from the drill hole. Rotate the timber around the surface of the concrete, scribing two lines with a masonry pencil. Use these two curves as a guide when laying the blocks. Also mark guidelines for the centre walls and chimney. Adjust how far the curved arms project by moving the fixed timber in as desired (in the barbecue opposite, the timber was moved in 150 mm for a courtyard depth of 1250 mm). Fix it firmly in place and leave it at least until the end blocks have been laid.

CUTTING THE STONE

6 Cut all the blocks for the curved wall to shape before you begin laying. Begin by

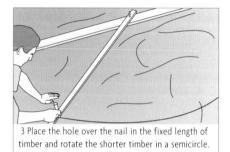
3 Place the hole over the nail in the fixed length of timber and rotate the shorter timber in a semicircle.

making a template of the required shape. Lay a 600 x 400 mm piece of plywood on the concrete footing over the drawn lines. Rotate the timber to scribe the curved lines onto the plywood. Again using the rotating timber, mark the lines for the ends of the blocks square to the curve and 500 mm apart, so that a complete block shape is created. Cut out the shape with a jigsaw.

7 Prepare a good solid bench (there should be no bounce) at a height that will allow you to stand up straight with an undressed stone beneath the stone being cut. Ensure the surface and blocks are clear of dust and grit.

8 Place the template on top of a block of stone and mark the shape with a green masonry pencil. Using a power wet saw with a 300 mm diamond-tipped blade, cut along the two end lines.

9 Square two lines from the marked curves down each cut end of the block. Turn the block over and place the template so it is in line with the vertical end lines before marking around the template again. Use a club hammer and bolster chisel to cut the curved faces. Turn the block over regularly and work back gradually to the marked lines.

CHIMNEY TAPER

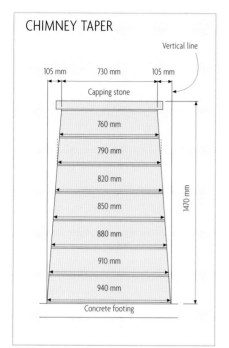

Vertical line

105 mm · 730 mm · 105 mm

Capping stone

760 mm

790 mm

820 mm

850 mm

880 mm

910 mm

940 mm

1470 mm

Concrete footing

Originally designed for wood firing with metal plates for the hotplate and base of the firebox, this barbecue has been converted to natural gas.

MATERIALS*

Concrete for slab: 0.8 m³ ready-mixed, or cement, sand and 10 mm aggregate

Trench mesh: 7 m

Tie wire and bar chairs

Two 100 x 50 mm straight timbers 3600 mm and 2000 mm long

Timber formwork with pegs and nails for slab

Sixty sandstone blocks 500 x 200 x 140 mm

Plywood for block template

Ten sandstone cappers 500 x 380 x 50 mm and two 800 x 300 x 50 mm

Portland off-white cement, white bricklayers, sand, lime and plasticizer for mortar

Steel plate 800 x 400 x 10 mm

Steel rod 200 x 8 mm diameter

Non-silicone water seal to protect stone

Two steel plates 930 x 700 x 12 mm

Copper pipe or steel bolts

* Finished size: 3320 mm wide and 1675 mm deep; chimney is 1470 mm high.

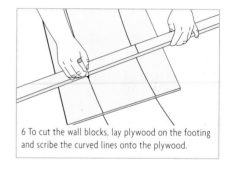

6 To cut the wall blocks, lay plywood on the footing and scribe the curved lines onto the plywood.

each block. This work must be done carefully and cannot be hurried.

LAYING THE STONE

10 Mix the mortar using white sand, lime and off-white cement, matching the colour of the stone as closely as possible. Use a plasticizer if you want to make the mortar more pliable (see step 13 on pages 409–410).

11 Start laying the first course at one end by putting a bed of mortar on the footing inside the marked curve. Lay the blocks to the centre of the curve, making sure they are

Remove the sharp edges with the carborundum stone as you go. Cut sufficient blocks to complete the curved wall. It takes

a professional stonemason 40–50 minutes to complete each stone, so don't be surprised if you have to spend an hour or more cutting

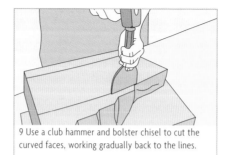

8 Place the plywood template on top of a block of stone and mark the shape with a green masonry pencil.

9 Use a club hammer and bolster chisel to cut the curved faces, working gradually back to the lines.

19 When laying the face blocks, place wedges in the notched areas to prevent movement while the mortar is drying.

vertical and level. Tap each into the correct position with the handle end of a club hammer, a rubber mallet or a block of 50 x 50 mm hardwood.

12 Lay from the other end to the centre. This means that any cut blocks in each course will occur in the centre, which will eventually be hidden by the firebox and

chimney. Complete the first three courses.

13 Repeat for the fourth course, but leave out the centre two blocks to form the flue opening and to tie in the chimney. Using a circular saw with a masonry blade, cut a notch (25 x 25 mm) along the top edge of the third course of the flue opening. This notch will support the firebox plate and

provide a seal to protect the stone from the smoke and soot.

THE CHIMNEY

14 Cut the blocks for the chimney in the same way as those for the curved wall. The chimney tapers 100 mm from vertical on each side when measured from the base to the top (see diagram opposite). To achieve this, the outside end of the end blocks for each course tapers 15 mm. Set a sliding bevel at the appropriate angle to taper 15 mm for every 200 mm of block height. Using the bevel, mark a cutting line. Cut the blocks for the chimney, and then dry-stack them to make sure that you are happy with the fit and the taper.

15 When you are satisfied, mortar the blocks for four courses in position. The first three courses butt against the curved wall, and the fourth is tied into it with two blocks.

16 Use the block template to mark the shape on the steel lintel and take it to a shop that does oxyacetylene cutting. Position the lintel on the overlapping blocks to create a flue opening and support the upper courses of the chimney. The lintel should be recessed 50 mm so that a ledge is left to support the hotplate.

17 Lay the remaining three courses of the chimney.

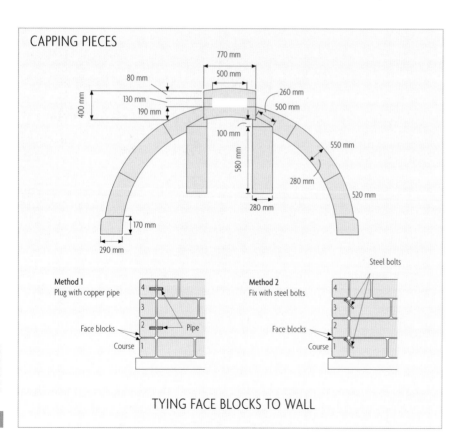

CAPPING PIECES

TYING FACE BLOCKS TO WALL

TO FINISH

18 Using the remaining stone blocks, construct the two straight arms in the centre. Butt the first two courses against the curved wall. Before laying the third course, cut a 25 x 25 mm notch from the inside top edge of each block as described in step 13. Repeat for the fourth course to accommodate the hotplate, and then lay the fourth course.

19 Lay the sixteen face blocks on the ends of the curved walls and centre arms. Those in the third and fourth courses of the arms are notched (50 x 25 mm) for the fireplate and hotplate. The face blocks are simply butted on. If you want to key them into the wall, drill 13 mm holes, which are then plugged with 12 mm copper water pipe, or you can drill holes at a 45-degree angle and secure the blocks with 125 mm long steel bolts. Place small timber wedges in the notched areas to prevent movement while the mortar is drying out.

20 Cut the capping pieces to cover the curved wall and centre arms. To cut the curved pieces, make a template for the capping pieces as in step 6, but make the capping pieces 250 mm wide. The two chimney capping pieces are each cut from one solid piece of 800 x 300 mm stone, curved at front and back as for the curved wall blocks.

21 Because sandstone is porous, it is best to seal it before you use the barbecue in order to protect it from grease and smoke stains. Check the sealant manufacturer's directions and conditions of use before applying it.

22 Allow the mortar to set for at least two days, remove the wedges and insert the fireplate and hotplate.

LAYOUT AND FOOTING PLAN

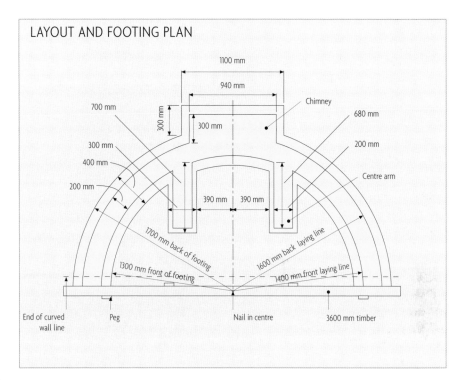

FRONT VIEW

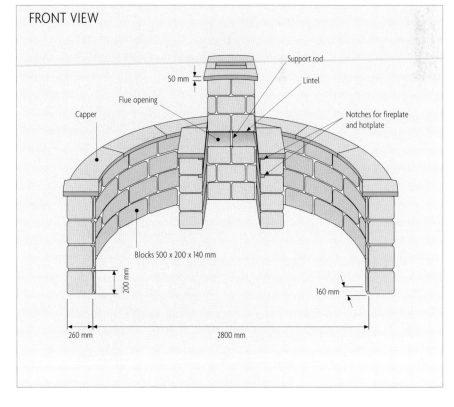

garden structures

garden structures

CHOOSING MATERIALS

Materials for your garden structures should be chosen carefully so that they will withstand exposure to all types of conditions and last for many years.

TIMBER

Many hardwoods are very durable and can be used for garden structures, but be sure they are well seasoned so they don't shrink or warp. Well-seasoned hardwood, however, can be difficult to work.

Pressure-treated softwood, usually pine, is generally most suitable for outdoor use. These timbers, which have a greenish look, are readily available. They have been treated with a compound of copper, chromium and arsenic (CCA) to withstand attack by insects, fungi and damp.

Treated softwoods come in a range of hazard levels from 1 to 5 (see page 370), with 5 being the most resistant and so also the most hazardous. Always take precautions when using treated timbers:

- Always wear gloves.
- Wear goggles and a dust mask when machining, sawing or sanding.
- Ensure there is good ventilation if you are working indoors.
- Wash your face and hands before eating.
- Never use treated timber for heating or cooking as the smoke and ash are toxic.

When treated timber is cut, planed or sanded, the broken surface should be resealed. Brush-on preservative is available.

When you are storing timber, keep it off the ground to prevent it being affected by moisture. Keep it in a covered area or under a tarpaulin to protect it from rain.

HARDWARE

Always use fastenings that will not corrode, usually galvanized ones. Use stainless steel fasteners in areas exposed to sea spray.

ERECTING POSTS

1 For 90 x 90 mm posts, dig holes 200 x 200 mm and 600 mm deep. In damp areas, dig 150 mm deeper and place 150 mm of coarse gravel in the bottom.

2 Stand the first post in the hole, lining up the face with a string line. Use a spirit level to check it is vertical both ways. Prop it upright with two timbers nailed to adjoining faces 900 mm from ground level. Stand the other posts in their holes the same way.

3 Mix concrete and pour it around the posts, packing it down with a piece of scrap timber. As soon as you finish packing the concrete, check the post hasn't moved. Let the concrete set for 24 hours and remove the props.

4 Find the lowest post and measure up it the required height. Mark this point and then transfer this level to the other posts.

- The most accurate way to transfer a level is with a water level. Fill a 6 m length of 12 mm clear plastic tubing with water and remove any air bubbles. It may be easier to see the water if you add a little food colouring. Hold one end of the tubing to the established mark and the other to the required point. Move the tubing up or down until the water level lines up with the established mark, then transfer the height of the water to the second point.

- A level can also be transferred over a straight line using a straight timber and spirit level. Drive a nail partway into the established point, and rest one end of the timber on it. Place the spirit level on the timber and raise the other end against the next post until the timber is level. Mark the position of the bottom of the timber.

5 Square a line around each post and cut it off square.

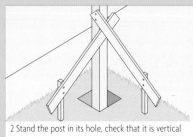
2 Stand the post in its hole, check that it is vertical and nail props to adjoining faces.

4 Rest the timber on top of the nail in the lowest post and raise the other end until it is level.

FINISHING THE STRUCTURE

Punch all nails below the surface and fill nail and screw holes with an exterior filler. Allow it to set and sand it smooth.

All timbers used outdoors need a protective finish to withstand the elements. Exterior-grade paint or clear finishes are suitable.

LATTICE SCREEN

Lattice panels are supported here by a post and rail frame. The frame can be fixed to a wall at one end, or both ends can be free-standing.

THE POSTS

1 On the front edge of the wall post mark out and cut the housings for the beam and rails (see diagram on page 430 and box on page 432).

2 Mark the centre of the outer face 300 mm from each end. If the wall is timber framed, adjust the marks to suit the framework. Using a 10 mm bit, drill the holes.

3 Hold the wall post against the wall. If the wall is brick, position the post so the fixings won't go into the mortar joints. Ensure the post is vertical. Run a pencil down the edge of the post so you can see if it moves. Drill through the holes into the wall, using a 10 mm masonry bit or a 6 mm bit for a timber frame. Insert a coach screw with washer, or a masonry anchor, into each hole.

4 Measure 5 m from the wall post and drive in a peg. Nail a clout nail into the wall post and a second into the top of the peg. Tie string to one nail and pull it tight to the other one; tie it off. To check that the line is square to the wall, measure along the wall 4 m and along the line 3 m. If the diagonal is 5 m, the string is square to the wall.

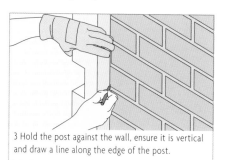

3 Hold the post against the wall, ensure it is vertical and draw a line along the edge of the post.

The closely spaced lattice makes this screen ideal when privacy is required. Here it is used to separate the living area of the garden from the driveway and the neighbouring house beyond.

MATERIALS*

PART	MATERIAL	FINISHED LENGTH	WIDTH	NO.
Beam	140 x 45 mm treated pine	4500 mm		1
Post**	90 x 90 mm treated pine	3000 mm		4
Wall post	90 x 45 mm treated pine	2090 mm		1
Rail	90 x 45 mm treated pine	2445 mm		2
Short rail	90 x 45 mm treated pine	1245 mm		2
Top trim	90 x 20 mm treated pine	4500 mm		1
Vertical trim	90 x 20 mm treated pine	1910 mm		4
Bottom trim	90 x 20 mm treated pine	1110 mm		2
Short trim	90 x 20 mm treated pine	1065 mm		1
Wall post trim	45 x 20 mm treated pine	1910 mm		1
Lattice panel	diagonal lattice	2000 mm	1200 mm	3
Arch panel	diagonal lattice	900 mm	350 mm	1

Other: Two 125 x 10 mm coach screws and washers or two 125 x 10 mm masonry anchors; 25 x 2.6 mm clout nails; 75 x 3 mm galvanized lost-head nails; 65 x 3 mm galvanized lost-head nails; 50 x 2.6 mm galvanized flat-head nails; timber peg; concrete; eight 1800 mm long timbers for props; abrasive paper.

* Finished size: 4500 mm long and 2090 mm high. Both the length and height can be adjusted as required. Use treated pine lattice.

**Use 4 rated treated pine. Length may vary according to the amount of slope on the site. All posts must finish at the same level as the wall post.

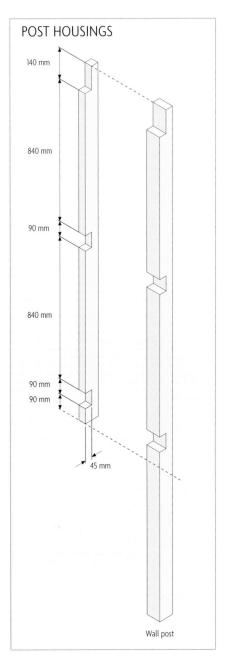

POST HOUSINGS

140 mm

840 mm

90 mm

840 mm

90 mm

90 mm

45 mm

Wall post

5 Along the string measure 1200 mm from the wall and dig the post hole (see box on page 428). Dig the second centred at 2400 mm, the third at 3300 mm and the fourth at 4455 mm. Erect each post so the face lines up with the string. Cut them off level with the top of the wall post.

6 On each post, mark out housings as on the wall post, measuring from the top of the post. Check they are on the same side as on the wall post. Cut the housings, starting at the top.

RAILS AND LATTICE

7 Cut the beam to length and lift it into the housings on top of the posts. Hold it to each post with a G-cramp. Skew-nail through the beam into each post with three 75 mm nails.

7 Cut the beam to length and use G-cramps to hold it in the housings on the top of the posts.

8 Cut the rails so the ends are flush with the posts at the opening and insert them into their housings. Skew two 75 mm nails into each post.

9 Place a lattice panel on the frame with the edges against the wall and flush with the top of the beam and the lower edge of the bottom rail. Fix it with 50 mm

flat-head nails at 200 mm spacings all round. Fix the other two panels so that the edge beside the opening is in the centre of the post.

10 Mark out the arch on the arch panel

outdoor

FRAMEWORK

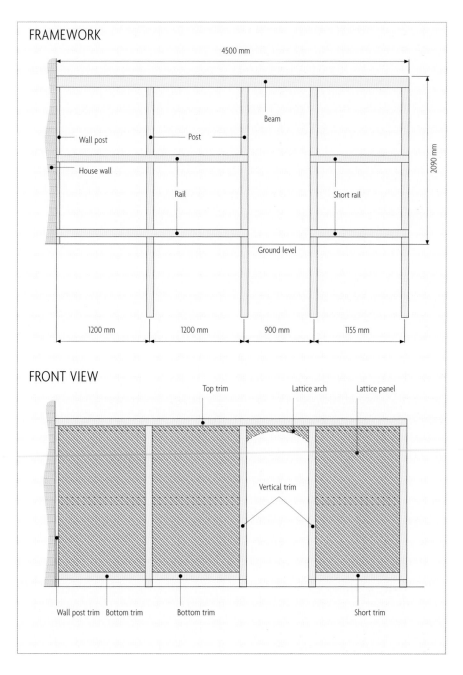

4500 mm

2090 mm

Beam

Wall post

Post

House wall

Rail

Short rail

Ground level

1200 mm   1200 mm   900 mm   1155 mm

FRONT VIEW

Top trim   Lattice arch   Lattice panel

Vertical trim

Wall post trim   Bottom trim   Bottom trim   Short trim

TOOLS

- Tape measure and pencil
- Marking gauge
- Square
- Tenon saw or jigsaw
- Circular saw (optional)
- Chisel: 25 mm
- Spirit level
- Electric drill
- Drill bits: 6 mm, 10 mm*
- Screwdriver
- Socket spanner (for coach screws)
- String line
- Post-hole shovel
- Water level (optional)
- Five G-cramps
- Hammer
- Cork sanding block

* Use a 10 mm masonry bit if you are fixing to a brick wall.

LATTICE ARCH

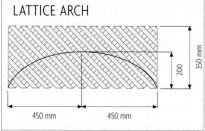

350 mm

200

450 mm   450 mm

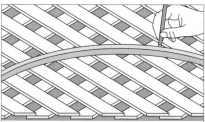

10 Bend a thin piece of timber or tubing to indicate the curve, and draw the curve onto the lattice.

(see diagram right) and use thin timber or tubing to draw the curve. Cut out the arch with a jigsaw or tenon saw, and sand the edge smooth. Fix it on the frame with the top flush with the top of the beam.

11 Fix the top trim over the lattice, with the top flush with the lattice edge, using 65 mm nails 300 mm apart. Fix a vertical trim over each post, flush with the sides of the posts. Add the wall post trim and the three bottom trims.

CUTTING A HOUSING

To mark out a housing, measure to the required point and square a line across the face. Then measure up the width of the housing and square a second line across. Continue these lines down each edge, set a marking gauge to the required depth and mark both edges between the lines. Or, if you are using a power saw, set it to cut the required depth.

Cut down the shoulders on the waste side of the marked lines to the required depth. Then make a number of relief cuts between the shoulders to the same depth. Space them about 6 mm apart. Use a 25 mm chisel and hammer to remove the waste

and clean out the housing, levelling and smoothing the bottom.

To cut a housing at the end of a timber, cut down the shoulder to the required depth, then cut along the timber from the end.

To make a housing, cut down the shoulders at either end and then make relief cuts between them.

When you use a power saw, the cut does not finish square to the surface it is running along, so finish the cut with a handsaw, keeping the saw square to the end of the cut. Clean and smooth the housing with a chisel if required.

Use a chisel and hammer to remove the waste, levelling the bottom of the housing.

GARDEN DIVIDER

Supported by two posts, this divider or screen consists of a panel with vertical battens attached to horizontal rails. A superstructure with cross-pieces placed over a pair of beams adds interest.

TOOLS

- Tape measure and pencil
- Square
- Marking gauge
- Tenon saw or jigsaw
- Circular saw (optional)
- Two 200 mm G-cramps
- Chisel: 25 mm
- Electric drill
- Drill bits: 3.5 mm, 12 mm long-shank speed bit
- Screwdriver and hammer
- Post-hole auger
- Spirit level
- Sliding bevel
- Spanner: 10 mm

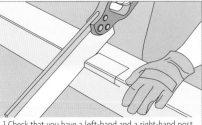

1 Check that you have a left-hand and a right-hand post, and cut the stopped housings for the bottom rails.

THE PANEL

1 With the ends of the posts level, clamp them together. Mark and cut one of the housings for the beam (see page 434 and box above). Roll the posts over and cut the opposite housings. Remove the cramps and roll each post in so two housings are facing and aligned. Clamp the posts together. Mark the through housing for the top rail and the stopped housing for the bottom rail. Check

4 Fix each batten, working into the middle with the spacing even and the batten against the spacer.

you have a left-hand post and a right-hand post. Cut the housings. Test the fit with the rails.

2 Cut the battens, making sure the ends are square so the joints will fit.

3 On a flat surface, lay the top rail on its edge and place a 45 mm thick timber as packing against the side of the rail. This will keep the battens at the correct height until they are fixed to the rail. Sit the bottom rail on the surface on its face, 1325 mm from the top rail and parallel to it.

4 Square a line across the face of the top rail 100 mm in from one end. Line up the edge of the first batten with the squared line, and drill two 3.5 mm pilot holes through the rail into the end of the batten. Insert a screw in each hole. Place a 90 mm wide timber spacer against the first batten and push the second up tight against it. Fix it to the top rail. In the same way, fix two battens at the other end of the top rail. Then, fix a third batten on each end. Continue, fixing one batten at a time on either end, working to the middle. Ensure the spacing is even and the batten is hard against the spacer before screwing it in place. As timber thicknesses vary slightly, check the space left when you get to the last few battens and adjust any gaps slightly..

5 Remove the packing piece and push the bottom rail up against the top rail, ensuring the ends are flush. Transfer the batten positions to the bottom rail by running a pencil down both sides of each batten.

6 Measure 70 mm from the bottom of each end batten. Slide the bottom rail down until the bottom edge lines up with this point. Position each batten and drill two 3.5 mm pilot holes through each, 85 mm and 145 mm from the bottom of the batten. Insert a screw in each hole.

ASSEMBLING THE FRAME

7 Lay the posts on the ground so the bases are close to where the holes will be. Ensure the rail housings face each other and the bottom housing is up. Place the panel upside down on the posts, with the bottom rail on top, and push each rail into its housing.

The beam and cross-piece superstructure gives an architectural quality to this elegant divider. The spacing of the battens can be altered to suit the amount of privacy required.

Check that the front edge of the top rail (the down side) is flush with the face of the post. Drill two pilot holes through the top rail into each post at an angle, and screw the rail to the posts. Fix the bottom rail into the housings in the same way, with two screws skewed through the rail into each post.

8 Dig 200 x 200 mm post holes 700 mm deep. Put 100 mm of coarse gravel in each.

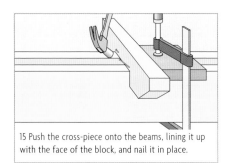

15 Push the cross-piece onto the beams, lining it up with the face of the block, and nail it in place.

With a helper, slide the assembly into the holes. Hold the posts vertical and use a spirit level to see if the rails are level: add more gravel under the lower post until they are. Use timber props to hold each post vertical. Fill the holes with concrete, and use scrap timber to pack it tight. Allow it to set.

9 On both ends of the beams, measure 200 mm from the bottom corner and 115 mm up at the end to create a splayed end. Cut the splay.

10 On the inside face of each beam, measure 315 mm from each end and square a line across the face. Lift the beams into the housings and line up the mark with the outer edge of the post. Clamp them in place. Using a 12 mm speed bit, drill holes through beam and post 50 mm in from each edge of the beam and centred on the post, keeping the drill level and square to the beam. Insert a coach bolt, with a washer, through the beam; tighten it with a spanner.

ADDING THE CROSS-PIECES
11 Cut the cross-pieces to length and clamp them together with the ends flush. Measure in 220 mm from each end and square a line across the edges. Cut a 10 mm deep housing across all pieces. Remove the cramps. Test the fit over the beams at the posts.

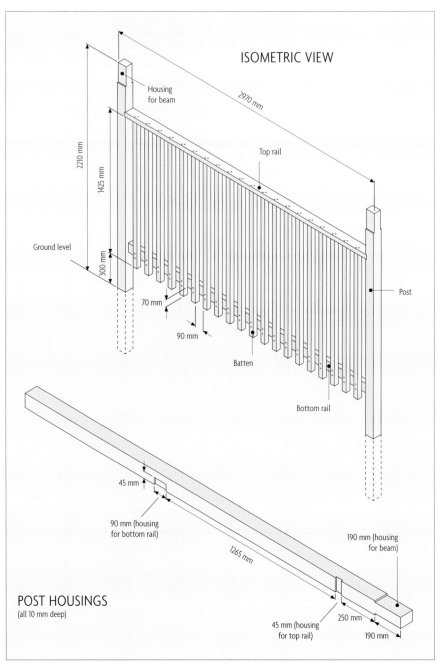

ISOMETRIC VIEW

2970 mm

Housing for beam

Top rail

2210 mm

1425 mm

Ground level

300 mm

70 mm

90 mm

Batten

Post

Bottom rail

POST HOUSINGS
(all 10 mm deep)

45 mm

90 mm (housing for bottom rail)

1265 mm

190 mm (housing for beam)

250 mm

45 mm (housing for top rail)

190 mm

12 Measure down 40 mm from the top corners of each cross-piece and, with a sliding bevel set at 30 degrees, mark a line back to the side with the housing. Cut along the line.

13 Take a cross-piece and push the housing over the beams, lining it up with the outer face of one post. Clamp a piece of scrap timber to the beam behind the cross-piece. With a 3.5 mm bit, drill a pilot hole at an

outdoor

MATERIALS*

PART	MATERIAL	FINISHED LENGTH	NO.
Post	90 x 90 mm treated pine	2810 mm	2
Batten	45 x 45 mm treated pine	1425 mm	20
Rail/packer	90 x 45 mm treated pine	2810 mm	3
Cross-piece	90 x 45 mm treated pine	600 mm	5
Beam	190 x 45 mm treated pine	3600 mm	2
Block	70 x 45 mm treated pine	180 mm	3

Other: 75 mm x No. 8 galvanized screws; four 175 x 10 mm galvanized coach bolts, nuts and washers; 75 x 3.8 mm galvanized lost-head nails; coarse gravel; four timber props 2.0–2.5 m long; concrete.

* Finished size: 3600 mm long and 2290 mm high.

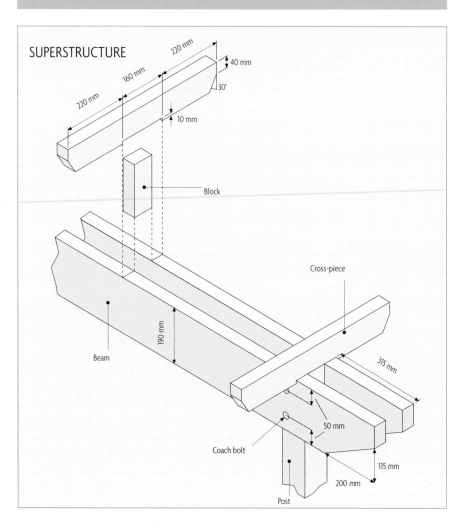

SUPERSTRUCTURE

angle though the cross-piece into each beam. Nail it in place. Move the cramp and block to the other side of the cross-piece, and drill and nail into the beams from the other side. Fix a cross-piece over the other post.

14 Square a line down each beam 1417 mm from one cross-piece. Push a block down between the beams, lining up the edge with the line and the top with the top of the beams. Clamp it in place. With a 3.5 mm bit, drill through each beam at an angle and skew-nail into the block.

15 Fit a cross-piece over the beams, lining it up with the block. Clamp scrap timber to the beams and nail the cross-piece in position as before.

16 In the same way, fix blocks and cross-pieces halfway between the centre and end cross-pieces.

GARDEN ARCHWAY

Construction of this garden archway is straightforward, with even the arch requiring no special skills, as the components are all screwed together. The structure can be extended on either side as desired.

THE POSTS

1 Using a straight edge and square, set out two parallel string lines 5500 mm long and 900 mm apart. Check they are parallel by measuring the diagonals—if they are the same, the lines are parallel. Measure 2500 mm along string line 1 for the centre. From there, measure and mark out 750 mm on each side.

2 Dig holes and erect posts A1 to line up with the 750 mm mark and the string line (see page 428 for erecting posts). Check they are 1500 mm apart. From the outer face measure 800 mm and erect posts B1. Erect posts C1 800 mm from the outer face of B1.

3 Place a 900 mm straight edge along the

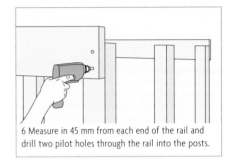

6 Measure in 45 mm from each end of the rail and drill two pilot holes through the rail into the posts.

inside face of one post A1 and post B1. Using a builder's square, transfer the position of post A1 to string line 2. Repeat for the other post A1. Dig post holes and erect the posts, ensuring the outer face is aligned with the line and the adjacent face with the matching post on string line 1. Erect posts B2 and C2 the same way. Allow the concrete to set.

4 Remove the props. Measure up 1800 mm on the lowest post, and square a line around it. Transfer this to the other posts. Cut off each post at the squared line. Measure down 100 mm from the top of each post and square a line around the outside.

SIDE STRUCTURES

5 Plane 3 mm chamfers on the ends of the end rails. Clamp a rail to each pair of posts A1 and A2, its ends flush with the outer face of the posts and the lower edge with the 100 mm line.

6 Measure in 45 mm from each end of the rail and square a line across the face. Using a 4 mm bit, drill two pilot holes 75 mm deep through the rail into the posts, 25 mm and 75 mm up from the bottom edge of the rail. Insert a bugle-head screw into each. (Bugle-head screws are self-drilling, but pilot holes

SIDE STRUCTURE EXPLODED VIEW

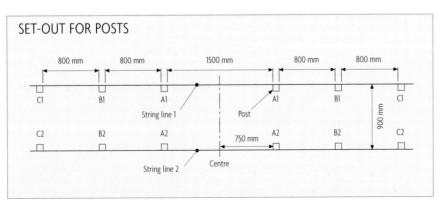

End rail · Post C1 · Side cleat A · Side rail · Post B1 · Side cleat B · Post C2 · Intermediate rail · Post B2 · Side cleat A · Side rail · Side cleat B · End rail · Post A1 · Post A2

SET-OUT FOR POSTS

800 mm · 800 mm · 1500 mm · 800 mm · 800 mm

C1 · B1 · A1 · A1 · B1 · C1
String line 1 · Post
C2 · B2 · A2 · 750 mm · A2 · B2 · C2
String line 2 · Centre · 900 mm

TOOLS

- Two string lines
- Tape measure and pencil
- Builder's square
- Post-hole auger
- Hammer and screwdriver
- Spirit level
- Shovel
- Water level (optional)
- Square
- Circular saw (optional)
- Handsaw
- Bandsaw or jigsaw
- Hand plane
- Two 200 mm G-cramps
- 1200 mm sash cramp
- Electric drill
- Drill bits: 4 mm, hexagonal bit to suit bugle-head screws
- Sliding bevel
- Spokeshave, belt sander or cork sanding block

This lovely archway can be used over a path or as a focal point in itself, perhaps with a seat installed under the arch. The lattice sides make ideal supports for climbing plants.

reduce the risk of the timber splitting.) Remove the cramps and repeat for posts C1 and C2.

7 Plane a 3 mm chamfer on the end of each side rail. Position each flush with the end rails and clamp it to the posts at either end. Measure 80 mm from each end and square a line across the face. Drill 4 mm pilot holes 35 mm and 85 mm from the bottom edge. Insert screws. Measure 970 mm from each end, and fix the rails to posts B the same way.

8 Fit an intermediate rail between the side rails against posts B (on the side facing

posts A), flush with the end of the posts. Skew two 75 mm nails into each post. Using 50 mm nails, fix side cleats to the inside of each side rail, flush with the tops of the posts.

THE LATTICE

9 Using a sliding bevel, mark a 45-degree mitre on each end of the lattice stiles and rails, with the short side of the mitre on the grooved side. Use two 75 mm nails to join each pair of rails to one stile. Cut the end

lattice to fit into the groove of the frames. Slide it into the frame and fix on the second stile. Centre a lattice panel between one pair of posts A, so the top is flush with the top of the posts. Fix it to the posts, using four 75 mm nails down each side. Fix the other panels between the other posts A and the posts C.

10 Place a horizontal lattice piece on top of each side structure and fix it to the cleats with 30 mm flat-head nails.

ARCH HALF SECTION AND HALF VIEW

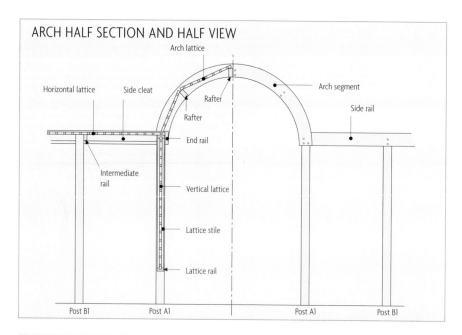

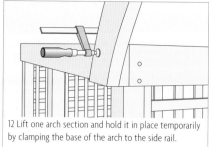

12 Lift one arch section and hold it in place temporarily by clamping the base of the arch to the side rail.

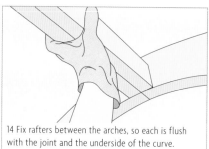

14 Fix rafters between the arches, so each is flush with the joint and the underside of the curve.

MATERIALS*

PART	MATERIAL	FINISHED LENGTH	WIDTH	NO.
Post	90 x 90 mm treated pine	2400 mm		12
End rail	140 x 35 mm treated pine	900 mm		4
Side rail	140 x 35 mm treated pine	1940 mm		4
Intermediate rail	70 x 35 mm treated pine	900 mm		2
Side cleat A	70 x 35 mm treated pine	800 mm		4
Side cleat B	70 x 35 mm treated pine	765 mm		4
Arch segment	290 x 35 mm treated pine	1155 mm		4
Rafter	90 x 45 mm treated pine	970 mm		4
Lattice stile	70 x 35 mm grooved surround	1400 mm		8
Lattice rail	70 x 35 mm grooved surround	720 mm		8
Vertical lattice**	Square lattice	1800 mm	900 mm	4
Horizontal lattice	Square lattice	1870 mm	900 mm	2
Arch lattice	Square lattice	970 mm	500 mm	4

Other: Four timber pegs; timber props 1800 mm long; concrete; 50 x 3 mm galvanized lost-head nails; 65 x 3 mm galvanized lost-head nails; 75 x 3 mm galvanized lost-head nails; 30 x 2.5 mm galvanized flat-head nails; 40 x 2 mm galvanized flat-head nails; 100 mm x No. 10 bugle-head screws; flexible timber, or plastic tubing 700 mm long (for drawing curves); abrasive paper: 60 grit.

* Finished size: 5310 x 900 mm and 2550 mm high. The lattice and surrounds should also be in treated pine or equivalent durable timber.

** Will be cut to length during construction.

THE ARCH STRUCTURE

11 Mark out the shape on each arch segment. Use a bandsaw to cut just outside the lines and smooth back to the lines by sanding. Plane a 3 mm chamfer along each edge.

12 Lift one arch segment into place, with the 50-degree cut lining up with the bottom of the side rail and the inside corner of the curve with the end of the side rail. Clamp it in place. Position a segment on the opposite side so the tops are together.

13 With a 4 mm bit, drill two pilot holes 75 mm deep and 30 mm from the bottom edge of the arch. Insert a screw in each. Measure up 80 mm from the screw nearest the opening for a third screw. Erect the second arch the same way.

TO FINISH

14 Slip a rafter between the arches flush with the joint and the underside of the curve. Place a sash cramp over the top. Drill two 4 mm pilot holes 75 mm deep through the face of the arch, 22 mm from the arch joint and 20 mm from each edge of the rafter. Insert a screw in each. Remove the cramp and fix the second rafter the same way. Use two G-cramps to hold the rafters together. Check the arch segments are flush, and fix the rafters together with 65 mm nails.

15 On the inside of each arch segment, measure down 450 mm and fix a rafter. Fix the arch lattice to the rafters with 40 mm flat-head nails, centring the joints on the rafters.

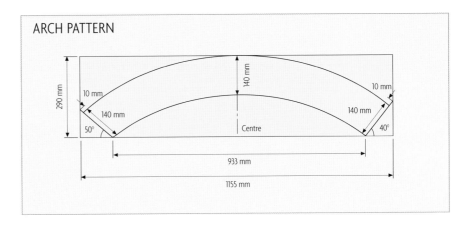

ARCH PATTERN

BEACON TRELLIS

Made from lengths of lattice strips, this trellis is easy to construct but requires precise cutting of the points for a good result. It can be fixed to any wall, whether timber or masonry.

THE MAIN FRAME

1 Carefully cut all the slats (A–G) to their finished length.

2 Take slat A. Mark the centre on one end and measure down each side 21 mm (see diagram on page 440). Connect the points and cut along the lines with a tenon saw. If you are using a mitre saw, set it to 45 degrees and clamp scrap timber to the fence 21 mm from the blade. Place the slat in the saw with one edge against the fence and the end against the stop. Cut through the slat, creating a 45-degree cut. Check that the end of the cut finishes in the middle of the square end of the slat. Turn the slat over, placing the opposite edge to the fence, and make a second cut.

3 Cut a point on one end of the two slats B. Lay the three slats A and B flat, side by side and with the square (bottom) ends flush. Measure up from the square end 434 mm and square a line across the faces of the slats. Measure and mark a second line 880 mm from the bottom and another 1350 mm.

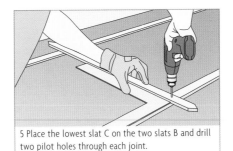

5 Place the lowest slat C on the two slats B and drill two pilot holes through each joint.

4 Cut a point on each end of the slats C. Measure 95 mm from each end, and square a line across the face.

5 Place the lowest slat C on the two slats B, lining up the 95 mm lines with the outside edge of the vertical slats and the lower edge

HINT

If you intend to make a number of these trellises, it will be worthwhile drawing out a full-size plan on a sheet of plywood or particleboard to make setting out and assembly much easier.

with the 434 mm line. Check that the joints are square. Apply a small amount of adhesive to the joints. Use a 2 mm bit to drill two pilot holes through each joint, and drive a 20 mm nail into each.

6 Fix the other two slats C to the slats B using the same method, lining up the lower edges with the 880 mm and 1350 mm marks.

7 Measure 359 mm from each end of each slat C. Slip slat A under slats C and line up the square end with the bottom of slats B and the edges with the 359 mm marks. Check that slat A is square with slats C and fix with adhesive and nails as before.

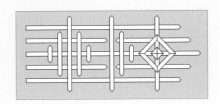

This lovely trellis makes a welcome change from lattice panels. It provides support for climbing plants or can be a decorative feature in its own right. Slats with rounded edges were used for a neat finish.

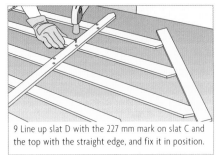

9 Line up slat D with the 227 mm mark on slat C and the top with the straight edge, and fix it in position.

SLAT POINT

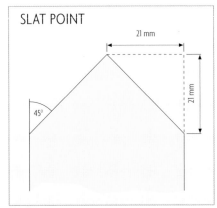

THE DIAMOND

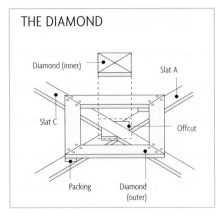

THE INTERMEDIATE SLATS

8 On the top and bottom slats C, measure in 227 mm from each point and square lines across the face. Cut a point on one end of each slat E. Place them under the lowest slat C, lining up the outer edge with the 227 mm line and the square end with the bottom of slats A and B. Fix each as before, so it is square /parallel to the outer members of the frame.

TOOLS

- Tape measure and pencil
- Mitre saw or tenon saw
- Square
- Electric drill
- Drill bit: 2 mm
- Hammer
- Cork sanding block
- Impact drill with 6 mm and 6 mm masonry bits (for fixing to a masonry wall)

MATERIALS

PART	MATERIAL	FINISHED LENGTH	NO.
Slat A	42 x 12 mm treated pine	1820 mm	1
Slat B	42 x 12 mm treated pine	1615 mm	2
Slat C	42 x 12 mm treated pine	760 mm	3
Slat D	42 x 12 mm treated pine	775 mm	2
Slat E	42 x 12 mm treated pine	855 mm	2
Slat F	42 x 12 mm treated pine	450 mm	3
Slat G	42 x 12 mm treated pine	176 mm	3
Packing	42 x 12 mm treated pine	60 mm	2
Diamond (outer)	42 x 12 mm treated pine	270 mm	4
Diamond (inner)	42 x 12 mm treated pine	90 mm	4

Other: Water-resistant epoxy adhesive; 20 x 2.6 mm galvanized flat-head nails; abrasive paper: 80 grit; exterior grade wood filler; 75 x 3.15 mm galvanized flat-head nails or 6 x 50 mm masonry anchors (plugs) and 65 mm x No. 6 galvanized screws for fixing to wall.

* Finished size: 1820 x 760 mm.

9 Cut a point on both ends of slats D. Slide a slat D under each side of the top slat C so the outer edge matches the 227 mm mark. Line up the top of slat D by placing a straight edge across the ends of slats A and B, then push slat D up until its end touches the straight edge. Glue and nail slats D in position as before.

10 Cut a point on both ends of the three slats F. Measure in from each point 72 mm and square a line across the face. Measure down 60 mm from the bottom of the lowest slat C and square a line parallel to it across slats A and E. Apply a small amount of adhesive to slats A and E just below the line and fix the first slat F in place with its upper edge lining up with the 60 mm line and the 72 mm lines flush with the outside edges of slats E. Drill and nail as usual.

11 Measure up 60 mm from the top of the lowest slat C and 60 mm from the top of the middle slat C and fix the remaining slats F in place in the same way, but line up the bottom of slat F with the 60 mm lines.

12 Cut points on both ends of the three slats G. Measure 60 mm from each slat F and fix slats G on slat A with an even overhang of 67 mm on each side.

THE DIAMOND

13 Cut two packing pieces 60 mm long with opposed 45-degree cuts on either end. Don't try to hold them with your fingers when you are cutting them: use a length of scrap to hold them down or cut them off a longer length. Glue them to slat A, 115 mm above and below slat C, with the wider side towards slat C.

14 Cut the four pieces for the outer diamond with a mitre cut on each end so that it measures 270 mm from long point to long point. Put the offcuts to one side.

15 Set the four pieces on top of the frame and line up the horizontal joints with the centre of slat C and the vertical joints with the centre of slat A. Apply adhesive under the joints, drill pilot holes and fix them in place with two nails at each end. The packing pieces should be hidden.

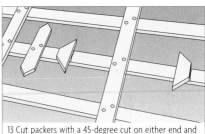

13 Cut packers with a 45-degree cut on either end and glue them to slat A, 115 mm above and below slat C.

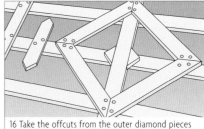

16 Take the offcuts from the outer diamond pieces and glue them to slat A, one on either side of slat C.

16 Take the triangular offcuts from the mitres and glue them to slat A, on either side of slat C (see diagram opposite).

The inner diamond consists of four pieces with 45-degree cuts on each end.

17 Cut the four pieces for the inner diamond with a 45-degree mitre on each end. Apply adhesive to the back of each piece and place it in the centre of the outer diamond. Drill one clearance hole in the middle of each piece and nail them in place.

TO FINISH

18 Sand the lattice smooth and fill gaps in the mitres with wood filler. Apply the finish of your choice.

19 Fix the trellis in place.

- To fix it to a timber fence, place it in the required position, ensuring it is standing straight. Use the 2 mm bit to drill a pilot hole in the centre of each joint between slats C and B, and fix it to the fence with

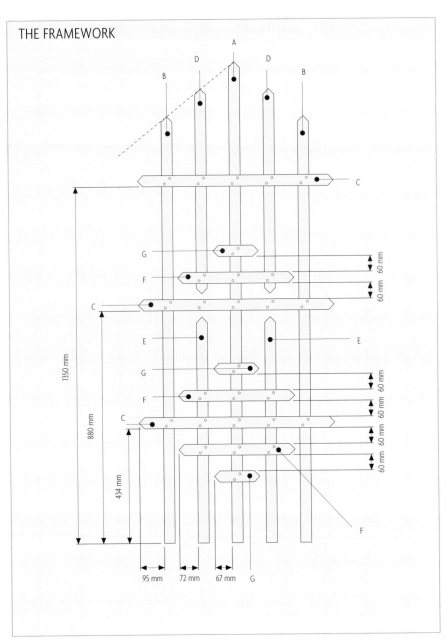

THE FRAMEWORK

a 75 mm flat-head galvanized nail at each joint.

- To fix it to a brick wall, use a 6 mm bit to drill a clearance hole through each joint between slats B and C. Sit it against the wall and mark the positions of the

clearance holes on the brickwork. Remove the frame. Install a 6 mm masonry bit in an impact drill and drill a 50 mm deep hole at each mark. Place a masonry plug in the hole. Sit the frame back against the wall and insert a 65 mm x No. 6 galvanized screw in each hole.

STORAGE LEAN-TO

A simple frame with housed joints is clad with boards and roofed with polycarbonate sheeting to make this multi-purpose garden lean-to. It is ideal for gardens where there is no room for a shed.

THE POSTS

1 Using a sliding bevel, mark a 15-degree angle on top of the back posts (see diagram on page 445). Cut the slope. Measure 2280 mm from the top of the slope and cut the bottom square. Prepare the front posts in the same manner so that they have a finished length of 2090 mm.

2 Lay the back posts on a flat surface, with the longer sides back to back and the square ends flush. Place one front post on either side, with the long side against the back posts. This way you will make a left-hand and right-hand set of posts. Clamp the four posts together with two sash cramps, keeping the bottoms flush.

3 Mark out and cut the housings for the bottom and two middle rails across all four posts, all 15 mm deep (see box on page 432). Test the housing width with a piece of 70 x 45 mm timber. If the fit is tight, cut one edge of the housing.

4 Remove the cramps. Take the left-hand pair (one front and one back post), line up the sloping cuts and clamp the posts together. Set a marking gauge to 74 mm and mark the housings on the ends of the posts. Cut the housings; remove the cramps. Repeat for the right-hand posts.

THE RAILS

5 Cut the six side rails to length. On one end of each side rail, mark and cut a 90 mm wide and 15 mm deep housing. Make a 45 mm wide and 15 mm deep housing on the other end of the rail.

This lean-to serves as a store for garden tools and materials, and doubles as a potting shed. A second shelf can be added on the upper rails, but don't make it too deep, or you may hit your head on it.

MATERIALS*

PART	MATERIAL	FINISHED LENGTH	NO.
Back post	90 x 70 mm treated pine	2280 mm	2
Front post	90 x 70 mm treated pine	2090 mm	2
Side rail	70 x 45 mm treated pine	685 mm	6
Top side rail**	70 x 45 mm treated pine	750 mm	2
Back rail	70 x 45 mm treated pine	1165 mm	4
Batten	70 x 45 mm treated pine	1275 mm	2
Shelf	190 x 45 mm treated pine	1195 mm	2
Fascia	90 x 20 mm treated pine	980 mm	2
Ridge capping	90 x 20 mm treated pine	1315 mm	1
Side capping	70 x 20 mm treated pine	875 mm	2
Cladding**	140 x 20 mm shiplap boards	2130 mm	18

Other: 65 mm x No. 8 galvanized cross-head screws; 75 mm x No. 8 galvanized screws; 50 mm x No. 12 roofing screws; 45 x 2.5 mm twisted-shank nails; 50 x 2.8 mm galvanized nails; two 900 x 820 mm pieces of polycarbonate roofing sheet (greca profile)

* Finished size: 1315 x 930 mm and 2370 mm high.

** Will be cut to length during construction. The reversible shiplap used had a coverage of 125 mm.

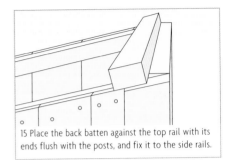

15 Place the back batten against the top rail with its ends flush with the posts, and fix it to the side rails.

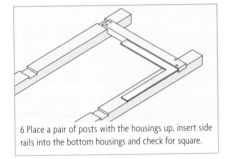

6 Place a pair of posts with the housings up, insert side rails into the bottom housings and check for square.

6 Lay a pair of posts (one front and one back) on a solid flat surface, with the housings facing up. Insert the 90 mm wide housing on one side rail into the bottom housing in the front post. The end of the rail should finish flush with the front of the post when the shoulder of the housing is hard against the back of the post. Check the rail is square to the post. Using a 3.5 mm bit, drill two pilot holes 20–25 mm in from each diagonal corner of the joint. Screw a 65 mm cross-

head screw into each pilot hole. Fix the middle and top rails to the front post in the same manner, keeping the fronts flush and the rails square to the posts.

7 Slip the back post under the rails and push each rail into its housing. Use a scrap piece of 45 mm thick timber to test that the ends of the rails are set in far enough to fit the back rails. Use the tape measure to check that the posts are parallel and the square to ensure the rails and posts are at 90 degrees to each other. With the 3.5 mm bit, drill two pilot holes through the rails, 15 mm in and 15 mm up from each edge. Fix the rails into the back post housings.

8 The top side rail has a 15-degree cut on each end. Using a sliding bevel, mark and cut one end, then measure 715 mm from the long point to mark the short point on the other

end. Cut it at 15 degrees. Test the fit of the rail in the top housings on the posts. The top of the rail should be flush with the tops of the posts, and the front end flush with the front post. The back end should finish 45 mm in from the outer edge of the back post.

9 Use a pencil to mark the position of the inside of each post on the top rail. Cut a 15 mm deep shoulder along each line, remembering to make a left-hand and a right-hand rail. Cut the housings and screw the rail in place.

10 Cut the back rails to length. With the help of a friend, stand the left-hand frame upright and insert a back rail into the lower housing on the back post, then stand the right-hand frame up and push the rail into that housing. Use a square to test that the back and sides are square to each other. If you have a 1500 mm sash cramp, place it across the back of the frame, level with the rail, and clamp the frames together. Otherwise, drill a 3.5 mm pilot hole through the back rail, 20 mm in from each end, into the ends of the side rails, and insert a 75 mm screw.

11 Place a back rail into the top housings. The top of the rail will be higher than the end of the back post, but this will be hidden when the roof is added. Using the 3.5 mm bit, drill two pilot holes and fix the side and back rails together at the corners with 75 mm screws. Repeat this on the opposite end of the rail.

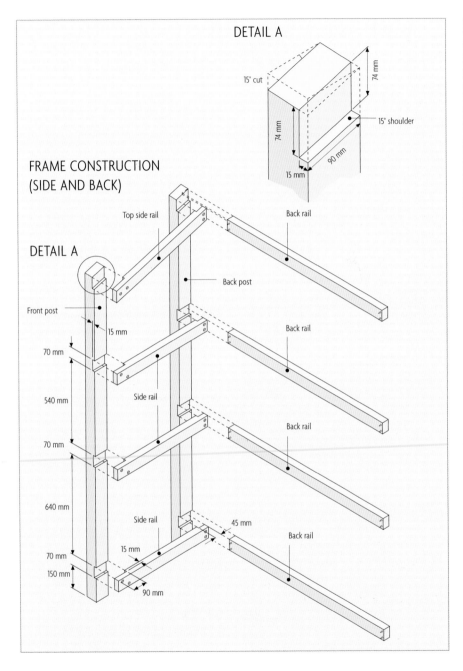

DETAIL A

15° cut

74 mm

74 mm

15° shoulder

90 mm

15 mm

FRAME CONSTRUCTION
(SIDE AND BACK)

Top side rail

Back rail

DETAIL A

Back post

Front post

15 mm

70 mm

Side rail

Back rail

540 mm

70 mm

Back rail

640 mm

Side rail

45 mm

Back rail

15 mm

70 mm

150 mm

90 mm

TOOLS

- Tape measure and pencil
- Sliding bevel
- Tenon saw
- Mitre saw (optional)
- Jigsaw
- Sash cramps
- Electric drill
- Drill bits: 3.5 mm, 8 mm masonry
- Screwdriver and hammer
- Marking gauge
- Cork sanding block
- Builder's square
- Hand plane
- Spanner: 8 mm

up against one post and line the bottom up with the lower edge of the bottom rail. Run a pencil along the top of the top rail to mark the length. Cut along the line. Put the piece back into position and nail it to each side rail with two 45 mm twisted-shank nails.

14 Place the second board in position against the first, with the tongue and groove joint up tight. Mark, cut and fix it as for the first board. Continue to work across each side until you reach the last board. Measure the distance to the front post and cut the board to fit (allow for the width of the tongue). Fix it in place. If necessary, plane the edge of the board to fit against the post. Repeat to clad the second side.

15 Cut the two battens to length. Place the back batten against the top back rail with its ends flush with the outer edge of the back posts, and screw it at an angle into the side rails using two 75 mm screws on each end. Fix the front batten in the same manner,

Place the two middle back rails in the remaining housings, and fix them at each end with two 75 mm screws.

12 Fix the bottom back rail with two screws either end and remove the sash cramp.

THE CLADDING

13 Trim the bottom end of each shiplap board square. Take the first board and use a hand plane to remove the tongue. Placing it against the side frame, on the outside of the structure, push the planed edge of the board

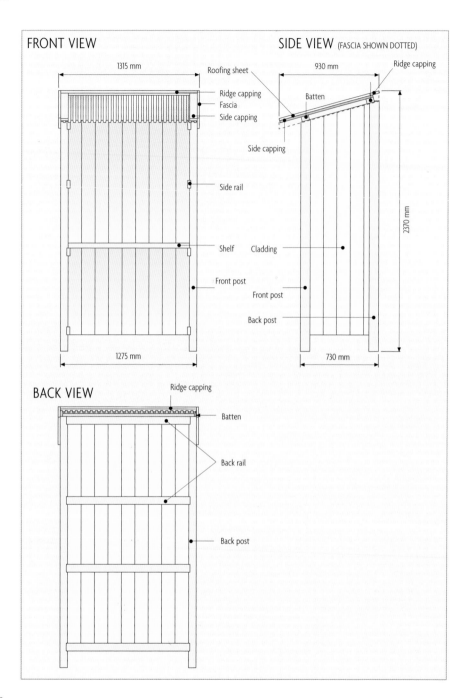

FRONT VIEW

1315 mm

Roofing sheet
Ridge capping
Fascia
Side capping

Side capping

Side rail

Shelf

Front post

1275 mm

SIDE VIEW (FASCIA SHOWN DOTTED)

930 mm

Ridge capping
Batten

Side capping

Cladding
Front post

Back post

2370 mm

730 mm

BACK VIEW

Ridge capping

Batten

Back rail

Back post

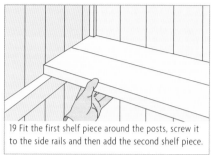

19 Fit the first shelf piece around the posts, screw it to the side rails and then add the second shelf piece.

17 Remove the tongue of the first board and cut it 2100 mm long (the distance from the underside of the top roof batten to the lower side of the bottom rail). Sit it in place and use a pencil to mark on it the top and bottom of the side rails. Lift it back out of the frame and use a square to transfer the lines 30 mm in from the edge. Set a marking gauge to 30 mm and gauge a line between each of the squared lines to mark a notch. Using a jigsaw, cut out the notch. Push the board back into place so it fits neatly around each side rail and against the post. Use two nails to fix it to each back rail.

18 Continue to clad the back wall, cutting each board to 2100 mm and fixing it with two nails at each rail. To make it easier to fit the last board around the side rails, leave the second-last board out until the last board has been fitted. Then push the tongue and groove joint between the last two boards together and spring them into position. Fix them in place as before.

TO FINISH

19 Cut the shelf pieces to length. Sit one piece on the middle side rails and push it up to the back posts. Use a pencil to transfer the inner edge of the back posts to it. Remove the piece and use a jigsaw to cut away the notch on each corner so that it will fit around the posts and against the back wall. Test the fit and adjust the notch if necessary. Use two 75 mm screws to fix each

keeping its front edge flush with the front of the posts.

16 The back wall is clad from the inside. Determine how many boards you require to cover 1135 mm (the distance between the back posts). If the boards don't fit precisely, the structure will look better if you cut the two end boards to the same width, rather than having just one board narrower.

end onto the side rails. Fix the second shelf piece to the side rails in front of the first piece, using two screws in the same manner.

20 Place a sheet of polycarbonate on the battens. Line up the side with the ends of the battens and let the front overhang by 100 mm. Using an 8 mm bit, drill clearance holes through the third ridge in from the edge, centring the holes over each batten. Use the spanner to fix a 50 mm roofing screw into each hole.

21 Place the second sheet to overlap the first one so that the valleys and ridges sit neatly over each other and the side of the second sheet is flush with the other end of the battens (trim the sheet with scissors if necessary). If the sheet falls a bit short,

don't worry, as the side capping will cover about 50 mm. Check that the lower edge of the sheets line up. Drill a hole through each ridge, directly above the battens, but don't drill holes in the first two ridges on either side as this will foul the capping. Insert screws as before.

22 Cut the fascia boards with a 15-degree angle on each end. Position them so that one end finishes flush with the back of the back post, the other end is in line with the edge of the polycarbonate, and the top is flush with the ridges of the polycarbonate. Use two 50 mm nails at each end to fix the fascia board to the posts.

23 Cut the ridge capping and skew-nail it to the top of the fascia boards, using two 50 mm nails and keeping the ends and back

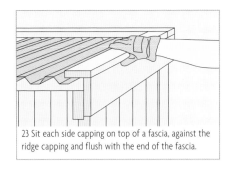
23 Sit each side capping on top of a fascia, against the ridge capping and flush with the end of the fascia.

edge flush with the fascia. Cut the side cappings, with the ridge end square and the lower end at a 15-degree angle. Sit each side capping on top of a fascia board, with the square end against the ridge capping and the other end flush with the end of the fascia. Skew 50 mm nails through the capping into the fascia at approximately 100 mm spacings.

PLANT HOUSE

The back walls of this structure are clad with weatherboards. The roof and front can be covered with clear polycarbonate to make a glasshouse, or with shadecloth for an effective shadehouse.

PREPARATION
To erect the plant house you will need a level area 1200 x 1200 mm. If the ground is not level, dig it out and install a flat base. A concrete slab or an area of clay or concrete paving would be suitable, or treated pine sleepers (200 x 75 mm) can be set into the ground under where the walls will be.

THE BACK FRAMES
1 Cut two back rails to length. On each end of both rails cut a 90 mm long and 17.5 mm deep housing (see box on page 432).

2 Using a sliding bevel, mark and cut a 22.5-degree cut on each end of a top rail (see page 449). Mark a line parallel to each

cut, 90 mm from the end. Cut a 17.5 mm deep housing.

3 Cut a corner stud with one end square and the other at 22.5 degrees. On the square end, cut a 90 x 17.5 mm housing. On the same face, measure along 1000 mm and square a line across, and then 90 mm for the middle housing. Cut a third housing at the top end, parallel to the angled end. Test the fit of each joint to ensure the rails and studs are flush. Adjust the fit if necessary by re-cutting the shoulders.

4 Cut the back frame end stud with the bottom end square and the top at 22.5 degrees. Make the three 90 x 17.5 mm housings.

5 Insert a back rail into the bottom and middle housing of each stud and then drill two pilot holes at opposite corners of each joint, using a 3 mm drill bit. Insert a 30 mm screw into each hole. Fix the top rail into the angled housings. Check the back frame is square and free of twist.

6 Make a second back frame the same way, but as a mirror image.

THE SIDE FRAMES
7 Cut a side frame end stud and a door stud to length. Take two plates and cut a 45-degree angle on one end of each. Measure 460 mm from the long point of the cut and square a line across. Cut along the line.

Designed to fit into a corner of your garden, this glass or shadehouse takes up little room but gives protection to your plants. It can be fitted out with pot stands or shelves, and baskets can be hung on the walls.

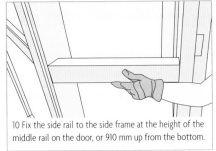

10 Fix the side rail to the side frame at the height of the middle rail on the door, or 910 mm up from the bottom.

8 Place the end stud on a flat, solid surface, resting on its edge. Hold a plate on each end of the stud with the end of the plate flush with the face of the stud and the edges level. Using a 3 mm bit, drill two pilot holes through each plate into the end of the stud, then insert a 75 mm screw into each.

9 Place the door stud with its edge flush with the outer face of the plates. Drill two pilot holes through each joint and insert 75 mm screws. Check the frame is square by measuring the diagonals, which will be the same length when square.

10 Make a 45-degree cut on one end of the side rail so it is 425 mm to the long point. Check the height of the middle rail on the door and position the side rail to match. (If there isn't a centre rail on the door, set the rail at 910 mm from the bottom.) Drill pilot holes and use two 75 mm screws through each stud into the ends of the rail.

11 Repeat steps 7–10 to make a second frame, the mirror image of the first so you have a right-hand frame and a left-hand frame.

ASSEMBLING THE FRAMES

12 The two back frames are held together with aluminium angle. Drill a series of holes 200 mm apart through each face of the aluminium angle, offsetting the holes 15 mm to prevent the screw heads fouling each other. Fix the angle to the edge of one

RAFTER

Compound cut

90 mm

70 mm

22.5°

Bird's-mouth cut

BACK FRAME

SIDE FRAME

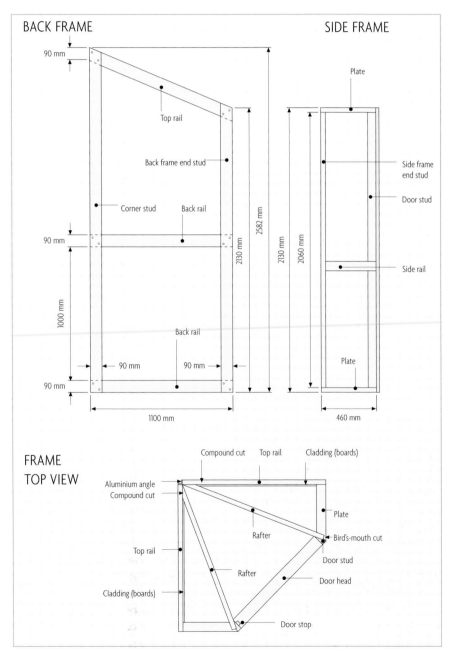

90 mm

Top rail

Back frame end stud

Corner stud   Back rail

90 mm

2130 mm

2582 mm

1000 mm

Back rail

90 mm   90 mm

90 mm

1100 mm

Plate

Side frame end stud

Door stud

2130 mm

2060 mm

Side rail

Plate

460 mm

FRAME TOP VIEW

Compound cut   Top rail   Cladding (boards)

Aluminium angle
Compound cut

Top rail

Cladding (boards)

Rafter

Rafter

Plate

Bird's-mouth cut

Door stud

Door head

Door stop

TOOLS

- Spirit level
- Tape measure and pencil
- Handsaw
- Jigsaw
- Power saw (optional)
- Sliding bevel
- Chisel: 25 mm
- Electric drill
- Drill bits: 3 mm, 6 mm
- Screwdriver
- Builder's square
- Two G-cramps
- Hammer
- Hand staple gun
- Utility knife
- Rasp
- Socket spanner: 8 mm

corner stud, keeping it flush with the inside face of the stud. Use a 40 mm hex-head screw in each hole.

13 Stand the two back frames in place. Keep them square at the base with the corners tight against each other, and screw the angle to the second corner stud.

14 Stand each side frame against the back frames, lining up the outer edge of the side frame end stud with the edge of the back frame end stud. Ensure the left-hand and right-hand frames are correctly placed with the door studs parallel. Use cramps to hold the frames in place and use the builder's square to check that they are square at the base. Drill four 3 mm pilot holes through the outside of the back frame into the side frame and use a 65 mm screw in each to fix them together.

MATERIALS*

PART	MATERIAL	FINISHED LENGTH	NO.
Back rail	90 x 35 mm treated pine	1100 mm	4
Top rail	90 x 35 mm treated pine	1227 mm	2
Corner stud	90 x 35 mm treated pine	2582 mm	2
Back frame end stud	90 x 35 mm treated pine	2130 mm	2
Door stud	90 x 35 mm treated pine	2130 mm	2
Door head	90 x 35 mm treated pine	826 mm	1
Side frame end stud	70 x 35 mm treated pine	2060 mm	2
Plate	70 x 35 mm treated pine	460 mm	4
Side rail	70 x 35 mm treated pine	425 mm	2
Rafter**	70 x 35 mm treated pine	1300 mm	2
Door stop	32 x 20 mm treated pine	2095 mm	1
Side frame cover strip (vertical)	30 x 6 mm treated pine	2130 mm	4
Side frame cover strip (horizontal)**	30 x 6 mm treated pine	400 mm	6
Door cover strip (vertical)**	30 x 6 mm treated pine	2000 mm	2
Door cover strip (horizontal)**	30 x 6 mm treated pine	800 mm	3
Roof cover strip	30 x 6 mm treated pine	1200 mm	4
Door head cover strip	30 x 6 mm treated pine	830 mm	1

Other: 30 mm x No. 8 galvanized screws; 65 mm x No. 8 galvanized screws; 75 mm x No. 8 galvanized screws; 40 x 8 mm hex-head screws; 40 x 2.6 mm galvanized flat-head nails; 25 x 2.6 mm galvanized flat-head nails; 2.5 m of 25 x 25 mm angle aluminium; 5.7 m² of timber cladding (weatherboards); ready-made timber flyscreen door (2040 x 820 x 20 mm); two 75 x 25 mm hinges and screws to suit; 7 m of 1 m wide 0.5 mm thick polycarbonate or shadecloth.

* Finished size: 1135 x 1135 mm and 2588 mm high.

** Will be cut to length during construction.

15 To prevent the door head slipping while you screw it in place, clamp a block of timber to each door stud.

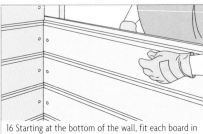

16 Starting at the bottom of the wall, fit each board in place on the frame and secure it using flat-head nails.

15 To prevent the door head slipping, clamp a small block of scrap timber to each door stud, 35 mm down from the top of the frame. Sit the door head on the blocks. On each end, drill two 3 mm pilot holes at an angle through the top of the head into the door stud, and insert a 75 mm screw in each. Remove the blocks and cramps.

FINISHING THE FRAME

16 Measure the inside width of one back wall and cut the timber cladding to length. Starting at the bottom of the wall and working upwards, fix each board to the back frame using 40 mm flat-head nails. Cut the last few boards at an angle so they finish flush with the top of the top rail. Measure the second wall; cut and fix the boards to it.

17 Cut the door stop to length and fix it to the left-hand door stud, 22 mm in from the front edge, drilling 3 mm pilot holes at 200 mm centres and inserting 30 mm screws.

18 On one end of each rafter, mark a bird's-mouth cut 90 mm long, using a pencil and sliding bevel set at 22.5 degrees (see diagram on page 449). Use a jigsaw to cut along each line.

19 On the other end of each rafter there is a compound cut. One has a left-hand cut and one a right-hand cut. Sit each rafter on the structure so that the bird's-mouth cut sits on the door stud. At the other end, line up the face of the rafter with the back corner. Run a pencil along the back wall of the frame, marking the underside of the rafter. Set a sliding bevel to 22.5 degrees and mark lines up each face of the rafter. Cut along these lines with a handsaw.

20 Fix each rafter in place by drilling two 3 mm pilot holes at an angle through the

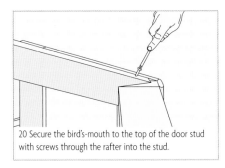

20 Secure the bird's-mouth to the top of the door stud with screws through the rafter into the stud.

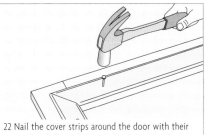

22 Nail the cover strips around the door with their inner edge flush with the inside of the door frame.

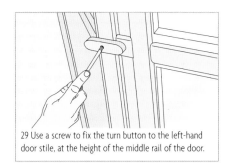

29 Use a screw to fix the turn button to the left-hand door stile, at the height of the middle rail of the door.

face of the rafter into the top rail and inserting a 65 mm screw. Secure the bird's-mouth to the top of the door stud by drilling holes into the stud, one through the top of the rafter and another through the bottom edge. Insert 65 mm screws.

THE DOOR

21 Lay the door down on a flat, solid surface with the outside face up. Cover the face of the door with polycarbonate sheeting or shadecloth. Use a staple gun to run a row of staples around the door frame near the inner edge. Using a utility knife, trim the edges of the polycarbonate or shadecloth to 25 mm away from the inside edge.

22 Make 45-degree cuts on both ends of the two vertical and two horizontal door cover strips so they fit neatly around the door, flush with the inside of the frame. Cut the remaining strip to fit across the middle rail of the door, between the two vertical strips. Fix them all in place with 25 mm flat-head nails.

23 Screw the hinges to the door, 250 mm in from each corner. Lift the door into the opening and screw the hinges to the right-hand door stud, allowing a clearance of 5 mm at the top of the door.

TO FINISH

24 Cut two 2190 x 500 mm sheets of polycarbonate or shadecloth. Place a sheet

against each side frame and staple along the door stud. Pull the sheet across the frame and staple the opposite edge to the side frame end stud. Then run a row of staples across the top and bottom plates as well as a row across the centre of the side rail.

25 For the roof, cut three triangular pieces of sheeting to fit, with 20 mm extra at the lower edge. Fix the lower edge to the front of the top plates and door head, and then drive a row of staples all the way around the edges to hold each sheet in place.

26 Take two roof cover strips and cut a 45-degree mitre on one end of each. Use six 40 mm nails to fix each to a top rail, covering the edge of the sheeting and lining up the mitre cut with the apex of the roof.

27 Place the other two roof cover strips on top of the rafters with the lower end flush with the front of the door stud. Use a pencil to mark the angle at the apex, and cut it with a jigsaw. Fix each strip on top of the rafters with 40 mm nails.

28 Fix cover strips to either side of the side frames. Measure the distance between them and cut the horizontal strips for each frame. Fix one to each of the top and bottom plates using three 40 mm nails, keeping the inside edge in line with the inside of the frame. Nail the third horizontal strip to the centre of the side rail.

29 To hold the door closed, make a turn button from a 70 mm long offcut of 25 x 12 mm timber. Round the ends with a rasp, and then drill a 6 mm hole through the centre of the turn button. The hole should be big enough so that a No. 8 screw can spin freely in it, but not so large that the head of the screw pulls through. Fix the turn button to the left-hand door stile, at the same height as the middle rail of the door, with a 30 mm screw. Leave the screw loose enough so that you can turn the button to hold the door closed.

HINT

You may find it easier to paint your plant house before fixing the polycarbonate shadecloth in place. If you do this, paint the cover strips before cutting them to length and then simply touch up the cut ends of the strips and nail heads once they are in place.

TROMPE-L'OEIL TRELLIS

This clever trellis 'archway' is made from lattice strips and is constructed in two parts for easy manoeuvring. The slats are glued and screwed together to produce a sturdy construction.

Ideal for a formal courtyard or small garden, this trellis is designed to give the impression of a three-dimensional archway. Matt black paint (blackboard paint) was used to complement the texture of the aged paint on the brickwork.

THE OUTSIDE SECTION

1 Make a 40-degree cut on one end of one slat C, using a sliding bevel and tenon saw, or a mitre saw. Place it side by side with a slat A and a slat B, with the square ends flush. Measure from the square end 180 mm and square a line across the face of each slat. Square a second line 50 mm further up. Repeat to make seven sets of lines.

2 Take five slats D, measure from one end 50 mm and square a line across. From this measure 50 mm and square a second line, then 170 mm and square the next pair of 50 mm lines. Square a line across the slat 25 mm from the opposite end.

3 Lay out slats A and B 170 mm apart. Place a little adhesive between each set of 50 mm lines. Place one slat D over the lowest set of lines (see diagram opposite). Using a 3 mm bit, drill two pilot holes 30 mm deep diagonally across each joint and insert a 30 mm screw into each. This is the method for joining all the slats. Fix the top slat D on the fifth pair of lines. Check that the frame is square by measuring the diagonals between slats D, and see that it sits flat. Fix on the remaining three slats D.

4 Set a marking gauge to 25 mm and mark a line along the back of slat C. Line up the ends of each slat D with the line and fix them to slat C.

5 Take slat E and measure 440 mm. With this as the short side of the point, cut a 40-degree angle. Measure 50 mm from the square end and mark across the face. Line up this with the outside edge of slat A and the short point of the 40-degree cut with the edge of slat C. Fix E in place, but use only one screw on the joint with slat C.

SIDES OF THE ARCH

6 Cut slat F with a 40-degree cut on one end. Take two pieces of timber 450 mm long and, using a panel pin on each end, fix them behind the frame, so slats F and C are 370 mm apart, with the square ends level.

7 Measure 290 mm from the bottom of slat F and mark. Place one end of slat G over the end of the lowest slat D, with the top edges flush. Line up the lower edge of the other end with the mark on F. Mark and cut the angle at each end. Fix G in place.

8 Place slat L against the angle cut on the end of E, with the other end overhanging F so the end of F is in the centre of L. Mark the angle at either end so L fits neatly against E and is flush with the outside edge of F. Cut the angles and fix L in place.

9 From the top edge of slat G, measure along F for 110 mm to find the position of slat H. Line up the lower edge of H with the lower edge of the second slat D and the 110 mm mark. Mark the angles on either end, and cut and fix slat H. Repeat for slats I, J and K, with the spacings as shown in the diagram at right

10 Cut slat M with a 40-degree cut at the top end. Place it under slats G–L, 80 mm in from slat F and with the angle cut centred on slat L. Glue and screw it into place. Cut slat N, also with a 40-degree cut at the top, place it under slats G–L, 90 mm across from slat M and with the angle cut centred on slat L.

11 Measure up 180 mm from the bottom end of slat F and, using a straight edge and pencil, mark a line back to the base of slat C. Cut along this line with a jigsaw.

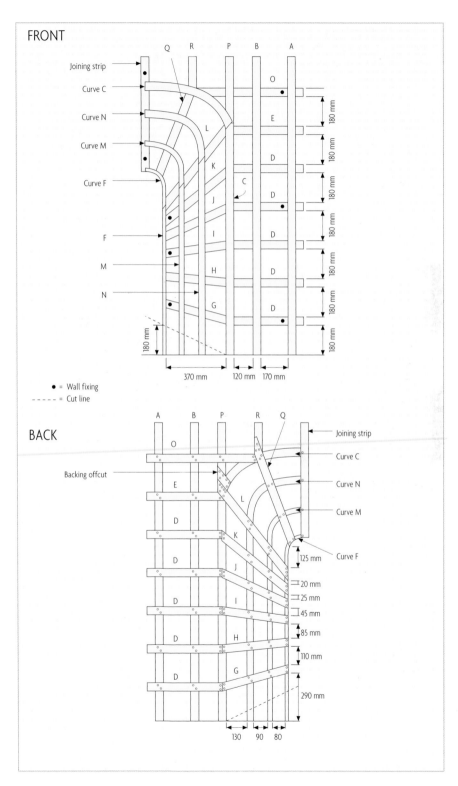

MATERIALS

PART	MATERIAL	FINISHED LENGTH	NO.
Slat A/B	50 x 20 mm treated pine	1800 mm	4
Slat C	50 x 20 mm treated pine	1400 mm	2
Slat D	50 x 20 mm treated pine	465 mm	10
Slat E**	50 x 20 mm treated pine	480 mm	2
Slat F	20 x 20 mm treated pine	925 mm	2
Slat G–J**	50 x 20 mm treated pine	500 mm	8
Slat K**	50 x 20 mm treated pine	600 mm	2
Slat L**	50 x 20 mm treated pine	750 mm	2
Slat M**	30 x 20 mm treated pine	1140 mm	2
Slat N**	40 x 20 mm treated pine	1330 mm	2
Slat O**	50 x 20 mm treated pine	730 mm	2
Slat P	50 x 20 mm treated pine	408 mm	2
Slat Q	50 x 20 mm treated pine	800 mm	2
Slat R	50 x 20 mm treated pine	185 mm	2
Joining strip	50 x 20 mm treated pine	665 mm	1
Backing offcut	50 x 20 mm treated pine	150 mm	2
Curves	190 x 20 mm treated pine	1200 mm	2
Cover strip	30 x 6 mm treated pine	665 mm	1

Other: Water-resistant epoxy adhesive; 30 mm x No. 8 galvanized screws; 25 mm panel pins; 20 x 2 mm galvanized lost-head nails; abrasive paper: 60 grit; 6 mm wall plugs and 65 mm x No. 6 screws for fixing to wall.

* Finished size: 2000 mm wide and 1800 mm high.

** Will be cut to length during construction.

TOOLS

- Tape measure and pencil
- Sliding bevel
- Tenon saw
- Mitre saw (optional)
- Jigsaw
- Electric drill
- Drill bits: 3 mm, 6 mm masonry
- Screwdriver and hammer
- Marking gauge
- Cork sanding block
- Square
- Spirit level

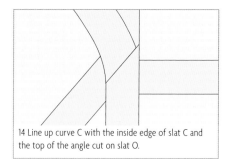

14 Line up curve C with the inside edge of slat C and the top of the angle cut on slat O.

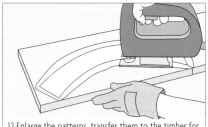

12 Enlarge the patterns, transfer them to the timber for the curves and use a jigsaw to cut out each piece.

THE ARCH

12 Enlarge the patterns opposite and transfer them to the timber for the curves. Using a jigsaw, cut out each piece and sand the edges smooth.

13 Make slat O, with a 70-degree cut on one end and a finished length to the short side of the point of 685 mm. Measure in 50 mm from the square end and mark. Fix O to the face of slats A and B, 180 mm up from E and with the 50 mm mark flush with the outer edge of A.

14 Line up the bottom edge of curve C with the inside edge of slat C and the top edge with the top of the angle cut on slat O. Fix curve C to slats L and O.

15 Take slat P and, with a pencil, scribe the shape of the top edge of curve C on its end. Cut it to shape with a jigsaw and then fix it to

slats L and O, keeping the edge in line with slat C. Place the backing offcut across the back of the joint at curve C and P, with its edge against L. Trace the edges of curve C and slat P onto the offcut and cut it to shape. Glue and screw the offcut across the joint in the usual way.

16 Fix curves N, M and F to slat L, with one end hard against slat N, M or F respectively. On curve F measure up 125 mm and place a mark. Place slat Q with its lower edge on this mark and the upper end against the 70-degree cut on slat O. On it, mark the inner edge of curve F and cut it to shape with the jigsaw. With a square resting on the edge of slat O, mark the cut needed on the top of

outdoor

Vertical slats of decreasing width are used to create perspective.

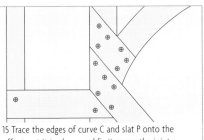

15 Trace the edges of curve C and slat P onto the offcut, cut it to shape and fix it across the joint.

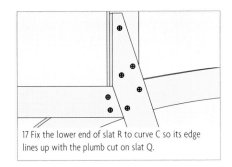

17 Fix the lower end of slat R to curve C so its edge lines up with the plumb cut on slat Q.

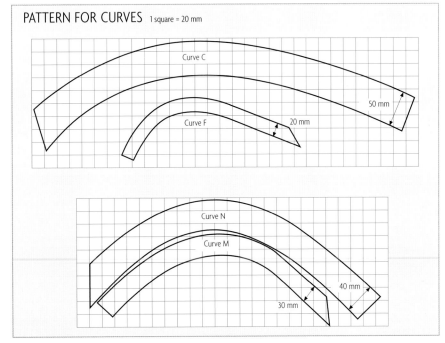

PATTERN FOR CURVES 1 square = 20 mm

Curve C

Curve F

50 mm

20 mm

Curve N

Curve M

40 mm

30 mm

slat Q and cut it. Fix slat Q to the back of curves C, N, M and F.

17 Take slat R, mark and cut the lower end to match the curve on curve C when its edge lines up with the cut on slat Q. Fix it to Q.

FINISHING PANEL 1

18 Place a straight edge across the ends of curves C, N, M and F and check that they line up. If they don't, mark and cut a straight line to ensure a good joint with the left-hand panel.

19 With a pencil, mark a line down the centre of the joining strip. Line up the centre line with the ends of the curves and the end of the strip with the inside of curve F. Apply adhesive to the joints, and drill a 3 mm pilot hole through each joint, fixing each with a screw.

20 Check the tops of slats A, B, P, R and the joining strip are level.

FINISHING THE TRELLIS

21 Make the left-hand panel in the same manner, following steps 1–18, but so that it is

a mirror copy of the right-hand panel. This is easiest if you assemble it on top of the first panel, face to face.

22 Sand all surfaces and edges smooth, and use wood filler in any gaps. Apply the finish of your choice.

23 Hold the panel with the joining strip against the wall. Use a spirit level to check that the top is level. To fix to a masonry wall, use a 6 mm masonry bit in an impact drill to drill eight 70 mm deep holes through the frame into the wall. Insert a masonry plug in

each hole and fix the frame to the wall with 65 mm screws.

24 Push the second panel against the first, lining up the ends of the curves. Fix it to the wall and then fix the end of each curve to the joining strip using a 30 mm screw.

25 Cut the cover strip to length so it finishes flush with the top and bottom edges of the curves. Use adhesive and 20 mm nails to fix it over the joint, hiding any gaps.

garden furniture

garden furniture

MAKING OUTDOOR FURNITURE

Building outdoor furniture requires the same skills and tools as any other carpentry job, and as always, a little forward planning will make the work much easier. Careful choice of materials will also result in a beautiful and long-lasting piece.

SUITING YOUR GARDEN

Before you begin work, spend some time deciding exactly what sort of garden furniture you need. Do you need a table for food or drinks as well as seats? Is your garden very small so that folding furniture is most suitable? Do you want furniture that is easily moved around the garden?

There is nothing worse than having your garden full of beautiful furniture you never use, so plan your requirements carefully.

CHOOSING MATERIALS

Outdoor furniture is, by its very nature, subjected to the weather, and the materials you use must be able to withstand the elements if the item is to remain in good condition.

Suitable timbers include treated pine, Western red cedar and jarrah. The latter two are much more expensive than pine, but can be worth the expense as they are very attractive. All timbers used outdoors require a protective finish, and the finish you choose will also affect your choice of timber. For instance, using jarrah would be a waste if you are planning to paint the item, but if you are planning to use a clear, oil finish to achieve a natural look, it might be worth the expense.

The nails, screws and bolts you use for outdoor furniture should always be galvanized so that they don't rust.

WORK AREA

- A specific workshop area isn't a necessity to build any of the projects in this book. However, some pieces are quite large, and you will need space to store materials and

to have enough space to move easily around the project during construction. An undercover area such as a carport or garage might suffice, but if you don't have a fixed roof to work under, make sure you can keep the timber dry and clear of the ground while it is stored.

- Good lighting is a necessity, not only for comfort, but for safety. Take care where you position your lights so you are not working in your own shadow and the light isn't in your eyes.
- Adhesives and paints can give off dangerous fumes, so always work in a well-ventilated area. Open windows and doors when applying adhesives or finishing coats.
- While an old table may be strong enough to serve as a workbench for small items, you will need a strong bench for most of these projects.

EQUIPMENT

Most of these projects can be completed using basic hand tools, but portable power tools will make the job easier and faster. A circular saw, electric drill, jigsaw and router are the most commonly used power tools in the home workshop.

SAFETY PRECAUTIONS

When using any type of portable power tool, make sure you are wearing the right safety gear. Always wear safety glasses that completely enclose the eyes and a dust mask (the cartridge type is recommended if you have any respiratory problems). If you have long hair, tying it back is not enough

Outdoor furniture such as this arbour seat turns a garden seat into living space.

protection—a cap or hairnet is essential. Also consider what clothing you will wear: loose-fitting garments are dangerous when working with machinery.

BEFORE YOU START

Read right through the instructions before you begin a project. Check that you have the tools, timber and hardware specified. Practise any techniques you are not familiar with on scrap timber.

outdoor

BARBECUE TABLE AND BENCH

This sturdy outdoor setting is simple to make. The construction requires the minimum number of joints and is suitable for the less experienced woodworker.

MAKING THE TABLE TOP

1 Cut two side rails and two end rails to length, using a power mitre saw.

2 Cut a 20 x 20 mm rebate along one edge of each end rail using a router. Measure in 70 mm from each end and square a line across the rebated side and edge. Set a marking gauge to 20 mm, turn over the rail and, working from the rebated edge, mark a line from the end to the 70 mm line. This part will be removed to create a flat section

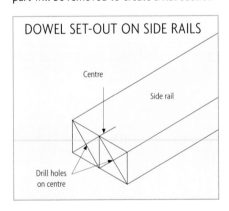

DOWEL SET-OUT ON SIDE RAILS

Centre

Side rail

Drill holes
on centre

A blue-on-white distressed finish gives this bench and table combo a contemporary look. It's perfect for dining al fresco with friends and family.

for the dowelled joint. Use a tenon saw to cut across the rebate and then a jigsaw to cut along the line. Round over the edge with abrasive paper.

3 Mark the dowel set-out on each end of the side rails (see diagram above). Use a 10 mm dowelling bit in an electric drill and bore the holes 26 mm deep. Place dowel centres in the holes and position the end rails at right angles to the side rails to mark the corresponding holes. Drill these holes 26 mm deep. Place adhesive in the holes and on the end of the rails. Insert the dowels and place the frame in sash cramps. Use scrap

timber between cramps and frame to protect the surface. Tighten the cramps and remove excess adhesive. Measure the diagonals for square. Leave to dry.

4 Cut eleven 1360 mm long slats and round over the ends and edges on the top surface with 120 grit abrasive paper. Lay the slats out upside down and fit the frame over the slats, allowing a gap of 3–5 mm between each board (a nail placed between the boards makes a useful spacer). For each slat drill one or two 4.5 mm clearance holes through the end rail, then 3 mm pilot holes into the underside of the slats. Hold each slat in

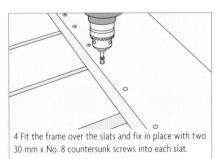

4 Fit the frame over the slats and fix in place with two 30 mm x No. 8 countersunk screws into each slat.

position and fix from beneath with 30 mm x No. 8 countersunk screws.

5 Using the End rail diagram (see page 460) as a guide, make a cardboard template to

MATERIALS*

PART	MATERIAL	FINISHED LENGTH	NO.
TABLE			
Side rail	70 x 35 mm treated pine	1360 mm	2
End rail	90 x 35 mm treated pine	900 mm	2
Slat	70 x 20 mm treated pine	1360 mm	11
Cleat	70 x 35 mm treated pine	760 mm	3
Spreader rail	70 x 35 mm treated pine	600 mm	2
Brace	70 x 35 mm treated pine	600 mm	2
Leg	70 x 35 mm treated pine	730 mm	4
BENCH			
Leg	70 x 35 mm treated pine	580 mm	4
Bearer	70 x 35 mm treated pine	450 mm	2
Back upright	70 x 35 mm treated pine	630 mm	2
Arm	70 x 35 mm treated pine	550 mm	2
Back slat (top)	90 x 20 mm treated pine	1350 mm	1
Back slat	70 x 20 mm treated pine	1350 mm	2
Seat slat	70 x 20 mm treated pine	1350 mm	1
Seat slat (front)	70 x 20 mm treated pine	1330 mm	5
Stiffener	70 x 35 mm treated pine	1260 mm	1
Rail	40 x 20 mm treated pine	450 mm	1
Cleat	25 x 25 mm treated pine	450 mm	2

Other: Epoxy adhesive; abrasive paper: two sheets of 120 grit; eight 50 mm long 10 mm diameter timber dowels; 30 mm x No. 8 galvanized countersunk screws; 40 mm x No. 8 galvanized countersunk screws; 50 mm x No. 8 galvanized countersunk screws; 65 mm x No. 8 galvanized countersunk screws; 50 x 2.5 mm galvanized decking nails; preservative; finish of choice.

* Finished size: table 1500 mm long x 900 mm wide x 750 mm high; bench 1400 mm wide x 600 mm deep x 840 mm high.

TOOLS

- Rule or tape and pencil
- Jigsaw and tenon saw
- Power mitre saw
- Router with 20 mm straight bit
- Marking gauge
- Electric drill
- Drill bits: 3 mm and 4.5 mm twist bit, 10 mm dowelling bit
- 10 mm dowel centres
- Sash cramps
- Screwdriver to suit
- Sliding bevel
- Combination square
- Builder's square
- Hammer
- Chisel: 25 mm

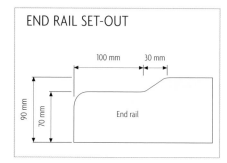

END RAIL SET-OUT

shape each end rail. Draw the shape onto the rails with pencil. Cut the shape with a jigsaw. Clean the edge with 120 grit abrasive paper.

6 Turn the top upside down and measure in 250 mm from each end. Square this mark across the bottom of the slats. Cut two 70 x 35 mm cleats to fit between the side rails. Bevel-cut the ends to 15 mm thick; round the edges over. Position the cleats on the inside

of the marked lines and drill a 4.5 mm clearance hole followed by a 3 mm pilot hole into each slat. Screw the cleats to each slat with a 40 mm x No. 8 countersunk screw. Fix a third cleat across the centre of the slats. Skew a 50 mm galvanized screw into the side rails from each side of the cleats.

ADDING THE TABLE LEGS

7 The legs are cut with a 5-degree parallel bevel on each end. Set the angle on a mitre saw or you may set a sliding bevel or create a pitch board (see diagram on page 463). To minimize waste, cut the legs from one length of timber. Bevel-cut one end at 5 degrees. Measure 730 mm, mark and cut parallel to the first cut. Mark and cut the other legs. The angle on the waste side is the same angle required for the next leg.

8 Cut two stretcher rails 600 mm long with 5-degree bevels (angled in opposite

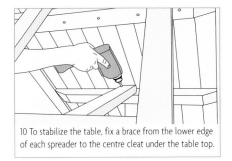

10 To stabilize the table, fix a brace from the lower edge of each spreader to the centre cleat under the table top.

directions, not parallel as for the legs) at each end. Measure up 300 mm from the bottom of each leg and square a line across the outside edge. Place the legs flat with the spreader rail on top. Line up the top edge of the rail with the squared lines. Keep the ends flush with the outside edge of the legs. Fix in position with two 50 mm x No. 8 countersunk screws on each leg. Use the pitch board or sliding bevel to ensure the rail is at the correct angle.

9 Stand the assembled leg frame upside down against the outside edge of an end cleat. Centre it against the cleat. Fix each leg with two 65 mm x No. 8 screws into the edge of the cleat. Repeat at the other end for the other leg frame.

10 To stabilize the table, cut a brace for each leg. Measure from the lower edge of the spreader rail to the centre cleat. Cut two braces to this length. Fix them with two 50 mm x No. 8 screws into the centre of the cleat and to the spreader. Turn the table right side up and lightly sand with 120 grit abrasive paper.

CUTTING BENCH PIECES
11 Cut the four legs 580 mm long. Bevel both ends of each at 5 degrees. Cut two bearers 450 mm long.

12 Cut an 80-degree angle on one end of each bearer. Measure and mark 70 mm in

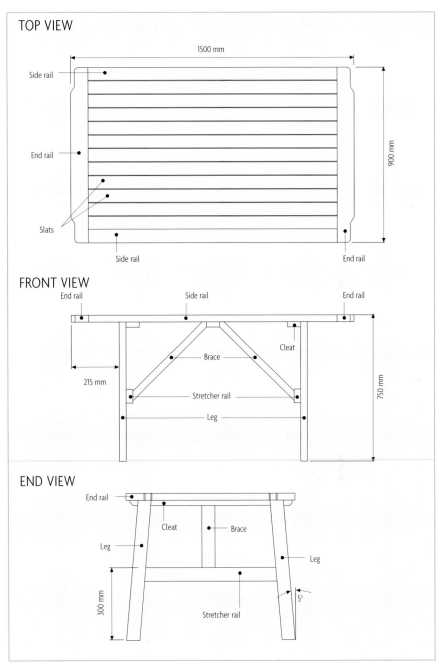

TOP VIEW

FRONT VIEW

END VIEW

from the opposite end of the bearer and square a line across the top edge (see diagram on page 462). Square a second line across the same end 10 mm down from the top. Join these points on the face and cut

the bevel. On the lower edge cut a 45-degree bevel. Cut two 630 mm back uprights, bevelling the top of each as for the bearers.

13 The arms fit around the back uprights and

This simply constructed bench is given an individual touch with a cut-out design in the top slat.

sit on top of the legs. Square-cut one end of an arm. Measure 70 mm from the end and, with a square and pencil, mark a line from the inside edge across the face.

14 Place a bearer on the edge of the arm and use it as a template to mark an 80-degree angle. Square the bevelled mark across the bottom of the arm. Use a gauge to mark 35 mm from the line to the squared end on each face. Remove this corner with a saw by cutting on the waste side of the line. Make the second arm in the same way but so you have one left and one right arm. Round the ends of the arms with abrasive paper.

15 Cut the back slats. Shape the ends of the top slat with a jigsaw to match the table top. Round the edges with abrasive paper. Cut a design in the centre of the top slat.

ASSEMBLING THE BENCH
16 Square a line 10 mm in from both ends across the back of the back slats. Position the top slat on the bevelled end of one back

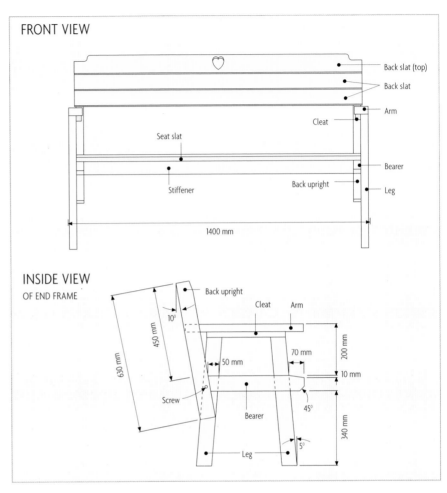

FRONT VIEW

Back slat (top)
Back slat
Arm
Cleat
Seat slat
Bearer
Stiffener
Back upright
Leg
1400 mm

INSIDE VIEW
OF END FRAME

Back upright
Cleat
Arm
10°
450 mm
630 mm
70 mm
200 mm
50 mm
10 mm
Screw
Bearer
45°
340 mm
5°
Leg

upright. Line up the squared line with the outside face of the upright and fix with adhesive and two decking nails. Check for square with a builder's square. Fix the other end of the slat to the other upright. Nail the other two back slats in place with a 10 mm overhang and a 4 mm gap between each. Cut two cleats from offcuts, turn the frame over and fix them across the back of the slats, 10 mm from the top (see photograph on page 459).

17 Cut the seat slats. The long slat goes at the front and overhangs the bearers 10 mm each end; the others sit flush on the bearers. Fix them in place as for the back slats. Turn

the seat over and cut the stiffener. It fits between the bearers, in line with the second slat. Fix it through the bearers with two 65 mm x No. 8 screws at each end. Fix a 40 x 20 mm rail across the centre of the slats.

18 Measure up 340 mm from the bottom of each leg on the inside face and mark a line across the face of the leg, parallel to the end. Position each leg against the bearer, lining up the set-out with the bottom edge. The front legs sit against the edge of the front slat. The back legs are fixed 50 mm in from the bevelled end (see diagram above) and secured with two 50 mm x No. 8 screws.

outdoor

19 The back is positioned so its top is 450 mm above the top of the bearer. Hold the upright against the end of the bearer and fix it in place with two 50 mm screws into the leg.

20 Cut two 450 mm cleats to fit against the inside of the legs at the top. Cut the ends at a 5-degree angle to match the outside of the legs. Fix in place, flush on top and ends, with two 50 mm screws into each leg.

21 Place the arm on top of the legs, against the back. Fix with 50 mm screws through the upright and cleat. Sand the bench and apply a finish to match the table.

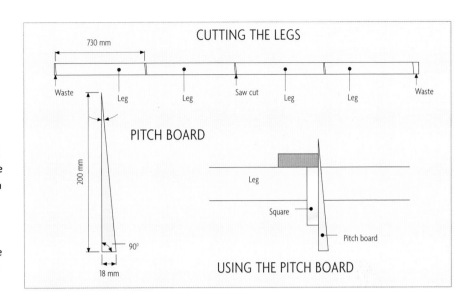

CIRCULAR SEAT

This circular seat is made in eight separate sections that can be joined to surround a tree trunk or other garden feature. Four sections make a semicircle to stand against a wall.

CONSTRUCTING THE FRAME

1 Cut sixteen front legs and sixteen back legs to length. Use a power mitre saw to ensure an accurate square cut. Measure 70 mm from the top of each front leg and square a line across the face and down each edge. Set the marking gauge to 17.5 mm and mark across the end and down each edge to the 70 mm mark to indicate the halving joint.

2 Place a front leg next to a back leg with the bottom ends flush. Transfer the set-out lines from the front leg onto the back leg to mark a corresponding joint. Mark a cross on the face between the set-out lines. Square the set-out lines across both edges and mark a depth of 17.5 mm between the lines. Repeat for the remaining legs. Adjust the depth of cut on the circular saw to 17.5 mm. Clamp each leg in turn on a set of trestles and cut the joints with the saw by lining up

the notch in the baseplate with the set-out line and cutting on the waste side. Place several intermediate cuts in the timber to help remove the waste. Chisel the waste from each joint, first removing the bulk of the timber by striking the chisel with a hammer or mallet, leaving approximately 3 mm of timber in the bottom of each joint. Clean the joint by paring in from each side down to the gauge line. Use the square to check the bottom is flat and adjust if required.

3 Cut the side rails to length. To cut the halving joints, measure 70 mm from each end and square a line across the face and down each side. Gauge the depth (17.5 mm); cut and remove the waste as before. Check each joint for accuracy of fit.

4 Place one front and one back leg on a flat surface with the recesses face up. Apply

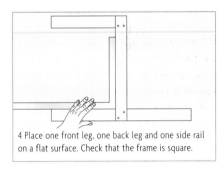

4 Place one front leg, one back leg and one side rail on a flat surface. Check that the frame is square.

preservative to each joint. Place a side rail in the recesses; check the inside of the frame for square. Drill two 4.5 mm holes 20 mm across from the inside of the front joint with 3 mm pilot holes into the leg and secure with 30 mm x No. 8 galvanized particleboard screws through the rail into the leg. In the back leg place a screw 20 mm in from the front edge and the other 20 mm in from the back edge. Check the frame for square. The side with screw heads

464

You can follow the sun or the shade all day with this clever seating arrangement constructed in treated pine and finished with paint designed for exterior use.

TOOLS

- Tape or rule and pencil
- Handsaw
- Circular saw
- Power mitre saw
- Jigsaw
- Builder's square
- Combination square
- Marking gauge
- Chisel: 25 mm
- Hammer
- Nail punch
- Electric drill
- Drill bit: 4.5 mm
- Screwdriver
- Sliding bevel
- Hand plane
- Trestles

will be the inside of the frame. Assemble the other legs and side rails, so that each seat section will have a left and right frame.

5 Cut the rails to length. To make housings for the front and back rails, measure 70 mm from the top of each leg and square a line across both faces and the front edge. Measure 35 mm from the front edge on the inside face and gauge a line from the top of the leg to the squared lines. Set a sliding bevel to 22.5 degrees and mark a line on the top of each front leg (see diagram on page 466). Hold the frame upright in a vice and cut down the line on the waste side with a handsaw. Rotate the frame 90 degrees and cut the shoulders down to the first cut. Check for accuracy of fit and adjust as required.

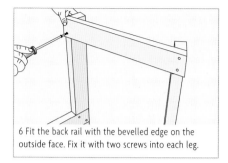

6 Fit the back rail with the bevelled edge on the outside face. Fix it with two screws into each leg.

6 The face of the back rail is bevelled to fit the vertical slats. Gauge a line 12 mm from the face along the top edge of the rail. Set the circular saw to cut at 10 degrees and use a rip fence to ensure a straight cut. Hold the timber firmly on edge in a vice and rip along the gauged line. Stand the rail on edge and cut the ends at 22.5 degrees using a power mitre saw. Apply a coat of preservative to the housings in the back legs and fix the rail flush on the outside face with two 50 mm x No. 8 galvanized particleboard screws into the leg. The front rail is cut 856 mm long and is fixed in the same manner.

7 The intermediate rail will need one edge bevelled to allow the back to be sloped. Gauge a line 12 mm from the front edge along the face. Tilt the circular saw to 10 degrees and set the rip fence to 58 mm. Hold the rail firm in a vice or skew-nail it on a trestle. Cut the bevel along the length. Place the rail flat on the mitre saw and cut the ends at 22.5 degrees so they finish flush on the ends. Place them against the back legs and drill two holes at each end into the top of each side rail. Fix with 50 mm x No. 8 galvanized particleboard screws.

ADDING THE SLATS

8 Cut the 90 x 20 mm vertical slats for the back. Position each slat over a side frame. Place a builder's square on the top rail and square up the slat so that the outside edge is flush with the end of the

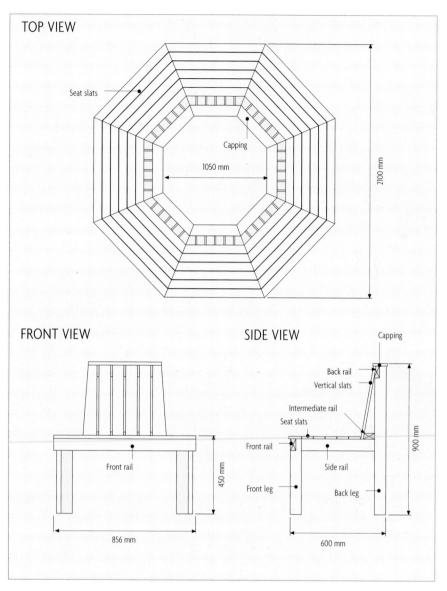

intermediate rail. With a pencil, mark the back of the vertical slat, the end and top edge of the top rail. Remove the slat and place it face down on the trestles. Mark a line along the length of the slat between these two points. Set your circular saw to 22.5 degrees. Hold the slats firm and rip along the line on the waste side. Ensure that the saw cut bevels the correct way. Remember, the set-out line is on the back

of the slat, therefore the face is wider. You will require one left-hand and one right-hand slat for each section. Stand the slat on edge and cut the top of the marked length with a 10-degree bevel. Use a hand plane to round the edge on the front corner of the bevelled side. Apply some preservative to the rail and to the back of the slat. Fix the slat with two 40 x 2.5 mm twisted-shank nails.

The individual sections are screwed together to form a complete circle.

9 Cut the remaining vertical slats to length with a 10-degree angle on top. Leave a gap of 10 mm between the slats. Fix as for the side slats.

10 The seat slats reduce in length from front to back. Select a straight slat to be cut for a starter board at the front of the seat. Cut one end at 22.5 degrees on the mitre saw. Position this slat with the bevelled end flush with the outside face of the frame. Allow 10 mm to overhang the front rail, and mark the length on the underside at the opposite end frame. Turn the board over and cut to this set-out using the

LEG BEVEL HOUSING

MATERIALS*

PART	MATERIAL	FINISHED LENGTH	NO.
Front leg	70 x 35 mm treated pine	450 mm	16
Back leg	70 x 35 mm treated pine	875 mm	16
Side rail	70 x 35 mm treated pine	600 mm	16
Back rail	70 x 35 mm treated pine	462 mm	8
Front rail	70 x 35 mm treated pine	856 mm	8
Intermediate rail	70 x 35 mm treated pine	520 mm	8
Vertical slat (side)	90 x 20 mm treated pine**	450 mm	16
Vertical slat (intermediate)	70 x 20 mm treated pine**	450 mm	32
Seat slat	70 x 20 mm treated pine**	870 mm	48
Capping	90 x 20 mm treated pine	480 mm	8

Other: 40 x 2.5 mm galvanized twisted-shank decking nails; 30 mm x No. 8 countersunk galvanized particleboard screws; 50 mm x No. 8 countersunk galvanized particleboard screws; abrasive paper: 100 grit; preservative; finish.

* Finished size: 2100 mm diameter x 900 mm high.

** The seat and vertical slats are cut from treated pine decking.

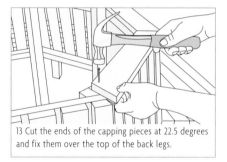

13 Cut the ends of the capping pieces at 22.5 degrees and fix them over the top of the back legs.

drop saw. Apply preservative, then fix the rail with two twisted-shank nails. As you are nailing close to the end, drill a pilot hole to prevent the timber splitting.

11 Cut one end of the next board. Position it on the seat, flush on the angled end. Use a 3 mm nail as a spacer between the boards at each end and mark the underside to determine the length. Cut and fix as for the starter board, ensuring the ends are flush with the outside of the end frames. Fix the remaining slats in the same way.

FINISHING

12 Apply a finish to each section of the project. If necessary, level the ground around the tree so the seat sits level and all sections line up with each other. Position each section in turn, joining them with 50 mm screws. Fix two screws into the front legs and three into the back legs, keeping the seat and backs aligned.

13 Cut the ends of the capping pieces at 22.5 degrees so that the shorter side fits on top of the back leg. Fix them with decking nails.

outdoor

ADJUSTABLE LOUNGER

The cross-rails of this elegant lounger are housed into the side rails, and the slats are set on edge for extra strength. The back adjusts to three different heights or can be laid flat.

This lounger is made from Western red cedar, a durable softwood for exterior use. It is also a lightweight timber, well suited to furniture that is often moved. You can, however, add wheels to the legs at one end if you like.

MATERIALS*

PART	MATERIAL	FINISHED LENGTH	NO.
Side rail	115 x 30 mm Western red cedar	2300 mm	2
Foot rail	115 x 30 mm Western red cedar	530 mm	1
Head/centre rail	70 x 30 mm Western red cedar	530 mm	2
Leg	115 x 30 mm Western red cedar	300 mm	4
Leg stretcher	70 x 30 mm Western red cedar	450 mm	2
Ledger	30 x 40 mm Western red cedar	450 mm	1
Fixed batten	70 x 30 mm Western red cedar	1200 mm	8
Short batten	70 x 30 mm Western red cedar	740 mm	7
Side batten	70 x 30 mm Western red cedar	760 mm	2
Back trimmer	70 x 30 mm Western red cedar	505 mm	1
Brace	30 x 30 mm Western red cedar	400 mm	2
Brace stretcher	30 x 30 mm Western red cedar	505 mm	1
Bearer	30 x 40 mm Western red cedar	307 mm	2
Block	30 x 40 mm Western red cedar	200 mm	2

Other: Two 540 mm pieces of 40 mm dowelling; abrasive paper: 80 grit; 65 x 2.5 mm galvanized lost-head nails; 50 mm x No. 8 galvanized particleboard screws; ten 75 mm x No. 8 galvanized particleboard screws; one 600 x 10 mm galvanized threaded rod with two dome nuts and washers to suit; natural decking oil or finish of your choice.

* All material sizes quoted are dressed measurements. For timber types and sizes, see page 199. Finished size: 2300 mm long x 580 mm wide x 350 mm high.

LEG HOUSINGS

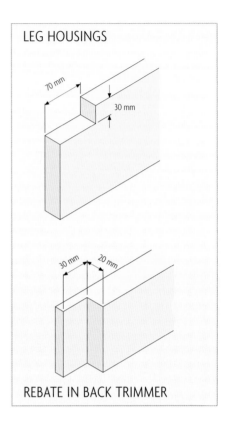

REBATE IN BACK TRIMMER

SIDE RAIL HOUSINGS

1 Cut two side rails. Watch for any bows in the timber, and keep them facing up. Measure 200 mm from each end and square a line across the face. Measure in 30 mm from these lines and square another line for the foot and head rail housings.

2 At the foot end square the shoulder lines across both the bottom and top face edges. Set a gauge to 10 mm and mark a line between the set-out lines on both edges to indicate the through housing.

3 Set the circular saw for a 10 mm cut. Hold the side rail firmly with a G-cramp. Cut the shoulders on the waste side. Make several cuts within the joint to make chiselling out the waste easier. Remove the waste with

a sharp 25 mm firmer chisel, working from both sides. Check the bottom of the joint for flatness and adjust it as required.

4 At the head end square the shoulder lines across the bottom edge. Using a marking gauge set to 10 mm, mark a line on the edge between these set-out lines. Then set the marking gauge to 70 mm and mark a line between the shoulder lines on the face side (to make a stopped housing 70 mm up from the bottom edge for the head rail). Use a tenon saw to cut the shoulders at an angle on the face to the gauge line on the face edge. Make several saw cuts within the joint, taking care not to go past the gauge lines.

5 Drill holes into the housing and remove the waste with a sharp chisel, cutting

across the grain by striking the chisel straight down on the shoulder lines. Turn the chisel around and hold the ground side down at about 45 degrees and strike it to sever the grain. Turn the chisel ground-side up and pare away the waste across the grain from the edge to the end of the housing. Remove a little at a time until the required depth is reached. Ensure the shoulders and the bottom of the joint are straight.

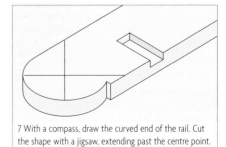

7 With a compass, draw the curved end of the rail. Cut the shape with a jigsaw, extending past the centre point.

TOOLS

- Tape or rule and pencil
- Circular saw
- Jigsaw
- Tenon saw
- Power mitre saw
- Combination square
- Marking gauge
- Chisel: 25 mm firmer
- Electric drill
- Drill bits: 4.5 mm, 10 mm, 40 mm forstner
- Hammer
- Nail punch
- Compasses
- Two G-cramps
- Screwdriver to suit
- Spanner to suit
- Cork sanding block

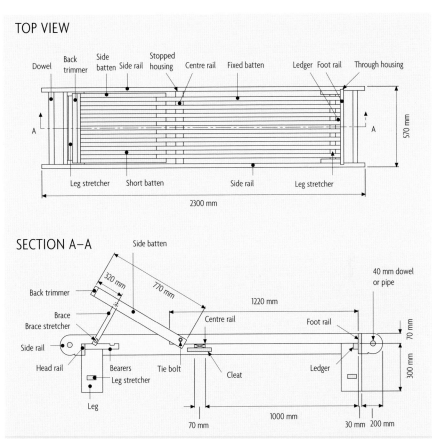

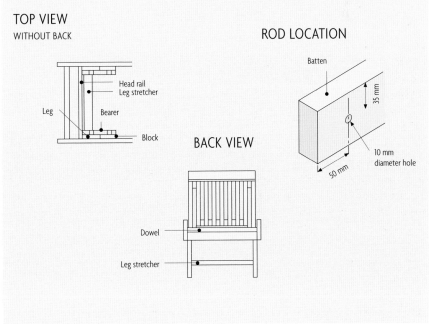

6 Make another stopped housing for the centre rail. Measure 1000 mm from the foot housing, then measure a further 70 mm. Square the lines across the face. Now measure 70 mm down from the top edge and mark the end of the housing between the shoulder lines. Square the lines across the bottom edge and mark a depth of 10 mm. Cut the stopped housing in the same manner as before.

FINISHING THE FRAME COMPONENTS

7 Use a combination square and pencil to mark a 45-degree line from each corner across the inside face of both ends of the side rails. Place the point of a compass at the intersection of these lines and draw the curved end of the rail. Cut the shape with a jigsaw, extending it a little way beyond the centre point. See diagram on page 468. Smooth the edges with 80 grit abrasive paper wrapped around a sanding block.

8 Dowelling is used at the head and foot of the lounger to create the handles. Drill a hole 20 mm deep at the intersection of the 45-degree lines using a forstner bit. Choose a bit that matches the diameter of the dowelling so that the hole is the correct size.

9 Cut four legs 300 mm long. Square the ends and, with square and marking gauge, set out a housing in the top corner of each leg, 30 mm in from the edge and 70 mm down from the top (see diagram on page 468). Hold the leg firmly with a G-cramp or vice and cut along the leg with a circular saw to the squared line, then cross-cut with a handsaw to remove the waste. Complete the rip cut with the handsaw.

ASSEMBLY

10 Before starting to assemble the lounger, apply a coat of preservative to all the joints if desired.

11 Cut the foot, head and centre rails. Place one side rail flat on a firm surface with the housing side up. Stand all the cross-rails in their housings. Skew a 65 mm nail through each cross-rail into the side rail. Place the other side rail flat, housing side up, then turn

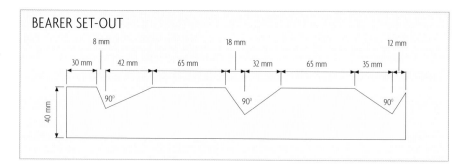

BEARER SET-OUT

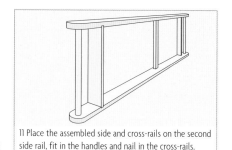

11 Place the assembled side and cross-rails on the second side rail, fit in the handles and nail in the cross-rails.

the assembled section over and stand it in the housings. Cut two 540 mm handles from dowelling. Fit them in the holes drilled at the ends, keeping all the pieces in position. Skew-nail the cross-rails to the second side rail as for the first side. Cut two cleats from offcuts, and fix them to the side rails beneath the centre rail.

12 Position the legs inside the frame with the head and foot rails sitting in the rebates. Drill two 4.5 mm holes through each leg and 3 mm pilot holes into the side rail. Fix the legs with 50 mm screws. For added strength, position a ledger 70 mm down from the top edge on the inside face of the foot rail. Fix it to the rail with three 50 mm screws. Skew-nail the leg stretchers between the legs.

13 Cut the eight fixed battens from 70 x 30 mm timber to the required length, using the mitre saw. Measure 50 mm in from one end on each and square a line across the face. Set a marking gauge to 35 mm and mark the centre of the line. At this set-out point drill a 10 mm hole right through each batten.

14 Lay one batten in position, against the inside of the side rails with the hole at the head end and bore a corresponding 10 mm hole right through the side rail. Repeat this procedure to drill a hole on the other side rail.

15 Use the offcuts from the battens as spacers. Place the spacers between the side

rail and the batten. Push the batten against the spacers, with the end of the batten against the inside of the foot rail. Position all the battens and insert the tie rod to help keep the holes in alignment. Nail through the outside of the foot rail into the end of the batten with two 65 x 2.5 mm galvanized lost-head nails. Nail the other end of the batten from underneath, through the centre rail. Remove the tie rod.

16 Cut the back trimmer 505 mm long from 70 x 30 mm timber. This should allow it to fit between the side rails with a little clearance. To cut a rebate joint to house each side batten, square a line across the face and down each side, 30 mm in from each end. Set a marking gauge to 20 mm and mark a line across the ends and along each side to the squared lines (see diagram on page 468). Cut the rebate on the waste side of the line with a circular saw. Remove the waste.

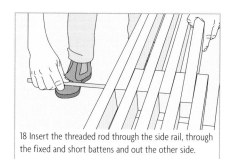

18 Insert the threaded rod through the side rail, through the fixed and short battens and out the other side.

outdoor

TIMBER

TIMBER CONDITIONS

Timber is sold in three conditions:

- sawn or rough-sawn: brought to a specific (nominal) size by bandsaw
- planed: either planed all round (PAR), planed on two sides (P2S) or double planed (DP)
- moulded: planed to a specific profile for architraves, window sills, skirting boards and so on.

Planed timber is sold using the same nominal dimensions as sawn timber, for example 100 x 50 mm, but the surfaces have all been machined down to a flat, even width and thickness so that the '100 x 50 mm' timber becomes 91 x 41 mm when planed. The chart on the right shows the sizes for seasoned timber in its sawn (nominal) state and after dressing.

Moulded timbers are also ordered by their nominal sizes. Their finished sizes will generally compare with those given in the chart for planed timber, but check them carefully at the timber yard as there will be many variations.

UNSEASONED TIMBER

The sizes for unseasoned timber will vary somewhat as the timber is still in the process of shrinking. This applies particularly for timbers measuring more than 100 x 50 mm. It is possible to have the supplier plane unseasoned timber to the required size.

SAWN (NOMINAL) SIZE (mm)	SIZE AFTER PLANING (mm)
25	19
31	23
38	30
50	41
75	66
100	91
125	115
150	138
175	160

TREATED TIMBER

Treated timber is, however, sold in its finished size. Some of the available sizes are:

70 x 35 mm	70 x 45 mm
90 x 45 mm	90 x 90 mm
120 x 45 mm	

TIMBER LENGTHS

Timber is now sold in stock lengths, beginning at 1.8 m and increasing by 300 mm to 2.1 m, 2.4 m and so on. Short lengths and offcuts are also usually available.

TIMBER FOR OUTDOOR USE

Garden furniture requires timber able to withstand the elements. Among the possible choices are treated pine, Western red cedar and hardwood. All these timbers will require some type of protective finish. If the timber has an attractive colour or grain, a natural oil finish will enhance its appearance.

---

17 Cut seven short battens 740 mm long and two side battens 760 mm long for the adjustable back. Set out and drill a hole at one end of each as for the fixed battens.

INSERTING THE TIE ROD

18 Insert a length of 10 mm threaded rod through the side rail and one 760 mm batten. Continue pushing the rod alternately through a fixed batten and a short batten, finishing with the remaining 760 mm batten inside the opposite side rail. Place dome nuts and washers on each end of the rod.

19 Position the back trimmer and fix it through each outside batten with three 65 x 2.5 mm galvanized lost-head nails.

Use the batten offcuts as spacers, and nail through the trimmer into the ends of the battens as before.

20 Cut two braces that will be used to adjust the angle of the back. Measure 30 mm from the end of each piece and drill a 4.5 mm hole in the centre. On the outside batten measure 320 mm from the trimmer and 30 mm up from the bottom edges. Drill a 4.5 mm hole.

21 Cut two bearers 307 mm long. Notches are cut on the bearers to determine the adjustable angle of the back. Refer to the diagram above left and mark the set-out on each bearer. Use a jigsaw to cut the three notches at 90-degree angles.

22 Position the bearers on each side against the leg, taking care to keep the top flush with the top of the leg. Place a timber block of the same thickness as the leg between the bearer and the side rail and fix with three 75 mm x No. 8 screws.

23 Fix the braces to the back with 75 mm x No. 8 screws. Cut a 505 mm long stretcher to fit between the braces. Position the stretcher 30 mm up from the bottom of the braces and fix with 50 mm x No. 8 particle-board screws.

FINISHING

24 Apply the protective finish of your choice to the lounger.

SWING SEAT

The A-frame construction of this appealing garden swing takes up relatively little space, making it suitable for large or small gardens. It is not difficult to make.

The ideal spot to while away your hard-earned leisure, this swing seat is constructed from treated pine and given a clear, natural finish.

TOOLS

- Tape or rule and pencil
- Power mitre saw
- Circular saw
- Jigsaw
- Handsaw
- Combination square
- Builder's square and rafter buttons
- Trestles
- Hand plane
- Marking gauge
- Hammer
- Electric drill
- Drill bits: 4.5 mm, 8 mm, 10 mm
- Screwdriver and spanners
- G-cramps
- Chisel: 25 mm
- Cork sanding block

MAKING THE FRAME

1 Cut the beam to length using a power mitre saw. Measure 150 mm from each end and square a line around the beam. This is the outside edge of the A-frame.

2 To mark the bevels at each end of the legs, set up a builder's square with rafter buttons. Fix one button to the blade of the square at 316 mm and the other on the stock at 97 mm. Place the leg on edge and mark the position of the stock on the timber (see diagram on page 474). This is the bevel for the foot cut. Then mark the position of the blade on the edge of the timber. Slide the square along the timber, lining up the stock with the previous blade position. Mark the blade length again and slide the square

along. Repeat until you have stepped the length six times. The last blade mark is the cut to go against the beam. Square these positions down each face of the leg; cut on the waste side. This is the leg template.

3 Clamp the timber on edge to the trestles and cut with a handsaw. Follow the set-out lines and regularly check both sides of the cut, especially the top cut. If necessary, plane the cut end to even the bevel. To cut the second leg, place the first leg on top of it, edge to edge, and trace the bevels and length from the first leg onto the second leg. Cut to match.

outdoor

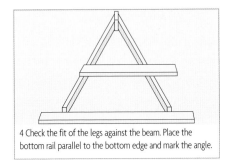

4 Check the fit of the legs against the beam. Place the bottom rail parallel to the bottom edge and mark the angle.

4 Place the two legs on edge with the top ends resting either side of an offcut of beam timber. Move the bottom of the legs 1200 mm apart. Check that the top fits neatly against the offcut and lay a straight edge against the feet to check the bevel. Adjust as required.

5 Measure 500 mm from the straight edge at the bottom of the legs and place a bottom rail over the legs. On the rail, mark the angle of the legs. On the legs, mark the top and bottom of the rail. Place a top rail across the legs, 150 mm down from the beam, parallel to the first rail. Mark as before. Remove the rails and join the set-out across the face. Cut the rails to length.

6 Check the fit. Use a square to transfer the marks down the inside face of the legs. Use these four pieces as a pattern for the other side frame. Construct it in the same way.

7 Set a gauge to 22 mm and mark a line on the inside face of each leg between the squared lines. Hold each rail on the gauged line, between the squared lines. Nail a 65 x 2.5 mm lost-head nail through the outside of the leg. When all the joints are fitted and the frame has been nailed, drill through the leg with an 8 mm bit down to the centre of the end of each rail. Drill a 4.5 mm pilot hole as deep as possible into the end of the rails. Put a 100 x 8 mm coach screw with washer into the hole and tighten. Repeat at the ends of all rails.

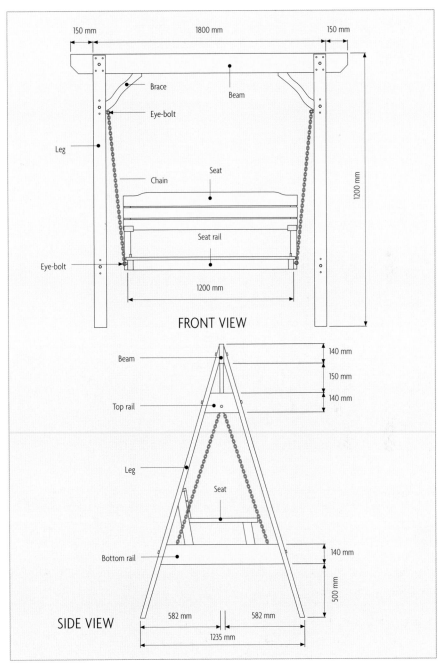

FRONT VIEW

SIDE VIEW

8 Place the frame on the face of one leg. Slide the beam in place at the top of the frame. Line up the outer edge of the frame with the square marks on the beam. Drill a 10 mm hole through the leg, the beam and the other leg. Fix with a 125 x 10 mm cup-head nut and bolt. Check the beam is square to the leg. Measure 30 mm up from the bottom of the beam and drill two 4.5 mm holes through the leg. Screw 65 mm screws through the leg, into the beam. Drill two 4.5 mm holes through the leg 30 mm from the top of the beam. Fix with 38 mm screws.

9 Fit the brace between the top rail and the beam. Fix the brace through the rail with a 65 mm screw. To fix the top of the brace to the bottom edge of the beam, drill a 4.5 mm hole near the end of the brace and fit a 38 mm screw into the beam.

CONSTRUCTING THE SEAT

10 Cut two bearers to length using the mitre saw. Square a line across the top edge, 200 mm from each end. Measure in another 70 mm and square a line as before (see diagram at right). Mark the centre of the bearer and square a line across the top edge and down the faces. Mark 10 mm down the centre line and tack in a small nail. To curve the seat, bend a thin piece of timber over the nail and out to the 70 mm lines. Trace the curve onto the bearer. Clamp the bearer to a trestle and cut the curve on the waste side with a jigsaw. Smooth with abrasive paper.

11 Square both 200 mm set-out lines across the inside face and both edges of the bearers. Measure in 35 mm from this and square a line around all sides. Set a gauge to 10 mm and mark both edges between the lines for the rail housings. Clamp the bearers to a trestle and cut on the waste side. Clean the joint.

12 Cut two back uprights to length with one end 10 degrees off square. For the halving housing, measure in 72 mm and mark a shoulder line across the face, parallel to the angle cut. Square this line down each edge. Set a marking gauge to 17 mm and mark a line along the edges of the timber and across the end. Make left and right uprights. Clamp the upright flat on a trestle and cut

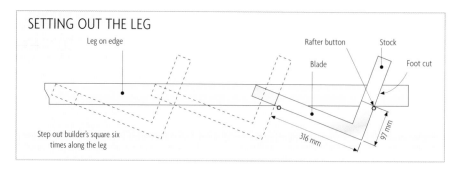

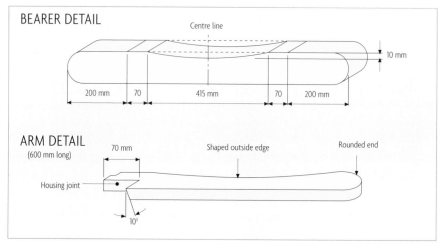

BEARER DETAIL

Centre line
10 mm
200 mm | 70 | 415 mm | 70 | 200 mm

ARM DETAIL
(600 mm long)
70 mm
Shaped outside edge
Rounded end
Housing joint
10°

the housing on the waste side. Make several cuts across the joint. Remove the waste; level the housing bottom.

13 Cut two arm supports, each end angled at 10 degrees. Set out and cut a housing at the bottom end as for the back uprights (see diagram opposite). Cut one left and one right. Cut two seat rails 1200 mm long on the mitre saw. Apply preservative to the housing and the end of the rails. Position the rails in the housing on the side of the bearers. Drill two 4.5 mm holes through the outside of the bearer. Fix the rails with 75 mm x No. 10 screws. Fix the back uprights and arm supports to the bearers with three 50 mm x No. 8 screws at the 200 mm set-out lines.

14 Cut two arms. Measure in 70 mm on one end and square a line across the face. Mark

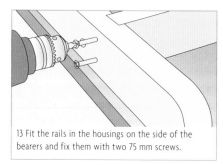

13 Fit the rails in the housings on the side of the bearers and fix them with two 75 mm screws.

a line on the inside edge 10 degrees off square and square a line back across the bottom. Gauge a line 35 mm in from the edge, from the squared line on the face across the end and back to the squared line on the opposite face. Cut out the corner with a handsaw. Round the front end of the arm with a jigsaw. Smooth with 120 grit abrasive paper. To fix the arm, measure 205 mm from the top of the bearer up the

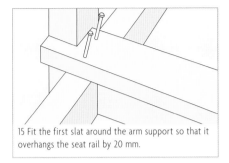

15 Fit the first slat around the arm support so that it overhangs the seat rail by 20 mm.

SEAT SIDE VIEW

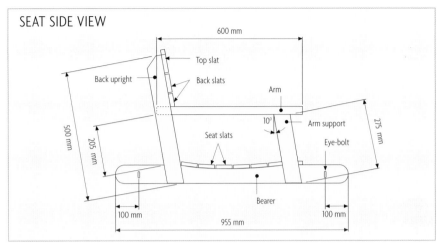

back upright. Hold the arm on top of this mark and drill a 4.5 mm hole. Fit two 50 mm x No. 8 galvanized particleboard screws through the back upright into the centre of the arm. Place another two screws through the top of the arm into the arm support.

14 Place the first rafter on a flat surface. Stand the ridge on end and align the rafter with the gauged line.

ADDING THE SLATS

15 Cut eight seat slats with the mitre saw. The two front slats fit around the arm support. Hold the first slat with the ends flush on the outside face of the arm supports. Mark the position of the inside face of the support on the edge of the slat. Square this line across the face of the slat. The slat overhangs the seat rail by 20 mm. Set a gauge to 20 mm to mark a line parallel to the front edge, from the squared line to the outside edge. Place a cross on the opposite side of the line to indicate the section to be removed. Hold the slat on a trestle and, with a handsaw, rip down the grain to the squared line then across the slat on the waste side. Clean the cut with a chisel. Sand the sharp edge with 120 grit abrasive paper and apply preservative to the ends and underneath.

16 Fix the slat to the bearer with two 40 x 2.5 mm decking nails at each end. Evenly space two more nails into the rail. Fit the second slat with a 15 mm cut-out in the front

MATERIALS*

PART	MATERIAL	FINISHED LENGTH	NO.
FRAME			
Beam	140 x 45 mm treated pine	2100 mm	1
Leg	90 x 45 mm treated pine	1987 mm	4
Bottom rail	140 x 45 mm treated pine	960 mm	2
Top rail	140 x 45 mm treated pine	230 mm	2
SEAT			
Bearer	70 x 35 mm treated pine	955 mm	2
Back upright	70 x 35 mm treated pine	600 mm	2
Seat rail	70 x 35 mm treated pine	1200 mm	2
Arm support	70 x 35 mm treated pine	275 mm	2
Arm	70 x 35 mm treated pine	600 mm	2
Seat slat	70 x 25 mm treated pine	1284 mm	8
Back slat	70 x 25 mm treated pine	1300 mm	2
Top slat	90 x 25 mm treated pine	1300 mm	1

Other: 65 mm x No. 8 galvanized particleboard screws; twenty-four 50 mm x No. 8 galvanized particleboard screws; 38 mm x No. 8 galvanized particleboard screws; eight 75 mm x No. 10 galvanized particleboard screws; 40 x 2.5 mm galvanized decking nails; 65 x 2.5 mm galvanized lost-head nails; eight 100 x 8 mm galvanized coach screws and washers; two 125 x 10 mm galvanized round-head bolts and nuts; abrasive paper: 120 grit; two 380 mm long wooden corner braces; six 100 mm galvanized eye-bolts with washers and lock nuts; six 5 mm galvanized snap hooks; 4.4 m of 20 mm galvanized chain; preservative; finish of choice.

* Finished size: 2100 mm wide x 1235 deep and 1900 high.

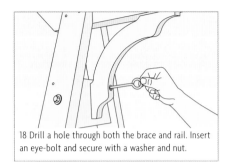

18 Drill a hole through both the brace and rail. Insert an eye-bolt and secure with a washer and nut.

edge to fit the back of the support. Leave a 5 mm gap between the slats. Nail the other slats to the bearers, overhanging 17 mm each end and with 5 mm between. Set out and cut the last seat slats to fit the upright.

17 Cut the top slat to length. Square a line 100 mm from each end. Gauge a line 70 mm in from the edge to the squared line. Use a can or jar to draw an inside and outside curve. Cut on the jigsaw. Place the slat on the back uprights, overhanging the top and ends by 5 mm. Fix with 40 x 2.5 mm decking nails. Cut and fix the second and third slats with a 5 mm gap between. Fit the third slat around the arms as before.

FINISHING

18 On the bearers measure 35 mm from the top edge and 100 mm from each end. Drill an 8 mm hole through the bearer and place

a 100 mm eye-bolt through each hole. Secure it with a washer and lock nut, with the eye square to the bearer. On the frame measure 100 mm up from the bottom of the top rail and drill an 8 mm hole through the rail and brace. Place a 100 mm eye-bolt through the hole and secure it with a washer and lock nut. Cut four 1100 mm lengths of chain. Attach the chain to the eye-bolts with a 5 mm snap hook.

19 Apply a suitable outdoor finish of your choice to the project to protect the timber from the weather.

ARBOUR SEAT

The lattice sides and roof of this sturdy arbour seat provide shelter from the sun while still letting through breezes to keep you cool. The construction is straightforward and does not require special skill.

PREPARING THE POSTS AND RAILS

1 Cut the four corner posts to length with a circular saw. Place the posts side by side with the ends flush and measure 350 mm from the bottom, then a further 90 mm. Use a builder's square to transfer these marks across all the posts. Mark a cross between the set-out lines to represent the housing for the bottom rails. Select two back posts and square the set-out onto a second side of each. Remember, you will need one left-hand and one right-hand post. For the side intermediate rail housing, measure up 1000 mm from the top of the bottom rail housing then a further 90 mm, square the lines and mark with a cross as before (see diagram on page 478). Set a gauge and mark a line 10 mm in from the edge between each shoulder line.

2 Clamp one back post firmly on the trestles. Set the circular saw to cut 10 mm

deep. Line up the notch in the baseplate of the saw with the squared lines and slowly cut a through housing (cutting on the waste side of the set-out). Make several other cuts in the housing to make it easier to remove the waste timber, and clean the bottom of the housing with a 25 mm chisel. Take care not to go past the gauged lines. Use an offcut of rail material to check the bottom of each housing for flatness and width. Cut the remaining housings in the back posts in the same way, and then cut the housings in the front posts.

3 Cut the side bottom and intermediate rails and the back bottom rail to length.

4 Cut two side top rails. To enable these two rails to overhang the posts, measure 150 mm and then a further 90 mm from each end, and square lines at these points across the face and 10 mm down each edge. Gauge a line 10 mm

deep and cut the housings for the post. Determine the front and back of the rail. Square the set-out lines of the rear housing across the inside edge and opposite face of each rail. Set a marking gauge to 30 mm and mark a line between these set-out lines and in the bottom of the housing (see diagram on page 478). You will need a left-hand and a right-hand rail. Hold the timber on edge and cut down the set-out lines of the housing with a handsaw to the gauge lines.

5 Cut the back top rail to length. Square a line across the face and down each side 30 mm from each end. Set a marking gauge to 10 mm and mark a line from the squared line along the edge and across the end. Cut and clean the housings.

ASSEMBLING THE FRAME

6 Apply preservative to all joints. Place the posts on a flat surface and position the side

outdoor

ASSEMBLED FRAME

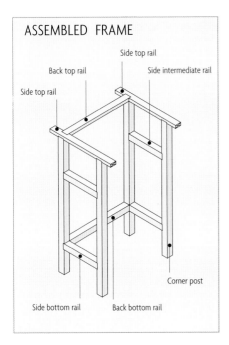

Side top rail

Back top rail

Side intermediate rail

Side top rail

Corner post

Side bottom rail

Back bottom rail

bottom rails one at a time in the housings with the outside faces flush. Drill two 4.5 mm holes at an angle through the bottom face of the rail. Hold the rail in the housing at 90 degrees to the post and fix it in place with two 65 mm screws. Additional screws placed through the top will add strength to the joint. Position the side intermediate rails and fix them as before. Take care to keep the frame as close as possible to square while you are assembling it. If you have sash cramps, place them over the frame to pull the joints tight. Place the top rail over the ends of the posts (ensure you have one left-hand and one right-hand frame) and drill four 4.5 mm holes through the face into the top of each post. Secure with 65 mm screws.

7 You may require a helping hand for the next step. Stand each side frame on its front edge and position the two back rails in the housings. The top rail is screwed through the top face into the ends of the post with 65 mm screws. Fix a nail plate over the top of each joint. The bottom rail

An asset to any garden, this arbour seat is constructed in treated pine and then given a protective coating of clear decking oil for a long life of year-round use.

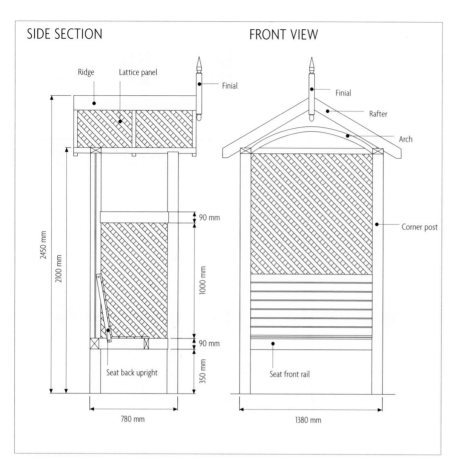

SIDE SECTION

Ridge · Lattice panel · Finial

2450 mm
2100 mm
90 mm
1000 mm
90 mm
350 mm

Seat back upright

780 mm

FRONT VIEW

Finial

Rafter

Arch

Corner post

Seat front rail

1380 mm

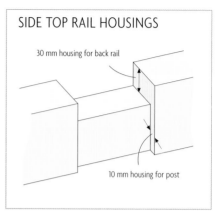

SIDE TOP RAIL HOUSINGS

30 mm housing for back rail

10 mm housing for post

CONSTRUCTING THE ROOF

10 Set up a builder's steel square with a pair of rafter buttons attached. Set the button on the blade to 345 mm (span) and that on the stock to 175 mm (rise). Place the square on a piece of rafter timber and pencil in the angle of the stock at the top (see diagram opposite). Mark the position of the blade button. Slide the square along the rafter and line up the stock with the mark. Mark the blade button point for a second time and slide the square along once again to line up the stock with this point. Mark the line of the stock at this location. This line will represent the edge of the bird's-mouth housing. Measure 25 mm up this line and slide the square along the rafter to line the blade up with this mark and mark the line of the blade. Measure out 150 mm along the blade from the line. Slide the square along the rafter and mark yet another line along the stock at the point. This is the bottom cut of the rafter.

has four screws skewed into the post as before. If necessary, nail a temporary brace over the front side to keep the frame steady and parallel while you work.

ADDING THE LATTICE

8 To determine the size of the lattice panel, measure the inside of the frame and reduce the measurement by 3 mm on all sides for clearance. Mark the required measurements on the face of the lattice and place a straight piece of timber on each mark. Draw a line the length of the cut along the straight edge. Place two 100 x 50 mm lengths of timber on a flat, firm surface. Position the lattice on top of the timber with the cutting line between the timbers. Nail or clamp the straight piece of

timber on top of the lattice to serve as a guide for a circular saw. Check the blade will line up with the marked line and cut the lattice, taking care to keep the base-plate against the straight edge and to support the offcut.

9 The lattice panels are beaded into the frame. Gauge a line 20 mm in from the back around the back opening. Cut the 18 x 12 mm bead to fit around all sides of the opening and fix it on the gauged line with 25 x 2 mm galvanized lost-head nails. Place the lattice in the frame and secure it in position by cutting and nailing another layer of bead around the opening on the other side of the lattice. Repeat the process for the side panels.

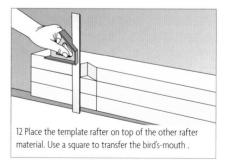

12 Place the template rafter on top of the other rafter material. Use a square to transfer the bird's-mouth .

outdoor

TOOLS

- Tape measure and pencil
- Circular saw
- Handsaw
- Builder's square
- Marking gauge
- Chisel: 25 mm
- Electric drill
- Drill bit: 4.5 mm
- Sash cramps
- Screwdriver
- Hammer
- Rafter buttons
- Trestles

SETTING OUT THE RAFTER

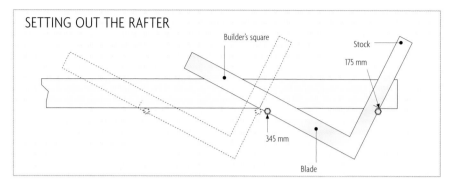

Builder's square

Stock

175 mm

345 mm

Blade

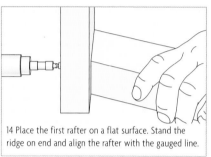

14 Place the first rafter on a flat surface. Stand the ridge on end and align the rafter with the gauged line.

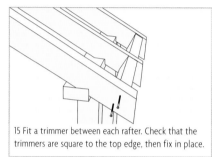

15 Fit a trimmer between each rafter. Check that the trimmers are square to the top edge, then fix in place.

11 The line for the top cut now needs to be repositioned by half the thickness of the ridge (17 mm) before it is cut. Position the square at the top of the rafter and slide down 17 mm. Cut the rafter to shape. Use a circular saw for each end and a handsaw for the bird's-mouth cuts. Take care with the cutting of this rafter, as it will be used as a template for all the rafters.

12 Place the template rafter on another piece of timber. Trace around the template and cut a second rafter to match. Place these two rafters in position with a piece of ridge material in between to test your set-out. Adjust as required. Place the template rafter on top of the other rafter material (three for each side). Use a square to transfer the set-out onto the remaining rafters and cut as before.

13 Cut the ridge to the same length as the side top rails. Set a marking gauge to 20 mm and mark a line on the faces parallel to the top edge. Find the centre of the ridge. Place

a rafter against the centre and mark the position, squaring the lines around to the opposite side. Place the ridge on one side top rail with the ends flush. Mark the front end so the set-out will be accurate. Transfer the centre rafter position onto the side rail. Repeat for the other side.

14 Place the first rafter on a flat surface. Stand the ridge on end and align the top edge of the rafter with the gauged line. Drill two 4.5 mm holes through the ridge. Fix the ridge to the end of the rafter with two 65 mm x No. 8 screws. Fix the other rafters on this side to the ridge with two screws in each, ensuring they line up with the gauge line and the end one is flush with the ridge. Hold the opposite rafters in position and drill a 4.5 mm hole through the top edge. A 65 mm x No. 8 screw is used to fix each to the ridge. Drill another screw hole through the other side of the ridge at an angle to hold the lower edge of the rafter.

15 Lift the assembled roof frame into position. Check the outside rafters are flush on the ends and the centre rafter lines up with the previous set-out. Fix the frame in place through the top rails with 65 mm x No. 8 screws. Cut a trimmer to fit between each rafter. Fix each trimmer with two screws, 30 mm from each end of the rafter and square to the top edge. Cut and bead in a lattice panel between each rafter in the same manner as for the sides and back.

FITTING THE SEAT

16 Cut two back uprights and one top rail for the seat. Square each end. Measure 100 mm from the back on the top of the side bottom rail and mark with a pencil on the inside edge. Hold the upright with the back edge on the 100 mm mark and the top end over the lattice bead on the corner post. Trace around the top on the bead. Cut the bead away with a sharp chisel so the upright sits flat against the

MATERIALS*

PART	MATERIAL	FINISHED LENGTH	NO.
Corner post	90 x 90 mm treated pine	2100 mm	4
Side rail	90 x 90 mm treated pine	620 mm	4
Back bottom rail	90 x 90 mm treated pine	1220 mm	1
Side top rail	90 x 45 mm treated pine	1080 mm	2
Back top rail	90 x 45 mm treated pine	1260 mm	1
Rafter	90 x 45 mm treated pine	925 mm	6
Trimmer	90 x 45 mm treated pine	423 mm	4
Seat trimmer	90 x 45 mm treated pine	480 mm	1
Seat front rail	90 x 35 mm treated pine	1200 mm	1
Seat centre upright	90 x 40 mm treated pine	700 mm	1
Seat back upright	40 x 40 mm treated pine	700 mm	2
Seat top rail	40 x 40 mm treated pine	1200 mm	1
Cleats	40 x 40 mm treated pine	to fit	2
Ridge	140 x 35 mm treated pine	1080 mm	1
Arch	140 x 45 mm treated pine	1200 mm	1
Seat/back slat	90 x 20 mm treated pine	1200 mm	12

Other: 65 mm x No. 8 galvanized particleboard screws; 25 mm x 2 mm galvanized lost-head nails; 40 x 2.5 mm twisted-shank decking nails; two 75 mm nail plates; four metal joint connectors; lattice: one sheet 1800 x 1200 mm and one sheet 2400 x 1200 mm; about 50 m of 18 x 12 mm bead; abrasive paper: 80 grit; ready-made finial; preservative; finish of choice.

* Finished size: 1380 mm wide x 1080 mm deep x 2450 mm high.

post. Repeat on the other side. Fix the seat top rail to the top of each upright with the end flush, using one 65 mm x No. 8 screw in each. Fix the assembled section in place with the top into the bead and the bottom aligned with the 100 mm mark.

17 Cut the seat front rail to length and fix it in place with a metal joint connector 480 mm in from the back posts. Cut a seat trimmer, fit it between the front and back rail and secure it with screws. Add a joint connector to each end for extra strength. Fix the centre upright to the side of the trimmer and under the top rail. Cut two seat cleats to

fit between the back upright and the front rail. Screw flush with the top edge of the side rail.

18 Cut twelve slats for the back and seat. Fix the back slats first with 40 x 2.5 mm twisted-shank nails, allowing a 3 mm gap between each board. Start at the bottom and work towards the top, keeping the ends flush with the uprights. Use two nails in each slat. Check periodically for parallel. Fix the seat slats in the same manner. The last board overhangs the front rail.

FINISHING

19 Measure the opening between the side

top rails. Cut the piece of timber for the arch to fit between them. Square a line at the centre. On each end, measure up the thickness of the top side rails (45 mm) and tack a nail at this point. Tack another nail at the top of the centre line.

20 Bend a piece of beading around the three nails and trace on the inside of the curve. At the centre line measure down 45 mm and tack in another nail. Bend the beading around this nail and down to the bottom corners of the timber to make a parallel curve. Cut the curve on the waste side of the line with a jigsaw. Sand smooth with 80 grit abrasive paper.

21 Fix the arch in place with a 65 mm x No. 8 screw through the bottom of the arch into the edge of the rail. A second screw should be skewed through the back to prevent the arch twisting around.

22 As a finishing touch screw a ready-made finial to the top of the roof through the back of the rafters.

23 Complete the arbour seat by applying your chosen finish.

TRADITIONAL GARDEN CHAIR

Designed on traditional lines to furnish your outdoor living area with style, this comfortable chair is constructed in jarrah with a natural oil finish.

CONSTRUCTING THE FRAME

1 Cut two back legs using a power mitre saw. Select and mark the face side and face edge. On one leg measure up 340 mm from one end and square a pencil mark across the face side and edge to represent the bottom of the side rail mortise (see diagram on page 482). Mark the side rail height (66 mm) up from this and square a pencil line on the face side and edge. Set a mortise gauge to mark a 12 mm wide mortise 14 mm in from the face edge between these two set-out lines. Measure up a further 200 mm and then an additional 50 mm for the arm. Set out a mortise (12 x 50 mm) for the arm. Repeat this set-out for the second leg.

2 Cut two front legs. Select and mark the face side and face edge and cut the bottom end square. Place a back leg flat on the bench, face side up. Place a front leg on top, face side down, with the bottom ends and face edges flush. Use a square to transfer the side rail mortise position onto the face edge of the front leg. Use the mortise gauge to complete the set-out. Repeat for the other leg.

3 Using a pencil, mark the top of the back leg 200 mm above the arm mortise and square a line around the timber. Set a marking gauge to mark a line 66 mm from the front edge on the face side and draw a line to the top of the side rail mortise. Draw a straight line from this intersection to the square top line at the back edge of the timber. Measure and mark 40 mm in from the back edge at the top. Place a rule from the 40 mm mark to the top of the side rail mortise on the front edge of the timber. Mark with a pencil.

This project for experienced woodworkers is sturdily constructed with mortise and tenon joints. The traditional styling suits any setting, and the seat is slightly curved for comfort.

BACK LEG SET-OUT

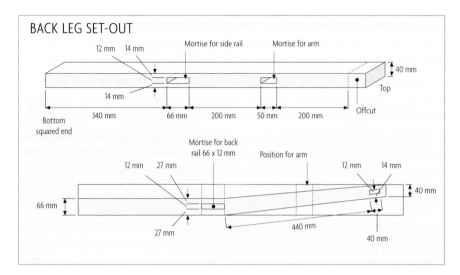

FRONT LEG SET-OUT

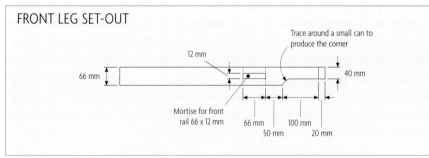

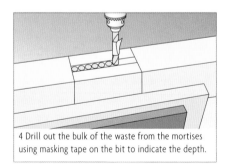

4 Drill out the bulk of the waste from the mortises using masking tape on the bit to indicate the depth.

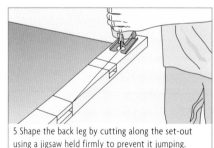

5 Shape the back leg by cutting along the set-out using a jigsaw held firmly to prevent it jumping.

4 To remove the bulk of the waste from the mortises, use an electric drill with a 10 mm bit. Place masking tape around the bit to indicate the depth to be bored (40 mm). Hold the timber over a solid point of the bench using a G-cramp or vice. Cut away the remaining waste with a 12 mm mortise chisel to finish 40 mm deep. Trim the mortise sides with a 25 mm firmer chisel.

Take care chiselling out the mortise. Hold the chisel upright so the recess is straight and true to size.

5 Clamp the back leg flat on a solid surface with the cutting line on the face side overhanging the edge. Place the jigsaw on the surface and hold it firmly. Cut slowly along the line on the waste side. Take it easy

as the timber is thick and the saw may jump. Use a new, sharp blade for the best result. Place the cut leg on edge in a vice and true up the edges with a hand plane. Check the face side is square. Round over the tops of the legs with abrasive paper.

6 For the top rail mortise, measure up the face edge of the back leg 440 mm from the back rail mortise. Then measure up 40 mm (the length of the mortise) and square a line across the face side at these points. Set the mortise gauge to mark a 12 mm wide mortise, 14 mm in from the front edge. Repeat for the other leg, remembering you need one left-hand and one right-hand leg. Drill and chisel the mortise 20 mm deep.

7 To shape the front legs, measure up 50 mm from the top of the side rails and square a pencil line around the leg. Measure 40 mm in from the back edge on this line. Pencil a parallel line from this mark to the top of the leg. With a small can or jar, trace a curve between the parallel line and the front edge of the leg. Cut the curve with a jigsaw. Clean up the edge with abrasive paper.

8 On the front leg measure 150 mm up from the top edge of the side rail mortise and square a shoulder line right around the leg. This will leave 20 mm above the line for a tenon. Set the mortise gauge as for the side rail (12 mm wide and 14 mm in from the edge) and mark from the shoulder line on the face edge, up across the end and down to the other shoulder line.

9 Hold the leg upright in a vice and, with a tenon saw, cut down both sides of the tenon on the waste side to the squared shoulder lines. Place the leg flat on the bench. Hold it firmly with a cramp or bench hook, and cut across the shoulder lines to remove the waste.

TOOLS

- Measuring tape and pencil
- Power mitre saw
- Jigsaw
- Tenon saw
- Mortise gauge
- Marking gauge
- Combination square
- Router with 3 mm rounding and 18 mm straight bit
- Electric drill
- Drill bits: 3 mm, 4.5 mm, 10 mm, countersink
- Two G-cramps
- Chisels: 12 mm mortise, 25 mm firmer
- Hand plane
- Builder's square
- Hammer and nail punch
- Three sash cramps
- Screwdriver to suit

MATERIALS*

PART	MATERIAL	FINISHED LENGTH	NO.
Back leg	90 x 40 mm jarrah	900 mm	2
Front leg	66 x 40 mm jarrah	580 mm	2
Side rail	66 x 40 mm jarrah	510 mm	2
Front/back rail	66 x 40 mm jarrah	560 mm	2
Top rail	66 x 30 mm jarrah	560 mm	1
Arm	140 x 40 mm jarrah	600 mm	2
Back slat	66 x 18 mm jarrah	455 mm	4
Back slat (centre)	90 x 18 mm jarrah	455 mm	1
Seat slat	66 x 18 mm jarrah	600 mm	6
Seat slat (short)	66 x 18 mm jarrah	520 mm	1
Cleat	35 x 20 mm jarrah	484 mm	2

Other: 25 mm x 1.5 mm galvanized lost-head nails; 30 mm x No. 8 galvanized countersunk screws; ten 50 mm x No. 8 galvanized countersunk screws; abrasive paper; 120 grit; epoxy adhesive; preservative; finish of choice.

*   All material sizes quoted are dressed measurements. For timber types and sizes, see page 471. Finished size: 600 mm wide x 620 mm deep x 850 mm high.

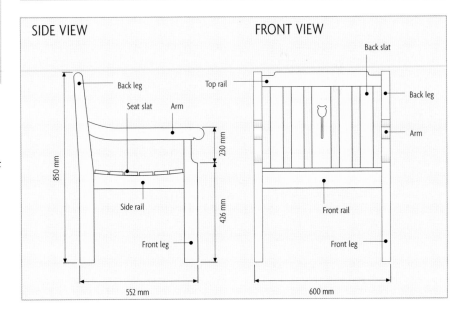

SIDE VIEW   FRONT VIEW

10 Using the mitre saw, cut the side rails 510 mm long. Measure in 40 mm from each end and square a shoulder line all around the timber. Mark the tenons 12 mm wide out from these shoulders and around the end. Hold the rails upright in a vice and cut as before. Check for fit in the legs and adjust by paring a little at a time away from the face of the tenons. Take care to remove any waste from the correct side to ensure the faces remain flush.

MAKING THE ARMS

11 Position the legs on the side rail and secure with a sash cramp. Use a builder's square to check each leg is square to the side rail. Cut the arms to length and hold one under the leg frame with the top edge in line with the top of the arm mortise in the back leg. Place the arm about 20 mm past the face edge of the back leg to allow the tenon to fit into the mortise in the back leg. The bottom edge should be in line with the shoulder of the front leg tenon. Trace around the tenon at the front and mark the shoulder line at the back. Square the tenon tracing around the bottom edge of the arm and use the mortise gauge to set out the mortise.

484

BACK RAIL END SECTION

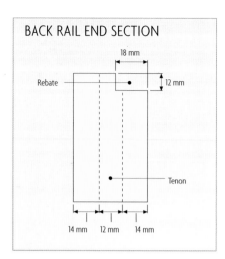

18 mm

Rebate

12 mm

Tenon

14 mm   12 mm   14 mm

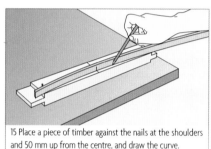

15 Place a piece of timber against the nails at the shoulders and 50 mm up from the centre, and draw the curve.

Drill out and cut the mortise 20 mm deep.

12 The tenon at the back of the arm has a bevelled shoulder to correspond to the slope on the back leg (see diagram on page 483). Square the marked shoulder line across each edge with a pencil. Turn the arm over and use a rule to line up each squared line and mark the shoulder with a pencil. Use the mortise gauge to mark the tenon and cut it as before. Reposition the arm under the legs and mark the width of the tenon on the face side of the arm.

13 Place the arm flat on the bench. Measure 235 mm from the front mortise along the lower edge and mark across the face side and down the lower edge. Place a thin piece of timber from this point to the bottom of the tenon and mark the curved line with

a pencil. Cut the curve with a jigsaw. Mark a parallel line 50 mm up from the lower edge to the squared line. Continue marking parallel to the curved line up to the top of the tenon. Round over and shape the front end of the arm with a jigsaw and abrasive paper.

14 The side rail has a slight curve in the top edge, 15 mm deep in the centre, sloping up to each end. Use a thin piece of timber and a pencil to shape the curve. Cut with a jigsaw.

15 Cut the three rails. Cut a 20 mm tenon either end of each rail, with 9 mm shoulders for the top rail and 14 mm for the front and back rails. To curve the upper edge of the top rail, fix nails 50 mm up from the lower edge and 175 mm in from each shoulder. Use

a thin piece of timber and pencil to create the curve and cut along it with a jigsaw. Sand with 120 grit abrasive paper. Place a 3 mm pencil rounding bit in a router and run a small round along the top of the rail. Router a groove 10 mm deep and 18 mm wide in the lower edge for the back slats.

16 To reduce the top rail tenon from 50 mm to 40 mm, place an 18 mm straight bit in the router. Set the fence on the base so the cutter will run in the centre of the rail, 6 mm in from the edge. Hold the rail firmly upside down in a vice and run the router from left to right with the fence held against the face of the rail.

17 Place the back rail in the vice and adjust the router to cut a rebate in the top edge

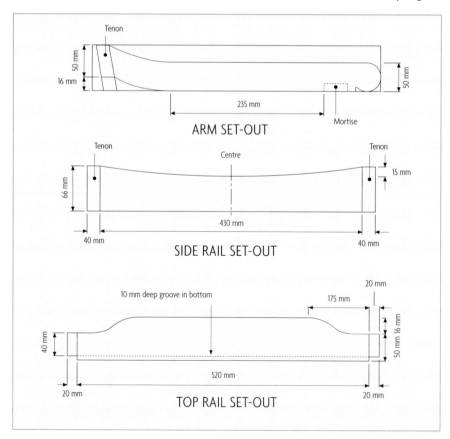

ARM SET-OUT

SIDE RAIL SET-OUT

TOP RAIL SET-OUT

outdoor

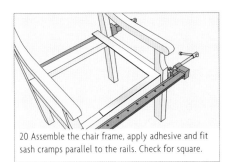

20 Assemble the chair frame, apply adhesive and fit sash cramps parallel to the rails. Check for square.

21 Hammer two 25 x 1.5 mm lost-head galvanized nails through the back of the slat into the top rail groove.

The centre slat can be decorated with your own cut-out design, or a ready-made baluster can be purchased.

12 mm deep and 18 mm wide. Check the fit of all the joints, adjusting as required. At the end of the tenons, cut a mitre with the long face towards the outside.

ASSEMBLING THE CHAIR

18 Assemble each side frame in sash cramps without adhesive. Place a scrap block between the job and the cramps to prevent marking the timber. Adjust it as necessary. Sand with 120 grit abrasive paper.

19 Use a small brush or stick to apply epoxy adhesive to the joints, taking care to follow the directions provided. Coat the sides of the tenons and shoulder with the adhesive and smear a little around the inside of the mortise before bringing the joint together. Assemble the frame with two sash cramps underneath, closing up the side rail joint and the arm joint. Use another cramp over the top of the front leg to close the joint under the arm. Place a builder's square on each leg and side rail to check for square. Adjust as required. Sight across the job to ensure there is no twist. If necessary, adjust the cramps to correct this. Additional weights or cramps placed on top of the frame can also help. Remove any excess adhesive. When the adhesive has dried, remove the frame from the cramps and use a hand plane to make the surface of the joints flush. Sand the face with 120 grit abrasive paper.

20 Check the remaining rails for fit, with

the back rail rebate on the top inside edge. Once satisfied, apply the adhesive and place the sash cramps across the chair parallel to the rails. Lay a builder's square inside the frame to check for square. Also check under the leg, between the front and back rails. Remove any excess adhesive. Once the adhesive has dried, remove the cramps and sand the frame to remove any adhesive or pencil marks.

FIXING THE SLATS

21 Cut four back slats to fit between the groove in the top rail and the rebate in the back rail. Cut a wider slat for the centre and cut out a design in the centre. Turn the chair over and position each slat. Maintain a 28 mm space between each slat. Hammer two 25 mm nails through the back of the slat into the top rail groove. Fix the slats into the back rail rebate with two 30 mm screws.

22 Cut two cleats to fit between the front and back rails. Hold one in position against the inside of the side rail, and trace the curved shape of the side rail onto the face of the cleat. Cut the curve with a jigsaw and fix the cleat with four 30 mm screws. Repeat for the second cleat.

23 Cut the seat slats. Position them with the short slat between the front legs, to check the accuracy of the fit. The 600 mm slats overhang each side by 3 mm. Working from the back rail, fix them to the cleats from

underneath with two 30 mm screws at each end. Use a nail to keep an even gap between each slat. Round over the front edge of the short slat. Position the front slat between the front legs and counter-bore from underneath the front rail. Fix with two 50 mm screws.

24 Strengthen the corners with scrap timber blocks approximately 150 mm long. Cut each end at 45 degrees to fit against the rail. Fix with a 50 mm screw at each end.

25 Sand out any marks and apply a protective finish so that the chair can be left outside if desired.

USING A ROUTER

- Read the manufacturer's instructions before operating.
- Always secure the work with cramps or a vice, leaving both hands free to operate the router.
- Wear safety glasses, hearing protection and a dust mask when operating the router.
- Use a scrap of timber to test the router setting before cutting into your project.

FOLD-UP TABLE AND CHAIR

This table and chair are simply made with slats glued and nailed to the rails. For ease of folding the chair seat swivels on steel rods; the table legs are held in place against a timber block.

MAKING THE TABLE TOP

1 Cut two side rails to length. Square a line 10 mm in from each end around the rail. Round the ends with abrasive paper to the set-out line.

2 Cut sixteen slats 450 mm long. Use abrasive paper to round the top edges of the slats along both sides and ends. Measure in 6 mm from each end of the slats and square a pencil line across the face edges.

3 Stand the rails on edge and about 350 mm apart. Apply PVA adhesive along the top edge of one rail. Place one slat at a 90-degree angle across the rails, lining up the outside edge with the 10 mm line on the glued rail. The slat should overhang the rails by 6 mm on each side (use the squared line as your guide).

4 Fix the slat to the rail with two 25 x 2 mm panel pins. Place the second slat at the other end and fix it in the same manner. Apply PVA adhesive to the other rail and nail the slats in place, taking care to keep the overhang in line and the rails and slats parallel. Position the remaining slats on the rails and fix with a 3.5 mm gap between

each slat. A spare nail makes a handy spacer to keep the gaps between the slats even.

ADDING THE LEGS

5 On the bottom of each leg use a set square to mark a 60-degree angle on the face (see diagram on page 489). Square a line down each face edge. Clamp the leg on a firm surface and cut the angle with a tenon saw. On the inside legs, measure 615 mm from the bottom on the longest side. Mark a 60-degree angle parallel to the first and cut it. Mark the centre across the width (see diagram Detail A on page 489), place a try square on the end and mark a 90-degree angle across the face from the centre. Continue the line down the edge and end. Cut with a tenon saw.

6 Cut the two outside legs 610 mm long, measured along the longest side, and square the top. Measure 15 mm from the top; drill a 6 mm hole through the centre. Round off the top with abrasive paper. Measure 320 mm from the bottom along the longest edge on all four legs and drill a 4.5 mm hole through the centre.

7 Cut a pair of stretcher rails 268 mm long. On each end of one stretcher rail, mark diagonals across the ends and then drill a 3 mm pilot hole in the centre.

8 Place the outside and inside legs together, with the 60-degree angles facing one way on the inside legs and in the opposite direction on the outside legs. Screw a 65 mm x No. 8 countersunk screw through one pair of legs into the pilot hole at the end of the stretcher. Place a washer under

the screw head and between each part. Turn the screw enough to hold the legs together but still allow movement. Repeat for the other side.

9 The other stretcher is fixed at the top of the inside legs. Drill a 4.5 mm hole through the leg 10 mm from the top. Line up the rail with the angle on top of one leg and drill a 3 mm pilot hole through the leg into the end of the rail. Countersink the top of the hole if desired. Apply a little PVA adhesive to the end of the rail and fix it with a 40 mm x No. 8 screw. Just across from the screw, drive a 25 x 2 mm panel pin through the leg into the rail. This will prevent the rail turning. Repeat on the other side.

ASSEMBLING THE TABLE

10 With the table top upside down on

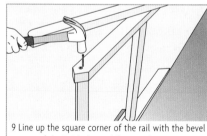

9 Line up the square corner of the rail with the bevel on top of the inside leg and fix it in place.

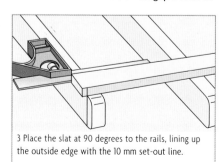

3 Place the slat at 90 degrees to the rails, lining up the outside edge with the 10 mm set-out line.

11 Centre the stop block between the rails underneath the second slat and fix it in place with 25 mm screws.

outdoor

a firm surface, measure 70 mm from the end of one side rail and square a line across the edge and side of the rail (see Side rail detail on page 489). Measure 20 mm from the lower edge and drill a 6 mm hole through the rail. Repeat on the other rail.

11 Cut a stop block 265 mm long. Drill a 4.5 mm hole through it, 25 mm from each end. Centre the block between the rails underneath the second slat. Screw in place with 25 mm x No. 8 screws.

12 Stand the legs within the rails. Place a washer between the leg and rail. Insert the 45 x 6 mm machine screws through the outside leg and out through the side rail. Secure with a dome nut and washer.

13 Check the action of the folding legs and adjust as required. Turn the table right way up and check that the top is level. If not, adjust the stop block. Sand and apply the finishing coat of your choice.

MAKING THE CHAIR LEGS

14 Cut two front legs to length. Measure 150 mm from one end (top) and square a line across the face (see Front leg detail on page 491). Set a marking gauge to 40 mm and mark from the squared line down the length of the leg.

15 At the top end, mark 40 mm from the opposite edge. Select a thin piece of timber (ply is ideal) and bend it from this mark to the 150 mm line on the edge. Trace the curve onto the leg with a pencil. Mark a pencil line 40 mm parallel to this curve, lining up with the gauged line. Clamp the leg firmly to the bench or trestles so the curve overhangs the end. Cut the curves on the waste side with a jigsaw. Smooth the curve with 80 grit abrasive paper. Mark

There when you need them, folded away out of sight when you don't, this table and chair are made from planed hardwood and then given a colourful finish with a gloss paint designed for exterior use.

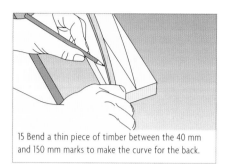

15 Bend a thin piece of timber between the 40 mm and 150 mm marks to make the curve for the back.

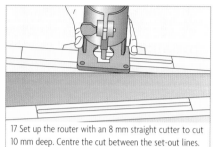

17 Set up the router with an 8 mm straight cutter to cut 10 mm deep. Centre the cut between the set-out lines.

21 When fixing the back rail, angle the screw slightly to ensure it goes into the rail.

and cut a 60-degree angle on the bottom of the leg. Repeat for other leg.

16 Cut two back legs to length. Measure 180 mm from the bottom and then a further 230 mm (see Back leg detail page 491). Square these two marks across the face of the leg. Position one leg in a vice (or clamp it to trestles) so that both square marks are on the same side and are kept clear of the vice jaws. Make certain the face is above the surface of the bench.

17 Set up a router with an 8 mm straight cutter to cut 10 mm deep. Fasten the guide fence to the router at 8 mm from the edge of the cutter. Test on a piece of scrap 25 x 18 mm timber and check the set-up. The cut should be in the centre of the timber. Hold the router up from the surface of the leg between the set-out lines, with the guide fence against the side. Start the router and slowly lower the cutter onto the leg. Machine the groove along the leg, taking care to stop at the squared set-out lines. Repeat the process on the other leg. Round each end of the legs slightly with abrasive paper.

MAKING THE SEAT
18 Cut the side rails to length. Measure 50 mm from each end and square a line across the face. Mark the centre point between the lines (160 mm) and square another line across the timber. To produce

the curved seat, measure 10 mm from the top edge of the side rail and tack in a small nail, leaving the head standing up around 15 mm. Bend a thin piece of timber around the nail to line up on the top edge with the squared lines. Trace the curve with a pencil. Hold the rail firmly in a vice or cramp, remove the nail and cut the curve on the waste side of the line with a jigsaw. Smooth with abrasive paper. Use the first rail as a template to cut the other rail. At the front ends of the side rails measure 25 mm from the bottom edge and cut off the top corner at 45 degrees.

19 Cut a back rail to length. Measure in from each end the thickness of the side rail (18 mm) and square the line across the face and down each side. Set a gauge to 12 mm and, working from the face, mark from the squared line across the end and down the other. Hold the rail face-up in a vice or cramp and cut the shoulder to the gauge line. With a 25 mm chisel, remove the bulk of the waste by chiselling down the grain. Clean and level the bottom of the joint by chiselling across the grain of the timber.

20 Cut the front rail to length. In either end cut rebates 18 mm wide and 12 mm deep for the side rails in the same way as in the back rail.

21 Place one side rail in the rebates in back and front rails and drill a 4.5 mm clearance hole through the side rail, approximately

10 mm in from each end. Countersink the holes if required. Drill a 3 mm pilot hole into the back and front rails. The hole at the back is drilled at a slight angle to ensure the screw goes into the rail, but not at too much of an angle or it will go out the side. Repeat for the other side rail. Apply PVA adhesive to the rebate joints and screw the frame together with 40 mm x No. 8 screws.

22 Cut fifteen seat slats to length. Round the top edges and ends with abrasive paper. Apply adhesive to the 45-degree angle on the side rails. Place the first slat on the angle so it rests against the front rail. Nail through the face into the side rail with 25 x 1.5 mm panel pins. Glue and nail the second slat so it touches the first. Glue and nail the remaining slats, using a 2.5 mm nail as a spacer. Check the slats lie parallel and adjust if required. Sand the outside edges flush with the rail and slightly round over the top edge.

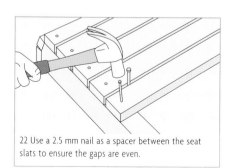

22 Use a 2.5 mm nail as a spacer between the seat slats to ensure the gaps are even.

TOOLS

- Tape measure and pencil
- Tenon saw
- Power mitre saw
- Jigsaw
- Cork sanding block
- Try square
- Builder's square
- Hammer and nail punch
- Set square 60/30
- Vice or cramps
- Screwdriver
- Electric drill
- Drill bits: 3 mm, 4.5 mm, 6 mm, 8 mm, countersink
- Adjustable spanner
- Marking gauge
- Router
- Router bit: 8 mm straight
- Bevel
- Chisel: 25 mm
- Trestles (optional)

ADDING THE BACK SLATS

23 The back slats are attached to the top of the front legs. Cut the two slats to length, and slightly round over the edges with abrasive paper. Measure 25 mm in from each end and approximately 12 mm from each edge and drill two 4.5 mm clearance holes. Countersink the top of the hole. Place a slat on one front leg, 20 mm down from the top with a 12 mm overhang on the outside. Line up the holes with the centre of the leg. Drill 3 mm pilot holes into the leg and fix with 25 mm x No. 8 screws. Use a builder's square to ensure the job is square. Fix the second slat parallel to

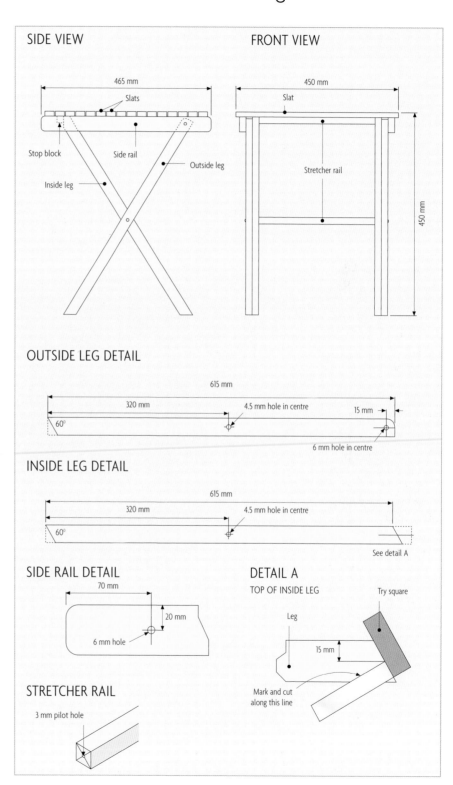

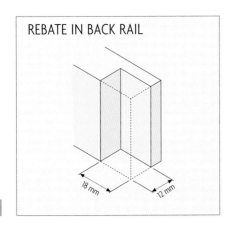

The shaped side rails of the chair allow the seat to be curved for comfortable seating.

the first with the same overhang. Place the two slats over the opposite leg. The gap between the legs must be 415 mm. Screw-fix as before.

24 Cut the front stretcher rail to length. Drill a hole approximately 25 mm in from each end and fix it 150 mm from the bottom of the front legs with a 25 mm x No. 8 screw into each leg as before. Sand and slightly round over the top.

ASSEMBLING THE CHAIR

25 Measure up 455 mm from the bottom of each front leg and square a line across the

MATERIALS*

PART	MATERIAL	FINISHED LENGTH	NO.
TABLE			
Inside leg	30 x 18 mm hardwood	630 mm	2
Outside leg	30 x 18 mm hardwood	610 mm	2
Side rail	40 x 18 mm hardwood	465 mm	2
Slat	25 x 13 mm hardwood	450 mm	16
Stretcher rail	18 x 18 mm hardwood	268 mm	2
Stop block	18 x 18 mm hardwood	265 mm	1
CHAIR			
Front leg	65 x 18 mm hardwood	900 mm	2
Back leg	25 x 18 mm hardwood	605 mm	2
Side rail	40 x 18 mm hardwood	420 mm	2
Back rail	40 x 18 mm hardwood	370 mm	1
Front rail	30 x 25 mm hardwood	370 mm	1
Seat slat	25 x 13 mm hardwood	370 mm	15
Back slat	65 x 13 mm hardwood	480 mm	2
Front stretcher rail	30 x 13 mm hardwood	480 mm	1
Back stretcher rail	30 x 13 mm hardwood	455 mm	1

Other: Abrasive paper: 80 grit and 120 grit; PVA adhesive. For table: 25 x 2 mm panel pins; four 65 mm x No. 8 countersunk screws; two 40 mm x No. 8 countersunk screws; two 25 mm x No. 8 countersunk screws; two 45 x 6 mm machine screws; two dome nuts; washers. For chair: four 40 mm x No. 8 countersunk screws; twelve 25 mm x No. 8 screws; two 50 x 6 mm countersunk machine screws with dome nuts and washers to suit; 25 x 1.5 mm panel pins; 388 mm length 8mm plain steel rod; 450 mm length 8 mm threaded steel rod with 20 mm thread each end or fully threaded; dome nuts and washers to fit rod; finish of choice.

* All materials quoted are dressed measurements. Finished size: table 400 mm wide x 465 mm deep x 510 mm high; chair 480 mm wide x 500 mm deep x 840 mm high.

REBATE IN BACK RAIL

18 mm

12 mm

outside face. To fit the threaded rod, drill an 8 mm hole, 12 mm in from the front edge. In each side rail drill another hole 160 mm from the back and 12 mm up from the bottom edge.

26 Carefully drill another 8 mm hole 25 mm in from the back of the side rail and 20 mm up from the bottom edge for the plain rod.

27 To fix the back legs to the front legs, drill a 6 mm hole through the front leg 650 mm up from the bottom and 12 mm in from the back edge. Measure 20 mm from the top of the back leg and drill a 6 mm hole in the centre. Countersink this hole on the inside (grooved) face. Place a washer between one front and one back leg and thread a 50 x 6 mm machine screw through. Fix with a dome nut and

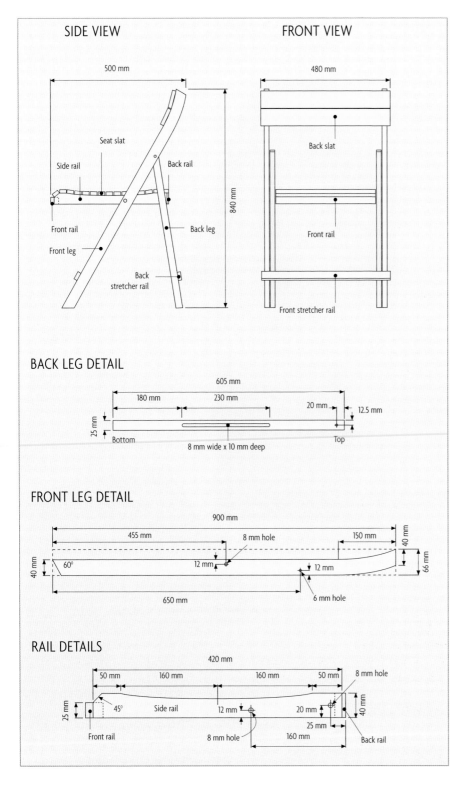

SIDE VIEW

500 mm

Seat slat

Side rail

Back rail

840 mm

Front rail

Back leg

Front leg

Back
stretcher rail

FRONT VIEW

480 mm

Back slat

Front rail

Front stretcher rail

BACK LEG DETAIL

605 mm

180 mm   230 mm   20 mm   12.5 mm

25 mm

Bottom   Top

8 mm wide x 10 mm deep

FRONT LEG DETAIL

900 mm

455 mm   8 mm hole   150 mm   40 mm

40 mm   60°   12 mm   12 mm   66 mm

650 mm   6 mm hole

RAIL DETAILS

420 mm

50 mm   160 mm   160 mm   50 mm   8 mm hole

25 mm   45°   Side rail   12 mm   20 mm   40 mm

25 mm

Front rail   8 mm hole   160 mm   Back rail

washer on the outside. Do not fix the other legs yet.

28 Position the seat frame against the joined legs and push the 8 mm plain rod through the seat into the groove in the back leg. Fit the other back leg so the rod is in the groove. Fix the top of this back leg to the other front leg with a machine screw as before. Insert the threaded rod through the front leg, the seat frame and the opposite front leg. Fit a dome nut on each side.

29 Measure 100 mm up from the bottom of the back legs. Open out the chair so the seat is flat and fix one end of the back stretcher rail with a 25 mm x No. 8 screw, allowing a 12 mm overhang. Check the legs are parallel and then fix the other side to the opposite leg.

FINISHING
30 Check the seat folds smoothly. Adjust it, if necessary, by tightening or loosening the screws.

31 Sand the chair and apply a protective finishing coat of paint.

birdhouses
and feeders

birdhouses and feeders

SHARING YOUR GARDEN WITH BIRDS

If you want native birds to visit—and enliven—your garden, it is important to provide them with an environment that supplies appropriate food, shelter and nesting sites. Birdhouses and feeders must be carefully planned and maintained.

PLANNING A BIRDHOUSE OR FEEDER

Britain's native birds include a variety of thrushes, tits, warblers and finches. In order to survive successfully in the wild, these species need trees, flowers and shrubs that provide them with fruits, seeds, insects and shelter. The natural habitat for many of these birds is deciduous woodland. In recent years many of them have adapted to living among human habitation. Many people believe that for this reason it is important to provide birdhouses and feeders in our gardens. However, these structures must be carefully planned and monitored—and impeccably maintained—if they are going to be of benefit to native birds.

Before deciding on the site and style of your birdhouse or feeder, spend some time investigating your neighbourhood and your own backyard. Find out what types of birds visit your local area—there are many books available to help you identify the different species. If possible, take a few weeks to study the habits of visiting birds. Try to find out what they may be feeding on: are they fruit-eaters or seed-eaters, or do they scavenge for insects? Check for nests in the garden, without disturbing them, and take note of the height at which they are built.

BIRD-FRIENDLY GARDENS

The best way to attract desirable bird species (and provide them with a constant food supply) is to include a variety of trees, shrubs and other plants—particularly native plants—in your garden. Gardens simply planted with roses, azaleas and gardenias may look attractive and smell nice, but they do not contain the diversity required to support a healthy ecosystem.

To encourage seed-eaters, plant seed-bearing plants such as lavender, sunflower and teasel. Birch and beech are good seed-bearing trees—plant them to attract finches. Birds such as thrushes love berries and fruit—suitable fruit- or berry-bearing plants include rowan, cotoneaster and hawthorn. Many birds feast on spiders and aphids, thereby acting as a form of natural insect control. Avoid using pesticides; if you must, apply a pyrethrum-based spray sparingly.

A large number of British birds live close to and feed on the ground, making good use of the natural cover and shelter offered by logs, thick grass and shrubs. Brambles and climbers such as honeysuckle provide good cover.

SUPPLEMENTARY FEEDING

If the food-bearing plants in your garden haven't reached a stage where they are attracting birds yet, then providing supplementary food for the birds is an option.

Many wildlife experts object to the idea of supplementary feeding, based on the idea that a constant supply of artificial food makes birds dependent and lazy, and increases the risk of predation by larger animals and other birds. Supplementary feeding may cause dietary problems, and could increase the risk of disease because of the concentration of birds around a particular feeding point. Aggressive species, such as magpies and crows, and even starlings and sparrows, are encouraged into gardens by bird feeders, at the expense of other native birds. Research and carefully consider both pro- and anti-feeding arguments before providing a bird feeder.

If you want to feed the birds, a mixture of foods and seed is recommended—make sure you use the right seed mix for the species in your area. Your local aviary supply shop can often give you advice on the use of vitamin supplements and the right seed choices. Fresh kitchen scraps such as apple cores and vegetable peelings can be given as a dietary supplement. Give only small amounts of food that will be quickly eaten up, and do not feed birds every day. In spring and summer, a time when birds rest more often, reduce the amount provided.

You must keep the bird feeder spotlessly clean to prevent the spread of disease. Uneaten and spilled food left on or near the feeder could also attract vermin and other pests.

A permanent, reliable source of clean water is just as important in attracting birds to the garden as a supply of food and a sheltered habitat. Any birdbath or bowl of water to be used by birds should have sloping sides and must be no more than 5 cm deep.

DESIGNING AND SITING A BIRDHOUSE

The best time to install birdhouses is in winter, before the breeding season begins.

outdoor

If you decide to provide supplementary food, it is important to find out what seed mix is the correct one for the particular bird species in your garden. This practical and economical feeder dispenses the seeds by means of a seed spreader.

Birdhouses should be situated in quiet, well-protected areas, sheltered from the wind, out of direct summer sun and attached firmly to their support. (On pages 509–511 you will find directions for building a post that will suit most types of birdhouses and feeders.)

If you are using a wooden pole, make sure it has a smooth surface, and don't place it adjacent to fences or trees that a cat can climb in order to reach the birdhouse. A galvanized water pipe also makes a good pole. If you place the birdhouse in a tree, be sure to cat-proof the tree: a galvanized sheet metal collar can be wrapped around the trunk to prevent animals from climbing up it (a collar can also be fitted to a wooden pole). If you are fixing the birdhouse to a wall, use suitable brackets and anchors.

Birdhouses that are particularly deep should have a piece of wire mesh attached to the inside face leading up to the entrance hole, to help the fledgling birds climb out. Alternatively, you can use saw cuts to form a type of 'ladder' on the inner face of the birdhouse.

The designs in this book can be modified to suit the requirements of many different native birds. Contact the RSPB for information about building a suitable birdhouse for the species you want to attract.

HOLLOW LOGS

Hollow logs provide ideal nesting sites for some bird species. They can look attractive in a garden and will provide shelter for many

Basic carpentry skills and lots of imagination are all you require to build a purely decorative birdhouse. A functional birdhouse for the garden must be specially designed and built with the needs of the feathered residents in mind.

These birdhouses, made in traditional 'folk art' style, are meant for use as interior decoration only.

of the animals on which birds love to feed.

Do not remove logs from woodland in order to relocate them in your garden: this upsets the natural balance of forests and woodland, as it deprives many birds, insects and animals of their habitat. An arboriculturist should be able to supply you with an offcut from a tree with a decayed heart.

BIRDHOUSE MAINTENANCE

Keep the birdhouse relatively clean. It is a good idea to place a couple of handfuls of wood shavings or sawdust at the bottom to help with moisture control. Many designs in this chapter include hinged lids or removable bases to make cleaning easier. After every breeding season, when the fledgling birds have left, inspect the inside of the birdhouse and clean out any unwanted pests and insects. Most nests can be removed after

each breeding season, as many birds will not build on top of old nests or use the same nest twice. Even so, you should find out about the nesting habits of the particular bird species before removing nests. Use warm water and a mild detergent to clean inside the birdhouse. Wiping out the birdhouse with a cloth soaked in disinfectant will keep most bird parasites under control.

The most important thing is to enjoy the birds in your garden. Watch them flutter among the trees and bushes, and listen to their songs. You will learn much about the unique wildlife around you and come to better understand your own relationship with the environment.

DECORATIVE BIRDHOUSES

Birdhouses also have a place indoors as quaint decorative items. Without the constraint of providing the correct habitat for a specific

bird, you can let your imagination run free and create houses of any shape, colour or size. Design ideas include birdhouses with steep-pitched shingled roofs, spires, front fences and several rooms.

HANGING BIRDHOUSE

This diamond-shaped birdhouse is designed to be suspended from a tree or from a tall garden structure such as a pergola. An optional false floor can be fitted inside the birdhouse to provide a flat, stable surface for nesting birds.

CUTTING OUT

1 The material should already have surfaces planed square and smooth. Check that the edges are straight and square. If necessary, plane one edge.

2 Use the combination square and pencil to set out the parts along the timber. Leave a 5 mm space between each part to allow for saw cuts and planing back. Square the lines around the timber with a pencil. Use a combination square and utility knife to score over the lines to cut the cross-grain fibres.

3 Use a jigsaw (or alternative saw) to cut the components to rough sizes. Temporarily nail the front and back pieces together using two 30 mm nails, then place the pieces in a vice and plane them to the marked lines. The finished width will be 200 mm. Make sure the edges are square.

4 Following step 3, bring all the remaining components to the correct lengths specified in the instructions and in the diagram on page 498.

5 Take the front and back pieces and mark the bottom corner with a cross. Measure

This birdhouse was built with durable Western red cedar, which will mellow with age to an attractive silver shade. The timber was finished with two coats of vegetable oil—the oil should be reapplied once every four to six months.

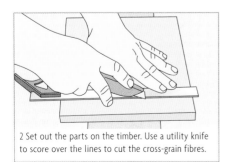

2 Set out the parts on the timber. Use a utility knife to score over the lines to cut the cross-grain fibres.

out 70 mm each way from the marked bottom corner—this measurement is for the two screws seen on the front and back. At the 70 mm points, drill a 5 mm hole 9 mm in from the edge, then countersink the holes.

6 Take the 181 mm long side piece and cut and plane it to a width of 142 mm. Next,

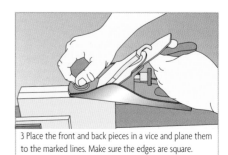

3 Place the front and back pieces in a vice and plane them to the marked lines. Make sure the edges are square.

take the 200 mm long side piece and cut and plane it to a width of 142 mm. Mix a small amount of epoxy resin adhesive and apply a little to the short edge. Start two 40 mm nails 9 mm in from the edge and about 25 mm in from each side. Bring the two side pieces together to form a 200 x 200 mm right angle, then finish nailing the pieces together.

7 Separate the two nailed front and back pieces. Apply some adhesive to the edges of the right-angled piece and place the front piece in position, aligning it with the sides. Fix the front piece with a 40 mm nail near the outer end. Use two 35 mm screws to complete the attachment of the front piece. Repeat for the back piece, to create a basic box shape.

ADDING THE ROOF
8 Turn the box so that it sits on the workbench with its roofless top face

TOOLS

- Combination square
- Pencil
- Measuring tape or fold-out rule
- Utility knife
- Jigsaw (or portable circular saw, tenon saw or panel saw)
- Smoothing plane
- Hammer
- Vice
- Electric drill
- Drill bits: 3 mm, 5 mm, 8 mm, countersink; 50 mm hole saw
- Screwdriver (cross-head or slotted)
- Nail punch
- Cork sanding block or electric sander

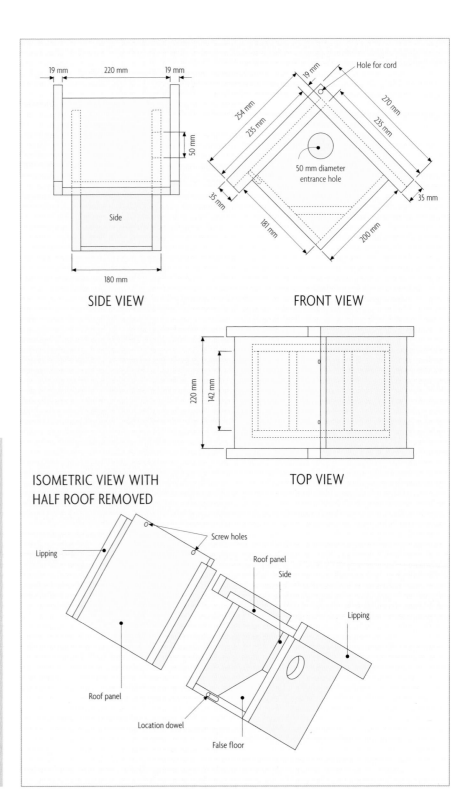

SIDE VIEW

FRONT VIEW

TOP VIEW

ISOMETRIC VIEW WITH HALF ROOF REMOVED

MATERIALS*

PART	MATERIAL	LENGTH	NO.
Front/back	225 x 25 mm timber PAR	200 mm	2
Side	175 x 25 mm timber PAR	181 mm	1
Side	175 x 25 mm timber PAR	200 mm	1
Roof panel	250 x 25 mm timber PAR	254 mm	1
Roof panel	250 x 25 mm timber PAR	235 mm	1
Lipping	50 x 25 mm timber PAR	235 mm	2
Lipping	50 x 25 mm timber PAR	270 mm	2
False floor (optional)	150 x 25 mm timber PAR	142 mm	1

Other: Two 30 mm nails; eighteen 40 mm nails; six 35 mm x No. 8 brass countersunk screws; epoxy resin adhesive; water-based wood filler; one 38 x 8 mm timber dowel; one sheet of 180 grit abrasive paper; vegetable oil (or 250 ml clear acrylic varnish); 6 mm sash cord.

* Finished size: 258 mm long; 380 mm wide; 330 mm tall. Timber sizes given here are nominal.

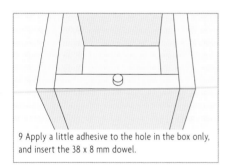
9 Apply a little adhesive to the hole in the box only, and insert the 38 x 8 mm dowel.

upwards. Apply a little adhesive to the three exposed edges. Place the 235 mm long roof panel flush with the top edges of the box, ensuring there is a 20 mm overhang at each side. Fix this panel to the box using three 40 mm nails, one in the front piece, one in the back and one in the side piece.

9 Turn the box over so the open side faces up. To insert the dowel, first locate the centre of the side piece along the top edge and drill an 8 mm hole to a depth of 30 mm. Take the 254 mm roof panel and lay it in position on the box. Along the top edge, measure in 50 mm from each side and 9 mm in from the edge for the screw holes. Drill a 5 mm hole at each point and countersink the holes. On the underside, mark the position for the dowel hole and drill an 8 mm hole to a depth of 10 mm. Apply a little adhesive to the dowel hole in the box only, and then insert the 38 x 8 mm dowel. Do not apply any of the adhesive to the hole in the roof panel.

10 Fit the roof panel in position and fasten it down with two 35 mm brass screws. Do not use adhesive—you will need to remove this roof panel later in order to insert the false floor (see step 17) and to clean the birdhouse.

11 Lay the box face upwards and apply a little adhesive to the front edge of the removable roof panel. Take a 235 mm long lipping, which should be cut to a width of 35 mm, and attach it to the roof panel. Keep it flush with the inner face and outer edge of the roof. Use 40 mm nails to fasten the lipping, which should be flush with the upper edge of the roof. Apply some adhesive to the other edge of the box and attach a 270 mm long lipping (which should be cut to a width of 35 mm). Turn the box over and repeat the process for the lippings on the opposite side.

12 With a combination square, measure vertically upwards 215 mm from the bottom apex of the box, then mark the position. Use a 50 mm hole saw to make the entrance hole in the front of the birdhouse.

FINISHING THE BIRDHOUSE

13 Use a combination square to mark vertical lines 14 mm down from the top apex of the lipping. Mark these lines on both the front and back of the box. Drill an 8 mm hole at these positions.

14 Punch all the nails below the surface and fill them with wood filler. Sand the unit well with 180 grit abrasive paper, working in the direction of the grain.

15 This birdhouse is finished with two coats of vegetable oil applied with a pad of steel wool soaked in the oil. Wipe off any excess with a clean, dry cloth. Leave the birdhouse for a few days to allow the oil to soak into the timber before applying a second coat of oil.

16 To finish, pass a piece of 6 mm sash cord through the holes and secure with

HINT

When planing the end grain, plane from each edge towards the centre first, and then plane from the centre towards the edge. Avoid planing over the end of the timber, as this will cause the timber to chip out.

a 'figure 8' knot. The birdhouse is now ready to hang. You may also want to fit a false floor in the birdhouse at this point.

ADDING A FALSE FLOOR

17 A false floor can be inserted in the birdhouse to give the birds a more stable and even place to nest. This false floor simply rests inside the birdhouse and is not nailed in place. Don't insert it until after you have sanded, stained and found a position for the birdhouse. Take the 142 mm long timber for the false floor and cut it to 125 mm wide. Use a smoothing plane to bevel the two long edges to 45 degrees, so that the floor sits

neatly in the base of the birdhouse.

18 Drill four or five drainage holes in the false floor, unscrew the roof panel as discussed in

step 10, and insert the false floor. If you want, you could also drill drainage holes in the bottom apex of the birdhouse.

FINISHING PRODUCTS

Water-based finishing products have been used in the projects in this chapter wherever possible. When oil is used, vegetable oil is recommended, rather than some of the commercially available finishing oils such as teak oil or Danish oil. Vegetable cooking oils are a good substitute, but may not protect the timber for as long. Even so, they won't damage the birds' health, and they are kept in most kitchens.

Water-based acrylic paints are recommended, as they outperform oil-based paints. Avoid the use of glossy paints, as they do not seem to be as attractive to birds as the flat or low sheen types.

OPEN-SIDED FEEDER

The design of this charming feeder is simple but effective. The roof, which is bevelled and planed to a pitched shape, keeps the seed dry. Raised side rails prevent any food falling out.

CUTTING OUT

1 Take the 225 x 16 mm timber for the base, and using a combination square set at 193 mm and a pencil, mark a line along the length of the board. Use a power saw or tenon saw to cut the piece close to this width. Square a line near one end of the timber and mark off the length to 193 mm. Square all lines over the edges and across the faces. Cut the piece to length.

2 Take the 50 x 16 mm material for the side rails and mark off four rails 255 mm long, leaving 5 mm spaces between each of them to allow for saw cuts. Cut the side rail pieces slightly overlength.

3 Measure in 19 mm from each end of the side rails, mark with a pencil, then square a line across one top edge and over the sides to half the width. Use a piece of scrap timber to mark the 12 mm wide halving joint. Hold the material so that it nearly covers the line and mark the thickness on the other side. Square this line across the edge and over the face to about halfway down. With a utility knife, trace over the marked lines in order to cut the surface fibres. Mark the waste area.

4 Use a combination square to mark a depth of 20.5 mm for the halving joints on each face. Clamp all four pieces in a vice or cramp, and use a tenon saw to cut on the waste side of each line to the depth mark.

MATERIALS*

PART	MATERIAL	LENGTH	NO.
Side rail	50 x 16 mm timber PAR	255 mm	4
Post	25 x 25 mm timber PAR	165 mm	4
Base	225 x 16 mm timber PAR	193 mm	1
Roof	75 x 75 mm timber PAR	300 mm	3

Other: Four 20 mm panel pins; four brass cup hooks; four 38 x 8 mm timber dowels; masking tape; epoxy resin adhesive; water-based timber filler; abrasive paper: one sheet of 100 grit and one sheet of 180 grit; 250 ml exterior acrylic paint of your choice; required length of brass chain.

* Finished size: 290 mm long (roof); 290 mm wide (roof); 240 mm tall (from base of feeder to top of roof). Timber sizes are nominal. For timber types and sizes see page 471.

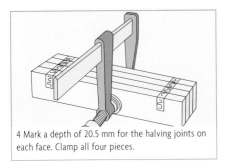

4 Mark a depth of 20.5 mm for the halving joints on each face. Clamp all four pieces.

Use the 12 mm chisel to remove the waste from the joint. The joints should fit snugly, not too tightly. Measure the diagonal distances to check that the frame is square.

ASSEMBLING THE FRAME, POSTS AND BASE

5 Mix a little adhesive and assemble the frame on a flat surface. Use scrap material and 20 mm panel pins to temporarily brace the frame diagonally, then leave to dry.

6 While the assembled frame is drying, use a smoothing plane to bring the base piece to fit neatly in the frame. When planing the end grain, always plane from the outer edges towards the centre to avoid chipping the timber.

7 On the 25 x 25 mm timber, mark off four posts each 165 mm long. Cut the posts with a tenon saw. Place all four pieces end upwards in a vice and mark the centre of each end. With an 8 mm drill bit, drill a 29 mm deep dowel hole.

8 Mix some adhesive and then apply it sparingly to the edges of the base piece. Insert the base in the frame, flush with the bottom of the frame. Use a 20 mm panel pin in the centre of each side to fasten the base.

9 Place adhesive in the outside corners of the frame and tape the posts in position with dowel holes at the top. With a square, check the posts are plumb. Leave to dry.

This feeder is suspended from weather-resistant brass chains, but it can also be mounted on a post—at least 2 m above the ground—as a 'bird table'. Feeders should be placed in a sheltered location within a short flying distance of cover.

TOOLS

- Combination square
- Pencil
- Measuring tape or fold-out rule
- Utility knife
- Marking gauge
- Safety glasses
- Jigsaw
- Tenon saw
- Portable circular saw
- Portable power plane or smoothing plane
- Cork sanding block or electric sander
- Vice
- Two 300 mm quick-action cramps or two sash or adjustable cramps
- Chisel: 12 mm
- Trestle (optional)
- Hammer
- Electric drill
- Drill bit: 8 mm
- Sliding bevel
- Nail punch

MAKING THE ROOF PIECES

10 Cut the 75 x 75 mm timber for the roof into three pieces 300 mm in length. Use a combination square and pencil to mark a centre line down the length of one face. On scrap board, mark out the roof pitch: 66 mm high and half the roof width (142.5 mm). Set up a sliding bevel to this pitch. Transfer the angle to the ends of the piece marked with the centre line.

11 Lay the centre piece down flat and place the other two pieces on either side of it. Mark the position where they meet the roof bevel. Use the sliding bevel to transfer the

13 Set the foot of the circular saw to the angle of the roof bevel. Cut on the waste side of the line.

roof bevel to these two pieces so that the slope continues. Mark the waste side.

12 Use a portable power plane or the smoothing plane to plane the roof bevel on the centre piece.

13 Set the foot of the portable circular saw to the angle of the roof bevel. Secure the second piece to a suitable work surface, such as a trestle with stops on one side and at the end. Set the depth of the blade so it only just passes through the timber, then cut on the waste side of the line. Repeat this step for the third piece of timber. The waste pieces will be turned over and used for the two outer pieces. (If you cannot cut the full depth with the power saw, turn the material over and cut carefully from the other side on the waste side of the line.)

ASSEMBLING THE ROOF

14 Hold all the roof pieces together and check the fit of the joints. Plane to adjust if necessary. Mix some adhesive and apply to

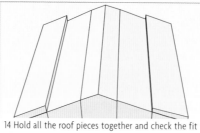
14 Hold all the roof pieces together and check the fit of the joints. Plane to adjust if necessary.

each joining face, then rub the joints together so a little adhesive squeezes out. Repeat this process until all five pieces that make up the roof have been glued. Lay the glued pieces down flat and then leave them to dry completely.

15 When the roof is dry, use an electric plane to remove some of the waste material. When using the electric plane, wear safety glasses, and keep the waste chute pointing away from your face. Mark the centre of the ridge and square a line down the roof and over the bottom face. Square a line down to the bottom at each end and join the points along the bottom. Using these centre lines, mark out the roof size on the underside of the roof. Before cutting, you should check that the roof shape is square by measuring the diagonal distances.

16 Use a jigsaw to cut out the square shape of the roof from the underside. Cut out the shape on the waste side of the line. Turn the roof over and use a straight edge to draw lines from the centre of the apex to the outer corners (these will serve as guidelines for planing across the grain).

17 Secure the roof to a flat surface, with one edge overhanging. Nail timber stops to the work surface as a jig, so the roof won't move as you plane. Plane along the length of the grain first, to within 1–2 mm of the roof bevel. Use a smoothing plane to finish the

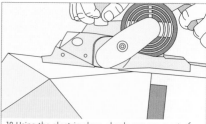
18 Using the electric plane, slowly remove most of the waste from the remaining side of the roof.

FRONT VIEW

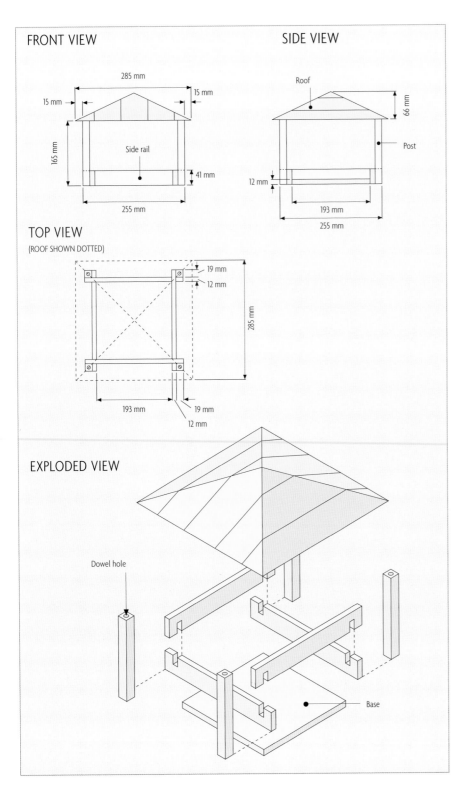

285 mm

15 mm

15 mm

165 mm

Side rail

41 mm

255 mm

SIDE VIEW

Roof

66 mm

Post

12 mm

193 mm

255 mm

TOP VIEW
(ROOF SHOWN DOTTED)

19 mm

12 mm

285 mm

193 mm

19 mm

12 mm

EXPLODED VIEW

Dowel hole

Base

bevel, keeping the edge of the roof about 2 mm thick.

18 Turn the roof panel around in the jig. Using the electric plane, slowly remove most of the waste from the remaining side of the roof. Remove the last lot of material with the smoothing plane.

FINISHING THE FEEDER

19 Measure the centre to centre distance on the posts and transfer the measurements to the underside of the roof. On the roof, drill 8 mm holes 9 mm deep at the marked dowel centre positions. Check the fit of the roof, then mix some adhesive and glue the holes. Press the roof into place and leave it to dry overnight.

20 Punch in all nail holes and fill gaps with wood filler. Use 100 grit abrasive paper to sand the roof, then finish the entire feeder with 180 grit abrasive paper.

21 Apply a coat of paint to the body of the feeder and use a clear acrylic finish for the roof. For the best finish, apply three coats and sand well between each coat. A regular coat of clear finish should be applied to the roof every four to six months to keep it looking its best.

DOVECOTE

A dovecote is the ultimate romantic garden feature. This project requires precision and patience, especially in the assembly of the roof with its overlapping slats and mitred ridge capping.

SIDE ASSEMBLY

1 Use the 60/30 degree set square to tilt the base of the portable power saw to a 60-degree angle. Place the plywood for the sides across the work surface. Set up a straight edge parallel to one long edge, far enough in to cut the angle on the edge of a sheet of plywood. Clamp the straight edge to the board, and make an angled cut along one edge.

2 Cut the next angle in the opposite direction. Turn the plywood over and set the straight edge parallel to the angled edge, at the necessary distance in to produce a piece 310 mm wide. The distance set from the line will be determined by measuring the distance from the inner edge of the saw blade to the outside edge of the foot (cut a piece of scrap material to check). Cut the second side piece.

3 Working from one square end of the plywood, use a combination square and pencil to mark out the length of the first side piece (750 mm) on the inside face. The inside face is the narrow face. Position a straight edge parallel to the line so that the saw will cut underlength on the outside face. Set the saw to a 45-degree angle and carefully make the cut. Square off the end of the plywood before you set out the next side piece. Use the combination square to square the line across the end and cut with a jigsaw or a handsaw. To finish, use a smoothing plane to smooth and square the end. Repeat this process to cut the other five side pieces.

4 Lay the sides down with the outside face

In a contemporary take on the traditional all-white dovecote, only the basic unit has been painted. The timber roof has been finished in a clear exterior acrylic to emphasize the intricacy of the design.

up, then place them next to one another with joint edges tightly aligned and bottom edges flush. Apply one strip of masking tape along the length of each joint, and at least four pieces of tape across. Fold the hexagon up and tape the remaining joint.

5 Loosely tie the two pieces of rope around

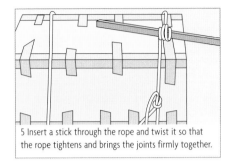

5 Insert a stick through the rope and twist it so that the rope tightens and brings the joints firmly together.

MATERIALS*

PART	MATERIAL	LENGTH	WIDTH	NO.
Side	18 mm exterior plywood	750 mm	310 mm	6
Base	18 mm exterior plywood	800 mm	800 mm	1
Support bracket	18 mm exterior plywood	250 mm	250 mm	4
Internal floor	18 mm exterior plywood	600 mm	600 mm	1
Roof panel	4 mm exterior plywood	504 mm	420 mm	6
Base lipping	100 x 25 mm timber PAR	440 mm		6
Fascia	75 x 16 mm timber PAR	400 mm		6
Roof slat**	50 x 10 mm timber wedge	2200 mm		—
Ridge capping**	12 x 10 mm timber	580 mm		12

Other: Four 25 mm panel pins; eighteen 40 mm nails; eighteen 15 mm panel pins; eleven 50 mm x No. 8 brass countersunk screws; scrap material for perches/supports; masking tape; two pieces of rope 2.4 m long; epoxy resin adhesive; twelve 50 mm wide strips of cotton cloth; paintbrush; abrasive paper: one sheet of 120 grit and one sheet of 180 grit; water-based wood filler; 500 ml exterior acrylic paint of your choice; 250 ml clear exterior acrylic finish.

* Finished size: 880 mm long; 880 mm wide; 1042 mm tall. Timber sizes given are nominal. For timber types and sizes see page 471.

** Cut roof slat and ridge capping material from one piece 2400 x 100 x 50 mm timber PAR.

the hexagon. Insert a small stick through the rope and twist it so that the rope tightens and brings the joints firmly together. Ensure the joints come up neatly and the angles are even. Use a smoothing plane to adjust if necessary.

6 Mix adhesive for the joints. Undo the rope and lay the side pieces flat, inside face up. Glue the face of each joint, reassemble the hexagon and tighten the ropes. Allow to dry.

MAIN ROOF ASSEMBLY

7 On the plywood for the roof panels mark a triangle with a base length of 440 mm and with a perpendicular height of 504 mm. Use a jigsaw to cut the shape slightly oversize and a smoothing plane to bring the triangle back to size.

8 Use this triangle as a template for marking out the other five triangles, then cut them out. Nail all triangles together with two 25 mm panel pins, the template piece to the

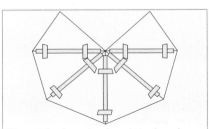

9 Lay out the plywood roof panel triangles and use masking tape to tape the joints.

outside. Place the triangles in a vice and plane to the template size. Remove the nails and plane a 15–20-degree bevel on each of the long edges.

9 Lay out the triangles and tape the joints together. Fold the triangles up and tape the final joint to form a neat hexagonal pyramid with the sides sloping in at 45 degrees. Unfold the pyramid, glue each joint, then refold. Place it base upwards, check the shape is even and leave it until dry.

10 Cut six strips of cotton material to the length of each joint. With a paint brush, apply adhesive inside the roof along each side of a joint. Place the cloth strip on top of the adhesive, pushing the cloth into the joint (paint more adhesive over the cloth if needed). Repeat for each joint. Stand

the pyramid base downwards to dry.

BASE ASSEMBLY

11 Take the plywood for the base and use a compass with an extension arm to draw a circle 800 mm in diameter. Without changing the radius, place the point of the compass on the circle and mark off six equal distances around the circle, ending up where you started. Use a straight edge to join the points to form a hexagon. Cut out with a jigsaw and plane back to the lines, keeping the edges straight and square.

12 Set up a sliding bevel to 60 degrees. Hold the timber for the base lippings against one edge of the base and mark off the inside length on the top edge of the timber (400 mm). Mark off the angle to the outside face. Square the lines across each face and

TOOLS

- Set square: 60/30 degree
- Measuring tape or fold-out rule
- Combination square and pencil
- Two quick-release cramps
- Portable power saw
- Jigsaw or handsaw
- Tenon saw
- Smoothing plane
- Hammer
- Vice
- Compass with extension arm, or a protractor
- Two sliding bevels
- Utility knife
- Bench hook
- Side cutters or pliers
- Screwdriver (slotted or cross-head)
- Electric drill
- Drill bits: 3 mm, 5 mm, 8 mm, countersink; 25 mm spade bit or hole saw
- Nail punch
- Cork sanding block or electric sander

use the bevel to return them across the remaining edge (they should meet up). Number the lipping corresponding to the edge on the base. Score the lines, then use a tenon saw to cut the mitres on each end. Clean up with a smoothing plane. Repeat for all lippings.

13 Glue the edge of the base and attach one lipping flush with the top of the base, using 40 mm nails—punch the nails below the surface. Repeat for all lippings. Use the smoothing plane to make a 10 mm chamfer around the top edge of the lipping.

FASCIA ASSEMBLY

14 Use the sliding bevel set at 60 degrees to mark a mitre across the edge of the fascia timber, near one end. Measure out 400 mm on the outer face and mark the opposite mitre on the other end. Mark out five more pieces the same way.

15 Plane the top edge to a 45-degree angle. Use the combination square to check the angle and ensure you are planing parallel to the bottom edge.

16 Trace the mitre lines with a utility knife. With the bottom edge facing up in the bench hook, cut the mitres, keeping the cut square. Insert two 15 mm panel pins in one face of each adjoining mitre and cut the heads off to leave 6–7 mm exposed. Push the mitres together to check the fit. Repeat for all joints. Take the frame apart and glue each joint, then reassemble and leave to dry.

ENTRY HOLES AND PERCHES

17 Mark out entrance holes 225 mm high and 150 mm wide. With an 8 mm bit, drill holes near the bottom corners of the upper entrance holes. Use a jigsaw with a fine-toothed blade to cut the holes, and smooth with 120 grit abrasive paper. Take the waste material, square across, and cut off the curved end of three pieces for the perches. Use a smoothing plane to plane the square end.

18 Make the internal floor now. Stand the dovecote on the 18 mm plywood and trace the inside shape of the unit. Cut out the shape with a jigsaw. Insert the floor level with the bottom edges of the top entrance holes and fix with six 40 mm nails.

19 Place two 15 mm panel pins 8 mm down from each upper hole, 80 mm apart. Nail in to half their length, then cut off the heads.

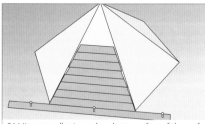

24 Mix some adhesive and apply to one face of the roof. Place the bottom slat on the roof, then attach the rest.

Push the perches into place. Remove the perches, then glue and reposition them. For the perch supports, mark a 120 mm diameter circle on a waste piece, then quarter it. Cut out with a jigsaw, glue and tape them in place, then leave to dry.

CUTTING ROOF SLATS

20 Set up a marking gauge to 4 mm and mark a line down one wide face of the roof slat timber. Square the line over the ends. Mark a line from the gauged line to the opposite corner on the end of the material: this is the angle of the roof slat. Plane the angle on the edge of the timber.

21 Clamp the roof slat timber to the bench, gauged line upwards. Using a jigsaw, cut a slat 10 mm thick. Plane the edge again to make the angle. Use a marking gauge to mark the line on the face and repeat the cut. Repeat until the 2400 mm piece has been turned into wedge slats.

22 Place the roof 'pyramid' on a flat surface, base down against a stop. Hold a slat up to the base and mark the bottom length. Set the sliding bevel to the ridge angle—hold the base of the bevel against the bottom edge, position the blade to align with the angle and tighten the screw. Transfer the angle to the slat at the length marks. Cut to length and use as a template for the other sides.

23 Tape the first roof slat piece in place.

Mark the length of the second row of slats and use the sliding bevel to set the angle. Use this as a template for the second row of slats, then tape the second piece in place. Repeat to cut all the roof slats.

24 Mix some adhesive and apply to one face of the roof. Place the bottom roof slat on the roof, then attach the rest, ensuring that each piece touches the one below. Work on one side at a time until all sides are covered. Allow to dry.

ADDING RIDGE CAPPING

25 Mark a centre line down the face of one side of the roof, from the roof tip to the centre of the base. Place the butt of the sliding bevel in line with the ridge, align the blade with the centre line and tighten the screw. This angle will be the mitre angle for the ridge capping. Set a second sliding bevel to the angle used for cutting the ends of the roof slats. This will be the angle of the foot cut for the ridge capping.

26 Take the ridge capping timber and with a marking gauge mark a line 4 mm wide along the face side. Use a jigsaw to cut to thickness. Plane the edge and repeat the step to cut twelve pieces 600 mm long. Bevel one long edge of each piece to the angle in step 25 and check the edge fit of the pieces on the ridge.

27 Mark the foot cut close to one end of a ridge capping piece. Ensure the bevelled edge will face in the right direction. With a utility knife and the sliding bevel, make the foot cut. Tape the piece in place, with the foot of the ridge capping touching the bench. Repeat for the capping on the opposite side of the same roof panel. Tape in place with the top ends of the two pieces overlapping. Use a pencil to mark the point of overlap on each piece. With the second

Nail holes and gaps in the roof have been filled with wood filler that matches the colour of the timber.

sliding bevel mark the mitre angle on each piece, then cut the angles with a utility knife. Adjust the bevels, then tape back into place. Use the two cut ridge pieces as guides for the remaining pieces and repeat the process, taping each one into place. When finished, remove each piece, glue it and tape it back in place (one at a time). Leave to dry.

28 Place the roof on the fascia frame, with an even overhang all round. Turn the roof on to one face to check the bevelled angle of the frame. Glue the bevelled edge of the

frame and tape the roof in place. Turn right way up and leave to dry.

ASSEMBLING THE DOVECOTE

29 Turn the roof upside down and support with packing material. Next, turn the main unit upside down, and locate it evenly within the roof. Trace around the inside of the unit. Remove the unit, apply adhesive to the top edges and relocate it on the roof. Use three strips of cotton cloth wetted with adhesive to join the roof to the main unit. Leave to dry.

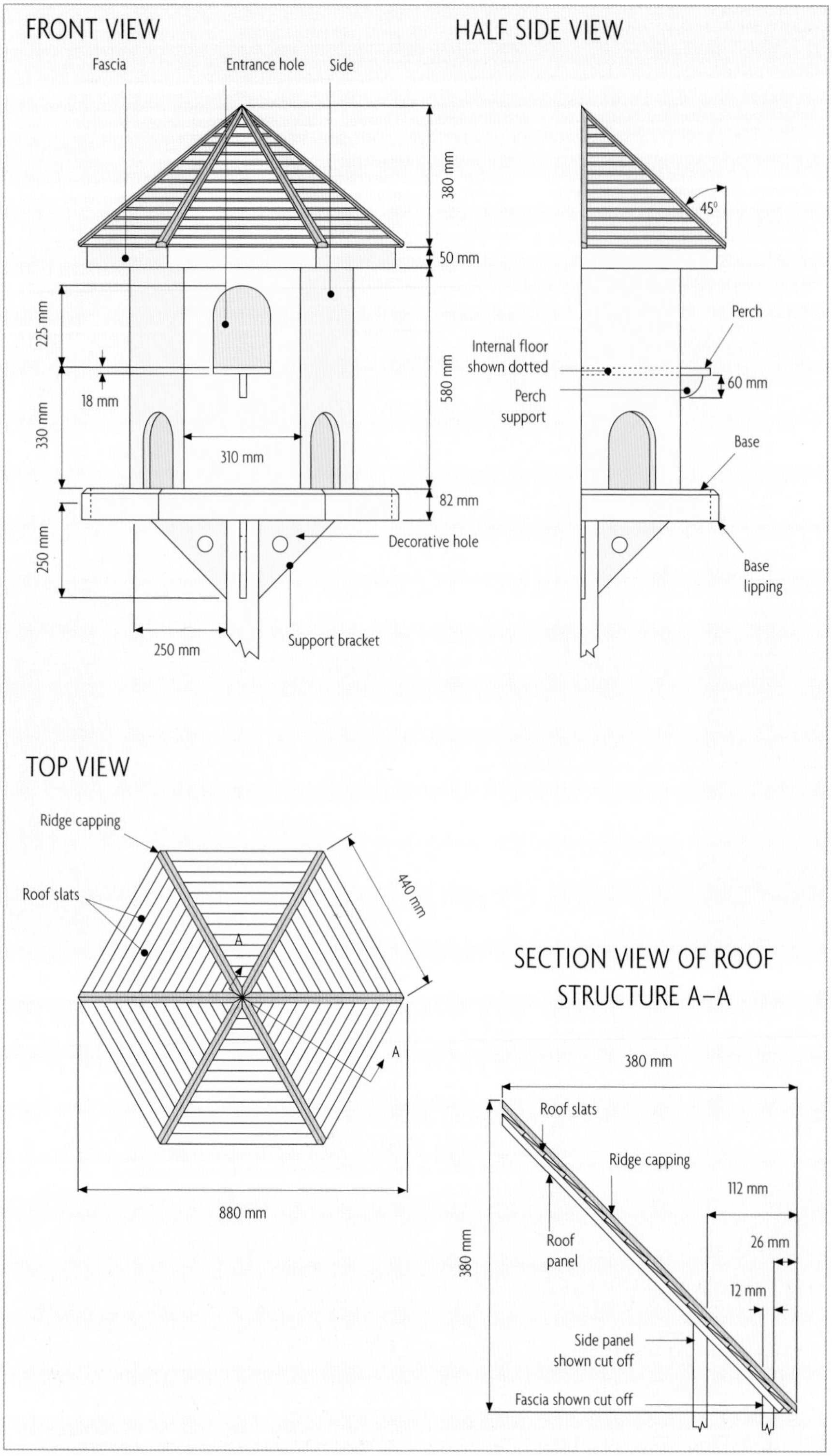

FRONT VIEW

Fascia   Entrance hole   Side

380 mm

50 mm

225 mm

18 mm

330 mm

310 mm

250 mm

250 mm

Decorative hole

Support bracket

HALF SIDE VIEW

45°

580 mm

Perch

60 mm

Internal floor
shown dotted

Perch
support

Base

82 mm

Base
lipping

TOP VIEW

Ridge capping

Roof slats

A

A

440 mm

880 mm

380 mm

SECTION VIEW OF ROOF
STRUCTURE A–A

380 mm

Roof slats

Ridge capping

112 mm

26 mm

12 mm

Roof
panel

Side panel
shown cut off

Fascia shown cut off

380 mm

30 On the top of the base, draw lines from each corner to the opposite corner. Set the unit on top of the base and align its corners with the marked lines. Ensure the unit is centred, then trace around the outside on to the base. Drill three 5 mm holes through the base, 8 mm inside the traced lines on the sides without low-set entrance holes. Turn the base over and countersink the holes. Position the base over the unit. Drill three 3 mm pilot holes through the 5 mm clearance holes into the unit, and use three 50 mm x No. 8 screws to attach the base.

MAKING SUPPORT BRACKETS

31 From the plywood cut two squares 250 x 250 mm. Cut them diagonally, then plane smooth. From the square corner, measure in 50 mm and down 130 mm to find the centre of the decorative holes. Use a spade bit or hole saw to cut the holes. In the centre of the base, set out the dimensions of the post (it should be made of 100 x 100 mm timber PAR). Use an offcut from the post to locate brackets centrally on the faces of the post. Drill 5 mm countersunk clearance holes 25 mm in from the ends of the brackets, then fasten the brackets to the bottom of the base with adhesive and four 50 mm screws. Use same-size screws to fix brackets to the post. Concrete the post into the ground, setting it at least 750 mm deep.

32 Fill and sand the dovecote, then apply your chosen finish.

POST FOR BIRDHOUSE OR FEEDER

This sturdy, stylish post is designed to be portable, and is anchored in position with steel tent pegs.
An optional fixing plate provides an extra-strong fastening for a birdhouse or feeder.

MAKING THE BASE

1 Take the base leg timber and mark out two pieces 600 mm long. Cut to length with a tenon saw, then mark the centre on one face. Measure out 33 mm from one side of centre. Square the line across the face and over each edge, down to half the timber thickness. Place one piece on the marked line on the other piece, and pencil the width of the halving joint. (The post must be modified for use with the Dovecote on page 504.)

2 Repeat the step for the other piece, squaring the lines over the edge to halfway down. Set a marking gauge to half the thickness of the timber. On both base leg pieces, mark a line between the two pencilled marks.

3 Use a utility knife to trace the lines for the halving joint, and mark the waste. Clamp the timber to the workbench and cut it with the tenon saw on the waste side of the line down to the gauged line. Make a number of cuts in between the lines, about 10 mm apart. Repeat the process for the other half of the base.

4 Use the 25 mm chisel to remove the waste down to the gauged line. Check the depth of

the recess as you chisel. Make sure the bottom of the recess is flat, with no high spots (the edge of the chisel makes a useful straight edge). Check the fit and adjust if necessary.

5 With the halving joint assembled, measure in 20 mm from each edge of the joint to form a 26 mm square in the centre of the joint. Do this on both faces of the halving joint. (You can also use a marking gauge set to 20 mm to mark the correct distance in from each edge of the material, on two edges, if you take the joint apart.) Use a pencil to mark the centre of the 26 mm square with a cross. With the joint assembled, use the 25 mm spade bit to drill a hole through the centre of the joint—drill from both sides of the material to be sure you are drilling straight. Use the 25 mm chisel to remove any remaining waste from the mortise, working from both faces towards

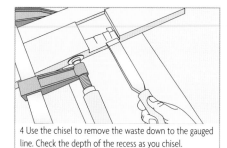

4 Use the chisel to remove the waste down to the gauged line. Check the depth of the recess as you chisel.

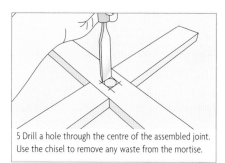

2 Set a marking gauge to half the thickness of the edge. Mark a line between the two pencilled marks.

5 Drill a hole through the centre of the assembled joint. Use the chisel to remove any waste from the mortise.

All edges of the post are chamfered for a finely detailed finish. The Western red cedar timber has been treated with a clear exterior sealer; it should retain its original colour if treated every few months and kept in a shaded position.

the centre to avoid breaking out the material on the bottom face.

MAKING TENON AND BRACES

6 Make sure the pole is 66 mm square. Use a combination square and pencil to square a line around the timber for the pole, 32 mm up from one end. Set the marking gauge to 20 mm. On the marked end of the pole, working from each face, mark a line across the bottom and down each face to the shoulder line of the tenon. Use the utility knife to trace over the shoulder lines of the tenon.

7 With the pole well supported, use a tenon saw to cut squarely down the shoulder lines on the waste side to the 20 mm marks on each face. Use the chisel to remove the waste from the shoulders of the tenon.

8 Test the fit of the tenon in the mortise. It should be a snug fit, but not too tight. Use the tenon saw to make a diagonal cut down the length of the tenon to accommodate the wedge that will be used to reinforce the joint.

9 Take the timber for the braces and use the combination square set to 45 degrees to mark out the four brace pieces at 310 mm long on their longest edge. It is best to mark them out opposite one another to save some cutting, leaving 5 mm between each piece to allow for the saw cuts. Trace over the lines with the utility knife to cut the cross-grain fibres, then make the mitre cuts with the tenon saw. Hold each piece in a vice and use the smoothing plane to smooth the mitre cuts back to the 45-degree knife lines. Before assembly, sand all the pieces with 120 grit abrasive paper.

10 From a scrap piece of 75 x 38 mm material, cut a fine wedge to fit into the saw cut in the tenon.

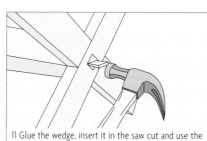

11 Glue the wedge, insert it in the saw cut and use the hammer to drive the wedge in to tighten the joint.

MATERIALS*

PART	MATERIAL	LENGTH	WIDTH	NO.
Base leg	75 x 38 mm timber PAR	600 mm		2
Pole**	75 x 75 mm timber PAR	2700 mm		1
Brace	75 x 38 mm timber PAR	310 mm		4
Fixing plate (optional)	18 mm exterior plywood	160 mm	90 mm	1

Other: Sixteen 40 mm nails; four 6 x 300–450 mm long steel tent pegs; two 50 mm brass countersunk screws; four 32 mm brass countersunk screws; abrasive paper: one sheet of 120 grit and one sheet of 180 grit; epoxy resin adhesive; paint brush; 500 ml exterior water-based clear finish.

* Finished size: 600 mm long (base); 600 mm wide (base); 2.7 m high (will vary). Timber sizes given are nominal. For timber types and sizes see page 471.

** Pole for dovecote (page 504) must be made of 100 x 100 mm timber PAR.

TOOLS

- Combination square and pencil
- Measuring tape or fold-out rule
- Tenon saw
- Marking gauge
- Utility knife
- G-cramp
- Chisel: 25 mm
- Vice
- Smoothing plane
- Hammer
- Router or spokeshave (optional)
- Sanding cork
- Screwdriver (cross-head or slotted)
- Electric drill
- Drill bits: 3 mm, 5 mm, 8 mm; 25 mm spade bit
- Nail punch

11 Mix a little epoxy resin adhesive, apply some to each halving joint and then bring the two halves together. Apply some adhesive to the tenon and the shoulders of the tenon, then fit the base over the tenon—make sure the base sits tightly against the shoulders. Apply a little adhesive to the wedge, insert it in the saw cut and use the hammer to drive the wedge in far enough to tighten the joint (be careful not to split the timber pole). Cut or plane off any excess wedge and tenon.

CHAMFERING THE BASE LEGS, POLE AND BRACES

12 Use a smoothing plane to plane a chamfer on the ends of each of the four base legs. Lay the pole on a suitable work surface. From the base, measure up 250 mm and then measure up a further 1500 mm. With a combination square, square the marked lines

outdoor

around the pole. Using a pencil and your fingers as a gauge, mark lines 5 mm in, parallel to all the edges between the lines. At the end marks, use a chisel at 45 degrees to make small cuts in the edges of the pole. With the ground cutting edge down, working from about 25 mm in from each of the previous marks, make a chamfer back to the original mark. Use a smoothing plane or spokeshave to finish the chamfers between the marks. (Using a router with a chamfering bit is a faster method, or you could use an ovolo moulding bit for a fancy finish.)

13 For the braces, start the chamfer 50 mm in from each end on the outside edge only. Use the same process as for the pole, but reduce the chamfer width to 3 mm.

FINISHING

14 Sand the pole and braces with 180 grit abrasive paper. Paint the underside of the braces with the exterior clear finish. Start a 40 mm nail about 25 mm in from each end of the brace and apply a little adhesive to each joint face of the brace. Locate the brace centrally on the base leg and the pole, then finish nailing the brace to the base and pole. Repeat this step for all braces and then place another nail in each joint. Measure 30 mm in from the end of each base leg and, in the centre at this point, drill an 8 mm hole through the timber. When positioning the post, a 6 mm steel tent peg about 300–450 mm long should be driven through this hole into the ground to stabilize the post.

15 Determine the height at which you will place the birdhouse or feeder, and cut the pole to the required length.

16 Take the optional fixing plate and drill two 5 mm holes so it can be attached to the post, countersinking the holes to ensure the birdhouse will sit flat. Align the fixing

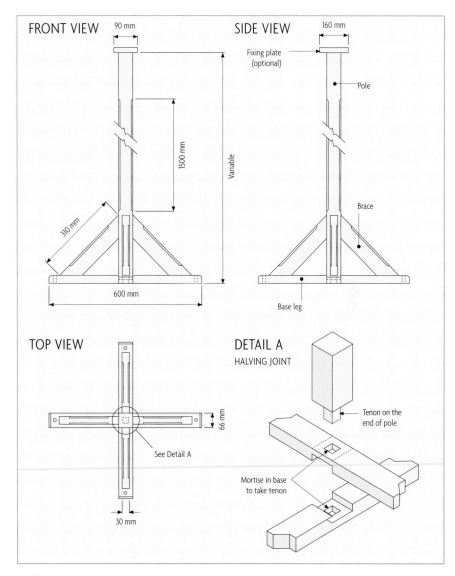

FRONT VIEW — 90 mm — 1500 mm — 310 mm — 600 mm

SIDE VIEW — 160 mm — Fixing plate (optional) — Pole — Variable — Brace — Base leg

TOP VIEW — 66 mm — 30 mm — See Detail A

DETAIL A
HALVING JOINT — Tenon on the end of pole — Mortise in base to take tenon

plate and drill two 3 mm pilot holes for the screws. Attach the fixing plate with a little adhesive and two 50 mm countersunk screws. Drill a 5 mm hole near each corner, ready for fixing the birdhouse in position. Most birdhouses will require four 32 mm x No. 8 brass countersunk screws to secure them to the fixing plate.

17 Punch all the nail heads below the surface and use a suitable wood filler to fill any

holes or gaps. Allow to dry before sanding with 180 grit abrasive paper.

18 Apply the first coat of exterior clear finish and leave to dry. Sand all the surfaces between each coat with 180 grit or finer abrasive paper—for the best results and the longest protection from the elements, use a minimum of three coats.

BIRDHOUSE WITH BEVELLED ROOF PANELS

With its small entrance hole, this snug design offers smaller birds a haven from larger predators.

CUTTING OUT

1 With a combination square and measuring tape, mark out the parts, leaving 5 mm between each for saw cuts. Keep at least one edge of each part to the outer edge of the sheet.

2 With a circular saw or jigsaw, cut the parts—use a fence or rip guide to keep the saw travelling straight.

SETTING OUT THE FRONT AND BACK PIECES

3 Take the front and back pieces and temporarily nail them together with 40 mm nails, aligning bottom edges. Both should be just over 240 mm long by 220 mm wide. Mark the centre of the shorter bottom edge, then square a line up the centre of the length. Mark off 160 mm and 240 mm along this line. Square the lines from the 160 mm mark to the outer edges of the boards.

4 Place the attached front and back pieces together in a vice, then plane the sides straight and square to the bottom. Use a combination square, as well as the 30-degree angle and the 45-degree angle on the set squares, to set out a 15-degree angle down from the 240 mm mark at the top centre position (or use a compass or protractor to set out the angles).

5 Using the 45-degree set square and the combination square, draw a line from the 160 mm marks on the outer edges to the 15-degree angle. This makes the intersecting angle. Repeat for the other side. Along the bottom edge, mark out 90 mm each side of the centre. Working from these marks, draw

lines to join the 160 mm marks.

6 Keep the front and back pieces nailed together and clamp them to the workbench. Use a jigsaw to cut out the shape of the two pieces. Place them in the vice and plane them back to the lines with a smoothing plane, ensuring that the edges are square.

MAKING THE SIDE PIECES, ROOF PANELS AND BASE

7 Set the sliding bevel to the angle of the side, using the front/back pieces as a guide. Transfer this angle to the bottom edge of the side pieces at each end. With a marking gauge, mark the width of angle along the edge to be planed. Place the side piece in a vice and plane back to the gauged line. Repeat for the other side panel. Plane the side pieces back to their correct size, 164 x 160 mm, keeping the edges square.

8 Plane the roof panels to their correct size, 240 x 115 mm, keeping the edges square. Using the front/back pieces as a guide, set

the sliding bevel to the mitre angle at the apex of the pieces. Transfer this angle to the edges of two of the roof panels and mark the width of the angle along the edge to be planed. Place the panel in a vice and plane the angle. Repeat this process for the other panel.

9 Using the front/back pieces as a guide, set the sliding bevel to the intersecting angle. Transfer this angle to the edge of the two remaining roof panels. Use a marking gauge to mark the line along the length of the panels, and then plane the angle on the pieces.

10 Plane the base back to its correct size of 220 x 240 mm, keeping the edges square.

ASSEMBLY

11 Mix up some adhesive following the manufacturer's instructions. Separate the nailed front and back pieces, and on the front piece where the sides are to be attached start two 40 mm nails 9 mm in

MATERIALS*

PART	MATERIAL	FINISHED LENGTH	WIDTH	NO.
Front/back	18 mm exterior plywood	240 mm	220 mm	2
Side	18 mm exterior plywood	164 mm	160 mm	2
Roof panel	18 mm exterior plywood	240 mm	115 mm	4
Base	18 mm exterior plywood	240 mm	220 mm	1

Other: Twenty 40 mm nails; four 35 mm x No. 8 brass countersunk screws; one 50 x 8 mm timber dowel for the perch; small amount of epoxy resin adhesive; wood filler; one sheet of 180 grit abrasive paper; 500 ml exterior acrylic paint of your choice.

* Finished size: 240 mm long (base); 350 mm wide (roof); 280 mm high (from bottom of base to top of roof).

outdoor

4 Use a combination square, and the 30 and 45-degree angle on the set squares, to set out a 15-degree angle.

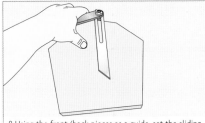

8 Using the front/back pieces as a guide, set the sliding bevel to the mitre angle at the apex of the pieces.

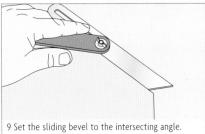

9 Set the sliding bevel to the intersecting angle. Transfer this angle to the edge of the roof panels.

from the edge. Take one side piece, glue the joining edge and then bring the front and side pieces together. Check to make sure that the bevelled edge of the side piece is flush with the bottom edge and side of the front piece. Finish by nailing the front piece to the side. Repeat this process for the remaining side and back pieces, to make a box shape. Ensure that the box is square.

12 Glue the lower angled edges at the top of the front and back pieces. Take the corresponding roof panels and start one 40 mm nail 29 mm in from each end of the panel. Align the roof panel on the box so it

These bevelled roof panels were carefully marked out using set squares and a sliding bevel. This birdhouse is made from waterproof exterior plywood, and has been painted in contrasting colours that highlight its distinctive shape.

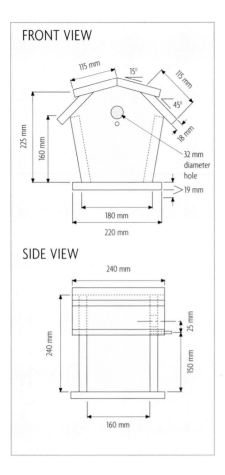

FRONT VIEW

115 mm · 15° · 115 mm

45°

18 mm

225 mm

160 mm

o

32 mm diameter hole

19 mm

180 mm

220 mm

SIDE VIEW

240 mm

240 mm

25 mm

150 mm

160 mm

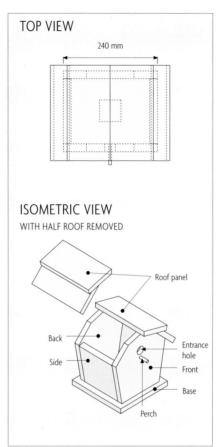

TOP VIEW

240 mm

ISOMETRIC VIEW
WITH HALF ROOF REMOVED

Roof panel

Back

Side

Entrance hole

Front

Base

Perch

TOOLS

- Measuring tape or fold-out rule
- Combination square
- Pencil
- Portable circular saw or jigsaw
- Compass or protractor (optional)
- Set squares: 60/30 degrees, 45 degrees
- G-cramp or quick-release cramp
- Vice
- Hammer
- Smoothing plane
- Sliding bevel
- Marking gauge
- Electric drill
- Drill bits: 3 mm, 5 mm, 8 mm; 32 mm spade bit or hole saw
- Screwdriver (cross-head or recessed)
- Cork sanding block or electric sander
- Nail punch

overhangs by 20 mm at each end. The bevelled edge must be flush with the top angle on the front and back pieces (see diagram above). Hammer in the nails. Repeat for the opposite roof panel. If the roof panels are not perfectly flush, wait until the adhesive sets and smooth them off with a smoothing plane.

13 Before fixing the remaining roof panels, check the fit. Ensure the mitre joint fits neatly. Glue the remaining joint edges and nail on the last two roof panels, keeping the ends flush and the mitres tight.

14 Lay the box face upwards. Measure 175 mm up the centre and mark the entrance hole position. Next, measure up 150 mm and

mark the perch position. Use a 32 mm hole saw or a spade bit to make the entrance hole. For the perch, use an 8 mm drill bit to drill a hole 10 mm deep. Apply adhesive to the hole and insert the dowel.

15 Align the box on the base. Trace around the box to mark the outer edges on the base, then remove the box. Measure in 29 mm from the front and back edge of the base to centre the screw positions, then measure in 55 mm from each side edge. Where these points intersect, drill a 5 mm hole. On the underside of the base, countersink the holes. Rest the box on its roof and align the base on the box. Drill 3 mm pilot holes, then fasten the base to the box using four 35 mm screws. Drill four drainage holes in the base.

16 Punch all nails below the surface and apply filler to all holes and gaps, then sand the entire birdhouse with abrasive paper. Apply a coat of paint, then leave to dry before sanding and applying a second coat. A third coat of paint is advisable.

outdoor

HOLLOW LOG BIRDHOUSE

This rustic thatched birdhouse will blend into the general garden scenery. Obtain a log from a saw mill—removing logs from woodland deprives many native animals of their natural habitat.

Keep in mind that the twigs or straw you have used on the roof will eventually be broken down by the elements or, most likely, be taken by birds to build their nests. You may need to mend the thatching a couple of times each year.

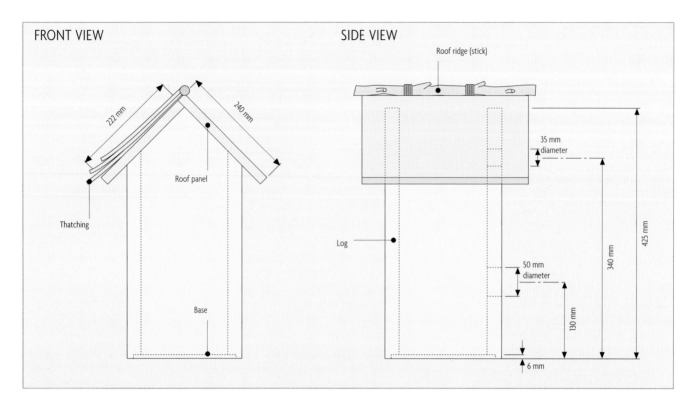

FRONT VIEW

222 mm

240 mm

Roof panel

Thatching

Base

SIDE VIEW

Roof ridge (stick)

35 mm diameter

Log

50 mm diameter

425 mm

340 mm

130 mm

6 mm

CUTTING OUT

1 Take the drawing of the birdhouse to a saw mill. Ask the proprietor to use a bandsaw to square up one end of the log and to cut the gable ends on the other end.

2 Wearing protective gardening gloves, use a banister brush to clean the inside of the log.

3 Turn the log bottom upwards, and support it so it is stable. Set the router to cut a

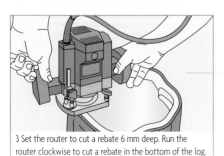

3 Set the router to cut a rebate 6 mm deep. Run the router clockwise to cut a rebate in the bottom of the log.

rebate 6 mm deep. Working from the inside of the hollow, run the router in a clockwise direction to remove the waste and create a rebate in the bottom of the log about 12–15 mm wide.

4 Lay the cardboard over the rebated hole. With a pencil, rub over the edge area to create a template of the hole outline. Cut out the template.

5 Lay the template on the plywood for the base and trace around it. Use a jigsaw to cut the base to fit into the rebate. Fasten the base with three ⅝ inch x No. 6 brass screws, then drill four 5 mm drainage holes.

6 Lay the log on the bench and mark positions for a small entrance hole 85 mm from the top and a large hole 130 mm from the bottom. Cut out with 35 mm and 50 mm hole saws.

7 Mark out the plywood for the two roof panels to the sizes given. Use the jigsaw to cut the panels slightly oversize, then plane the edges back to the lines with a smoothing plane, ensuring they are straight. Mix some adhesive and apply it to one long edge of the 222 mm wide panel. Use two 40 mm nails to fasten the other roof panel to the first roof panel, making an angle of 90 degrees.

THATCHING THE ROOF

8 Choose several long, straight twigs. Hold them so the ends are roughly flush, then trim the ends with scissors or secateurs. Apply a 20 mm wide layer of hot adhesive at the top and about 200 mm down, and position the twigs on the roof, near one end. Using scrap timber, press the twigs on to the roof until the adhesive begins to set.

9 Repeat until you reach the opposite end, then repeat for the other side. Fill any gaps,

outdoor

MATERIALS*

PART	MATERIAL	FINISHED LENGTH	WIDTH	NO.
Log	Hollow tree offcut	425 mm	200 mm diam.	1
Roof panel	18 mm exterior plywood	280 mm	240 mm	1
Roof panel	18 mm exterior plywood	280 mm	222 mm	1
Base	6 mm exterior plywood	200 mm	200 mm	1
Roof ridge	Stick	280 mm	20 mm diam.	1

Other: Three $^5/_8$ inch x No. 6 brass screws; six 40 mm nails; two 35 mm x No. 8 brass screws; a piece of thin cardboard; crayon or pencil; epoxy resin adhesive; eight hot-glue sticks; dried reeds or willow twigs (obtainable from craft or homewares stores) or straw; 900 mm copper wire.

* Finished size: This will depend on the size of the log obtained. The example shown here is 240 mm in diameter and 450 mm high (from the bottom of the log to the top of the twig roof ridge).

TOOLS

- Measuring tape or fold-out rule
- Banister brush
- Gardening gloves
- Electric router
- Router bit: 12 mm
- Jigsaw (or portable circular saw or handsaw)
- Scissors or secateurs
- Electric drill
- Drill bits: 2 mm, 3 mm, 4 mm, 5 mm; 50 mm and 35 mm hole saws
- Hammer
- Nail punch
- Screwdriver (cross-head or slotted)
- Smoothing plane
- Hot-glue gun
- Blunt-nosed pliers

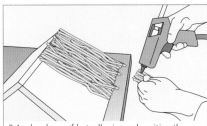

8 Apply a layer of hot adhesive and position the twigs on the roof, near one end.

USING A ROUTER

- Use cramps to secure the work.
- Always do a test cut on a scrap piece to check the settings.
- Wear safety glasses, hearing protection and a dust mask.
- Don't cut to the required size the first time. Always make two or three passes with the router.
- If the router sticks, wipe the fence with soap or candle wax.

and trim the ends of the twigs so they overhang the roof by 40 mm. Attach twigs to the front and rear edges of the roof.

TIMBER

Western red cedar and exterior plywood were used extensively in this chapter. Exterior plywood is a waterproof product made up of laminations of timber veneers—18 mm thickness has adequate insulating properties. For a good surface finish requiring little filling, use a B-grade veneer face. Western red cedar is the recommended timber for projects with a clear exterior finish—it outperforms other timbers used outdoors because of the resin, oils and tannins it contains. Never use treated pine for birdhouses or feeders, as it contains arsenic—many birds gnaw on timber, and the toxins in treated pine may eventually kill them. Particleboard and medium density fibreboard will not withstand outdoor conditions.

FIXING THE ROOF RIDGE

10 Take the roof ridge stick and drill two 2 mm holes, 20 mm apart and about 50 mm in from each end, right through. Place the end of the wire in one hole and bind it around the stick until you reach the other hole. Push the end of the wire through the second hole. Pull it tight with pliers. Repeat

for the other end of the stick. Glue the wire to hold in place.

11 Drill two 3 mm holes in the roof, one on either side near the centre of the ridge. Bind the wire around the middle of the roof ridge stick, then push the ends through the holes on each side of the roof ridge. Turn the roof over and use pliers to pull the stick tightly to the roof. Twist the wire tight, cut off any excess wire and push the ends out of harm's way.

ATTACHING THE ROOF

12 Find a place on the roof to fasten the two 35 mm x No. 8 screws that secure the roof to the log. Drill a 5 mm clearance hole through the roof and a 3 mm pilot hole into the log. Glue the gabled end of the log, put the roof on and insert the screws.

window boxes
and planters

window boxes and planters

PLANNING YOUR PROJECT

Window boxes and planters are simple woodworking projects that are ideal for beginners or quick weekend projects. Making your own planter is very satisfying, and you'll be able to tailor-make it to suit a particular space or purpose.

MATERIALS

Window boxes and planters will always be subject to water damage, especially those used outside. Even those kept on a covered deck or patio may be exposed to extremes of weather. The materials used in their construction—timber, adhesive and paint—should be chosen accordingly.

If water can sit on a surface, paint and timber will break down and rot very quickly. As much as possible, timbers should be sloped to shed water. Also remember to fill all gaps and cracks before painting to stop water penetrating into the timber.

TIMBER

Planters and window boxes should be constructed of a timber that is resilient in external conditions, for example cedar, or a hardwood such as European oak. Plywoods should be of exterior quality.

ADHESIVE

An epoxy adhesive is much better than PVA for external conditions.

PAINT

Using an exterior paint will help prolong the life of a planter, whether it is placed inside

Environmental conditions are an important factor in timber selection.

or outside. Most exterior paints contain UV protection as the sun contributes to paint breakdown quite considerably.

BASES

Most window boxes and planters are designed to contain plants in plastic pots or boxes, which are very easy to replace when a new flower display is desired. Keeping the plants in plastic pots also helps to prolong the life of the wood, as there is no contact with soil and moisture. If you do want to fill the box with soil, you will need to waterproof the timber with a bitumous product.

TIMBER IS SOLD IN THREE CONDITIONS:

- sawn or rough-sawn: sawn to a specific (nominal) size
- planed, either planed all round (PAR), planed on two sides (P2S) or double planed (DP)
- moulded: planed to a specific profile for architraves, window sills, skirting boards and so on.

Planed timber is mostly sold using the same nominal dimensions as sawn timber, for example 100 x 50 mm, but the surfaces have all been machined to a flat, even width and thickness so the '100 x 50 mm' timber is actually 91 x 41 mm. The chart shows the actual sizes for seasoned timber; unseasoned timber such as pine will vary in size.

Moulded timbers are also ordered by nominal sizes, but check them carefully as there will be variations.

SAWN (NOMINAL) SIZE (mm)	SIZE AFTER PLANING (mm)
19	15
25	19
38	30
50	41
75	66
100	91
125	115
150	138

FIXING WINDOW BOXES

Always use external fasteners—stainless or zincalumed screws—when securing a window box in place. The method of fixing will vary according to the material to which it is being attached. If attaching a window box to bricks or concrete, you will need wall plugs for the screws.

- Window boxes that fit into the window reveal can be fixed through each end, or you could screw metal angle brackets to the window frame—these will be hidden by the box. Allow for a slight fall to the front edge to keep the water away from the window and house.

- Window boxes that fit against the house in front of a window can be fastened directly to the wall, through the back of the box, at each end. Metal angle brackets can be used behind or below the window box.

- Some window boxes have a base with drainage holes drilled in each front corner.

When fixing the box in place, make sure it has a slight fall to the outside front edge, to keep the water draining away from the window and the house.

- If the window isn't protected by an eave or overhang, and the window box is sitting on the sill of the window, it may be worthwhile packing the box up slightly (about 12 mm) to allow air flow, so water doesn't collect and cause a problem between the two timbers.

SLATTED WINDOW BOX

This sturdy window box consists of horizontal slats fixed to corner posts. It is an ideal project for a beginner, or for a quick weekend project.

This window box was constructed from cedar and given several coats of exterior acrylic paint. The length can be easily adjusted to fit your window sill.

METHOD

1 Measure your window and decide on the appropriate length for your window box. Adjust the length of the long rails accordingly. Using a tenon saw, cut the posts, long rails, end rails and bottom slats of the window box. When cutting the rails, cut the first piece and use it as a template to mark out and cut the other pieces—this helps ensure a more accurate cut.

2 Lay the eight long rails together on the bench, face up and side by side. Do the same with the eight end rails. At each end of each rail, half hammer in two nails, one roughly 10 mm in from the end, the other 25 mm in, positioned diagonally. Placing the nails diagonally will help prevent the timber splitting when the nails are hammered in.

3 Lay two of the posts on the bench. Lay one end rail across the top of the posts, making sure it is flush at the top and sides. Mark the position of the rail with the aid of a square, then remove the rail, apply adhesive, reposition the rail on the posts and hammer in

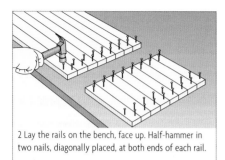

2 Lay the rails on the bench, face up. Half-hammer in two nails, diagonally placed, at both ends of each rail.

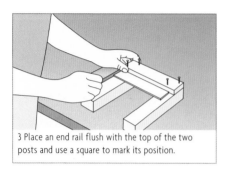

3 Place an end rail flush with the top of the two posts and use a square to mark its position.

the two nails at each end. Glue and nail the bottom rail in place in the same fashion. Leaving a 6 mm space between each rail, glue and nail on the two middle rails. This piece will be one end of the window box. Repeat with the remaining posts and end rails to make the other end. Use a nail punch and hammer to hit the nails just below the surface.

4 Glue and nail the long rails into position, using the same method as for the end rails, keeping the ends flush, and spacing them the same distance apart as the end rails.

5 Check that the two bottom slats fit between the bottom end rails. If the slats are too long, trim them to size using a mitre or tenon saw. Apply adhesive to the ends of the slats and nail them into place, flush with the bottom of the window box and about 50 mm apart.

6 Fill any holes with filler, then sand all over using a sanding block and 120 grit abrasive paper. Apply the finish of your choice.

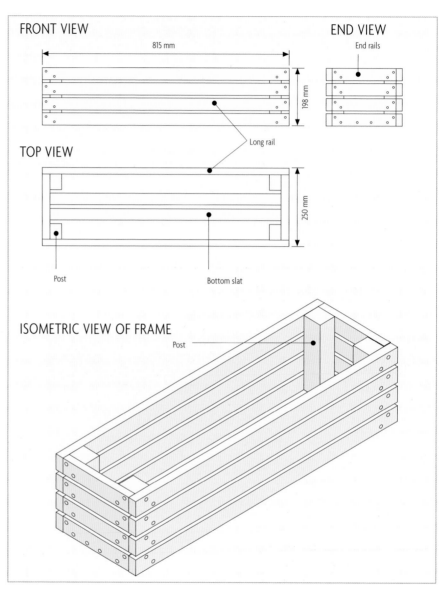

FRONT VIEW

815 mm

198 mm

Long rail

END VIEW

End rails

TOP VIEW

250 mm

Post

Bottom slat

ISOMETRIC VIEW OF FRAME

Post

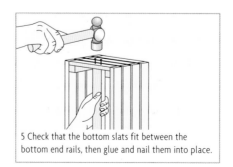

5 Check that the bottom slats fit between the bottom end rails, then glue and nail them into place.

HINTS

- When working with timber, identify the 'best face' and mark it for use as the outside face of the project.
- If you intend to varnish rather than paint a finished window box or planter, be sure to thoroughly clean off any excess adhesive as you work, as the adhesive will discolour the wood and show through the varnish.

outdoor

MATERIALS*

PART	MATERIAL	LENGTH	NO.
Post	50 x 38 mm timber PAR	183 mm	4
Long rail	50 x 25 mm timber PAR	815 mm	8
End rail	50 x 25 mm timber PAR	210 mm	8
Bottom slat	50 x 25 mm timber PAR	777 mm	2

Other: PVA or epoxy adhesive; 40 mm nails; abrasive paper: two sheets of 120 grit; water-based wood filler; finish of choice.

* Finished width 250 mm, length 815 mm. Timber sizes given are nominal. For timber types and sizes, see page 520.

TOOLS

- Tape measure
- Pencil
- Tenon saw
- Square
- Rule
- Hammer
- Fine nail punch
- Cork sanding block

PICKET WINDOW BOX

Cutting out and nailing on the pickets is the most labour-intensive part of constructing this window box, but the striking effect is worth the effort. They are fixed to a plywood box.

METHOD

1 Mark out a blank (250 x 90 mm) front picket and cut it out using a jigsaw. Use it as a template to mark out and cut fifteen more front and back pickets. Using a circular saw fitted with a ripping guide, or a panel saw, cut the plywood front and use it as a template to cut the back. Cut the bottom, two ends and the divide (if applicable).

2 To make the box, clamp the bottom to the bench, apply adhesive and nail the ends onto the bottom using three 40 mm nails on each edge. Turn it onto its back, then glue and nail

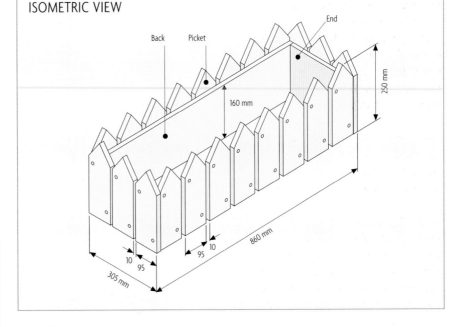

ISOMETRIC VIEW

2 Clamp the bottom of the box to the bench, then glue and nail on the ends using three nails along each edge.

on the front piece, spacing the nails 150 mm apart. Turn again and glue and nail on the back. If you need to use a divide, mark the centre line across the middle of the planter,

then glue and nail the divide in place.

3 To cut the pointed top on the front and back pickets, mark the centre of the top

3 Cut the pointed top of the first picket and finish the cut edges with a smoothing plane.

edge of one picket, then measure 60 mm down each side. Join these points and cut off the corners using a jigsaw. Plane the cut edges smooth using a smoothing or block plane, and use the picket as a template to mark out and cut the other front and back pickets. Plane all the cut edges smooth. Take off the sharp edges on all the face edges and the inside edge of the picket top using a plane or sanding block.

4 To position the front and back pickets, cut a 14 mm scrap of timber as a spacer. Glue and nail the first picket on the back of the box, flush with the end and bottom. Slide the spacer next to the picket, and glue another picket into place, hard up against the spacer; nail the picket home

TOOLS

- Steel or fold-out rule
- Pencil
- Jigsaw
- Adjustable cramps
- Block or smoothing plane
- Circular saw with adjustable ripping guide, or panel saw
- Hammer
- Nail punch
- Cork sanding block

This row of pickets with a distressed finish adds a delightful touch to a long window sill. The box has been reinforced with a divider because of its length.

HINT

CUTTING A LARGE PIECE OF PLY CAN BE A PROBLEM.

- First cut a 75 mm strip from the long edge of the ply to act as a straight edge. Clamp it to both ends of the ply to guide the saw.
- The straight edge may also need fastening in the middle to prevent movement while sawing.
- To support the tail end of the ply during cutting, slide a piece of timber through the cramps and lift the tail end of the ply on top of the timber while finishing the cut.

outdoor

Using one picket as a template to cut the others ensures they are all a uniform shape.

MATERIALS*

PART	MATERIAL	LENGTH	WIDTH	NO.
Picket	100 x 19 mm timber PAR	250 mm		22
Front/back	15 mm exterior ply	818 mm	170 mm	2
Bottom	15 mm exterior ply	788 mm	200 mm	1
End	15 mm exterior ply	200 mm	170 mm	2
Divide**	15 mm exterior ply	200 mm	155 mm	1

Other: PVA or epoxy adhesive; 20 mm nails; 40 mm nails; abrasive paper: three sheets of 120 grit; water-based wood filler; finish of choice.

* Finished width 259 mm, length 848 mm. Adjust the length to fit your window—that shown opposite is 1796 mm long. Timber sizes given are nominal. For timber types and sizes, see page 520.

** Include a divide if your window box is over 1000 mm long.

and continue along the back. Adjust the spacing so that the last picket sits flush with the end. Use the same method to glue and nail the pickets along the front. Punch all the nails just below the surface of the timber prior to filling.

5 Mark and cut out a 250 x 77 mm end picket and use it as a template to cut out another five. Cut the picket shape as before. Attach the end pickets to the box as before, positioning the outside edges flush with the front and back pickets and the bottom.

6 Fill any holes with filler, then sand the box all over using a sanding block and 120 grit abrasive paper. Apply the finish of your choice.

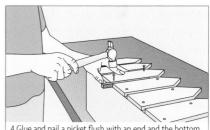

4 Glue and nail a picket flush with an end and the bottom, then use a spacer to position the other pickets.

WINDOW BOX WITH MOULDING

A scotia moulding adds interest to this simple window box, which is made from exterior plywood. The window box could also be made without the moulding.

METHOD

1 Mark out and cut the front, back and bottom using a panel saw or circular saw. To cut the ends, mark a 210 x 170 mm rectangle. Measure in 20 mm from the bottom left-hand corner of a 210 mm edge and draw a line to the top left-hand corner. Measure 10 mm in from the bottom right-hand corner and draw a line to the top right-hand corner. Cut away the waste and plane the edges straight with a plane. Use as a template to mark and cut the other end.

2 To make the box, place the ends upright on the bench and position the back piece onto the ends. Glue and nail the back onto the ends using three 30 mm nails on each side. Turn the structure on its back and glue and nail the front onto the ends in the same manner. Check that the bottom will fit—if it

3 Using wooden blocks to protect the timber, clamp the box to the bench and plane the joining edges flush.

A stencilled design adds an attractive finish to this simple window box, which can be used outside or inside the house. Here it decorates an open verandah.

TOOLS

- Pencil
- Tape measure
- Fold-out rule or 300 mm steel rule
- Square
- Jigsaw
- Panel saw, or circular saw fitted with a ripping guide
- Smoothing or block plane
- Hammer
- Nail punch
- Two adjustable cramps
- Cork sanding block
- Tenon saw and mitre box or mitre saw
- Pincers

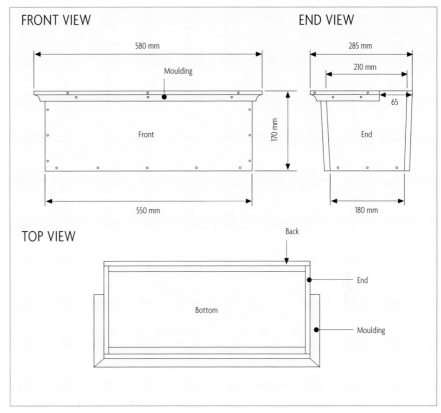

FRONT VIEW

580 mm

Moulding

Front

170 mm

550 mm

END VIEW

285 mm

210 mm

65

End

180 mm

TOP VIEW

Back

End

Bottom

Moulding

doesn't, plane it to fit, then glue and nail the bottom in place from the outside, flush with the sides and ends. Clean up excess adhesive and allow to dry.

3 Clamp the box to the bench, protecting it with wooden blocks, and plane the edges flush. Sand all over with 100 grit abrasive paper, paying particular attention to the top edge to get it straight and even.

4 To mark the mitres on the moulding, place it along the top front edge of the box, with one end of the moulding protruding 25 mm past the end. Mark the moulding at each end of the box and draw a rough line in the

STENCILLING

Photocopy the stencil on page 528; enlarge to suit your window box. Cover it with a sheet of acetate and cut around the design with a craft knife. Position the stencil with low-tack tape. Apply the paint and leave to dry.

direction of the mitres. Cut the two mitres using a mitre saw or mitre box. Mark the moulding for the ends in the same way. They were finished 65 mm in from the back edge to suit the depth of this particular window. Adjust the length to fit your window.

5 Using pincers, cut seven nails to a length of 10–15 mm. To attach the moulding to the front, fix a block of wood to a vice, then rest the front of the box on the wood to support the timber. Tack the front moulding in place using three 30 mm nails along the top, and three shorter nails near the bottom. Fit the side mouldings in place in the same way and tack them with two 30 mm nails along the top and two shorter nails along the bottom. Glue and nail the front moulding into place, then the end ones. Cover the corners with plastic, and use

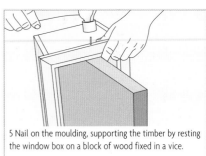

5 Nail on the moulding, supporting the timber by resting the window box on a block of wood fixed in a vice.

a cramp to pull the mitres flush while the adhesive dries.

6 Clean up any excess adhesive and allow to dry, then sand the box using a sanding block and 120 grit abrasive paper. Apply the finish of your choice.

The scotia moulding on the box has mitred corners.

MATERIALS*

PART	MATERIAL	LENGTH	WIDTH	NO.
Front/back	12 mm exterior ply	550 mm	172 mm	2
Bottom	12 mm exterior ply	526 mm	180 mm	1
End	12 mm exterior ply	210 mm	170 mm	2
Moulding	25 mm scotia	1200 mm		1

Other: PVA or epoxy adhesive; 25 mm nails; 30 mm nails; abrasive paper: one sheet each of 100 grit and 120 grit; heavy-duty plastic; water-based wood filler; finish of choice.

* Finished width 255 mm, length 580 mm. Timber sizes given are nominal. For timber types and sizes, see page 520.

STENCIL FOR WINDOW BOX
WITH MOULDING

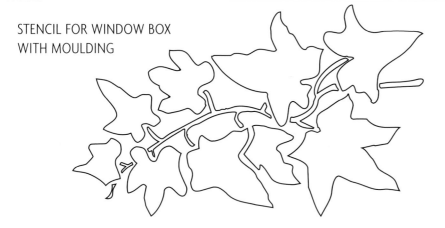

HINT

If the ply is pitted, fill the entire surface with water-based wood filler before sanding—mix the filler with a little water first to make it easier to use.

CLASSIC PLANTER

This handsome planter is characterized by panels with a raised centre, but less expert woodworkers may prefer to use plain flat panels.

THE FRAMES

1 Measure out a rail and cut it out using a tenon saw. Use this piece as a template to cut out the other seven rails. Repeat this process to cut the posts and uprights, then cut one panel (297 x 257 mm) and use it as a template to cut another three.

2 Place the rails and uprights roughly in position as four frames on the bench. Take the uprights from one frame and place them together in a vice, end grain up. Drill two 6 mm holes, 17 mm deep, into the end of each upright roughly on the centre line, then drill the other end. Repeat with the remaining uprights and reposition them on the bench. Place centre points into the holes, and use a square to guide the rail and upright into position. Fit all the rails and uprights in this way, making marks to help during assembly. If the holes are too tight for the dowels, re-drill them using a 6.5–7 mm bit.

3 Glue each frame together, working the adhesive into the holes and onto the dowels and joining surfaces. Using two sash or G-cramps, and some plastic between the cramps, timber and bench, pull each frame together, using a square to check that the structure is square, and ensuring it doesn't bow up under the pressure of the cramps. If necessary, clamp the frames to the bench to keep them flat. Clean up any excess adhesive. Leave to dry.

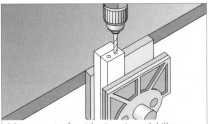

2 Secure a pair of uprights in a vice and drill two holes into the end of each, roughly in the centre.

4 Using a sharp chisel, carefully clean away any dried adhesive from the internal corners of each frame.

4 Remove the cramps and use a very sharp block plane to remove excess dried adhesive, and to make the joins flush. Using a fine belt in the belt sander or 100 grit abrasive paper, sand the edges and the front and back faces. Use a very sharp chisel to clean any dried adhesive from the internal corners of the frames.

POSITIONING DOWELS

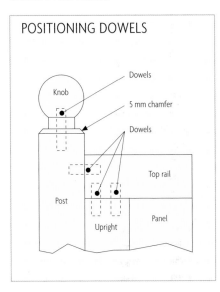

This planter was crafted from oak and was varnished to display the beautiful grain in the timber.

5 Cut a rebate into the inside edge of the frame for the panel. Use a router fitted with a 10 mm rebating bit with a bearing wheel, set to a depth of 10 mm. Check the setting on some scrap and measure the cut for accuracy. Clamp the frame face side down to the bench. Cut the rebate, working carefully and making three or four runs, rather than one heavy one. Chisel out the corners, working across the grain to remove the bulk of the timber and make the corners square.

THE PANELS

6 Fit the four panels into the frames, choosing the best side for the face. If necessary, plane the panels back to fit, then mark each frame and its corresponding panel.

7 To cut away the panel border and leave the raised centre, you will need to use a table

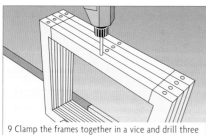

9 Clamp the frames together in a vice and drill three holes along the two side edges of each frame.

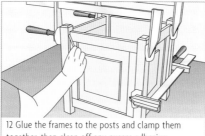

12 Glue the frames to the posts and clamp them together, then clean off any excess adhesive.

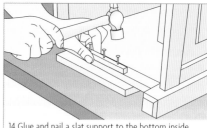

14 Glue and nail a slat support to the bottom inside edge of each side of the planter, roughly in the centre.

saw for the best results. Omit this step if you prefer plain, flat panels. Carefully cut 60 mm wide borders 10 mm deep around each panel.

8 Fit the router with the cove bit set at a depth of 8 mm, with a guide set at 60 mm from the centre of the bit. Clamp each panel to the bench and router the cove all round each raised centre. Sand smooth, using 100 or 120 grit abrasive paper.

ASSEMBLY
9 Clamp the four frames together, uprights facing up. Drill three 6 mm holes, 17 mm deep, into the two side edges of each frame, one in the end grain of the top and bottom rails, and one in the centre of the upright. Put centre points into the holes.

10 On two adjacent sides of each post, draw a line 25 mm from the top to indicate the top of the frame. Place the posts on the bench; lay the panels next to them, placing 10 mm packing pieces underneath the panels so they sit against the middle of the post. Mark the holes from the frames onto the posts. Drill holes, as before, checking each side for fit.

11 To chamfer the top of the posts, draw a line on the top face, 5 mm in from the edges, all the way round. Draw another line on the side of the posts, 5 mm from the top, all the way round. Place one post in a vice and using a sharp block plane, chamfer the top of the post, using the lines as a guide. Repeat with the other posts. Find the centre of the top of each post and drill a 6 mm hole, 17 mm deep,

for the dowel. Drill a hole the same size and depth into the shaft of each knob.

12 Apply adhesive to the rebate and fit the panels into the frames, clamping them in position with the G-cramps. Clean off any excess adhesive and leave to dry, then sand

TOOLS
- Fold-out rule or steel rule
- Tape measure
- Pencil
- Table saw or jigsaw
- Vice
- Electric drill
- Drill bits: 6 mm, 6.5 mm, 7 mm high-speed steel (HSS)
- Square
- Tenon saw
- Four adjustable cramps (500 mm)
- Four G-cramps (500 mm)
- Block plane
- Belt and orbital sanders (optional)
- Medium and fine sanding belts
- Chisel
- Electric router or laminate trimmer
- Router bits: 12 mm cove bit; rebating bit with a 10 x 10 mm bearing wheel
- Cork sanding block

MATERIALS*

PART	MATERIAL	LENGTH	NO.
Rail	50 x 25 mm timber PAR	320 mm	8
Upright	50 x 25 mm timber PAR	280 mm	8
Cross-slat	50 x 25 mm timber PAR	335 mm	2
Post	50 x 50 mm timber PAR	425 mm	4
Panel	300 x 25 mm timber PAR	297 mm	4

Other: PVA or epoxy adhesive; 6 mm centrepoint kit; 30 mm nails; sixty 32 x 6 mm dowels; abrasive paper: four sheets of 100 grit and two of 120 grit; masking tape; heavy-duty plastic; thinners; four 40 mm wooden knobs; finish of choice.

* Finished size 400 mm square, height 470 mm. Timber sizes given are nominal. For timber types and sizes, see page 520.

HINT

If you are making an outdoor window box or planter, it is preferable to use epoxy or waterproof adhesive during construction, especially if there is any likelihood of contact with water. Epoxy adhesive also provides greater strength than PVA adhesive and may be preferred for heavier projects.

with a sanding block and 120 grit abrasive paper if necessary. Insert dowels, glue the frames to the posts and clamp together with two cramps on each side while the adhesive dries, ensuring all is square. Insert dowels and glue the knobs in place, holding them secure with masking tape. Clean off any excess dried adhesive.

13 Cut the cross-slats for the bottom, then mark and cut a cross-halving joint (see box on page 536) to join the slats together where they cross, so both pieces are level.

14 Take a 200 mm long offcut from the 50 x 25 mm timber and cut it in half lengthways. Cut each strip into two shorter strips, so you have four pieces about 100 mm long. These will be the slat supports. Lay the planter on its side and position a support along the inside bottom edge, centred between the sides, and flush with the bottom. Glue and nail the piece into place from the inside. Repeat with the remaining strips on the other sides. When the adhesive is dry, fit the slats to sit on the supports.

15 Sand with 120 grit abrasive paper. Apply the finish of your choice.

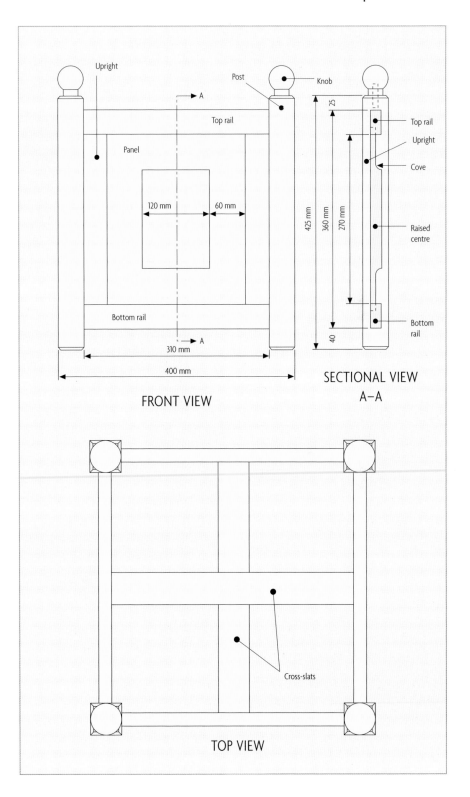

FRONT VIEW

SECTIONAL VIEW
A–A

TOP VIEW

LONG PLANTER

Sturdy yet stylish, this planter is relatively simple to construct. It consists of a frame of posts and rails with lining boards fixed to the inside. Beads along the top of the boards give a neat finish.

THE FRAME

1 Measure and cut the beads, posts, top rails and bottom rails using a mitre saw, or if you have one, a compound mitre saw. Mark out and cut twenty-six lining boards. From the decking, cut the slats.

2 Place the six posts on the bench together, using a square to ensure the ends are flush. Measure and draw a line 25 mm in from the right-hand end of the posts for the top of the rails. Draw a line 50 mm in from the other side for the base of the bottom rail. Pull the posts apart, and carry the line around one corner on four of the posts. Carry the line around two corners on the remaining two posts—these will be the middle posts.

3 On the two middle posts, mark out the housings for the rails—place a top rail on the 25 mm line and mark its bottom edge onto the post; place a bottom rail against the 50 mm line and mark its top edge onto the post. Measure down the edges 20 mm and mark the depth of the housings. Using a tenon saw, make a series of cuts 5–10 mm apart along the housing, then, working from each side, chisel out the housing.

4 In each end of the rails, drill two 6 mm holes, 17 mm deep, for the dowels, placing them close to the top and bottom on the long rails, and closer to the middle on the end rails. The dowel holes need to be at different heights so that when the planter is assembled, the dowels don't intersect.

5 Place two corner posts on the bench and position a top and bottom rail against the

Tongue and groove lining boards make this project quick to assemble, once the basic frame is in place. This planter was constructed from oak, with cedar beads.

marks on the posts. Put centre-point markers into the two holes in the top rail. Position the top of the rail at the 25 mm line, using a square to check that the timbers are square as they come together. Mark the post with

the bottom rail in the same way. Repeat with the other rails and corner posts, making distinctive marks at each join so that the timbers will be assembled in the correct position. Drill holes into the posts on the

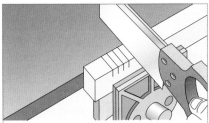

3 Cut the housing on the two middle posts by making a series of cuts 20 mm deep using a tenon saw.

MATERIALS*

PART	MATERIAL	LENGTH	NO.
Side bead	19 x 19 mm timber PAR	1110 mm	2
End bead	12 x 12 mm timber PAR	276 mm	2
Post	50 x 50 mm timber PAR	425 mm	6
Top side rail	50 x 25 mm timber PAR	1110 mm	2
Bottom side rail	75 x 25 mm timber PAR	1110 mm	2
Top end rail	50 x 25 mm timber PAR	300 mm	2
Bottom end rail	75 x 25 mm timber PAR	300 mm	2
Lining board	110 x 12 mm tongue and groove lining boards	280 mm	26
Slat	75 x 25 mm hardwood decking	1080 mm	4

Other: PVA or epoxy adhesive; 6 mm centre-point kit; 20 mm nails; 40 mm x No. 8 screws; abrasive paper: two sheets of 100 grit and two of 120 grit; finish of choice.

* Finished width 385 mm; length 1190 mm. Timber sizes given are nominal (except for lining boards). For timber types and sizes, see page 520.

centre-point marks. Position all the dowels and check the fit. If the dowels are tight or don't line up exactly, use a 6.5 or 7 mm drill bit to make the holes a little looser.

6 Apply adhesive to the holes, dowels and housing on the middle post. Assemble one side of the planter, using sash cramps to pull the posts and rails together, and checking it is square and parallel. Measure the centre line of the rails and position it against the middle post. Clamp it into place with G-cramps until dry. Assemble the other side of the planter in the same way. Clean away any excess adhesive before it dries.

7 Remove the cramps and sand off any dried adhesive. Insert the dowels, then glue and cramp the end rails to the corner posts, using two G-cramps at each end. Clean off any excess adhesive, then leave to dry and sand off as before.

8 Using a block plane, plane a slight bevel on the top edge of the beads to shed water.

Turn the planter on its side and nail a long bead 10 mm down from the top edge of one top side rail. Repeat with the other top side rail and top end rails.

ADDING THE BOARDS

9 Drill two holes 10 mm in from the top and bottom end of each lining board, using a 1.5 mm drill bit. Plane the tongue off four of the lining boards using a block plane. (The planed edges will butt against the end rails.)

10 Place the planter on its side. Apply enough adhesive to the rail (under the bead) to position a few lining boards at a time.

Butt a planed lining board against the bead and the end rails and nail it into place. Working towards the centre, glue and nail four more boards into place. Repeat the process from the opposite end, working back towards the centre. There will be a gap in the middle behind the posts. Repeat with the other side.

11 To make the ends, place three lining boards together on the bench and mark the centre point. Turn the planter over onto one end and measure the distance across the end between the lining boards. Halve this measurement and, working from the

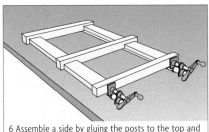

6 Assemble a side by gluing the posts to the top and bottom side rails and clamping them together.

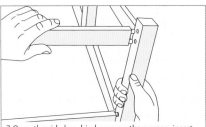

7 Once the side has dried, remove the cramps, insert the dowels and glue the end rails to the corner posts.

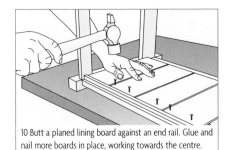

10 Butt a planed lining board against an end rail. Glue and nail more boards in place, working towards the centre.

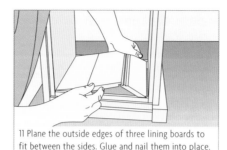

11 Plane the outside edges of three lining boards to fit between the sides. Glue and nail them into place.

The end lining boards are planed flat for a tight fit between the posts.

centre of the three lining boards, measure out either side and mark a line down the outer edges of the boards. Plane off the excess timber, then glue and nail the boards in place—it will be a tight fit. Repeat with the other end.

12 From the leftover 50 x 50 mm timber, cut two support blocks for the bottom slats, each 250 mm long. Turn the planter upside down and, using a 4.5 mm drill bit, drill two clearance holes through each bottom end rail, 75 mm in from each corner post, then countersink from the face side. Glue and screw the support blocks onto the rails, flush with the bottom. Rest the bottom slats on the support blocks.

13 Fill any holes with filler and sand all over with a cork sanding block and 120 grit abrasive paper. Apply the finish of your choice.

TOOLS

- 300 mm steel rule or fold-out rule
- Tape measure
- Pencil
- Square
- Panel saw
- Tenon saw
- Chisel
- Electric drill
- Drill bits: countersunk, 1.5 mm, 6 mm, 7 mm high-speed steel (HSS)
- Two 1.2 m sash cramps
- Four G-cramps
- Rubber mallet
- Belt sander (optional)
- Orbital sander (optional)
- Block plane
- Hammer
- Nail punch

OCTAGONAL PLANTER

Made from thirty-six identical pieces threaded together with sash cord, this delightful hanging planter is easy to make and is perfect for hanging from a tree or verandah. Cross-pieces hold the sides in shape and support the pot.

METHOD

1 Measure out and cut one side, measuring 210 mm long, then use this piece as a template to mark along the timber the remaining thirty-five sides. Using a mitre saw or a mitre box set at 45 degrees, carefully cut off the pieces—note that the marks indicate the long point of the cuts. Working one piece at a time, cut the mitre at the opposite end, discarding the offcuts. Long point to long point should measure 205 mm.

2 On one piece, measure 40 mm in from one end and draw a line parallel with the mitre. Repeat with the other end. Within the quadrilaterals, draw lines from corner to corner to make a cross. The position for the holes is at the centre. Drill right through with a 7 mm bit. Place this piece on top of each other piece, ensuring all the edges are flush, and drill through to make a mark, holding tightly so the timber doesn't move. When you have marked all the pieces, drill a hole through each mark—you may want to

protect the surface of your workbench. Countersink the holes from each side to remove any splinters and make it easier to thread the rope.

3 Smooth all the edges with a sharp block plane, being careful on the end grain of the long point, which will need support to stop it splitting away. On the end grain, use the plane in a slicing motion. If the timber on the end grain is too hard to plane, sand it instead. Apply the finish of your choice.

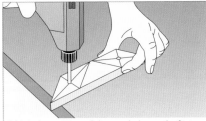

2 Mark the positions of the rope holes on the first piece of timber and drill the holes right through.

TOOLS

- Pencil
- 300 mm steel rule
- Mitre saw, or mitre box and tenon saw
- Combination square
- G-cramp
- Electric drill
- Drill bit: 7 mm high-speed steel (HSS)
- Block plane
- Utility or marking knife
- Tenon saw
- Chisel
- Hammer

4 Using a utility knife, cut the cord into four 2 m lengths. Apply a little instant adhesive to the ends to stop them fraying and to make them easier to thread through the holes. Thread a piece of cord up through one hole and down through the other on one side piece, making sure the cord is an equal length on both sides. Repeat with three more pieces. Place these four in position on the workbench, rope ends up, and thread on four more pieces for the next layer, offsetting each piece. Continue with the remaining pieces.

5 Tie a loose knot in the end of each rope. Turn the planter over and pull the rope through so the knots are on the bottom.

This useful and attractive planter was constructed from cedar and given a coat of oil to protect the timber.

4 Thread separate cords through four pieces as a base. Continue threading the layers, offsetting each piece.

6 Cut the bottom cross-pieces. Mark and cut a 15 x 9 mm rebate on the bottom ends of each piece, then mark and cut a cross-halving joint to join the pieces together where they cross, so they end up level. Pull the side pieces apart slightly and put in one cross-piece. Repeat with the other. The cross-pieces will lock together and won't move once the pot is in place.

7 Hang the planter and adjust the knots so the planter hangs level. Cut off any excess rope.

HINT

If the planter is to be hung outdoors, make the pieces from hardwood for extra durability.

TOP VIEW

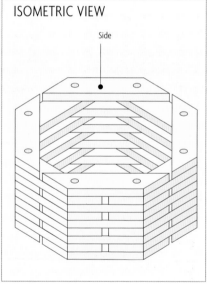

ISOMETRIC VIEW

CROSS-HALVING JOINT

1 Find the centre on the top face of one piece. Measure out either side half the width of the other timber. Square lines across the face.

2 Lay the two pieces together as they are to finish, and square lines across each the width of the other piece. Square the lines down both edges of both pieces for half the thickness of the timber. Mark the waste.

3 Using a tenon saw, make a series of cuts along the joint, cutting only to the marked line. Chisel out the waste and check that the pieces fit together neatly.

ISOMETRIC VIEW OF CROSS-HALVING JOINT

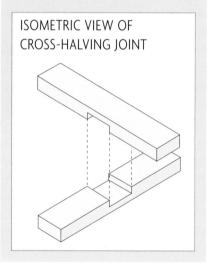

MATERIALS*

PART	MATERIAL	LENGTH	NO.
Side	50 x 25 mm timber PAR	210 mm	36
Cross-piece	50 x 25 mm timber PAR	250 mm	2

Other: Instant adhesive; wood oil; 8 m x 6 mm sash cord; finish of choice.

* Finished width 300 mm; length 300 mm. Timber sizes given are nominal. For timber types and sizes, see page 520.

MINIATURE PLANTERS

These miniature planters make a striking feature on stairs or along a verandah edge. They are simply constructed with plywood sides set into angle timber.

The plywood decorations on these pretty planters are often sold in art and craft shops, in a wide range of shapes. Alternatively, make your own from offcuts.

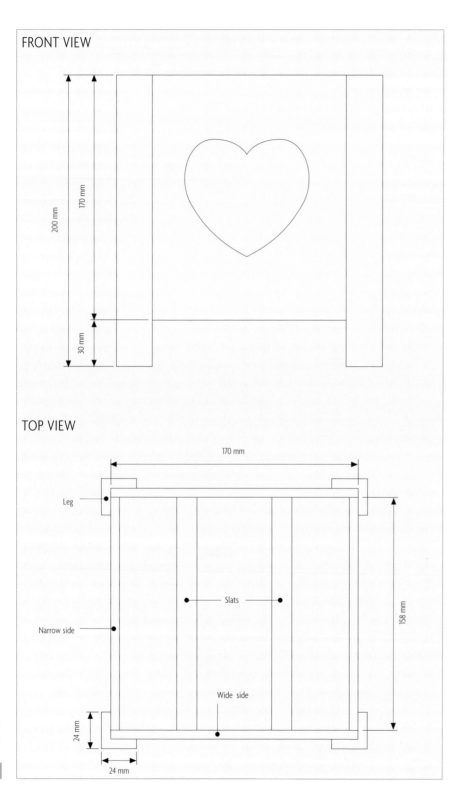

FRONT VIEW

200 mm

170 mm

30 mm

TOP VIEW

170 mm

Leg

Slats

158 mm

Narrow side

Wide side

24 mm

24 mm

TOOLS

- Pencil
- Fold-out or steel rule
- Tape measure
- Square
- Jigsaw
- Block plane
- Cork sanding block
- Tenon saw or mitre saw
- Two adjustable or G-cramps
- Chisel
- Hammer
- Eight small G-cramps or hand-held spring clamps

METHOD

1 To make the sides, take a sheet of ply. Using a jigsaw, cut two lengths, each 915 x 170 mm, so that they both have a factory edge (mark these for later identification); this will be the top edge of the planter. Plane one cut edge of the remaining ply and cut another piece 170 mm wide. The planed edge will be the top. Cut two lengths 170 mm wide from each side of the remaining sheet, again marking the factory edges. Discard the remaining ply.

2 Choose the best sides of the ply for the face and sand them smooth using a sanding block and 120 grit abrasive paper. Sand the external angle timber and cut the legs to length. From the ply strips, and using the jigsaw, cut the twelve wide sides and the twelve narrow sides, keeping them in separate piles with the factory edges together.

3 Position a wide side into two of the angles, with the factory or planed edge at

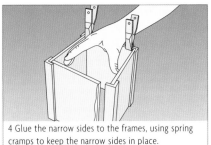

4 Glue the narrow sides to the frames, using spring cramps to keep the narrow sides in place.

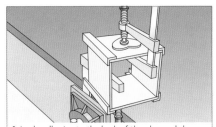

5 Apply adhesive to the back of the plywood shapes. Centre on the box and clamp in place.

HINT

If you are intending to paint the planters, it may be easier to paint the box and the plywood shapes separately before fixing the shapes onto the planter.

the top and flush with the top of the angle, leaving a 30 mm overhang below for the legs. Glue the side in place and clamp together with a small G-cramp or spring clamp in each corner, using heavy-duty plastic to prevent sticking, and keeping the top edges flush. Clean off excess adhesive and leave to dry. Remove the cramps. Repeat until all the wide sides are glued.

4 Take two glued frames and cut away any dried adhesive from the joining edges with a sharp chisel. Apply adhesive to the edges of two narrow sides and to the joining edges of the frame. Glue together, using small cramps or spring clamps to hold the narrow sides in position. Check for square, then clean away excess adhesive and leave to dry.

5 Position the plywood hearts and stars on two opposing sides of each planter, ensuring they are centred. Apply adhesive to the back of the shapes and clamp them in position.

6 Position the bottom slats flush with the bottom of the planter and fix them in place with adhesive and nails. Support the bottom edge of the ply with a small offcut when nailing.

7 Clean up the adhesive; leave to dry. Sand with 120 grit abrasive paper. Apply the finish of your choice.

MATERIALS* (MAKES 6)

PART	MATERIAL	LENGTH	WIDTH	NO.
Wide side	6 mm exterior ply	170 mm	170 mm	12
Narrow side	6 mm exterior ply	170 mm	158 mm	12
Leg	31 x 31 mm external angle timber	200 mm		24
Slat	19 x 19 mm timber	158 mm		12

Other: PVA or epoxy adhesive; abrasive paper: two sheets of 120 grit; six plywood hearts; six plywood stars; 25 mm x 1.25 mm panel pins; heavy-duty plastic; finish of choice.

* For six planters you will need two 915 x 610 mm sheets of plywood.
  Finished size 185 mm square; height 200 mm. Timber sizes given are nominal.
  For timber types and sizes, see page 520.

playhouses
and sandpits

playhouses and sandpits

BUILDING FOR CHILDREN

Few do-it-yourself enthusiasts can resist the joy of making play equipment for the children in their lives. It is, however, essential that attention is paid to the safety of the equipment.

A level, grassy area is the perfect location for play equipment, as it is clean and the grass will cushion falls.

Think carefully about whether you need to put glass in a playhouse window, as it can be dangerous if broken.

The handrail on this playhouse provides a neat, attractive finish but, more importantly, it is a safety feature that will help prevent your little ones falling off the edge of the verandah.

SAFETY

Safety is always the key consideration when building for children. They will climb into and over everything and never use things in the way they are intended to be used.

- Never leave edges sharp or rough as children might fall against them.
- Make sure there are no small, detachable pieces on which small children can choke.
- Always erect handrails on stairs or raised areas.

LOCATION

Before you begin to build your sandpit or playhouse, think about where it is to be placed.

- Always set up sandpits, playhouses or other play equipment where you have them in clear view at all times. Accidents can take only a few seconds to happen.
- Build outdoor houses and play equipment on a level, grassy area where falls will be minimized. If a suitable grassed area is not

outdoor

available, surround the feature with bark chips or other impact-absorbent material.

- Make sure playhouses are sited away from possible hazards such as prickly or irritating plants or furniture with sharp edges.

MATERIALS

Give some thought to the materials you will be using to build the playhouse or other play equipment. Remember that young children may chew or lick any surface.

- Avoid using glass in playhouse windows as it can easily be broken. Use plastic or simply cover the opening with insect screen.
- Treated timbers are toxic. They may be necessary for components that are in contact with the ground to prevent rot and attack by insects, but they should be avoided where children may come in contact with them. Also ensure that any paints or other finishes you use are non-toxic.

MAINTENANCE

Children's play equipment can be subjected to very rough treatment, and so regular checks are essential if it is to remain safe.

- Make sure houses are anchored securely when they are set up. A serious accident could result from one tipping over.
- Check every so often that all screws and other fixings are tight.
- Regularly check outdoor playhouses for insects, snakes or other animals, and remember to keep them clean.

BASIC SANDPIT

This sandpit is easy to build, and the dimensions can be modified to suit your needs. The bottom is covered with anti-weed mat to keep out insects and vegetation.

CUTTING OUT

1 Use a square and straight edge to mark out four 1200 mm long end boards. Cut the boards and place them side by side in pairs, ensuring the best match. If there are gaps in the joints, straighten the edges and plane the boards square. Mark out and cut the 2200 mm side boards and prepare them in the same manner.

2 Cut the timber for the end trims lengthwise to a width of 50 mm. Plane the edges smooth and square.

3 Cut a 45-degree diagonal splay at one end of each corner cleat. Plane a bevelled edge from the lower end of the splay to the base of the cleat and sand with abrasive paper. Using a 6 mm bit, drill and countersink four holes through each cleat. Repeat through the other sides, offsetting the holes.

ASSEMBLY

4 Join the side boards into pairs by placing adhesive on the top edge of one board. Butt the boards together and hold them in place using sash cramps. Glue the end trims to the end grain of the side boards; fix with

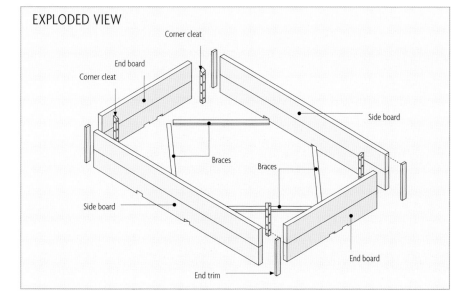

EXPLODED VIEW

Corner cleat

End board

Corner cleat

Side board

Braces

Braces

Side board

End board

End trim

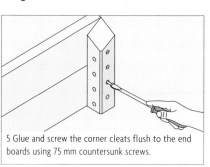

5 Glue and screw the corner cleats flush to the end boards using 75 mm countersunk screws.

TOOLS

- Square
- Straight edge
- Tape measure
- Pencil
- Handsaw
- Plane (hand or electric)
- Sash cramps
- Screwdriver
- Hammer
- Portable electric drill
- Drill bits: 2 mm, 3 mm, 6 mm, countersink
- Chisel
- Disc sander
- Dust mask
- Safety glasses
- Hearing protection

8 Position the braces in the housings and attach with a screw. Cut the overhanging ends so they finish flush.

This durable sandpit is made from treated pine and is finished with a timber undercoat and exterior paint to withstand the elements. Use a plastic cover when the sandpit isn't in use to keep the sand dry.

30 mm nails. Glue and clamp the end boards together.

5 Glue the corner cleats to the end boards and fix them with 75 mm countersunk screws. Ensure the cleats are flush with the ends of the boards.

6 Plane the ends of the side boards flush with the end trims. Spread adhesive on the ends and cleats of the end boards and butt them against the sides. Ensure the structure is square and screw the ends to the sides with 75 mm countersunk screws through the cleats.

7 Turn the frame over and place a brace at a 45-degree angle across each corner, with an overhang of about 50 mm at each end. Then mark the position of the braces on the edges of the frame and set the braces aside.

8 Using a handsaw and chisel, cut housings for the braces. Reposition the braces and screw them to the frame with 40 mm countersunk screws. Carefully cut the overhanging edges of the braces at an angle so they finish flush with the edges of the frame.

outdoor

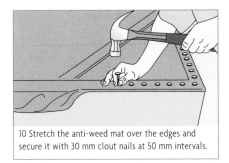

10 Stretch the anti-weed mat over the edges and secure it with 30 mm clout nails at 50 mm intervals.

MATERIALS*

PART	MATERIAL	LENGTH	NO.
End board	200 x 50 mm treated timber	1200 mm	4
Side board	200 x 50 mm treated timber	2200 mm	4
End trim	70 x 35 mm treated timber	400 mm	4
Corner cleat	35 x 35 mm treated timber	375 mm	4
Brace	70 x 35 mm treated timber	900 mm	4

Other: Abrasive paper; epoxy-resin adhesive; 30 x 2 mm helical thread nails; thirty-two 75 mm x No. 10 countersunk galvanized screws; fourteen 40 mm x No. 10 countersunk galvanized screws; 2.4 x 1.5 m anti-weed mat; 30 mm galvanized clout nails; medium sanding discs; 0.75 m³ sand; finish of choice.

* Finished size: 2238 x 1300 mm and 400 mm high. For information about timber sizes and conditions see page 520.

MAINTAINING A SANDPIT

To ensure your sandpit has a long life, invest in a canvas cover. Place a bucket in the centre of the sandpit and stretch the canvas over the frame to prevent rainwater settling on the cover. Secure the ends to the ground with hooks and eyes or a weight on each side. This will keep the sand clean and dry and protect the frame from the elements.

FINISHING

9 Plane small bevels on all edges of the sandpit and sand all surfaces using a medium sanding disc. Apply an exterior finish of your choice.

10 Turn the sandpit over and stretch anti-weed mat over the edges. Fold the fabric edges over three or four times and secure with 30 mm clout nails at 50 mm centres.

11 Remove any vegetation and the topsoil from the area where you will put the sandpit and level it. Position the sandpit and fill it with sand.

BASIC PLAYHOUSE

This traditional playhouse is straightforward to make. The walls are made from plywood and are self-bracing, while the roof is a simple king post truss construction covered with hardboard.

CUTTING OUT

1 Mark out the floor, sides, front and back on the plywood, using a tape measure, pencil and straight edge. Check that the pieces are square (measure the diagonals). Clamp a straight edge to the board and use a circular saw to cut out the parts. Mark and cut out the other pieces.

2 Plane the edges of each piece to the finished size, and ensure all are straight and square. Select the best face of each; mark it as the outside.

3 Using a tape measure and straight edge, mark out the windows on the side walls (see diagram on page 548). Drill a hole in one corner of each opening and cut out with the jigsaw. Smooth the edges with abrasive paper.

4 Mark and cut out a 40 x 50 mm notch in the top corners of the front and back panels and a 470 x 880 mm doorway in the front. Cut the floor to 1150 mm wide except for the porch (see diagram on page 548).

THE FLOOR FRAME

5 Turn the floor upside down and lay out the bearers on it. Starting at one end, position the joists between the bearers at intervals of 500 mm.

6 Nail galvanized metal brackets in each corner of the floor frame. Ensure the frame sits flush with the outside edges of the floor board, excluding the 25 mm overhang at the front and sides of the porch.

TOOLS

- Square
- Straight edge
- Tape measure
- Pencil
- Cramps
- Circular saw
- Handsaw
- Jigsaw
- Smoothing plane
- Hammer
- Nail punch
- Notched trowel
- Spirit level
- Screwdriver
- Portable electric drill
- Drill bits: 3 mm, 10 mm
- Utility knife
- Cork sanding block
- Dust mask
- Safety glasses
- Hearing protection

The neat shape and green colourway of this playhouse allow it to fit unobtrusively into the garden, where it will provide years of pleasure. It has a door with cut-out design and a window in each side wall.

7 Turn the frame upright and apply adhesive to the top, using ample amounts around each intersection. Place the floor onto the frame, ensuring it is square, and nail it in place. Seal the underside of the structure with an exterior finish.

8 Choose a level location for the playhouse, so the porch faces the sun. Place house bricks at each corner and in the middle of the long sides to raise the frame at least 75 mm off the ground. Use a spirit level to ensure the brick piers are level. Position the floor frame on the bricks.

ATTACHING THE WALLS

9 Place adhesive along the sides of the bearers and edges of the floor board and firmly press the side walls against them. Ensure that the bottom edge of the walls is flush with the bottom of the bearers and

that the wall projects 12 mm at the back. Brace the walls in place.

10 Attach the back wall to the floor frame in a similar manner, ensuring that it sits firmly between the side panels and that

MATERIALS*

PART	MATERIAL	FINISHED LENGTH	WIDTH	NO.
Floor	12 mm plywood	2225 mm	1200 mm	1
Side	12 mm plywood	1712 mm	1200 mm	2
Front	12 mm plywood	1150 mm	1113 mm	1
Back	12 mm plywood	1150 mm	1200 mm	1
Window lining	12 mm plywood	500 mm	25 mm	4
Window head	12 mm plywood	470 mm	50 mm	2
Window sill	12 mm plywood	470 mm	50 mm	2
Door lining	12 mm plywood	880 mm	25 mm	2
Door head	12 mm plywood	1150 mm	50 mm	1
Gable	12 mm plywood	1200 mm	688 mm	2
Roof sheet	5.5 mm hardboard	2376 mm	920 mm	2
Floor bearer	70 x 45 mm timber**	2200 mm		2
Floor joist	70 x 45 mm timber**	1070 mm		5
Door ledge	50 x 25 mm timber	470 mm		2
Door brace	50 x 25 mm timber	950 mm		1
Door jamb	50 x 25 mm timber	880 mm		2
Floor plate	50 x 25 mm timber	340 mm		2
Packer	50 x 25 mm timber	469 mm		8
Roof beam	75 x 38 mm timber	2376 mm		2
End beam	75 x 38 mm timber	1072 mm		2
King post	75 x 38 mm timber	450 mm		2
Ridge	75 x 38 mm timber	2376 mm		1
Roof brace	75 x 38 mm timber	600 mm		2
Rafter	100 x 25 mm timber	900 mm		10
Porch post	50 x 50 mm timber	1063 mm		2
Door cladding	T&G boards*	880 mm		4
Interior trim A	19 mm quarter angle	1063 mm		2
Interior trim B	19 mm quarter angle	1044 mm		2
Eaves stiffener	19 mm quarter angle	2376 mm		2
Exterior trim A	25 x 25 mm plastic angle	1150 mm		2
Exterior trim B	25 x 25 mm plastic angle	1063 mm		2
Roof trim	25 x 25 mm plastic angle	2376 mm		1
Gable trim	25 x 25 mm plastic angle	920 mm		4

MATERIAL DETAILS

Other: Epoxy-resin adhesive; two-part acrylic adhesive; twenty-four small galvanized steel right-angle brackets; 30 x 2 mm helical thread nails; 30 mm panel pins; 30 mm x No. 6 countersunk screws; 50 mm x No. 10 countersunk screws; wood filler; abrasive paper; two 75 mm T-hinges with 20 mm screws; 40–45 mm doorknob; house bricks; exterior grade finish of choice.

* Finished size: 2400 x 1400 mm and 1700 mm high without brick piers. Timber sizes given are the nominal size. For a note on timber sizes and conditions, see page 520. Four 2400 x 1200 mm sheets of plywood were used.

** Use treated timber.

* Use tongue and groove lining boards. They come in various widths. Boards 130 mm wide with double 'V' rebates were used for this project, but other sizes can be easily adapted.

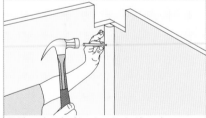

12 Glue a length of interior trim inside each corner and secure it with panel pins.

TIMBER

STRESS GRADINGS

Timber is stress graded and given a C or D rating (followed by a number that indicates the bending stress of the timber). The higher the number, the greater the stress the timber can withstand.

For general use in playhouse construction you should choose timber that has a stress rating of C24 or greater.

---

the corners are flush. Nail the sides to the back.

11 Glue and nail the floor plates to the floor frame on each side of the door position and inset 12 mm from the front ends of the side walls. Glue and nail the front between the sides and flush against the floor plates. Glue and nail the door jambs against the ends of the floor plates and the edges of the doorway.

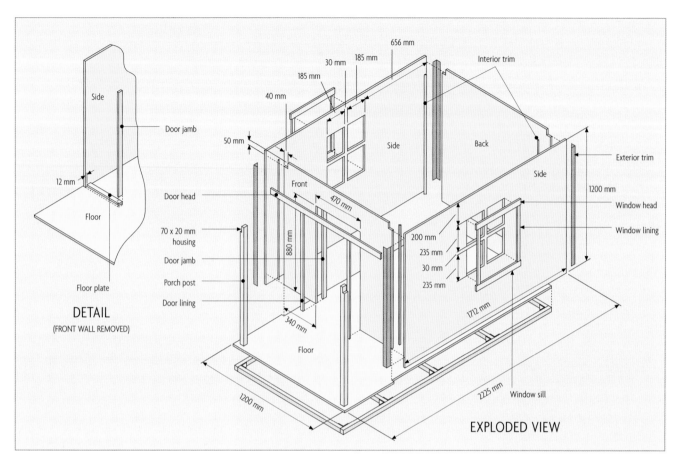

Side

Door jamb

12 mm

Floor

Floor plate

DETAIL
(FRONT WALL REMOVED)

Door head

70 x 20 mm housing

Door jamb

Porch post

Door lining

50 mm

40 mm

185 mm

30 mm

185 mm

656 mm

Interior trim

Side

Back

Side

Exterior trim

1200 mm

Window head

Window lining

Front

470 mm

880 mm

200 mm

235 mm

30 mm

235 mm

340 mm

Floor

1712 mm

1200 mm

2225 mm

Window sill

EXPLODED VIEW

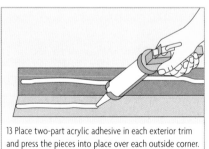

13 Place two-part acrylic adhesive in each exterior trim and press the pieces into place over each outside corner.

12 Glue a length of interior trim A inside each back corner. Secure the trim with panel pins. Punch them below the surface and fill with wood filler. Attach the lengths of interior trim B in the front corners as before.

13 Apply two-part acrylic adhesive in each exterior trim and press it into place over the

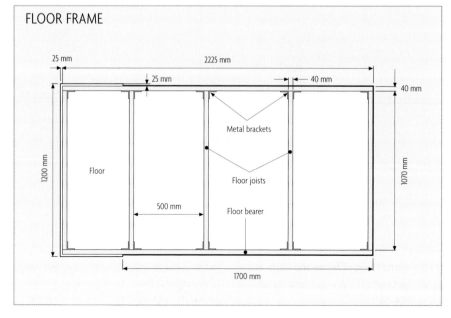

FLOOR FRAME

25 mm

25 mm

2225 mm

40 mm

40 mm

1200 mm

Floor

Metal brackets

Floor joists

500 mm

Floor bearer

1070 mm

1700 mm

A nail hammered partway into the bottom of the post is fitted into a hole drilled in the porch floor.

THE DOOR

16 Position the door linings so they overlap the opening by 10 mm. Glue and nail them in position. In the same way fix the door head in position, ensuring that it sits flush against the top of the linings. Sand the edges of the doorway and door jamb smooth.

17 Apply adhesive to one side of the door ledges and nail the tongue and groove door cladding to them. Glue and nail the door brace between the ledges on a diagonal.

18 Mark out a decorative design on the door. Carefully cut out the design with the jigsaw, and then smooth the edges with abrasive paper.

19 Screw the strap of the T-hinges to the door ledges, then screw the butt of the hinges to the jambs. Attach the doorknob.

FINISHING

20 Before fixing the roof to the walls, smooth all surfaces with abrasive paper. Use fine abrasive paper on the plastic trim. Apply an undercoat and finished gloss coat of paint. Allow the paint to dry well.

21 Lift the roof into place, ensuring the roof beams rest in the notches of the front and back walls with an 80 mm overhang at the back. Use 30 mm screws to fix them through the side walls near each corner.

22 In the top of each porch post cut a 70 x 20 mm housing to take the roof beam.

23 Hammer a helical shaft nail into the base

outside corners. Hold the trim until the adhesive sets.

THE ROOF

14 Construct the roof frame and fix on the roof sheet following the instructions on pages 564–565.

WINDOWS AND DOOR

15 Glue the window linings to the exterior wall on each side of the window and secure them with panel pins. Punch the pins below the surface and fill the holes with putty. Attach the window head and window sill at the top and bottom of the linings in a similar manner.

of each post, leaving a 10 mm projection. The posts should sit near the front corners of the porch. Drill 3 mm holes for these nails in the porch floor so that the posts will fit under the beams. Fit the posts in position, with the nails in the holes. Screw the posts to the roof beams with 50 mm screws and skew-nail them to the floor.

PLAYHOUSE WITH VERANDAH

This spacious playhouse has a verandah with decorative timber railing and brackets along the front. The construction, however, is not complex. It has windows in the front and one side wall, and another can be added in the back wall if desired.

CUTTING OUT

1 Following the materials list on pages 553–554, mark out the floor, front, back and side walls on the plywood and ensure the pieces are square. Clamp a straight edge to the board and cut out the parts using a circular saw. Mark and cut out all the other parts. Cut the verandah rails lengthwise to a width of 35 mm and the baluster support to a width of 25 mm. Plane the edges of all boards to the finished size and ensure they are straight and square. Select and mark the outside of each.

2 Cut a 40 x 50 mm notch in the top corners of the side walls. Mark and cut out the door and windows (see diagram opposite). Plane and smooth the edges of the windows and doorway.

FLOOR AND FOUNDATION

3 Lay the three floor joists parallel to one another, leaving a 515 mm space between each, then lay the floor sheet over the joists. Ensure the joists are square and flush with the edge of the floor. Remove the floor and apply adhesive to the top of each joist. Replace the floor and fix it in place with 30 mm countersunk-head screws or helical thread nails.

The traditional verandah on this playhouse offers children an extended play area protected from the elements. It is finished with exterior gloss paint and timber decking paint to ensure it will withstand the weather.

outdoor

EXPLODED VIEW

DETAIL OF BALUSTRADE

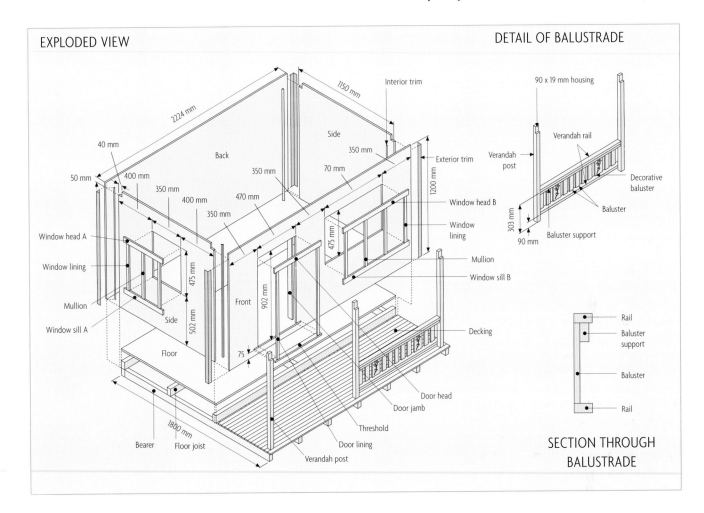

SECTION THROUGH BALUSTRADE

4 Choose a level location for the play-house and place the three floor bearers 1040 mm apart to support the floor base. Place the floor base on the bearers, with the back aligning with the back of the bearers. Fix it with a 50 mm bracket at each inside corner. Level the bearers with a few bricks under each end.

5 Place verandah bearers 320 mm apart between each bearer (see diagram on page 552) and fix with brackets. Place a 12 mm spacer against the floor joist and nail the verandah decking to the bearers using 30 mm flat-head nails.

ATTACHING THE WALLS

6 Place two ribbons of adhesive along the outsides of the front and back floor joists and the edges of the floor board, and firmly press the front and back walls in place against them. Ensure that the bottom edge of the walls is flush with the bottom edge of the joists and that the walls project 12 mm either end. Erect temporary braces to hold the walls in place until the side walls are fixed.

7 Attach the side walls in a similar manner, ensuring that they sit firmly between the front and back walls. Nail the sides in place through the front and back walls using 30 x 2 mm galvanized helical thread nails.

8 Glue a piece of interior trim in each internal corner and secure the trim with panel pins. Punch the pins below the surface and fill the holes with filler.

9 Place a ribbon of glue in each piece of exterior trim. Press it firmly in place on the outside corners.

WINDOWS AND DOORWAY

10 Fix the window linings to the exterior walls on the vertical edges of the windows using adhesive and panel pins. Use panel pins to fix the mullions vertically across the windows (two across the front window and one across the side window). Punch the pins

15 Remove the roof and cut off the excess overhang at an angle so that it will fit over the verandah.

below the surface and fill with filler. Fit the window sills and heads in a similar manner, ensuring they are flush with the linings.

11 Use a router to cut a 38 mm deep and 12 mm wide groove across the bottom of the threshold and notch the ends so they fit around the sides of the doorway. Glue and pin the threshold in place so that the notches fit around the wall. Glue and pin the door jambs in place so that they rest on the sill.

12 Attach the door linings in the same way as the window linings, ensuring they rest on the door sill and stop flush with the top of the door. Attach the door head in the same way.

THE ROOF

13 Construct the roof frame as on pages 564–565. When the gables have been cut to shape, centre the circular vent on one of the gables, mark and cut out the circle. Fit the vent. Glue and nail the gables to the frame.

14 Proceed as on pages 564–565, fixing on the packers, eaves stiffener and roof sheets but fix the stiffener only to the back of the playhouse. Fix on the roof and gable trims.

15 Lift the roof into place with the roof beams fitting into the notches in the side walls. Mark the rafters on the verandah side so they overhang the front wall by 30 mm

TOP VIEW OF BEARERS AND JOISTS

Bearer · Floor joist · Bearer · 1150 mm · 1800 mm

Floor joist · Verandah bearer · Verandah bearer · 700 mm

320 mm · 320 mm · 320 mm · 320 mm · 320 mm · 320 mm · 40 mm · 40 mm · 2200 mm

SIDE VIEW WITH FLOOR AND VERANDAH DECKING

640 mm · 12 mm · 1150 mm · 40 mm · 40 mm · 12 mm · 515 mm · 40 mm · 515 mm · Decking · 75 mm · 75 mm · Brick or paver · Bearer · Floor joist · Floor · Floor joist · 1800 mm

measured horizontally. Square off the wall at this point to mark a horizontal line on the rafters. Remove the roof and cut the rafters along the line.

16 Smooth all surfaces using abrasive paper. Use fine abrasive paper on the plastic trim. Apply the finish of your choice and allow to dry well.

17 Lift the roof into place with the side frames resting in the notches of the side walls. Attach the roof with a screw at each corner.

THE VERANDAH

18 The verandah roof fits below the 30 mm projection of the main roof. To allow for the thickness of the rafters and roof sheet locate

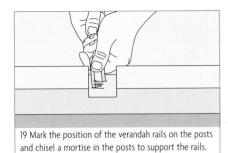

19 Mark the position of the verandah rails on the posts and chisel a mortise in the posts to support the rails.

the top edge of the wall plate 35 mm below the top of the wall. Screw the wall plate in position.

19 Cut a 50 x 19 mm housing into the top of each post. Mark the positions for the rails on the posts, measuring up 90 mm from the post base for the bottom of the bottom rail and 303 mm for the bottom of the top rail (see diagram on page 551). Chisel mortises in the posts to take the rails. Drive a nail into the bottom of each post, allowing 10 mm to project. Mark the position of the posts on the decking so they'll be approximately 20 mm from the verandah edge, 1047 mm apart and sit over the bearers. Drill a 3 mm hole in the decking at the centre of each post position.

20 Erect the posts by placing the nails in the post bottoms into the holes in the decking and skew-nail the posts to the decking. Fit the verandah beam into the housings and fix it with screws. Fix the corner brackets to the posts and the beam using both adhesive and panel pins.

21 Place a rafter at each end of the wall plate and beam. Position the remaining rafters between these two end rafters, approximately 576 mm apart. At each joint drill two holes and insert 30 mm countersunk screws. Fix an eaves stiffener to the ends of the rafters using panel pins.

MATERIALS*

PART	MATERIAL	FINISHED LENGTH	WIDTH	NO.
Floor	12 mm plywood	2200 mm	1150 mm	1
Front/back	12 mm plywood	2224 mm	1200 mm	2
Side	12 mm plywood	1150 mm	1200 mm	2
W. sill/head A	12 mm plywood	450 mm	50 mm	2
W. sill/head B	12 mm plywood	800 mm	50 mm	2
W. lining/mullion	12 mm plywood	475 mm	25 mm	7
Threshold	12 mm plywood	570 mm	50 mm	1
Door lining	12 mm plywood	890 mm	25 mm	2
Door head	12 mm plywood	570 mm	50 mm	1
Gable	12 mm plywood	1200 mm	685 mm	2
Roof sheet	5.5 mm hardboard	2400 mm	920 mm	2
Verandah roof	5.5 mm hardboard	2400 mm	720 mm	1
Floor joist	70 x 45 mm timber**	2200 mm		3
Floor bearer	70 x 45 mm timber**	1800 mm		3
Verandah bearer	70 x 45 mm timber**	700 mm		4
Decking	40 x 12 mm timber**	2200 mm		16
Roof beam	75 x 38 mm timber	2376 mm		2
End beam	75 x 38 mm timber	1080 mm		2
King post	75 x 38 mm timber	450 mm		2
Ridge	75 x 38 mm timber	2376 mm		1
Rafter	100 x 25 mm timber	900 mm		10
Packer	50 x 25 mm timber	469 mm		8
Verandah rail	50 x 25 mm timber	1044 mm		2
Baluster support	50 x 25 mm timber	1044 mm		1
Verandah beam	50 x 25 mm timber	2400 mm		1
Verandah rafter	50 x 25 mm timber	720 mm		5
Wall plate	50 x 25 mm timber	2424 mm		1
Door jamb	50 x 25 mm timber	890 mm		2
Door ledge	50 x 25 mm timber	470 mm		2
Door brace	50 x 25 mm timber	960 mm		1
Door cladding	T&G boards*	780 mm		4
Verandah post	38 x 38 mm timber	1000 mm		3
Baluster	50 x 16 mm timber	200 mm		9
Baluster	Decorative pieces	200 mm		2
Eaves stiffener	19 mm quarter angle	2376 mm		2
Interior trim	19 mm quarter angle	1063 mm		4
Exterior trim	25 x 25 mm plastic angle	1150 mm		4
Gable trim	25 x 25 mm plastic angle	920 mm		4
Roof trim	25 x 25 mm plastic angle	2376 mm		1

MATERIALS*

PART	MATERIAL	FINISHED LENGTH	WIDTH	NO.
Barge board	90 x 19 mm decking	1150 mm		2
V. barge board	90 x 19 mm decking	720 mm		2

Other: Epoxy-resin adhesive; two-part acrylic adhesive (for plastic); abrasive paper; 30 mm x No. 6 countersunk screws; 50 mm x No. 10 countersunk screws; 30 x 2 mm galvanized helical thread nails; 30 mm panel pins; 30 x 2 mm galvanized flat-head nails; twelve 50 mm galvanized steel right-angle brackets; two 150 x 30 mm galvanized steel straps; eight small galvanized steel right-angle brackets; wood filler; circular window for door; two 75 mm T-hinges with 20 mm screws; 40–45 mm knob for door; house bricks; round ceiling vent; finish of choice.

* Finished size: 2400 x 1820 mm and 1900 mm high. Timber sizes given are the nominal size. For more information on timber sizes and timber conditions see page 520. V = verandah; W = window.

** Use treated timber.

* Use tongue and groove lining boards. They come in various widths. Boards 130 mm wide with double 'V' rebates were used for this project, but you can use other widths and adapt the instructions as necessary.

TOOLS

- Square
- Straight edge
- Tape measure
- Pencil
- Cramps
- Circular saw
- Handsaw
- Jigsaw
- Smoothing plane
- Hammer
- Nail punch
- Notched trowel
- Spirit level
- Screwdriver
- Portable electric drill
- Drill bits: 3 mm, 10 mm
- Router
- Utility knife
- Chisel
- Cork sanding block
- Dust mask
- Safety glasses
- Hearing protection

MAKING THE DOOR

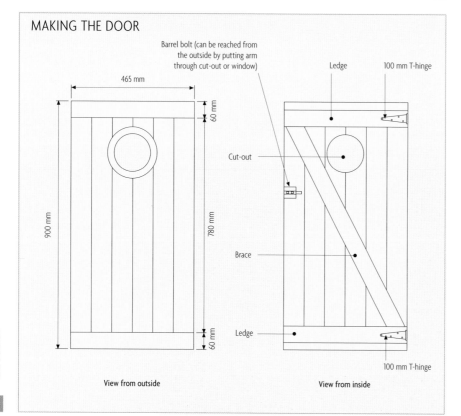

Barrel bolt (can be reached from the outside by putting arm through cut-out or window)

465 mm

60 mm

Ledge

100 mm T-hinge

Cut-out

900 mm

780 mm

Brace

60 mm

Ledge

100 mm T-hinge

View from outside

View from inside

22 Spread adhesive over the top surface of the rafters and align the back edge of the roof sheet with the ends of the rafters. Weight the sheet in place until dry.

23 Centre the baluster support on the bottom of the top rail and glue it in place. Fix the rails to the posts. Space the balusters evenly between the rails, and glue and nail them to the baluster support and bottom rail.

outdoor

ROOF STRUCTURE
(ROOF SHEETING NOT SHOWN)

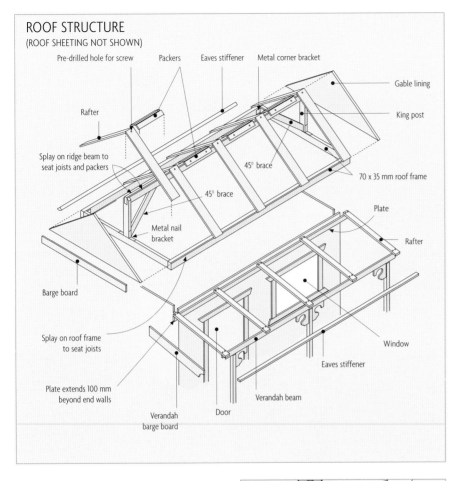

Pre-drilled hole for screw · Packers · Eaves stiffener · Metal corner bracket

Rafter

Splay on ridge beam to
seat joists and packers

Metal nail
bracket

Barge board

Splay on roof frame
to seat joists

Plate extends 100 mm
beyond end walls

Verandah
barge board

Door

Verandah beam

45° brace

45° brace

Gable lining

King post

70 x 35 mm roof frame

Plate

Rafter

Window

Eaves stiffener

the plastic trim. Apply the finishes of your
choice and allow them to dry well.

28 Position the barge boards and mark the
angle between the level barge board on the
main roof and the sloping barge board on
the verandah roof. Cut the barge boards to
length and add a quarter-round cut-out at
the front end.

29 Screw the barge boards in place using
30 mm countersunk screws and fill the
holes with filler. Give the barge boards
an undercoat and finish coat of paint.

30 Lightly sand the verandah timbers and
apply the finish of your choice. Hang
curtains in the windows.

THE DOOR

24 Glue and nail the door cladding to the
door ledges. Apply adhesive to the door
brace and nail it in position diagonally
between the ledges (see diagram opposite).

25 Position the circular window on the front
of the door so that it misses the diagonal
brace. Mark its position with a pencil and cut
out the circle with the jigsaw. Smooth the
edges of the cut-out with abrasive paper and
fit the window into the door.

26 Screw the strap of the T-hinges to the
door ledges, then screw the butt of the
hinge to the door jambs. Attach the door
knob and, if desired, a barrel bolt where it

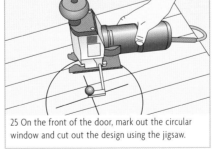

25 On the front of the door, mark out the circular
window and cut out the design using the jigsaw.

can be reached through the cut-out
or window.

FINISHING

27 Smooth all the surfaces on the building
that have not had a finish applied with
abrasive paper. Use fine abrasive paper on

MUSHROOM PLAYHOUSE

Constructing the fibreglass roof of this novelty playhouse is a two-person job but the result is well worth the effort required. A plywood floor forms the base of the circular room.

CUTTING OUT

1 Firmly hold two sheets of 12 mm plywood together lengthwise. For the floor and inner circle pieces, use a nail to mark a centre 1025 mm from one end and 175 mm from the joint. Tie a piece of string to the nail and to a pencil. Draw two concentric circles: one with a 1025 mm radius, the other with a 725 mm radius (see diagram opposite).

2 Mark out a circle with 250 mm radius for the roof top. For the inner circle pieces and fishplates B, mark out an arc with 725 mm radius, then another arc with 650 mm radius from the same centre. Mark out fishplates A, then cut out the pieces using a jigsaw.

3 Join the eaves circle pieces by gluing a fishplate A at each joint; screw the fishplates in place with ten 20 mm countersunk screws. Join the inner circle pieces in the same way using three fishplates B.

THE FLOOR AND WALLS

4 Lay the floor joists on a flat surface at 400 mm centres, the longer joists in the centre. Spread adhesive on top of them and lay the floor segments on them with the join at right angles to the joists. Screw the floor in

The walls of this mushroom playhouse are made from pine palings and given a coarse sanding to achieve a stalk-like texture. Like the fibreglass 'cap', they are painted with exterior gloss paint to guard against weathering.

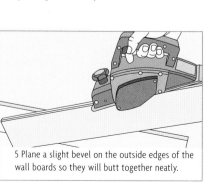

5 Plane a slight bevel on the outside edges of the wall boards so they will butt together neatly.

place using 30 mm countersunk screws. When the adhesive sets, cut the floor joists flush with the edge of the floor.

5 Plane a slight bevel on the outside edges of the wall boards so they will butt together neatly when fitted around the floor.

6 Nail four wall boards to the floor and joists, spaced evenly around the circle. Place the inner circle inside the top of the boards. Ensure it is level; nail it in place. Butt another board against one of the four and use a square on the floor to ensure it is vertical. Glue and nail it to the floor and inner circle.

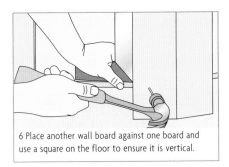

6 Place another wall board against one board and use a square on the floor to ensure it is vertical.

16 Turn the upside down dome and mark and cut around the overhang

Apply adhesive along the bevelled edge and attach the other boards in turn.

7 Plane the joints of the wall boards and fill any gaps with filler. When the filler is dry, sand the wall surface with abrasive paper so that the texture resembles a mushroom stem.

8 Mark out a door (575 x 400 mm) and window (280 x 240 mm), and round the corners. Drill a hole to start the jigsaw and cut out the openings. Sand around the edges.

THE ROOF FRAME

9 Nail the rafter supports to the roof top at the four cardinal points (see diagram on page 558) so that they extend beyond the edge.

10 Cut a bird's-mouth notch in each end of the rafters. Screw-fix each against the edge of the top and a support. Let the rafters project out at 45 degrees.

11 Position the frame so the rafters rest on the inside of the eaves circle. Screw the rafters to the eaves with 30 mm screws.

12 Cut bird's-mouth notches at one end of each strut. Position the struts between two rafters with the notch at the base and screw them in place to stabilize the frame.

SHAPING THE DOME

13 Centre one dome form A over the top and screw in place with 15 mm pan-head screws. Bend the sides down and temporarily nail them to the outside of the eaves. Ensure the top is fairly flat and the sides curve symmetrically like a mushroom cap. When the shape is satisfactory, secure the ends with three 30 mm x No. 6 bugle-head screws. Attach the other form A at 90 degrees to the first.

14 Cut a 90-degree point into one end of each dome form B; the pointed ends should fit into the angle of the existing forms. Attach the top of the forms with three 15 mm x No. 8 pan-head screws. Bend the ends down and screw them to the eaves circle with three 30 mm x No. 6 bugle-head screws.

15 Position forms C so the tops slide under forms A and B; attach them with two 15 mm screws. Screw the ends to the eaves circle. Place forms D and E between them where appropriate and screw them in place.

16 Turn the dome and mark a line around the overhang 75 mm from the eaves circle and cut with a jigsaw.

17 Curve an eaves stiffener around the inside edge of the overhang and temporarily screw or clamp it in place. Butt a second eaves stiffener against the first, and temporarily

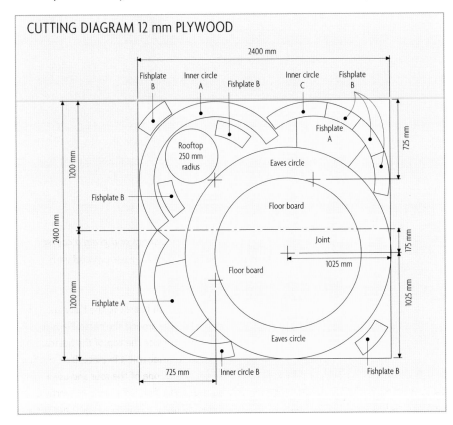

CUTTING DIAGRAM 12 mm PLYWOOD

2400 mm

Fishplate B — Inner circle A — Fishplate B — Inner circle C — Fishplate B

Fishplate A

Rooftop 250 mm radius

Eaves circle

Fishplate B

Floor board

1200 mm

2400 mm

Joint

1025 mm

Floor board

Fishplate A

725 mm

175 mm

1025 mm

Eaves circle

725 mm — Inner circle B — Fishplate B

ROOF FRAME DETAILS

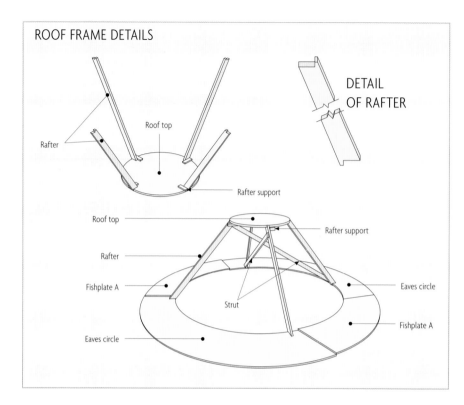

DETAIL OF RAFTER

Rafter

Roof top

Rafter support

Roof top

Rafter support

Rafter

Fishplate A

Eaves circle

Strut

Fishplate A

Eaves circle

---

attach it. Put each subsequent eaves stiffener in place in the same way to form a double layer of support for the eaves. Screw the stiffeners in place through the outside of the dome with 15 mm x No. 8 pan-head screws at 200 mm centres. Sand the edges using coarse abrasive paper.

18 Attach a piece of masking tape to the outside bottom edge of the dome and run a continuous length around the dome. Fold the tape down to cover the edges of the eaves

support. Repeat this on the inside edge of the dome, folding the tape back over the first piece. Use a third length to cover the other two.

19 Turn the dome upright and fill any large gaps with strips of cardboard taped into place. Tape over any remaining gaps. Turn the dome upside down again.

SMOOTHING THE SURFACE

20 Mix 400–500 ml of resin with 5–6 ml of catalyst. Gradually stir in approximately

1 litre of microsphere to form a smooth paste. Apply the paste quickly around the dome where the eaves stiffener rests on the eaves circle. Shape the paste with the 30 mm filling knife and remove any excess filler before it hardens. Turn the dome right way up.

21 Mix 1 litre of resin with 10–12 ml of catalyst and gradually stir in 2 litres of microsphere. Apply the paste to the top of the dome, filling in any irregularities, and smooth it with a spatula. Continue this process, mixing small amounts of filler, until the dome is smooth. Allow the filler to harden and then sand off any edges, leaving a smooth surface.

LAYING THE FIBREGLASS

22 Turn the dome again. Hold a straight edge against the fibreglass mat and fold up and tear off seven 1000 x 300 mm sections (the fibres should form a ragged line).

23 Lay each section lengthwise over the edge of the dome, leaving about 125 mm over the outside of the dome and about 100 mm across the eaves circle. Make a few 75 mm tears in the edge that covers the eaves so the fabric can bend around the curve; allow a 100 mm overlap of each piece of fabric. Bend the fabric into shape and then remove it and put it aside within easy reach.

24 Mix 2 litres of resin with 20 ml of catalyst, depending on the climate and conditions in which you are working (see box on page 560). Working quickly, pour and spread the resin with a paintbrush where the first section of fibreglass is to be laid. Put the fibreglass mat in place and brush resin over it. Continue this process, occasionally using the ribbed roller to smooth the fabric down and remove air bubbles before the resin dries. Turn the dome over and support it securely on the inner part

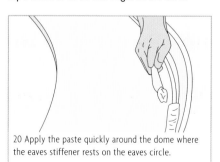

20 Apply the paste quickly around the dome where the eaves stiffener rests on the eaves circle.

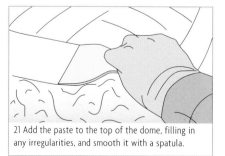

21 Add the paste to the top of the dome, filling in any irregularities, and smooth it with a spatula.

MATERIALS*

PART	MATERIAL	FINISHED LENGTH	WIDTH	NO.
Floor board	12 mm plywood	1450 mm diameter		1
Eaves circle	12 mm plywood	2050 mm diameter		1
Inner circle	12 mm plywood	1450 mm diameter		1
Fishplate A	12 mm plywood	1300 mm diameter segments		2
Fishplate B	12 mm plywood	1450 mm diameter segments		7
Roof top	12 mm plywood	500 mm diameter		1
Dome form A	3 mm plywood	2700 mm	200 mm	2
Dome form B	3 mm plywood	1350 mm	200 mm	4
Dome form C	3 mm plywood	1200 mm	200 mm	8
Dome form D	3 mm plywood	900 mm	125 mm	8
Dome form E	3 mm plywood	800 mm	125 mm	8
Eaves stiffener	3 mm plywood	2700 mm	75 mm	5
Floor joist A	90 x 35 mm timber**	1000 mm		2
Floor joist B	90 x 35 mm timber**	1450 mm		2
Wall board	90 x 13 mm timber**	900 mm		46
Rafter	45 x 19 mm timber**	710 mm		4
Strut	45 x 19 mm timber**	1250 mm		2
Rafter support	45 x 19 mm timber**	150 mm		4

Other: Epoxy-resin adhesive; fifty 20 mm x No. 8 countersunk screws; twenty-five 30 mm x No. 8 countersunk screws; 200 15 mm x No. 8 pan-head self-drilling screws; 100 30 mm x No. 6 bugle-head self-drilling screws; 30 x 2 mm flat-head galvanized nails; wood filler; three rolls of wide masking tape; abrasive paper or discs: coarse and medium; 15 m² chopped strand mat fibreglass with a weight of 450 g/m²; 21 kg drum of fibreglass laminating resin; 500 g bottle of methyl ethyl ketone peroxide (MEKP) catalyst; 4 kg bag of microsphere filler; acetone; plastic containers of various sizes; cardboard off-cuts; eight house bricks; finish of choice.

* Finished size: 1550 mm high; 2100 mm diameter. All the 12 mm plywood pieces can be cut from two 2400 x 1200 mm sheets. For more information on timber sizes and conditions see page 520.

** Use treated timber.

TOOLS

- Pencil
- String
- Tape measure
- Straight edge
- Jigsaw
- Handsaw
- Screwdriver: cross-head
- Square
- Smoothing plane
- Hammer
- Spirit level
- Cramps
- Portable electric drill
- Electric sander
- Filling knife: 30 mm
- Spatula: 100 mm
- Paint brushes
- Ribbed roller: 12 mm
- Dust and fume mask
- Safety glasses
- Hearing protection
- Disposable rubber gloves

of the eaves circle to avoid damaging the fibreglass.

25 Tear off two 2500 x 1000 mm sections of fibreglass. Lay them across the middle of the dome so they overlap the rim 100 mm on either side. Tear off several 1000 x 1000 mm sections for the rest of the dome.

26 Prepare another batch of resin and catalyst. Apply the resin to the dome, beginning on one side, working up towards the top and down the opposite side. Put a 2500 x 1000 mm section of fibreglass in place and brush resin over the mat. Smooth the mat with the roller as before. Repeat this process with the other 2500 x 1000 mm mat, placing it at 90 degrees to the first.

27 Begin laying the other sections of fibreglass so they lap the edges of the dome and extend upward. Ensure each section overlaps the adjoining section. Keep applying freshly made resin and smoothing the surface with the roller as the job proceeds. There should be at least two layers of fibreglass over the whole dome.

USING FIBREGLASS

- Most large hardware stores stock DIY fibreglass kits.

- Fibreglass comes in different weights and measures. The weight determines the amount of laminating resin required: generally 2–2½ times the weight of the fibreglass mat.

- Fibreglass cannot be formed into corners, and so you have to smooth out any sudden changes of direction.

- Acetone is used to clean fibreglass equipment, but if you are only doing one job, it is better to dispose of the materials when you have finished.

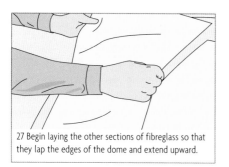

27 Begin laying the other sections of fibreglass so that they lap the edges of the dome and extend upward.

28 Leave the dome in a cool, shaded area to set for at least twelve hours. Inspect the fibreglass closely; smooth any stray fibres with abrasive paper.

FINISHING

29 The spots on the dome were marked out using cardboard templates in two sizes and a pencil. Apply the finish of your choice to the walls and dome.

30 Position bricks under the floor joists to level the playhouse and keep it off the ground. Lift the dome onto the walls and position it carefully. Using four fishplates B, and adhesive and 30 mm screws, fix the eaves circle to the inner circle.

DOME DETAIL

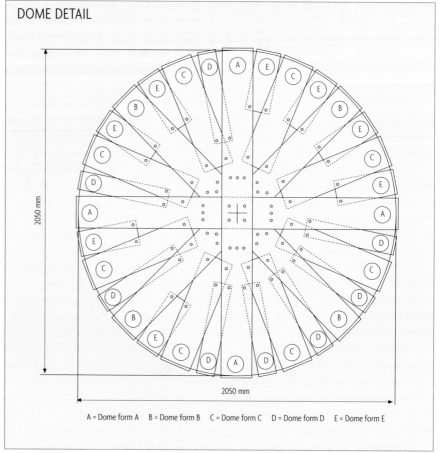

2050 mm

2050 mm

A = Dome form A   B = Dome form B   C = Dome form C   D = Dome form D   E = Dome form E

RESIN AND CATALYST

- Never use resin and catalyst without wearing rubber gloves, full skin cover and protective glasses; avoid breathing the fumes.

- Resin is manufactured for use in specific climatic conditions, so choose one for your climate.

- Resin needs a catalyst to activate it so that it will set. The amount depends on the temperature: about 2 per cent of catalyst at 15–18°C, 1–1.5 per cent at 18–22°C and 1 per cent at 22–27°C.

- Work with manageable quantities because resin remains workable for only a short time after being catalysed.

- Use the minimal proportion of catalyst to lengthen setting time.

- Assemble tools and containers before mixing material. Large plastic ice-cream containers are suitable, and tiny glass jars with volume marks make suitable catalyst measuring pots.

- Work in a shaded and cool area to maximize resin setting time.

SANDPIT WITH ROOF

The simple pitched roof on this sandpit will give protection to children from the sun as well as reducing maintenance by helping to keep off falling leaves and other debris.

PREPARING THE BOARDS

1 Use a square and straight edge to mark out four 1200 mm long end boards. Cut the boards and place the lengths side by side in pairs ensuring the best match. If there are gaps in the joints, straighten the edges and plane the boards square. Mark out and cut the 2200 mm side boards and prepare them in the same way.

2 Cut the timber for the end trim lengthwise to a width of 50 mm and plane the edges smooth and square.

3 Cut a housing 400 mm long and 30 mm deep on the bottom of each roof post. Cut another housing, also 400 mm long but only 20 mm deep, at right angles to the first; on two posts cut the second housing to the right of the first, and on the other posts cut the second housing to the left of the first (see diagram on page 565). Drill two holes into the face of each housing, through the post. These will be used when attaching the posts to the frame.

JOINING THE FRAME

4 Join the pairs of side boards by placing epoxy adhesive on the top edge of one board and butting them together. Clamp the

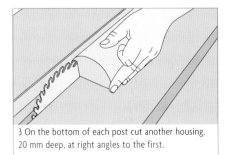

3 On the bottom of each post cut another housing, 20 mm deep, at right angles to the first.

The seaside theme used to decorate this sandpit will bring back memories of holidays at the beach, but the sandpit would provide just as much fun if given a simple paint job. The waves were created with a cardboard template.

boards together and allow to dry. Use adhesive to fix the end trims to the ends of

the boards. Nail them in place with 30 mm nails. Glue and clamp the end boards together.

5 Plane across the ends of the side boards to create a neat, flush joint with the trims and ends. Apply adhesive to each end of the end boards and butt them against the side boards. Temporarily nail the ends in position. Measure the diagonals to check that the structure is square and adjust if necessary. Finish nailing.

6 Turn the frame over and place a brace at a 45-degree angle across each corner so that it has an overhang of 50 mm at each end. Mark the position of the braces on the edges of the frame and set the braces aside. Using a handsaw and chisel, cut housings for the braces in the edges of the frame.

7 Reposition the braces; fix with 40 mm countersunk screws. Cut the overhanging edges of the braces at an angle so that they sit flush with the edges of the frame.

8 Stretch anti-weed mat over the edges of the frame. Fold the edges of the fabric over

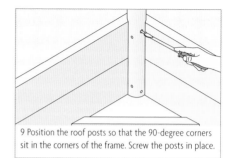

9 Position the roof posts so that the 90-degree corners sit in the corners of the frame. Screw the posts in place.

a few times and secure them to the frame with 30 mm clout nails at 50 mm centres.

THE ROOF

9 Position the posts so that the 90-degree corners sit in the corners of the frame. Apply adhesive and screw the posts in using 100 mm countersunk screws in the holes.

MATERIALS*

PART	MATERIAL	LENGTH	WIDTH	NO.
End board	200 x 50 mm timber**	1200 mm		4
Side board	200 x 50 mm timber**	2200 mm		4
End trim	70 x 35 mm timber**	400 mm		4
Brace	70 x 35 mm timber**	900 mm		4
Roof post	90 mm timber poles**	1450 mm		4
Roof beam	75 x 38 mm timber	2376 mm		2
End beam	75 x 38 mm timber	1070 mm		2
King post	75 x 38 mm timber	450 mm		2
Ridge	75 x 38 mm timber	2340 mm		1
Roof brace	75 x 38 mm timber	600 mm		2
Rafter	100 x 25 mm timber	900 mm		10
Roof sheet	5.5 mm hardboard	2400 mm	920 mm	2
Gable	12 mm plywood	1200 mm	685 mm	2
Packer	50 x 25 mm timber	200 mm		8
Eaves stiffener	19 mm quarter angle	2376 mm		2
Roof trim	25 x 25 mm plastic angle	2376 mm		1
Gable trim	25 x 25 mm plastic angle	920 mm		4

Other: Epoxy-resin adhesive; two-part acrylic adhesive (for plastic trim); 30 x 2 mm helical thread nails; 30 mm panel pins; 30 mm x No. 6 countersunk screws; 50 mm x No. 10 countersunk screws; sixteen 100 mm galvanized countersunk-head screws; eight galvanized steel right-angle brackets; 2.4 x 1.5 m anti-weed mat; 30 mm galvanized clout nails; abrasive paper; medium sanding discs; 0.75 m³ sand; masking tape; cardboard; exterior acrylic gloss paint in yellow, white and blue or finish of choice.

*   Finished size: 2238 x 1300 mm and 1900 mm high to the roof ridge. Timber sizes given are the nominal size; see page 520 for information about timber sizes.

** Use treated timber.

TOOLS

- Tape measure
- Straight edge
- Square
- Pencil
- Handsaw
- Smoothing plane
- Electric plane (optional)
- Circular saw and saw table (optional)
- Portable electric drill
- Drill bits: 4 mm, 6 mm, countersink
- Sash cramps
- Hammer
- Chisel
- Screwdriver
- Notched trowel
- Utility knife
- Disc sander
- Dust mask, safety glasses, hearing protection

EXPLODED VIEW

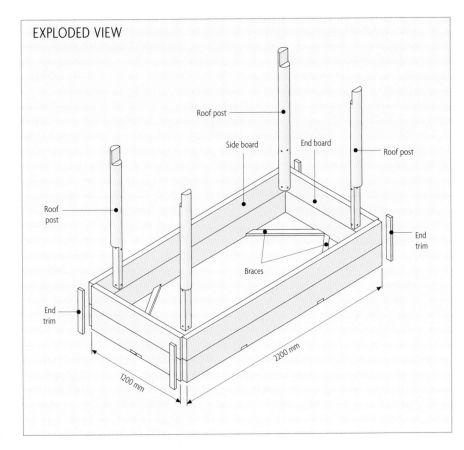

Roof post

Side board

End board

Roof post

Roof post

Roof post

End trim

Braces

End trim

2200 mm

1200 mm

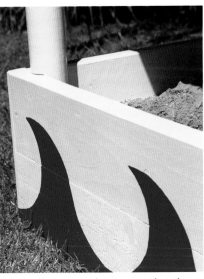

Housings are cut in the posts so that they fit neatly into the corners.

CHOOSING SAND

- Sand is usually delivered moist and its weight may vary, so it is best to order by volume.
- For these projects, you will need three-quarters of a cubic metre of sand to fill the sandpit to a depth of 300 mm. The dry weight is 1.25 tonnes.
- There are many varieties of sand, and it is wise to check the workability and cleanliness before ordering. Washed beach sand or river sand free of clay particles is most suitable.
- Special fine-grade sand that is less irritating to young skins and has been specially cleaned is available from some larger toy and baby stores.

10 Mark out and cut a 50 mm long housing 30 mm deep at the top of each post to hold the roof beam. Cut a 50 mm wide, 45-degree splay on the outside of each post, opposite the housing. Place the roof beams in the housings and measure the distance between them to determine the length of the end beams.

11 Remove the beams. Construct the roof (see box on pages 564–565).

FINISHING

12 Plane small bevels on all the edges of the sandpit frame and then sand all surfaces using a medium sanding disc (when sanding the roof structure, use fine abrasive paper on the plastic trim). Apply two coats of exterior acrylic gloss paint to the base, posts and gables. Paint the roof sheets white.

13 On a 440 x 300 mm piece of cardboard make a template for the wave pattern. Starting at one corner of the sandpit, mark out the design on the sides with a pencil. Paint the design using a small-detail brush to fill in the edges; fill in the rest of the pattern with a larger brush.

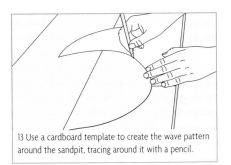

13 Use a cardboard template to create the wave pattern around the sandpit, tracing around it with a pencil.

14 To make the stripes on the roof, start at one side of the roof sheet and lightly mark eight vertical lines 266 mm apart. Apply masking tape on the outside edges of each second stripe and paint the blue stripes. Remove the masking tape before the paint dries.

CONSTRUCTING THE ROOF

FRAMING

1 Place the roof beams on a level surface and position the end beams between them at each end. Ensure the frame is square and nail right-angle brackets in each corner. Attach temporary braces in two corners to hold the frame square.

2 In the centre top of each king post cut a housing 35 mm wide and 70 mm deep. Centre a king post on each end beam and fix it in place using right-angle brackets. Set the ridge in the housings in the king posts. Apply adhesive and fix it in place using 50 mm screws. Cut 45-degree splays on both ends of each roof brace and screw them in place between the king post and bottom of the ridge.

3 Position five rafters on each side of the roof frame, one at each end and the others evenly spaced. Mark their position on the ridge and roof beam. Remove the rafters. Plane 45-degree splays on the ridge and beams to provide a seat for the rafters. Reposition the rafters and screw them in place using 30 mm screws. (Drill holes for the screws at the ridge end of the rafters to prevent the timber splitting.)

FRAMING GABLES AND ROOF SHEETS

4 Position the gables on the ends of the roof frame. Mark the roof slope on the back of the gables and cut them to shape. Plane the edges smooth. Apply adhesive and fix them with 30 mm nails.

5 Position the packing pieces on the splayed edge of the ridge midway between each rafter. Nail them to the ridge.

6 Attach the eaves stiffener to the ends of the rafter overhangs using panel pins. Punch them below the surface and fill with filler.

7 Ensure the roof sheets sit snugly on the frame and that the finished edges line up. Using a notched trowel, apply adhesive to the rafters, packers and eaves stiffener on one side of the roof frame. Turn the frame over and lay it on the roof sheet. Weigh down the rafters and leave until the adhesive sets. Repeat with the other roof sheet, then plane along the ridge to make a neat edge for the roof trim.

ROOF STRUCTURE

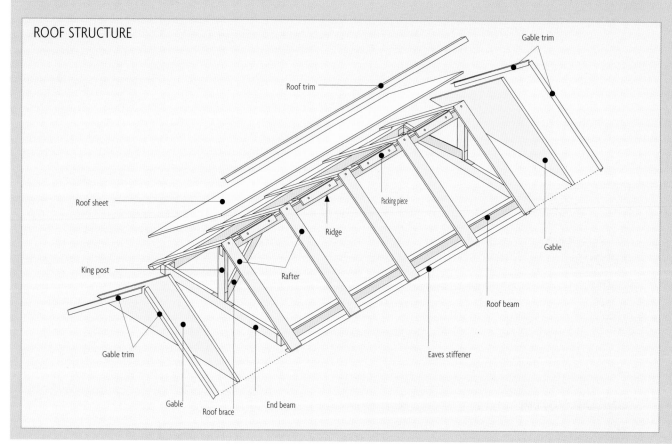

Gable trim

Roof trim

Roof sheet

Packing piece

Ridge

King post

Rafter

Gable

Roof beam

Gable trim

Eaves stiffener

Gable

Roof brace

End beam

outdoor

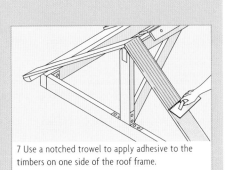

7 Use a notched trowel to apply adhesive to the timbers on one side of the roof frame.

8 Glue the roof trim along the ridge to cover and seal the joint in the roofing. Cut the ends of the trim with a utility knife to fit neatly with the gable ends. Position the gable trims and cut them to fit where they meet the roof trim at the ridge, then glue into place.

8 Glue the plastic roof trim along the ridge. Cut the ends flush with a utility knife.

Plastic angle serves as roof trim, covering the join between the roof sheets and gables.

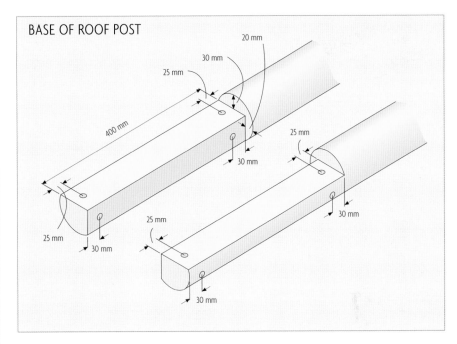

BASE OF ROOF POST

15 Decide where the sandpit will be placed and mark out the ground. Remove any vegetation and the topsoil and level the area. Place the sandpit in the prepared area and fill it with sand.

16 Lift the finished roof structure onto the posts, ensuring that the beams fit in the housings. Screw the roof to the posts using 50 mm countersunk screws.

NOVELTY SANDPIT

The construction of this sandpit is fairly straightforward; the frame of exterior-grade plywood is joined with corner cleats and braced in opposite corners by a seat and storage box.

PREPARING THE BOARDS

1 Using a tape, square, pencil and straight edge, mark out the pieces on the plywood sheets (see diagram on page 568). Cut them out and then cut the 12 mm deep rebates on the sides, ends and box front. Label each piece. Cut the timber pieces. Cut the 340 mm cleat lengthwise diagonally to make two triangular cleats.

2 Plane and smooth the edges of all pieces to the finished size and ensure they are straight and square.

ASSEMBLING THE FRAME

3 Glue and screw the corner cleats to the inside of the ends, using 25 mm screws and ensuring the cleats line up with the top and bottom edges of the ends (see diagram below). Apply adhesive to the outside edges of the cleats and the ends and position them between the sides. Fix through the side into each cleat using three or four 25 mm screws.

4 Place the seat in the corner rebate; fix it with adhesive and 30 mm nails. Turn the frame over and attach the storage box base in the same way.

5 Cut the ends of the edge stiffeners at 45 degrees. Centre the edge stiffeners on the side panels, 150 mm from the corners with the diagonally cut cleats. Apply adhesive and screw them in place. Once the adhesive has set, plane bevels on the edges.

CLEATS

MATERIALS*

PART	MATERIAL	FINISHED LENGTH	WIDTH	NO.
Side A	12 mm plywood	2100 mm	340 mm	1
Side B	12 mm plywood	2100 mm	500 mm	1
End A	12 mm plywood	1200 mm	500 mm	1
End B	12 mm plywood	1200 mm	340 mm	1
Seat	12 mm plywood	500 mm	500 mm	1
Seat ramp	12 mm plywood	600 mm	100 mm	2
Box base and lid	12 mm plywood	612 mm	600 mm	2
Box front	12 mm plywood	880 mm	488 mm	1
Box ramp	12 mm plywood	806 mm	160 mm	1
Ramp side	12 mm plywood	700 mm	400 mm	2
Ramp back	12 mm plywood	400 mm	136 mm	1
Corner cleat A	38 x 38 mm timber	340 mm		1
Corner cleat B	38 x 38 mm timber	328 mm		1
Corner cleat C	38 x 38 mm timber	476 mm		1
Seat cleat	38 x 38 mm timber	100 mm		2
Support bracket	38 x 38 mm timber	260 mm		4
Edge stiffener	38 x 38 mm timber	1200 mm		2

Other: Epoxy-resin adhesive; 25 mm x No. 10 countersunk cross-head self-tapping screws; 20 mm x No. 10 countersunk cross-head self-tapping screws; 30 x 2 mm helical thread nails; medium and coarse abrasive paper; two 75 mm T-hinges with 12 mm screws; 2.4 x 1.5 m anti-weed mat; 12 mm galvanized clout nails; 0.75 m³ sand; finish of choice.

* Finished size: 2100 x 1224 mm and 512 mm high. You will need one sheet of plywood 2400 x 1200 mm and one 1800 x 1200 mm. Timber sizes are the nominal size; for more about timber sizes and conditions see page 520.

This sandpit resembles a garage with a ramp and tunnel (make sure the sand is at the right height for access to the tunnel), but it can be painted to suit your child's taste. A plastic bowl half under the seat allows for water play.

CUTTING DIAGRAM

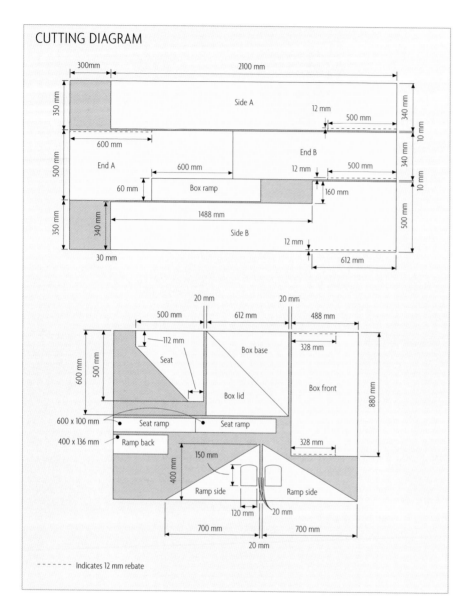

- - - - - - Indicates 12 mm rebate

outdoor

TOOLS

- Tape measure
- Straight edge
- Pencil
- Square
- Circular saw
- Saw table (optional)
- Handsaw
- Jigsaw
- Smoothing plane
- Screwdriver
- Portable electric drill
- Drill bit: 3 mm
- Rasp
- Hammer
- Sanding block
- Dust mask
- Safety glasses
- Hearing protection

Attach the ramps to the relevant end or side board by screwing through these support brackets.

THE STORAGE BOX

9 Using a handsaw, cut a 45-degree bevel along the side edges of the box front so it fits against the frame. Do the same on the vertical edges of the raised corner of the frame. Fit the box front in place. Ensure the bevels match. Trim the edges with a rasp or coarse adhesive paper for a smooth fit. Apply adhesive and screw the box front to the frame using 25 mm screws positioned 18 mm from the edge of the box front. When the adhesive sets, rasp and sand the joint.

10 Use a jigsaw to cut the 120 x 150 mm tunnel openings in the ramp sides 20 mm

THE SEAT AND RAMPS

6 Cut a 30-degree splay on one end of two support brackets. Position each bracket vertically just under the outside edge of the seat with the splay at the top and pointing outwards to support the ramps (see diagram opposite). Apply adhesive to the two brackets and attach them to the sandpit frame with 25 mm screws.

7 Place the seat cleats under the seat at right angles to the support brackets. Attach them the same way.

8 Position the seat ramps on the support brackets and mark a bevel on the ramps so that they will meet the seat neatly. Cut the bevels. Apply adhesive to two support brackets and screw one under each ramp, on the edge that will rest against the frame.

SEAT AND RAMP DETAIL

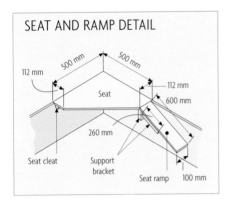

from the back of the ramp and 100 mm from the base. Put a slight curve on the top of the opening. Glue and screw the ramp back to the centre of the box front with four 20 mm screws, then glue and nail the ramp sides to the edges of the ramp back.

11 Put the box lid in place. Fit the ramp in place and mark a bevel where it meets the lid. Cut the bevel; rasp and sand smooth the edges. Glue and screw the ramp to the sides.

12 Sand the corners of the box lid to match the front and frame. Screw the strap of the T-hinges on one side of the lid and the butt to the side or end of the sandpit frame.

13 Apply the finish of your choice and decorate the box as desired. Fix on anti-weed mat and prepare the area as on page 545.

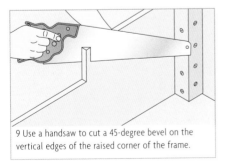

9 Use a handsaw to cut a 45-degree bevel on the vertical edges of the raised corner of the frame.

EXPLODED VIEW

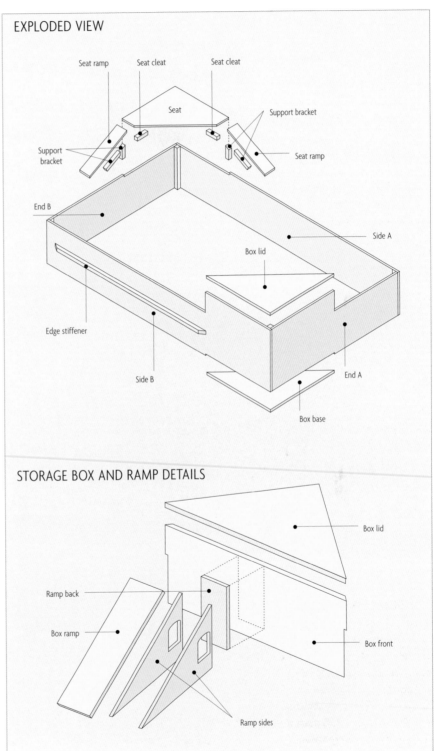

STORAGE BOX AND RAMP DETAILS

CASTLE PLAYHOUSE

This versatile playhouse can be used indoors or out. Built-in seats provide bracing and, when they are removed, the playhouse folds up and stores easily.

CUTTING OUT

1 Mark the front and back walls and four side panels on the MDF using a tape, pencil and straight edge. Measure the diagonals to check the pieces are square. Cut the parts. Plane the edges to the finished sizes.

2 Place two side panels side by side. Measure 125 mm from the outside edge of the board and mark the castellations across the top (see diagram on page 573); then mark

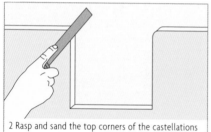

2 Rasp and sand the top corners of the castellations to a 3 mm radius, and sand all the cut edges.

out the front and back panels. Drill holes in the corners to turn the jigsaw and cut out the castellations. Save the offcuts for use as arch stones. Round off the top corners of the castellations with a rasp. Sand all the cut edges.

3 Drive a nail into the centre of the front panel, 400 mm from the base. Using string and a pencil, mark a semicircle with 200 mm radius to form the top of the

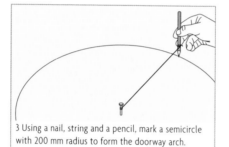

3 Using a nail, string and a pencil, mark a semicircle with 200 mm radius to form the doorway arch.

doorway. Mark the sides of the doorway using a straight edge. Mark the windows the same way, with a 75 mm radius arch and the nail 575 mm up and 200 mm in from the edge. Cut the door carefully for use as the drawbridge. For the windows, drill a 10 mm hole in the window to start the jigsaw.

4 Cut out the seats. On offcuts, mark the window arches with inside radius of 75 mm and outside radius of 125 mm. Cut out the pieces.

BRACING

5 Centre a seat stiffener on the underside of each seat (see below). Apply adhesive and fix in place from the top with three 20 mm screws.

6 Screw the door stiffener across the front of the drawbridge 400 mm from the base using two 20 mm countersunk screws. It will prevent the drawbridge hitting the floor.

7 Plane the door sill to 40 mm wide. Mark out and cut a 50 x 12 mm notch in each end so it fits into the opening flush with the outside face of the wall. Glue and screw the door sill to the frame at each end with two 30 mm countersunk screws.

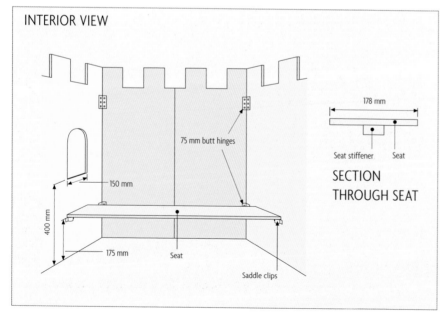

INTERIOR VIEW

75 mm butt hinges

150 mm

400 mm

175 mm

Seat

Saddle clips

178 mm

Seat stiffener   Seat

SECTION THROUGH SEAT

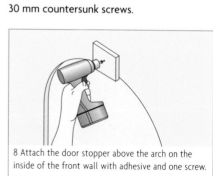

8 Attach the door stopper above the arch on the inside of the front wall with adhesive and one screw.

This fun castle playhouse was made from MDF and radiata pine. It is painted in a bright colour scheme that highlights the decorative detailing, and will appeal to its young owners.

MATERIALS*

PART	MATERIAL	FINISHED LENGTH	WIDTH	NO.
Front and back	12 mm MDF	1420 mm	1020 mm	2
Side	12 mm MDF	1020 mm	450 mm	4
Window arch	12 mm MDF	250 mm	125 mm	2
Door stopper	12 mm MDF	50 mm	50 mm	1
Seat	12 mm MDF	900 mm	178 mm	2
Seat stiffener	50 x 25 mm timber	900 mm		2
Door sill	50 x 25 mm timber	500 mm		1
Door stiffener	50 x 25 mm timber	400 mm		1
Corner stiffener	42 x 9 mm timber	1020 mm		4
Corner quoin	42 x 9 mm timber	100 mm		20
Corner infill	20 mm cove moulding	1020 mm		4

Other: String; PVA adhesive; abrasive paper; forty-eight 10 mm x No. 8 countersunk screws; ten 20 mm x No. 8 countersunk screws; twelve 10 mm x No. 10 dome-head screws; 15 x 1 mm panel pins; wood filler; two 900 mm piano hinges with 10 mm screws; eight 75 mm butt hinges with 15 mm screws; two 50 mm butt hinges with 10 mm screws; eight 25 mm double-sided saddle clips; one small barrel bolt; 1.5 m metal or plastic chain; two metal cabinet handles; finish of choice.

* Finished size: 1460 x 940 mm and 1020 mm high. Timber sizes given are the nominal size. For more about timber sizes and conditions, see page 520.

TOOLS

- Tape measure
- Pencil
- Square
- Panel saw
- Circular saw (optional)
- Jigsaw
- Smoothing plane
- Rasp
- Cork sanding block
- Hammer
- Nail punch
- Portable electric drill
- Drill bits (various sizes)
- Screwdriver
- Cramps
- Chisel: 18 mm
- Dust mask
- Safety glasses
- Hearing protection

8 Glue the door stopper to the inside above the doorway and fix it with one 12 mm dome-head screw.

9 Glue the strips of corner stiffener lengthwise to the front edges of the front and back panels. Glue and nail the corner infill in place using panel pins (see corner detail opposite). Punch the pins below the surface and fill with filler.

DECORATIVE ELEMENTS
10 Glue and clamp the window arches above each window.

11 Place the side panels together in pairs. On the outside edge of one panel, start at the base and position five quoins 104 mm apart. On the other panel, start at the top and position the quoins in

the same way. Glue and clamp them in place.

12 Use nine castellation offcuts to make the arch 'stones'. Centre the first above the arch and make splay lines by pivoting a straight edge from the arch centre (see diagram opposite). Mark the curve of the arch on the bottom end of the stone. Remove the stone and cut to shape, planing a 10 mm bevel on the top and sides. Glue and clamp the stone in place. Mark and prepare the other stones in the same way.

FINISHING
13 Apply the finish of your choice; allow to dry well. Butt the sides together in pairs; fix piano hinge on the outside face of each pair.

14 Screw two saddle clips to the interior under each window with the outside edge of each clip 175 mm up and apart. Attach corresponding clips on the back wall. Fold the sides together and place them against the front and back. Mark the positions of the clips. Chisel out 7 mm deep recesses for the clips.

15 Join the walls with two 75 mm butt hinges in each corner, placing each hinge behind a quoin on the side wall.

16 Secure the drawbridge to the door sill using two 50 mm butt hinges. Fix two equal lengths of chain to the inside of the doorway, 400 mm up from the base and at the same point on the drawbridge, using

ARCH DETAIL

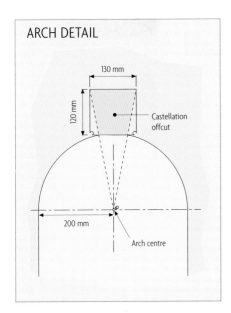

130 mm

120 mm

Castellation offcut

200 mm

Arch centre

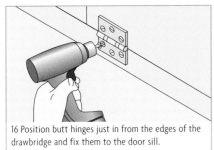

16 Position butt hinges just in from the edges of the drawbridge and fix them to the door sill.

a 10 mm x No. 10 screw through the end link of the chain. Attach the barrel bolt to the inside front wall just above the chain fixing so the drawbridge can be held closed.

17 Rest the seats on top of the saddle clips. Mark the position of the clips on the underside of each seat. Remove the seats and partially screw 12 mm cup-head screws into the seat, so the head sits in the clips.

18 Fix two cabinet handles to the outside back wall at the same height as the window arches to make transport of the folded playhouse easier.

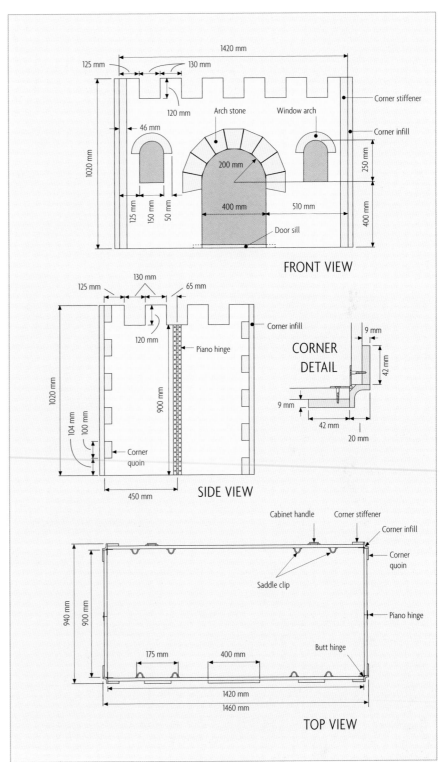

FRONT VIEW

1420 mm
125 mm
130 mm
120 mm
Arch stone
Window arch
Corner stiffener
Corner infill
1020 mm
46 mm
250 mm
125 mm
150 mm
50 mm
200 mm
400 mm
510 mm
400 mm
Door sill

SIDE VIEW

125 mm
130 mm
65 mm
120 mm
Piano hinge
Corner infill
1020 mm
900 mm
104 mm
100 mm
Corner quoin
450 mm

CORNER DETAIL

9 mm
42 mm
9 mm
42 mm
20 mm

TOP VIEW

Cabinet handle
Corner stiffener
Corner infill
Corner quoin
Saddle clip
Piano hinge
940 mm
900 mm
Butt hinge
175 mm
400 mm
1420 mm
1460 mm

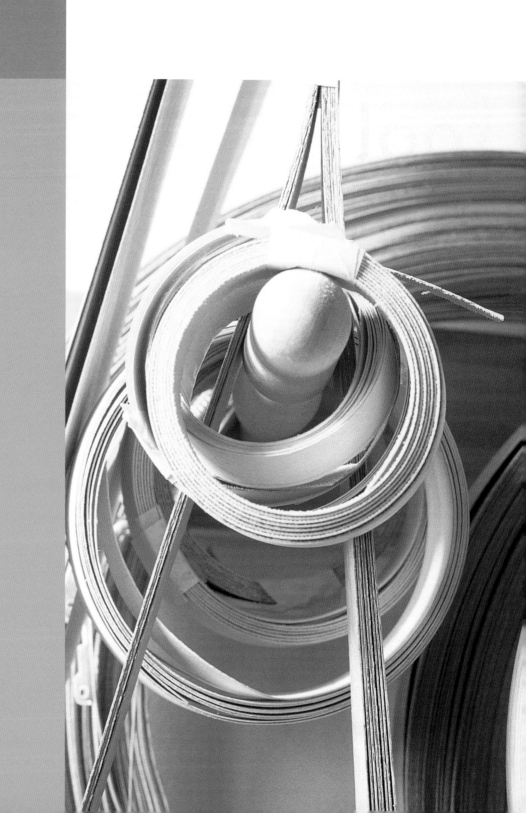

glossary and tool kit

glossary

Abrade To sand a surface using abrasive material

Acrylic paint Water-based liquid containing suspension of solid pigment particles

Additive or admixture Any substance added to concrete to modify its standard properties

Aggregate Hard, inert solid material such as sand, or crushed stone

Alkyd A resin used in oil-based paint to increase hardness

Allowance Extra material included in a panel for sewing or attaching

Antique Artificially create the appearance of age, usually by rubbing dark brown paint over the surface and wiping it back with a cloth

Arris Sharp edge where two flat surfaces meet at an angle

Background Surface to which a render coating is to be applied

Back-tack To attach a cover using cardboard strips to create a crisp, straight edge

Bagging Applying a thin layer of mortar that is finished with a hessian bag or plastic sponge

Baluster Timber that supports a handrail

Balustrade Series of balusters supporting a handrail

Barge capping Metal weatherproof strip covering the gap between the roofing and the barge board

Base Background surface

Base material Finely crushed gravel that compresses to a hard, solid base when compacted

Bat A half or part brick

Batten Narrow piece of wood

Battlement Parapet with indentations for shooting through

Beam Horizontal timber that supports the roof frame

Bearer Timber that supports the (deck) floor joists

Bed joint Mortar joint between courses of bricks

Bedding sand Coarse-grained material, such as washed river sand, that packs beneath paving

Bevel Surface that meets another at an angle other than 90 degrees

Bevel/chamfer To remove right-angled edges of timber by planing to a slope

Bird's-mouth housing A notch cut in a rafter so it sits over the wall plate

Bleaching The process of whitening or blonding timber to remove unwanted dark stains or lighten timber to even out the colour

Blistering Eruption of paint or varnish film forming bubbles on the surface

Blooming A whitish appearance on the surface of varnish sometimes accompanied by loss of gloss

Bond Overlapping pattern of bricks that holds brickwork together

Bonding agent Substance used to improve the strength of adhesion between two surfaces

Brace Diagonal member that stops movement of a structure

Bracket Support fixed to a wall to hold a shelf

Bridle ties Loops of twine sewn into foundations to hold flock in place

Butter Use trowel to put mortar on a brick before laying it

Capital An adornment sitting on the top of a post

Capping Protective covering on top of a fence

Cement Dehydrated powder made of limestone and shale; on addition of water it binds the aggregate to form concrete

Chamfer Flat surface on an edge, normally at a 45-degree angle

Cissing Failure of paint or varnish coating to form a continuous film on the surface. The film rolls back in globules, leaving round bare patches

Clearance hole Hole drilled right through a timber in preparation for screwing it to another

Cleat Small piece of timber used to connect two parts of a structure

Collar tie Horizontal member tying a pair of rafters together

Commons Bricks for internal work

Composition mortar Mortar that includes lime

Compound cut A cut in two directions, angled through both the width and thickness of the timber at an angle other than 90 degrees

Counterbore A large hole drilled over a pilot hole so that the screw may be hidden by a plug

Countersink Make a tapered recess so that a screw sits flush with the surface

Creosote Coal tar substance that protects wood from decay

Cross-cut Cut made in timber at right angles to the grain

Cross-joint Vertical joint between bricks in a wall

Curing The process of keeping concrete wet for a time to ensure maximum hydration and strength

Cut in Use brush tips to paint right up to an edge

Cutting in The careful painting of an edge to avoid spreading paint onto an adjacent area

Dado mould Decorative mould fitted around a post

Distress Age a painted surface by using abrasive paper and steel wool to rub back areas of paint so the item has the appearance of being older than it is

Door head Top part of a door frame

Dowel Wooden pin used to reinforce a joint by being inserted into each of the two joined pieces

Drag Pull a stiff bristle brush through wet glaze to create an impression of fine lines

Drumming A term used to describe the hollow, drum-like sounds of poorly adhered tiles or render.

Dust cover Any material, usually calico, on the underside of a piece

Efflorescence White, powdery discolouration caused by salts rising to the surface of paving bricks

Enamel paint Oil-based liquid containing suspension of solid pigment particles

End grain Timber surface that is cut at 90 degrees to the longitudinal grain

Face Dressed surface from which measurements are taken

Face brick Brick used for external or exposed brickwork

Face mark Mark made to indicate face side or edge of timber

Face side/edge Planed face or edge from which measurements are taken

Fascia board Board fixed to ends of joists to provide a neat finish

Fence Adjustable guide to keep a tool running parallel and at a set distance from the edge

Ferrule Metal ring placed over the end of the paintbrush to give it added strength and to hold the bristles together

Filler A smooth paste used for filling slight surface imperfections

Finish Coating used to enhance the appearance of furniture

Firebox A fire chamber or opening

Fixing Means of attaching one thing to another

Flashing Strip of impervious material fitted over a joint to prevent the entry of water

Float Hand tool used for shaping and finishing plaster

Floating coat Coat applied to straighten the wall

Flue Chimney shaft

Flush Level with another surface

Footings Part of the construction used to transfer a load to the ground

Form box Simple box used to hold wet concrete in place until set

Formwork Removable timber frame used to contain a wet concrete slab

Foundation Materials used in the supporting base of a furniture piece

Frame The supporting structure, usually made out of timber, of a furniture piece

French polish Finish made by dissolving shellac in spirit and applying by rubbing

Gable Triangular end of pitched roof structure

Glaze Paint mixed with water and scumble medium

Grout Mixture of fine sand and cement used for filling joints in tiles and other paving surfaces

Hard finish plaster Plaster used for finishing coat on a mortar base

Header Brick set through or across the wall

Header course Border of bricks, usually laid side by side, to give strength to the edge of the path

Housing A recess in a piece of timber cut as part of a joint

Jamb Side piece of doorway

Jig Device to hold and guide tools

during their use

Joist Timber to which flooring is fixed

Key A slightly rough surface that has been sanded to provide a bond for paint or paper

King post Vertical timber used to connect roof ridge and end beam

Lacquer A hard glossy coating made by dissolving cellulose or resins in solvent

Lap marks Marks caused when a fresh coat of paint overlaps and blends with a previously applied coat that is still wet

Lay off Work over the painted surface to eliminate or reduce brushmarks

Laying off Making final light brushstrokes over a wet film of paint to smooth and even it out

Ledger Horizontal timber fixed to a wall to support cross-timbers

Lintel Horizontal support over an opening

Lipping Decorative edge material

Lug Projection on the sides or backs of tiles to aid in spacing or to provide grip for the adhesive

Mask off Use low-tack tape or card to isolate an area while you are painting near it; this prevents one colour from contaminating the other

Masonry wall Wall of brick, stone or concrete

MDF Medium-density fibreboard

Mesh or bars Used to give concrete tensile strength and help control shrinkage

Mitre Joint made by cutting the ends of two pieces to 45 degrees

Mortar Mix of sand, cement and water, used to bond bricks or stones, or to give a path strength

Mortise Rectangular recess cut in timber to receive a tenon

Mullion Vertical member dividing a window frame

Off form The state of concrete immediately after formwork has been removed

Offset Angled positioning, not in a straight line

Oil Smooth, sticky liquid insoluble in water

Opacity The ability of a paint to completely cover the surface or colour over which it is applied

Paint wash Paint diluted with water to give soft finish

PAR Planed all round; term applied to timber planed to size

Particleboard A panel made of wood chips, also known as chipboard

Pediment Low-pitched, triangular part of pitched roof structure

Pier Column supporting the bearers and floor of the deck

Pilot hole Small hole to allow the thread of the screw to cut in and pull the joint tight

Plate Top or bottom member of a framed wall

Plinth A supporting structure at the base of a fence

Plumb Vertical

Polyurethane A durable, clear coating for timber, cork or vinyl that is easily cleaned

Post Timber or steel vertical used to support the bearers and floor of a deck

Prime Precoat with stain or paint

Profile Pegs and batten to which string lines are tied during setting out

Rack out Step out brickwork

Rafter Member that supports a roof; runs from ridge to roof beam

Rail Horizontal component of a frame; fits between stiles

Raised grain Swollen grain in timber resulting from moisture absorption

Rampart Embankment or walkway around a fort

Rebate Stepped recess along an edge; forms part of a joint

Reinforcement Steel welded

Render Coat a background with mortar (usually cement based and applied as one coat)

Resilient floor tiles Tiles made from flexible PVC, linoleum, cork or rubber

Resin Compound that exudes from a plant, or synthetic version

Ridge Highest point of a roof

Ridge capping Metal strip formed over the ridge to provide a seal

Rip cut Cut made in timber in the direction of the grain

Riser Vertical board under the tread of a stair

Ropiness Heavy brush-marks in the surface of the paint coating. This will reduce gloss level and dirt retention

Routing Cutting grooves and patterns within the timber face

RS Rough-sawn timber

Screed Narrow band of mortar used as a guide when ruling off and finishing a render coat

Screeding Process of dragging back sand or mortar to a level finish prior to laying paving material

Scumble medium Medium that extends the drying time of paint

Set-out Measurements marked on the timber

Setting coat Finishing coat of plaster, usually thin and smooth

Shiplap Interlocking panels

Shoulder The rise at the side of a housed joint where the cut is made

Sinking Failure of a paint or varnish film to maintain its potential or original sheen or shine

Size A sealer applied to a wall to decrease its porosity and help wallpaper adhere

Skew Nail or screw at an angle

Slab-on-ground Slab poured onto and supported by the ground

Slurry Wet mix of six parts cement to one part sand and water, often used to improve the bonding between a surface and pavers

Snug plug A round wooden plug or dowel glued into a counterbored screw hole and levelled to the surface of the timber with a chisel

Solvent The base that makes up the coating solution and evaporates as the coating dries; can be water, mineral turpentine or thinners

Span Distance between supports

Splay cut Cut at an angle other than 90 degrees

Spray paint Paint using an aerosol can or spray gun

Square Edges meet at an angle of 90 degrees

Square a line Draw a line at 90 degrees to the edge of the timber

Stain Penetrating dye or pigment

Stencil plastic/Mylar Strong but easy-to-cut clear film used for making stencils

Stile Vertical component of a frame

Stipple Apply paint to, or remove it from a surface using many light dabs

Stirrup Metal bracket fixed to the footing to support the post

Stop mortise A hole cut partially into a post

Stopper A stiff material, which dries with a minimum of shrinkage, used for making good large holes and cracks

Straight edge Any piece of material with a reliable straight edge

Stretch To apply directional tension to attach fabric or foundation material to a furniture piece

Stretcher Brick set along a wall

String Diagonal timbers used to support the treads of a staircase

Strip Remove old finishes back to bare timber

Stud Vertical member of a timber-framed wall

Support Small piece of timber connecting two parts of a structure

Support rail Part of the furniture

frame not usually seen on the exterior of the piece

Suspended slab Slab supported by formwork rather than by the ground

Tack cloth Specially treated cloth used to remove dust from surfaces prior to painting them

Template Pattern made so a shape can be reproduced accurately

Tenon Projecting end of a timber that fits into a mortise; a stub tenon does not go right through the other timber; a barefaced tenon is cut into only one side of the timber

Tensile strength Measure of the ability of a material to resist failure when subjected to bending forces

Tessellating Interlocking pattern that leaves no gaps

Timber frame construction Wall with thin cladding on frame of vertical and horizontal timbers

Timber rail Any piece of timber used as a support or decorative feature on an upholstered piece of furniture

Tint Shade of a colour, especially a lighter shade

Tone Shade or tint of a colour

Tongue Projecting part of a timber that fits into a groove

Top coat Final layer of finish

Tread Horizontal part of each step

Trimmer Timber cross member fitted between two rafters

Undercoat Layer of paint used to choke the timber grain before top coat is applied

Varnish Clear, protective coating made with polyurethane resin

Vitrified Highly fired ceramic material that has a high glass content and low porosity

Wax Natural substance, usually solid, lustrous and insoluble in water

Wax polish Beeswax polish, sometimes containing silicones to improve water-resisting properties. Produces a matt finish which does not resist abrasion

Weep hole Opening in mortar joint so water can escape

Welt The excess material, sometimes also called the allowance, from the edge of the

fabric to the stitching line on machine-sewn panels

Wetting in Satisfying the suction of a masonry surface by slightly dampening it before filling its holes

tool kit

If you are a woodworker with experience you will already have a set of tools, but if you are starting this journey you will need to begin by purchasing some basic tools. It is good practice to extend your tool kit by purchasing reasonably priced tools as they are needed for a particular job, and also to have a long-term plan for expensive tools, power tools and machine tools.

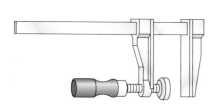

Adjustable cramp Holds parts together; both attachment and screw are adjustable

Bevelled-edge chisel Cuts grooves or pares slivers from wood

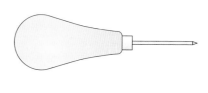

Bradawl An awl used to pierce timber for inserting screws or brads

Airless spray Small, electric spray gun for painting fences or lattice work

Block plane Small, lightweight plane ideal for small projects and fine trimming

Brick bond guage Used to calculate brick placement when setting out

Angle grinder Power tool with wheel for cutting or grinding metal or masonry

Bolster chisel Cold chisel with a broad splade used for cutting pavers, bricks or stone

Bricklaying chisels Used to remove dried mortar from brickwork

Bricklaying raker Is dragged along a joint to give a raked shape

Bull float Used for levelling and smoothing the surface of concrete

Clamshell digger two-handled spade for digging holes

Bricklaying trowel Used to spread mortar for the joints

Chalk line Stretch it tightly between two points and pluck it to leave a straight chalk line

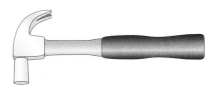

Claw hammer The round head drives in nails, the split claw pulls them out

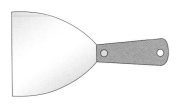

Broad knife Used to apply bedding and topping cement when finishing plasterboard

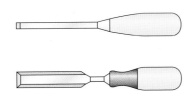

Chisels A mortise chisel (top) has a square edge with no bevelled faces; a bevelled-edge chisel cuts grooves or pares slivers from wood

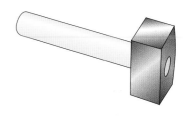

Club hammer Small, heavy mallet used with a straight edge for compacting pavers

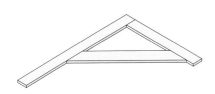

Builder's square Flat, right-angled device for determining 90 degree angles

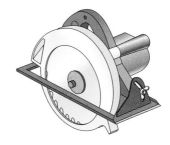

Circular saw Electric saw with circular blade for heavy cutting work

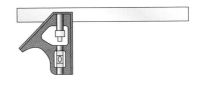

Combination square Measuring and marking tool for checking if joints are square

Coping saw Saw for cutting curves and scribing joints

Craft knife Used for cutting stencils

Electric drill Variable speed drill with a set of bits ranging from 2 to 10 mm diameter

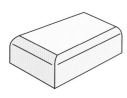

Cork sanding block Block around which abrasive paper is wrapped

Dowelling jig Ensures dowel holes are vertical and exactly opposed

Electric plane Used to level the tops of joists

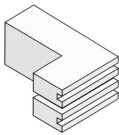

Corner block Fits on the corner of brickwork to hold a string line in place

Drill press Drills holes absolutely vertically (an electric drill and stand can be used instead)

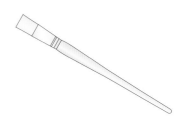

Fitch brush Small brush used for delicate tasks

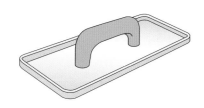

Cove float Steel float with turned up edges used for finishing concrete

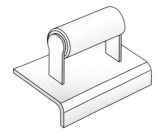

Edger Used to round off and strengthen the edges of concrete slabs

Flat brush Available in 50 mm, 75 mm and 100 mm sizes for general paint work

glossary

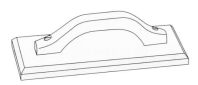

Float Wooden or metal tool used to smooth and compress concrete

Hand-stapler Medium weight, for staples up to 10 mm in size

Jigsaw Electric saw with thin blade for making curved cuts

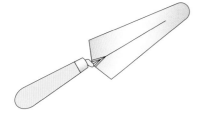

Gauging trowel Used for mixing small quantities of plaster and for applying mortar to awkward positions

Hot-glue gun Glues foam and finishes

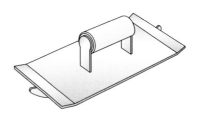

Jointing tool Used for making control joints in concrete to allow for expansion

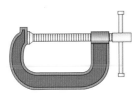

G-cramp Holds work firmly to a surface between the adjustable screw and the end of the cramp

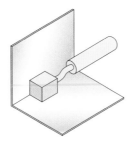

Internal angle tool Used to finish internal corners

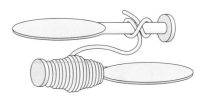

Line pins Anchor string lines and can be driven into mortar joints

Grass brush Also known as a water brush; used for splashing water on walls and cleaning

Jack plane Longer than a standard plane; used for long lengths of timber

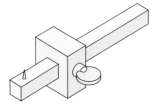

Marking gauge Scores a line parallel to an edge; the stock is adjustable

Measuring tape Used for measuring and setting out the concreting site

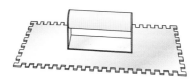

Notched trowel Used to spread adhesive so as to ensure better cohesion

Pincers Used to grip nails and tacks to pull them out

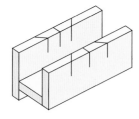

Mitre box Box with ready-cut slots to guide a saw when making mitre cuts

Orbital sander Electric sander used for small areas such as corners or awkward areas

Plasterer's hawk Used to hold plaster or mortar during work

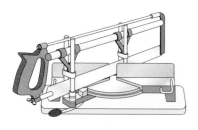

Mitre saw Used to cut moulding at an angle to make neatly fitting corners on a frame

Paint roller Frame with a replaceable sleeve; used to cover large areas with paint

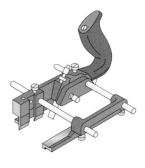

Plough plane Specialty plane for planing grooves

Nail punch Fits on a nail and when hit by a hammer drives the nail below the surface

Panel saw Saw for cutting plywood and other thin manufactured boards

Plumb line A metal weight attached to string used to ensure vertical lines are straight

Post-hole auger Used to dig holes for circular posts

Round iron jointer Is dragged along a joint to give a rounded shape

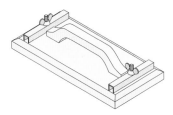

Sanding float Used with abrasive paper when finishing plasterboard joints

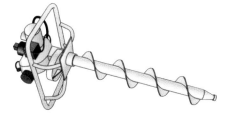

Power auger device for drilling holes in the ground

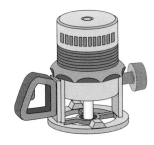

Router Hollows out or cuts grooves in timber

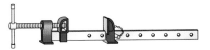

Sash cramp Long, adjustable cramp with screw tension at one end and adjustable sliding stop

Putty knife Knife with blunt blade used to work and smooth fresh putty

Rubber mallet Hammer-like tool with rubber head used to compact pavers into place

Scraper Scraper with stiff blade used to remove paint or old adhesive

Rebate plane Specialty plane with blade the full width of the sole; used for cutting rebates

Rubber squeegee Spreads grout over tiles

Skutch hammer Hammer with comb-like teeth on one end for chipping bricks

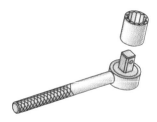

Sliding bevel Measuring and marking tool; its adjustable blade can be set at any angle. Used to set out or test a bevel or slope on timber

Socket and rachet Rachet onto which socketed heads, varying in size, can be fitted; tightens bolts and coach screws

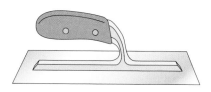

Spokeshave A plane with two handles for smoothing cylindrical wooden surfaces

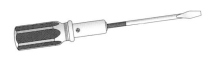

Slotted screwdriver Drives in screws with a single slot

Spanner Used to tighten bolts and nuts

Straight trowel Also known as a laying trowel, setting trowel, plasterers trowel, steel float and floating trowel; used to apply plaster or mortar

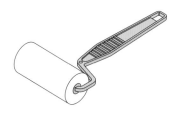

Small foam roller Used for applying paint to stencils

Spatula Used to apply tiling adhesive

Stud finder Electronic implement for locating studs in timber-framed walls

Smoothing plane A blade set in the centre of the plane smooths the surface of the timber

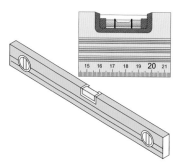

Spirit level Used to ensure string lines and brick courses are level and vertical

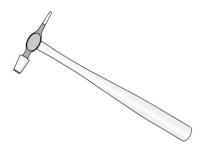

Tack hammer Used for tacks or upholstery studs

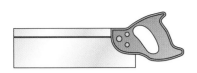

Tenon saw General purpose woodworking saw with metal backbone to keep the blade straight

Upright sander Used to sand floors over a large area such as a room; can be hired when needed

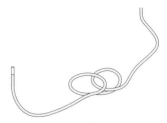

Water level Used to check for level over long distances or around corners

Tile cutting machine A heavy-duty cutter for cutting hard tiles

Utility or marking knife Sharp knife with disposable blade for cutting and marking

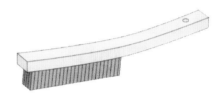

Wire brush Used for cleaning formwork or scrubbing concrete surfaces

Tile scorer Scribes a line on the tile to score the surface where a break is required

Vice Screws to the edge of a workbench to hold timber secure

Wooden float Also known as a hand float; used to finish mortar or to put a sandy finish on concrete slabs

Try square Used to check work for square or to mark right angles

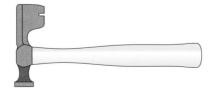

Wallboard hammer Has rounded driving face to make a depression without tearing the plasterboard liner

Wooden mallet For stripping covers and frame repairs

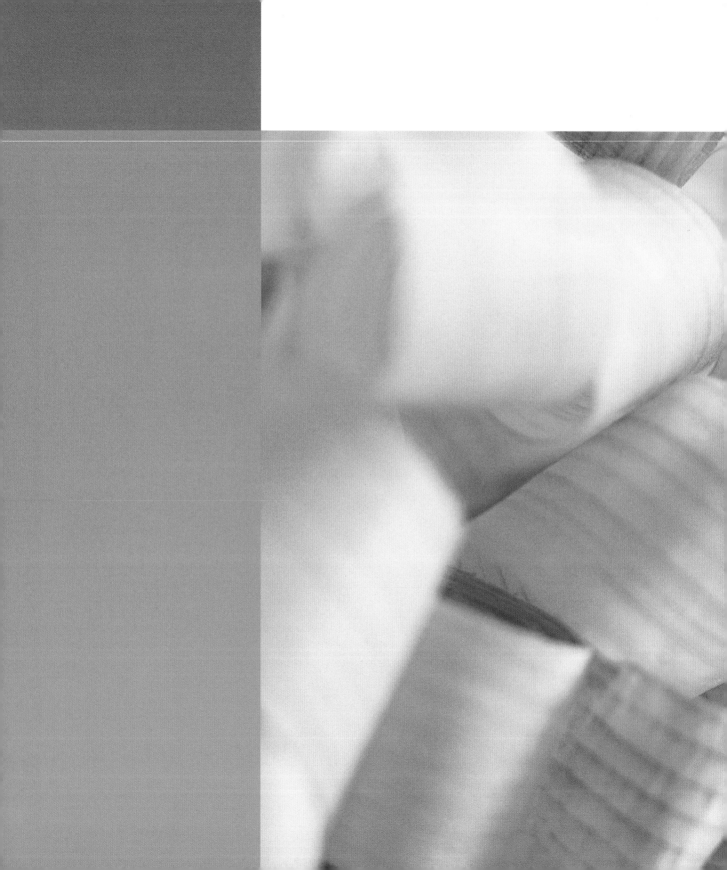

using timber

BUYING AND STORING TIMBER

When buying wood, it is best to visit a timber yard personally in order to examine the boards for defects and to select the best pieces to suit your needs.

BUYING HARDWOODS

Hardwoods are cut from the tree into planks and the stated thickness of the board is the sawn size. However, the maximum dimensions you have to work with must allow for planing the plank all around so it is flat and square. For example, a sawn plank purchased at 25 mm will finish between 2 and 15 mm, depending on how much has to be removed in order to make it flat, straight and square. In order to arrive at a specific dimension of 25 mm, a thicker board would have to be purchased, thus giving more waste. You also need to consider how much width you will get out of a plank.

When buying hardwoods in planks, there may be some resistance to turning over too many boards in a stack to find the best grain characteristics or colour, especially if you require only a small amount. However, if you are reasonable, generally timber dealers will be happy to oblige.

BUYING SOFTWOODS

You will encounter a similar situation regarding measurements of sawn softwoods, but the dealer will normally allow you to pick out the pieces yourself. Sometimes softwoods can be purchased 'planed all round' (PAR) or 'dressed all round' (DAR)—that is, planed or dressed on all four sides. But the size given would be expressed in the original sawn size—for example, a board labelled 50 x 25 mm will actually be about

41 x 19 mm, but it will not be to an exact measurement. It will be to the nearest size that the timber yard can plane in order to achieve a reasonable finish on all faces. As a result, a purchase made on one occasion may differ on another.

GENERAL POINTERS

Finished sizes also vary according to the country of origin and the milling standards in that country. Some countries have standard thicknesses and widths, allowing for a consistency of product from one yard to another. This tends to be the case particularly with common building and carpentry grade timber and machined sections such as mouldings and base boards.

The more exotic timber for fine cabinet work is generally supplied rough sawn. If it needs to be planed, then the maximum thickness and width will be provided.

When purchasing timber in large quantities the cost is often calculated by its cubic content, although in smaller volumes it may be sold by the length or piece. Be aware of how the dealer makes the calculations. Some dealers may want to charge you by the cubic foot, which can become quite confusing, particularly if you are used to dealing in cubic metres. Remember there are approximately 35 cubic feet in a cubic metre. So ask the dealer for the cubic metre rate in addition to the cubic foot rate and then make sure they both add up correctly.

If you live a long way from a dealer there are mail order companies that will supply a large range of timber in varying sizes. The product is obviously more expensive but often there is no alternative, especially if you need a specific species. Generally, however, suppliers have a reputation to maintain and give a good service.

STORAGE IN THE WORKSHOP

Once you have obtained your timber, you must ensure that it is stored under suitable conditions. Hardwood planks are best stored in a similar way to that found in a good timber yard—horizontally with spacers in between each board and away from sunlight and direct heat sources. It is sometimes the case that softwoods are stored vertically at the suppliers, but this is best avoided, unless it is absolutely necessary as a result of space constraints. In general, make sure that your workshop is dry and well ventilated.

You will find that as you undertake more projects there will be material left over. Not all of this will be waste and you should store any scraps that may be useful to use in later projects. Ensure, however, that this is undertaken methodically so that you know where to find different types.

MANUFACTURED BOARDS

Even though the natural characteristics of wood are a major part of its attraction, they also tend to cause problems including shrinkage during mass manufacturing. Therefore, the industry has developed a number of ways of using timber to make board materials that are much more dimensionally stable than natural timber and are readily available to the home woodworker.

BOARD SIZES

Manufactured boards are usually produced to standard thicknesses, which are precise and expressed either in imperial or metric sizes. The sheet size is generally made to a standard 2440 x 1200 mm. Larger sheets can be made available to special order—that is, approximately 3600 x 1800 mm. Some of the thinner thicknesses may be sold at a different size—for example, 3 mm aeroply may be found 150 cm square. Many outlets, however, will cut standard sheets into smaller sizes, normally increments of the standard sheets—for example, 1200 x 1200 mm.

TYPES OF MANUFACTURED BOARD

There are various types of manufactured board available on the market today. These include plywood, particleboard or chipboard, fibreboard and blockboard. Manufactured board can be used on its own, but also forms a base for wood veneer.

Plywood

Plywood is made from constructional veneers, which are laminated and glued together, with the grain alternating along and across the board. Usually there is an uneven number of layers so that the outside grain directions on the faces of the finished boards are the same. Plywood is available in a range of different thicknesses—from a flexible 3 mm sheet to a hefty 30 mm board.

Plywood can have various numbers of layers—the thinnest, three-ply, has three layers. As its name suggests, three-ply is made from just three laminates—two face veneers and a core that is sometimes the same thickness.

Thicker boards, or multi-plies, are made of more sheets of laminates—always an odd number finished to the standard board thicknesses. The performance of plywood is determined by the quality of the laminates and the type of adhesive used in the manufacturing process. Interior grade plywood is normally bonded with a urea-formaldehyde adhesive. These are suitable for most interior work, but other types should be chosen if they are to be used for kitchens and bathrooms. Exterior grade plywood—termed weather and boil proof or WBP—is bonded with phenolic adhesives, which are highly resistant to weather, wet and dry heat, insects and fungi. Marine plywood has laminates that are selected so that they are fault-free. For very special applications resorcinol adhesive can be used.

Particleboard or chipboard

Particleboard, also known as chipboard, is made from small wood chips, which are glued together under pressure. It is stable but can be affected by moisture if a waterproof adhesive has not been used. Some boards are made from similar-sized particles, but often you will find boards with outside layers of high-density particles sandwiching a coarser core, such as in graded-density particle board. Decorative particle board is also available with faces of wood veneer or plastic laminates.

Other boards with greater tensile strength are available, but more for building work than furniture making. Oriented-strand board is made from long strands of wood. Flakeboard or waferboard is made from big chips of wood, bonded in layers with random grain direction.

Fibreboards

Fibreboard is made out of tiny particles of wood (finer than sawdust) that are fixed together with a tough resin. For many years, the best-known material was standard hardboard, which normally has one smooth and one textured face. Standard hardboard is available in a large variety of thicknesses—from 2–10 mm. Fibreboard is often used for making cabinet backs and toys.

One problem with hardboard, as well as chipboard and other particleboard, is that lippings, either solid or veneer, have to be applied to the edges. To overcome this problem, medium-density fibreboard (MDF) was developed. MDF has a dense, smooth surface texture that is ideal for routing or painting. The edges can be polished so that there is no need to use lippings. It has now become a standard material for much furniture making and also has certain applications for some interior trim. MDF comes in thicknesses ranging from 5–30 mm.

Blockboard

Blockboard is constructed of solid wood strips between laminates. They are particularly suited for worktops and shelves. Boards are normally sold as full boards in various sizes, with thicknesses ranging from 10–25 mm.

Laminboard is a top-quality block construction board. The core strips of solid wood are quite narrow—approximately 2mm wide. It is usually edge-glued with two laminates on either side of the core, commonly with the grain of the outside in line with the direction of the core strips. This is probably the most stable manufactured board available.

Standard blockboard has core strips that are wider than laminboard—approximately 20 mm. The core strips are not necessarily glued, and are sandwiched between outside laminate faces in one or two layers on each side. A problem with this board is that the strips can show through the outside veneers, particularly if there is only one on each face.

Battenboard is a cheaper blockboard where the interior strips are much wider— from 30–40 mm. Obviously show-through is much more likely.

In addition to these boards, solid boards made from wood strips, joined end to end and glued together to make a wide board, have been used in the furniture industry and are available in many do-it-yourself outlets. If you can visually accept the pattern of the board's strips, they are stable and are a useful alternative to other boards and solid wood.

Buying and storing manufactured board

When you wish to depart from the sizes of the projects as given or want to develop your own designs, always remember at the planning stage to reduce waste as much as possible by checking that the components needed can be economically cut from the standard-size sheets.

Unless you are purchasing from a company that carries a large range, the selection available from local outlets may be limited. When buying plywood, birch ply is best for making furniture because of its quality and birch veneer faces. Often the plywood available locally uses low-quality veneers. With blockboard and particleboard, the local quality can also be variable. There are several grades of specialized boards that use different adhesives or resins as bonding agents. The best can be entirely waterproof if required; if you need a high-performance variety, you will need to order from a company that specializes in high-grade board.

Manufactured boards can be stored vertically as long as they are well supported to ensure that they do not bend or warp. Support the boards in a strong shelf rack along one side of the workshop. They

must also be stored under dry conditions because they can soak up moisture.

PREPARING THE TIMBER

Before measuring and marking the timber for a project, it is important that it is perfectly flat, square and straight.

CHECKING TIMBER

1. Check to see if the surface is free of pits or bumps by running a straight-edge across it. If the surface is not flat, it should be planed true—perfectly flat— before the wood is measured and marked.

2. You can check if the board is straight by positioning two steel rulers across each end. Now sight along the board and, if the two rules appear parallel, the wood is straight.

MARKING THE FACES OF TIMBER

1. Make the face-side mark (usually a scroll shape) on the timber surface, toward the edge to be planed next.

2. Plane the edge straight and at right angles to the face side. Check with a straight edge and try square.

3. Apply the edge mark, conventionally a 'V' shape, on the face edge.

using timber

VENEERS

A veneer is a thin sheet of wood that is used for structural or decorative purposes. With many types of wood now hard to find in solid form, the use of veneer for decorative purposes is becoming more common.

Many types of wood have such interesting and unique characteristics that, in order to conserve and extend their use, they are made into veneer.

There is a vast range of veneer available to the woodworker today. This is the case with woods that exhibit highly decorative grain patterns, such as curly mahogany.

For structural use they tend to be known as constructional veneers and they are usually cut to thicknesses of between 1 and 3 mm.

HOW VENEERS ARE PRODUCED

In early times, veneers were produced by sawing, which resulted in thick veneer— as much as 3 mm—and a very high waste element from the sawdust. Veneer-slicing machines were developed in the 18th century to produce thin veneers.

Sliced veneers

Flat slicing is where the log is supported on a carrier and a series of slices is produced. This can be standard flat slicing, quarter-cut slicing, or flat-sliced quartered. Quarter-cut slicing is used to produce veneer with a more varied grain pattern than flat slicing. Flat-sliced quartered veneer is produced when quartered logs are cut across the log. Sometimes when slicing, fine cracks, known as knife checks, can occur on the back face of the veneer. This is called the open or loose face. If possible lay this face down, although when using book-matched veneers this will not be possible.

Rotary-cut veneers

The rotary cut is used for constructional veneers and some decorative veneers. The trunk of the tree, after the bark has been removed and softened by steaming, is set on a machine similar to a huge lathe. As the machine revolves, a continuous sheet is cut from the log. The cutting knife reduces in radius to give a sheet of even thickness.

For decorative veneers, the log can be positioned in different ways so that various grains and figures are emphasized. Rotary cutting can be off-centre, half-round or back-cutting. Both off-centre cutting and half-round cutting produce a figure similar to flat-slicing. The back-cutting method is used to make the most of curly and burl veneers.

VENEER TYPES

Many types of veneer are available today and have been made from a wide variety of hardwoods, with varying colours, grains, figures and textures. The specific type of veneer is obtained by slicing the log in various ways. The part of the tree that the veneer comes from—for example, the main trunk, burls or the fork—will also determine the type of veneer that is produced.

Some of the most common types of veneer are described below.

Crown-cut veneers are the most common veneers used to decorate tables and other traditional furniture. They are produced using the flat-sliced quartered method of veneer slicing.

Curly veneers are produced from the fork of a tree where the trunk divides.

Striped veneers are produced using the quarter-cut flat-slicing method. This results in a radial cut being made across the width of the tree's growth rings.

Burl, or burr, veneers are often used for pieces such as jewellery boxes. Some types of burl veneers are highly figured.

Some interesting veneers are created from hardwood timber with irregular grain. These are called freak-figured veneers.

Artificial dyes are also used to make veneers in various colours.

BUYING AND STORING VENEER

Veneers are available from specialized suppliers. The most common types are normally to be found in fairly long lengths— 3650 mm or more—and between 250 and 350 mm wide. Thicknesses vary, depending on the intended use. Where exotic veneers are needed, the size will be smaller and will depend on the log from which they are cut. Calculate how much veneer you need and allow 15 per cent for waste. Every veneer is different, so finding a match may be tricky.

Veneers are fairly brittle, so take care when opening your rolled up sheet or it may crack. If the veneer has end splits, then repair it with paper veneer tape.

Veneers should be stored flat, in a cool and dry environment. Store away from bright light. If using matched veneers, the leaves should be numbered.

WOODFINISHING

Woodfinishing is sometimes viewed as the final but brief operation of a woodwork project. However, it actually needs to be carefully considered at the outset in order to decide on the most appropriate finishing method and when it is best to apply it. Make sure that you leave enough time for finishing, and prepare and plan thoroughly before you start any project.

Even though finishing is generally the final process that you will undertake in any woodworking project, it can often be useful—and sometimes essential—to pre-finish your wood components before assembly. This is so that the finish can be applied to all the nooks and crannies that cannot be reached after assembly.

Finishing technology has developed to satisfy two criteria for when the object is in use—practicality and appearance.

Use may often dictate the finishing strategy—for example, the amount of physical or environmental wear that the piece will have to resist. Will it be used indoors or outdoors, or will it be subjected to continuous wear?

There is a wide range of finishes available today: natural clear, synthetic-coloured, as well as some unusual surface finishes. Before you apply finish though, it is important to prepare the wood surface as necessary.

FILLERS

You will often have to fill small cracks and holes in order to prepare the wood for finishing. There is a range of filling materials available.

Filler knife

A filler, or putty, knife is used to apply a filler. A filler knife is a thin, flexible piece of stainless steel fixed to a handle. It is used to work the filler or putty into the defect within the surface of the work before sanding and applying a finish.

Filler

Small cracks and holes can be filled with a filler as near as possible to the wood's colour.

You can also use preparations based on shellac. Shellac sticks come in wood colours and are ideal for repairing small cracks or knotholes.

Wax sticks

Wax sticks are made from carnauba wax and mixed with resin and colouring pigments. Wax sticks are normally used for repairing small hairline cracks in the wood surface. Remember that you should use wax sticks only when you intend to use a wax finish on the work.

Wood filler

Wood filler is made from natural and/or synthetic materials, and is normally used to fill wood defects, such as splits and knotholes. It can be readily sanded down to provide a smooth surface for a polish. It is available in a variety of colours to match almost any wood, and can also be mixed with lighter or darker filler or paint pigments for a perfect colour match. Most filler for cabinet work is water-based, although alcohol-based types, which dry more quickly, are also available.

Grain filler

Grain fillers are much the same as wood fillers, except that they are more watery. Grain fillers are rubbed into the surface with a cloth, left to dry, and then fine sanded. Even though powdered grain fillers are available, it is preferable to use successive coats of lacquer cut down between each application.

Shellac

The resin in softwoods can bleed, especially from knotholes. Shellac—a resin dissolved in denatured alcohol—prevents bleed.

PREPARING THE SURFACE

Decisions made as to the practicality and appearance of wood finishes are closely linked.

1 Before applying any finish, be sure that the surface is well prepared by planing, scraping, and using abrasive papers.

2 Ensure the surface is free of dust or other particles by wiping it with a tack cloth.

3 In some situations you may need to fill the grain, or any defects, with a filler. Place the filler between the filler knife and the defect. Apply pressure with the knife while dragging it across the surface. This forces the filler into the defect. As with any filler or putty, slightly overfill the defect. When dry, sand back to a flush finish.

If you are using a softwood with knots, you may need to use shellac at this stage.

NATURAL CLEAR FINISHES

When quality wood is used nowadays, there is generally no need to change the colour, but only to bring out the natural qualities of the wood species. It is worth remembering that on exposure to light the colour of most will usually tend to darken anyway. For this reason, the clearest finish possible is often the most desirable.

French polish

French polish is made out of shellac, a natural substance made from beetles dissolved in denatured alcohol. It has been used for many years and used to be the furniture maker's standard finish during the 19th and early 20th centuries. It can be finished to a very high gloss, but unfortunately is vulnerable to both water and alcohol. There are various types of French polish available today.

Button polish is the highest grade of French polish and is a golden-brown colour.

Garnet polish is a dark red/brown and is used on wood to make it look like mahogany.

White polish is made from bleached shellac and is used for pale-coloured woods.

Transparent polish is used where minimum colour change is required on light woods such as ash and sycamore.

Coloured polish contains an alcohol-based stain and is used in order to modify the colour of the wood.

Penetrating oils

Oils soak into the wood, giving it a beautiful rich finish that enhances the grain rather than simply coating the surface. When applying oil finishes, it is best to thin the first coat to encourage penetration into the wood, and then follow this with several coats to build up a good finish. This is better than simply flooding on a thick coat. Oil is the most easily repaired of all wood finishes. Simply sand down and re-oil. A range of oils is available today.

Linseed oil can be raw or boiled. Raw oil takes a long time to dry, boiled less so. Since drying has to be done naturally, the resulting finish is not as hard as with other oils. Its performance can be improved by adding dryers, such as gold size or terrabin.

Danish or teak oils have dryers already added. Different formulations will give good results in terms of penetration and hardness.

Tung oil is from the tung tree, and is also known as Chinese oil. It is very durable and is also heat and alcohol resistant.

Waxes

Wax polish is made from beeswax or carnauba wax in turpentine. Each of these waxes can be used alone but it is generally better to seal the grain with a thin lacquer or with white shellac before building up wax coats. Wax is often used as a final finish on top of other materials. A very fine steel wool is used to apply a soft wax, giving a semi-matt surface. The surface is then buffed with a soft cloth. With so many ready-made preparations available, waxes are no longer as popular.

Applying French polish, oils and waxes

Some of these finishes are combustible and prone to self-ignite, so after you have applied the finish, be sure to unfold the cloth or pad and leave it out to dry completely.

Application by cloth pad

French polish is applied with a thick, soft pad.

Other finishes such as oils can also be applied in the same way.

1 Make the pad from a square of white linen cloth with a ball of batting cotton placed over the cloth. Fold the cloth over the batting, and then turn in the edges. The pad is then held in the palm of the hand.

2 The batting can be charged with shellac, oils, or some of the other finishes.

3 Dip the pad in the finish, letting it soak up a reasonable amount of the finish; it should not be dripping wet.

Application by cloth

A cloth is usually used for applying waxes and oil. Cotton is best for this process.

1 When applying oil, soak the cloth thoroughly in a finish of your choice.

2 Rub the cloth over the wood surface with even strokes.

It is very important when you have finished with the cloth to unfold it and leave it outside to dry to avoid spontaneous combustion.

Application with steel wool

This method is used for applying wax.

1 Wax can initially be applied with a pad of very fine steel wool, rubbing in the general direction of the grain.

2 Subsequent burnishing is made with a lint-free cotton cloth formed into a pad. This is then used to rub the wax to a dull shine.

SYNTHETIC CLEAR AND COLOURED FINISHES

With the rapid developments that have taken place in the manufacturing processes in recent years, there is now a wide range of different types of synthetic finish available: stains, resins, lacquers, and paints. Each is suitable for a particular purpose, so be sure to choose carefully.

Stains

Staining was traditionally done to modify the colour of wood when the original did not suit the maker's requirements. More recently, makers have chosen woods for their specific virtues, and a small range of other colours has been developed. They add an overall finish that will colour the wood but still show the grain. These stains are available in water-, alcohol- and oil-based forms.

Water-based stains have been formulated to give results as close as possible to traditional products, without using dangerous substances.

There are a variety of effects that you can achieve by applying the same stains to different base woods.

Lacquers (varnishes)

Lacquers, or varnishes as they are sometimes called, also have a long history, but are not as popular today. They create a fairly hard, resistant surface and can be used in clear form over another surface or as a flat, opaque colour that disguises the grain. They are available in gloss, semi-gloss and matt finishes and can be water- or solvent-based.

Water-based lacquers have the same benefits as water-based stains.

Paints

Interesting effects can also be produced with paint, either completely disguising the grain, allowing some hint of wood to show through, or with a broken finish. Traditional paints have been oil-based, but water-based and, more recently, plastic-based paints have become very familiar, and all come in a wide range of colours. When completely dry, finish the effect with wax for a soft finish or a clear lacquer for a more durable finish.

Applying lacquers, stains and paints

These finishes are often applied with a brush, although stroking a stain on with a cloth is also effective. Taking care to achieve an even finish is always a priority.

Application by brush

1 Take a scrap piece of the same wood as that used in the project you are working on and apply your chosen stain to check if it gives a suitable result. You can create a deeper colour by applying more coats.

2 When you are happy with your test piece you can then proceed with your project.

3 Apply the finish with straight strokes of the brush along the grain and let the film settle naturally. When using paint you need to brush initially in different directions, finishing off with light strokes in one direction. This should be with the grain if the piece is solid wood. If you are painting up to an edge, always brush outwards.

4 Wipe off any excess with a cotton cloth. Lightly take the brush across the grain again to avoid leaving any cloth marks.

5 When it is dry, rub down with self-lubricating silicon-carbide paper.

6 Remove any sanding dust and apply additional coats of finish as needed.

7 When you have achieved the colour that you want, a clear finish can be applied.

UNUSUAL SURFACE FINISHES

If you are after an interesting finish for your work, many options are available, including fuming, blasting, scrubbing and scorching.

Fuming oak

Oak and other woods that contain a proportion of tannin can be fumed effectively when exposed to ammonia, which makes the wood darken. Take an airtight container into which the project can be placed after final finishing. Place some saucers of strong ammonia in the compartment with the project and seal it. After a time the oak will change colour to an attractive grey. When the desired colour is obtained, remove the ammonia and apply a transparent finish. Take the utmost care when using ammonia, because the fumes are very toxic. Always wear a face mask and goggles.

Sandblasting

Sandblasting is an industrial method of cleaning components prior to other finishing treatments. When wood is sandblasted the softer grain is removed and the hard grain remains. It is then usual to apply a transparent finish. This process should be carried out by a specialist.

Scrubbing

Until recently, wooden work surfaces in kitchens were scrubbed for cleaning purposes. The resulting finish was a light, bleached wood surface. As with sand-blasting, this is because the soft grain was worn away. For the right piece of woodwork this can be a very interesting effect.

Scorching

Scorching is not normally a method that is used on fine furniture because this finishing technique uses a blowtorch in order to burn the surface of the wood. The resulting charred material is then carefully wire brushed away. Subsequent finishing with a lacquer or an oil gives an unusual finished effect, particularly when used on softwood species of wood.

SPRAYING WOOD FINISHES

Setting up spray equipment in a proper working environment is expensive. It is essential that the area is clean, that there is adequate extraction/ventilation for the noxious chemicals and that lighting is suitably flameproof. Unless you already have experience in spraying or want to turn your hobby into something more, it is preferable to use the other techniques described here.

SAFETY FIRST

- Make sure that during the finishing process the area is well ventilated. When using the toxic materials wear protective clothing and gloves, a face mask and a respirator.

- It is a good idea to use barrier creams.

- Your surroundings must be clean. Remember that most materials are flammable, so keep only enough for the work at hand.

- Store bulk finishes in a separate building away from your home and workshop.

- Make sure that an extinguisher and/ or fire blanket are readily available nearby.

- Do not smoke.

- Keep finishes away from children.

- Always follow the manufacturer's instructions.

index

index

index

Published in 2007 by Murdoch Books Pty Limited
www.murdochbooks.com.au

Murdoch Books Australia
Pier 8/9, 23 Hickson Road
Millers Point NSW 2000
Phone: +61 (0) 2 8220 2000
Fax: +61 (0) 2 8220 2558

Murdoch Books UK Limited
Erico House, 6th Floor
93–99 Upper Richmond Road
Putney, London SW15 2TG
Phone: +44 (0) 20 8785 5995
Fax: +44 (0) 20 8785 5985

Chief Executive: Juliet Rogers
Publishing Director: Kay Scarlett

Design Concept: Heather Menzies
Design: Heather Menzies and Craig Peterson
Project Manager: Emma Hutchinson
Editor: Gordana Trifunovic
Production: Monique Layt

ISBN 978 1 92120 879 9

A catalogue record for this book is available from the British Library.

Text, design and photography © Murdoch Books 2006
Front cover photography by Sue Stubbs

Readers of this book must ensure that any work or project undertaken
complies with local legislative and approval requirements relevant
to their particular circumstances. Furthermore, this work is necessarily
of a general nature and cannot be a substitute for appropriate professional advice.

Printed by Toppan Hong Kong in 2007. PRINTED IN CHINA